OXFORD STUDIES IN MEDIEVAL
EUROPEAN HISTORY

General Editors
CAROLINE GOODSON   AMY REMENSNYDER
and
JOHN WATTS

The Making of Lay Religion in Southern France, c. 1000–1350

JOHN H. ARNOLD

OXFORD
UNIVERSITY PRESS

Great Clarendon Street, Oxford, OX2 6DP,
United Kingdom

Oxford University Press is a department of the University of Oxford.
It furthers the University's objective of excellence in research, scholarship,
and education by publishing worldwide. Oxford is a registered trade mark of
Oxford University Press in the UK and in certain other countries

© John H. Arnold 2024

The moral rights of the author have been asserted

All rights reserved. No part of this publication may be reproduced, stored in
a retrieval system, or transmitted, in any form or by any means, without the
prior permission in writing of Oxford University Press, or as expressly permitted
by law, by licence or under terms agreed with the appropriate reprographics
rights organization. Enquiries concerning reproduction outside the scope of the
above should be sent to the Rights Department, Oxford University Press, at the
address above

You must not circulate this work in any other form
and you must impose this same condition on any acquirer

Published in the United States of America by Oxford University Press
198 Madison Avenue, New York, NY 10016, United States of America

British Library Cataloguing in Publication Data
Data available

Library of Congress Control Number: 2023947282

ISBN 978–0–19–287176–3

DOI: 10.1093/oso/9780192871763.001.0001

Printed and bound in the UK by
Clays Ltd, Elcograf S.p.A.

Links to third party websites are provided by Oxford in good faith and
for information only. Oxford disclaims any responsibility for the materials
contained in any third party website referenced in this work.

*This book is dedicated to Joe Canning and to Alex Webb,
for many walks, long conversations, and their
supportive friendship during lockdown.*

Acknowledgements

I am very grateful to the Leverhulme Trust who funded a year's fellowship in 2010–11 for a project then entitled 'Communities of Belief in Southern France', which laid the foundations for this book. In the following decade, a year of sabbatical leave from Birkbeck, University of London, and, later, another from the Faculty of History and King's College, University of Cambridge, further allowed its progress and completion. I am also very grateful to Sam and Philippa Price for allowing me to borrow Gull Cottage on several occasions when the only way forward was a bit of monastic solitude, and Sean Matthews similarly for La Cabanie.

I am indebted to a host of archivists and archival staff in southern France, among whom I should in particular mention Emmanuel Moreau in Montauban, who expended notable labour to bring various materials to my attention. I am similarly indebted to librarians and staff in the University Library in Cambridge, the British Library, the Institute of Historical Research, the Warburg Institute, the Bibliothèque nationale in Paris, and the bibliothèques/médiathèques municipales in Albi, Perpignan, and Toulouse. A particular salute also to the many unknown but heroic French colleagues who digitize a wide variety of materials for Gallica and for the CNRS's Bibliothèque virtuelle des manuscrits médiévaux (BVMM), whose generous labours made it possible to continue work on the book during the pandemic. Miklós Földváry provided me with access to the excellent Usuarium website, Rowan Dorin did similarly for his amazing Corpus Synodalium project, Régis de la Haye kindly granted me permission to use his unpublished collection of acts relating to the abbey of Moissac, and the late Noël Coulet generously supplied me with a photocopy of the transcription of the visitation of Aix discussed in Chapter 6. At a very early stage of research I benefited from practical help regarding certain archives from Jamie Corner, and at the very final stages from digital photos supplied by Ryan Low and by Matthias Bryson. I am also most grateful to Héléna Lagreou for assistance in locating the rights holders of various images. My deepest gratitude to them all.

A number of colleagues have very kindly read and commented upon draft material at various stages, including Nicole Archambeau, Wendy Davies, Adam Davis, Paul Fouracre, Caroline Goodson, Felicity Hill, Adam Kosto, Gregory Lippiatt, Rory Naismith, Nicholas Orme, and Sethina Watson. Pete Biller and Ian Forrest both read an almost-complete draft, friendship taking them well above and beyond the call of duty; this was true also of a kind and generous anonymous reader for the press. I am very grateful to Joe Canning and Pete Biller for checking Latin translations, and similarly to Giulia Boitani and Stefano Milonia for

Occitan. With regard to the latter language, I should also note various moments of assistance rendered by Bill Burgwinkle and Catherine Léglu. Any remaining errors, linguistic or otherwise, are of course entirely my own responsibility. Edwin Pritchard did sterling service copyediting the book, and I am very grateful to all at OUP for their efforts in its production.

I have benefited hugely from specific advice and discussion of particular points with many colleagues, among whom I should note in particular David Bates, Myra Bom, Elizabeth Comuzzi, Sean Curran, David d'Avray, Rowan Dorin, Hélène Debax, Jean Dunbabin, Caroline Goodson, Felicity Hill, Florence Journot, Adam Kosto, Florian Mazel, Leah Otis Cour, Sylvain Piron, Rebecca Rist, Lucy Sackville, Claire Taylor, Steve Watts, Tessa Webber, Ben Wiedemann, and Elisabeth Zadora-Rio. The project was more generally assisted by conversations with a host of academic friends in various formal and informal settings, over the last decade and more. In addition to all those mentioned above I would like to thank in particular Scott Bruce, Marie Déjoux, Simon Ditchfield, Filippo de Vivo, Claire Judde de la Rivière, Anne Lester, Charles de Miramon, Bob Moore, Eric Palazzo, Eyal Poleg, Miri Rubin, John Sabapathy, Lucy Sackville, Dan Smail, Julia Smith, Julien Théry-Astruc, Alessia Trivellone, and Alex Walsham. A workable shape for the book came into view following a key conversation with Andy Wood, and the challenge of the project was brought into focus by Frances Andrews asking me difficult questions at an early stage. (Without her intervention—'I hope that you are going to think seriously about change over time?'—the book would have been shorter, simpler, and finished much sooner; my profound thanks to her nonetheless!) I am very grateful to the editors of the book series for their encouragement and their patience as the project has slowly developed. There are undoubtedly many others to whom I also owe a debt of gratitude for conversations and thoughts, across the decade that the project has progressed; I hope any whom I have left unmentioned will forgive my blurred memory.

Finally, as ever, I am profoundly grateful to my family—my partner, Victoria Howell, and my children, Zoë and Alex—for their patience, their support, and their love.

Contents

List of Figures	xi
List of Maps	xiii
Abbreviations	xv
Conventions	xvii
Introduction	1

PART I

1. Christianity and Local Churches, c. 1000–c. 1150	23
2. Peace, Violence, and Saints, c. 1000–1150	55
3. A Re-formed Landscape, c. 1100–c. 1200	77
4. Towns and the Holy, c. 1100–c. 1250	117
5. Papal Interventions, c. 1200–c. 1320	162

PART II

6. Space and Materiality	201
7. Instruction and Storytelling	270
8. The Discipline of Belief	334
9. Negotiations of the Faith	381
10. Being Christian	430
Conclusion	468
Appendix: The New Cathar Wars	475
Bibliography	487
Index	517

List of Figures

6.1.	Campo Santo, urban burial ground, Perpignan (author's own photograph)	215
6.2.	Lady Boneta burial plaque, Campo Santo (author's own photograph)	224
6.3.	La Roquebrussanne, chapel Notre-Dame d'Inspiration (Photo © Russ—ProvenceBeyond)	229
6.4.	La Roquebrussanne new church (Saint-Saveur) (Photo © Karayuschij|Dreamstime.com)	230
6.5.	Laroque-d'Olmes old church (chapel of Saint-Roch) (author's own photograph)	233
6.6.	Laroque-d'Olmes new church (Saint-Sacrement) (author's own photograph)	234
6.7.	Retable with Virgin and Child, Angoustrine (Saint-André), 12th century (Photo © Ministère de la Culture (France), Médiathèque du patrimoine et de la photographie (objets mobiliers), tous droits réservés)	241
6.8.	Antependium, Angoustrine (Saint-André), 12th century (Photo © iMAGE Maker)	242
6.9.	Crucifix, Angoustrine (Saint-André), 12th century (Photo © Ministère de la Culture (France), Médiathèque du patrimoine et de la photographie (objets mobiliers), tous droits réservés)	245
6.10.	Crucifix, Perpignan cathedral, 13th century (Photo © iMAGE Maker)	246
6.11.	Stone capital, church of Saint-Martin, La Plaisance (author's own photograph)	249
6.12.	Christ in Majesty/Last Supper, apse, Angoustrine (Saint-André), 12th century (Photo © iMAGE Maker)	250
6.13.	Bell, Saint-Guillaume-de-Combret, 11th or 12th century (Photo © iMAGE Maker)	261

List of Maps

1. Map of the region   xviii
2. Cistercian abbeys founded in the twelfth century   95
3. Hospitaller and Templar houses founded in the twelfth century   96

(All maps created by Matilde Grimaldi; to whom, many thanks.)

Abbreviations

AASS	J. Bolland, et al., eds, *Acta sanctorum quotque toto orbe coluntur, vel à Catholicis scriptoribus celebrantur* (Antwerp: apud Ioannem Meursium, 1643–1940), 68 vols
A&B	J. H. Arnold and P. Biller, eds and trans., *Heresy and Inquisition in France, 1200–1300* (Manchester: Manchester University Press, 2016)
AD Aude	Archives départementales de l'Aude, Carcassonne
AD BdR	Archives départementales des Bouches-du-Rhône, Marseille
AD HG	Archives départementales de la Haute Garonne, Toulouse
AD P-O	Archives départementales des Pyrénées-Orientale, Perpignan
AD Tarn	Archives départementales du Tarn, Albi
AD T-et-G	Archives départementales du Tarn-et-Garonne, Montauban
AM	Archives municipales
Arnold, *Inquisition and Power*	J. H. Arnold, *Inquisition and Power: Catharism and the Confessing Subject in Medieval Languedoc* (Philadelphia: University of Pennsylvania Press, 2001)
BL	British Library, London
BM	Bibliothèque municipale
BnF	Bibliothèque nationale de France, Paris
Cart. Apt	N. Didier et al., eds, *Cartulaire de l'église d'Apt* (Paris: Libraire Dalloz, 1967)
Cart. Béziers	J. Roquette, ed., *Cartulaire de Béziers (Livre noire)* (Paris: Picard, 1918)
Cart. d'Aniane	L. Cassan and P. Alaus, eds, *Cartulaires des abbayes d'Aniane et de Gellone* (Montpellier: Jean Martel Ainé, 1900)
Cart. de la Selve	P. Ourliac, ed., *Le cartulaire de la Selve: la terre, les hommes, et le pouvoir en Rouergue au XIIe siecle* (Paris: CNRS, 1985)
Cart. Lézat	P. Ourliac and A.-M. Magnou, eds, *Cartulaire de l'abbaye de Lézat*, 2 vols (Paris: CNRS, 1984–87)
Cart. Mas-d'Azil	D. Cau-Durban, ed., *Abbaye du Mas-d'Azil. Monographie et cartulaire, 817–1774* (Foix: Veuve Pomiès, 1897)
Cart. Moissac	R. de la Haye, 'Recueil des actes de l'abbaye de Moissac, [680]–1175' (2011), unpublished pdf housed at author's website https://www.academia.edu/40493765/Recueil_des_actes_de_labbaye_de_Moissac_680_1175
Cart. Notre-Dame de Nîmes	E. Germer-Durand, ed., *Cartulaire du chapitre de l'église cathédrale Notre-Dame de Nîmes (834–1156)* (Nîmes: A. Catélan, 1874)

ABBREVIATIONS

Cart. Sainte Foi de Morlaas	L. Cadier, ed., *Cartulaire de Sainte Foi de Morlaas* (Pau: L. Ribaut, 1884)
Cart. Saint-Sernin	*Cartulaire de l'abbaye de Saint-Sernin de Toulouse (844–1200)*, ed. C. Douais (Toulouse: Privat, 1887)
Cart. S. Étienne d'Agde	R. Foreville, ed., *Cartulaire du Chapitre Cathédrale Saint-Étienne d'Agde* (Paris: CNRS, 1995)
Cart. Silvanès	P.-A. Verlaguet, ed., *Cartulaire de l'abbaye de Silvanès* (Rodez: Imprimerie Carrère, 1910)
Cart. Saint-Victor	M. Guérard, ed., *Cartulaire de l'abbaye de Saint-Victor de Marseille*, 2 vols (Paris: C. Lahure, 1857)
Cart. Templiers de Douzens	P. Gérard and E. Magnou, eds, *Cartulaires des Templiers de Douzens* (Paris: Bibliothèque nationale, 1965)
CCCM	Corpus Christianorum Continuatio Mediaevalis
CCSL	Corpus Christianorum Series Latina
CdF	*Cahiers de Fanjeaux* (Toulouse: Privat, 1966–)
Doat	BnF Collection Doat, MS number then following
Fournier	J. Duvernoy, ed., *Le registre de l'inquisition de Jacques Fournier, évêque de Pamiers (1318–1325)*, 3 vols (Toulouse: Privat, 1965)
HGL	C. Devic and J. Vaissète, eds, *Histoire générale du Languedoc*, 16 vols (1730–45. Re-edition, Toulouse: Privat, 1872–1905)
Inquisitors and Heretics	P. Biller, C. Bruschi, and S. Sneddon, eds, *Inquisitors and Heretics in Thirteenth-Century Languedoc: Edition and Translation of Toulouse Inquisition Depositions, 1273–1282* (Leiden: Brill, 2011)
Mahul, *Cart. Carcassonne*	M. Mahul, ed., *Cartulaire et archives des communes de l'ancien diocèse et de l'arrondissement administratif de Carcassonne*, 6 vols (Paris: V. Didron et Dumoulin, 1857–71)
Mansi	G. D. Mansi, ed., *Sacrorum conciliorum nova et amplissima collectio*, 53 vols (1759–98; repr. Graz: Akademische Druck- und Verlagsanstalt, 1961)
MGH	Monumenta Germaniae Historica
PL	J.-P. Migne, ed., *Patrologiae cursus completus. Series Latina*, 217 vols (Paris: J.-P. Migne, 1844–55)
RHGF	Recueil des Historiens des Gaules et de la France
W&E	W. L. Wakefield and A. P. Evans, eds, *Heresies of the High Middle Ages* (New York: Columbia University Press, 1969)

Conventions

Medieval southern France had various currencies in circulation, structured on the standard model of 12d (*denarii*, pennies) to a *sou* (a shilling, *solidus* in Latin, usually abbreviated to 'sol.' in contemporary documents), and 20 *sous* to one *livre* (*libra* in Latin, a pound in English). In the text I use d, *sous*, and *livres*, usually indicating the place of issue (most commonly Melgueil or Toulouse) where a document points it out, also noting 'marks' and other denominations of value when they are specified. It is generally understood that silver pennies and *sous* were the main coins actually in circulation, increasing in volume across the twelfth century.

In this region, notaries and other scribes usually took the year to have changed on 25 March; in the text I have attempted to regularize the ascription of year according to the modern convention of 1 January.

Place names are given in their modern French equivalent unless I have been unable to locate them, in which case they are left italicized. Personal names (almost always appearing in Latin in the archives) are for the most part given also in modern French, because this best allows cross-referencing with francophone scholarship. I do recognize that there is a counter-argument for providing Occitan names (Peire rather than Pierre, Guilhem rather than Guillaume, Joan rather than Jean, etc.), but I have opted for utility over potential authenticity. In a few instances I have rendered a name in English, where failure to do so in an anglophone text might otherwise confuse the reader over whether or not I am referring to a particularly famous figure, such as the Blessed Virgin Mary, Peter the Venerable, or Bernard of Clairvaux. I have otherwise aimed to give saints' names, including those of the apostles, in the French form, so as to harmonize with related place and church names.

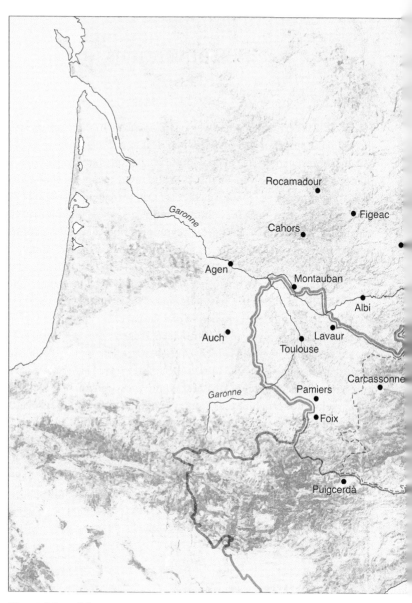

Map 1 Map of the region

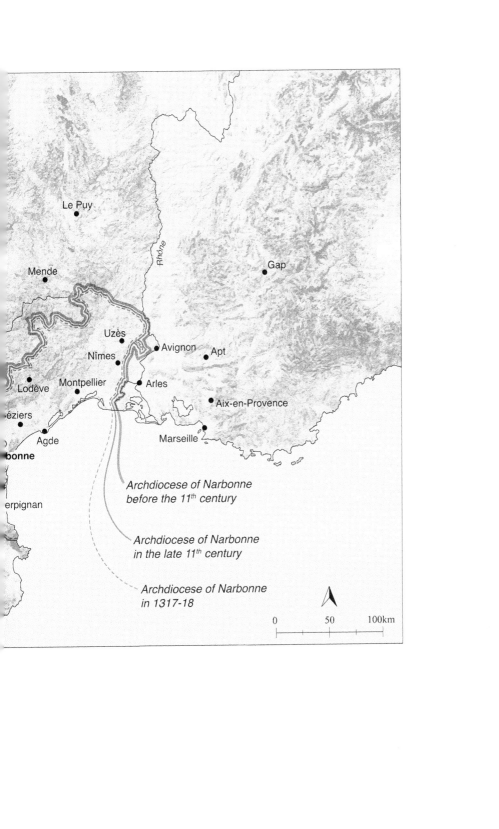

Introduction

How did Christianity change for ordinary people between the turn of the millennium and the coming of the Black Death? That is to ask, not how did the institutional structures of the Catholic Church develop, nor how Christian theology was elaborated in regard to the sacraments and morality, nor what new forms of enthusiastic piety become visible—though all of these have some bearing on the topic. It is to ask, rather, how did the fundamental experience of 'being Christian' unfold across those centuries for the vast majority of ordinary people? What changed and what continued in terms of the material contexts, the embodied experiences, the habits, ideas, norms, and expected behaviours, and the frameworks of ecclesial governance, by which non-elite lay people knew themselves to be Christian?

This book attempts to provide an answer to that opening question, for one specific region in western Europe at least. Such a project sits at the intersection of two distinct historiographical inheritances.[1] The first is the scholarly study of Christian popular religion, in works that have analysed a range of source materials within a particular time period in order to fashion a multifaceted but largely synchronic picture of the spiritual life of the laity.[2] Such studies have tended to be

---

[1] Beyond and around the strands of scholarship discussed below there are also a host of important thematic approaches to medieval religious culture. These are areas I have written about at some length elsewhere, and I shall not rehearse them in detail here: J. H. Arnold, *Belief and Unbelief in Medieval Europe* (London: Bloomsbury, 2005), particularly pp. 7–20; J. H. Arnold, 'Histories and Historiographies of Medieval Christianity', in J. H. Arnold, ed., *The Oxford Handbook of Medieval Christianity* (Oxford: Oxford University Press, 2014), pp. 23–41.

[2] Attempts to write about the dynamics of ordinary people's faith in a particular medieval time and place have a pedigree that goes back to the mid-twentieth century at least: for example, Paul Adam's *La vie paroissiale du XIVe siècle* (Paris: Sirey, 1964), based on a 1946 thesis, focused primarily on northern France; Jacques Toussaert's *Le sentiment religieux en Flandre à la fin du moyen-âge* (Paris: Plon, 1963); some portions of Emmanuel Le Roy Ladurie's famous *Montaillou* (Paris: Gallimard, 1975); Robert Brentano's *A New World in a Small Place* (Berkeley: University of California Press, 1994), a study of the diocese of Rieti, albeit one which, despite his desire to find 'the color of men's souls' (p. 4), pursues an ecclesiastical history as much as a study of popular religion; Andrew Brown's *Popular Piety in Late Medieval England* (Oxford: Oxford University Press, 1995), focused on Salisbury, important in particular for its integration of (Lollard) heresy into the mix; Katherine French's *The People of the Parish* (Philadelphia: University of Pennsylvania Press, 2001), a social history of the diocese of Bath and Wells; and, most recently, we could perhaps include Arnved Nedkvitne's *Lay Belief in Norse Society, 1000–1350* (Copenhagen: Museum Tusculanum Press, 2009). To these one might add a couple of important earlier, albeit briefer forays—Eileen Power's chapter on 'Bodo, a Frankish peasant' in her *Medieval People* (Harmondsworth: Penguin, 1924), Margaret Deanesley's 'Religion and Lay People' in her *The Pre-Conquest Church in England* (London: Oxford University Press, 1961)—and various influential early modern studies such as Michel Vovelle's *Piété baroque et dechristianisation en Provence au XVIIIe siècle* (Paris: Plon, 1973), William Christian's *Local Religion in Sixteenth-Century*

focused on the later middle ages, when written sources become richer in local detail.[3] Within this genre, since its publication in 1992, Eamon Duffy's *The Stripping of the Altars* has remained an influential example, for anglophone historians in particular.[4] Duffy's principal aim was to disabuse historians of the English post-Reformation period of the idea that late medieval Christianity was moribund, superstitious, and priest-ridden, and to present instead a vibrant picture of lay enthusiasm and engaged worship (which was then, as Duffy saw it, swept away by the upsets of the Henrician Reformation). His book has subsequently informed and inspired other medievalist work, notably prompting Augustine Thompson's substantial study of Christianity in the towns of northern Italy, which covers a similar period, and a not dissimilar region, to that addressed in this book.[5] As with those two works and others, *The Making of Lay Religion* attempts to provide a textured and detailed study of the content and practices of medieval lay Catholicism for a particular period and place.

However, whilst drawing inspiration from such studies, the current work also departs from them in important ways. There are two main issues arising with Duffy and with Thompson: in common with some other examples of the genre, neither really addresses change over time (other than in Duffy's gesturing toward a Henrician Reformation that he sees descending, undesired, from on high); and both tend to read the complexities of lay faith through the most pious lens available. 'Traditional Christianity', as they present it, is a uniform and deeply devout Catholicism that stretches back, smooth and unchanging, from the Reformation watershed, almost unmarked by internal divisions of doctrine, material resource, or social status. This stream of 'tradition' is presented as one of consistent lay enthusiasm, spiritual yearning, and observant obedience; knottier issues of doubt, disobedience, and heresy are kept largely external to the tale. In contrast, this book encompasses the heretical and the orthodox, and perhaps more importantly the quotidian, the disengaged, and the doubtful as well as the devout and enthusiastic lay Christian. It seeks to fashion a social history of religion, to think, that is, about how the practice of Christianity varied, both communally and individually,

---

Spain (Princeton: Princeton University Press, 1981), David Sabean's *Power in the Blood: Popular Culture and Village Discourse in Early Modern Germany* (Cambridge: Cambridge University Press, 1984) and David D. Hall's *Worlds of Wonder, Days of Judgement: Popular Religious Belief in Early New England* (Cambridge, Mass.: Harvard University Press, 1989). I should note also Jörg Oberste's *Religiosität und sozialer Aufstieg in der Stadt des hohen Mittelalters, Band 2: Städtische Eliten in Toulouse* (Cologne: Böhlau, 2003), the second half of which addresses the civic elite in Toulouse and some of their religious practices, albeit with 'heresy' the predominant focus.

[3] But for an important picture of ordinary people's Christianity across the high middle ages, see S. Hamilton, *Church and People in the Medieval West, 900–1200* (Harlow: Pearson, 2013); and, for an earlier period and different geography, J. Tannous, *The Making of the Medieval Middle East: Religion, Society and Simple Believers* (Princeton: Princeton University Press, 2018).

[4] E. Duffy, *The Stripping of the Altars: Traditional Religion in England, 1400–1580* (New Haven: Yale University Press, 1992; 2nd edn, 2005).

[5] A. Thompson, *Cities of God: The Religion of the Italian Communes, 1125–1325* (Philadelphia: University of Pennsylvania Press, 2005).

in its material settings. By a 'social history', I mean also that my core focus is not upon the Church as an institution, nor the spiritual extremes of Christian experience (though both may intermittently enter the frame), but rather the broad mass of people who understood themselves to be Christian. To quote the influential social historian of early modern religion John Bossy, my aim has been to write a book 'about a body of people, a way or ways of life and the features of Christian belief which seemed most relevant to them'.[6] But I have sought also to reflect further as to how we might understand a 'way of life', by exploring not only the specific propositional beliefs and associated practices with which the laity were presented, but to examine also the *modes* of belief experienced by the Christian laity; that is, to uncover the embodied practices and the range of varied material contexts, within which lay people 'did' belief.

The second historiographical inheritance for my study does address change over time, taking a diachronic and usually more geographically expansive approach: scholarship that has addressed the profound changes that the institutions of medieval Christianity underwent across the central middle ages. A host of modern studies have traced changes in ecclesial structure, and in particular the balance of ecclesiastical and secular power and authority, across this key period of 'reform'.[7] Particularly pertinent to the current study are those works which have sought to address changes in Christian piety as well as institutional change. Foundational among these is Herbert Grundmann's *Religious Movements in the Middle Ages*, first published in 1935, revised by the author in 1955, and translated into English in 1995.[8] In his analysis of the various 'new religious movements', both orthodox and heretical, Grundmann pointed in particular to how Christian symbols and ideas—those around apostolicity, most importantly—were differently adopted, interpreted, and turned into lived expressions of faith by various groups; suggesting also that such phenomena must be set within the socioeconomic developments of the twelfth and thirteenth centuries. Another study of extraordinary, and perhaps still somewhat untapped, power was Gabriel Le Bras's two-volume contribution to Fliche and Martin's *Histoire de l'Église*, concerning what Le Bras called 'institutions ecclésiastiques', meaning however not a dry 'institutional' study in the anglophone sense, but a sociological examination of

---

[6] J. Bossy, *Christianity in the West. 1400–1700* (Oxford: Oxford University Press, 1985).
[7] Within a huge bibliography, see in particular A. Fliche, *La réforme grégorienne et la reconquête chrétienne (1037–1123)*, Histoire de L'Église vol. 8 (Paris: Bloud & Gay, 1944); A. Fliche, *Du premier concile du Latran à l'avènement d'Innocent III (1123–1198)*, Histoire de L'Église vol. 9 (Paris: Bloud & Gay, 1944); M. D. Chenu, *La théologie au douzième siècle* (Paris: J. Vrin, 1957); G. Tellenbach, *The Church in Western Europe from the Tenth to the Early Twelfth Century*, trans. T. Reuter (Cambridge: Cambridge University Press, 1993); G. Constable, *The Reformation of the Twelfth Century* (Cambridge: Cambridge University Press, 1996).
[8] H. Grundmann, *Religious Movements in the Middle Ages*, trans. S. Rowan (Notre Dame, Ind.: University of Notre Dame Press, 1995). See also now J. K. Deane, ed., *Herbert Grundmann (1902–1970): Essays on Heresy, Inquisition and Literacy*, trans. S. Rowan (Woodbridge: York Medieval Press, 2019).

every aspect of the Christian Church and its constituent parts. The chronology addressed by Le Bras in those volumes is left somewhat vague, but generally hinges around the twelfth and thirteenth centuries.[9] This broad line of inheritance can be further traced across studies by Marie-Dominique Chenu, Giles Constable, Colin Morris, and others, and of particular importance is André Vauchez's characterization of the period following the Fourth Lateran Council as marked by the 'campaign of interior conversion', meaning both the extension of pastoral reform within the geographical interior of Christendom (as against the external crusading movement), but also alluding to the sense in which lay Christianity might be seen as coming eventually to engender a more 'interiorized' spirituality.[10] Most recently, Florian Mazel has produced a powerful re-analysis of the various changes that took place across western Europe between the eleventh and thirteenth centuries, and has provocatively argued that 'la réforme grégorienne' should be seen as a 'total social phenomenon' (drawing here on the anthropologist Marcel Mauss), during which were transformed not only religious ideas and institutions but political power structures and fundamental social relations.[11]

Again, my own project draws direct inspiration from these works, but also from some critique of certain approaches. Whilst they do directly address change over time, some historians have found it difficult to avoid the combination of teleology and value judgment essential to the 'reform' narrative: that what was 'reformed' was necessarily in some innate sense 'better' than what preceded it, and that the path of reform was thus an inevitable stage along the road of Christianity's predestined internal development.[12] Vauchez's 'campaign of interior conversion', for example, implicitly presents itself as the next step onward from the crusades and the Gregorian reform, a necessary and inevitable unfurling of Christianity in its historical development. Thus the 'pastoral revolution' associated with the Fourth Lateran Council tends to be seen by later historians as Christianity getting better at properly being 'Christianity'.

---

[9] G. Le Bras, *Institutions ecclésiastiques de la Chrétienté médiévale: préliminaires et 1ère partie, livre I* (Paris: Bloud & Gay, 1959); G. Le Bras, *Institutions ecclésiastiques de la Chrétienté médiévale: première partie, livres II à VI* (Paris: Bloud & Gay, 1964).

[10] Chenu, *La théologie*; G. Constable, *The Reformation of the Twelfth Century* (Cambridge: Cambridge University Press, 1996); C. Morris, *The Discovery of the Individual, 1050–1200* (London: SPCK, 1972); A. Vauchez, *La spiritualité du Moyen Âge occidental, VIIIe–XIIIe siècle* (Paris: Seuil, 1994).

[11] F. Mazel, 'Amitié et rupture de l'amitié : moines et grands laïcs provençaux au temps de la crise grégorienne (milieu XIe–milieu XIIe siècle)', *Revue historique* 307 (2005), 53–95; F. Mazel, 'Pour une redéfinition de la "réforme grégorienne"', *CdF* 48 (2013), 9–38. See further discussion in Chapter 3 below.

[12] For a useful overview and critique, see L. Melve, 'Ecclesiastical Reform in Historiographical Context', *History Compass* 13 (2015), 213–21. A number of recent anglophone studies have emphasized continuity as much as change across the central middle ages, albeit with a strongly northern European focus; for a useful overview see C. Leyser, 'Review Article: Church Reform—Full of Sound and Fury, Signifying Nothing?', *Early Medieval Europe* 24 (2016), 478–99.

Moreover, when analysis of reform moves from issues of papal/imperial power or monastic spirituality to the wider terrain of lay faith, in their attempts to explain change over time historians have not infrequently found themselves gesturing toward an inchoate and collective 'desire' or 'appetite' on the part of the laity for greater spiritual engagement. Such allusions implicitly suggest a lurking Christian *Zeitgeist*, simply awaiting its moment to be made manifest. At best, the description of emergent phenomena ('enthusiasm', 'desire', 'spiritual yearning') imply their own circular account of causation: the desire for a new mode of spirituality is somehow the sufficient cause for the new mode of spirituality, and the emergence of the new mode is itself evidence for the antecedent desire. From some avowedly Catholic modern interpretive perspectives, a key factor appears to be the workings of the Holy Spirit itself, as an 'evangelical reawakening' in the ordinary Christian population is proffered as the agent of historical change.

Such accounts certainly take *homo religiosus* seriously, as John van Engen has long encouraged medievalists so to do, and set the laity, if not centre stage, then at least actively adjacent to monastic and episcopal reformers.[13] But they will not really do from the perspective of the social historian. I am absolutely in agreement that the needs, desires, and activities of the ordinary laity mattered in the changes seen across this period, and that, indeed, there was a dialectical dynamic between ecclesiastical reform on the one hand, and lay negotiation and demand on the other, that is fundamental to how change plays out in a particular region. But there is nonetheless a danger in assuming that *homo religiosus*, in something like the form taken by later Christianity, lurks immanently in every period and place; and a tendency to take for granted that what one means by the laity being 'religious' or being engaged in 'religion' is transparent and transhistorical.

With regard to this latter point, two overlapping issues arise. One is that, as various historians have previously discussed, 'religion' and 'religious' are words that have had varied meanings in different historical and cultural contexts, and within a pre-modern lexicon do not indicate an abstract 'system' or sphere of human experience. In medieval Latin, *religiosus* used as a noun refers primarily to a member of the monastic orders; and as an adjective, in a continuation from its earlier classical sense, means something like 'rightly and diligently spiritually directed' or 'worshipful'.[14] As Pete Biller pointed out some decades ago, this does not necessarily mean that medieval people lacked any sense of an elaborated system of faith (to take one potential modern meaning of 'religion'). By the late twelfth century it is clear that words like *fides* (faith) and *lex* (law) could be used in something like that fashion, to talk about faiths other than Christianity:

---

[13] J. van Engen, 'The Christian Middle Ages as an Historiographical Problem', *American Historical Review* 91 (1986), 519–52.
[14] J. Bossy, 'Some Elementary Forms of Durkheim', *Past & Present* 95 (1982), 3–18; P. Biller, 'Words and the Medieval Notion of "Religion"', *Journal of Ecclesiastical History* 36 (1985), 351–69.

Judaism, Islam, and on occasion divergent Christian heresies.[15] So we need not be imprisoned by a historical vocabulary here, any more than if we wish to discuss 'society' or 'gender' or 'politics'. But we may still wish firstly to note the likely emphasis of all such medieval terminology, which tends toward a sense of exterior performance, thus retaining something of the antique meaning of 'right worship'. We can also recall that Biller further suggested that the twelfth and thirteenth centuries may constitute a hinge point in western Christianity's awareness of itself as one faith confronted by others, and thus that there might be change over time within the period addressed here. We need moreover to be wary of allowing a modern conception of what 'religion' encompasses and involves—a conception of what it *ought to* encompass and involve—covertly to colour our understanding of what pertains in past centuries.

The second issue, leading on from that last point, is that, as again various scholars have noted, 'religion' as a second-order abstraction (of the kind that allows the comparative study of 'religions', for example) is a modern category, and one that can be argued to invent the scholarly boundaries of the thing it purports to describe.[16] Moreover, modern conceptions of 'religion' tend to be marked in western European scholarship by a perspective that defaults to Christianity and perhaps to certain aspects of modern, western Protestant Christianity in particular (regardless of the personal faith convictions of any specific author). They thus often take certain abstract features almost for granted: that a faith's address to all people 'of that religion' will aspire to be universal and uniform (other perhaps than regarding issues of gender); that whilst 'religious' tenets may enjoin certain positive social acts of engagement or care for others, religion itself is a sphere of human activity separable from other aspects of society, economy, and politics, 'religion' being the opposite or counterpoint of the 'secular'; that it thus in some sense belongs to, or constitutes, a kind of private sphere, distinct from other aspects of law and governance; and that at its core is an individual and interiorized spiritual experience, something either deeply experienced or at least persistently immanent to all people 'of that religion'.[17] It is not that historians of the middle ages necessarily assume all of these features to be present in medieval Christianity, but rather that these features lurk in a dispositive mood, as conceptualizations of what religion 'should be', mapped teleologically toward their future unfolding.

---

[15] Biller, 'Words', pp. 363–69.

[16] J. Z. Smith, 'Religion, Religions, Religious', in M. C. Taylor, ed., *Critical Terms for Religious Studies* (Chicago: University of Chicago Press, 1998), pp. 269–84; J. Z. Smith, '"Religion" and "Religious Studies": No Difference At All', *Soundings: An Interdisciplinary Journal* 71 (1988).

[17] See among various wider discussions P. Collinson, 'Religion, Society and the Historian', *Journal of Religious Studies* 23 (1999), 149–67; D. R. Peterson and D. Walhof, eds, *The Invention of Religion: Rethinking Belief in Politics and History* (New Brunswick, NJ: Rutgers University Press, 2002); C. Caldwell Ames, 'Medieval Religious, Religions, Religion', *History Compass* 10 (2012), 334–52; B. Nongbri, *Before Religion: A History of a Modern Concept* (New Haven: Yale University Press, 2015).

The 'Making' of 'Lay Religion'

In response to these issues, some historians and anthropologists have called for a clearer definition of what one means by 'religion' when attempting such analyses; Gavin Langmuir, for example, suggests distinguishing between 'religion' as the explicit sets of practices and beliefs which people in authority prescribe and require of others, and 'religiosity' as the 'dominant pattern or structuring of non-rational thinking' and the 'conduct associated with it', which 'the individual trusts to establish, extend and preserve consciousness of his or her identity'.[18] This has the potential benefit of distinguishing between a system (that can itself change over time) and the complexities of human experience in any given social situation. In my use of 'religion' in the title of this book I am in part gesturing toward the conceptualization he proffers regarding authority: that it is across this period that Christianity as a system comes to establish sustained and elaborated prescriptions and requirements for ordinary lay people; that the Christian 'religion' thus comes to embrace them and to demand things of them in a way largely not seen hitherto.

However, it seems to me that in Langmuir's distinction between religion and religiosity, the presence of a modern set of ideas about what 'religion' fundamentally is (or ought to be) still lurks, albeit relabelled: 'religiosity' is presented as a universal and transhistorical dynamic that is individual, interiorized, and concerned with identity. I am not arguing that medieval Christianity could not have those dynamics; rather, that we should not assume that they are always already present, but that part of what 'religion' may do is precisely to evoke and inculcate such elements and bring them into play. One contention of this book is that such an interiorized, individualized dynamic—focused in part on the dangers of 'sin' but also on engendering an increasingly affective (sensory, emotional) faith—did indeed become extended to the whole Christian laity, from around the later twelfth century onward. Some historians would see such a historical shift to 'religious interiority' as not occurring until the fifteenth or sixteenth centuries; others might object that it can exist very much earlier, as most obviously in the writings of Augustine of Hippo. In response, one might note that phenomena can long exist marginally and *in potentia* before they become, or are made, a more general and thus 'social' feature. Moreover, the extension to a wider community of believers of such dynamics does not imply subsequent stasis: the 'making of' does not imply 'completion'. Nor, importantly, are either 'interiority' or 'individuality' binary choices necessarily set against 'externality' and 'community': the former are elements that Christianity *gains* in particular ways for the great mass of believers; they do not necessarily displace other existent dynamics. There certainly are

---

[18] G. I. Langmuir, *History, Religion and Antisemitism* (Berkeley: University of California Press, 1990), p. 162.

further shifts in late medieval, and of course post-medieval, modes of Christian piety.[19] None of these periods saw 'the discovery of the individual' in a teleological sense. The point is that they each developed their own discursive structures and practical regimes within which interiorized (and in some sense 'individualized') Christian selfhood was manifested.[20]

My thinking about how to conceptualize 'religion' is further influenced by the anthropologist Talal Asad, whose work on Christianity (including medieval Christianity) and Islam has occasionally informed some other notable discussions of the issues.[21] Asad emphasizes that any attempted universal definition of 'religion' is necessarily prey to a circularity that fails to recognize the conditions of its own possibility: that the phenomena one may attempt to gather together within such a definition are themselves produced and policed by the institutions, cultural schema, and power structures that set about constituting a particular 'religious' system. For example, deciding what is 'religious' rather than 'secular' will turn out always to be dependent on some antecedent idea of how 'the secular' or the 'non-spiritual' or so forth is constituted in a particular time and place. Moreover, Asad suggests, these are not emergent natural or random features, but are essential elements within particular power dynamics, 'power' understood not as 'repressive authority' but in a more supple Foucauldian sense as discursive regimes which generate demands and possibilities, seek to produce classifications and knowledge, and thus make possible—sometimes imposing, but perhaps as often *proffering*—particular identities (or 'subjectivities' in a Foucauldian sense). For Asad, then, 'religion' is always a discursive field of power, and our use of it as a term must recognize it as something brought about—'made'—in a particular historical and cultural context.

In an Asadian mode, this book argues, then, that the period under study did indeed see a growth in lay enthusiasm, and moreover a notable growth in certain interiorized and individualized experiences of belief for the ordinary laity; but, however, that these were not straightforwardly pre-existent features, awaiting the right historical moment to be made manifest, but were an extension to the whole mass of the laity of a discourse of Christianity that evoked, framed, and thus made possible such features. It was equally, and by the same process, a period that saw the growth of 'heresies'—divergent choices driven by enthusiasm for apostolic models of holiness and the promise of salvation, labelled heretical by orthodox authority. But perhaps most importantly it was a period that brought to

---

[19] Particularly influential on later scholarship is the work of Jean Delumeau, who identified medieval roots for what he nonetheless sees as an early modern development toward interiority: J. Delumeau, *Le péché et la peur: la culpabilisation en Occident (XIIIe-XVIIIe siècles)* (Paris: Fayard, 1983).
[20] For an important similar argument for late medieval religion in England, see J. Bryan, *Looking Inward: Devotional Reading and the Private Self in Late Medieval England* (Philadelphia: University of Pennsylvania Press, 2007).
[21] T. Asad, *Genealogies of Religion: Discipline and Reasons of Power in Christianity and Islam* (Baltimore: Johns Hopkins University Press, 1993); see, for example, Caldwell Ames, 'Medieval Religious, Religions, Religion'.

the whole mass of believers a framework within which they could be 'worse' or 'better' Christians, or indeed could locate themselves—or be located by others—within a spectrum of implied gradations therein. As the period unfolded, ordinary people could attempt to be *good* Christians, in terms of their obedient practice but also increasingly in terms of their inner disposition. These elements moreover changed over time, due to a confluence of factors. These include, for example, 'reformist' ideas within the Christian church hierarchy, the extension of papal authority, the reworking of relations between ecclesial authority and political power (the latter having a particular importance for southern France). Thus elements of an ecclesiastical history necessarily inform the study, particularly in Part I of the book. But I also argue that across the period, changes to the features of Christianity were themselves, in part at least, *social* in nature. That is, the material conditions, embodied experiences, and individual or collective agency of ordinary people were part of what prompted and constituted changes in the nature of Christianity as a lived faith, between the millennium and the Black Death.

Thus the process by which such change came about was not purely a top-down imposition of a particular power structure or governing discourse. Those elements were certainly present; this was, as we shall see, a period in which 'inquisition into heretical wickedness' intervened into the lives of ordinary lay people on a notable scale in southern France. But such interventions from 'above' met particular conditions on the ground, and were confronted by various desires, negotiations, and challenges from 'below'. As western Christianity extended the depth of its engagement with every lay Christian, so did it encounter the varied complexity of those people and their responses; and those people, most frequently encountering 'the Church' in its more specific representative of the local priest, not only engaged with but further elaborated upon and chose within the available forms and meanings of Christian worship. Their choices and challenges fed back into the ecclesiastical hierarchy, prompting further response. At one extreme that response might involve further inquisitorial discipline, but more broadly could inform the elaboration of spiritual and pastoral advice that bishops provided to parish priests, better to serve their flocks. It is in this sense then that I address the 'making' of lay 'religion': not as a new stage on an inevitable journey toward a pre-ordained *telos*, but an enquiry that adopts a particular definition of a critical term ('religion' defined in an Asadian sense) in order to explore the contours of how it came about across a particular period.

...in 'Southern France'

In pursuing this project, I have restricted myself to a geographical region: what we would now call southern France, but which in the central medieval period had no clear, singular designation. The area studied reaches up from the Mediterranean, and it is important to note that it was very much part of the wider Mediterranean world, something sometimes elided by some modern scholarship that has been more focused on the emergence of 'France' as a nation. The people of southern France shared a common vernacular language, 'Occitan' or 'Provençal' in modern parlance, which itself transmitted a common courtly culture and was used comfortably alongside Latin in a host of administrative documents from an early date.[22] In my studies I have mostly stayed beyond the borders of Gascony to the west (just occasionally straying into the eastern part of that region when a particular set of sources have proved too tempting) and have kept my analytical focus primarily within about 150 km of the Mediterranean coast, going no further north than Rocamadour, Mende, Le Puy, and Valence, in each case briefly lured that far by particularly useful textual material. To the east, the areas around Marseille, Aix, Montpellier, Manosque, and Gap provide a necessarily indistinct border. The modern regions of Languedoc-Roussillon and Provence cover most of the area traversed overall; in the medieval period much of it was within the archdiocese of Narbonne, though politically (up to the mid-thirteenth century at least) it was further fragmented between various different counts. (See Map 1.)

Further below, I will say a bit more regarding that landscape—its political, socioeconomic, and literal features—but I will firstly set out why I have chosen a regional focus. Having written in a previous book about the Christian laity across a wide but mostly undifferentiated geography and chronology, one aim here is to allow a more detailed focus that can incorporate specific socioeconomic features, and can address change over time with regard to particular sociopolitical circumstances. Part of what I suggest is that whilst what I have chosen to call the 'making of lay religion' occurred across all of western Christendom, those 'makings' varied in their precise details, timings, and emphases. This is likely most visible within a particular region, more than within a kingdom or 'nation' (the latter almost certainly importing a modern geography and assumptions about statehood onto a medieval landscape). In the case of southern France, a very clear variant factor was the papacy's apprehension of 'heresy', in the form of the Albigensian Crusade (1209–29) and the subsequent imposition of inquisition into heretical wickedness. But other local factors also pertained, including, for example, the continuous presence and growth of mercantile activity both within and to markets beyond the region, the fragmented nature of local lordship, and—from the later twelfth century onward—the strong degree of a self-consciously 'civic' ideology found even in very small settlements. These features are not unique to southern France, but they do combine in a particular way in that region.

The point is in any case not to single out southern France as a unique case, but rather to seek to demonstrate that a regional focus may bring certain dynamics

---

[22] I am aware that there are fine gradations made by linguistic scholars between and within these vernaculars; but would note that vernacular materials travelled easily across the whole region, and that the distinctions were probably not hugely present to medieval Occitan speakers themselves.

into clearer view. Thus whilst we are no longer in the post-antique world of 'micro-Christendoms' memorably described by Peter Brown, there is a utility to emphasizing what regional variation still pertains, as the Christian Church extended its dominion.[23] I have therefore attempted intermittently throughout the book to indicate briefly how certain features found in southern France might compare or contrast with other regions with which I have some familiarity, such as England, northern France, Catalonia, and northern Italy. Such comparisons, it should be emphasized, are meant only suggestively, as an invitation to further reflection. There is, moreover, a rich existing scholarship, almost entirely in the form of articles and chapters, on orthodox religion in southern France in this period, much of it the product of the annual 'colloque de Fanjeaux', and I am deeply indebted to that body of work. My hope is also in part to make it more visible to scholarship elsewhere in Europe, further to facilitate more collective comparative analysis.

I noted 'heresy' as a particular feature in southern France (though we should recall that it is by no means the only part of western Christendom to have certain pious enthusiasms thus labelled). Additional motives for focusing on this region arise from that topic. One is to try to provide a broader context for 'heresy' within the orthodox religious ideas and practices of the region, to show indeed that 'heresy' thus named is not the only element of popular religion that one might address when considering southern France in the high middle ages. Within anglophone historiography on southern France, the study of heresy has very strongly predominated, something also true albeit to a lesser extent in francophone study. But there is more that can be said, as this book attempts to show. This is not intended to diminish or marginalize the importance of heresy and its repression, however interpreted; but it is intended to make more visible additional topics that can be studied from the rich documentary sources, including, indeed, the sources produced by inquisition.

A word then about sources. These are, as noted, very rich, though they have their own lacunae. There are almost no diocesan visitation records extant within the region until the 1340s, and whilst there are some very useful (and in the cases of Ste Foy and Our Lady of Rocamadour, very famous) sets of twelfth-century *miracula*, the only canonization materials I have used are those relating to St Louis of Toulouse. Archaeological studies have been invaluable, though in comparison to some other areas of Europe, it has been frustrating that the remains of material culture are often very hard now to locate. The available sources of course vary across time: before the late twelfth century, the vast bulk of documentary material is drawn from monastic cartularies, saints' *vitae* and the aforesaid *miracula* collections, and ecclesiastical councils. When trying to reconstruct the experience of

---

[23] P. Brown, *The Rise of Western Christendom: Triumph and Diversity, A.D. 200–1000* (Oxford: Blackwell, 1996).

Christianity in local churches, we are particularly dependent on monastic collections of charters; as we will see in Chapters 1 and 3, in particular, it is possible to use such cartularies to glean important glimpses about local experience, but the archival frame undoubtedly conceals much from our view.

From the late twelfth century onward similar materials still pertain, but others come also to the fore, including chronicle accounts connected to the crusade, inquisition registers, civic customs and other records, and a variety of notarial documents recording inquiries and the conclusion of disputes. Wills exist, sparsely in the early centuries but in much greater number by the late thirteenth century. By the mid-thirteenth century, a variety of other pastoral materials grow in considerable profusion, from short guides for confessors to collections of preaching *exempla* collated in southern France, to great treatises that seek to address all manner of issues regarding the Christian faith. Every genre of source, and to some extent every individual document, of course has its own 'source-critical' questions, requiring the historian to think carefully and imaginatively over how best to read for nuance and how one might discern multiple voices behind the written record. My aim throughout has been to make such issues visible, but not overwhelming; to create a synthesis from this profusion of materials, but a synthesis which communicates the complex texture therein.

Religious Change in Southern France

Part I of this book addresses in some detail how Christianity changed in various ways in southern France across the period 1000–1350, taking the arrival of the Black Death (in truth perhaps arriving as early as 1347 in this region) as a terminus. This does not imply that the coming of the plague necessarily ended or altered the previous situation; rather, it recognizes that to extend the picture much beyond that point would require considerable further exploration of post-plague continuity and change, and that this is impractical within the confines of one already somewhat lengthy book. Similarly, to take the year 1000 as a beginning point does not imply that no changes precede that moment, but rather that the same issue of scope pertains: a full discussion of the shifts from Carolingian to post-Carolingian Christianity would require yet further space.

It may be helpful to set out some important features of the region, and it is important also to address briefly some existing narratives regarding historical change that affect it. Geographically southern France is an area of quite notable contrasts, between major mountain ranges—bordered on the west by the Pyrenees, the east by the Alps, and with *les montagnes noires* in the middle—and riparian flat lands. Major rivers connect the Mediterranean basin northwards, and the region was familiar with a high degree of extra-regional traffic, from trade networks to the major pilgrimage routes into the Iberian and Italian peninsulas and on to the Holy Lands. The lands in between were home to farming of various kinds—animal husbandry, cereal growing, arboriculture—and then, as now, it was peppered with thousands of small vineyards, providing a regional, and then in the thirteenth century international, trade in viticulture.[24] In addition to the great cities—Marseille, Narbonne, Toulouse, Perpignan, each with a past reaching back to Roman antiquity—there were many smaller towns and villages, some (from perhaps the eleventh century onward) encircled by stone walls and self-designating as *castra* (*castrum* in the singular), a term which I retain in its Latin form throughout the book, to avoid the confusion arising if one translates it inaccurately as 'castle'. As with elsewhere in Europe, major population growth in the twelfth and thirteenth century saw both the expansion of existing settlements, and the creation of many new ones; there are a plethora of places called 'Villeneuve' throughout the region, and other towns also—such as Montauban—that we know were founded by lordly fiat in that period. Such towns and *castra*, even when really quite small, frequently adopted a self-consciously 'civic' identity, with elected 'consuls' facilitating local self-governance, under the higher auspices of lordly dominion.[25] Trade and commerce were commonplace and widespread, and were probably a factor in the swift adoption of aspects of Roman law. *Lo codi*, an Occitan translation of Justinian's *Institutes*, dates from the later twelfth century, for example, and it is from around that date that we see the rapid spread of notaries within the region, making documentary culture quite readily available, even fairly far down the social scale, by the first quarter of the thirteenth century.

The region did not belong to one kingdom nor did it have any independent political unity. At different points various monarchs laid the claim of overlordship over various parts, including the kings of England, France, Aragon, and Mallorca, whilst the German emperor exercised notional suzerainty over Provence, a region more directly ruled (until 1245) by a cadet branch of the counts of Barcelona. The situation further changed in the mid-thirteenth century, in the aftermath of the 1229 treaty that concluded the Albigensian Crusade, in which the count of Toulouse, whilst allowed to retain comital authority, surrendered control of the county after his death (which came in 1247). Thus the Capetian monarchy extended its reach southwards: fairly directly in the case of the south-west, indirectly via Charles d'Anjou (who became count of Provence in 1246) in the south-east. But different parts of the region came under direct Capetian control at different specific dates, and the extent of that control—for example, the ability of the French crown to raise tax from certain cities—remained, in practical terms, rather uncertain even into the following century. For much of the period under

---

[24] P. Wolff, *Commerces et marchands de Toulouse (vers 1350–vers 1450)* (Paris: Plon, 1954), première partie.
[25] Fundamental works include J. H. Mundy, *Liberty and Political Power in Toulouse, 1050–1230* (New York: Columbia University Press, 1954); M. Bourin-Derruau, *Villages médiévaux en Bas-Languedoc*, 2 vols (Paris: L'Harmattan, 1987).

study here, political power was held at a regional level by a number of different counts, predominantly the counts of Toulouse in the south-west and the counts of Provence in the south-east, but also others, including the counts of Foix, of Orange, of Comminges, of Forcalquier, and the Trencavel family who were at various points viscounts of Carcassonne, Albi, Béziers, Nîmes, and Razès. Particularly in the eleventh and twelfth centuries but to some extent thereafter also, the archbishop and bishops of the region were also major political actors, as indeed were some abbots, in the earlier period through their family connections to the great comital houses, in the thirteenth century sometimes through their relations to the papacy. Finally, the great cities also gained independent stature (with, admittedly, some major setbacks) in the twelfth and thirteenth centuries. None of this political fragmentation, one should note against some earlier historiography, was the cause or facilitator of heresy. It did, however, complicate how bishops could exercise their authority, how the papacy intervened, and indeed how effectively or otherwise inquisition into heretical wickedness could operate at various points in time (as is explored further in Chapters 4 and 5).

Because of the wider social frame to my analysis, it is useful to address briefly a further set of influential historiographical narratives that relate particularly to the earlier period here studied. These narratives are not limited to southern France, but—particularly in some earlier francophone scholarship—have extended a particular embrace to the region. They can be presented as three interlocking 'big stories': the Crisis of Feudalism; the Peace of God; and the Gregorian Reform. The way in which these stories interlock can be related as follows (here adopting, I should emphasize, an element of caricature). Firstly, 'Feudalism': once there was the Carolingian Empire, which provided central rule and justice, and supported the Church. But in the tenth century, that empire fell, and, it has been claimed, the loss of central authority led to a kind of anarchy, as local powerful laymen came to style themselves as 'knights' and 'lords', built castles, and exercised forms of local jurisdiction that subjugated the local peasantry, making those who were previously freeholders into unfree 'serfs' (*servi*). This loss of central authority has sometimes been seen as peculiarly visible either side of the Pyrenees, in Catalonia and Languedoc.

Two things, it is further claimed, then came to ameliorate this sorry and frequently violent situation. One was the formation of affective bonds between lords and vassals, where the former would grant the latter land or office in the form of a 'fief' (*feudum*) in exchange for service, their special relationship sealed by a ritual of homage, thus binding men of this class together in a pyramidal hierarchy. The other (to turn to our second story, 'The Peace of God') was the intervention of the Church, which in the eleventh century in particular forged a new form of 'Peace' by holding large assemblies at which, in part through the presence of holy relics and in part through popular demand, knights were forced to swear oaths to limit their violence. The want of central authority continued to be a problem, but further steps toward a better situation were made when (to invoke the third story) the reforms implemented by Pope Gregory VII in the later eleventh century empowered the Church to wrest back from the hands of these lay lords the various local churches they had usurped and unjustly seized. Through these means, it is suggested, a more uniform and civilizing Christian ideology could be disseminated once again, bringing moral reform to society. The threat and use of violence, including violence against the people and possessions of the Church, was fundamental within this emerging system; and it is the widely distributed and unregulated use of violence that distinguishes this 'feudal' system from the 'monopoly' that earlier and later states held over the legitimate use of physical force (as Max Weber influentially put it). The Church's efforts therefore to regain its autonomy and to promote 'peace' are the necessary and equally fundamental complement, and a key stage 'onward' in 'western civilization'.

As said, I here somewhat caricature the historiographical tradition; but with some justification, and in order to point up the following issues that have a bearing on what follows in this book. In regard to the first narrative, that of 'feudal revolution', or 'mutation' or 'anarchy': whilst lordship, landholding, and changes in social structure are not my primary focus, they cannot be ignored, for they are intimately connected to a number of aspects of how Christianity operated within this landscape. But there are interpretive problems here also. The first is that whilst some elements of the sociopolitical changes described above are present in our region, it is not clear that they all come together into a new social 'system' as such, nor that they necessarily show us a world notably more or less fragmented than it was previously.[26] On the one hand, one can definitely see the growth of defensive towers, fortified settlements, and the like throughout the region, the appearance in the eleventh century of people named as *milites* in the surviving sources, some such people 'having men' in a way that implies some oath-forged relationship. Whilst north of the Pyrenees (in contrast to Catalonia) charters in the early eleventh century still sometimes mention 'the king', it is true that they record the settlement of disputes via horizontal agreements made in the hands or presence of one or more mediators, such as bishops, rather than via royal

---

[26] The fundamental critique of 'feudalism' as a reified system is S. Reynolds, *Fiefs and Vassals* (Oxford: Blackwell, 1994), and the most important recent intervention is C. West, *Reframing the Feudal Revolution* (Cambridge: Cambridge University Press, 2014), following various important contributions by Dominic Barthélemy. A spirited attempt to make southern France fit the feudalism model is presented by H. Débax, *Le féodalité languedocien: serments, hommages et fiefs dans le Languedoc des Trencavel (XIe-XIIe siècles)* (Toulouse: Presses universitaires du Mirail, 2003), where the weight of her discussion has to rest mostly on the 'oaths' element of her title, in the absence, as she notes, of much homage or fief-holding. For a subtly different view, see F. L. Cheyette, *Ermengarde of Narbonne and the World of the Troubadours* (Ithaca, NY: Cornell University Press, 2001) and the nuanced emphasis on varied sociopolitical structures presented in F. Mazel, *Féodalités, 888–1180* (Paris: Belin, 2010). Without subscribing to the central thesis of the book, I find very useful the concept and discussion of 'lordship' in T. Bisson, *The Crisis of the Twelfth Century* (Princeton: Princeton University Press, 2009).

authority. We see clear evidence of people of servile status who can be given as donations to monasteries, and eleventh-century charters tend to record land transfers via 'surrenders' or gifts rather than via straightforward contracts of sale.[27] On the other hand: southern France is notable for the growth of *castra*—walled settlements—as much as 'castles', and many of these had two, three, or even four co-lords, which at the very least complicates the notion of rapacious individual lordship.[28] Moreover, the walling or fortification of settlements occurs across the whole period, with a lot happening in the late twelfth century, rather than in the classic period of 'feudal crisis'. As already noted, a number of important cities founded in the classical period continued to operate as centres of political power. Moreover, in southern France in particular, it has been suggested that Carolingian royal authority had already fragmented by the late ninth century, whilst leaving in place a fair degree of its legal and fiscal apparatus, albeit operated at a more local level in a more diffuse fashion. It is thus not clear to what extent a further transition was happening in the eleventh century.[29]

'Surrenders' of land and gifts do suggest a different notion of recording property transfer, but the presence of counter-payments 'in charity'—what modern anthropologists might call counter-gifts—plus the possibility of later reclaiming or indeed re-gifting the same bit of land, do not support a straightforward notion of a 'feudal' relationship, with the lesser party dependent entirely on the whims of the person bestowing the land. The word *feudum* ('fief' in modern English translation) is found infrequently in southern French documentation, and I have most often encountered it applied to the bundle of rights and lands associated with a local church, rather than land given for military or labour service. *Honor* (plural *honores*) is probably the most common label applied to parcels of lands, properties, and rights, and its meaning is extraordinarily flexible.[30] A similar point could be made regarding the peasantry: the term 'serf' (*servus*) is almost never found in southern France, and a study by Mireille Mousnier identified such a range of words, attached to a great variety of situations, that no clear taxonomy of 'freedom' or 'unfreedom' seems possible. Most frequently, when making a gift of another human being, charters talk of 'my man/woman' (*homo meus*), very often

---

[27] M. Bourin-Derruau, 'Le Bas-Languedoc', in M. Zimmermann, ed., *Les sociétés méridionales autour de l'an mil* (Paris: CNRS, 1992), pp. 55–106; Pierre Bonnassie, 'L'espace "Toulousain" (Toulousain, Comminges, Quercy, Rouergue, Albigeois)', ibid., pp. 107–45.

[28] See now H. Débax, *La seigneurie collective: pairs, pariers, paratge, les coseigneurs du XI au XII siècle* (Rennes: Presses Universitaires de Rennes, 2012).

[29] A. R. Lewis, *The Development of Southern French and Catalan Society, 718–1050* (Austin: University of Texas Press, 1965), pp. 104–13; Lewis argues for a further turn to knightly domination in the late tenth century, but notes that this flows on from the same families that had been dominating the region in the later Carolingian period (though some of his analysis of change also rests upon mistakenly interpreting all mentions of *castra* to indicate lordly 'castles').

[30] See E. Magnou-Nortier, *La société laïque et l'église dans la province ecclésiastique de Narbonne (zone cispyrénéenne) de la fin du VIIIe à la fin du XIe siècle* (Toulouse: Associations des Publications de l'Université de Toulouse-Le Mirail, 1974), pp. 350–51.

then naming them.[31] These are clearly not 'free' men and women, and often their existing or future offspring are also gifted, indicating that their lack of freedom is understood to persist beyond their individual person. But what their servile status further implies—agricultural labour, annual payments in kind or in money, supporting military service directly or indirectly, ability or inability to alienate their own property, and so forth—is often unclear, and certainly varied greatly from person to person and place to place. Moreover, other charters in which servile people are mentioned are more clearly gifts of the *land*, on which the named unfree person resides—making it less clear whether they were forever bound to that servitude, or whether they were more like a sitting tenant. To give one example of the complexities, we can note a charter from the third or fourth decade of the twelfth century, in which Raimond de Marliac gave to Guillaume, abbot of Lézat, a man called Amiel de Marliac, the gift of this Amiel said to be 'with the counsel and will of the same Amiel', who then 'confirming the gift in this same hour, placed his hands in the hands of the abbot...and gave himself to the aforesaid abbot'.[32] It is not clear whether Amiel was a servile labourer or someone of a higher social rank who would provide service to the abbot—perhaps more probably the latter, since across the course of one sentence Amiel apparently turns from someone who is 'given' to someone who can 'confirm' the gift that he himself comprises.

In short, whilst there clearly was change from the period of Carolingian rule, it is not clear that what subsequently arose can be characterized as a singular social system, and it is certainly not well described by an appeal to a notion of a 'feudal' pyramidical hierarchy, to which a mirrored conception of 'the Church' can be either opposed or integrated. This is the key point with regard to the focus of this book: we cannot simply see 'the Church' as an indisputably sovereign entity that was always heroically struggling to gain its rightful independence from rapacious secular powers and to mitigate their secular misbehaviour. If we look at the sociopolitical landscape of southern France in the period 1000–1150, we might ask, not 'how did the Church reform this fragmented society?', but rather 'what forms did Christianity take in this uneven landscape of lordship?' That is the concern of Chapter 1. To understand the nature of Christianity in southern France in the eleventh and early twelfth century, we are thus not particularly helped by adopting wholesale a notion of 'feudal mutation' or 'feudal anarchy' which Christianity had to tame and 'civilize'. The Peace of God movement, for example—further explored in Chapter 2—frequently involved the direct participation of major

---

[31] M. Mousnier, '*Dono unum hominem meum*: désignations de la dépendance du XIe au XIIIe siècle en Languedoc occidental', *Mélanges de l'École française de Rome: Moyen Âge* 111/1 (1999), 51–60. Nothing in her otherwise useful discussion appears to support her conclusion that 'La personnalité du lien est fortement affirmée: le rapport est établi entre deux personnes, en vertu de la naissance ou de la volonté.'
[32] *Cart. Lézat*, I, p. 83 (no. 108).

secular lords as well as bishops and saintly relics, and (to follow arguments made by some other modern revisionist historians) the protection of monastic and episcopal lands, and indeed the 'Peace' itself, in part involved the exercise of violent force in the service of the Church.

Moreover, the claims of later ecclesiastical reformers to be rescuing church property and worship from the hands of rapacious lords can obscure several important qualifications. One is to note how much of that 'property' comprised not places of worship but local agricultural resources such as fields, farms, mills, irrigation rights, and so forth, where the local monastery or priory or cathedral was one participant in what was essentially a struggle between different powerful agricultural producers. Another is that where the 'property' was a local church and its attached rights, these were frequently in fact created by local lords themselves (as we shall further explore in Chapter 1); the 'surrenders' of such goods were a particular way of presenting what we might otherwise see as gifts, relating to churches that were never previously held by the local monastery or cathedral. Moreover, as Stéphen Weinberger pointed out some decades ago, where we do see ecclesiastical properties 'seized' by local lords, these could often constitute disputed inheritances, where a parent or grandparent had gifted to the Church goods that their descendants saw as part of a familial inheritance.[33] I shall return to the issue of reform in Chapter 3, in part following Florian Mazel's analysis of how it dislocated ties between the aristocracy and the older monastic orders, then exploring what new features this permitted to appear within the landscape of southern France.

At this point we might usefully reflect upon yet another historiographical 'big story', the Capetian domination of the south. This is a tale that tends to follow one of two well-worn lines: as part of the necessary story of French nationhood, uniting a people who were always destined to be joined; or as a colonial project that erased a precious but somewhat fragile 'foreign' culture that it neither valued nor understood.[34] That the Capetians *did* come to dominate the south is of course true, but as already noted above it did not happen at a stroke in 1229 nor even upon the death of Raimond VII of Toulouse. Motivation for crusade—most notably in the case of its initial co-leader, Count Simon de Montfort—clearly included the desire to acquire new lands, alongside more pious elements; but the outcomes in the longer term were not straightforwardly 'colonial' in the full sense of importing new settlers (unlike, for example, England's domination of Wales).[35]

[33] S. Weinberger, 'Les conflits entre clercs et laïcs dans la Provence du XI siècle', *Annales du Midi* 92 (1980), 269–79.
[34] Contrast P. Belperron, *La croisade contre les Albigeois* (Paris: Pion, 1942); M. G. Pegg, *A Most Holy War: The Albigensian Crusade and the Battle for Christendom* (Oxford: Oxford University Press, 2008).
[35] M. Aurell, G. Lippiatt, and L. Macé, eds, *Simon de Montfort (c. 1170–1218): le croisé, son lignage et son temps* (Turnhout: Brepols, 2020), chapters by Lippiatt and Vincent in particular; J. Given, *State and Society in Medieval Europe: Gwynedd and Languedoc under Outside Rule* (Ithaca, NY: Cornell University Press, 1990), particularly chapter 4.

And whilst the papacy, via crusade and then inquisition, did intervene very directly in the region, the practical exercise of ecclesiastical authority following the crusade—the activities of bishops and mendicants in particular—was not so much imposed by northern French from 'without' but in the main conducted by those indigenous to southern France itself. What all of this meant for the experience of the ordinary laity, in the context also of increased urbanization, the emergence of new pious foundations and the like, is explored in Chapters 4 and 5. The chapters in Part I of the book thus trace a series of changes across the period c. 1000–c. 1320, looping back over some of the chronology where necessary to bring a theme more clearly into view, in each area keeping the main focus on the effects of these changes on local Christianity and ordinary people, and vice versa.

Lived Christianity in Southern France

Part II of this book adopts a more fully thematic approach, and whilst it ranges broadly across the centuries covered, the greater focus rests upon the thirteenth and early fourteenth centuries. In pursuing a social history of Christianity, I am informed by the wider legacy of works that have addressed the cultural and embodied aspects of faith. To adopt a term that originates in francophone scholarship (the work of Gabriel Le Bras in particular), we might call this approach a focus on *la religion vécue*, 'lived religion'. As developed by later US scholars such as Robert Orsi and David Hall, the concept of 'lived religion' has operated as a means by which to allow one to explore distinctions between what organized religion mandates and what its ordinary adherents, in their sociocultural settings, choose then to do, to embrace, to elaborate upon, and to reject, but without drawing an absolute line between 'official' and 'folkloric', 'elite' and 'popular'.[36] For recent francophone scholarship on medieval religion, it has somewhat faded from view as an animating concept, in part perhaps because such works have tended to orient themselves more toward the structural than the experiential.[37] But it has invigorated a series of interesting works and collaborations by medievalists elsewhere in Europe.[38]

---

[36] R. A. Orsi, *The Madonna of 115th Street: Faith and Community in Italian Harlem, 1880–1950*, 3rd edn (New Haven: Yale University Press, 2010); D. D. Hall, ed., *Lived Religion in America: Toward a History of Practice* (Princeton: Princeton University Press, 1997).
[37] For interesting reflections on past and recent dynamics, see F. Mazel, 'Histoire et religion, entre pratique historiographique, principes épistémologiques et enjeux de sociétés', *Recherches de science religieuse* 109 (2021), 701–16.
[38] In particular S. Katajala-Peltomaa and R. M. Toivo, eds, *Lived Religion and the Long Reformation in Northern Europe, c. 1300–1700* (Leiden: Brill, 2017); S. Katajala-Peltomaa, *Demonic Possession and Lived Religion in Later Medieval Europe* (Oxford: Oxford University Press, 2020); S. Katajala-Peltomaa and R. M. Toivo, *Lived Religion and Gender in Late Medieval and Early Modern Europe* (Abingdon: Routledge, 2021).

For my purposes the point is not only the sense of popular elaborations and divergences, but that being 'lived' they are necessarily embodied: sensory, emotional, performed. These are the aspects of 'lay religion' that Part II seeks to address. Chapter 6 begins with the spatial and the material, whilst Chapter 7 turns to the programme of 'beliefs' that ordinary lay Christians were encouraged to acknowledge, accept, and—toward the end of the period—actively and explicitly embrace. Chapter 8 focuses on the most 'disciplinary' of these areas, relating to practices of inquisition into heresy, and the parochial management of sin, confession, and penance. Chapter 9 brings centre stage a theme that threads through the other chapters, namely the collective and individual ways in which lay people negotiated the demands of Christian religion; it focuses on local communities' relationships with their parish priest, on the sometimes fraught context of confraternities and their worship, and through one particular case study, on the choices made within testamentary culture. Finally Chapter 10 focuses largely on one individual layperson and his experience of both orthodox and heretical faith, drawing links out to other aspects of difficult or problematic belief.

I have suggested elsewhere that the social historian might productively think about belief as operating performatively, in the linguistic sense of 'speech acts'; or rather, that is, as a series of 'belief acts' that are both individual and collective, embodied and social, most often framed, structured, and prompted by ecclesiastical authority but experienced and negotiated by individual people in their particular social setting.[39] In the following pages I have not insistently repeated that argument, though an engagement with the anthropological and other theoretical scholarship that inspired it occasionally rises to the surface of the text. My theoretical tools, in other words, have tended to stay a little submerged in what follows, in order that the voices of the medieval sources can predominate, the ordinary lay voices in particular. Those voices are never simple, never 'pure', and always positioned and partial. But they are rich, and the book seeks also to make them more accessible to others and to give them the attention that they deserve.

[39] J. H. Arnold, 'Believing in Belief: Gibbon, Latour and the Social History of Religion', *Past & Present* 260 (2023).

PART I

1
Christianity and Local Churches, c. 1000–c. 1150

Very soon after the year 1000, at the market in the settlement of Baziège some 25 km south-east of Toulouse, a number of donkeys got loose. They had been brought to market by certain 'Goths' (meaning, possibly, people from the north of the Iberian peninsula, or perhaps simply those who lived on the Mediterranean coast in Languedoc) who had unloaded them onto the open road. The uncontained donkeys promptly set about eating the corn which had been brought to market, and, moreover, 'did bad things' (*faciebant malum*). In response, someone called Odolric Auruz 'and his men' took possession of the donkeys, and refused to hand them back until paid a measure of salt. We know this because of a document which survives copied into the cartulary of the monastery of Saint-Sernin in Toulouse. The monastery owned the market, and Rodgar (the leader of the monastery) and Grimaud (its dean) were extremely annoyed that Odolric had taken this action on his own recognizance. Because of this Grimaud, who probably had financial responsibility for the monastery and its extensive holdings, 'stayed in great discord with Odolric Auruz' until Raimond, bishop of Toulouse, brokered an agreement. Henceforth, Odolric was to be paid part of the market sales tax (*ledda* or *leuda* in Latin, *leude* in modern French scholarship) in salt, up to two pack-loads when there was a full, large market; and he was granted two men, Aribert Samuel and Stephan Samuel (presumably brothers, and possibly Jews, judging by their family name) who were exempted from the sales tax if selling their own goods, and who could pass on this exemption to their sons. 'All others, whatever they arranged or sold, whether in the market or in the outdoor market, had to pay the sales tax, just as Goths and other men. Such an agreement was made and confirmed in the hands of Raimond, the bishop, such that never more would Odolric or his [men] do badly to people coming to the market, and never have salt other than the two pack-loads, nor have other men exempt from taxes other than those two above.'[1]

I like the vignette of the donkeys, making mischief and being disruptive; they are a tiny snatch of unruly life amidst the somewhat repetitive and formulaic body of charter evidence which constitutes the main textual material available for

---

[1] *Cart. Saint-Sernin*, p. 100 (no. 135), undated, but mention of Bishop Raimond of Toulouse puts it between 1004 and 1010.

the eleventh and early twelfth century. Of course, they may never have existed: the charter could be relating a little 'Just-So' story invented to account for a particular economic and political arrangement. It may well have been rewritten when copied into the cartulary at a later date, or even forged entirely.[2] But even if only fictional and functionally mnemonic, they were doing what donkeys will do. We may hope that other aspects of the surviving cartularies, even if not always truthful in their specifics, communicate some generic truth: that even where there is invention, boilerplate repetition, or convention, the outlines still provide material that is true *enough*—that is, that tells us things which would have seemed reasonable and not unexpected at the time. And we may hope that on occasion, like the donkeys, some interesting details break free of their expected bounds and reveal a little bit more of the world around them that otherwise remains obscure.

But I have not only begun with this charter because of the donkeys. In trying to think about Christianity in the eleventh and early twelfth century, and to think about it not only as a set of theological propositions but as something situated in time and space and life, we are quickly confronted by an uneven landscape. What we can see—where the evidence survives—is particularly uneven. A monastery like Saint-Sernin, which had existed since late antiquity and which had been a site of international pilgrimage ever since Charlemagne had bestowed various relics upon it, not only accumulated land and wealth but also memory.[3] Its presence looms large in the surviving documents, and the nature of those materials encourages us to think of it, and other foundations like it, as sitting at the centre of networks of land, property, flows of taxation, and influence. Saint-Sernin mattered, as did various other major and long-standing foundations in southern France, such as Lagrasse (roughly equidistant from Carcassonne and Narbonne), Gellone (north-west of Montpellier), Saint-Victor in Marseille, and Moissac (north-west of Montauban). These places, and the documents they created and kept, cast important light on the region and its history. But in this book I want, whenever possible, to try to get close to what was happening in less exalted localities—what 'Christianity' was not so much in the choir of a richly endowed basilica during

---

[2] See P. Gérard and T. Gérard, eds, *Cartulaire de Saint-Sernin de Toulouse*, 4 vols (Toulouse: Amis des Archives de la Haute-Garonne, 1999), II, pp. 714–16 (no. 135). In this re-edition of the cartulary, it is argued that this document was forged in the late eleventh century, in the context of the later contest over the market between Saint-Sernin and Guillaume de Baziège; though I would venture to suggest that the purely linguistic evidence for re-dating it would support seeing it as a later rewriting of an earlier document (the charter's incipit making clear that it is a 'brief commemoration' rather than claiming to be the actual act of agreement, and the tense of some key verbs indicating that it records a past event).

[3] For insight into the potential dynamics around gifts and both secular and monastic memory in an Iberian setting, see W. Davies, *Acts of Giving: Individual, Community and Church in Tenth-Century Christian Spain* (Oxford: Oxford University Press, 2007), pp. 61–64; and for France and Italy, various essays in F. Bougard, C. La Rocca, and R. Le Jan, eds, *Sauver son âme et se perpétuer: transmission du patrimoine et mémoire au haut moyen âge* (Rome: École française de Rome, 2005).

the office of the mass, but what it was in a smaller settlement like Bazière, on a busy day during market time, for example. It would also be interesting to know if the experience in those localities was always predicated on their position as one node in some wider network, at the heart of which sat a monastery or cathedral; or whether what flowed along the lines of that network was primarily a stream of goods and wealth, and that spiritual experience and instruction could be a more local affair, rather than just something disseminated from these great centres.

The social landscape is also uneven. Odolric Auruz has 'men', those that do his command and who are prepared to act physically against the property of others. We might decide to call him a local 'lord'; certainly that term would make sense later in the eleventh century, when we would see a lot more men like him, using organized force to extract monetary wealth from other entities, and surplus value from peasant labour. His ability to mobilize the threat of physical violence—though quite restrained in nature in this particular instance—makes him someone that the monastery needs to buy off with a regular payment of salt, which is being used effectively as a form of currency. That salt, and the 'Goths', remind us that there is travel across this landscape, associated most of all with trade; but some also, as noted above, for the purposes of pilgrimage. Beyond the bustle and occasional hubbub of the market, there are many more people in this landscape who are unlikely to travel far from their fields much of the time, and who are in various ways subject to the lordship of others. The men of the Church are themselves not socially uniform: those in the named positions of power, where identifiable, overwhelmingly come from the same stratum as secular lords. The position of a rural priest—where and when we can find a rural priest in the evidence—is undoubtedly more lowly, and at this point in time more likely to be subject to, rather than wielding, lordship.

These social, political, and economic aspects are tremendously important, and loom large in the surviving evidence. It would be unwise to decide, a priori, that they are something 'other' than part of the history of religion; of, that is, the history of making aspects of shared and individual belief, singular and collective practice, everyday hopes and extraordinary concerns into something that approximates to our modern notion of 'religion'. But we should also note that these charters tell us a little bit about those beliefs and hopes and fears, even if not in ways that are separable from the economic and political negotiations they primarily record. According to the Saint-Sernin cartulary, the monastery possessed the market at Bazière (meaning that it drew some income in dues from the business conducted there) because it had been a gift from one Donatus and his wife Rixende 'for the salvation of the souls and bodies of him and his forebears (*parentes*)'. Donatus gave the market, with the permission of other powerful figures in the region, 'to the Lord God, and to Saint Sernin of Toulouse, where his body lies, and his clerics, Rodgar the *prepositus* and Grimaud the dean and all others both present and future there who serve God'.[4] Gifts of land and income were important, as they were what made somewhere like Saint-Sernin into a powerful edifice; they were what helped to ensure that it endured, and in its perdurance—its apparent promise of unchanging permanence—underwrite its claims to a privileged spiritual position. Gifts and counter-gifts were what bound the monastery to families of lordship, allowing some of that perdurance to rub off on them, and perhaps to connect themselves more loosely with the exalted role of serving God. And by giving such a gift in such a service, it would appear that Donatus and Rixende wished to save their souls, and the souls of their parents— though what this meant to them more precisely is not yet apparent. Their gift is one pious act among the many recorded in the cartularies; one among the many more that must have been left unrecorded, particularly for the more humble. How we reach toward that larger history is the primary aim of this book. Nonetheless, in that particular recorded moment we can start to see how lordship, social status, networks of power, and the promise of heaven were connected—for those with land, at any rate. In this chapter we will begin by addressing some aspects of Christianity and lordship (the lordship of the Church and ecclesiastics as well as that of the nobility), before turning to the experience of Christianity in localities, via what we can discern of local church buildings, their priests, and the laity's interactions with both.

Christianity and Lordship

If we want to understand Christianity in a particular locality in western Europe in the eleventh and twelfth century, it is impossible to ignore the question of lordship—of its nature in the secular world, of its means of operation and legitimation, and its relationship to the Church. The experience of Christianity in any rural locality depended in very large degree upon lordship of one kind or another, for the basic provision of a place of worship and an officiating priest. As discussed in the Introduction, we may not wish to embrace the idea that southern France in particular experienced 'feudalism' in the mode classically presented by an older historiography, particularly because this does not very accurately capture the nature of landholding and associated rights and duties in the region. But the region most surely had a range of lords within it, each of whom exercised claims upon the wider resources of the land and people. It does seem useful to think

---

[4] *Cart. Saint-Sernin*, p. 99 (no. 134); Gérard and Gérard, *Cartulaire de Saint-Sernin*, pp. 712–13, no. 134, who again argue from the language used—particularly the phrase *clerici...Deo ibi servientes*— that this is a forgery (or at least a rewriting of an earlier charter) produced in the late eleventh century. This may be correct, though one notes that the notion of 'serving God' survives in tenth- and eleventh- century charters elsewhere, as one would expect given that it is a biblical phrase, taken up and further developed by Augustine.

about the dynamics of this in the mode proffered by Thomas Bisson, who suggests that the power exerted by lordship is best understood not as 'governance' (in the sense of a top-down, strategic management of a landscape) but as 'effluent', that is, flowing out from a central point, its 'power' an aspiration and ambition to exert control and influence, but however almost always butting up against the 'flow' of claims from other similar entities in a region.[5]

With this in mind, it is important to emphasize that in southern France the Church did not sit 'outside' lordship but was very much part of it. I will suggest some ways further below, and again in subsequent chapters, of how the dynamic of lordship might be seen to inform spiritual matters. But in the first instance, that the Church was part of lordship needs to be noted in a practical sense: in almost all the major cities (Toulouse being the main exception), bishops exercised secular lordship, sometimes in combination with a lay lord, and this could include the administration of secular justice. The grand monastic houses held large amounts of property, not only in the forms of subject churches and their accompanying lands, but also towns and *castra*, and other agricultural holdings; and within those holdings they similarly exercised secular lordship over a subject peasantry. Indeed, this is one point to take from my opening example: the monastery of Saint-Sernin 'owned' the market at Bazière in that it exerted lordship over it, drawing income from it and to some degree regulating its business. Since the ninth century, some archbishops, bishops, and abbeys had taken possession of Carolingian castles, and those same archbishops, bishops, and monastic *prepositi* came from the same noble families as the secular counts and viscounts in each region.[6] An example from the very far south: a charter from around 1034 records the agreement of the division of lordship between Peire, bishop of Girona (now in northern Spain), and his nephew Roger I, count of Foix; this agreement is accompanied by a second document recording an oath of fidelity made by Roger to Peire. From later in the same century we have other oaths of fidelity—where the main point is to agree not to trespass against the other party's rights and holdings—made to the archbishop of Narbonne by Guillaume II, count of Besalu, and Peire, the son of Garsen, viscountess of Narbonne.[7]

This marks a feature that remains largely continuous throughout the period covered by this book: senior ecclesiastics very often came from noble families, and in southern France very often continued to exercise political and secular as well as ecclesiastical power, well into the mid-thirteenth century, and to some degree beyond. Bishops and monastic *prepositi* (as the leaders of monasteries were often termed in the eleventh and early twelfth centuries) were usually

---

[5] Bisson, *Crisis of the Twelfth Century*, particularly introduction and chapter 1.
[6] Lewis, *Development*, p. 134; Magnou-Nortier, *La société laïque*, pp. 344–48.
[7] C. Brunel, ed., *Les plus anciennes chartes en langue provençale: recueil des pièces originales antérieures au XIIIe siècle* (Paris: Picard, 1926), pp. 1–7 (nos 1, 2, 3, and 4).

referred to as 'Lord', and whilst this was strictly speaking an honorific title, it was far from a dead letter: to be in charge of a diocese and a city, or to have control of a wealthy monastery, was to exercise lordship in a very real sense. Moreover, ecclesiastical institutions and their leaders could receive unfree people as property donations.[8] For example, in 1100 the cathedral canons of Saint-Nazaire in Carcassonne received from a man known as Pela the gift of a woman called Ugberga 'with her children', Pela 'surrendering and relinquishing' all claim to her (the canons giving in return 3 *sous*).[9] Similarly in 1146 one Bertrand gave to Saint-Étienne-d'Agde 'the man Stephan Rainard Bumbel with his wife and with all of their descendants who issue from them, and with all usages (*usatica*) which they are given to make me'.[10] An undated charter, possibly from the 1120s or 1130s, records an agreement between the abbot of Saint-Sernin and Géraud, prior of the hospital of Vacquiers (22 km north of Toulouse), setting out what Géraud 'retained' in the town, the rest going to the abbey; Géraud was to keep a third part of the tithe, but also a third part of *iusticie* (the income generated by holding a court), a third of the *census* (an annual exaction on property), and a third part of the lands 'which the abbot will work within his lordship (*in dominio*)' namely so that Géraud received a third of what was cultivated and sown there.[11] Even in the absence of the keyword *dominium*, the rights that both ecclesiastics gained would quite clearly indicate lordship as we now understand it.

Studies of medieval religion have often not been very good at incorporating these phenomena into their histories; or rather, such matters tend to be presented only from the perspective of particular reformers who wanted to draw a clear line between secular affairs and the world of the Church. The ideological and spiritual struggle of 'reform' was to become an important factor in southern France, and we turn to it in Chapter 3; but it should not obscure the extent to which the Church had long exercised lordship over land, resources, people, and justice. We may wish to try to consider, wherever possible, what that lordship looked like to the ordinary laity, and how it fitted into or affected their experience of Christianity. In 1109 Pierre de Luc, *prepositus* of the cathedral canons at Nîmes, gave to the cathedral a manse in his home village of Luc (which appears to have been a canton of Nîmes), 'which manse holds Stephana, wife of the late Bernard Silvestri, and her children. And this manse gives as *census* a pig worth two shillings, and two good focassia loaves, and two capons, and 6d at the feast of Saint Michel, and

---

[8] Magnou-Nortier sees evidence of this appearing in the eleventh century for the first time (in this explicit form; earlier gifts of land may well have implied people as well): *La société laïque*, pp. 226–27.
[9] Doat 65, fol. 24r–v. No land is mentioned in this case, and it seems very clear that it is a person and not a property being transferred.
[10] *Cart. S. Étienne d'Agde*, p. 136 (no. 42), 6 June 1146. See similarly *Cart. Saint-Sernin*, p. 154 (no. 216), August 1100, gift of a man called Pons Trossa de Savardu.
[11] *Cart. Saint-Sernin*, p. 32 (no. 46); p. 311 (no. 433) records the same charter. Dating via the name of the abbot, Raimond; if Raimond Guillaume, then active in the first decades of the twelfth century.

provisions for four knights, and a sheep at Easter or 12d.'[12] Would Stephana have felt any difference arising from the ultimate destination of the livestock, bread, and pennies? One can imagine both a positive—a sense of connection to a grander edifice in the city—and a negative—that a more distant authority now claimed rights over your labours. But in both cases we are reminded that lordship extracted material goods and time from people within their *dominium*, and that the Church was an innate part of this system.

Christianity in the Localities

The big stories of 'feudal anarchy', 'the Peace of God', and 'Gregorian reform', as outlined in the Introduction, present a particular methodological problem: they tend to fill up the space of discussion, and thus prevent other questions being asked about Christianity in this period and region. Regardless of how one views the post-Carolingian centuries in southern France, a moment's reflection makes it obvious that even when violence and conflictual lordship were common, they were not the experience of each and every day. Life necessarily went on in the spaces in between the fighting, and all that life involved: having babies, rearing children, forming and sustaining marriages, caring for old people, farming, trading, and some form of cultural activity (even if irrecoverable in its detail today). And, beyond the more extraordinary kinds of events that periodically occurred at major shrines or as part of a 'Peace of God' event—topics to which we shall turn in Chapter 2—there would be many more, less dramatic, forms of Christian worship in the localities. What we can say about the latter is my main interest in this chapter.

A good place to begin is in church—that is, in the physical building that medieval Catholicism designated as central to acts of worship. We can see stone survivals from this period incorporated into the surviving fabric of various of the large monasteries and cathedrals, and we know that episcopal churches existed in various population centres from late antiquity and the Carolingian period, for example at Elne, Carcassonne, Narbonne, Béziers, Agde, Lodève, Loupian, Maguelonne, Nîmes, and Uzès.[13] A number of these were rebuilt on a larger scale in the twelfth century, with architectural elements from that period still visible within later expansions—this is the case with substantial parts of the nave of Carcassonne cathedral, for example. Various monastic churches were also constructed on an impressive monumental scale: at Saint-Michel-de-Cuxa in the

---

[12] *Cart. Notre-Dame de Nîmes*, pp. 311–12 (no. 196), 13 Mar 1109.
[13] C. Pellecuer and L. Schneider, 'Premières églises et espace rural en Languedoc méditerranéen (V–Xe S.)', in C. Delaplace, ed., *Aux origines de la paroisse rurale en Gaule méridionale (IVe–IXe siècles)* (Paris: Errance, 2005), pp. 98–119; see fig. 1, p. 99, and accompanying discussion.

diocese of Elne, for example, even at the beginning of the period the nave measured 30 m long, and the choir another 12 m.[14] But for most people in the period, the majority of whom did not live in or near to the urban centres or monastic centres, these fairly grand spaces would be experienced on rare occasion, if indeed ever.

In recent decades, archaeologists have been able to expand greatly our knowledge of local churches in more rural areas in the south. There are some physical legacies from late antiquity, though more often in terms of sites (at one point abandoned, and then revived) than surviving monuments. Rural church building did occur in the early middle ages, possibly more in the south of France than in other parts of the empire.[15] Studies of particular sites suggest that these were usually quite small and simple structures, often comprising a fairly narrow nave that ended in a square space comprising the choir and apse—though they may well have originally been the only *stone* structure in their environs, and therefore perhaps more impressive within their contemporary milieu.[16] Christophe Pellucuer describes in detail such a church, that of Saint-Sébastien in Maroiol near Aniane. Here the nave is 3.6 m wide and about 10 m long—just about wide enough for four or five people to stand comfortably side by side, rather less if one aimed to make a central aisle for a priest to walk down. This nave opens into the apse, here 5 sq m. However, at the transition between nave and apse there is an arch which narrows the width of the building to only 2 m. This suggests a strong division of space, both symbolically and in terms of sight lines, between that of the altar, at which the priest would perform the mass, and the nave in which the lay congregation would stand or sit (unsurprisingly we have no archaeological evidence from this period to indicate whether people expected benches or other forms of seating). The church was built at some point between c. 650 and c. 850, on a site which had already been used for burials (one tomb was incorporated into the church building itself). *Who* built the church is not known: the nearby monastery at Aniane may well have been involved, and certainly the agrarian production associated with the monastery prompted the growth of the settlement at Maroiol. By the eleventh century some local 'noble' men associated themselves with the church in surviving charters, though whether their forebears were involved in its earlier creation we cannot say.[17]

---

[14] G. Mallet, 'Entre traditions et innovations: l'espace liturgique de deux églises romanes du diocèse d'Elne, Saint-Michel de Cuxa et Sainte-Marie d'Arles-sur-Tech', *CdF* 46 (2011), 37–57, floorplan at p. 38.

[15] Though see the warning note sounded by E. Zadora-Rio, 'L'historiographie des paroisses rurales à l'épreuve de l'archéologie', in Delaplace, ed., *Aux origines*, pp. 15–23, at p. 18.

[16] L. Schneider, 'De l'archéologie du monument chrétien à l'archéologie des lieux de culte: propos d'introduction et repères historiographiques', *Archéologie du Midi médiéval* 28 (2010), 131–45; note particularly fig. 1 (p. 135) setting out a number of floorplans.

[17] Pellucuer, 'Premières églises', pp. 108–9. See also L. Schneider, 'Le site de Saint-Sébastien-de-Maroiol', *Archéologie médiévale* 25 (1999), 133–81.

This, then, is the kind of material legacy that people of the eleventh and early twelfth century most often received from the preceding Christian centuries. But what of monumental production within the period itself? There was a lot of it, particularly in the twelfth century. Pellucuer notes that within the diocese of Lodève, which by the early fourteenth century contained 121 identifiable churches, some 45% were built in the eleventh and twelfth centuries (of the remaining 55%, roughly half pre-date 1000, and half were built after 1200).[18] These churches were similar in their basic layout to the Carolingian inheritances, with simple rectangular naves that led onto either square or—increasingly commonly—semicircular apses. The size of structure was generally bigger than that of Saint-Sebastien-de-Maroiol, but not that much greater: lots of churches have a nave less than 10 m long, and less than 5 m wide; in almost all cases the nave is less than 15 m long and 6 m wide; and the division between nave and apse often narrows somewhat.[19] These churches almost always have only one or two very small slit windows in the south wall of the nave, and sometimes one other tiny window at the head of the apse. They were thus spaces of darkness, into which light could be brought; a topic to which we will return in a later chapter. In terms of decoration, at some (but by no means all) sites there are some extant carvings on stone capitals, and slightly more exterior to certain churches.[20] These should not be discounted, and I will also discuss some of these elements in a later chapter; but they are far from extensive. For understandable reasons modern art historical work has focused upon the extant examples, but tends to ignore the rather larger number of churches which lack any surviving decoration.[21] It seems unlikely that any extensive wall painting ever existed, and it would have been extremely hard to discern in the dark interiors had it ever done so.

At some point in the twelfth century most churches had gained what modern French architectural historians sometimes call 'un clocheton' but more accurately

---

[18] Pellecuer, 'Premières églises', p. 111.

[19] My characterization here is based upon personal visits across the Toulousain, and the analyses in G. Durand, 'Les églises rurales du premier âge roman dans le Rouergue méridional', *Archéologie du Midi médiéval* 7 (1989), 3-42 and E. Zadora-Rio, 'Archéologies des églises et des cimetières ruraux en Languedoc: un point de vue d'"Outre Loire"', *Archéologie du Midi médiéval* 28 (2010), 239-48. Among other specific studies note: L. Bayrou et al., 'L'église Sainte-Marie de Peyrepertuse', *Archéologie du Midi médiéval* 8-9 (1990-91), 39-98; P. Chevalier, 'Topographie et hiérarchie au sein de l'édifice ecclésial: l'espace du choeur et l'aménagement de ses limites (XIe–XIIe siècles). Quelques réflexions', *CdF* 46 (2011), 59-78; A. Michelozzi, 'L'église romane Saint-Laurent à Jonquières-et-Saint-Vincent (Gard)', *Archéologie du Midi médiéval* 22 (2004), 27-44; A. Michelozzi, 'L'église Saint-Pierre-de-Campublic à Beaucaire', *Archéologie du Midi médiéval* 25 (2007), 19-34.

[20] For example, V. Lassalle, 'Le décor sculpté de l'église romane Saint-Michel de la Garde-Guérin à Prévenchères (Lozère)', *Archéologie du Midi médiéval* 22 (2004), 77-102; C. Balagna, 'L'église romane de Croute à Lasserrade (Gers): un édifice inachevé de Gascogne centrale autour de 1125', *Archéologie du Midi médiéval* 26 (2008), 59-91.

[21] For a more positive reading of Catalan examples, emphasizing the appearance in the eleventh century of images of Christ-as-authority (potentially over the space surrounding the church building) see A. Trivellone, 'Le développement du décor monumental et la conquête de l'extérieur des églises: *sagreres* et façades catalanes au cours de la première moitié du XIe siècle', *CdF* 46 (2011), 175-227.

'*un clocher-mur*' (the closest British equivalent is a 'bell-cote', though this tends to denote something a bit more structural): a small free-standing brick wall on the roof, above the west end, with an opening or openings to hold a bell or bells. These would not support the kind of large cast bell one would find in larger churches from later centuries, but instead would hold a small bell, most probably beaten out from two sheets of iron, likely to make a sound more like a cowbell than a sonorous chime. A remarkable example of such a bell survives from the very rural church of Saint-Guilhem-de-Combret.[22] Such *clochers-murs* are still extant however on a number of rural churches, as at the 'chapelle' de Sainte-Madeleine outside Pezens, Aiguillon (where the 'mur' holds three bells), Peyrolles, Pomas (designed for two bells), Serres (ditto), and Sainte-Marie-de-Vilarmila on the outskirts of Llupia, to name just some examples from the further south-west of the region.[23] As churches gained bells, the Christian soundscape changed in each locality. This is a topic to be explored further in Chapter 6, but for the moment we can note that it would have affected the sonic 'reach' of the church into its immediate surroundings.

We thus also need to consider where these churches were located. One phenomena was the formation of settlements around older churches, sometimes with the church sat exactly central to a circular village (as at Villar Saint-Anselme, Gueytes-d'en-Haut, Mouthoumet, Loupia, La Digne-d'Amont, La Digne-d'Aval, Airoux, Carlipa, Saint-Martin-Lalande, Paulhan, Fabrège, Balaruc, and Abeilhan), sometimes with the church ending up at one end of a settlement which had grown more longitudinally (as at Peyrens).[24] It is very unlikely that these were *new* settlements around churches which previously stood alone in the landscape: on a site where stone buildings have been erected it is essentially impossible to discern whether any wood structures were previously present, but since we know elsewhere (for example at Maroiol) that that was the case, it is likely to have been so in these localities also. Moreover, as Anne Parodi has demonstrated, the notion that antiquarians previously held of churches frequently standing alone in a field or wood is challenged by recent archaeological research: although certain documents may, apparently perversely, describe a particular church and its lands as if it sat in the middle of nowhere, clear archaeological evidence of nearby

---

[22] An image is available via <https://fr.wikipedia.org/wiki/Ermitage_Saint-Guillem_de_Combret#cite_ref-AssoMobilier_36-0> (accessed 21 Mar 2018) and <https://fr.wikipedia.org/wiki/Ermitage_Saint-Guillem_de_Combret#cite_ref-AssoMobilier_36-0> (accessed 21 Mar 2018) and another is reproduced in Chapter 6 below. The bell is apparently now held in the Centre de Conservation et de Restauration du Patrimoine at Perpignan, though I have not seen it directly.
[23] Personal observation from site visits.
[24] D. Baudreu and J. P Cazes, 'Les villages ecclésiaux dans le bassin de l'Aude', in M. Fixot and E. Zadora-Rio, eds, *L'environnement des églises et la topographie religieuse des campagnes médiévales*, Document d'archéologie francaise 46 (Paris: Éditions de la Maison des sciences de l'homme, 1994), pp. 80–97; K. Pawlowski, 'Villes et villages circulaires du Languedoc: un des premiers modèles de l'urbanisme médiévale?', *Annales du Midi* 99 (1987), 407–27.

settlement often exists.[25] That said, as we shall see in Chapter 3, there were *some* churches built at a real distance from villages, established as hermitages and/or pilgrimage waystations; such is the case with the chapel of Saint Martin outside the village of Camelas, and the aforementioned church of Saint-Guilhem-de-Combret (a few miles from the town of Le Tech), both of which perch dramatically amidst the foothills of the Canigou mountains.[26] As already noted, some other surviving churches may have been built at a shorter distance from the nearest village, but equally the village may have moved away from the original foundation; one wonders if this was the case, for example, with the so-called 'chapelle de Saint-Roch' that sits about 600 m outside the village of Laroque-d'Olmes, understood by the local tourist board to be a fourteenth-century chapel dedicated to Roch for protection from plague, but which looks very much to have originally been a standard early twelfth-century local church.[27] It is in the eleventh and more particularly the twelfth century that settlements start to become fortified, often gaining stone walls and sometimes defensive towers; and as noted, this was also a period in which a lot of new churches were built, perhaps sometimes as 'chapels' that sat within a few miles of a 'mother church' (though in fact this language is fairly rare in southern French records), but also a large number of entirely new buildings.

It is very hard to estimate in any clear way the overall geographical spread and density of rural churches in this period, and thus try to glean a sense of how wide an area each one aimed to serve. A few clues can be found. One comes from a donation in 1085 of the church of Saint-Pierre in Lastonar with its appurtenances, which specifies among other things that the burial rights (*cimiterii*) extended 30 *stadii* all around the church. If we decide that a 'stade' should be understood in its classical meaning, this indicates a radius of about three and a half miles.[28] Should we describe this as the church's 'parish'? The word *parrochiam* appears intermittently through the documents of the eleventh century, more frequently indicating a kind of 'right' than a basic unit of an ecclesial or spiritual network. The word is used a number of times in eleventh-century charters in the cartulary of the monastery of Saint-Victor in Marseille, for example, essentially as a loose geographical description, often though not always linked to a particular named church. For instance, the testamentary charter of the powerful lord Gombáu de Besora from 1041 describes various lands as being 'in the parish of St Minat... in the parish of

---

[25] A. Parodi, 'Les églises dans le paysage rural du haut Moyen Age en Languedoc oriental (IX–XIIe s.)', in Fixot and Zadora-Rio, eds, *L'environnement des églises*, pp. 107–21, at p. 109. Why a charter would not mention a nearby settlement is unclear, but might be to do with uncertainty over adjacent landownership, a problem bypassed by reference to geographical features in the locality.
[26] Visited by the author. There is an excellent guide to romanesque churches in this region: G. Mallet, *Églises romanes oubliées du Roussillon* (Montpellier: Presses universitaires du Languedoc, 2003).
[27] Visited by the author; site discussed further in Chapter 6.
[28] *Cart. Moissac*, p. 183 (no. 125). Classically a 'stade' = c. 600 feet.

St Pierre de Bigas' and so forth, but also mentions 'those fiefs and parishes' which he held in the county of Barcelona, and 'those fiefs and parishes and allods and *bailias*' in various other *castra*—'parish' thus looking rather like one kind of area among others over which a lord could lay claim to income.[29] From the same cartulary, a charter recording gifts by the viscount of Marseille from 1044 mentions, amidst other lands bestowed, 'a parish or tithing' alongside other lordly rights of exaction, 'parish' thus again suggesting a meaning primarily connected to income; though whether that was income directly connected to spiritual services, or another land-based exaction, is unclear. Yet another charter, from a year later, donates two churches in the town of Gigors (c. 23 km south of Gap) 'with all parish [rights] and a full half of the tenths' (*cum omnia parrochia et tota medietate decimi*), in this case indicating a clearer distinction over the nature of the rights (and thus perhaps suggesting that the 'parish rights' were connected to ecclesial activity, such as oblations); though clearly still focused on income.[30] Around 1055 Bishop Bertrand of Fréjus donated to Saint-Victor a certain '*presbiteratum* or *parrochiam*, with all ecclesiastical appurtenances...that is, with all church rights, firsts, vigils, oblations, and...a third of the tenths on all things', again clearly demonstrating a strong link with income (as well as an interesting choice of precise terminology), though in this case, in concert with many donation charters of this period, focused as much on the income produced through liturgical and sacramental activity as on the tithing rights over the surrounding area.[31] Collectively, these usages suggest that in this period we should not imagine 'the parish' as a component in a top-down organizational grid imposed from on high, but as the geographical area that the particular church could lay claim to in terms of tithes and dues—the area over which it could hope to extend its particular form of *dominium*, one might say.[32]

In addition to the model discussed above, where an older church comes to sit centrally within a *castrum*, two new patterns started to emerge when contemporary church building occurred in the eleventh and twelfth century. One was to make the church itself part of the emerging castral defences, incorporating its stonework into the walls of the town or village (as happened at Pégairolles-de-Buèges, Aumelas, Montarnaud, Fouzilhon, Laroque-Aynier, Assas, and elsewhere). The other—presumably where the foundation of a church occurred after a settlement had fortified—was to build the church beyond the *castrum*, as a separate space entirely (as at Montalba le Chateau, Mourèze, Cornus, Neffies,

---

[29] *Cart. Saint-Victor*, II, appendix, pp. 517–21 (no. 1048).
[30] *Cart. Saint-Victor*, I, pp. 47–51, at p. 49 (no. 32); II, p. 33 (no. 691).
[31] *Cart. Saint-Victor*, I, pp. 536–37 (no. 537). See similarly II, pp. 565–66 (no. 1091), where in 1096 Gauzfredus relinquished 'ecclesiam vel parrochiam' of the castle of Grimal.
[32] The essays in C. Delaplace, ed., *Aux origines de la paroisse rurale en Gaule méridionale (IVe–IXe siècles)* (Paris: Errance, 2005) are very useful but collectively tend to take for granted what a 'parish' implies, in a somewhat teleological fashion; I return to the topic in Chapter 5.

Castries, Bellegarde, Calvisson, Lunel, and Maugio).[33] As ever, we have no contemporary witness to tell us how these various spaces were experienced, but one may reflect on what the different arrangements might encourage. A church that sat in the very heart of a *castrum* could not help but be a symbolically important presence, the literal centre of the community, and perhaps providing a sense of additional refuge; but at the same time could not accommodate burial, which would have to occur in a separate cemetery. A church that sat outside the walls of the village could much more easily have an adjacent cemetery—though this would not automatically be the case—whilst also necessarily being a site one had to go *out* to, demanding a move from the de facto secular space of the *castrum* to the holy space of the church. Maybe this made little difference to the regular experience of Christian worship, but one would have to admit that we start to see, at the very least, a further range to that experience (to set alongside the wider range which incorporates the grander cathedral buildings in the larger cities).

Who was building these new churches in the eleventh and early twelfth centuries? The surviving charters provide numerous examples of lay people—sometimes, but not always, those styled 'knights' or 'noblemen'—giving land and wealth to support the creation of churches (or the rebuilding of old ones) which are then, or subsequently come to be, under the control of monasteries. For example, an undated charter, but likely to be from the eleventh century, records that Aladaicia and her sons Jean and Guillaume gave a field to a monastery 'to make a church', appearing to mean not just that the land would supply income but would be the actual place of erection. This sort of arrangement is made explicit in a charter from 1122, when three brothers (who note also the support and agreement of two other named men, 'and all my forebears and friends') gave the abbey of Moissac an allod on which they wished a church to be built, 'in honour of our Lord Jesus Christ and the Blessed Mother of God Mary, and the Blessed Apostles Pierre and Paul, and Saint Sacerdos and all the saints of God'.[34] We can also sometimes see a more 'top-down' approach in regard to the building of churches. In the late eleventh century, the abbot of Moissac and another monk who was also prior of the church of Ségur gave a hill at Camalières to a priest called Vivien 'and to Amiel his relative, and all their relatives and kin', such that they should 'go forth and take possession' of it, in order to build a church there. A few decades earlier a charter records that the bishop of Couserans, together with the greater landowners of the

---

[33] M. Bourin and A. Durand, 'Église paroissiale, cimetière et castrum en bas Languedoc (Xe–XIIe s.)', in Fixot and Zadora-Rio, eds, *L'environnement des églises*, pp. 98–106; Parodi, 'Les églises dans le paysage rural', p. 110.

[34] *Cart. Lézat*, I, pp. 50–51 (no. 65); *Cart. Moissac*, p. 300 (no. 216). We can find elsewhere people giving diverse land which is likely to be providing income rather than the foundation place itself, for example *Cart. Saint-Victor*, I, p. 237 (no. 214), 1018: 'Hi sunt donatores: Barnardus, quartairatam I de vinea; Constantinus quoque minus, alia quartairada; Sisfredus quippe, sestairatam I; Pontius autem clericus, alia sestairada; Rotbertus vero, sextairatam I; porro Ricarthus, modiatam I; Spiranthue ergo, sextairada I.... Confirmatum est hoc a supradictis donatoribus. Consona voce dixerunt: sic fiat.'

region of Lézat, decided to build the church of Saint-Antoine and to repair the church of Saint-Pierre.[35] Sometimes the high and the local could combine: some time around 1065, Bernard Pelet, bishop of Couserans and abbot of Lézat, consecrated the church of Saint-Pierre in Mont. He provided some financial support himself, as did another monk called Hugues, a deacon called Bertrand de Saint Jean, a priest called Étienne, and another (the first appointed to the church) named Bernard Amiel. The charter however also records a large number of other donors giving land or income, all apparently from the locality: another twenty-six men and three women (other women also named as confirming certain donations made by brothers or fathers). That they had land to give indicates that they were not lowly—but none of them are styled as 'noble' or 'knight'.[36]

As the example of Saint-Pierre in Mont demonstrates, it is important to note that the creation of churches was often a collective act, rather than simply one lord acting alone. From some time in the 1070s, a charter notes that Raimond Arnaud and Guillaume his brother, 'most noble men', had given the monastery of Lézat some land to support the building of a church at Saint-Christaud-de-Volvestre, this gift subsequently supplemented by further donations by eight other people 'with the counsel of all the good men (*boni homines*) of the same parish'. At some point in the 1060s three brothers gave two farms (*casales*) and other lands in Daumazan, either to build or (more likely) to rebuild the church there, 'for the soul of our father Étienne and our mother Arsinde, and for their burial'—this appearing to mean burial at the church rather than at the monastery to which it was donated.[37] Co-ownership of churches was extremely common.[38] To cite just a few of the many examples: in 1081, four different people each gave one-quarter of the church of Saint-Cyr at Caumont to the monastery of Moissac, possibly indicating that they or their forebears had originally built it. From around the same period, ten men and their wives gave two churches, plus various other bits of land, to the same monastery, apparently indicating the previous collective ownership of all of them.[39] Slightly later—in 1108—the knights of the *castrum* of *Ritalans* gave support from their goods for a new church to Ste Marie, ten named knights plus other unnamed brothers. This included the gift, by Pierre de Durban and his mother, of half of the church of Carla-Bayle (*Castlar*): this might indicate that they were sharing a holding that they had previously enjoyed alone,

---

[35] *Cart. Moissac*, p. 187 (no. 129). *Cart. Lézat*, I, pp 80–82 (no. 106).
[36] *Cart. Lézat*, I, pp. 377–8 (no. 500).   [37] *Cart. Lézat*, I, p. 170 (no. 218), p. 603 (no. 833).
[38] D. Panfili, 'Transferts d'églises, de dimes et recomposition des seigneuries en Languedoc (vers 1050–vers 1200)', *CdF* 48 (2013), 581–602, at pp. 582–83 notes the fact of complex multiple ownership, citing the church of Saint-Pierre-d'Elt which was donated by seventeen named men *et alteri homines multi*. For some comparative comments on tenth-century foundations in northern Iberia, see Davies, *Acts of Giving*, pp. 50–52.
[39] *Cart. Moissac*, p. 174 (no. 120), p. 175 (no. 121).

but equally likely indicates that the church at Carla-Bayle had also been in co-ownership.[40]

These churches are visible to us because they become part of the monastery's holdings, but we can presume that the patterns here would be replicated in other localities. The overall picture given by the cartulary of the abbey of Saint-Lézat is instructive in this regard. For the period up to 1199, the cartulary contains 161 charters in which a church or churches are specifically noted, most often gifts or surrenders of churches to the monastery.[41] Of these, forty-eight appear to indicate a single family in possession of the church or churches under discussion (that is, 29%); or, if we decide to include occasions on which two or more adult brothers jointly donate churches as also constituting a 'single family', fifty-four charters (34%). If one focuses on the churches rather than the occasions which prompted a charter (the same churches sometimes of course appearing multiple times), the proportion of 'single-family possession' rises a bit, but not that much. There are roughly 120 churches named or noted across the charters, and the proportion of these held at *any* point by one family is still only 40%. That is, even by the most capacious estimate for single-family ownership—ignoring any earlier or later occasions on which a particular church came to be held by multiple people—the evidence still shows this to be a minority of cases. Thus overall the evidence strongly suggests that more than half of the churches were frequently held by several different people, sometimes large groups of people. A similar picture emerges from a shorter and more closely focused cartulary, that of the Hospitaller foundation at Saint-Clar (c. 40 km south of Agen), which contains charters of donation for thirty-one churches, all from the early twelfth century. Nine of the charters record donations by one person or close family group, but the rest are again held by a wider number of people. In fact sixteen of the churches list four or more separate donors. For example, the church of Toumoustin (a small village c. 25 km south-west of Toulouse) was donated by Dodo de *Flacedet* and his brother Roger, Pierre de *Flacedet*, Bernard and Urset de Puy, Raimon Bernard, Rossa de *Flacedet*, the Lady of Le Pin-Murelet and Gualhard her son, Pierre d'*Exarto*, and Guillaume de Puy; and the donation was made 'with the counsel of Aymeric de Murelet and Calvet de *Vezad* and his brothers'.[42] These are obviously interconnected people,

---

[40] *Cart. Lézat*, I, pp. 29–30 (no. 38). The editorial apparatus gives the date as 1118, but the transcription as 1108. The editors identify Carla-Bayle (17 km south of Lézat) for *Castlar* though there is also a *castrum de Castlar* some 80 km to the east, near Durfort.

[41] It is difficult to be utterly precise with the data discussed here, as one cannot always be certain that a named church, and another unnamed church in the same location, are identical or not; I have erred however toward a conservative reading in each case, that is, assuming concurrence of churches. I have ignored the few occasions on which a bishop donates a church, and have ignored occasions on which tithes are donated, but with no mention of a specific church.

[42] Cartulaire de Saint-Clar, no. v, edited in P. Ourliac, *Les sauvetés du Comminges: étude et documents sur les villages fondés par les Hospitaliers dans la région des coteaux commingeois* (Toulouse: Boisseau, 1947), pp. 86–118.

as you would expect if they all held part of the same church, and from the place names that can be identified, they are also relatively local (Murelet and Le-Pin-Murelet are both less than 10 km from Toumoustin; there is a Pouy-de-Touges—perhaps home to the Bernard and Urset mentioned above—even closer). But they also obviously do not constitute one 'feudal lord' or family.

The picture is admittedly not quite so strong as we look to the east of the region via the large cartulary of the abbey of Saint-Victor in Marseille, though collective ownership is nonetheless clearly still present. There we find about 56% of churches donated by a single person or a couple, or a couple plus either their children or a parent, and a further 11% donated by brothers or by an uncle and nephew. Only 33% were thus given by multiple groups (or a few charters where a single individual donated what was clearly only a portion of the rights to the church, the other portions by implication held by others).[43] In that cartulary in particular one sees a number of very powerful lords donating churches. But at the same time, we do still find some more lowly groups handing over a church; and, on a few occasions, multiple people giving land to a newly established church as an endowment (a *sponsalicium*).[44] So, across the whole region, although we undoubtedly do find the 'classic' situation of a single lord building or inheriting a local church (almost always only becoming visible in the written record when handed over to a religious foundation at a later date), we also find some examples of collective foundations, and substantial evidence for collective subsequent 'ownership'. And we should note that, as we saw above, there is on occasion mention of the 'good men'—the *boni homines*—of a locality who exist, rhetorically at least, to indicate a wider communal investment in the issue. Thus, whilst local lords clearly did draw income from the church (or the part of the church, or churches) that they possessed, this was not always as straightforward as one single figure dominating the local landscape, adding the tithe to his other exactions.

It is important also to note that local churches, just like monasteries, could continue to receive substantial pious donations after their initial foundation. There are a few rare occasions when the written evidence tells us about gifts of land to an existing local church. In 1038 it is recorded in the cartulary of Saint-Victor of Marseille that two men called Vualdrad and Teotfred, plus Teotfred's wife Scocia and their children, donated some land to the church of Saint-Pierre in Brignoles; a couple of years later Silvius and his wife Agcelina, with his brother Pons and sister-in-law Poncia, similarly donated land to the church of

---

[43] By my count 162 churches mentioned in charters of the eleventh and twelfth centuries, though in this cartulary it is particularly difficult to identify repeated occurrences of the same church across different charters.

[44] For example *Cart. Saint-Victor*, I, pp. 237 (no. 214, from 1018, re *sponsalicium*), 374 (no. 368, from 1042); II, pp. 126–28 (no. 779, from 1042); I, pp. 142–43 (no. 114, from 1050), pp. 568–70 (no. 578, from 1058).

Saint-Étienne.[45] A charter from the mid-eleventh century records that Atilius Bucaniger, on his deathbed, gave some land to the church of Saint-Martin-de-Magrens, so that the clerics there could sing masses and celebrate divine office during Lent.[46] Another moment is recorded in an act made sometime in the 1120s or 1130s, by which Raimond Datfredi gave his body and his soul, and all things that pertained to the church of Sainte-Constantia, to the monastery of Saint-Sernin. In recounting what this gift contained, the charter notes that at an earlier point in time 'a certain man called Bernard Gauzfredi gave to God and to the church of Sainte-Constantia, for the redemption of his soul, a piece of land; and on that land I, R[aimond] Datfredi, planted a vineyard to the honour of God and to the church of Sainte-Constantia'.[47] Pious donation could therefore continue at a local level as well as flowing in toward the larger monastic centres—but is of course now almost invisible, as the local churches did not sustain archives like those of the monasteries.

As one example above has already illustrated, the local lords may well have had a further investment in the church and its appurtenances in a different sense: as a place of burial (whether near the church, or in a geographically separate cemetery) for their forebears, and eventually for themselves. Quite a few of the gifts related to burial recorded in monastic cartularies for this period are hoping to gain interment within the monastery itself.[48] For fairly obvious reasons, that does not indicate an overall preference in society, but the bias of the evidence: monastic cartularies record gifts to themselves, and only incidentally tell us about other localities. There are some elements to these monastic choices that may however tell us something more broadly about the place of burial. One is mention of being buried 'honourably', which would seem to imply 'with some ceremony', and where for some donors the point of giving to the monastery was to ensure that, should poverty later befall the donor, the monks would nonetheless still provide an honourable burial. For example, Guillaume Amiel, his wife, and sons handed over another son to the monastery, and a quarter share in three churches, in exchange for which the monastery guaranteed that they would be received 'with all charity' if they should fall into poverty, and that 'if in truth we do not have either resources or lands (*honores*) and we are reduced to poverty, they will bury us honourably in

---

[45] *Cart. Saint-Victor*, I, pp. 376–77 (no. 371), 334–35 (no. 318).
[46] *Cart. Lézat*, II, pp. 118–19 (no. 1163).
[47] *Cart. Saint-Sernin*, I, pp. 150–1 (no. 211); undated, but the prior named in the charter gives us the rough period. See also *Cart. Saint-Sernin*, II, pp. 53–54 (no. 1060), and p. 54 (no. 1061), both c. 1060, recording gifts of land to the existing church of Saint-Pierre in Padern (mentioned above in my text); II, pp. 59–60 (no. 1071), c. 1060, again to the same church specifies the gift 'to Eicard, priest, and all gathered at that place', making clear that the donations are for the souls of all his relatives.
[48] N. L. Taylor, 'The Will and Society in Medieval Catalonia and Languedoc, 800–1200', unpublished PhD (Harvard, 1995), pp. 213–14 (and p. 330, tables 5.4 and 5.5) notes that place of burial becomes a more common element in wills across the eleventh and twelfth centuries, and that a donation is de rigueur for burial within monastic grounds.

the monastery of St-Pierre or in the cemetery of St-Germier'.[49] This suggests that, on the one hand, some ceremony around burial was generally desirable, but that, as in later periods, the extent of that ceremony might be constrained by poverty or other logistical reasons.

It may be that 'honourably' primarily meant 'with prayers and blessings', but one will from the mid-twelfth century indicates that provision might be made for something like a wake also: 'For burial and all other things which are necessary for me... I leave 100 *sous*; and if there is grain and wine in my house, whatever is needed should be given over to a feast.' The same donor goes on to specify a more religious element: 'And I leave 9 gold coins in oblations for masses, thereby that whichever priests celebrate mass on the obit of my death should be given one gold coin each, and the bishop two.'[50] This, it should be noted, is a will from 1155, clearly made by someone of wealth; how widely one infers a similar set of practices or plans, and whether they would have occurred in the preceding century, is not certain. I have found only a very few wills or charters from the eleventh century that specify masses to be said for the dead, but rather more, and with more elaborate or precise ambitions, by the middle of the twelfth century. This might indicate a real change in practice, in terms of which lay people—albeit mostly socially elite lay people—could hope to gain this kind of specific intervention from a monastery, beyond those who had made themselves formal *confratres* of the order.[51] (Pious elements in wills from the eleventh and twelfth century, including burial choices, are discussed in greater detail in Chapter 3).

---

[49] *Cart. Lézat*, I, p. 232 (no. 295), c. 1072 × 81. For other examples of 'honourable' burial, see similarly *Cart. Moissac*, p. 3122 (no. 226); *Cart. Lézat*, I, p. 404 (no. 537), pp. 406–07 (no. 540), p. 408 (no. 543), all eleventh century. Note also pp. 594–95 (no. 819) where should the donors (a husband and wife) fall into dire poverty they are to be allowed to live on 'alms' at the monastery for the rest of their lives, and where broad geographical bounds are specified wherein the abbey takes responsibility for their burial; a similar kind of use of the monastery as 'insurance'.

[50] *Cart. S. Étienne d'Agde*, pp. 114–15 (no. 17); Guillaume Rainard, who also makes other donations to the chapter. For a more religious parallel, see *Cart. Lézat*, II, pp. 120–1 (no. 1166), 1130 × 37, where a woman called Ava makes gifts of people and land, arranging that after her death her brother, a monk, will provide the 'senior' monks with 'bread and wine and fish' on the day of her obit, and that they will sing mass and visit her tomb and the tombs of her parents.

[51] Eleventh-century evidence: *Cart. Saint-Sernin*, p. 214 (no. 298), undated but probably early eleventh century, donor gives the church of *Colobers* so that they sing 'a thousand masses' for the salvation of his soul; *Cart. Lézat*, I, pp. 532–33 (no. 721), c. 1010; pp. 244–45 (no. 307), promise to sing three trental masses in exchange for donation; *Cart. Lézat*, II, pp. 118–19 (no. 1163), 1032 × 60, though here it is not clear that the masses are being said specifically for the donor; *Cart. Notre-Dame de Nîmes*, pp. 216–18 (no. 135), 1043 × 60, which includes (p. 218) provision for an anniversary mass for the donor's mother, to be given by one of the 'senior' canons. Twelfth century, for example *Cart. Lézat*, I, pp. 27–28 (no. 35), 1113 charter, four men giving in perpetuity one-tenth of the grain, flour, and fish associated with the mill at Vernet in exchange for the monks celebrating a trental mass every year for forty years, for their souls and the souls of their parents; I, p. 217 (no. 277), 1122, a man donates tithes so that monks will celebrate a 'full trental mass' for his soul for thirty days. *Cart. S. Étienne d'Agde*, pp. 368–69 (no. 340), 3 Apr 1147, will of Bernard de Roujan, in which complex and detailed provision is made for masses for his soul in a variety of ways, via specifically subdivided donations.

Those with substantial land and funds to give had greater choice over where they might be buried; whether or not the knightly few chose to use the cemetery linked to the local church, it is clear and unsurprising that others did.[52] On several occasions the burial rights of local churches are noted as part of the gift that they collectively comprise. A priest called Deusdet Cabocud—one of a group of donors who handed over the 'fief' of the church of Saint-Fructueux in Mirandol to the abbey of Moissac—specified that he held, and was now donating, the burial rights; that is, the income that payments for burial generated locally.[53] Mention of burial rights does not mean that a cemetery had to be adjacent to the church, but does imply one within the locality, linked liturgically at least to the church and its priest. We also occasionally see gifts made specifically to the cemetery, as at the church of Saint-Pierre at Mont mentioned above, where one of the many donors, Raimond Sicfred of *Texoneras*, gave income from a vineyard in Mont to support the altar 'and to the cemetery works' (*ad ista opera ciminterium*).[54]

Later in this book I will return to the topic of burial and associated issues across a longer period of time, but it is useful to note here the important archaeological work that has been done on rural cemeteries in southern France over the last twenty years, which has greatly illuminated our understanding of burial in the early and central middle ages. Excavations have been carried out in a number of contrasting sites, sometimes preparatory to a modern building project (as at Saint-Laurent-de-la-Cabrerisse, east of Lagrasse) or, for example, where an abandoned medieval village has been identified (as at Vilarnau, on the outskirts of Perpignan).[55] The volume of published work is still relatively small, and its findings open to future revision by further excavations, but a number of features can be remarked. There is a little evidence that suggests the existence of some isolated rural cemeteries, though whether these are continuances of classical Roman burial practices or a trick of the evidential light (that is, apparently 'isolated' because evidence of accompanying settlements has not survived) is uncertain.[56] As discussed further above, churches situated centrally within tightly packed *castra* had to have separate cemeteries beyond the walls, though as far as I have been able to ascertain, to date there has been little archaeological investigation of this kind of

---

[52] As we will see in Chapter 3, from the mid-twelfth century onward the choices of the nobility could be constrained also by the agreements made between different religious foundations regarding burial rights.

[53] *Cart. Moissac*, p. 128 (no. 87). The use of 'fief' (*feudum*) indicates, if anything at all, nothing more than that it is a parcel of rights (here in fact a bundle of rights possessed by a number of different people) that are being discussed; the very fact that it can be gifted indicates how little the word speaks to the received notion of 'feudalism' in this context.

[54] *Cart. Lézat*, I, pp. 377–78 (no. 500).

[55] A. Giallard, S. Kacki, C. Puig, J. Bénézet, and A. Corrochano, 'Premiers résultats concernant le site des Jardins de Saint-Benoît (Saint-Laurent-de-la-Cabrerisse, Aude), pôle religieux et funéraire des Corbières', *Archéologie du Midi médiéval* 28 (2010), 209–18; O. Passarrius, R. Donat, and A. Catafau, 'L'église et le cimetière du village médiéval déserté de Vilarnau à Perpignan', ibid., pp. 219–38.

[56] Schneider, 'De l'archéologie du monument chrétien à l'archéologie des lieux de culte', p. 138;

arrangement. Where the church was situated in a larger plot of land, there is good evidence of substantial burial around the outside of the structure, sometimes clustering around the east end—thus near to the altar—but more often on the south side of the church—most probably therefore the area through which the priest and worshippers would enter the church.[57] A few graves have been found within twelfth-century church buildings, though this may be because the church itself was built over an existing burial site; it does not seem to be a common feature for rural churches generally.[58] (The situation would be different with a larger monastic church, where burial within the structure seems more likely). As one would expect, bodies were almost always buried in roughly west-to-east alignment. In some cases, it would appear that burial expanded outward concentrically from the church, preserving the earlier inhumations, and the current studies have not found substantial reuse of existing space (though this is certainly something which can be attested for later periods textually).[59] Thus whilst burials from this period do not include any use of permanent individual memorials above ground—no headstones or tombs—they do seem to have kept graves protected. This is more clearly notable where we find the practice of burial under board or tiles, or—in what appears to be something more particular to this region—old mill stones.[60]

We therefore have a sense of the cemetery as a distinct and somewhat demarcated space, not gaining stone or brick walls until the thirteenth century but perhaps marked out in other ways prior to that, for example, by the use of free-standing crosses.[61] (We shall return to the space of the cemetery in Chapter 6). There are some eleventh-century injunctions to create a 'sanctuary' space around churches, which *might* be understood to be coterminous with its cemetery. A letter from perhaps 1049 makes a specific link in that regard, as Archbishop Pons of Aix relates the consecration of a local church and its cemetery in the village of Tourves (east of Aix) and forbids anyone from using force or

---

[57] East of church, for example A. Bergeret, 'L'église Saint-Martin-de-Castries (La Vacquerie-et-Saint-Martin-de-Castries, Hérault), dépendance de l'abbaye de Gellone sur le Larzac', *Archéologie du Midi médiéval* 28 (2010), 193–208. South of church, for example Passarrius et al., 'L'église et le cimetière...de Vilarnau', 225–26; Giallard et al., 'Premiers résultats...Saint-Laurent-de-la-Cabrerisse', 212–13 (though also north and west in this case).

[58] Bergeret, 'L'église Saint-Martin-de-Castries', fig. 3.

[59] M. Ott, 'Saint-Nazaire-de-Marissargues à Aubais (Gard): une église et son cimetière du VIIIe au Xe siècle', *Archéologie du Midi médiéval* 28 (2010), 147–59, at p. 152; roughly similarly Y. Ardagna, D. Blanchard, E. Pélaquier, L. Vidal, and M. Seguin, 'Aux marges de l'ancienne agglomération antique du Camp de César: Saint-Jean de Todon *alias* Saint-Jean de Rousigue (Laudun-L'Ardoise, Gard)', *Archéologie du Midi médiéval* 28 (2010), 161–80, at p. 176.

[60] E. Zadora-Rio, 'Archéologies des églises et des cimetières ruraux en Languedoc: un point de vue d'"Outre Loire"' *Archéologie du Midi médiéval* 28 (2010), 239–48 ; Passarrius et al., 'L'église et le cimetière...de Vilarnau', pp. 226, 228.

[61] *Cart. Saint-Victor*, I, pp. 477–80 at p. 478 (no. 474), c. 1074: 'sicut cruces de cimiterio stant usque in fluvium Colobrarie'; cf. Y. Codou, 'Le paysage religieux et l'habitat rural en Provence de l'antiquité tardive au XIIe siècle', *Archéologie du Midi médiéval* 21 (2003), 33–69, p. 50.

raiding those spaces.[62] How we should understand the protection given to the space around the church buildings? This is a novel development found in some of the church councils associated with the 'Peace of God' movement (discussed further in Chapter 2). The protection is usually described in the councils as extending 'thirty paces' (*passus*) outward from the church. This we meet first at the council of Toulouges in 1027, where its meaning is fairly specifically linked to the protection of church property: that nobody should dare to 'violate or assault' a church, or any house located within a radius of thirty paces of a church.[63] By 1041, the next council of Toulouges subtly extends the potential meaning—'no man will violate (*infringat*) a church, nor its space, nor cemetery, nor houses which are in the circuit of a church'—though it also includes an interesting exception: those churches which have been or will be made into strongholds (*in quibus castella facta sunt aut erunt*), because those are churches within which thieves and robbers gather together before or after their evil deeds.[64] Around the same period, the council of Saint-Gilles similarly excludes churches which are considered to be used for warfare and produces another subtle variation: that all churches should be protected from anyone carrying off goods within thirty 'dexters', nor should anyone seek to do ill to another within that space.[65] Perhaps one should interpret 'dexter' as another version of 'pace', though it is intriguing to note that in Barcelona in this period it would appear to indicate a rather greater unit, suggesting that 'thirty dexters' could be equivalent to something like 80 m.[66] The council of Toulouges in 1064 × 66 moves most clearly beyond the specific protection of property to a more general point: that nobody should violate a church or a cemetery or sanctuary (*sacraria*) within thirty paces of the church, by doing any injury to another within that space.[67]

It is important to note the detail from these councils because, although they do clearly share a common purpose, the variations have not been much noted in modern discussion. Several French and Catalan archaeologists, for example, have taken 'the Peace of God' injunctions and the creation of a 'sanctuary' of thirty paces around the church as a repeated and coherent plan that exercised great cultural force, and have used it to interpret the archaeological record for apparent changes to settlement patterns in the eleventh century, and for buildings

---

[62] *Cart. Saint-Victor*, I, pp. 339–43 at p. 340 (no. 325): 'ut infra terminos istius ecclesie vel cimiterii, nullus hunquam hominum neque ulla feminarum, cujuscumque dignitatis, ullo unquam tempore, vim inferre audeat aut predam facere...', there dated to 1019, but subsequently re-dated on basis of bishop's reign—see M. Lauwers, *Naissance du cimetière: lieux sacrés et terre des morts dans l'Occident médiévale* (Paris: Aubier, 2005), p. 14 and p. 278 n. 8.

[63] Mansi 19, cols 483–84.   [64] Toulouges 1041, c. 2; RHGF XI, pp. 510–11.

[65] Mansi 19, col. 843. See similarly council of Toulouges 1064 × 66, Mansi 19, col. 1041.

[66] P. J. Banks, 'Mensuration in Early Medieval Barcelona', *Medievalia* 7 (1987), 37–56. As noted above, the burial rights of the church of Saint-Pierre in Lastonar extended '30 *stadii*' around it (*Cart. Moissac*, p. 183 (no. 125)), indicating a much larger area; though another possibility is of course that all these measurements of '30 somethings' are to be understood symbolically rather than precisely.

[67] Mansi 19, col. 1041.

constructed near to the church.[68] But there are problems with this model, at least as a general interpretive template. As we have seen, it is not the case that all nucleated settlement in the period placed the church building at its centre or even within its walls, suggesting that the 'protected circle' around the church was not something one relied upon too optimistically. And as we have also seen, many churches were built by local figures, often local lords, and thus it is not helpful to see 'lordship' on one side of the equation and 'the Church' on the other. Moreover, as Michel Lauwers discusses in his monograph on the birth of the cemetery, we do not have evidence for southern French bishops taking a more directly active role in sacralizing the cemetery in the tenth and eleventh centuries, unlike their northern French counterparts (who in this period were already performing acts of consecration on the surrounding land as well as the church building itself).[69] It seems likely, therefore, that whilst ordinary people may have turned to the church building on occasion for physical protection—not least because it was made of stone, and because it was sometimes additionally fortified—there is not any very strong evidence that they would have felt a sense of sanctuary, in the modern meaning, when *close* to it but still outside.[70]

In any event, the community of the dead were remembered and protected, kept within a boundary that, by the twelfth century at least, was marked out as 'sacred' through consecration and ritual (another topic to which we will return in Chapter 6). But it seems that to a large extent the dead exist for the community as a collectivity, not marked or remembered as individuals in ways which would outlast personal remembrance.[71] This is not to suggest that people were not treated as individuals when they were first buried or for a period thereafter. Clearly, as noted above regarding 'honourable' burial, they were, and there is some archaeological evidence of hierarchical distinctions also, as a few graves in certain sites seem to indicate a greater investment in time and resources than

---

[68] For example, P. Bonnassie, 'Les *sagreres* catalanes: la concentration de l'habitat dans le "cercle de paix" des églises (XIe siècle)', in M. Fixot and E. Zadora-Rio, eds, *L'environnement des églises et la topographie religieuse des campagnes médiévales*, Document d'archéologie française 46 (Paris, 1994), pp. 68–79; A. Catafau, 'Paroisse et *cellera* dans le diocese d'Elne Xe–XIIe siècles', *Les cahiers de Saint-Michel de Cuxa* 30 (1999), 91–100; A. Catafau, 'Les *celleres* du Roussillon, mises au point et discussions', *CdF* 40 (2006), 17–40. See also D. Baudreu and J. P Cazes, 'Les villages ecclésiaux dans le bassin de l'Aude', in Fixot and Zadora-Pio, *L'environnement*, pp. 80–97, at p. 88; D. Carraz, 'Églises et cimetières des ordres militaires: contrôle des lieux sacrés et *dominium* ecclésiastique en Provence (XIIe–XIIIe siècle)', *CdF* 46 (2011), 277–312, at p. 282.

[69] Lauwers, *Naissance du cimetière*, p. 151.

[70] There are a few later occasions when one can find mention of seeking sanctuary *within* a church: see, for example, cases from the 1330s in J. Shatzmiller, ed., *Médecine et justice en Provence médiévale: documents de Manosque, 1262–1348* (Aix: Uni de Provence, 1989), pp. 187, 195, 199, 213. Some town statutes address the issue by the late twelfth century: see agreement between bishop and the *pros omes* of Albi in 1188, Doat 105, fol. 107, edited in E. d'Auriac, *Histoires de l'ancienne cathédrale et des évêques d'Alby* (Paris: Imprimerie impériale, 1858), p. 200; customs of Carcassonne, c. 1205, no. 104, edited in A. Teulet, ed., *Layettes du trésor des chartes* (Paris: Henri Plon, 1863), I, pp. 272–81 at p. 281.

[71] Lauwers, *Naissance du cimetière*, particularly pp. 10, 127.

others.[72] But in the eleventh and early twelfth century, it would appear that the social memory of the community did not attempt to preserve the individual identity of those who had died, in regard to their place of rest at least.

Local Priests

The 'rights' of the local church over burial are possibly one of the strongest indicators for the presence of a local clergy in this period, even if not necessarily always a resident priest linked to just the one church.[73] For such rights to be exercised, someone had to officiate over a burial, and collect the relevant donation, and it seems unlikely that this would happen without at least some liturgical and ceremonial business being enacted around the fact of burial. (We saw above, of course, a greater degree of post-mortem liturgical activity linked to knightly burial and commemoration when linked to a major monastery.) The assumption in much past historiography has been that local churches in this period, 'unreformed' and in lay hands, would necessarily lack proper pastoral provision. The available evidence is very sparse, but there is some indication that this is too minimalist a view. Whilst I am also a little sceptical as to whether the much more energetic picture some recent scholars have painted of earlier Carolingian pastoral provision necessarily applies to all areas of the empire (as there is much less evidence for episcopal enthusiasm or parochial implementation in a southern French setting), I am sympathetic to the idea that we should imagine the local church as a place of meaningful worship, not simply a stone edifice.[74]

---

[72] Zadora-Rio, 'Archéologies des églises', p. 241.
[73] A number of charters note, alongside mention of first-and-tenth tithing rights, the presence of an *ecclesiasticum* attached to a church, which may indicate a portion of land that is supposed to support the priest (though one wonders if it could indicate rights to other dues and donations). However, as these become visible often at the point that a church is being donated, as part of the valuable bundle of rights and properties attached to the church, it does not seem particularly safe to assume that the presence of an *ecclesiasticum* necessarily indicates the presence of a resident priest.
[74] For the more energetic picture, see particularly C. van Rhijn, *Shepherds of the Lord: Priests and Episcopal Statutes in the Carolingian Period* (Turnhout: Brepols, 2007); S. Patzold and C. van Rhijn, eds, *Men in the Middle: Local Priests in Early Medieval Europe* (Berlin: De Gruyter, 2016); C. van Rhijn, *Leading the Way to Heaven: Pastoral Care and Salvation in the Carolingian Period* (Abingdon: Routledge, 2022). However, see comments by Magnou-Nortier, *La société laïque*, p. 124 on 'the Carolingian renaissance' in this region compared with the Rhinelands; and elsewhere Patzold and van Rhijn themselves note that many local churches were materially quite poor (S. Patzold and C. van Rhijn, 'The Carolingian Local *Ecclesia* as a Temple Society?', *Early Medieval Europe* 29 (2021), 535–54). We may also note the relatively small number of extant Carolingian manuscripts originating in or connected to southern France identified in the corpus of material compiled by Susan Keefe in her important work on baptism and creedal instruction: S. A. Keefe, *Catalogue of Works Pertaining to the Explanation of the Creed in Carolingian Manuscripts* (Turnhout: Brepols, 2012) which lists ten southern French manuscripts (mostly now held in the Bibliothèque municipale in Albi); and S. A. Keefe, *Water and the Word: Baptism and the Education of the Clergy in the Carolingian Empire*, 2 vols (Notre Dame, Ind.: University of Notre Dame Press, 2002), noting four (some of which overlap with those

Those who appear to be local clerics—rather than clerics directly attached to a cathedral or monastery—do appear in the charter evidence, sometimes as donors (including some cases noted already above), or mentioned within donations.[75] More rarely we catch sight of them in relation to a particular local church: a gift of the church of Saint-Pierre at Padern from around 1060 lists the six priests attached to it, and notes that one of them (Ato) has been chosen by the others to take a position of seniority after the death of another (Raimond, his father).[76] That being a priest was a family business should not surprise us in this period; and if anything, it suggests a reasonably strong mechanism for 'instruction' in duties, just as would be the case with more artisanal trades handed down from father to son. A further implication with this particular case at Padern would appear to be to note that the priests are resident and must be supported as part of the donation. One way in which this could work is shown in a charter from 1101, recording a dispute over a donation made some decades earlier wherein the lay donor seems to have specified that his son should become the priest of one of the churches he was donating.[77] Another charter from the later eleventh century shows a local lord handing over a portion (but not the entirety) of the tithing income from a church as a 'fief' to a priest; this is a rare piece of evidence, but perhaps indicates a more standard practice.[78]

previously noted in regard to the creed). See similarly my comments further below regarding penitential manuals as discussed by Rob Meens.

[75] See also *Cart. Moissac*, p. 141 (no. 95), 1072/73: a donation by Hugues Estève, priest, of the church of Saint-Pierre at Sermur, with much detail on his various other lay relatives (via whom he holds the church); *Cart. Lézat*, I, pp. 64–65 (no. 87), c. 1010 where Benoît Alabert, priest, gives various lands that he holds in a place called *Laner*, except for those lands which he had given to two other priests; *Cart. Lézat*, I, pp. 156–57 (no. 201), c. 990, a priest gives various lands, reserving the usufruct of some of them to his two sons (one of whom is also a priest); *Cart. Lézat*, I, pp. 188–89 (no. 240), late eleventh century, where Raimond Eic, *clericus*, gives half of the church of Saint-Sernin d'*Asclamundi*; *Cart. Lézat*, I, pp. 208–09 (no. 267), Hugues, *clericus*, gives himself to the monastery plus half of the altar of Saint-Felix; *Cart. Lézat*, II, pp. 492–93 (no. 1707), late tenth century, Dato, priest, gives the church of Saint-Mamet-Despust; *Cart. Lézat*, II, p. 494 (no. 1710), late tenth century, Gaston, priest, gives half and sells half of church of Saint-Nazaire-de-Galié; *Cart. Lézat*, II, pp. 497–98 (no. 1717), late tenth century, Garsias Raimond, priest, gives the church of Saint-Paul-d'Artigues to one Raimond Eti; *Cart. Lézat*, II, pp. 500–01 (no. 1724), Auriol, priest of Saint-Martory, gives half the church of Saint-Médard; *Cart. Saint-Victor*, I, p. 609 (no. 614), c. 1020, Étienne Pèlerin, priest, and another man give land for the souls of their forebears and for a light before the altar of St Julien the Martyr.

[76] *Cart. Lézat*, II, pp. 35–6 (no. 1039). Similarly *Cart. Mas d'Azil*, pp. 157–58 (no. 1), 1081, where the surrender or sale of the church of Saint-Hippolyte-d'Ortals is done partly with the 'counsel and authority' of four named clerics, who also 'praise and confirm' the exchange.

[77] *Cart. Moissac*, p. 234 (no. 162). For a parallel case, see pp. 331–34 (no. 241), 1129 × 35, at p. 332 for a church at Lunel apparently pledged (that is, mortgaged) to the monastery by a couple and their son, the witness list revealing that the son was also the priest.

[78] *Cart. Lézat*, II, p. 407 (no. 1577), 1061–90: Roger de Muret and Serena his wife give a third of the tenths, and half of the firsts, to Bernard Amiel, cleric, and Guarmund his son-in-law in fief; Guarmund had to become Roger's 'man' (*homo de duobus manibus suis*), and he and Bernard had to pay 5 sous in good wine to make amends for a previous dispute they had had with Serena. The relative complexity of the agreement perhaps explains why a charter was made, and included in the cartulary. For another example, see *Cart. Lézat*, II, p. 478 (no. 1668), eleventh century, where a family hands over three-quarters of the church of Saint-Martin-d'Ox and its holdings to Pierre Auriol, priest, to then be passed on to his children or nephews.

Elsewhere a priest is more clearly *given* as part of the donation itself, and is thus by implication 'unfree'. Guillaume Mancip, his wife Uga, and his sons gave the church of Maurent to the monastery of Saint-Sernin, along with the gift of a man and his land, and 'Bernard Durand, cleric'; it is not clear whether Bernard was a priest linked to the church building itself or not.[79] Priests are also occasionally mentioned in regard to a portion of tithing that would be handed over to their bishop, including in one eleventh-century charter where some of these financial rights were passed over to a layperson in exchange for a donation of land to the cathedral chapter, but with the clear injunction that the priests continue to 'sing' in the churches.[80] We also see priests appear in charters conducting business more generally, such as buying or selling land, and just occasionally appear *inter alia*, as with 'Centullus the priest' whose vineyard happened to be adjacent to one that was being gifted, along with the church of Saint-Étienne-d'Ardac, by a local lord—though whether Centullus had anything to do with that church is not specified.[81] Another priest, Lauterius, is mentioned as cultivating (*excolit*) a manse in Forcalquier which another man, Guillaume, donated to the monastery of Saint-Victor in Marseille in 1025.[82]

So there were some churches not only in towns but in or near rural *castra*, though they were often quite small in size; and there were some clergy who could be providing services at such churches—though whether every church had a permanently resident priest is not demonstrable. What about the material culture within the churches in this period? It would be wonderful at this point to turn to surviving objects, but for want of a French version of the Portable Antiquities Scheme, it is extremely difficult to locate extant examples. We know more, of course, about the large cathedral churches in major cities, all of which had or came to possess important relics, and which would undoubtedly have possessed a range of impressive liturgical objects; though even here, it is only in the later twelfth century that anything much of this kind of thing starts to become visible in the surviving sources.[83] But there are some details in charters that indicate either what objects came with local churches or, at least, were generally expected to be there.

---

[79] *Cart. Saint-Sernin*, pp. 131–32 (no. 181).

[80] *Cart. Apt*, pp. 228–29 (no. 84): charter of 1053, in which Pons Pulverel confirmed an earlier contract made by his grandfather (*avus*) with an earlier bishop, in which he gained the tithe income formerly given to the bishop, in return for a vineyard and lands that he donated to the cathedral, that tithe income (in part at least) paying for priests to sing mass.

[81] Buying (albeit presented as a 'surrender', but with a price of 4 *sous* clearly given), *Cart. Lézat*, I, p. 64 (no. 86); Centullus in *Cart. Lézat*, I, p. 121 (no. 156). Other priests visible as adjacent landowners: *Cart. Lézat*, I, pp. 104–05 (no. 139); 109–10 (no. 143); 115 (no. 150); 121 (no. 156); 125 (no. 161); 359 (no. 476), all late tenth/early eleventh century; 377–78 (no. 500), 1060s; 469–70 (no. 628), later eleventh century; 519–20 (no. 699), c. 1000; 529–30 (no. 718), late tenth century; 598 (no. 826), 990; *Cart. Lézat*, II, pp. 160 (no. 1251), 926; 210 (no. 1337), late tenth century.

[82] *Cart. Saint-Victor*, I, pp. 461–62 (no. 456).

[83] The material culture of churches in later centuries is discussed further in Chapter 6.

Very unusually one charter notes an occasion in the early twelfth century at which the bishop of Barbastro consecrated a church to Ste Marie in the *castrum* of a place called *Ritalans*, 'and placed in the altar relics of the holy martyrs Pope Cornelius and Artemisia the virgin'.[84] Having relics in each altar was certainly the expected practice for all churches by a later stage, but it seems unlikely that we can extrapolate from this lone example to all other local churches in this earlier period. We find more quotidian, but liturgically important, objects mentioned a bit more frequently. In 1075 a record of the 'donation' (in exchange for 180 *sous*) of the church of Saint-Pierre-de-Padern (a small village once near Saint-Ybars, now disappeared) to the monastery of Lézat, includes mention not only of its tithing and burial rights and the land owned by the church, but that it is handed over 'with the books and bells (*signi*) and chalice and thurible and all ecclesiastical ornaments which the same church is seen to possess'; another donation of a church from a similar period specifies 'books and bells (*signi*) and vestments and oblations, and with its altars and whatever pertains to them' (the latter phrase possibly indicates other unnamed liturgical objects, but more likely implies income previously directed toward a specific altar).[85] When consecrating the church of Saint-Pierre-de-Mont, mentioned further above, the bishop enjoined the priest to expend the donations to the church on finishing its construction, and then on 'crosses and bells (*signi*) and books and robes (*pallia*)'—both an indication of the integral importance of these liturgical objects, but also that they were not simply handed out by the diocese but had to be financed and purchased by the locality.[86] Just a couple of references also indicate that churches—as one would expect, given the practicalities if nothing else—had lights, in the form of either candles or oil lamps; though these only start to become a visible focus for *lay* patronage by the mid-twelfth century.[87]

---

[84] *Cart. Lézat*, I, pp. 29–30 (no. 38); see above my earlier comment re dating this charter. Cornelius was a third-century pope and martyr; Artemisia is possibly Artemia, daughter of Emperor Maximian (c. 250–c. 310), executed as a Christian convert in the early fourth century. It is not entirely clear where this church (Sainte-Marie-de-Roudeille in the *castrum* of 'Ritalans') was located, though the donors are identified with *castra* relatively close to Lézat. The bishop had been in Toulouse earlier and may have been en route back to his diocese when performing this task.

[85] *Cart. Lézat*, II, pp. 43–44 (no. 1048); I, p. 41 (no. 51). See also I, pp. 174–75 (no. 223), donation in 949 of church of Saint-Christaud 'cum signis et libris' and its various lands; I, pp. 208–09 (no. 267), donation of half of altar of Saint-Félix 'with offerings, chalices, thuribles, burial rights, bells, vestments, receipts, tenths, firsts'; I, pp. 235–36 (no. 299), church at Sabonnères 'cum signis et libri, cum chalicem et turribulum, videlicet cum omne ornamentum ecclesiastici ministerii'.

[86] *Cart. Lézat*, I, pp. 377–78 (no. 500). NB charter of one Henri, who was planning on entering the religious life, giving the various properties he owned in Apt to the works of the cathedral, and 'if the works of the church have been completed, these resources should be directed either to the writing of books and document or to making bells (*signis*) or for alms for the poor'; *Cart. Apt*, pp. 237–38 (no. 89), 1048 × 80.

[87] For example, from the will of Guillaume Bordel of Conas, 1141, a bequest of some land to the church of Sainte-Eulalie (probably in Montblanc) 'for lamp oil'; see *Cart. S. Étienne d'Agde*, p. 339 (no. 298). We return to this topic in Chapter 3 below.

From these scant references we may infer that the expectation for local churches was that they would have the key objects necessary for performing the mass and the wider liturgy—some books (*which* books are almost never specified, though one might presume a sacramentary, a missal, or a lectionary),[88] a chalice for the wine (but only a couple of extant mentions at this stage of a paten for the bread),[89] robes for the priest, at least one cross, at least one bell (though this may mean handbells for use during services, rather than a suspended church bell), and some candles or oil lamps providing light for the altar at least. Given the expectation that these objects should be provided for locally, and that the charters in which they are specifically mentioned talk about 'a chalice' or 'a thurible' in the singular, this also suggests that there would be a degree of fragility to the local set-up, where loss or damage could potentially disrupt the local liturgy until replacements could be procured.

To understand how people used churches at this time, and what their experience of Christianity would be via that local provision, we have to provide hugely suppositional interpretations, the contours of which depend much upon the way in which we view the period as a whole. If one sees the eleventh and early twelfth centuries as marked, above all else, by rapacious and fragmented secular lordship, and 'the Church' as fighting a desperate battle to ward off lay encroachments and violence, then the picture looks pretty bleak, the local church as perhaps little more than a means of providing revenue to a secular lord. It might have a priest, but one of servile status, utterly dependent on the lord for his livelihood, possibly illiterate, distracted by his marriage and offspring from any strong focus on spiritual things, able to provide only a rudimentary form of liturgy at best, and nothing in the way of real pastoral instruction. This is how some past historians have seen the situation across much of Europe, their view echoing that of various 'reformers' within the period.

However, this may not be the case. It rests upon a received concept of how 'the Church' *ought* to be structured and governed, one which is not very adept at capturing varied dynamics within the period itself. Some decades ago Elizabeth Magnou-Nortier argued that a different canon-legal tradition, dominant in southern France, distinguished between 'authority' and 'ownership' of ecclesiastical lands. She thus presented lay lords in this region in this period as 'patrons, protectors and defenders' of churches, rather than struggling with ecclesiastical

---

[88] The will of Hugues, bishop of Toulouse (undated, but probably Hugues II, and therefore mid-eleventh century), specifies a missal, and a missal with a lectionary, among other bequests; *Cart. Saint-Sernin*, pp. 191–94 (no. 280). *Cart. Mas d'Azil*, pp. 177–78 (no. 27), 1150: oath taken by one Bernard, who surrenders the tithe on the church at Paris (a small village nearby); he takes the oath in the hands of Guillaume the chaplain of the aforesaid church, touching the missal.

[89] *Cart. Lézat*, I, pp. 243–44 (no. 306), surrender of church of Saint-Michel in *Monte*, c. 1035, with 'signis et libris et turribulis et vestmentis necnon et calicem et patenam'; I, p. 288 (no. 364), 1058 donation of Saint-Paul-de-Lussan, similarly.

authorities over power.[90] Her rather optimistic perspective perhaps swings too far in the other direction; it is in any case more focused on monastic and episcopal matters than the local church. Nonetheless it is a useful corrective. Even in the 'worst case' picture sketched in the preceding paragraph—one to which, to be clear, I do not myself subscribe—it seems inescapable that one thing the priest would be doing was providing some form of service in relation to burial. The very common mention of burial rights must surely indicate the provision of some form of clerical rite—because if not, what would occasion any monetary donation when families buried their dead?[91] (As we shall see at the end of this chapter, one might also suspect that baptisms were regularly available also; though in truth 'rights' relating to baptism are not mentioned very often in the charter evidence.) Other things flow from this. The nobility, as we have noted, sometimes opted for burial at a monastery or cathedral rather than at a local church or cemetery, which suggests another way in which the community of the dead echoed the social stratification among the living. Those nobles, donating to monasteries in regard to their burial, could make provision for trental masses and the like. The provision of a more elaborate liturgical service unavailable at a local level might be part of the attraction of the monasteries to the laity; but it could be taken also to indicate some wider knowledge of such elements, such that these provisions were what the nobility sometimes sought out. It might therefore suggest that in some places, the local priest (or indeed priests, as we have noted at least one church which possessed several) was able to perform a similar duty, even if on a lesser scale.

A couple of eleventh-century 'Peace' councils also include a stated desire to get people to attend church, as they stress the importance of abjuring work on Sundays. The period of truce set out at Toulouges 1027 is framed such that 'everyone would render the honour owed to the Lord's day'. A letter of the archbishop of Arles in 1041 frames the need for its peace injunction in part because of the generally bad state of things, such that nobody is observing the Sabbath but are instead doing 'servile' works; the archbishop and bishops have therefore established four special days, namely the Thursday (because of Ascencion), Friday (because of Christ's passion), Saturday for the veneration of his burial, and Sunday to celebrate the resurrection. On these four days nobody was to do any 'rural work', nor to attack his enemies; by implication this was to apply each week, though a specifically Lenten context is strongly evoked.[92] The strong assumption is therefore that people would be able to attend church at which they would find liturgical services being performed regularly, if nothing else.

---

[90] Magnou-Nortier, *La société laïque*, pp. 344–45, 392–94, 445–46.

[91] See in general Lauwers, *Naissance*, and discussion further below. Burial rights are mentioned in about one-quarter of all church donations in the cartulary for Lézat, and in over half the charters where any details regarding rights are provided.

[92] Toulouges: Mansi 19, cols 483–84 (trans. Buc in Head and Landes, eds, *Peace of God*, p. 334); Arles: Mansi 19, cols 593–96.

These concerns recur in a broader context in other texts, including some saintly *vitae* from the period. The *miracula* given in the *vita* of St Vivian, whose shrine was in the monastery at Figeac, emphasize the observance of Sundays at several points: a local 'cripple' called Étienne came to the shrine for healing on many days 'except for the Sabbath, which is named for repose'. In contrast, a man called Guitbert refused to stop his work on the Sabbath, and was punished by finding his pickaxe stuck to his wrist bracelet. Only when he had come to the shrine and prostrated himself in prayer for the whole day, to seek to propitiate the holy confessor for his crime, was he freed—and this freedom was granted on a Sunday. As a more positive example, a knight called Ugo from Cardaillac came to the monastery to pray on a Sunday (accompanied by an old man who was mute, who was then cured).[93] It is of course hard to know what audience was imagined or intended for a Latin text that recorded *miracula* in this period, though it is not unreasonable to assume that the short and vivid tales could have had a wider dissemination, as part of promoting the shrine; and in their details, could therefore have aimed at instruction, just as later preaching stories ('*exempla*') would do. We should also bear in mind however that telling tales of lax observance by the laity was something that probably helped monks emphasize their own monastic identity. Of course, it is not the case that the mid-eleventh century was the first time in which the Christian laity were told to abstain from work on Sundays and feast days, and to attend mass; there were Carolingian injunctions to do just this.[94] But it is an interesting moment at which to see it being emphasized, alongside other matters of public order; a possible indication of a renewed desire to regulate lay behaviour that is not otherwise visible in the available sources.

But in any case, as I have argued above, the image of the lone nobleman exercising arbitrary and solipsistic lordship does not fit well with the southern French evidence: as with *castra*, churches were often created by, or depended upon donations from, a number of powerful local people, and on occasion a wider group of *boni homines* also. Linked to the importance of burial practices, one might presume that these people had some ongoing investment in the structure of a spiritual as well as an economic nature. One should not, in any case, too readily separate those two elements. It is worth reflecting on the fact that the various 'rights' associated with churches, as listed in charters when they were created or donated, simultaneously indicated a flow of income to the church but also a provision of some form of spiritual benefit. Tithes—the firsts and tenths mentioned most frequently—were a form of taxation, but one which, in theory at least, partly

---

[93] 'Translatio et miracula Sancti Viviani', pp. 268–69.
[94] For example, in the capitulary compiled by Ansigisus in 827, c. 75, *Capitularia regum Francorum* I, ed. A. Boretius, MGH (Hanover: Hahn, 1883), p. 404. More broadly see W. Thomas, *Der Sonntag im frühen Mittelalter* (Göttingen: Vandenhoeck & Ruprecht, 1929); S. Jurasinski, *The Old English Penitentials and Anglo Saxon Law* (Cambridge: Cambridge University Press, 2015), pp. 100–09; and NB Magnou-Nortier, *La société laïque*, p. 108.

went to the maintenance of a locally identifiable structure, often (at least for the earlier part of the eleventh century) the most impressive structure in the locality; and the provision of tithes might perhaps have led local residents to feel some investment and involvement in the sacred duties performed within that building.

Sometimes, in addition to those associated with burial, other rights are also mentioned: for example, in a donation, made probably in the late eleventh century, by a priest (who perhaps had a greater interest in specifying this level of detail), the church of Saint-Sernin in *Asclarmundi* is specified as coming not only with firsts and tenths and burial rights, but 'receipts, penitences, [and] offerings' (*recepti, penitencie, offerenda*).[95] What is meant by 'receipts' is not certain, but perhaps is about financial dues from lands owned by the church. 'Offerings' surely indicates ongoing local donations, perhaps to the altar, perhaps linked to the regular performance of the mass, as one would expect for later periods. 'Penitences' is in some ways the most intriguing thing in this list. It is mentioned in at least one other church donation in the charters associated with the monastery of Moissac, and is found also in an early eleventh-century charter recording the sale of the episcopal church of Sainte-Cecile in Albi.[96] One might see it as a money payment made in lieu of performing some other form of penance; or perhaps as a donation made to a priest for having bestowed a penance, which would put it more in line with the other forms of income listed. There is passing evidence from other early twelfth-century sources that sinful knights and others might seek out 'penance' for their wrongs. For example, a young 'Gascon' (possibly meaning a mercenary) is reported to have entered the Marian shrine at Rocamadour without having first received penance and absolution (*sine penitentia et sacerdotali beneficio adiit*). This prompted divine punishment: he was possessed by the Devil. Later he did seek penance from his own local priest, also restoring tithes that he had misappropriated.[97] Maybe, unlike this particular figure, other sinners more dutifully sought out penance with sufficient regularity for it to constitute a 'right' held by a church. Alternatively, we might interpret 'penitences' as an expected oblation associated with a more general act of confession made by the priest on behalf of his community during the mass (a topic to which we will return briefly in Chapter 8). However, reflecting on the fact that the tale from Rocamadour subsequently explains that the young Gascon had been

---

[95] *Cart. Lézat*, I, pp. 188–89 (no. 240); the priest, Raimond Eic, gave half of the church. Dated by the editors to c. 1096 presumably on the basis of his mention of hoping to return from Jerusalem (where he was headed); but actually Jerusalem is mentioned in other charters prior to the First Crusade. See also p. 560 (no. 762), 1085 × 96, re donation of church of Saint-Geniès in Marens, where *penitencie* are mentioned alongside tithes and burial rights.

[96] *Cart. Moissac*, p. 191 (no. 133), donation of three-quarters of church of Saint-Séverin de *Meisme* in 1085; *HGL*, V, cols 432–33 (no. 214). The latter also mentioned *sacrationes* and *missas*, in both cases implying payments (for blessings and saying masses, one presumes); this however in an episcopal context.

[97] E. Albe, ed., *Les miracles de Notre Dame de Rocamadour au XIIe siècle* (Paris: H. Champion, 1907), pp. 79–81; translation in M. Bull, ed., *The Miracles of Our Lady of Rocamadour: Analysis and Translation* (Woodbridge: Boydell, 1999), pp. 104–5.

excommunicated for withholding tithes, one might also interpret income associated with 'penitence' as moments at which people made recompense to free themselves from excommunication. In any event, in any of these scenarios, it indicates at least a notion of the provision of penance at a local level, in a sufficiently regular form for it to be worth listing as an associated 'right', in at least a few cases.[98]

It also surely implies some degree of instruction regarding sin—for which penance is the necessary response, and which is thus not only linked to reflection at the deathbed—though what form this would take and with what level of detail is utterly unknowable for most local churches. In a much more civic context, we do have, from the late eleventh century, a charter recounting the establishment of the hospital of Saint-Raimond in Toulouse by Guillaume IV, count of Toulouse (d. 1094). The donors (the count plus the bishop and a few others) specified that the hospital should be equipped with all that it needed, for the poor and all people who stayed there; as with other such foundations, it was perhaps as much a hostel as a hospital. The necessary provision of the establishment included sending to the hospital all the burial garments or sheets that arrived with bodies that were to be interred at Saint-Sernin, and that there should be an altar in the hospital dedicated to St Jean, 'where the poor, and all other Christians, could hear the ministry of God'.[99] What one takes 'ministry' (*ministerium*) to mean is not certain. It could simply indicate 'hear the mass being performed', but might also suggest the provision of the sacraments and the possibility of some religious instruction, as one would more clearly find as a regular part of the provision that hospitals made for their residents later in the middle ages.

Lack of evidence for local pious instruction and activity is not evidence that such things did not exist, and I am perhaps being overly cautious in not magnifying further the picture that can be drawn from the tiny fragments gleaned from monastic cartularies.[100] One fairly rich example, from the end of the period discussed here, does suggest a greater amount of activity directed toward and involving the laity. This is a letter from Bermund, bishop of Béziers, written in 1148, announcing that the church of Saint-Sernin, outside the town of Béziers, had been given to the Knights Hospitaller. The letter describes the things that people can *no longer* expect to do in the church, because it was now in the sole possession of that order: that the church could not receive other parishioners without the agreement of the bishop, or make a cemetery there; people could not be assigned penance, nor view (or possibly receive) the Eucharist, nor have tombs in

---

[98] For discussion of penance in this period, see S. Hamilton, *The Practice of Penance, 900–1050* (London: Royal Historical Society, 2001) and R. Meens, *Penance in Medieval Europe, 600–1200* (Cambridge: Cambridge University Press, 2014). Evidence for southern France is relatively sparse: in the appendices to his book, Meens identifies between seven and nine relevant manuscripts of penitential manuals which might have been produced in southern France, out of a total corpus of over 180 manuscripts. For further discussion, see Chapter 8 below.
[99] *Cart. Saint-Sernin*, pp. 380–82 (no. 547).
[100] For judicious comments south of the Pyrenees, see Davies, *Acts of Giving*, p. 49.

the church unless they had a prior connection to the Hospitallers. Major masses could not be performed there except on the feast of Saint-Sernin, nor could the hours be sung on the day before the Sabbath, nor could the cross be worshipped, nor baptisms or marriages performed there, 'nor can women get up from their beds following childbirth to sing mass' (that is, the practice later called 'churching' in England), nor can the bell be rung whilst the bell of the church of Sainte-Marie-Madeleine is ringing, nor the hours be rung during Lent.[101] This particular church was adjacent to a major civic centre, and might not speak to the experience in other, more rural, regions. Nonetheless, the wider array of things which Bishop Bermund ordered to cease in 1148 clearly *did* occur before that date—and it is possible that they were regular practice long before, both near Béziers and elsewhere across the region.

But as a final caveat, we can perhaps usefully contrast what Bermund ordered with another moment at which things were forbidden, about a century earlier: around 1059 Berengar, the viscount of Narbonne, petitioned a gathering of bishops against various alleged misdeeds perpetrated against him by Guifrid, archbishop of Narbonne. Among many other things, Guifrid had excommunicated the viscount and his lands, 'so cruelly that no-one was baptized there, nor did anyone receive communion, nor was anyone properly buried'.[102] This suggests, in happier times, a regularity of local provision for at least these three things across a wide geography. What the viscount of Narbonne laments as forbidden are essentially sacramental provisions for the beginning and the end of life, but perhaps not quite so much in between (unless we decide that 'receive communion' refers to Easter worship and not only to the last rites). What was actually available in any specific rural locality would perhaps vary somewhere between these two poles, the relatively rich picture we get from 1148 and the more limited provision emphasized around 1059. Moreover, that variation could very likely have continued well beyond 1148 in some more rural places.

A final thought: Berengar's petition against Guifrid was a highly rhetorical piece of political theatre. The things listed as forbidden under excommunication are what he chose to emphasize, and perhaps do not give us the whole picture. But that emphasis is in itself telling: it focuses upon what local priests were understood essentially to provide, namely entrance into Christianity, and the provision of a proper ending to this life. If these were the priorities not only of Berengar but of his subjects, they fit fairly well with the picture of local churches that this chapter has tried to build up. They are, in other words, very largely what Christianity essentially *was* for most people in this period.

---

[101] Martene and Durand, *Thesaurus Novus Anecdotorum* I, pp. 406–07.
[102] *HGL*, V, fols 496–502 (no. 251): 'tam crudeliter ita ut nullus ibi baptisetur, nec communicetur, nec sepeliatur'. See J. A. Bowman, 'Do Neo-Romans Curse? Law, Land, and Ritual in the Midi (900–1100)', *Viator* 28 (1997), 1–32, p. 25.

2
Peace, Violence, and Saints, c. 1000–1150

As in every period of history, the most quotidian and immediate focus for most people's pious activity would of necessity be their immediate locality. For many, this would form the entirety of their devotional experience. If one lived in a major city like Toulouse, Narbonne, or Marseille, there would be some variety and competition between different shrines, perhaps some awareness of different rhythms of liturgical service, and one could possibly experience some contrasting settings for both worship and religious instruction. If one was in a smaller town or a much more rural locality, the range of activity and opportunity for contrast would hugely diminish, and it seems likely that the conjunction between locality, the local power dynamics, and communal worship would be very strong.

But there was of course a larger Christendom beyond, both literal and conceptual. There was a larger geographical Christendom to which one might travel through pilgrimage (a topic to be explored a little further in Chapter 6) or for other reasons such as trade. As importantly there was a larger Christendom to which one might try to connect oneself symbolically rather than practically, a Christendom that we might conceive as a web of interlinked but also competing centres of holiness, the main nodes in that network being a combination of monasteries, cathedrals, and shrines. Access to such a wider Christendom, whether in practice or in theory, inevitably tended to be much easier for lay elites than for the masses, particularly prior to the later twelfth century (as we will see further in Chapter 3). But the worship associated with regional saints did in particular provide a wider dynamic available on occasion to non-elites. In this chapter, by looking at interactions with saints—particularly through the notional 'Peace of God' movement—we can explore what a lay experience of Christianity in the eleventh and early twelfth centuries might involve *beyond* the immediate experience of the local church. We will also attempt to think about what abstract ideas and Christian concepts might have been available beyond the local.

The Peace and Violence of God

At some point in the late tenth century—perhaps as early as 980—there was a major gathering of bishops from various cities in the Auvergne, who came together at a rural place called Coler, somewhere near Aurillac.[1] They congregated in order to hold a council, seeking to establish the solidity of the political order (*pro statu res publicae*) and an 'inviolable peace'. To that end, relics of saints from across the region were gathered, coming in procession from various monastic and cathedral shrines. Among the throng of saints was the early church bishop St Vivian, whose relics were brought out of the monastery at Figeac, further to the south. En route to the council, the Figeac monks stopped at a place near a wood.[2] There they gathered up branches and greenery to make a canopy to cover the statue of the saint, so that it would not get wet from the rain. But as the monks laboured in the wood, the entourage of a local knight called Géraud came across them, and tried to get them to stop. They were not initially deterred, but then Géraud's men 'drove them off, cruelly smitten by many insults and wounds'. In response to this attack upon his people, the saint delivered rightful punishment: that wood henceforth bore no fruit and became a total wasteland, until the time of Géraud's eventual death; whereafter it again returned to fecundity.[3] The monks in any case recovered from their assault, and continued on to Coler, where many great miracles then took place.

The council at Coler is one of the earliest examples of what historians have come to call the 'Peace of God' movement. Although the narrative *vita* of St Vivian from which the story comes is not the most straightforward source— among other things, it recounts an almost identical set of details for another peace council some years later at Limoges,[4] the monks again beaten away in their attempts to gather wood, and Vivian punishing the local lord in exactly the same fashion—it contains nonetheless a key conjunction of elements found in a variety of other texts of the period. We have bishops from a region congregating to reform a social situation (however we choose to translate *res publica*, it clearly indicates a set of concerns beyond the purely ecclesiastical); the relics of saints, plural, are gathered in order to make a particularly impressive display; an important context is the violent action to which local lay lords, such as Géraud, are wont to turn; and a saint punishes such behaviour.

---

[1] There are different possible sites identified: see discussion in C. Lauranson-Rosaz, 'Peace from the Mountains: The Auvergnat Origins of the Peace of God', in T. Head and R. Landes, eds, *The Peace of God: Social Violence and Religious Response in France around the Year 1000* (Ithaca, NY: Cornell University Press, 1992), pp. 104–34, at pp. 122–23. Lauranson-Rosaz's suggestion of Cueilhes, very near Aurillac, is persuasive.

[2] Lauranson-Rosaz suggests that the 'Nuntemdinem' of the text could be an orthographic mistake for 'in Antuenedinem', that is Antuéjouls, which is en route between Figeac and Aurillac: C. Lauranson-Rosaz, 'La paix populaire dans les montagnes d'Auvergne au Xe siècle', in P.-R. Gaussin, ed., *Maisons de Dieu et hommes d'église* (Saint-Étienne: Publications de l'Université de Saint-Étienne, 1992), pp. 289–333, at p. 314 n. 72.

[3] 'Translatio et miracula Sancti Viviani Episcopi', *Analecta Bollandiana* 8 (1889), 264.

[4] 'Translatio et miracula Sancti Viviani', p. 273. A detailed critique of other aspects is given in D. Barthélemy, *L'an mil et la paix de Dieu: la France chrétienne et féodale 980–1060* (Paris: Fayard, 1999), pp. 312–22.

For the purposes of this chapter, the particular interest of the Peace of God movement is the apparently abundant presence of ordinary lay people. In the *vita* of St Vivian they come together in an 'infinite number' at Colers, forming a group with the many saints who had been brought there. Other texts relating similar events emphasize the involvement of many of the laity, of 'an innumerable multitude of people' at Limoges in 994, and acts constituted by the bishops 'along with all the clergy and the faithful people' at Toulouges in 1027.[5] What these councils proposed, and hoped to enforce, also had implications that were potentially profound for all Christians, the ordinary laity included: they sought to prevent nobles from committing acts of violence against ordinary peasants; to protect the space of the church and its cemetery and the houses immediately around (as noted in Chapter 1); and to impose a total ban on fighting for half of each week.[6] Indeed for some modern historians, the Peace movement marks *the* moment at which ordinary people become crucial participants in not only a political movement, but a profound religious revolution. As outlined in the Introduction, various historians have seen the late tenth century as a period which witnesses a swift collapse of centralized order, and the rise of local lords competing in their attempts to dominate the local landscape through violence, seizing control of both lay and ecclesiastical lands. It has been argued that, inspired by the potential for radical change heralded by the millennium (the year 1000), the masses responded eagerly to—or indeed, petitioned for—episcopal intervention into the otherwise unchecked ravages of feudal lordship. In this interpretation, the unbeatably powerful conjunction of saints, bishops, and people provided a means by which noble violence could be brought into check; and, in the most radical telling of this narrative, it is only with this conjunction that Christian theology starts really to influence how all of European society functioned.[7]

The Peace of God is also an area of considerable interpretive debate, only some of which however has the potential to illuminate issues of local, lay religious practice.[8] A key part of its importance is the eventual geographical spread of the 'Peace', by the late eleventh century reaching into northern France, the Low

---

[5] R. Landes, 'Popular Participation in the Limousin Peace of God', in Head and Landes, eds, *Peace of God*, p. 186 n. 11; Mansi 19, cols 483–84 ('Acts of the Council of Toulouges, 1027', trans. P. Buc, in Head and Landes, eds, *Peace of God*, p. 334).

[6] Here drawing on the councils of Nice/Arles (1041) and Toulouges (1041): Mansi 19, cols 593–96; RHGF XI, pp. 510–11.

[7] R. Landes, 'Can the Church be Desperate, Warriors be Pacifist, and Commoners Ridiculously Optimistic? On the Historian's Imagination and the Peace of God', in K. L. Jansen, G. Geltner, and A. E. Lester, eds, *Center and Periphery: Studies on Power in the Medieval World in Honor of William Chester Jordan* (Leiden: Brill, 2013), pp. 79–92.

[8] Key critiques in D. Barthélemy, 'La paix de Dieu au temps du millénaire', in his *La mutation de l'an mil a-t-elle eu lieu? Servage et chevalerie dans la France des Xe et XIe siècles* (Paris: Fayard, 1997), pp. 297–361; *L'an mil et la paix de Dieu* (Paris: Fayard, 1999). For an earlier perspective on southern France, Magnou-Nortier, *La société laïque*, pp. 292–312. See now G. Koziol, *The Peace of God* (Leeds: ARC Humanities Press, 2018).

Countries, and central Italy. These examples clearly move us beyond the geographical bounds of southern France, as is really also the case with Aurillac and Limoges; although the participants from Figeac do keep us more directly connected to the culture of the south. In short, my concern here is not with the whole edifice, real or imagined, of 'the Peace'. Instead, I want to focus only on those materials that come from the south of France (taking Mende, Figeac, and Cahors as my northerly limits) in an attempt to see what this corpus of texts suggests about the laity's involvement in a less 'localized' form of Christian worship, beyond the local church, in the eleventh century in particular. In what follows, I am going to rehearse and slightly elaborate upon some existing critiques of 'the Peace of God' as a historiographical edifice, in order to try to loosen the rather emphatic grasp it has had particularly on some scholarship regarding local religion in southern France. But I do not wish to abandon the topic as a whole. As we shall see, the materials relating 'the Peace' *can* provide interesting evidence for one way in which ordinary lay people encountered saints and the powers of the holy; and, as we shall see in Chapter 5, an ecclesial sense of 'Peace' continues to inform wider dynamics in southern French society in later centuries.

The recognized sequence of episcopal councils and edicts for the south demonstrates a fairly strong degree of legislative unity and development: the councils of Narbonne (990), Toulouges (1027), Mende (sometime between 1030 and 1048), Nice or Arles (1041), Toulouges (1041), Saint-Gilles (1042 × 44), four different councils at Narbonne (17 March and 1 August 1043; 1054; and 1055), Toulouges once again (1064 × 66), Mende (1102 × 12), and Toulouse (1114).[9] In the documents produced by, or reporting the activities of, bishops and others there are some recurrent themes, and some precise repetitions of content. There is an emphasis upon the unrestrained violence of the nobility, their depredations against the Church and its possessions (thus Narbonne 990, Toulouges 1027, Saint-Gilles 1042 × 44, Narbonne 1043), but also a broader sense of 'peace', that attempts to limit the days, and later the period of the year, in which fighting can be done *at all*—the earliest example from these materials being Toulouges 1027, which orders such a ban between the ninth hour on Saturday to the first hour on Sunday 'so that everyone renders the honour owed to the Lord's day'.[10] Other elements of 'the Peace' found recurrently in the south, and similarly in other areas, include making nobles swear oaths not to fight in certain periods or to

---

[9] Editions in the order cited in the text above: Mansi 19, cols 103, 483–84; C. Brunel, 'Juges de la paix', *Bibliothèque de l'École des Chartes* (1951), 41–42; Mansi 19, cols 593–96; RHGF XI, pp. 510–11; Mansi 19, cols 843, 599–604, 827–32; O. Pontal, *Conciles de la France capetienne jusqu'en 1215* (Paris: Cerf, 1995), 139; Mansi 19, cols 1041–44; C. Brunel, *Les Miracles de Saint Privat, suivi des opuscules d'Aldebert III, évêque de Mende* (Paris: Picard, 1912), pp. 14–15; *Cart. Lézat*, II, pp. 211–12 (no. 1342). To these, one could potentially add the councils held in Vic in 1030 and 1033 as they were convened by the same Bishop Oliba of Vic; see J. A. Bowman, 'Councils, Memory and Mills: The Early Development of the Peace of God in Catalonia', *Early Medieval Europe* 8 (1999), 105.

[10] Mansi 19, cols 483–84; trans. Buc in Head and Landes, eds, *Peace of God*, p. 334.

otherwise break the peace; a general ban on fighting on holy days, and on building castles during holy periods of the year (Lent, Ascencion, Pentecost); protection of women and other non-combatants; protection of church property, and more precisely, protection of the physical building of the church and the land around—as we saw in Chapter 1, anything sat 'within 30 paces' of the church. However, in contrast to some suggestions in more northerly evidence, particularly chronicle accounts, there is no 'millennial' theme apparent in any of the southern material.[11]

As several historians have argued at least some of the councils can be shown to have quite specific and locally directed agendas.[12] This must be borne in mind also when considering the councils' attempts to limit violence against peasants: monasteries and cathedrals owned land to which peasants were tied, and owned property for which they paid dues. Some of the concern expressed for peasants can thus be seen as a further attempt to protect 'church property'. As noted in the preceding chapter, we can see some direct gifts of unfree people to monasteries (sometimes but apparently not always with land as well) by the very local lords who are otherwise understood to be the target of these injunctions.

All of this has been debated within the wider understanding of the Peace of God movement and the much larger arguments about 'feudal revolution' or 'feudal transformation', which are not my main concern here. But elements of this matter also with regard to the issue of the experience of Christian worship in southern France. If we see a region beset by constant local violence in the late tenth and eleventh centuries, with no recognition of higher authority, where the Church is the only possible source of intervention and restraint, and where the local church building (following the injunction of these councils) is the only 'safe space', then the experience of Christianity would be inextricably linked to attempts to establish some degree of sociopolitical order.[13] As noted, for some historians, the importance and process of these transformations qualify the Peace of God as a 'popular' mass movement, and colour a host of other associated features in the religious landscape of the period. But if, on the other hand, things are not quite so fraught and so lacking in structure and law, then the question of 'order' becomes more situated politically, more clearly a programme of episcopal reform.[14] As Geoff Koziol argues, having emphasized the nuanced allowances of legitimate violence contained within many of the Peace council clauses,

---

[11] See similarly comments on the evidence in general by Koziol, *Peace of God*, p. 46, and on 'the Peace' having rather different regional emphases, pp. 3, 56–62.

[12] Most brilliantly, see Bowman, 'Councils, Memory and Mills'.

[13] A picture embraced by Pierre Bonnassie in various publications, and to varying degrees informing the analysis of a number of regional historians and archaeologists, for example A. Catafau, 'Les celleres du Roussillon, mises au point et discussions', *CdF* 40 (2006), 17–40.

[14] See now M. W. McHaffie, 'Law and Violence in Eleventh-Century France', *Past & Present* 238 (2018), 3–41.

'[t]he Peace of God was therefore not a repudiation of lordship. It was a regulation of lordship that implicitly accepted lords' rights.'[15]

Seen in this light, there are implications for how ordinary Christians in particular localities might have experienced the exciting, but in fact relatively rare, convocations at which 'Peace' was proclaimed. It may also suggest that the involvement of 'the people' in the councils needs to be seen, at least in part, as something more orchestrated than spontaneous, and perhaps also as something amplified narratively by ecclesiastical authors. To begin with the latter point: from the eleventh-century evidence regarding the councils held *in* the south, it is really only at Toulouges 1027 that we see the presence of the ordinary laity invoked— though admittedly southern clergy and relics also attended councils held further north, at Colers, Le Puy, and Limoges, at which crowds of laity were present. Lauransan-Rosaz makes the subtle point that '[u]ltimately, whether the poor were actually there may be less significant than the emphasis placed on their presence in the document'.[16] However, if sticking to a strict southern French frame, 'the poor' are for the most part absent, even rhetorically. Instead we see archbishops, bishops, counts, and viscounts—sometimes closely related, as at Narbonne in 990 (the presiding archbishop having among those present his brother the viscount of Narbonne), usually acting together (most clearly in the case of the 'peace judges' appointed in Mende in the second quarter of the eleventh century) and in any case, as we know from copious other sources, all coming from the same noble background.[17] Bishops in this period are nobles, and exercise lordship; modern historiographical interpretations that have sought to make them into something like eleventh-century versions of liberation theologians in twentieth-century Latin America are ultimately unconvincing.[18]

Nonetheless some of the stories and narratives of the period *do* suggest various ways in which lay people might interact with the saints, sometimes with dynamics similar to those suggested in the accounts of the grand 'Peace' gatherings. A late eleventh-century *vita* of St Isarn, abbot of the monastery of Saint-Victor in Marseille who died in 1048, relates various tales of how the saint posthumously punished noblemen who aggressively attempted to extend their lordship against the abbey's possessions.[19] One particular story is illuminating in multiple ways.

---

[15] Koziol, *Peace*, p. 70.
[16] Mansi 19, cols 483–84; Lauranson-Rosaz, 'Peace from the Mountains', p. 120.
[17] Mansi 19, col. 103; C. Brunel, 'Les juges de la paix en Gévaudan au milieu du XIe siècle', *Bibliothèque de l'École des Chartes* 109 (1951), 32–41.
[18] For Carolingian precedents for episcopal orchestration and an emphasis on the role of the bishop as public authority, see K. F. Werner, 'Observations sur le role des évêques dans le mouvement de paix aux Xe et XI siècles', in *Mediaevalia christiana XIe-XIIe siècles: hommage à Raymonde Foreville* (Brussels: Éditions universitaires, 1989), pp. 155–95; and H.-W. Goetz, 'Protection of the Church, Defense of the Law, and Reform: On the Purposes and Character of the Peace of God, 989 × 1038', in Head and Landes, eds, *Peace of God*, pp. 259–79.
[19] AASS Sept. VI, cols 737–49.

A peasant 'sworn to the monastery' who lived in the town of Trets (c. 40 km north-east of Marseille) had a cow stolen from him by the inaptly named 'Redemptus', the *viguier* of the local lord. The peasant came to the monastery and asked the saint to answer his woes. The next day, as it happens, Redemptus also visited the monastery, to pray at the shrines of the saints. As he was doing this ('but not in perfect prayer', the text hastens to emphasize) he entered the shrine of St Isarn, where the peasant was still prostrate in supplication. Redemptus, seized by a devilish spirit, kicked the peasant. At this impious action, the saint (we are perhaps to understand a statue or an apparition), his head covered by a cowl and without saying a word, immediately left the shrine and entered the church. The *viguier*, much alarmed, leaped on a horse to get away, doing this within the cemetery bounds of the abbatial church. At this 'sacrilege' he was struck by divine vengeance in his foot. This caused an excruciating wound which medical attention could not assuage or heal; and after three days of agony, he chose to amputate 'the most impious foot'. And, the anonymous author of the *vita* says, this illustrates the way that the Lord protects his servants (for as his prophet said, 'Whoever touches you, touches the apple of my eye' (Zach. 2: 8)); when the *viguier* kicked the peasant, 'he struck the holy man in his heart'.[20] It is clear that the cemetery is here figured as a holy space, associated with the spiritual charge of the shrine and the church, and somewhere that is profaned by actions such as kicking peasants and leaping onto horses. But it is also important that the *viguier* had sinned multiply against the saint and his church: doing wrong within these bounds occasions the punishment, but the wider wrong is done to the church's interests through the earlier theft of the cow (from a peasant who perhaps, in some sense, also belonged to the church). It is thus not clear whether the space of all churches and cemeteries would receive quite such a direct intervention; the story depends upon its proximity to the wronged saint's shrine. There are issues of a hierarchy or graded arrangement of 'sacred space' here, rather than straightforward evidence for all churches and their surrounding lands enjoying spiritual protection.

The laity's relationships toward the saints is a very broad area, and there is more to be said in a future chapter when we come to look at later periods as well. But a few points can usefully be made here regarding the eleventh and early twelfth centuries. We briefly met two other encounters with saints in Chapter 1: the injured sabbath-breaker Guitbert, who sought healing at the shrine of St Vivian, and the knight Ugo who came to the same shrine simply 'to pray' one Sunday. We have just seen the unnamed peasant, wronged by Redemptus, come to seek restitution for a wrong (the stolen cow). In each case, the lay people act on their own recognizance, without specific prompt or orchestration by a priest or

---

[20] AASS Sept. VI, col. 742.

bishop or monk. With Guitbert and the peasant, the motive is an individual hope for intercession, but in the case of going to pray there is a suggestion—since Ugo was accompanied by the blind man—that this might be a more collective activity. This is more clearly so in another story from the *miracula* of St Gilles, where one healing miracle is said to have been witnessed not only by monks and clerics but by 'innumerable ordinary people (*plebes*) who had gathered there from many different places in order to pray'.[21] Another tale from the same collection makes clear a potential difference between specific petition and general prayer. A *sénéchal*, desperately in need of supernatural protection, came to the shrine to make petition: 'Saint Gilles, confessor of Christ, at whose tomb I have once before desired to pray, although not worthily or fittingly, aid me in this hour...'.[22]

Now, all of these things are brought dramatically together in the peace of God assemblies, where in some of the classic accounts we see people seeking individual healing miracles, the invocation of the saints in pursuit of the 'peace', and collective worship on a notably large scale. Such is the case at Colers and Limoges (according to the *vita* of St Vivian) and Le Puy (from the *vita* of St Enimie).[23] How should we read lay involvement in these extraordinary events? It is clear from the *vitae* that the pursuit of healing miracles, at the councils but also en route there and back, is a common motive; in that sense a key factor is likely to be the relative accessibility of the relics, as the shrine is temporarily made mobile and peripatetic. Thus the large-scale events could be seen as part of a broader continuum. But does the collective nature of the assemblies make a difference?

Bernard Töpfer argued some years ago for a highly intentional and monastically directed orchestration of lay worship at shrines in general in this period, and in the Peace of God in particular.[24] As he points out, collective worship on a large scale was a feature (narratively at least) of other occasions as well, notably when a saint's relics were translated. In case of St Vivian, the eleventh-century narrative of the ninth-century translation of the saint to Figeac certainly imagines that the abbot involved set out to gain maximum publicity: he sent messengers to tell all the people of the area to congregate. This prompted 'an infinite multitude of clergy and people carrying candles and crosses to come to that place, and so as to carry them off from there, with great rejoicing and jubilant hymns the relics of the

---

[21] *Livre des miracles de Saint Gilles*, ed. and trans. M. and P.-G. Girault, G. Duhil, and A. Chupin (Orléans: Paradigme, 2007), p. 40 (no. 1b): an event from 1088 written up in the 1120s. See similarly p. 70 (no. 8).

[22] *Livre...Saint Gilles*, p. 44 (no. 2).

[23] We should note that evidence for the presence of relics at various of the other councils is tangential at best: in the case of Toulouges 1027, for example, it rests upon the closing injunction 'In the presence of God and of his saints, we forbid all the canons of the aforesaid see...' (forbidding them from absolving anyone of disobedience to the council, unless given authority so to do), and in several of the other southern French cases is not visible at all in the surviving texts.

[24] B. Töpfer, 'The Cult of Relics and Pilgrimage in Burgundy and Aquitaine at the Time of the Monastic Reform', in Head and Landes, eds, *Peace of God*, pp. 41–57.

saints were borne by them and made to be carried to the appointed place'.[25] The narrative then describes how other peasants noticed the procession and decided to join in, suggesting both an element of spontaneity, but also a sense of established recognition from previous experience: the same *vita* relates that a peasant couple observed the *translatio* as it moved through the countryside, the wife then saying to her 'most beloved' husband that they ought to go and worship. A question then arises as to quite how novel the peace of God assemblies were, and to what extent the lay people coming to those assemblies were focused on the 'peace' part.

There is certainly an important blurring between those gatherings understood by modern historians to constitute 'the Peace of God movement' and other events. In 1114 there was a procession and assembly in the Toulousain, orchestrated by the archbishop on the orders of Duke Guillaume de Poitiers, who had temporarily taken control of the county (the count of Toulouse being absent on crusade). This does mention 'peace' in vague terms: it was done, according to the surviving text (an extract from what appears to be a now-lost *vita et miracula* of St Antoine made at Lézat), 'to restore the faltering peace of the people of Toulouse' (*ob reformandum pacem Tholosani deviam*). The obvious context here was clearly high political rather than 'feudal anarchy'. The archbishop ordered all the clergy to assemble, bringing with them their relics from chests and parish churches. A great troop assembled with their relics, setting up tents outside the walls of Toulouse so as to be able to accommodate the huge number of 'the blind, the dumb, the deaf, the barren, those having demons, the insane and the frenzied'. But it is not clear that any oaths are sworn, warriors present, or other decisions made—the assembly of relics, and the miracles they perform, would appear to be the main point.[26]

One wonders similarly about a rather more famous occasion a century earlier, near Rodez, recorded in the book of Ste Foy, where Bernard of Angers noted that relics were carried to councils 'according to the custom of this province' (*secundum morem illius provincie*, a statement which, if taken at face value, indicates a practice stretching back well before the millennium). There were secular lords 'deliberating at a distance' from the relics—this being assumed by modern historians to be a peace council, though the text does not in fact make use of the word.[27] The same text mentions in passing another occasion when, on account of 'some calamity', the monks took the reliquary of Ste Foy out in procession, 'followed by

---

[25] 'Translatio et miracula Sancti Viviani', p. 260.
[26] *Cart. Lézat* II, pp. 211–12 (no. 1342); cf. G. Pradalié, 'Une assemblée de paix à Toulouse en 1144', *Annales du Midi* 122 (2010), 75–82.
[27] A. Bouillet, ed., *Liber miraculorum sancte fidis* (Paris: Alphonse Picard, 1897), pp. 71–72 (I. 28), translation in P. Sheingorn, ed., *The Book of Sainte Foy* (Philadelphia: University of Pennsylvania Press, 1995), p. 98. Cf. D. Barthélemy, *Chevaliers et miracles: la violence et le sacré dans la société féodale* (Paris: Armand Colin, 2004), p. 76.

an enormous crowd of people of both sexes'.[28] Nor is 'peace' mentioned by the *vita* of St Vivian when it relates 'a meeting of bishops and innumerable people, to which were carried the bodies of many saints' held at a place called Lalbenque, near Cahors, some time around the year 1000.[29] The *vita* of St Enimie, which emphasizes 'peace' in connection to the council held at Le Puy, fails to do so later in the text regarding a more recent (that is, early twelfth-century) council at Mende. The sense of orchestration remains strong however: 'It is not all ancient history to which I refer, for indeed there are living and able witnesses, who assert that at the most recently completed council at Mende, they observed the miraculous power of the most glorious virgin Enimie. They say indeed that having finished the meeting, the bishops went up to the pulpit, and in the final sermon were blessing the people who were gratefully returning to their own homes', when the body of the saint began to perform more miracles.[30]

The important point here is not so much to critique the historiographical reification of 'the Peace of God' but rather to note that these examples suggest that the peace assemblies worked in part by adapting an *existing* form of interaction between paraded saints and the gathered laity. Such an interaction was not in any sense regular or quotidian, but it was comprehensible, repeated, and aimed to gather the faithful in the company of the saints from across a region. This, for the eleventh and early twelfth centuries, adds a very important element to what we might understand by 'lay worship', beyond the bounds of the local church (the dynamics of which I shall return to further below).

As noted in the Introduction, there is a tendency within some of the scholarship on the Peace of God, and on the Reform movement, to place 'the Church' and 'violence' at opposing poles. The ecclesiastical sources of the period encourage this, through their self-depiction of church property being 'seized unjustly' by rampaging nobles. There is also an echo within modern historiography of earlier scholarship that saw a starker contrast between 'civilization' and 'barbarism'. But it is ultimately not helpful to separate the Church from violence. In the first place, monasteries in particular were embedded in the practical demands of lordship, which could involve them not as victims of but participants in lordly dispute. In disputes over land, southern French monasteries could participate in the recognized mechanisms of dispute settlement preferred by the nobility, such as the use of trial by battle by champions—such as we find, for example, by the monks of Moissac around 1083, and several examples involving the monks of Lézat in the

---

[28] Bouillet, *Liber miraculorum*, pp. 50–51 (I. 15); Sheingorn, *Book*, pp. 80–81.
[29] 'Translatio et miracula Sancti Viviani', p. 274.
[30] C. Brunel, ed., 'Vita, inventio et miracula Sanctae Enimiae', *Analecta Bollandiana* 57 (1939), 236–96, at p. 296.

first half of that century.[31] Around the end of the eleventh century Lézat made an agreement with a local lord, Guillaume Enard, that he would provide a certain degree of protection in future disputes with enemies of the monks, including the provision of either judges and oathmakers (*judices et fidejussores*) if they were involved in a judgment meeting (a *placitum*) or else a champion if called to a duel (*duella*) 'which is called in the vernacular a "battle"' (*que vulgo batala dicitur*); all of which tends to confirm that involvement in legal violence was something the monastery expected and planned for.[32] Violence in a legitimate cause—defence of monastic landholding rights—was part and parcel of the ecclesiastical world, and perhaps unsurprising given the close familial connections between abbots and lay lords.[33]

Beyond this, we must also recognize the ways in which saints and shrines (particularly those with a strong episcopal backing) made use of a different kind of 'violence' to counter secular encroachments. We have met already some saintly violence: the punishment of the *viguier* Redemptus by St Isarn, and the punishment of the local lords who objected to monks pillaging their woods by St Vivian—this latter example being presented, as I noted above, not once but twice within the same narrative. Such saintly behaviour was quite common; indeed, in some of the *vitae et miracula* of the eleventh and early twelfth centuries, the *main* role of saints would appear to be exacting revenge on those who have wronged 'them' (that is, the cathedral or monastery that possessed their relics). A collection of miracles performed by St Privat in the first half of the twelfth century, in the far north of the region in and around Mende, provides a particularly clear example. These *miracula* tell repeatedly of how the saint violently punished those who had trespassed against him. A knight called Gaucelm had been laying waste to lands owned by the saint, and died impenitent of these crimes—his body was then consumed by 'great balls of fire' that issued from the tomb. Gui, count of Auvergne, who had also failed to treat the saint's lands properly, was mortally wounded by a lance blow, his failure to defend himself from this fatal attack being attributed to St Privat's intervention. Another knight attacked the city of Mende and killed eight inhabitants; eight days later he was killed by his enemies, again by the saint's power. Yet another knight usurped a village belonging to the saint. In revenge, fire sprang up from the earth and burned all his vines and chestnut trees. An archdeacon, in dispute with bishop, had various goods of St Privat's stolen, but his men who were trying to carry them off were fought by animals all day long,

---

[31] *Cart. Moissac*, p. 184 (no. 126)—the opponents being people connected to the same lord of Lomagne who later burnt down the town, as noted above; *Cart. Lézat*, I, pp. 316–18 (no. 409), 1026, the process proposed but refused; I, p. 318 (no. 410), 1026 × 1031; II, pp. 177–79 (no. 1295), 1031 × 40.

[32] *Cart. Lézat*, I, pp. 310–11 (no. 400).

[33] For an excellent analysis, see E. Magnani Soares-Christen, *Monastères et aristocratie en Provence milieu Xe-début XIIe siècle* (Münster: Lit, 1999), particularly pp. 411–29.

and eventually gave the stuff up. Occasionally the saint was rather less forceful: a lord who tried to take over the village of La Roche, in the lands of the saint, then went to offer alms to Privat. Three times his offerings were rejected by the hand of a statue of the saint, and as a consequence he repented, and handed the village back.[34] I write 'the lands of the saint', following the language of the source. They were of course more clearly the lands of the bishop and chapter. But the sense of counter-lordship embodied in the saint, his supernatural violence meeting the (real or perceived) depredations of secular violence, helps to clarify how much the saint is 'in' the system, rather than an alternative to it.

This is a point which Dominique Barthélemy has nicely explored in regard to Ste Foy, whose famous shrine at Conques housed one of the most visually extraordinary and 'embodied' reliquary statues, and whose miracles contained a variety of attacks against those who had harmed 'her' monastery.[35] Barthélemy emphasizes that Ste Foy does not represent an alternative to warrior society, but is embedded within the world of knightly violence—that she is indeed a participant who favours some and is an enemy to others. Thus (he argues) her *miracula* do not provide an alternative theology of peace, nor any idea of making war 'moral', but rather—for those whom she favours—a means of 'sacralizing' certain kinds of violence, including the war of one lord against another.[36]

This is a powerful analysis. However, characterizing the violence as 'sacralized' may be a step too far. It is important to note the *arbitrariness* intrinsic to the power struggles of lordship, an arbitrariness echoed by Ste Foy's interventions. This is well illustrated by a tale about a knight called Géraud from near Conques, who travelled to Rodez to ask his lord to lend him a prized falcon; the lord acquiesced, but on the agreement that Géraud would forfeit all his property if he lost the bird (an outcome that the cunning lord would apparently favour, at any rate according to Bernard of Angers when he narrated the tale). Stopping off on his way home in the countryside near Albi, Géraud decided to fly the bird—and promptly lost it. At home, bewailing his fate, his wife encouraged him to seek intercession at Ste Foy's shrine. Before he got a chance to do so, a 'tame goose' flew in through the window, and was then followed by the falcon; thus all was saved. It's a good story when told in full, and Bernard of Angers does his best to give it spiritual meaning—but the randomness of fate, and the uncertain nature of Ste Foy's 'jokes' (as apparently the people of the area called them) is the clearer message.[37]

---

[34] Brunel, *Miracles de Saint Privat*, pp. 5, 6, 8, 9, 18, 19.
[35] For example, Bouillet, *Liber miraculorum*, miracles I.5, I.6, I.10, I.11, I.12, I.24, I.26.
[36] Barthélemy, *Chevaliers et miracles*, chapter 2, particularly pp. 72–113; note, for example, Bouillet, *Liber miraculorum*, pp. 158–59 (III.18), where the saint sides with a knight called Fredol, from the region near Nîmes, in his war against another local knight, in return for Fredol having donated a manor to the monastery.
[37] Here I diverge slightly from Amy Remensnyder, who explored Ste Foy's *joca* as part of a more folkloric culture; though the point about arbitrariness remains. See A. Remensnyder, 'Un problème de cultures ou de culture? La statue-reliquaire et les *joca* de Sainte Foy de Conques', *Cahiers de civilisation médiévale* 33 (1990), 351–57.

Thus it seems more fitting to say that Ste Foy does not make violence sacred, but rather participates in violence—and in the arbitrary flow of favour and disfavour intrinsic to lordship—from her supernatural position; the point being that in a world in which violence is a recurrent option, it is beneficial to have a particularly powerful figure on 'your side'.

The miracles of St Gilles recorded by Pierre Guillaume in the 1120s include several where a knight is freed from captivity thanks to the saint, Gilles apparently having such a knack for this kind of miracle that his shrine was festooned with 'fetters and iron manacles' donated afterwards in thanks.[38] Another miracle recorded late that same century makes more explicit how one might understand this kind of intervention. Raimond Féraud, a knight from Tarascon (just northeast of Saint-Gilles), was captured during conflict between Raimond V of Toulouse and Raimond Berengar, count of Barcelona, and was brought to the town of Saint-Gilles as a prisoner, bound in irons. He invoked the saint's protection: 'I know that it is because of my sins that I am handed into your power, and must submit to any number of torments. But you labour in vain: I am a servant of the Blessed Gilles, and you do not have the power to do anything to me except that which he permits. It is therefore pointless to bind me, as he will free me from your hands.' And indeed, after a certain amount of hardship, he was released from his prison by miraculous intervention.[39] Getting a saint 'on your side' could itself be achieved through violence and trespass: the *vita* of St Vivian relates, in approving and gleeful detail, how the abbot arranged the theft of the relics from their original home in Saintes. He sent men to the shrine, one of them pretending to be demonically possessed in order to gain entrance. He then told the locals that their town was under attack by 'Norman pirates' causing them all to run out—at which point the rest of the abbot's men could break into the tomb with iron bars.[40] That is an eleventh-century text relating ninth-century events, but even in the early twelfth century kidnapping a saint via his relics was still a possibility. The narrative relating the peace council at Toulouse in 1114 notes toward its end that the many miracles performed by the relics of St Antoine brought him to the attention of the count of Poitiers; in response, the abbot of Lézat ensured that there was a large armed guard posted around the relics, and had the saint guarded 'day and night'.[41]

These stories place the saints in a world of knights and nobles, where intervention within armed disputes or for prisoners of battles are part of an important but relatively elite milieu. But some elements of saintly violence perhaps resonated more widely. In the story regarding Redemptus, we should remember that the unnamed peasant whom he had wronged was at the shrine seeking recompense

---

[38] *Livre...Saint Gilles*, p. 68 (no. 8).   [39] *Livre...Saint Gilles*, pp. 94–101 (no. 13).
[40] 'Translatio et miraculi Sancti Viviani', pp. 258–59. See P. Geary, *Furta Sacra: Thefts of Relics in the Central Middle Ages* (Princeton: Princeton University Press, 1978) for wider discussion of relic theft.
[41] *Cart. Lézat*, II, p. 212.

from the saint directly, and would presumably not have been unhappy at the *viguier*'s fate. Or rather, perhaps we should say, any lay audience who heard this miraculous tale might include those who identified more directly with the wronged peasant than the sinner, and take from it the lesson that attaching oneself to a powerful patron such as St Vivian might provide a means of vengeance if not always prior protection. A story told in verse in the *vita* of St Enimie tells of an even worse despoiler of the poor, one Teodard who 'did injury to rustics and to women' and was an avaricious thief. He ransacked and burned a farm which belonged to the saint; as a result he was punished by a terrible burning rash and a variety of other bodily afflictions, eventually dying 'scabby, itching and with putrid flesh'.[42] It is his depredation of the saint's lands that occasions this horrible end, but the tale could clearly present some comfort—and hope?—to those peasants and others who found themselves subject to the violence of lordship. But it was the comfort of vengeance rather than protection: the saints in this period for the most part do not offer an alternative to lordly violence, but are part of its spiralling and arbitrary dynamic.

Ideas of Faith

Whilst, as noted, the various 'Peace' councils can often be interpreted in terms of rather specific political situations, as they sought to protect church property they did so via the promotion of wider legitimating ideals. This propositional content was elaborated and extended in scope and conception across various councils. Thus we have the descriptions of councils seeking to establish 'the Peace' in a general sense, as reported in certain saints' *vitae* and some (more northern) chronicles. We find an increasing emphasis upon 'peace' being the right ordering of relations between Christians, both 'friends and enemies, neighbours and strangers' as the council convened by the archbishop of Arles put it in 1041.[43] This conceptual element reaches a kind of apogee in the south at the council of Narbonne in 1054. The council was convened by the archbishop of that diocese, and was one of the largest affairs: it involved the bishops of Béziers, Agde, Lodève, Maguelonne, Nîmes, Girona, Barcelona, and Albi, along with the count of Carcassonne, the viscount of Narbonne, and various other nobles, abbots, and clergy. This gathering produced a much lengthier and more detailed set of statutes than any preceding event, and begins with a canon framed unequivocally as a general principle: 'We warn and order...that no Christian should kill any other Christian; because whoever kills a Christian without doubt spills the blood of Christ.'[44]

---

[42] Brunel, ed., 'Vita...Sanctae Enimiae', pp. 289–90.
[43] Mansi 19, cols 593–96.
[44] Narbonne 1054, c. 1 (Mansi 19, col. 827).

This is a truly radical statement. It carries with it a number of fundamental claims: that *Christians* should not kill each other (a slight amendment to the Sixth Commandment, but a much smaller amendment than we would find for much of the middle ages); that all Christians are one in Christ, with some implied sense of equality of worth (one may note that the image of 'Christ's blood' being shed is deployed in a number of late medieval and early modern revolts to assert a radical social equality);[45] and the very fact that the Church, as embodied by the archbishop and bishops, could pronounce so bluntly over an issue that sat at the heart of political life, as fighting 'wars' against other knights was, and would for centuries continue to be, a normal part of noble conduct.[46] At the same time, one has to ask what the bishops really intended and expected. The first canon immediately continues, 'If, against our injunction, someone in fact unjustly kills a man, he should be amended by law'—which would appear to take away quite a large part of what the preceding statement had given. (As Barthélemy and others have noted, we do not seem to be dealing with a total absence of secular legal authority.) Nonetheless, we should not diminish the radical *potential* of this discourse of Christian peace, and the sense in which it perhaps proffered a wider conceptual frame within which the laity—possibly not only the noble laity—were invited to consider their conduct.

As I have been exploring in these first two chapters, if we wish to understand what 'Christianity' was within a localized landscape, we must realize how it entwined with lordship, along with various other practical and social contexts. But it was of course always also a set of ideas and stories that reached beyond the local. In Chapter 1 I noted some occasions when a few more wealthy or elite people opted to be buried in a monastery rather than a local church, at which point we can see a little bit more of the choices they made regarding memorial masses, place of burial, and so forth. We have to remember that, whilst visible to us, this was a decision made by a tiny minority within this period. This was not only because of differences in material resource—poor people lacking the financial donations that would secure burial and commemoration in grand institutions—but surely also by personal choice: although we can see those who 'gave their bodies' to the monasteries such as Saint-Sernin or Moissac, there are others from the same social strata who did not, the majority of whom must surely also have been buried locally. For many of the people recorded in the cartularies, contact with the monastery thus marks out some connection or ambition *beyond* the local—not only in terms of immediate geography, but as a means of connecting to a larger network, and a more powerful spiritual grid. A wider 'idea' of

---

[45] J. H. Arnold, 'Religion and Popular Rebellion, from the Capuciati to Niklashausen', *Cultural and Social History* 6 (2009), 149–69, at p. 156.
[46] See J. Firnhaber-Baker, *Violence and the State in Languedoc, 1250–1400* (Cambridge: Cambridge University Press, 2014).

Christianity is thus present, alongside more specifically political factors; as I suggested in the last chapter, the donations made to monasteries could be seen as a means by which families might seek to associate themselves with their perduring power, and their promise of closer access to God.

This does not necessarily draw a strong distinction between how donors and the general Christian faithful related to a local, rural church and relations between lay elites and a monastery or cathedral. But one might think of the more powerful ecclesiastical centres as exercising a kind of *spiritual* 'lordship' which operated with a similar dynamic to that which, as I noted above, Thomas Bisson has outlined in a more secular context: the power and dominion of that lordship flowing outwards from its centre, reaching out into a landscape that already contains other, similarly competing, points of power. An influential interpretation of pious gift-giving for this period, focused on northern France, was provided by Barbara Rosenwein in her monograph *To Be the Neighbor of St Peter*, which argued, among other things, that monastic donations provided a social 'glue' for elite families in a time of feudal anarchy.[47] Whilst I am not persuaded by the overall 'feudal anarchy' argument, I do see value in the notion that donation forges links that can act to foster cohesion—but perhaps cohesion across *time* in particular (for those belonging to higher social strata at least). It is then important to note that the long-term survival of monasteries—their perdurance, as I called it in Chapter 1—is a major part of what both facilitates this strategy and makes them attractive recipients for gifting. However, this cohesion-over-time is potentially also a form of social differentiation, as the strategy is not open to all.[48]

A mixture of things is therefore going on within these gifts (and the sales, surrenders, temporary donations, and the like—the terms are used much less precisely, and with much more overlap, than some historians would have one imagine). One is the linkage of land with salvation: many charters contain a 'pro anima' clause, noting that something is given 'for my soul' and very often 'and for the souls of my forebears (*parentes*)'.[49] On occasion, it is explicitly noted that this land is available to be given precisely because of those 'forebears': in the late 1070s, Eicio and his wife Gitberga gave 'for the respite of our souls and the souls of all our forebears, our allod that has come to us from the allod of our forebears or through purchase'.[50] That the land which people gave had come to them via

---

[47] B. H. Rosenwein, *To Be the Neighbor of St Peter: The Social Meaning of Cluny's Property, 909-1049* (Ithaca, NY: Cornell University Press, 1989).

[48] An important contrast to the predominant donations are two charters in the cartulary of Lézat which emphasize that the land they describe is sold (to the church of Sainte-Marie at Peyrissas, owned by the monastery) because of famine: 'we sell this because of our necessity, because we do not have that which we can eat'. *Cart. Lézat*, I, p. 325 (nos 421, 422), c. 1100.

[49] It is possible that one might translate *parentes* even more generally as 'relatives': in two charters which ask for burial, a clause indicates that this depends upon 'my friends or *parentes*' carrying the body to the monastery. *Cart. Lézat*, I, pp. 406-07 (no. 540), 408 (no. 543), both from 1059.

[50] *Cart. Lézat*, I, pp. 594-95 (no. 819).

inheritance was of course commonly the case, and it suggests a particular nuance to the bundle of things going on in the *pro anima* and *ad parentem* clauses: that this was not simply about making an individual choice to focus on 'family memory' as one particular kind of pious investment among others, but rather that the spiritual benefit of making such a gift remained in some sense attached to the land, and to those others who had also held that land.

Pro anima and *ad parentem* clauses are part of the formulaic vocabulary of charters, but the variable fact of their presence or absence in different charters from the same cartulary and period suggests that they do speak generally to the wishes—often, one should remember, the collective wishes—of those having the document made. What, then, of the wider framing language of such charters, the pious phrases and religious images that they sometimes also deploy? Can we use any of this material to get at the pious ideas and motivating beliefs of the laity?[51] Salvation may be rooted in the local, and in particular connected with the gifting of land that has collective memory and value associated with it; but the framing sense of *time* associated with salvation may remind us that it is also a reaching out past the immediate and the local, to something 'beyond'.

For this period at least, a monastic voice overwhelmingly predominates. A number of charters, some decades either side of the year 1000, preface a donation by reference to 'the end of the world drawing near'. Rather than a sign of strong apocalypticism within the period this is however a demonstrably formulaic opening: a warning about the neglect of spiritual things, leading on most often to a statement about the desirability of giving alms for the good of one's soul (with frequent reference to the Gospel passages 'give alms and behold, all things are clean to you' (Luke 11: 14) and 'he who reaps, receives wages and gathers fruit unto everlasting life' (John 4: 36)).[52] In these and other prefatory passages in such charters, particularly those from before 1100, the voice is general and abstract: an overall statement of the state of the world, the general desirability of almsgiving, the collective hope of a future salvation. This does not make them empty letters. One might imagine that such ideas and passages were spoken out loud at the point of donation, and at least understood to frame the act of giving in that moment (much as with the separate, final clauses that often threatened damnation to anyone who, at a later point, dared to go against the agreement).[53] They are perhaps akin to the practice of collective confession, where the priest would make a general statement about the fallen nature of humankind and sinful

---

[51] For interesting thoughts in comparative regions, see Davies, *Acts of Giving*, pp. 100–06, and M. Bull, *Knightly Piety and the Lay Response to the First Crusade: The Limousin and Gascony, c. 970–c. 1130* (Oxford: Clarendon Press, 1993), pp. 155–56.

[52] For example, *Cart. Notre-Dame de Nîmes*, p. 74 (no. 44), 943; *Cart. Lézat*, I, pp. 171 (no. 219), 1032 × 35; 576–77 (no. 788), 990 × 95; 584–86 (no. 803), 1026 × 31; 588–89 (no. 812), late tenth century; 590–91 (no. 814), 1032 × 60; II, p. 172 (no. 1285), c. 1000.

[53] On the latter, see Bowman, 'Do Neo-Romans Curse?'

behaviour, all of which was understood to apply to those present, but without the specificity that individual confession would bring.

On occasion the pious prefatory clauses could be more expansively didactic in content, as with an unusual and quite lengthy preamble from a charter produced around 1060, which begins by noting that all men, 'rich and poor, noble or non-noble', will see that the Day of Judgment is near, and then starts to rehearse elements of the Creed, recounting that God descended to earth to free us from the rule of the Devil, by he who was born of a virgin, who suffered captivity, humiliation, and death. 'Know, brothers', the preamble continues, as if in the voice of a preacher making a monastic sermon, 'that no-one was redeemed through gold or silver, nor from precious gems, nor earthly things, but from His own blood', and that through doing good works when we can, we may help to atone for our sins. This preface finishes with a telling change of voice from the one who addresses his audience, to the donor: 'I, moreover, in my extremity hearing these words...', this linking clause then leading on to the specifics of the donation.[54] Another charter from 1093 has a similarly lengthy and didactic preamble directed toward the works of mercy, and the importance of charity for salvation.[55]

From the late eleventh century, whilst charter preambles continue to be highly formulaic and often quite general in tone and address, we start to see more frequent statements in which the individual lay donor is placed as the specific focus of the theological points made regarding sin and redemption. A donation charter by Rostagnus and his sister Biliardis, giving land to the cathedral church of Nîmes in 1078, states that they were 'considering the day of our deaths and our many sins, by which we have gravely offended God... and recognizing that after death a greater punishment is provided for us in hell', noting that they can make some recompense through 'true penitence', prayer, and good works.[56] A will from December 1103 begins: 'I, Pons Hugues, the fear of sin and Hell pricking my heart, and for the salvation of my soul and remission of my sins and [the sins] of my forebears, give and relinquish to the Lord God and to the monks of Saint Peter of Lézat...'.[57] Another charter from 1124, recording a gift of lands that had previously been given but then revoked, has an even greater sense of self-accusation:

> I, Olivier de Bensa, recognize myself to be guilty and to be a sinner against God and against the canons of the church of Saint Sernin of Toulouse, in regard to

---

[54] *Cart. Lézat*, II, pp. 59–60 (no. 1071).   [55] *Cart. Mas d'Azil*, 170–71 (no. 17), 1093.
[56] *Cart. Notre-Dame de Nîmes*, pp. 247–48 (no. 155).
[57] *Cart. Lézat*, II, pp. 380–81 (no. 1535). For similar language, see *Cart. Templiers de Douzens*, pp. 50–51 (29 Mar 1133). I have found two earlier examples of similar language, in deathbed wills: that of the count of Comminges, dated 1032 × 35, which begins with reference to the 'sins and negligence and crimes that I have committed against God' (*Cart. Lézat*, I, pp. 186–87 (no. 237)); and that of Atilius Bucaniger, 1031 × 60, 'for remedy of my soul and because of love of the celestial Father, and in order to evade the fires of Hell' (*Cart. Lézat*, II, pp. 118–19 (no. 1163)). Scholarship on Catalonia has tended to find many more examples.

myself, and the *honor* which my father gave to Saint Sernin for me, and for the salvation of my soul and the souls of my forebears. And I, just like the bad son, stole it from them...and just like a thief, I held it until today. And because of fear of death and Hell, and love of God, I myself return all of that *honor* which my father held in the church of Peyrepertuse...[58]

This is perhaps a change in documentary practice rather than a change in lived experience; a change, that is, to the *style* of rhetoric with which the combination of gift, donor identity, and ideas about sin and salvation are recorded. However, as we shall see in Chapter 3, there is a slight initial shift in evidence after c. 1100 for some of the laity to have burial and memorial mass wishes recorded in their wills; thus we do cumulatively get a sense of lay people—*powerful* lay people, that is— moving more clearly centre stage in their gifting. Peyrepertuse does however seem to have made people feel particularly guilty. Immediately after the charter just mentioned, an extraordinary document appears in the cartulary, dated from a few months later. In it a priest from Carcassonne records that he was called to the deathbed of a man called Bernard Pierre, who had turned up in the house of one his parishioners. Bernard made his deathbed confession, which the priest (Pons) recorded as if in the first person: 'I, guilty sinner, confess to God and to the Blessed Virgin Mary, and to all the saints, and to you brother, all the sins which I have done...', going on to admit that he and his brothers had long 'unjustly' held and 'despoiled' the church of Sainte-Marie at Peyrepertuse.[59]

Across all the charter material, we find a handful of mentions of pilgrimage to Jerusalem, not only from the twelfth century, when those practices of armed pilgrimage we now called 'crusades' were well under way, but earlier too.[60] If not heading directly to Jerusalem, the donor could nonetheless make symbolic gifts in its direction. Odilo, son of Radulf, gave a parish church to the abbey of Moissac in the mid-eleventh century, giving it 'to the Lord God and to the Holy Sepulchre and in honour of the Holy Resurrection'.[61] The charter which tells us about the church of Saint-Pierre-de-Mont, mentioned several times above, was brought into being sometime in the 1060s by a particular priest, because, as a rather touching prayer which concludes the charter explains, he was planning what would probably be a final pilgrimage:

---

[58] *Cart. Saint-Sernin*, pp. 349–50 (no. 501). See various in *Cart. Mas d'Azil* with a similar language.

[59] *Cart. Saint-Sernin*, p. 351 (no. 502), 14 Dec 1125. I discuss the confession in greater detail in Chapter 8.

[60] Post-1095 examples: *Cart. Apt*, pp. 248–49 (no. 96), c. 1097, mention made amidst donation that donor is going to Jerusalem; *Cart. Aniane*, pp. 300–1 (no. 369), 1104, passing reference to earlier landholder having done similarly; *Cart. Silvanès*, p. 14 (no. 11), 1132 donation from Bernard Guillaume de Versols, 'wishing to go to Jerusalem'; *Cart. S. Etienne d'Agde*, pp. 307–08 (no. 258), 1147, will made by Étienne, chaplain of Mezoa; Brunel, *Les plus anciennes chartes*, pp. 75–76 (no. 75), c. 1155, Rouergue; inventory of possessions of Raimon de Cassagnes 'when he set out overseas'.

[61] *Cart. Moissac*, p. 96 (no. 60). See also c. 1120: Brunel, *Les plus anciennes chartes*, pp. 24–26 (no. 20).

And I, Bernard Amiel, wish to go to Jerusalem, and commend my body and my soul to God, and my household (*mia mainada*) and my parishioners, men and women, and my friends, that they may be blessed and absolved on the part of God and the Holy Mary and St Pierre and all the male and female saints of God. Amen.[62]

Here the local parish, the holy lands of pilgrimage, and the salvational hope for the next life combine rather movingly. It is not entirely certain from the Latin whether Bernard Amiel intended to draw a distinction between 'my parishioners' and 'my friends'; the possibility that the two categories at least overlapped is clearly present, not least in his explicit care for *their* salvation, as he takes his final leave of a spiritual community that he had founded and fostered. We catch the briefest sense of what was perhaps the most important and yet inevitably elusive aspect to local Christianity: the affective relationships between the people who made it.

Conclusions

As I have argued above, there is a different kind of picture of lay experience visible within the Peace of God sources, one which need not be understood as apocalyptic and which probably should not be seen as totally spontaneous or notably autonomous, but rather as a pre-existing practice, in which the mass worship of relics was orchestrated on particular occasions. This is not to say however that lay involvement was of no importance or interest. A few particular elements are worth emphasizing. One is that the saints operated as powerful local figures, notably in a world in which other local figures competed—including other saints. Competition between shrines, often narratively presented as being between the relative intercessory or protective power of individual saints, is a common feature in the *vitae et miracula* sources of the eleventh and twelfth centuries, and must to some degree have been part of the laity's understanding of the world the saints inhabited. It also echoed something of the experience of those subject to secular lordship, where different figures of power attempted to dominate—through force, intercession, exaction, and protection—the landscape around them, in competition with other similar figures. Saints and lordship sit closely together.

---

[62] *Cart. Lézat*, I, pp. 377–78 (no. 500). See also *Cart. Saint-Sernin*, pp. 98–99 (no. 131), 1076–77, document recording a dispute within which mention is made of evidence of Raimond Ebonis, former *prepositus* of Saint-Sernin and bishop of Lectoure, 'and who now as an old man wishes to go to Jerusalem'. Nor was Jerusalem the only destination for long-distance pilgrimage, as we see from a will c. 1000: Amiel 'wished to walk to Rome in the service of omnipotent God and St Pierre the Apostle, and he fears therefore that death will overtake me [*sic*], I wish to distribute my acquired inheritance'. *Cart. Lézat*, I, pp. 144–46 (no. 189).

And just as a peasant's experience of lordship might vary from the quotidian—labouring in the lord's fields, regularly seeing a fortified tower at a distance, observing the passage of social superiors about their business—to the more extraordinary and eventful—such as the gathering of a massed army, occasions of armed combat, perhaps attendance at a festivity organized by the lord's household for Christmas—so was the experience of relics and saints not *one* thing, but a range of both regular and more unusual events. As noted above, there is some evidence of people going to pray at shrines, to worship more generally, without any particular petition or occasion. There is of course evidence for communal worship at shrines, associated particularly with the feast day of the saint. There is talk of the saint and their doings within the region, the *fama* of the saint, one might say, shared between the laity as much as communicated to the laity by monks or bishops.

Not everyone participated actively, and, as we would also find in later canonization records, the eleventh- and twelfth-century *miracula* contain examples of those who sceptically rejected the saint's power, then punished for their insubordination (and thus entering the record). I mentioned above a peasant couple who observed the translation procession of the relics of St Vivian. The wife, having heard the 'praising songs' of the multitude, suggested to her husband that they should go and worship. The husband's response was in fact unenthusiastic. He told his wife to get back quickly to her work and to ignore the furore, as 'it is probably just the bones of some dead person or other, which are gathered together to be venerated by the foolish beliefs of the people' (*fortasse ossa sunt alicujus mortui, que collecta in unum stulta veneratur opinio populi*).[63] The book of Ste Foy tells somewhat similarly of a servant girl, a weaver, who instead of rushing to worship at a passing procession of the saint's reliquary, stayed obstinately at her work. The girl was 'unmoved by the fear of God and took no pleasure in the sound of those singing divine praises'.[64] So one might be immune—prior to the imposition of divine punishment—to the charisma of the saint. At the other end of the scale of experience were occasions of massed worship drawing together the relics from a number of shrines, housed in reliquaries fashioned (in the south of France in particular) into the likeness of human form and decorated with gold, silver, and jewels.[65] These might draw huge crowds of people from different social levels, many hoping for healing cures and other intercessions, with bishops orchestrating and instructing the multitude. Moreover, lay members of that multitude were able to participate practically. It is notable that several *miracula* from these collections are modelled on Christ's feeding of the multitude with the loaves and the

---

[63] 'Translatio et miracula Sancti Viviani', p. 260.
[64] *Liber miraculorum sancte Fidis*, p. 158 (1.15).
[65] On the reliquaries, see D. F. Callahan, 'The Cult of the Saints and the Peace of God in Aquitaine in the Tenth and Eleventh Centuries', in Head and Landes, eds, *Peace of God*, pp. 165–83, at pp. 167–69.

fishes; the point being not just the parallel with Christ, but the active role of lay people in the logistical element of the gathering.[66] Such involvement may not have been so available when the saints were sequestered within their shrines. Large-scale events of this kind, we must remember, were extraordinary, at once both legible because of their adaptation and amplification of pre-existing practice, and rendered powerful by their distance from quotidian experience.

What I have thus tried to make visible, across these first two chapters, is not only a patchwork of examples showing us what lay Christianity might include—baptism, worship, saints, miracles, burial—but that these form a landscape of contrasts. This, in two senses: what one might experience or have available might vary considerably with material circumstance. This could depend on where one lived, the most obvious contrast being between civic centres and more remote rural locales; but also on who one was, where those with status and money clearly had additional options open to them. The second sense of contrast: that each individual Christian might themselves undergo contrasting experiences at different times. These might range from occasions of highly charged moments of public participation such as we have met in this chapter, to quiet and quotidian experiences in a small local church on a Sunday. They might include occasions in which certain spiritual claims were rejected or diminished, alongside moments at which they were fervently embraced. The nature of the sources available for the eleventh and twelfth centuries has required that one builds up a picture from fragments, as if assembling a rather battered and incomplete jigsaw puzzle. The landscape that is revealed is not flat and uniform. It has one visible and recurrent dynamic—that which I have, for convenience, called 'lordship'—and at times a strong flavour of hierarchy, accompanied by symbolic or literal violence. Its most frequently visible actions are key rituals around birth and death, the moments in between perhaps less clearly addressed. But it is also a landscape that contained other kinds of human interaction and spiritual aspiration, glimpsed only in very fleeting but precious moments, such as Bernard Amiel's blessings bestowed upon his friends; a Christianity of communal care.

---

[66] See, for example, 'Translatio et miracula Sancti Viviani', p. 274.

3
A Re-formed Landscape, c. 1100–c. 1200

At some point in the first few decades of the twelfth century, a papal legate wrote to Amiel, bishop of Toulouse. The preamble to his letter recounts that when he had been with the bishop at Toulouse for the recent council they had held there, the legate had set out the instructions which the pope had previously issued at the council of Troyes regarding tithes, oblations, and ecclesiastical possessions. It is the latter point that is the main focus: in the letter, the legate goes on to excommunicate several named lay people, and then lists over sixty churches which were to be placed under interdict until those who 'unjustly hold them' returned them to the abbey of Saint-Sernin.[1] The sharp end of reform had come to the south. But what we really mean by 'reform' and what implications it may have had for the ordinary laity requires some further careful analysis.

The decades at the end of the eleventh and the beginning of the twelfth centuries are, for ecclesiastical historians, overwhelmingly associated with 'reform', particularly with the reforms propounded by Pope Gregory VII and a larger circle connected to him, where the Church's desire to separate itself from secular domination, and to reinvigorate its spiritual provision, was fought out in a variety of settings. In a broader sense, the south had been experiencing the Gregorian reform for some decades prior to the legate's letter, through papal intervention in episcopal elections, through monasteries connecting themselves to Cluny—most importantly the monastery of Saint-Victor in Marseille—and through the choice of language deployed in certain charters.[2] The western Church as a whole underwent considerable change across this period, and the highly fraught political battles between pope and emperor in Italy were of fundamental importance to the

---

[1] *Cart. Saint-Sernin*, pp. 196–98 (no. 282). Undated; the council of Troyes was presumably the one held in 1107, but we are not aware of an episcopal council at Toulouse until 1119, which seems perhaps a little late. (In Chapter 2, we also saw the assembly orchestrated in 1114 by Duke Guillaume de Poitiers; but no evidence for the presence of a papal legate attending.) Note also *Cart. Lézat*, II, pp. 73–74 (no. 1096), dated 1079, where the bishop's earlier bestowal 'in fief' of the church of Sainte-Julienne, and an allod called Verzil, to a layman, his mother, brothers, sisters, and children—made in return for various goods, presumably rendered annually—was then revoked at a later point 'propter excommunicationem Romani seu Tholosani consilii'. Again which council(s) are here evoked is not at all clear. The revocation was under Bishop Izarn of Toulouse, who died in 1105.

[2] Within a huge field, see in particular the contributions to *La réforme 'grégorienne' dans le Midi*, CdF 48 (2013). For a classic account of some ecclesial and political elements, E. Magnou[-Nortier], *L'introduction de la réforme grégorienne à Toulouse* (Toulouse: Association Marc Bloch, 1958).

wider issues at stake. As Colin Morris has noted for the period in general, the notion of reform was predicated more on an ideal of purity of worship than the sort of inner, moral improvement a later period might assume.[3] But that purity of worship—a primarily liturgical emphasis—required a wholesale shift in control, away from potential local variation, toward something more centralized, in aspiration at least. To achieve this, reformers pursued a separation of ecclesiastical practice from worldly power, making the clergy into a more clearly distinct group in appearance, social position, and practices. 'Simony'—the selling of church offices for profit—was for a period of time figured as the most appalling of all sins, itself a form of 'heresy' for some polemicists (a form of language which turns up occasionally in charters recording the surrender of churches).[4] It was also a usefully labile category: allowing a married clergyman to pass on a church to a son could be seen as a form of simony, as could lay ownership of churches that they themselves had built and endowed, as could various of the political aspects of wheeling and dealing that tended to come with the role of being a powerful bishop or abbot.

I point to the legate's letter above as a key marker of 'reform' for the south because of its specificity of action and practicality of consequence: this is not purely rhetorical, nor confined to some internal reorganization within a monastic order, but evidence of a large-scale, top-down intervention in the control of resources. Florian Mazel and Pierre Chastang have provocatively argued that one might see the Gregorian reform as a 'total social phenomenon' (here referring to the sociological theory of Marcel Mauss), in which 'the Church' as a whole, and the social order of which it was a part, were remade across the period.[5] The importance of the social consequences of reform, and the brio with which they pursue the argument, are inspiring. But this interpretation depends simultaneously upon seeing the reform movement as something dynamic and ideologically focused, whilst also pulling into the analysis a number of phenomena from various areas of western Europe across a very 'long' twelfth century. How it played out in particular regions does matter rather substantially; for instance, southern France did not experience anything like the Patarene movement in northern Italy, where groups of inspired lay people called, sometimes violently, for the Church to

---

[3] C. Morris, *The Papal Monarchy: The Western Church from 1050 to 1250* (Oxford: Clarendon, 1989), pp. 80–82, 100.

[4] For example, *Cart. Moissac*, pp. 237–38 (no. 164), dated 1101, where Viscount Raimond gives churches, having admitted to his ancestors having held through 'simoniac heresy'; *Cart. Moissac*, pp. 287–88 (no. 206), copy of letter of Pascal II in either 1099 or 1118, denouncing Simony, linking it explicitly with heresy, making mention of 'Arians, Sabellians, Fotinians, and Manicheans'.

[5] F. Mazel, 'Pour une redéfinition de la "réforme grégorienne"', *CdF* 48 (2013), 9–38; P. Chastang, 'Réforme grégorienne et administration par l'écrit des patrimoines ecclésiastiques dans le Midi de la France (Xe–XIIIe siècle)', *CdF* 48 (2013), 495–522.

be remade afresh.[6] As we shall see further below, it is absolutely the case, as Mazel and others have demonstrated, that relations between the major lords and the monastic and episcopal churches changed across the late eleventh and twelfth centuries, and perhaps particularly so in Languedoc and Provence. But what followed from that for the experiences of the wider populace requires further investigation, and it may not ultimately be helpful to subsume various other areas, such as the exclusion of non-Christians and the birth of new religious orders, into a singular 'reform' narrative.

The modern historian also needs to be wary of being pulled into the contest as an accidental participant: wary, that is, of the quite considerable gap between the all-encompassing rhetoric of reform and its specific local realities; wary of assuming that the period in which a reforming pope issues dictates is necessarily the period in which change actually occurs; and particularly wary that 'reform' can tell us about things that were innately worse being made better. Thus whilst this chapter explores the effects of 'reform' in southern France, the question of local experiences for the non-elite continues to sit centre stage, and whilst I argue below (in concert with others) that the reform agenda brought about a substantial change in the overall landscape of possibility, my focus is to explore ways in which the local experience of Christianity adapted to these possibilities from a bottom-up perspective. 'Reform', in other words, was primarily a rearrangement of lordship and ecclesial control. Its spiritual aspirations should not be assumed to have a direct impact—or perhaps indeed *any* impact—on the provision of Christian worship in local churches; though its effects (as discussed further below) on the relations between aristocratic families and religious orders did lead to the establishment of new foundations, these opening up some new possibilities for the non-elite laity also in due course.

The Landscape of Local Reform?

Whilst papal pressure exerted particularly around the turn of the twelfth century did produce a number of lay 'surrenders' of churches and tithes, these had in fact occurred also in earlier periods, went on very much later (well into the thirteenth century), and seigneurial churches remained a feature of the southern French landscape long after the Gregorian period. The desire to enforce clerical celibacy, and to reform clerical dress and behaviour such that they would be more clearly distinguished from their lay neighbours, is found in the south. But it is not a particular feature of regional ecclesiastical legislation in the eleventh or early twelfth century. There are recurrent aspects of wider 'reform' found in the councils

---

[6] See J. Norrie, *Urban Change and Radical Religion: Medieval Milan, c. 990–1140* (Oxford: Oxford University Press, forthcoming).

associated with the 'Peace of God' movement addressed in the previous chapter. These have not played a central role in discussions of 'the Peace', but are as much a feature as the more dramatic inventions those councils made, and probably just as central to the episcopal aims of the movement.[7] There is concern expressed over armed clergy (councils of Toulouges, 1027, 1041 and 1064 × 66, Narbonne 1054), who were explicitly *not* afforded the protection of the Peace. Incestuous marriage 'up to the sixth degree' was forbidden at Toulouges 1027. The council of Narbonne in 1054 forbade lay ownership of church property and rights (with some interesting caveats in canons 12 and 16 relating to occasions when they had been sold or gifted by churchmen). Amy Remensnyder has previously emphasized the elements of 'reform' of lay lordship in the peace councils, to which these elements in part relate; but it is clear in the latter case that the councils were legislating toward a wider agenda that included elements of the behaviour and Christian responsibilities of the ordinary laity.[8]

If we turn to other southern French councils, we find some further, though by no means extensive, elements of 'reform'. The council of Toulouse in 1056 condemned simony (it specified that bishops should not accept payment for ordinations, nor demand payment for consecrating churches, nor should anyone attempt to sell church offices), and enjoined clerical celibacy. It condemned lay people who had directed ecclesiastical goods to their own benefit and lordship. But the council expressed no particular concern regarding clerical dress or comportment, beyond a desire that bishops, abbots, and priests not be ordained as such until they were 30 years old, unless their 'sanctity and wisdom' were sufficient to warrant an earlier elevation.[9] The council of Toulouse in 1119, presided over by Pope Calixtus II early in his pontificate, was a bit more expansive. It announced various prohibitions in line with reform legislation: it forbade the purchase of ordinations or ecclesiastical promotions, the lay appropriation of ecclesiastical incomes, the passing on of ecclesiastical offices to sons or other relatives, and any cleric from demanding payment for anointing with holy oil or for burial. (To be clear: oblations for such things were permitted and indeed strongly expected, but demanding payment was not.) From the surviving records—which are admittedly incomplete—the council had three main things to say about the clergy. Firstly, that no free man could be bound to service by another and most of all no cleric thus bound by a layperson; secondly, that no cleric should be compelled to serve a layperson in a benefice. (Both prohibitions suggest, in line with a smattering of evidence noted in Chapter 1, that there were indeed 'unfree' priests who were expected to exercise their office as a kind of 'labour service', and who

---

[7] See similarly Goetz, 'Protection of the Church', pp. 274–76.
[8] A. Remensnyder, 'Pollution, Purity and Peace: An Aspect of Social Reform between the Late Tenth Century and 1076', in Head and Landes, eds, *Peace of God*, pp. 280–307.
[9] Mansi 19, cols 847–49.

were tied to the particular parish.) Finally, the council ordered that any monk or cleric who returned to the world and cut his beard or hair like a layperson would be held outside the Christian communion until they had amended themselves.[10] In the passage of years between the two Toulousan councils we do therefore see an amplification of concerns. But elsewhere in Christendom one would find in much more extensive discussion of how clerical dress, hair, celibacy, moral behaviour, and public comportment should set them clearly aside from the laity, and this whilst they were clearly still otherwise satisfactorily fulfilling their office and station.[11] At Toulouse, even by the early twelfth century, the issue is focused on those *leaving* religion and abandoning the tonsure; a rather more limited prohibition, and one focused more on monks and canons than parish priests.

As we move across the decades of the late eleventh and early twelfth centuries, the south's practical experience of reform was predominantly focused on two different aspects that would restructure the lay elite's relationship to ecclesiastical establishments. One was a shift away from local control and income: as we see in the letter to the bishop of Toulouse with which I began, pressure was put on lay lords to hand over the ownership of churches and tithes, so that the many small churches came into the possession of larger ecclesiastical structures, predominantly the large monasteries but also some bishops and cathedral chapters. The other aspect was more political: monasteries were 'reformed' such that, among other things, the appointment of abbots moved out of the hands of the major magnates. These were changes that restructured relations between the powerful in the medieval world, but as we will see they had consequences and created opportunities much lower down the social scale.

We will focus initially on the first aspect. As said above, it is important to note that churches and tithing income were periodically gifted or 'surrendered' or indeed sometimes sold to monasteries and cathedral churches both before and after the period most associated with the Gregorian reform. We find plenty of churches gifted to monasteries in the tenth and early eleventh centuries, and conversely, for example, a charter from 1174 appears to record the 'sale' of tithes to the abbey of Saint-Sernin, albeit for an unspecified amount. One can also find tithes 'held in fief' by a number of different lay people—who paid the abbey of Lézat an annuity for them—up until the Albigensian Crusade.[12] Some cartularies

---

[10] Mansi 21, cols 225–26; for its context within wider reform legislation, see M. Stroll, *Calixtus the Second, 1119–1124: A Pope Born to Rule* (Leiden: Brill, 2004), pp. 72–74.

[11] M. C. Miller, *Clothing the Clergy: Virtue and Power in Medieval Europe, c. 800–1200* (Ithaca, NY: Cornell University Press, 2014).

[12] *Cart. Saint-Sernin*, pp. 34–35 (no. 49), where the verb 'vendere' is used very clearly; *Cart. Lézat*, I, pp. 147–50 (no. 192). See similarly *Cart. Béziers*, p. 248 (no. 183), 1154: the bishop allows Raimond de Boujan to retain all the tithes he holds, and promises that he will not be excommunicated; Raimond to give six *setiers* of grain annually. *Cart. d'Aniane*, pp. 355–56 (no. 225), 1170: Pierre de Agnatico surrenders, for a cash counter-gift, the tithe of tenths that he holds in the parish of the church of Saint-Pierre-de-Gignac.

deploy emphatically 'reformist' language in the donation charters they record from later eleventh and early twelfth centuries, whilst others do not. The cartulary of Mas-d'Azil, for example, frequently prefaces donations of churches as things 'held unjustly' by lay people—though sometimes still then allowing that the donation is made 'for the souls of their forebears' or similar, and providing a financial counter-gift or recompense.[13] In comparison, the charters for the same period surviving for the abbey of Moissac do not frame donations in this guise, and indeed the language of 'injustice' appears there only as part of a legal formula to cover future eventualities, regarding various things 'held justly or unjustly' (*iuste vel iniuste*).[14] So whilst there clearly was an important 'top-down' element to these changes, this did not precisely dictate or guarantee local outcomes.

As local churches moved from lay to ecclesiastical hands, did this make any substantial difference to the parishioners and the local priest? The 1056 council of Toulouse had sought to ensure that for those churches held by lay people, at least one-third of tithing income went to the service of the church, as directed by the bishop and clergy; though it is not clear that this differed proportionately from churches held by monasteries or the cathedral (though perhaps they were less likely to need the threat of anathema to ensure compliance).[15] It could be the case that the ecclesial tithing rights, and the produce or money generated by the lands held by a church (often termed its '*honor*'), were treated as a source of personal income when owned by the lay lords and others—often, we must remember from Chapter 1, multiple others. It could be that a shift to monastic or episcopal possession redirected those funds to make better provision for an incumbent priest and the upkeep of the church, this being the view held by a number of influential historians for western Christendom generally.[16] But as we can quite clearly see from records relating to the secular lands they owned, the monasteries and cathedrals were also accustomed to extracting wealth from a landscape of distributed possessions, drawing income to the centre to support their primary activities and buildings. The cartularies occasionally contain brief 'inventories' of churches

---

[13] See, for example, the complex case of the church of Saint-Hippolyte-de-Ortals, held 'unjustly' by six men as a 'fief' from four other men (described as 'the most noble and famous and valiant within the world'); this nonetheless given for the souls of the six men, and those of their forebears; for which they received in recompense 270 *sous* 'in precious things' (*in res preciatas*); Cart. Mas-d'Azil, pp. 157–58 (no. 1).

[14] For example, Cart. Moissac, pp. 161 (no. 110, 1079), 191 (no. 133, 1085), 306 (no. 220, 1125). There is one exception: p. 70 (no. 41, 1024 × 32), where Arnaud Odo, viscount of Gascony, is said to hold two churches 'unjustly'; but this is a papal letter intervening directly in the matter.

[15] Toulouse 1056, c. 11 (Mansi 19, col. 849). Canon 10 specified that churches held by monasteries or by the cathedral should pass one-third of income over to the bishop; assuming that they were also taking a cut of income, it seems likely that 'one-third of tithing' was assumed to be the proportion usually assigned to the running of the actual parish church, regardless of owner.

[16] For an optimistic view (somewhat dependent on the example of Cluny), see G. Constable, 'Monasteries, Rural Churches and the *Cura Animarum* in the Early Middle Ages', *Settimane di studio* 28 (1982), 349–89, particularly p. 359.

held by a monastery or cathedral in the eleventh and twelfth centuries, but in comparison to the sorts of surveys we would find in the thirteenth century, these record simply the fact of possession and the income-generating lands associated with them, not anything about the fabric or liturgical resources of those churches.[17] Their visible interests and activities, that is, remain primarily that of lordship; ecclesiastical rather than secular lordship, but as argued in the preceding two chapters, not really different in its fundamental dynamic.

Very occasional vignettes from the charters can provide some potential sense of how much an ecclesiastical centre concerned itself with the provision of worship in the localities. It is possible that some monasteries might themselves provide aspects of the care of souls: in 1154 Pope Adrian IV wrote to the monks, clergy, and people of Béziers to tell them to respect the authority of their bishop and pay him the due portion of all tithes and oblations, and further warned that certain monks, against the requirements of their professed rule, had been baptizing little children, and presuming to give penance and the Eucharist to lay people, all of which were strictly forbidden.[18] This active-but-unregulated exercise of the *cura animarum* might have been proffered by other monastic communities, though of course it could only have an effect in the area local to such a foundation; Adrian's dictat did not seem to be addressing an increased monastic presence in local churches, but the activities of a renegade few. And, to hammer the point home, a monastic community that did not contain ordained priests (not at all unusual in this period) was not in a strong position to supply canonically approved pastoral care to local communities. Bishops were those with the key responsibility. In an influential article from 1982 Giles Constable noted that the council of Nîmes (1096), overseen by Pope Urban II, had apparently required bishops to install priests in those 'parish' churches which had ended up in monastic hands, something which might suggest that 'reform' prompted a major shift in the provision of a more pastoral Christianity in local worship.[19] However, whilst that clause is present in Mansi's edition (*Sacra concilia* XX, col. 933), it is not in fact found in the earliest manuscript records of the council. In those, the opening canon focuses only on the issue of 'simoniacal' bishops who had sold the tithing rights of 'altars' to monasteries, something which the pope then forbade (although allowing monasteries to retain the rights if they had already held them for thirty years).[20] This rather suggests that the issue of local churches being left without pastoral provision—the concern addressed by the later interpolation—was not in

---

[17] For example, *Cart. Béziers*, pp. 63–64 (no. 56), some time after 1010, which lists both various lands held by the bishop and includes various churches, and their accompanying 'fields', among these.
[18] *Cart. Béziers*, p. 253 (no. 188).   [19] Constable, 'Monasteries, Rural Churches', p. 383.
[20] For example, BnF MS lat. 10402, fol. 81r–v. Fundamental for the issue of later interpolations in this period: R. Somerville, *Pope Urban's Council of Piacenza* (Oxford: Oxford University Press, 2011), pp. 121–22.

fact considered in the period of the original council; it seems rather to be a late twelfth-century addition.[21]

In general though we should probably not assume that monastic or episcopal control of churches would immediately lead to the better provision of training, materials, and personnel. Ecclesiastical control of local churches—and their lands—was first and foremost about the control of resources. That might provide a foundation for increased spiritual provision, but the equation is not automatic or assured, and there is little evidence of the change of ownership leading to much intervention in clerical behaviour at a local level (as the rhetoric for reform might otherwise lead one to suspect). A charter does survive from the second or third decade of the twelfth century, where the donor, a monk of the monastery of Magrens, transferred to the parish priest Bernard a third of the rights to the church of Sainte-Colombe, making this conditional on Bernard no longer associating with a woman called Belisen and her son (and one presumes also his child). But this is the *only* occasion that I have found where an aspect of reform ideology with regard to clerical roles—namely celibacy—leaves it mark in the charter evidence. And it is clearly a rather specific instance, prompted by the particular monk making the gift, who himself retained the other two-thirds of the church's income.[22] It does of course also show us another occasion in which local provision and monastic ownership might entwine, with a local priest allowed a portion—but only a portion—of the church's income to support his activities.[23]

Two examples from the records of the cathedral church of Saint-Nazaire in Béziers frame some further local possibilities. The first comes from 1069 and records a donation of four pieces of land in the village of Sauvian (*Salviano*) by one André and his brothers, done in recompense for André's faults:

> I, the aforesaid André, confess to have erred gravely, and to have heedlessly offended my Lord, because I have claimed to be a priest, when I have never received the blessing of the rank of priest, and many times have sung mass to the ignorant. And having for some time persisted in this deceit, and having falsely mocked many unsuspecting people, I recalled the beneficial words which said *Neither shall the wicked dwell near you, nor shall the unjust abide before your eyes. You hate all the workers of iniquity; you will destroy all that speak a lie* [Ps. 5: 6–7]; and the Apostle said: *who unworthily eats the bread and [drinks from] the chalice of the Lord, eats and drinks judgment to himself* [1 Cor. 11: 27/29].[24]

---

[21] It appears thus, in what looks to be a late twelfth-century hand, in BnF MS lat. 3860, fol. 138r-v.

[22] *Cart. Lézat*, II, p. 127 (no. 1174), 1120 × 37.

[23] See also *Cart. Moissac*, pp. 91–92 (no. 57), 1135 agreement between bishop and monks regarding church of Saint-Clar over division of oblations.

[24] *Cart. Béziers*, pp. 99–100 (no. 78): 'Ego quidem Andreas prescriptus confiteor me graviter errasse, et contra Dominum meum negligenter deliquisse, quia dicebam me esse sacerdotem, cum nusquam presbiteri gradus benedictionem sump[s]issem; et sepe ignorantibus missam cantabam, cum autem in hac fallacia multo perseveraverem tempore, et multos incautos falso ludificarem,

The second is from 1085, and records a complex agreement regarding the *honor* (constituting in this case the total tithing within the limits of a place called *La Marreschera*) of the church of Saint-Genès-de-Grézan, which had been mortgaged (apparently to the cathedral), and which a certain Raimond Bliger—apparently a layman—had redeemed for 250 *sous*. 'And Matfred the bishop understood this church of Saint Genès to be excommunicate, because a cleric had not sung [mass] in this church for three years' (*Et ista ecclesia Sancti Genesii Matfredus episcopus tenuit excommunicatam, quod non cantavit in ecclesia ista clericus de annis tribus*). The bishop and canons then agreed that Raimond would hold the *honor* for his lifetime, after which it would revert to the *dominium* of the church of Saint-Genès, 'and to the priest who will liturgically minister that church with all due care and without other deception' (*et ad ipsum presbiterem qui ipsam ecclesiam decantaverit cum omni deliberatione, et sine ullo inganno*).[25] The details here are more than a little confusing, but it would appear that 'the same priest' here means an as-yet-unspecified person who will be appointed to the benefice, and not Raimond Bliger (who would in any case by that point be dead).

In both cases, we have evidence of episcopal oversight of the proper provision of the liturgy, and a willingness to intervene in a locality. The fact that the church of Saint-Genès had been excommunicated suggests some degree of active engagement, though the reasons for this are not made clear (the phrase *tenuit excommunicatam* suggests not that the bishop had actively excommunicated the church himself, but that he believed that it was excommunicated). But the eventual reversion of the tithing is then linked explicitly to the management of the church by its cleric, a more positive sense of episcopal management of parochial provision. The other example—André the unordained priest—also indicates a fairly strong degree of episcopal engagement, and perhaps record keeping of ordinations, of a kind which we would expect to see in the thirteenth century but which is otherwise largely invisible to us in this period. So we might decide that an active bishop and cathedral chapter were paying reasonably close attention to liturgical provision in the localities (if not necessarily anything more than the regular performance of the mass), and would be more likely, and better equipped, to pursue such issues when churches came directly under their control.

On the other hand, both examples could also point in a rather different interpretive direction. André, whilst not fully ordained, *had* been performing the mass regularly, and there is no mention of a lack of personal ability; though also no mention of any priestly activity beyond singing mass. From the point of view of the bishop, the lack of ordination was a major issue; but from the point of view of

---

recordatus sum verbo profecie dicentis: Neque habitabit juxta te malignus neque permanebunt injusti ante oculos tuos; odisti omnes qui operantur iniquitatem perdes omnes qui loquuntur mendacium. Et Apostolus ait: qui calicem Domini et panem indigne sumpserit, judicium sibi manducat et bibit.' The case is briefly noted in Magnou-Nortier, *La société laïque*, p. 433.

[25] *Cart. Béziers*, pp. 111–12 (no. 87). My thanks to Felicity Hill in unravelling this charter.

the congregation, those 'many unsuspecting people'? The issue here is a change in what constitutes 'competency' rather than competency itself. Perhaps episcopal oversight did go along with some substantive differences in training and resourcing, but perhaps equally the local clergy, often trained up in the 'family business', had been performing their roles perfectly adequately from the viewpoint of the local laity. In contrast, the church of Saint-Genès, whilst excommunicated, lacked adequate provision, but the bishop's response here, in the short to medium term at least, seems to have been to further enforce that situation via temporary alienation of the church's *honor*. In other words, in both examples, in the short term at least, episcopal intervention seems to have meant that local liturgical provision ceased.

A further example again suggests that what was most immediately at stake was ecclesiastical control, whether monastic or episcopal, rather than consolidation or amplification of the *cura animarum*. This is a case recorded in the cartulary of Aniane from 1138, where the bishop of Maguelonne was called in to resolve a dispute over a church established at Valcrose by one Pierre Raimond, to which the monastery was laying claim. The bishop resolved that the church could continue to operate as a kind of small community, but under his episcopal jurisdiction. However, those who were based there should not have the temerity to claim reward for baptisms or visits (to the dying, presumably), or for burial services or 'penances'.[26] We have here, as previously explored in Chapter 1, a sense of things which might therefore in other circumstances be available from local churches—baptism, spiritual care for the dying, some form of penance (though what exactly the latter constitutes continues to remain unclear).[27] But we also have clear evidence of a combination of monastery and bishop shutting down that provision. What had apparently emerged locally was not to continue thus.

It may be that more happened locally, independent of top-down direction, than the majority of our sources can reveal. In May 1108 a man called Deusde Roger de Boujan and his niece Boneta gifted and surrendered that which they held of the church of Saint-Saturnin-de-Pouzac. Some of this (a quarter of the tithe) Deusde had previously gained as a mortgage from Boneta's father; more of it was part of an agreement with another relative called Matfred, from Abeilhan, who appears to be the incumbent priest. What is notable about this gift is that Deusde and Boneta gave these things not to a monastery or bishop, but to the church of Saint-Saturnin-de-Pouzac itself—specifically, 'to the Lord God, and to St Saturnin de Pouzac, and to you Matfred d'Abeilhan, and to your parishioners of the same church, to do <with it> whatsoever you wish and pleases you'. In return Matfred and the parishioners gave Deusde and Boneta 25 and a half *sous* of Béziers; this sum (the same charter explains) had been willed to the same church

---

[26] *Cart. d'Aniane*, pp. 260–62 (no. 118). [27] See Chapter 1, pp. 51–54.

of Saint-Saturnin-de-Pouzac by one Jean de Pouzac for the 'inheritance' of his soul.[28] So here we have a little snapshot of almost entirely local negotiations and provision for what would appear to be a very modest parish church (one which, as far as I can tell, no longer survives).[29] Matfred and his 'parishioners'—a very early occurrence of that term, we should note—are here present as active agents, using one donation—Jean's legacy—to sort out a separate deal—Deusde and Boneta's gift. In all of this, we have a much more tantalizing sense of a local priest and his flock engaged in the financial management of their church, not least in the ability of that priest to hang on to money willed to the church and use it for further parochial benefit.

We know about the transaction because it was witnessed by the head of the chapter of Saint-Nazaire in Béziers; and because a couple of weeks later, Matfred 'with the counsel of all his parishioners' donated half of the church to the chapter (this perhaps being the portion that Deusde and Boneta had previously held in agreement with him)—and thus both charters were recorded in the cathedral's cartulary.[30] And this is the point: if that had not been the case, it would have remained invisible to us. What we cannot know is how much else of the local remains invisible. As is so often the case for this period, we cannot easily escape from a monastic or episcopal viewpoint, because of the nature of the surviving evidence. Where we see change, we cannot also know whether it comes purely because of the 'reformist' policies from on high, or because of local decisions, choices, and enthusiasms.

As I said further above, the south's experience of top-down reform had a second strand, reconfiguring the political relationship (and other things which followed on therefrom) between the powerful lay lords and the long-standing monastic houses. Eliana Magnani Soares-Christen has demonstrated that in Provence there is a notable shift, beginning in the late eleventh century but most notable in the twelfth, from a monasticism strongly embedded in the familial and patronage networks of the aristocracy, to one which actively separated itself from the secular elite and became much less 'permeable' to donations.[31] A key shift is over the provision of abbots and bishops: as we saw in Chapter 1, from Carolingian times and well into the eleventh century, aristocratic families expected to provide all the major players in a region, and this quite obviously included bishops and the heads of the major monastic foundations. As 'reform' ideas began to take hold, this changed. In the second half of the eleventh century, a number of bishops

---

[28] *Cart. Béziers*, pp. 154–55 (no. 111).
[29] Whilst there is a church of Saint-Saturnin-de-Pouzac—still relatively modest—in the high Pyrenees, north of Bagnolles-de-Bigorre, Abeilhan and Boujan locate us a long way from there, somewhat east of Béziers, where there is a surviving 'rue de Pouzac' leading south-east of Abeilhan. It is most likely that the church in question has now disappeared or been renamed.
[30] *Cart. Béziers*, pp. 155–56 (no. 112).
[31] Magnani Soares-Christen, *Monastères et aristocratie*, p. 411.

were deposed by papal legates, usually following accusations of simony: in 1060 this befell Ripert, bishop of Gap, Pierre, bishop of Sisteron (who, at the age of 8, had been bought the bishopric by his father, Rambaud, co-lord of Nice), and Foulques, bishop of Cahors.[32] The case of Gap gives us perhaps the ideal model from the reformist perspective: as well as being bishop, Ripert was Lord of Mévouillon (a *castrum* halfway between Gap and Avignon), and was married. After his deposition, Pope Alexander II persuaded the cathedral canons to elect a man called Arnoux, who had been a child oblate in the monastery of Sainte-Trinité in Vendôme, was well educated in Latin, and would in fact go on to be recognized as a saint. Arnoux was himself from a noble background, as his *vita* emphasizes, but the import of this was that he was 'of free birth', and thus not tied to any other lord.[33] We should not imagine that the reform movement suddenly transformed ecclesiastical leadership into an egalitarian career path available to all, nor that such changes that were made came swiftly or universally. For example, not until around the third decade of the twelfth century did Alphonse-Jourdain, count of Toulouse, give up the right to appoint the 'secular abbot' (who problematically held office alongside the religious abbot) of the monastery of Moissac.[34] But over the longer term the changes did disrupt the tightly knit connections that had long existed between the great monastic estates and the great lords. Whereas previously the aristocratic families had expected, as a natural part of their regional lordship, to provide bishops and abbots to the major foundations, by the twelfth century it was increasingly the case that such figures would come from within the monastic orders themselves, and see their priorities as emerging firstly from that context (even if in fact still having familial ties to the nobility).[35]

These two strands—the (re)appropriation of lay property, including churches, into monastic and episcopal control, and the diminution of seigneurial connection to ecclesiastical hierarchy—were changes not only in regard to ideas of reform and ecclesiastical governance, but in wider sociocultural practice. Barbara Rosenwein has influentially described the earlier period as seen through the charters of Cluny, in which gifting and counter-gifting, and a hazy two-way flow of property, moved back and forth to weave ties of friendship and interdependence between the monastery and the lay elite. Florian Mazel has adapted and developed a similar picture for Provence, but importantly notes that this world was fracturing.[36]

---

[32] F. Mazel, 'Pour une redéfinition de la "réforme grégorienne"', *CdF* 48 (2013), 28; J.-H. Foulon and M. Varano, 'Réforme et épiscopat en Provence: étude comparée des cas de Gap et de Sisteron au milieu du XI siècle', *CdF* 48 (2013), 311–42.

[33] O. Hanne, 'La genèse médiévale d'une figure de l'épiscopat de Gap: saint Arnoux (c. 1065–c. 1079)', contribution to colloque *Les évêques de France au XXe siècle*, 2011; online publication 2016 <https://halshs.archives-ouvertes.fr/halshs-00995817/document> (accessed 19 July 2017).

[34] *Cart. Moissac*, p. 335 (no. 242, 1127 × 35).

[35] Soares-Christen, *Monastères et aristocratie*, p. 471.

[36] B. Rosenwein, *To Be the Neighbor of Saint Peter: The Social Meaning of Cluny's Property, 909–1049* (Ithaca, NY: Cornell University Press, 1989); F. Mazel, 'Amitié et rupture de l'amitié: moine et grands laics provençaux au temps de la crise grégorienne (milieu XIe–milieu XIIe siècle)', *Revue historique* 633 (2005), 53–95.

Under the pressure of reform ideas, lay gifts or surrenders of property to the Church were increasingly understood as acts of full and permanent alienation—or understood thus by the abbots and bishops and the papacy at least. It is this that underlies at least some of the violence of lordship explored in Chapter 2: what was presented in ecclesiastical sources as violent depredation against the Church may have been understood by the lay protagonists as efforts to reclaim familial inheritances.[37] There was, as Mazel has put it, a crisis of 'friendship' in the late eleventh to early twelfth century: where the interests of individual noble families and particular monasteries had previously seemed obviously entwined, there was now a difference in strategic aim, and consequent tension. Straightforward gifts to the old foundations began to dry up; the terrain was shifting.

A Changing Landscape of Piety

In the long term, probably the most fundamental change to western Christendom to emerge from the Gregorian reforms was the clearer demarcation between 'clerical' and 'lay' identity, at all levels of society, in terms of the physical appearance and dress of clerics, expectations regarding their personal moral conduct, and in regard to the role they played as ministrants of the sacraments. This might suggest that, across the later eleventh and early twelfth century, the Church successfully gathered all that was 'spiritual' to itself, producing a greater separation from the secular world where the laity could materially support the endeavours of the clergy but were to leave things otherwise well alone. It should be emphasized that this *was* precisely part of what was intended by 'reform'; a separation of spheres of authority. As Hugh of Saint-Victor wrote in his *De sacramentis*, 'There are two lives, one early, the other heavenly, one corporeal, the other spiritual... In order that justice may be served in both lives and prosperity flourish, men were first distributed on each side by zeal and labour the goods of each life... All things that are earthly and made for the earthly life belong to the power of the king; all things that are spiritual and attributed to the spiritual life belong to the power of the supreme pontiff.'[38] Thus the reformers sought to prise off the fingers of the aristocracy from the levers of monastic and episcopal power.

But this increased separation of spiritual and secular does not tell the whole story, for as the period of intense papal 'reform' came to fruition in the twelfth century, so too do we start to see certain lay people becoming more spiritually active, some making a bold transition from the one life to the other. It is thus important to see the relationship between the spiritual and the secular reconfigured

---

[37] S. Weinberger, 'Les conflits entre clercs et laïcs dans la Provence du XI siècle', *Annales du Midi* 92 (1980), 269–79.

[38] Hugh of Saint-Victor, *De sacramentis Christiane fidei*, PL 176, col. 418; trans. B. Tierney, *The Crisis of Church and State, 1050–1300* (1964; Toronto: PIMS, 1988), pp. 94–95.

rather than simply separated. Whilst donations to the older Benedictine foundations radically slowed, new opportunities for patronage emerged, accompanied and perhaps fostered by some new possibilities for intense spiritual engagement. This was something experienced by the very few, to be sure; but through their spiritual activities—notably public on occasion—they added to the complexity and potential choice of the wider landscape for the many.

Let us begin with a very dramatic case, in the public square in Lodève, on Palm Sunday, in a year perhaps soon after 1130. The bishop stood with his clergy 'on the step that was made for speaking', and a large crowd was gathered. A layman—a knight, no less—was led forward 'like a criminal', beaten with wooden staves as he went along undressed and barefoot, his neck encased in a wooden collar called a *redorta* in the vernacular. With him were companions, including another knight, a priest, and four other men, whom he had earlier converted by 'his word and example' (a phrase often associated with the expected behaviour of reformed cathedral canons in this period).[39] 'Coming to the bishop like a runaway slave (*servuum*) who had left a good master, he delivered himself to God through the hand of the bishop, [and] on his knees he begged forgiveness. He gave the bishop a letter that he brought in hand; in it he had described all his sins.' The bishop, after some demurral, agreed to read out the letter of self-accusation, whilst the man continued to be beaten around the square, weeping copiously; his tears prompted a similar, compassionate response from those around (*com-passio*—to suffer with). Eventually 'all who were present marvelled and revered him with great affection. They acclaimed his repentance and affirmed that the Lord had truly looked upon him.' Many others were moved to confession and penance by his example.[40]

This comes from the *vita* of Pons de Léras, not someone who achieved even informal sainthood, but the founder of a monastic institution at Silvanès, whose conversion to the religious life is described in detail in a narrative written by a monk there later in the twelfth century. Aspects of the narrative necessarily draw upon an established set of ideas and images, such as the echoes of Christ's humiliation prior to his crucifixion, and the importance of tears signalling inner penance. Very public acts of penance were a part of earlier Carolingian practice, though the instances of which we are aware usually come from higher up the

---

[39] C. W. Bynum, *Docere verbo et exemplo: An Aspect of Twelfth-Century Spirituality* (Missoula, Mont.: Scholars Press, 1979).

[40] The narrative is preserved in Dijon, BM MS 611, fols 1–28v, edited in B. M. Kienzle, 'The Works of Hugo Francigena: *Tractatus de conversione Pontii de Laracio et exordii Salvaniensis monasterii vera narratio; epistolae*', *Sacris erudiri* 34 (1994), 273–311. Whilst I have here rendered *servuum* (MS 611 fol. 8r) as slave rather than 'serf' (on the grounds that we do not otherwise find the language of 'serfs' in southern French materials), the translation here otherwise follows B. M. Kienzle, 'The Tract on the Conversion of Pons de Léras and the True Account of the Beginning of the Monastery at Silvanès', *Cistercian Studies Quarterly* 30 (1995), 219–43, at p. 231. I have not been able to consult V. Ferras, *Pons de Léras: un cistercien occitan au XII siècle*, 2nd edn (Toulouse: n.p., 1979).

social scale.[41] Pons was a knight, with a castle, and apparently a prime example of a rapacious lord; but his crimes were more on the level of sheep rustling than the major stand-off between pope and emperor that had famously led to Emperor Henry IV performing three days of penance at Canossa some fifty plus years earlier. Most importantly of all, Pons was turning the public performance of penance into a permanent act of conversion to a new life, rather than penance as a transitory rite, prefatory to the reassertion of social status.

Thus, whilst elements of the narrative draw upon familiar tropes, and existing patterns of penitential behaviour provided some model for whatever actions actually took place, there is nonetheless something new here: that a layperson of Pons's social standing—a local knight, clearly quite well connected but not a major player in the region—should experience and publicly proclaim a conversion to a radically new, religious way of life.

Three aspects of the nature of that conversion are notable. One is that Pons was not dying. It was not unusual for the pious consciences of noble people suddenly to quicken on their deathbed. We have seen as much above in various charters, and most explicitly in Chapter 1, in the record of Bernard Pierre's deathbed confession in which he made restitution of the goods of the church of Peyrepertuse. But Pons de Léras was not in this situation. His heart 'was pierced with the spear of the gracious Lord', and 'fear of the Lord transformed him completely from his earlier actions'. He contemplated his past evil deeds, and 'inwardly moved by his heart's pain he was totally converted to penitence', this being bodily expressed by a great outpouring of tears.[42] What kind of reparation could he make, and how could he appease the judge of all? 'Suddenly he resolved to leave behind everything of this world and henceforth to spend the remainder of his life doing acts of penance (*penitentie actibus*).'[43] This is a layperson undergoing a conversion experience, apparently unprompted by anything other than reflection on his own misdeeds. The focus on penance and atonement, their cognitive availability to a noble layman like Pons, must surely suggest that such ideas were in wider circulation than we might gather from other sources. But we must also then remember that Pons was doing something highly unusual. His was a conscience pricked well beyond the normal bounds, aiming at self-reform and the re-dedication of his life, something which apparently could not be carried out through the more normal channels of monastic gift-giving.

The second aspect picks up particularly on that last point. Pons felt remorse for his past misdeeds, and for the particular nature of those deeds, which are emphasized as being the acquisition of wealth and goods gained via trickery,

---

[41] M. de Jong, *The Penitential State: Authority and Atonement in the Age of Louis the Pious, 814–840* (Cambridge: Cambridge University Press, 2009).

[42] MS 611, fol. 4r-v: 'et tactus dolore cordis intrinsecus totus ad penitenciam est conversus'; Kienzle, 'Tract on the Conversion', p. 229, translation slightly amended.

[43] Kienzle, 'Tract on the Conversion', p. 229.

hard bargaining, and the threat of violence from his neighbours. Inspired by the Gospel passage 'If you wish to be perfect, go, sell all that you have and give it to the poor' (Matt. 19: 21) he put his wife and daughter (with an endowment) into a nunnery, gave his son to a monastery in Lodève, and exchanged all his property for livestock and foodstuffs. This provided him with a large amount of moveable goods, which he aimed to distribute to the poor and needy, churches and monasteries being mentioned initially, but also hospitals, the poor, pilgrims, widows, and orphans. 'But he believed that this act would perhaps be less acceptable to God if he did not first return those things that he had once taken by force.' To that end, he sent messengers around the towns and villages and *castra* and churches proclaiming that anyone to whom he owed anything, or from whom he had taken anything by force, should come to him in the village of Pégairolles (a few kilometres east of Lodève) in the days following Palm Sunday, and he would give back their goods.[44] This is all described in notable detail, and its focus on *restitution* is unusual, particularly restitution to other lay people. There are elements of something like this found in wills, particularly once we are into the twelfth century—for example, testators asking that their debts be settled by their executors, or surrendering ecclesiastical property having 'recognized' on their deathbed that they have sinned in previously holding it. But Pons's sins are not to be ameliorated simply by giving things to existing monastic institutions (though that is included, as noted, *en passant*). To make things right with God he must make restitution to, and gain forgiveness from, his neighbours. A very active step toward salvation is made by a layperson himself, and through the reactions of other lay people, whose eventual forgiveness is emphasized in the text.

The third unusual element is what came next. Pons and his companions set out on pilgrimage; not perhaps in itself unusual, and the places to which they went were existing centres of pilgrimage, firstly Saint-Guilhem-le-Desert (about 20 kilometres east of Lodève) where a fragment of the cross was worshipped, and then the much longer journey to Saint-Jacques-de-Compostelle. At Compostelle, the archbishop received them very enthusiastically, initially thinking to persuade them to settle and form a religious house there, before determining that they would be of more use to those who spoke the same vernacular language back in southern France. This focus on language suggests that they planned not only to live a holy life, but to instruct or preach more widely—something that places them in the company of some rather more contentious 'wandering preachers' from the same period (to whom we will turn below). Their journeys then became rather more remarkable: all the way up to the Normandy coast to Mont-Saint-Michel, then to the church of Saint-Martin of Tours, then to Limoges, and then back south to Rodez. Eventually they settled in a more remote region relatively

---

[44] Kienzle, 'Tract on the Conversion', pp. 230–32. This assumes Pégairolles-du-Buèges; there is also Pégairolles-de-l'Escallette to the north.

nearby, supported by a founding donation from a local nobleman, Arnaud du Pont, his wife Bouissonna, and their children, in 1133. Further donations followed immediately, with the notable assistance and orchestration of the bishop, 'in whose hands' various donations are said to have been made in the surviving charters for this early period. These first gifts are made 'to the Blessed Virgin Mary', to build a church in her honour, and subsequent donations are to her 'and to the brothers of Sainte-Marie of Silvanès'.[45] After a little while, the success of the foundation became such that 'it was said to be suitable for having an order and constructing an abbey' (the voice of the bishop perhaps audible here, behind the passive grammatical construction). This prompted considerable debate over what *kind* of order and rule to adopt: Cistercian or Carthusian? Pons went off to seek advice, and ended up adopting the Cistercian model. Silvanès formally becoming a Cistercian abbey in 1136.

To put all of this in context, let us note that there is another story—in fact, a short narrative poem—recorded in the *miracula* of St Enimie, written probably not that long before Pons had his conversion experience, but looking back to the previous century. This tale tells of an unnamed layman: a criminal, vicious, impious, someone full of bad works. 'Some time later he was converted, God give us clemency, and came to penance, and indeed to feel bitterness,' and was dressed in a hair shirt and bound in chains. To further his penance, he set off to venerate at the shrines of the saints, going thus to Jerusalem, Acre, Constantinople; and then to Rome, and St Mark's in Venice; to Germany, Flanders, Brittany, and to Mont-Saint-Michel in Normandy. Thereafter he travelled back to southern France and journeyed round all the famous shrines of the region: St Martial at Limoges, Mary at Le Puy, Ste Foy at Conques, St Gilles at Rodez, St Antoine at Vienne, St Sernin at Toulouse, and St Jacques at Compostelle—and of course eventually to St Enimie, who appeared to him in a dream, and freed him from his chains, which had by then caused him terrible wounds and bodily suffering.

This anonymous lay penitent thus provides another narrative precedent for Pons de Léras's conversion and extensive peregrinations. But we should notice how much is different here. The unnamed reformed criminal is a solitary figure, with no followers and no wider message to the world. The path narrated by his tale is one of expiatory suffering; it arrives at a destination and conclusion only through an act of divine clemency. His example to the world is the unending debt caused by sin, where the structure of the story implies that, without St Enimie's intervention, his peregrinations and sufferings would have known no end. In contrast, as we have seen, Pons has followers, a message, a new life following conversion. His journeying seems to be a spiritual quest more than an expiation for past crimes. His example provides a focal point for the creation of community.

---

[45] *Cart. Silvanès*, pp. 11–30, *passim*. The bishop is a witness in the vast majority of the donation charters in the 1130s.

And whilst he shares a criminal past with the unnamed penitent pilgrim, his conversion focuses much more on transformation by voluntary *poverty* rather than pain, explicitly linked to an apostolic model. Lay people—Pons, his immediate followers, but also those who then helped him—play a key role throughout the story of the foundation of Silvanès: the lengthy acts of pilgrimage, apparently in search of the ideal kind of religious life to adopt, the orchestrated foundation gifting by other noblemen, the ability initially to start a local monastery dedicated directly to the Virgin Mary, before being prompted to adopt more clearly an existing 'rule' and way of life. New forms of religious practice and expression, and new choices to be made among those forms, are clearly apparent at every stage.[46]

As Soares-Christen and others have pointed out, the fracturing of relations between the existing noble elites and the older religious orders created a space of opportunity. It is into this changing landscape that the new orders of Cistercians, Templars, and Hospitallers emerged; and moreover a resurgence of churchbuilding and the founding of hospitals and leper houses. The first two decades of the twelfth century saw six or seven new, local monastic foundations in the south of France that became Cistercian around the middle of the century, a similar number of foundations in the 1130s (Silvanès amongst them), and a further expansion from the middle of the century onward, resulting in over thirty Cistercian houses (six of them nunneries) by 1200. The bulk of these were located within 120 km of Toulouse, with a few more on the Mediterranean coast, but only one east of the Rhône (see Map 2).[47] The Hospitallers arrived in eastern Provence in the very early years of the twelfth century, the Templars in Languedoc a couple of decades later, in both cases depending initially on the support of major lords (the Trencavels in particular with regard to the Templars). From the 1140s onward more commanderies were founded for both orders. By the end of the twelfth century, there were over thirty Hospitaller foundations, and perhaps half as many Templar houses, spread fairly evenly across the region, and reaching further east, beyond the Rhône, than the Cistercian holdings (see Map 3).[48] Hospitals—or hostels, the distinction is not clear in this period—were local foundations, not part of monastic orders, and early examples are harder to track from surviving records, but many major foundations start to be visible by the later twelfth century, and some much earlier than that.[49] All of these provided a new outlet for the pious gifting of the nobility; indeed, one can say in a fairly literal sense that they

---

[46] On the choice of religious life, see C. W. Bynum 'Did the Twelfth-Century Discover the Individual?', *Journal of Ecclesiastical History* 31 (1980), 1–17.

[47] My analysis draws here upon the information in B. Wildhaber, 'Catalogue des établissements cisterciens de Languedoc aux XIII et XIVe siècles', *CdF* 21 (1986), 21–44; see also the map provided there (p. 22), but note that there all foundations are mapped, including those established in later centuries.

[48] D. Selwood, *Knights of the Cloister: Templars and Hospitallers in Central-Southern Occitania, 1100–1300* (Woodbridge: Boydell, 1999), pp. 48–71.

[49] See Chapter 4, below.

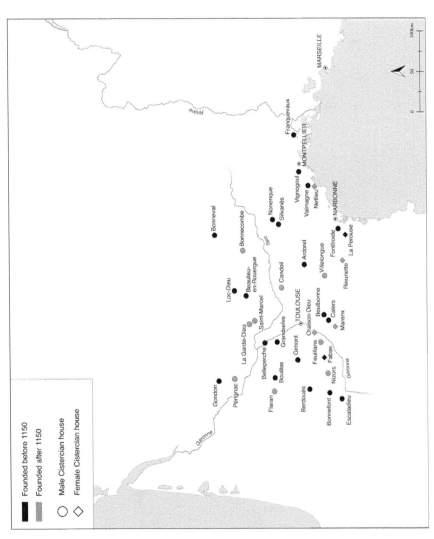

Map 2 Cistercian abbeys founded in the twelfth century

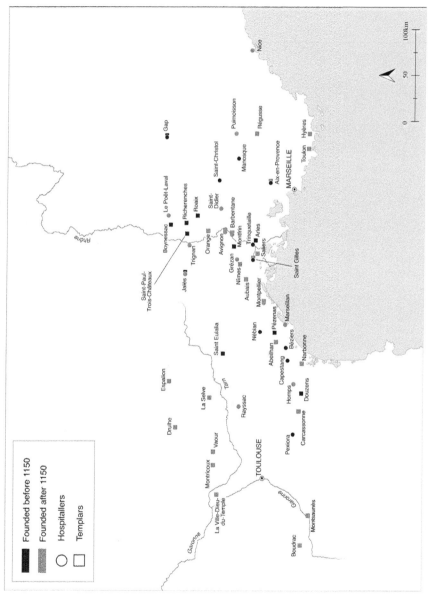

Map 3 Hospitaller and Templar houses founded in the twelfth century

were *created by* the redirected flow of lay donations, which provided the land and wealth to construct new churches, priories, commanderies, and hospitals. The relationship between aristocracy and these new forms of monasticism (and other pious foundations) did not replicate the older patterns, but produced a new set of interlinkages, where lay activity and choice was clearly apparent as they helped to found and sustain these fresh forms of piety, but where episcopal encouragement and canalization of donations is also apparent.[50]

Thus a long-standing intertwining of aristocratic interests and monastic institutions was being reformed, or perhaps more precisely one should write 're-formed'. Whilst older patterns of influence and connection were being shut down, so too were new opportunities and possibilities opening up for the most powerful laity in particular, allowing them to make active choices over whom and what they wished to support within a shifting spiritual landscape; this in turn then created new opportunities for more modest donations, once the foundations had taken place. The charters from this period and, increasing in frequency in the twelfth century, testamentary documents suggest that at a more local and less exalted scale there was also change, with a greater elaboration of choices and specific directions that lay donors might make. The aristocratic landscape did surely matter; as just noted, it is the combination of reformist ideas and aristocratic redirection of gifting that transforms the pious choices available in the twelfth century. But it is the more local and specific that interests me most, and it is in this direction that we now turn.

The various cartularies of course record pious donations from long before the twelfth century. These, it should be noted, are almost entirely donations of land, or churches, or the revenues derived directly or indirectly from both, and the donors or sellers rarely include any additional commemorative requests or pious contextual statements. Where such additional aspects do appear, they are occasionally in regard to burial—as discussed in Chapter 1—but more usually fairly general clauses about the transaction being done 'for the souls of our forebears', and also sometimes for the souls of the donors themselves. This is not to suggest that these are empty phrases. As we saw, they say something important about the nexus of land, memory, and the afterlife. But they are general and largely undifferentiated, and they place most of the specific interpretation in the hands of the monastic recipients of the gift. That is, the spiritual work that might arise subsequent to the transaction is something to be carried out, as best seen fit, by the monks. The fact of the gift and counter-gift, and the relationship they implied, mattered more than the specific details of the spiritual counter-gift of prayer.[51]

---

[50] Soares-Christen, *Monastères et aristocratie*, pp. 471ff. Damien Carraz, 'Templars and Hospitallers in the Cities of the West and the Latin East (Twelfth to Thirteenth Centuries)', *Crusades* 12 (2013), 103–20 at p. 113 on bishops encouraging knightly orders as part of formation of parochial care and reformed religion.

[51] See similarly, though with a different inflection, Mazel, 'Amitié et rupture', pp. 71–72.

There are occasional exceptions: a charter from the mid-eleventh century sets up various masses, including an anniversary mass for the mother of the donor, and an undated but probably even earlier charter from Urso Bernard (issued 'to all his friends') gifted the church of Colobers to Saint-Sernin 'for remedy of my soul, and such that a thousand masses are sung for my soul'.[52] But these are exceptions— and the rather optimistic 'thousand masses' suggests a rhetorical flourish in the direction of the monks rather than a specific accounting of pious provision. Leaving the details to the experts, as it were, perhaps explains also why certain donation charters—many of those for the eleventh and twelfth centuries, for example in the cartulary of Aniane—lack any pious clauses.[53] Here, in addition to noting the vagaries of scribal habits, one has to presume that the donors were simply confident that gifting to the monastery would produce some spiritual benefit, and did not feel the need to be specific.

In contrast, one of the things that starts to change in the twelfth century is a greater degree of specificity on the part of the donors, particularly but not only in cases where the donation has some testamentary quality. Donors and testators are more frequently specific about memorial masses and other such activities: Guillerm Stephan, in a testamentary charter made perhaps around 1120 in preparation for his departure to Spain, asked for an annual mass by the monks of Aniane, and that his heirs should provide wine for services in the monastery for the rest of their lives; Pierre Raimond de Murel requested a full trental mass in another testamentary document of 1122; in 1147, Bernard de Roujan left money for ten masses to be said every year for his soul, the souls of his father and his mother, and 'all the faithful dead', along with other pious provisions.[54] Demonstrating particular elaboration regarding certain aspects of the performance, at some point in the later twelfth century the Lady de la Tour gave land to the monks at Morlaàs for an anniversary mass for the souls of her husband Guillaume de la Tour and all his forebears, 'namely on Sunday in the middle of Lent, with cross and thurible, and sounding all the bells'.[55] One could easily continue to multiply the examples for the mid- to late twelfth century.

We also start to see donations made to new places or groups of particular spiritual interest, in addition to the ancient monasteries: to particular shrines and to local hospitals in various wills, for example, and to 'the poor'. By the latter we

---

[52] *Cart. Notre-Dame de Nîmes*, pp. 216–18 (no. 135), 1043 × 60; *Cart. Saint-Sernin*, p. 214 (no. 298). See also *Cart. Lézat*, I, pp. 532–33 (no. 721), c. 1010, setting up masses for the dead *pro anima mea et pro animas parentorum meorum* throughout Lent.

[53] This is surprisingly even the case with a donation charter made on donor's deathbed in 1110: *Cart. d'Aniane*, pp. 263–64 (no. 121). There are a few exceptions, particularly later in the cartulary when general *pro anima* clauses do intermittently appear (perhaps indicating a change in scribal practice), but they remain rare in comparison to other cartularies.

[54] *Cart. d'Aniane*, p. 280 (no. 138); *Cart. Lézat*, I, p. 217 (no. 277); *Cart. S. Étienne d'Agde*, pp. 368–69 (no. 340).

[55] *Cart. Sainte Foi de Morlaàs*, p. 343 (no. 34), 1140 × 75.

should understand not 'the poor' as a whole socioeconomic group, but rather particular clusters of the symbolically important poor, as in a charter from around 1120, wherein various properties connected to the church of La Capelle were bought by Raimond de Millau and Guiral d'Artal from a variety of other men, to support the Holy Sepulchre 'and all the poor of Jerusalem'; another from c. 1143, where Lady Ermessens of Montpellier, her son, and his wife gave land 'to the work of the poor lepers' (*ad opus pauperum leprosorum*), presumably in Montpellier; and far to the west, a charter from 1154 in which the bishop of Oloron and countess of Béarn gave permission that a chapel could be built in the hospital of Morlaàs, at the supplication of a certain Lady Juliana, that it be devoted to serving the needs of the poor and of pilgrims.[56] Gifts to well-established foundations also start to display more inventive pious detail on the part of the donor: again from around 1120, a charter which records various people giving up the rights they held in the church of Saint-Jean-de-Moras to the abbey of Saint-Sernin includes a particular requirement from one Jordan of Teruzan, in return for certain additional land, that the monks should set up an annual feast on the day of Mary's birth in the cloister of the monastery of Saint-Paul-d'Anerag, providing twenty-one loaves and a pack-load of wine.[57] It is of course possible that lay people—in these cases, almost certainly minor nobles (and in the case of Lady Ermessens, a very major noblewoman)—had previously been directing donations toward such specific aspects of worship; but it is only in the twelfth century that it starts to become visible in the written record, and this *might* in fact indicate a real shift in practice.

This is similarly the case with what look to be donors from much further down the social scale, making much smaller gifts. This is something which, again, might well have been an invisible presence in earlier times; but the arrival of new religious orders does seem to have both facilitated and recorded a more modest level of donation. There are several good examples of this from the later twelfth century in the cartulary of the Templar establishment at La Selve: in about 1180 Pons Raimon gave, for a 'charity' (that is, a monetary counter-gift or payment) of 3 *sous*, the produce from one sheep that he held at the manse of Domensol (*doni I. anell que avia el mas de Domensol*). Similarly, for a counter-gift of 10 *sous*, Uc de la Roque and his son Ratier gave a sheep 'to God and Saint Mary and to the knights of the Temple'; Bernois and his son Raimond At gave a sheep for 5 *sous* 'de caritat', with Raimond swearing on the 'Sanz Evangelis' that he would not later

---

[56] Brunel, *Les plus anciennes chartes*, pp. 24–26 (no. 20); A. Germain, ed., *Liber instrumentorum memorialium: cartulaire des Guillems de Montpellier* (Montpellier: Jean Martel aîné, 1884–86), pp. 282–83 (no. 150); *Cart. Sainte Foi de Morlaàs*, p. 323 (no. 9).

[57] *Cart. Saint-Sernin*, p. 360 (no. 515). In the following charter Jordan gave other lands, and it is clear that his family had a long association with Saint-Paul-d'Anerag, which appears to be a small foundation (now on the edge of the village of Isle-en-Dodon) with resident clergy, that is, the kind of 'hermitage' discussed later in this chapter.

dispute the deal; and Berart and his brother Arnal gave two sheep and the rights they held in the fields of Grèze 'for the love of God and to amend the damage which he had done to the house of La Selve' (the nature of the damage left unspecified).[58] A few shillings, some sheep: these very much look like non-elite donors, and this kind of small-scale gifting is a new feature of the documentary landscape at least.

As those counter-gifts 'for charity' indicate, the nature of these donations is not always straightforward patronage. They remain distinct from sales—which also exist—but include a range of inflections, from arrangements which emphasize the importance of the recompense given by the monastery, to those which suggest such recompense is indicative of a higher meaning. With regard to the former: one Pons Roger de Villalier made gifts of land to the Templar foundation at Douzens in 1144, receiving in return a payment of 20 *sous* of Carcassonne, and a measure of wheat and of barley; again in 1147, receiving 100 *sous* as 'alms'; and once again in 1162, receiving 'for charity' 2 sixteenths of wheat and one of barley. These are in one sense business transactions, and Pons Roger clearly had an ongoing relationship with the Templar commandery—he acted as a witness to another charter in 1147.[59] But only one of the amounts paid—the 100 *sous*—was of any real size, and by providing a counter-gift, and describing it as alms or charity, the Templars were perhaps further ensuring that the transfer of land would not be later disputed, and that the meaning of the transaction provided a sort of 'pious bonus' on both sides. A slightly different inflection of meaning appears in another charter from the same cartulary, where Serena and her children give to the Templars a vineyard, and two other vineyards which another man held from them. 'And it is true that because of this and good friendship (*bona amicicia*) you gave to us three measures of grain.'[60] Gifting and counter-gifting is here that which creates, marks, and sustains 'good friendship'—which we should understand not as an emotional connection but as an implicit promise of future mutual support.

A further variation is conditional counter-gifts or payments which were in themselves directed to pious purposes. A number of donations to the Cistercian foundation at Silvanès, organized by a parish priest called Deodat, ensured that the monastery reciprocated through aiding the parish in the practical provision of worship: in 1159 Deodat 'with the counsel and praise of my parishioners' freed the monks in perpetuity from rendering any tithes to his church over certain lands that they held; 'in payment and settlement, you paid us back in return three bells, and these you handed over to us such that it [*the agreement, presumably*]

---

[58] *Cart. de la Selve*, p. 133 (nos 16 and 17), p. 159 (no. 57), p. 254 (no. 197).
[59] *Cart. Templiers de Douzens*, p. 134 (no. 146), 1144; pp. 127–28 (no. 139), 1147; p. 131 (no. 143), 1162; as witness: pp. 130–31 (no. 142), 1147.
[60] *Cart. Templiers de Douzens*, pp. 125–26 (no. 136), 1156.

should remain firmly and securely for all time'.[61] Bells were not a cheap item, and having three of them was a fairly luxurious investment for a parish church in the mid-twelfth century. A year later he brokered another deal, handing over further tithing rights to the monastery, in return for various goods at different points of the year, such as two lambs on the birth of St John the Baptist.[62] A similar arrangement to the bells counter-gift was arranged by another cleric, Bernard the priest of Roquessels, who in 1162 donated the tithes of his church; in recompense and 'for charity' the monks gave a priestly garment (*unum vestimentum sacerdotale*).[63] (We are reminded, as we saw in Chapter 1, that the provision of liturgical objects was a local responsibility.)

There is a further key area of gifting which starts to intensify in the twelfth century, one long associated however with the laity: gifting for the provision of lights.[64] From the corpus of southern French material I have surveyed, we do find a few earlier charters which direct some or all of their donation toward this end: in 923, a donation of a vineyard and three fields '*in meis luminaribus vel sacrificium offerendum*' (this being the earliest example I have found); in 1020, a donation of land and part of a vineyard 'for lights before the altar of St Julien the martyr'.[65] But both of these donations were made by priests. The earliest example of lay people doing the same comes from 1089, when two brothers, Pons and Ato, gave a manse to the monastery of Mas-d'Azil 'so that the monks of that place can make lights before the altar of St Mary, for the remedy of our souls and all of our forebears, every night in perpetuity, and this is the altar in the same monastery of St Étienne'.[66] From around the same time, a charter donating the church of Salléles-d'Aude to the monastery of Moissac includes mention of the donation of rights regarding *spiculariis* (possibly meaning 'gleaning'?) for the upkeep of the lights in the church.[67] It is important to note in both cases the desire to provide income that would keep the lights burning 'every night', in line with an aspiration voiced in church councils since the late sixth century.[68] This is a subtly different form of gifting from some later examples from wills, where something more limited and specific is outlined: for example, in 1110 Étienne Udalger asked his nephews, as executors, to make provision for a lamp to Ste Marie Madeleine

---

[61] *Cart. Silvanès*, p. 64 (no. 76), 1159.   [62] *Cart. Silvanès*, pp. 97–98 (no. 122), 1160.
[63] *Cart. Silvanès*, p. 317 (no. 402), 1162.
[64] D. Postles, 'Lamps, Lights and Layfolk: "Popular" Devotion before the Black Death', *Journal of Medieval History* 25 (1999), 97–114; C. Vincent, *Fiat Lux: lumière et luminaires dans la vie religieuse du XIIe au XVIe siècle* (Paris: Cerf, 2004); P. Fouracre, *Eternal Light and Earthly Concerns: Belief and the Shaping of Medieval Society* (Manchester: Manchester University Press, 2021).
[65] *Cart. Notre-Dame de Nîmes*, pp. 42–44 (no. 23); *Cart. Saint-Victor*, I, p. 609 (no. 614).
[66] *Cart. Mas-d'Azil*, pp. 178–79 (no. 29).
[67] *Cart. Moissac*, p. 192 (no. 134), charter from 1087. See J. F. Niermeyer, *Mediae Latinitatis Lexicon Minus*, revised edn (Leiden: Brill, 2002), 'Spiculatura = gleanings'; C. du Fresne du Cange et al., *Glossarium mediae et infimae latinitatis* (Niort: L. Favre, 1883–87), 'Spiculator → Spigulator...Gall. Glaneur'.
[68] See Fouracre, *Eternal Light*, chapters 1 to 3.

throughout Lent, for the sake of his soul and those of his forebears; Guillaume Bordel of Conas, in a will from 1141, left the church of Sainte-Eulalie a piece of land 'for oil for the light'; in 1166, Guillaume Mantilini left a 'measure of oil to the work of the lights' to one church, and 6d similarly to another.[69]

Lights were also however another thing which could appear as a counter-gift, as in the donation charter from 1157 by Hugues, the priest of Cénomes, and his parishioners, who gifted four fields to Silvanès, and among various things received in return gained 18d of Melgueil to light their church on the feast of St André.[70] They also appear as counter-gifts from a religious establishment *to* a layperson. In 1136, Jordan de Lissac donated the church of Saint-Croix to the abbey of Saint-Sernin, with an interesting rider: that if it happened that Jordan should come to the feast of St Sernin in Toulouse, the abbey should give him a candle which he could offer at the altar (and feed him and three knights that day, if he requested it).[71] That one can ask the monastery to give the object which one then offers at an altar in the monastery suggests an interesting sense of gifting, perhaps that the donation to the saint rather than the institution is rather more present to the lay donor than the language of the charters usually makes clear. If my suggestion here is correct, this again indicates a shift away from the earlier habit of leaving the specifics of worship to the monastic experts. Another Jordan, this one of Verfeil, made a donation to Saint-Sernin sometime in the first half of the twelfth century, absolving them from the hospitality that they had been accustomed to give him on the annual feast of that saint, and similarly from the candles of a cubit's length that they had been giving him ('from depraved and iniquitous habit') every Sunday.[72] The element of lordly exaction here—now relinquished by Jordan—is clear; but one wonders about the purpose of the candles, whether they were being appropriated for ordinary domestic use (as the disapproving gloss perhaps suggests) or whether, as with the preceding case, they would have been used for personal acts of worship. Arnaud Pons gave a vineyard to either the altar or the church of Saint-Jean and to Bernard de *Montarigo* (someone closely connected with the monastery of Lézat, but whose role is not clear) in 1179; in return, Bernard 'or his successor' was to give him and all his future offspring two candles, one at Christmas, the other on the birth of St Jean—again possibly for domestic use, but given the dates specified, more likely for donation to a shrine.[73]

---

[69] *Cart. Béziers*, pp. 157–60 (no. 114); *Cart. S. Étienne d'Agde*, p. 339 (no. 298); *Cart. Templiers de Douzens*, pp. 281–83 (no. 10)—in both cases, this income was to come from dues owed to Guillaume Mantilini from others, namely Guillelma Fissona and Amiel Codleira. A charter (mentioned above n. 23) from c. 1135 regarding the division of oblations made to the church of Saint-Clar includes the provision that if candles were given, half would go to the monastery and half to lighting the church; *Cart. Moissac*, p. 354 (no. 257).

[70] *Cart. Silvanès*, pp. 272–73 (no. 344).   [71] *Cart. Saint-Sernin*, pp. 144–45 (no. 203).

[72] *Cart. Saint-Sernin*, pp. 59–60 (no. 81); undated, but given the named prior and praepositus, likely 1120s or 1130s.

[73] *Cart. Lézat*, I, p. 407 (no. 541).

I have used a few examples drawn from wills in the preceding paragraphs, and it is worth concentrating briefly on this genre of document for the eleventh and twelfth century, as aggregate changes in their contents provide some indication of the wider shift toward lay agency in pious directions that I have been exploring here. There is not a huge amount of material for southern France in this period: the cartularies and archives I have explored offer a corpus of just 103 wills between the late tenth century and 1199, of which only thirteen were made by women, and three or four men who seem fairly poor (these latter found only in the very late twelfth century). The vast majority come from socially elite figures—though 'elite' perhaps covers quite a range, with some from the ranks of the relatively modest local nobility as well as very major lords. There are also seven clergy (a priest, two deacons, a canon, and one or possibly two chaplains). Most of the wills survive as copies in ecclesiastical cartularies, with a few others from the secular cartulary of the lords of Montpellier, and a very few original documents in various *archives départementales*.[74]

Deciding what constitutes 'a will' in this period and from these documents is not always straightforward, but a charter in which there is mention of a sickbed, one's heirs, deposition of one's body and/or soul, or naming executors can provide a reasonable indication of testamentary intent, alongside those documents that are explicitly described as wills. A few other caveats should be noted. Some cannot be dated with certainty, or only within a range of years; in these cases, I have allocated them to the earliest possible date, since my purpose is to see how early on some features *could* appear. Particularly where 'wills' appear as charters, there is no guarantee that they constitute the entire testamentary output of an individual; nor, of course, that they were actually carried out. (I have not included charters which deal solely with a *specific* provision in an earlier will, on the grounds that those cases clearly do not give us a sense of the overall testament.) Scribal practice and local custom may affect the content of a will: indeed the opening testamentary statement of a will from 1170 notes that 'I leave my part of the *manumissio* [likely meaning the portion paid to executors for execution of their duties] to the church of Ste-Marie-de-Rivesaltes, just as is the custom in this town'.[75] South of the Pyrenees, a charter of rights from 1113 granted by the count of Urgell to the town of Agramunt included the provision that the goods of those who died intestate could be given by the good men of the town to the poor, and to the works needed on churches, bridges, and hospitals; it is possible that similar practices pertained in southern France similarly.[76] Both examples remind us that

---

[74] I have included in this corpus several pre-1200 wills calendared in appendix 8 to Mundy, *Society and Government*, where I had not already located the material elsewhere; these are mostly held in monastic materials in the AD T-et-G.
[75] AD P-O H1, will of Blancha Fina de Rivesaltes.
[76] Baluze, *Marca hispania*, pp. 1239–41 (no. 350).

we are not necessarily seeing 'individual' choices made in these documents, but something more collective—yet *choices* nonetheless.

So: this group of 103 wills is arrayed chronologically as follows: 4 come from the 990s (this being as far back as I spread my net), 21 from the eleventh century, and 78 (76%) from the twelfth century. Over half of the wills (58%) date from the period after 1150. An as yet unpublished PhD thesis by Nathaniel Lane Taylor demonstrates that a very much larger number of wills exist in Catalonia for this period, and it is useful to refer to his findings to contextualize those from this much smaller group.[77] Nonetheless, there is a fairly clear pattern to emerge from the southern French material I've amassed. In most areas where we might identify lay choice or agency—such as specifying place of burial, making gifts to the poor, providing monetary gifts for pious causes, provision for lights—the vast majority of examples come from later rather than earlier. Thus twenty-nine wills specify place of burial to some greater or lesser degree; all but one of those are from the twelfth century, and most—86% of this subset—are post-1150. (As said, post-1150 wills constitute 58% of the overall corpus; I am using percentages here only because they make comparisons easier, that is, to differentiate the chronological distribution of the overall sample from the chronological pattern of specific features.) Taylor's Catalonian evidence demonstrates a similar pattern: place of burial was rarely stated in earlier testaments, but became almost obligatory by the late twelfth century.[78] Twenty-one wills make some explicit provision for the poor; for example, Pons de Fenouillet in 1187 left, among other things, 'one sixteenth [of grain] for bread for the poor, one sixteenth for lepers'.[79] Of those twenty-one wills, one is from 991 and another from 1020; the rest are twelfth century, and in fact seventeen (81% of those making such provision) were post-1150. In the case of provision for lights, which we have seen above also in other kinds of donation charters and which would become very common in the thirteenth and fourteenth centuries (as we will see in a later chapter), only nine wills included such a request; one came from 1091, but the rest were spread across the twelfth century.

Another feature that would be common to later wills was the inclusion of monetary gifts, which (as Taylor notes for his wider sample) allowed a greater subdivision of legacy to a wider group of recipients. Some of these gifts could be vast—in

---

[77] N. L. Taylor, 'The Will and Society in Medieval Catalonia and Languedoc, 800–1200', unpublished PhD, Harvard 1995. He also includes wills from Languedoc within his study, and appears (p. 25) to have amassed perhaps twice as many wills from that region, albeit for a lengthier period, drawing upon some sources I have not accessed, such as the unpublished cartulary of the Trencavel family. Set alongside the very much larger body of material from northern Spain, he works with a corpus of 2,860 wills, the vast majority from Catalonia. Note also M. Roche, 'La société languedocienne d'après les testaments (813–1270)', unpublished PhD thesis, Toulouse 1986, 2 vols; this however addresses a smaller corpus of material for the eleventh and early twelfth centuries than I have located.

[78] Cf. Taylor, 'The Will and Society', p. 214, and p. 330, figs 5.4 and 5.5.

[79] *Cart. S. Étienne d'Agde*, pp. 169–70 (no. 83).

1180 Roger, the viscount of Béziers, aimed to leave 15,000 *sous* to the abbot and monks of Caunes—but some were smaller amounts, ranging from 6d to 50 *sous*.[80] Taylor's predominantly Catalonian evidence demonstrates bequests of money becoming common in the eleventh century;[81] from my corpus however there are only four examples prior to 1100, most (a further twenty-nine wills) appearing in the twelfth century. Once again the majority (82% of those making this provision) came from after 1150; this is similarly the case if one ignores the wills displaying vast wealth, and focuses only on those leaving more modest sums.[82]

Last of all, and following on in part from the practice of leaving smaller monetary gifts, we can look at how many *different* pious institutions (whether churches, hospitals, or monasteries) a testator might leave things to. Here the picture is complicated. Slightly under half of the wills (46) left things to just one, sole recipient—typically the monastery in whose cartulary the gift is recorded. These examples are spread fairly evenly across the time period and chronological distribution of the sample, with exactly half (23 wills) appearing earlier than 1150. This is also more or less the pattern for testators who left things to two or three institutions (typically a monastery, a local church, and a hospital; or a church, and the Hospitallers and Templars). Two wills left things to four institutions, both dating from the first half of the eleventh century. But above that number a clearer picture emerges. There are nineteen wills that leave things to five or more institutions— that is, seeking to distribute their pious donations notably widely. Two of these are very early: the will from 990 of Guillaume, viscount of Béziers, a major lord and landholder, who left bequests to twelve different institutions; and the will of a man called Arimanus from 991, who named five institutions (and also, unusually for this period, left half of his moveable goods to the poor).[83] One other comes from 1041, the will of the nobleman Gombáu de Besora, made in preparation for heading to Spain to fight 'the Saracens'; he distributed sums of silver to eighteen different institutions, including St Peter's in Rome—a blaze of performative piety. All the rest—fifteen wills (79%)—date from after 1150, and it is here that more modest examples are found, such as Ugo de Sallela, whose will from 1187 left 10 *sous* for burial to his parish church of Sainte-Marie, another 3 *sous* for the lights, to the Hospitallers a measure of wheat, a tunic to the church of Saint-Martin, and his pelisse to the leper house.[84]

The blur of numbers in the preceding paragraphs can be summed up fairly simply: the pious choices that could be made in wills become notably more varied

---

[80] Martene and Durand, *Thesaurus novus anecdotorum*, I, cols 597–99.
[81] Taylor, 'The Will and Society', pp. 224–25.
[82] Twenty-one wills leave sums of 100 *sous* or less, mostly amounts ranging from 6d to 20 *sous* (though in some cases the testator clearly holds considerable wealth in land). Of these, seventeen date from 1150 or later.
[83] *Cart. Béziers*, pp. 52–55 (no. 49), 55–56 (no. 50).
[84] AD Aude 10 J 287 (a seventeenth-century transcription).

and elaborated in the later twelfth century. This in part reflects exactly the same factors as those which affected elite donation and patronage, namely the appearance of new potential recipients—the new knightly orders, but also, particularly in the later twelfth century, the founding of charitable hospitals in various towns and cities; 'hospitals' here perhaps primarily meaning places that would provide lodging to those in need. (The earliest will I have found that mentions donation to a hospital dates from 1141; one notes also the will of Raimond de Foreville from 1157 in which he leaves a house to a certain Raimond Guidbaldi 'so as always to provide lodging for the poor there' (*ut hospitentur ibi semper pauperes*)).[85] But it also suggests that more lay people were materially in a position to make pious legacies—perhaps also that more coinage was available for this—and that this opened up further possibilities of lay activity, choice, and agency.

This should not be overemphasized: as noted, the majority of wills for this period come from demonstrably elite people, and the types of choices available tend toward certain norms. It is, as I said above, as much about collective choices as individual ones. But some particularly individual bequests do stand out. Thus, for example, the will of Pierre Tequit of Montagnac in 1173 gives, among other things, money to the altar of his local church and to individual priests, leaves his linen from the bed 'in which I lie' to the hospital of Montagnac, and asks that twelve paupers be dressed in tunics and shirts made out of cloth from Montpellier (among other things, an interestingly early attestation of that town's reputation as a production centre for high-quality textiles).[86] Guillaume Rainard, an apparently quite rich layman, made a will in 1155 in which he specified a number of pious provisions: burial in the cathedral church of Saint-Étienne-d'Agde, with 500 *sous melgoriensis* for the church buildings, another 100 *sous* for expenses around his burial, and 9 gold pieces for oblations, one to go to each priest that celebrated his obit mass, and two to the bishop; 'and I give my cape of precious cloth (*capam... de cisclatone*) to the church of St Étienne, and my silver goblet and two rings, one gold and the other silver, so that there should be a thurible for daily use'.[87] It is not certain whether the rings were to pay for the thurible, or to be fashioned directly into it, but the sense of personal connection is clear—*my* cape, *my* goblet, *my* rings being directed toward a key liturgical object. This is similarly the case on a few occasions when knights left martial possessions to the Templars or the Hospitallers: in 1159 Bernard de *Tonga* left his sword and his shield to the Templars, among many other pious bequests, and in the same year Guiraud de Touroulle likewise left them his palfrey; in 1166, Pautonnier de Preissan left the Hospitallers his saddle, his shield, and his lance.[88] In each of these and other similar cases, the testator turns personal objects into alms. The individual, possessive element cannot

---

[85] *Cart. S. Étienne d'Agde*, p. 339 (no. 298), will of Guillaume Bordel de Conas; pp. 244–45 (no. 171).
[86] *Cart. S. Étienne d'Agde*, pp. 174–75 (no. 87).
[87] *Cart. S. Étienne d'Agde*, pp. 114–15 (no. 17).
[88] *Cart. S. Étienne d'Agde*, p. 132 (no. 36); pp. 221–22 (no. 142); pp. 177–78 (no. 89).

be assumed to be erased by the act of piety. With 'my saddle, my shield, my lance' and other such objects, some element of personal commemoration can be assumed—at least as a hope projected forward by the dying legatee.

We also find some wills in which there is no pious provision at all. In nearly a fifth of the corpus (nineteen wills, mostly from the twelfth century) no pious institution is named, although a couple of wills do make some vague provision to give 'for charity'. Most of these wills deal only with the division of property within the surviving family. This is the case with the will of Gerauda de Labrigia in 1186, which, despite having a chaplain as one of the witnesses, simply hands over her land to her son. A rather more complex testament, made in 1196 by Pons de Monte Arago in the hands of the bishop of Comminges, similarly lacks any mention of his or any other soul, and contains no pious bequests.[89] In both cases one might decide that this means that there would be an additional document in a different form which made provision for alms and memorial masses. But this seems less likely with an intriguing will which survives as a single sheet of parchment from 1143. This was recorded at the command of Gauzbert de Château Roussillon 'who died on the journey to St Jacques [de Compostelle]', and who simply left all his *honores* to his children and his wife. The will records the extent and nature of these holdings in some detail, but includes no pious provisions or expressions whatsoever, beyond asserting that he willed these things 'in the power of omnipotent God and his friends' (the latter phrase probably indicating the witnesses and the scribe of the will, who were with him when he died).[90] Given the nature of his journey, to one of the most important shrines in all Christendom, Gauzbert clearly was engaged in worship; but in his case, his choice was to focus on familial ownership of land and income when dictating his testament. Was this perhaps because he was making the will *in extremis*, too aware that he was dying far from home and his usual social networks? In such a situation, in that time and place, it would appear that setting out the complexities of what would happen to familial property was more important than specifying acts of piety and remembrance.

There is one final 'testament' to note, one which is more of a memorial statement of practice than a will. It comes from sometime between 1135 and 1140, from Morlaàs (far to the west of the region), and records information about the church of Saint-André which Bernard de Beuste, priest of Morlaàs, built with the help of his neighbours. He was its first chaplain and, nearing death, he appears to have wanted to set out some of the important 'customs' he had been able to establish during his incumbency regarding the church's financial relationship with the nearby monastery of Sainte-Foi in Morlaàs. Among other things he noted that whatever people bring on the day after Easter as oblations—'namely bread, coins,

---

[89] *Cart. Lézat*, II, pp. 336–37 (no. 1475); pp. 162–63 (no. 1261). See also *Cart. Lézat*, II, pp. 107–08 (no. 1149); *Liber instrumentorum memorialium*, pp. 193–94 (no. 98), p. 572 (no. 395).

[90] AD P-O, 1 J 816.

candles'—was to be received by the chaplain, but then handed over to the monks.[91] As with the charter discussed further above, in which Matfred the priest and his parishioners became briefly visible to us, we have here a tiny flash of illumination over something which would otherwise remain invisible, and which might yet matter very much more. Another is given to us by a detail in the council of Narbonne in 1054. In canon 14 the council spells out various ecclesiastical rights that are not to be held by the laity: 'no layperson should retain for his own purposes tithes, nor oblations, nor burial payments, nor eggs or those things that they give during the aspersion of salt and water on Maundy Thursday, nor the payments for trentals which is rightfully given to the clergy for prayers for the faithful dead.'[92] These Easter eggs, as we might call them, 'or those other things' provides another precious glimpse of the modest, local donation to altars discussed in the conclusion to Chapter 1. The oblations noted here, and those described by Bernard de Beuste, probably formed a more important aspect of lay piety than anything the preceding paragraphs have discussed. His emphasis that these humble oblations, despite being destined for the monastic owners, should be received by the local chaplain at the local altar suggests a care for the feelings of his parishioners and their investment in the church that they helped to make. As I have suggested elsewhere, we might interpret this as a moment in which the priest attempts to maximize the chances that parochial oblations can engender a meaningful and affective experience of 'belief'.[93]

Donations, oblations, and gifts get written down in wills and charters because of the nature of the moment of giving. It is an important moment for pious giving; though as the examples of wills lacking pious clauses reminds us, perhaps not universally so. But giving happens on many other occasions as well, particularly around major feasts. If we were in very late medieval England, or any other area where things like church wardens' accounts survive, this would be clear and obvious. Here in the twelfth century, in the south of France, we have a single charter, alongside a couple of other references mentioned above. We may well imagine that we are looking here at the tip of an iceberg, whilst remembering that such oblations are evidence of lay choice and agency, not simply obedience.

The Extraordinary and the Everyday

As I noted above, Pons de Léras might be seen, in the journeying stage of his *vita*, as part of a wider movement apparent in the early twelfth century in various parts

---

[91] *Cart. Sainte Foi de Morlaàs*, p. 344 (no. 35).
[92] Mansi 19, col. 830: 'Monemus iterum, ut nullus laicorum in opus suum retineat primitias, neque oblationes, neque cimiteriorum pretia, neque ova, aut ea que ad eos dantur per aspersionem salis et aque in coena domini, neque trigintarios qui recte debentur a clericis recipi pro fidelium defunctorum orationi.'
[93] Arnold, 'Believing in Belief'.

of France, namely the appearance of charismatic wandering preachers, who brought a message of ascetic penance to wider audiences across their regions. Norbert de Xanten, Bernard de Thiron, Vitalis de Savigny, and Robert d'Arbrissel were active in various parts of northern France in this same period, Géraud de Salles perhaps coming further south. Each man underwent some form of conversion experience and subsequently followed, for a period, a more penitential and peregrinatory form of life, then going on to found monastic communities.[94]

In the south of France, the two figures associated with this pattern were both denounced as 'heretics'—a label which was also intermittently applied to some of those just mentioned. These were Henri de Lausanne (or Le Mans; his place of origin is not actually known) and Pierre de Bruys. Rather inevitably for this period, all we know about them comes from hostile sources; in the case of Pierre, solely from a treatise—*Contra Petrobrusianos*—written against his ideas by Peter the Venerable, abbot of Cluny, and with Henri a mixture of narrative sources, sermons, and letters written by his enemies. Neither began their careers in the south, but both spent some time there. Peter the Venerable addressed his treatise to the bishops of Die and Gap, and the archbishops of Arles and Embrun, in whose diocese he believed Pierre de Bruys was causing mischief. The preacher was then arrested by the archbishop of Arles, though it is unclear what then became of him. Henri de Lausanne came further west, preaching in the Toulousain, followed on by an irate Bernard of Clairvaux, who wrote letters and sermons against him, and warned Alphonse-Jourdain, count of Toulouse, not to be 'deceived' by Henri, who had (Bernard admitted) the 'appearance of piety'.[95] In 1145 Bernard himself travelled to the south to try to eradicate Henri's influence, preaching in Sarlat (60 km north of Cahors), Verfeil (east of Toulouse), and Albi.[96]

Recent historiography on Henri and Pierre has differed in its interpretations. It is generally agreed, with good reason, that 'the reform movement' is an important context for their careers; and it is notable in Henri's case in particular that his initial appearance at Le Mans as a preacher was welcomed by the local bishop, until he subsequently realized what a firebrand he had admitted to his city and chased him out. However, the preachers' relationship to Gregorian reform has been seen in very different ways: as revanchist radicals, calling for a return to the emphasis upon poverty that the earliest stages of reform had propounded; or as refuseniks, rejecting the newly priest-and-sacrament-centred world that a reformed Church sought to establish, understood by their audiences at least as a

---

[94] See Grundmann, *Religious Movements*, pp. 7–20; M.-D. Chenu, 'The Evangelical Awakening' (first publ. 1957), in his *Nature, Man and Society in the Twelfth Century*, trans. J. Taylor and L. K. Little (Toronto: PIMS, 1997); H. Leyser, *Hermits and the New Monasticism: A Study of Religious Communities in Western Europe, 1000–1150* (Manchester: Manchester University Press, 1984), chapters 3 and 4, and appendix II; B. Barriere, 'Les abbayes issues de l'érémitisme', *CdF* 21 (1986), 71–105.
[95] Bernard of Clairvaux, letter 241, PL 182, 434–36 (trans. W&E, pp. 122–24, doc. 14A).
[96] B. M. Kienzle, *Cistercians, Heresy and Crusade in Occitania, 1145–1229* (Woodbridge: York Medieval Press, 2001), pp. 97–101.

return to an older model of local holy men.[97] There is perhaps a danger in both cases of reifying 'the reform movement' into an overly coherent whole, against which these radicals fall into their heresy. It is not clear to what degree any specific message regarding poverty, for example, had been broadcast beyond monastic settings in the south of France; as we have seen, what is visible for a lay and predominantly noble community is a separation of ecclesiastical and secular possessions and influence. As said, we only know the contents of Henri's and Pierre's messages from hostile sources. This means not only that the reports of their message are negative, but that ideas and implications may have been projected onto the 'heretics' that they themselves never voiced. It certainly also means that in some cases their popularity and effects were hugely exaggerated, as we would find, for example, in Bernard of Clairvaux's letter when he claims that in the Toulousain 'churches are without congregations, congregations are without priests, priests are without proper reverence, and, finally, Christians are without Christ'. The first three things might be true in specific locations—we have indeed seen a few places earlier this chapter where the provision of worship was lacking or at least interrupted—but for the region as a whole, this is, as one would expect with Bernard, grandiloquent rhetorical flourish rather than accurate reportage.

Can the ideas that Henri and Pierre were propounding tell us anything about the expectations and experience of lay Christianity in this period? Peter the Venerable's treatise alleges that Pierre de Bruys had five key propositions (all 'heretical', all to be refuted in detail by the abbot): against child baptism, on the grounds that those below the age of reason were not capable of the cognitive reflection required for belief; against church buildings, on the grounds that 'the Church' was the community of the faithful and nothing more; against reverence for the cross, on the grounds that it was the instrument on which Christ suffered and was thus to be despised; against the Eucharist, on the grounds that the body of Christ had been eaten only at the Last Supper; and against any forms of funeral worship—oblations, prayers, masses—on the grounds that only the works carried out in this life could benefit a person.[98] Our fullest account of Henri's errors comes from a treatise written by 'Guillaume the Monk' that survives in a manuscript now held in Nice, which claims to record a debate between the author and the heretic. Monique Zerner has suggested that this may in fact be Guillaume Monachi, archbishop of Arles (d. 1141), writing contemporaneously. The treatise lists six areas of dispute: that bishops and priests should not have money or lands;

---

[97] See P. Jiménez-Sanchez, *Les catharismes: modèles dissidents du christianisme médiéval (XIIe-XIIIe siècles)* (Rennes: Presses universitaires de Rennes, 2008), p. 106; R. I. Moore, *The War on Heresy: Faith and Power in Medieval Europe* (London: Profile, 2012), pp. 125–26.
[98] Peter the Venerable, *Contra Petrobrusianos hereticos*, ed. J. Fearns, CCCM 10 (Turnhout: Brepols, 1968). Cf. D. Iogna-Prat, *Order and Exclusion: Cluny and Christendom face Heresy, Judaism and Islam (1000–1150)*, trans. G. R. Edwards (Ithaca, NY: Cornell University Press, 2002), p. 109 and ff.

that there is no Gospel command to go to a priest for penance; that priests do not have the power to bind and loose; that the ties of marriage are indissoluble except where someone has committed adultery; that no good can be done for the dead (by prayers, for example); and that the unbaptized children of Christians, Jews, and Saracens are saved, if they die prior to the age of reason.[99]

Assuming that these propositions engaged at least some of the laity—as the hostile sources allege, and as the fact of the preachers' travels would suggest—can they tell us anything about lay spiritual concerns more generally? What happens to children who die young is an interesting element, something which we can see caused great concern in a later period.[100] As mentioned in a previous chapter, there is very little *specific* reference to baptism in the early charters for southern French churches, though it was one of the things (in the conclusion to Chapter 1) that we saw specified as forbidden by a blanket excommunication of the lands of the viscount of Narbonne around 1059. The point about the age of reason might be taken to imply an interest in a more reflective piety, but should also be noted as a more quasi-legal qualification: having reason, 'discernment', would allow a free person to enter into contractual relationships with others, including the making of oaths, and perhaps the kind of spiritual relationships enacted in the various charters we have seen. It is not hard, in any case, to see an enticing comfort in knowing that children would be saved. The same is probably true with regard to marriage and adultery; it is pretty certain that a lay audience, particularly a noble lay audience, would be pleased to have their practices here confirmed.

It is less easy to see how Pierre de Bruys's apparent rejection of church buildings would be received by a lay audience—perhaps implicitly as a way of avoiding tithes (something that is not explicitly rejected in these particular accounts of the heretics' preaching, though it is suggested elsewhere)? Or, among the local elites, as a comfort for the loss of those 'possessions' that, as we have seen, were being 'reclaimed' by the monasteries as part of reform? This latter seems likely to be the case with Henry's proposition that bishops and priests did not need money or lands (*pecunias vel honores*)—the word *honores* suggesting in particular not a rejection of oblations or indeed tithing, but the wider lands and income-generating holdings that were the underlying financial base of lordship, and which provided an additional income for churches.

---

[99] M. Zerner, ed. and trans., *Guillaume Monachi: Contra Henri schismatique et heretique*, Sources chrétiennes 541 (Paris: Cerf, 2011), regarding authorship pp. 16–22;<b/> M. Zerner, 'Au temps de l'appel aux armes contres les hérétiques: du "Contra Henricum" aux "Contra hereticos"', in M. Zerner, ed., *Inventer l'hérésie? Discours polémiques et pouvoirs avant l'Inquisition* (Nice: Centre d'études médiévales de Nice, 1998), pp. 119–56, at pp. 125–30. An amalgam of the earlier and later versions is translated: W&E, pp. 115–17, doc. 12. However, as Zerner demonstrates, this version (from an edition by Raoul Manselli) elides important differences between the early text and a later version; she persuasively argues that the later text, in the Paris manuscript, comes from late in the 12th century and has a clearly different agenda from the earlier version.

[100] See Chapter 6.

It is again hard to know what to make of the rejection of worship of the cross, of prayers for the dead, and of the Eucharist. It seems likely that a form of *scriptura sola* was informing both heretics in their respective theological propositions (as is clearly the case in regard to the Eucharist), but it is doubtful as to how powerfully that could have been communicated to a wider audience, most of whom would probably only have met elements of the Bible aurally via lectionaries and other liturgical books, if at all. The cross was ubiquitous in Christian culture, for obvious reasons; perhaps a point about the mode of worship, to the spiritual truth beyond the material object, was here misinterpreted by the orthodox opponent? It is unlikely that a detailed account of eucharistic theology would be normally present in a parochial setting in this period, and what we can see of lay opinions later on suggests that what might seem deeply shocking to a learned clergyman might be met with more of a shrug by an average Christian. More interesting is the rejection, by both preachers, of prayers and other works for the dead. We are reminded that there is no single, clear theology on Purgatory in circulation at this point.[101] As I have argued above, in the eleventh century the spiritual work which monks did for the dead was, according to the detail of the charters at least, largely left up to them, but it is however precisely in the early twelfth century that donors were starting to be more specific about masses, prayers, obits, and the like. What Henri and Pierre were rejecting was something which, it would appear, had only recently come into the purview of the laity—and almost entirely the noble laity, we should remember.

This last point leads me to demur from R. I. Moore's interpretation that Henri and Pierre gained popularity because they rejected 'the ever wider distinction between the clergy and the laity' in favour of a pre-existent 'community-based worship'.[102] They were certainly attempting to intervene in a changing situation, but one in which a lay agenda regarding new spiritual possibilities was also present. One wonders in this regard similarly about Henri's proposition that there was no Gospel injunction to go to a priest for penance. Moore reads this as a rejection of private confession, as against 'the old practice of public confession'. In fact we cannot be certain that what Henri said necessarily implied the practice of regular, individual, private confession in the sense we would associate with later centuries. Something of that kind is clearly a possibility, though one which could well already have existed: we did see, in Chapters 1 and 2, and in an example above, 'penitences' as a right—presumably because carrying a financial element— explicitly held by a few local churches. But as previously discussed in regard to that topic, what kind of 'confession' prompted the bestowal of 'penance' is not entirely clear. The author Guillaume spends much of his rebuttal of this point

---

[101] J. Le Goff, *La naissance du purgatoire* (Paris: Gallimard, 1981); A. E. Bernstein, 'Esoteric Theology: William of Auvergne on the Fires of Hell and Purgatory', *Speculum* 57 (1982), 509–31.

[102] Moore, *War on Heresy*, pp. 125–26.

discussing the public identification of leprosy, and figures penances accordingly as a kind of 'cleansing', which might be suggestive of a more public process.[103]

In any event, what is certain is that in this period going to the priest for penance, whatever form it took, *had to* involve choice and agency on the part of the layperson who sought it out. Such a choice was admittedly made within a wider cultural system that might be making more or less effort to encourage and enjoin such an action—but crucially we have not seen much, if any, evidence of that kind of cultural encouragement by the twelfth century in this region of Europe. Even the spectacular penance undertaken by Pons de Léras, whilst overseen in its public orchestration by the bishop, appears to have been undertaken freely and without prompt, absent any specific clerical instruction or injunction; as his *vita* makes clear, Pons spontaneously presented himself to the bishop, having already written his letter of self-accusation. His penance was a choice, not an imposed punishment, and he seems largely to have orchestrated its details himself. The wider point is this: we are 100 years before the Fourth Lateran Council and its injunction requiring all Christians to make at least annual confession. We cannot see any religious authority at this point, in this region, instructing people that they had to make regular confession. There was certainly no ecclesial structure in place that could attempt to check on compliance or negligence. It seems likely therefore that Henri's words were prompted by occasions when members of the laity sought to seek out penance. Henri's 'heresy' did not decry an ecclesiastical injunction, and was thus less an attack upon 'the Church' as a reforming edifice than an encouragement toward a different form of lay penitential piety.

In trying to understand the laity's experience of Christianity in the twelfth century there is a temptation to seize upon the wandering preachers, heretical or otherwise, as key informants. They provide stories, beliefs, *faith*. But they were extraordinary figures performing within the landscape, not the landscape itself. What they preached certainly related to existing strands of worship, and they took those strands to create some new propositions and potentials, that shone out for a brief, bright period. But this is not to say that they provided the frame and experience for most worship or general understanding of the Christian message; any more than did their opponent Bernard of Clairvaux, whose charismatic preaching in the south may have struck his audience as rather similar to those he opposed, in its external elements of performance at least. For those who saw these figures—necessarily a small portion of the population—above and beyond the specific content of their sermons was the simple and powerful fact of someone fulfilling the culmination of Mark and Matthew's Gospels, preaching to the people in a broadly apostolic style. The dramatically public piety that they presented did have longer-term effects. But at this point at least it primarily operated, as with

---

[103] Zerner, ed., *Guillaume Monachi: Contra Henri*, pp. 170–81.

the occasions of large-scale worship of relics discussed in Chapter 2, to offset the quotidian experiences of worship. In a wider sense their example may be seen as one part of a wider landscape of reformed spiritual possibilities, as potential recipients of donation and engagement, whose simultaneous novelty and antiquity polished their innate individual charisma.

It is then important to note that rather less dramatic examples may also have existed, not so visible to us now because they were not so contentious at the time, and thus did not generate written commentary. Let us return to an example I cited earlier in this chapter: the case of the church at Valcrose from 1138, where the bishop of Maguelonne had to resolve a dispute between this local church and the monastery of Aniane. The church had been founded by one Pierre Raimond, whose status—lay or clerical—is not stated. It sits in a secluded valley, about an hour's walk west of La Boissière; therefore not a village church, but one which was nonetheless accessible from the nearby settlement. The bishop resolved that the church could continue to operate, rather than be handed over to Aniane, but that it would be under his episcopal jurisdiction, with a 'community' (*collegium*) of no more than seven men—this making a local church appear rather more like a small, hitherto independent, monastic foundation; a hermitage we might perhaps call it, which is certainly how the small surviving church building is remembered by some today.[104] The community, the bishop ruled, could keep up to 100 animals, either sheep or goats, and an ass or a mule, but could not have dogs or cats ('mousers', *murilegi*, to be precise). They could not receive any 'converts', whether lay or secular, without the bishop's express permission. As previous noted, they could not undertake those elements of the *cura animarum* they had previously practised.[105]

We do not know what happened subsequently to the community at Valcrose; we only know about it in this form at all because of the dispute with Aniane. But it is an indication that in the south of France, as elsewhere, small and apparently spontaneous foundations could start up, and could then play some role in the provision of Christian worship in the locality.[106] There are a few other examples of what appear to be similar small, local foundations, though they appear in the documentary record only rarely. One important example is a will that exists as an original single document; a glimpse of something resting beyond the view of the larger cartularies. It was made in 1173 by Pons Aribert, who appears to have been a relatively lowly landowner. In it he asks to be buried, with two sheets and what

---

[104] See image and text at <http://lesmulotsenbalade.blogspot.co.uk/2009/10/lermitage-de-valcrose-la-boissiere.html> (viewed 7 July 2017). See also <https://garrigue-gourmande.fr/index.php?option=com_content&view=article&id=5341&Itemid=506%22> which asserts that it was used as a hermitage by the abbey of Gellone in the 15th century (viewed 5 Oct 2017).
[105] *Cart. d'Aniane*, pp. 260–62 (no. 118).
[106] Leyser, *Hermits*; T. Licence, *Hermits and Recluses in English Society, 950–1200* (Oxford: Oxford University Press, 2011).

is possibly a pillow from his bed (*cum meo lecto unius falcate et unius lenteoli uniusque chapitalis*) in the cemetery of Saint-Martin-de-la-Rive, giving 'the Blessed Martin and the monks of the same place' some income from the parts that he held of three vineyards (or other land). He also passed on to his wife and children 'as much as I have or am given to have in the common fields' and his part of some other shared lands, as well as his cows and one ass; and he asked for an anniversary mass from the chaplain of Saint-Cyr, in nearby Canohès, to whom he also left a horse collar.[107] The church of Saint-Martin-de-la-Rive is now on private land and not visible to the public, but from descriptions available is small, built in the classic southern French style with a semicircular apse, and sits about a half mile outside the village of Saint-Féliu-d'Avall, west of Perpignan.[108] If there were monks there, they could not have been many in number, and we have no evidence of them being incorporated into any larger order. Nonetheless, someone as relatively ordinary as Pons—not a poor man, but certainly not noble and apparently not particularly wealthy—could form a sufficient link with them to be able to ask for burial.

As said, the documentary record does not furnish us with many more examples. But it is worth remembering that there are the physical remains of a number of other modest twelfth-century churches situated, like Saint-Martin-de-la-Rive and Valcrose, away from the main towns and villages, in valleys or on hills that made them more obviously places of retreat—though still visible to and in contact with local settlements.[109] Another such place was the church of Sainte-Marie-Madeleine—now known as the hermitage of Saint-Guilhem-de-Combret—which perches up in the Canigou hills, north of Saint-Féliu-d'Avall. Despite its remote location, there are two liturgical manuscripts still surviving associated with it, one a twelfth-century *mixtum* (a short compilation extracted from the breviary and missal) and the other a twelfth-century copy of the ninth-century sacramentary of Arles.[110] There is no mention of an eremitical monastic community based at this church, though a very late twelfth-century charter, copied into the sacramentary, records that Robert, abbot of nearby Arles-sur-Tech, 'donated' (that is, relinquished) to Guillaume, 'priest of that place', the annual *cens* of a chicken that was owed to the monastery for a certain vineyard.[111] But the combination of liturgical books and its remote location—a good three hours' walk from either of the two nearby villages of Le Tech and Prats-de-Mollo—suggests

---

[107] AD P-O, G 1007. The church of Saint-Cyr-et-Sainte-Julitte is in nearby Canohès. The will is written by a priest, also called Pons; perhaps from this church.
[108] See description at <http://pyreneescatalanes.free.fr/Villages/StFeliuDAvall.php> (accessed 4 Sept 2017). Mallet, *Églises romanes*, is unable to provide any additional detail.
[109] See comments in Chapter 1, pp. 32–33.   [110] BnF MS n.a.l. 557; Perpignan, BM MS 4.
[111] Perpignan, BM MS 4, fol. 8v: '...quod ego dom[i]nus Rotbertus abas d[e] arulis...dimitto a domino deo et s[an]cte marie magdalene d[e] cumbret[i] et s[an]cti guillelmi confessor xpi et tibi Guillelmi sacerdos de predicto loco I callina quatinus a dies de senso de ipsa vinea de les quareres...'

that it may formerly have been a small community. And in any case, Guillaume or any other priest regularly delivering services there would surely have felt himself to be leading a fairly eremitical existence.

With Valcrose and Saint-Martin and the remote chapel to the Madeleine we see nothing as dramatic as Pons de Léras's peregrinations, or Henri de Lausanne's denunciations. But the existence of remote chapels, some with small eremitical communities, provides as important an element in the experience of Christianity for these local areas. As we can see via Pons Aribert's will, they illustrate local enthusiasm and active spiritual choices; less dramatic but perhaps more important locations of more intense holiness, scattered around the local landscape, even if only visible to us on rare occasion now. It is also important to note that at Valcrose we see this local enthusiasm being met by a measure of episcopal control from above. This is a dynamic that we shall encounter in a variety of ways as we move on in time, as 'reform' came to exert further influence on the wider experience of Christian worship.

4
Towns and the Holy, c. 1100–c. 1250

In 1165, a group from Lombers, a very small town about 15 km south of Albi, came to a formal meeting convened by the bishop of Albi. The place where it was held is not actually specified in the surviving document. Historians customarily treat it as occurring in Lombers, given that the group had strong support from the people and knights of that place. But it seems as likely that it was convened in the city of Albi itself, given the presence of a large number of bishops and abbots from the region, Viscount Raimond Trencavel, Constance the wife of Count Raimond V of Toulouse, and 'many other people, indeed almost all the population of Albi and of Lombers, and people from other *castra*'. The meeting adapted a recognized legal process in the south, the formal 'arbitration' in which, under the aegis of a powerful figure (here, the bishop), both sides chose and agreed upon a number of judges to settle a dispute.[1] Bishop Gaucelin of Lodève took on the formal role of the opposing party to the group from Lombers 'who had themselves called "Good Men"' (*qui faciebant se appellari boni homines*)'. The very large audience strongly suggests that this was not however a straightforward arbitration, and indeed what followed largely comprised a theological debate, with the sustained trading of biblical authorities and interpretations. The 'Good Men' responded to some questions by Gaucelin, refused to answer some others, and also spoke at some length independently.

There are some clear elements to what the group believed: they did not accept the authority of the Old Testament, but only the New Testament's Gospels, Epistles, Acts of the Apostles, and the Apocalypse of St John. Following injunction in the Gospels and the Epistle of James, they would not swear an oath. They were highly critical of the clergy, who, they said, fell far short of the requirements set by Paul in his first letter to Timothy (1 Tim. 3: 2–7): 'they were not bishops or priests but rather rapacious wolves, hypocrites and seducers, lovers of salutations in the marketplace and the first seat at feasts, wishing to be called "Rabbi" and "master" [Matt. 23: 6–7] against the precepts of Christ, wearing shining white clothes, bearing jewelled gold rings on their fingers'.[2] They were questioned also

---

[1] P. Jiménez Sánchez, 'Les actes de Lombers (1165): une procédure d'arbitrage?', in H. Débax, ed., *Les sociétés méridionales à l'âge féodal (Espagne, Italie et sud de la France, Xe–XIIIe siècle): hommage à Pierre Bonnassie* (Toulouse: Presses universitaires du Midi, 1999), pp. 311–17.

[2] Mansi, XXII, cols 157–68, at col. 159: 'non erant episcopi neque presbyteri sed lupi rapaces, et hypocritque et seductores, amantes salutationes in foro, primas cathedras et primos accubitus in coenis; volentes vocari Rabbi et magistri contra praeceptum Christi, ferentes albas et candidas vestes,

on their beliefs regarding the efficacy of child baptism, whether the consecration of the Eucharist depended upon the character of the person performing it or receiving it, whether married couples who had sex could be saved, and various things regarding confession. Their responses appeared largely orthodox—so much as issues in these areas were fully clear at this point in orthodox theology— and they proffered to the assembled people a short statement of faith which also appeared orthodox. But they again refused to take an oath in support of their own statement, or to guarantee that they were not holding back any additional and less orthodox ideas, repeating their argument that oaths were against Christ's edicts, and saying moreover that the bishop of Albi had promised them that they would not be required to take an oath (something he then denied).[3] Gaucelin, bishop of Lodève, then 'proved and adjudged them to be heretics' on each of the areas covered, adducing his lengthy arguments on the basis of only the parts of the Bible that they themselves accepted (a reminder of how much of the process was a debate rather than simply a trial). The lengthy stream of biblical quotations he cited suggest that he saw himself rebutting heretical beliefs which went rather beyond those they had formally stated, for example going into some detail to argue that baptism did lead to children's salvation even if they were not old enough to have faith themselves, and that married sex and procreation were entirely licit and did not impede salvation—these both being areas where the 'Good Men' had not wished to answer questions in any detail. The whole meeting ended with the bishop of Albi agreeing with Gaucelin's judgment, warning the knights of Lombers that they should no longer support the group, and the various other witnesses similarly confirming this; but with no specific outcome for the 'Good Men' themselves.

As with various other twelfth-century encounters between religious authority and heterodox enthusiasm, the debate or arbitration has been much discussed within the disputed history of 'heresy' in southern France. On the one hand, the orthodox statement of faith and the anticlerical invective can suggest a 'reformist' context, at its most extreme not much more than a continuation of the positions held some decades earlier by Henri de Lausanne and Pierre de Bruys.[4] On the other, the insistence on being called 'Good Men' (a term which permeates later sources, appearing, as we shall see below, to be a self-designation also for some

gestantes in digitis aureos annulos gemmatos...'. I have departed slightly here from the translation in W&E, doc. 28.
 [3] On this and the surrounding issues, see H. Débax, 'Serments prêtés, serments contésté: pour une mise en perspective du refus du serment chez les hérétiques (Languedoc, XIIe siècle)', published online: <https://halshs.archives-ouvertes.fr/halshs-01981204/document> (accessed 3 Nov 2020, cited by permission of the author).
 [4] Thus Moore, *War on Heresy*, pp. 188–91, 199; though this does not address the rejection of the Old Testament, the potential implications of Gaucelin's more extended scriptural rebuttals, the elements of Henri's and Pierre's beliefs that were *not* repeated by the Lombers group, or their refusal to take an oath.

who were decried as heretics some decades after), the rejection of the Old Testament, the sense that they were concealing elements of their real faith, and the implications of the lengthier biblical passages cited by Gaucelin in rebuttal of potential heretical ideas,[5] could lead one to identify them with those heretics whom later historians have tended to call 'Cathars'.

I shall return to the issue of terminology, and other questions surrounding heresy, further below, but want firstly to emphasize a different element to what we have just seen, and position it within a wider frame. Beyond its similarity to a legal 'arbitration', the event in 1165, whether held at Albi or at Lombers, was essentially a public disputation in a civic setting. As a disputation, it was focused on scriptural interpretation and its implications not only for the role and behaviour of the clergy, but in regard to wider issues affecting all Christians: did baptism guarantee the salvation of children? Could married couples be saved, given that they were not celibate? Was contrition sufficient to amend sin or did one have to perform bodily penance? And how did these issues relate to the actual words of the New Testament and its wider injunctions? Thus whilst record of these events comes down to us as an occasion in which orthodox authority identifies 'heresy', the issues at stake and their playing out in front of a lay, civic audience were, in their own moment, not limited to a simple issue of binary allegiance or ecclesiastical authority. They explored the question of salvation, the relationship between the Bible and spiritual authority, and they set out for a broader lay audience fundamental issues regarding salvation. Thus, as the Lombers group prepared to set out their own creed, 'they turned to the whole people and said: "Listen good people to our faith which we will confess, and moreover we confess it now out of love for you and for your grace"'.[6]

The events of 1165 were moreover just the first in a series of similar encounters over the following five decades, a few of which were closer to being formal trials, but many of which were very clearly and explicitly public debates. In 1178, the papal legate Pierre de Pavia and the abbot of Clairvaux Henri de Marsiac, having forced a confession and abjuration of heresy from a leading citizen in Toulouse

---

[5] It may be worth noting that the extended passages are apparent only in the Mansi edition, not in RHGF 14, cols 431–34 or the translation in W&E, doc. 28. Mansi's version (and the earlier edition on which it is based, namely Ph. Labbé, ed., *Sacrosancta concilia* (Paris: Impensis Societatis Typographical, 1671), cols 1470–79) was based on a now-lost medieval manuscript originally held in the inquisition archives in Carcassonne. This was also separately copied into Doat 21, fols 2r–20r. The latter is now re-edited in P. Jiménez, 'Source juridiques pour l'étude du catharisme: les actes du "concile" de Lombers (1165)', *Clio et Crimen* 1 (2004), 365–79; see p. 365 n. 1 for discussion re other editions. A shorter account of the council appears in the chronicle of Roger of Howden, mis-dated to 1176. It is of course possible that this shorter account precedes the longer one, though it could equally be a briefer redaction. For further discussion re Howden and the manuscripts, see M. M. Bom, *Constance of France: Womanhood and Agency in Twelfth-Century Europe* (London: Palgrave Macmillan, 2022), chapter 6, n. 95; my thanks to Myra Bom for discussion and advance access to her text.

[6] Mansi, XXII, col. 165: 'Audite, o boni viri, fidem nostram quam confitemur, nunc confitemur autem propter dilectionem et gratiam vestri.'

(Pierre Maurand), managed to persuade two other 'false brethren and heresiarchs', Bernard Raimond and Raimond de Baimiac, to come to Toulouse to present their faith, under a promise of safe conduct from the count. This they did, again before a broad audience including laity. They brought with them a written document setting out their faith, and spoke in the vernacular, much to the contemptuous condescension of the legate. The beliefs they attested again appeared orthodox, but various of the local clergy and laity in the audience then claimed to have heard them preaching much more radical ideas, including explicit dualist beliefs (that is, 'that two gods existed, one good and the other evil; the good one who made invisible things and all that which could not change or be corrupted; the bad one who made the sky, land, men, and other visible things'). On this basis they were excommunicated.[7] Sometime in perhaps the following decade, another debate was held at Lombers, between Bishop Guillaume of Albi and 'an important heresiarch' Sicard le Cellerier, this time very much at the bidding of the knights and townspeople there.[8] Around 1190 the archbishop of Narbonne invited a group of Waldensians (a radical group begun in 1173 by Valdes, a citizen of Lyons) to debate with a group of lay and clerical people, overseen by a particular priest agreed upon by both sides as judge and with an audience of 'many other clerics and lay people'. We have a description of how such a debate worked, from the beginnings of an anti-heresy treatise written by Bernard de Fontcaude, a Premonstratensian abbot, who was present: the Waldensians 'were accused by the true Catholics regarding certain articles on which they thought wrongly, and on each of these they responded; thus at length it was disputed, with each party producing many authorities [*that is, biblical passages*]'.[9]

As we move into the thirteenth century, the occasions multiply. At Carcassonne in February 1203 two debates were organized by Peire II, king of Aragon, one between Waldensians and the Cistercian papal legates Raoul and Pierre de Castelnau, the other between 'the heretics' bishop Bernard de Simorre' and his companions on one side and a number of unnamed Catholics on the other. At the latter debate, the heretics, 'after much evasion and twisting of words... publicly confessed that there were three Gods and more, declaring that all visible things were made by a malign God, adding... that the giver of the Mosaic law [*that is,*

---

[7] As recorded in a public letter written by Pierre de Pavia, PL 199, cols 1119–24. At col. 1123: 'quod duo dii existerent, alter bonus et alter malus; bonus qui invisibilia tantum et ea que mutari aut corrumpi non possunt, fecisset; malus, qui coelum, terram, hominem et alia visibilia condidisset'.

[8] Guillaume de Puylaurens, *Chronique, 1145–1275*, ed. and trans. J. Duvernoy (Paris: CNRS, 1976), cap. iv, pp. 40–43. This bishop took office in 1185, which thus sets the earliest possible date for the event; it could be later, in the early thirteenth century pre-Crusade. English translation in William of Puylaurens, *Chronicle*, trans. W. A. and M. D. Sibly (Woodbridge: Boydell, 1999).

[9] Bernard de Fontcaude, *Adversus Waldensium sectam liber*, PL 204, cols 793–840, at col. 795: '... de quibusdam capitulis, in quibus male sentiebant, a veris Catholicis accusati sunt: eisque per singula respondentibus, hinc inde diu disputatum est, et ab utraque parte multae productae auctoritates'. I diverge somewhat from the translation in W&E, doc. 34.

the God of the Old Testament] was a malign God'.[10] According to the chronicler Pierre des Vaux-de-Cernay, Bernard de Simorre and another heretic called Theodoric frequently disputed with Gui, abbot of Vaux-de-Cernay (and later bishop of Carcassonne), when he was part of a preaching mission to the south led by Bishop Diego of Osma in 1206–07. The same Theodoric and another man called Baldwin debated with these preachers for eight days in the *castrum* of Servian (c. 12 km north-east of Béziers) in either 1206 or 1207.[11] Another such debate was held in Montréal in 1207, and was the occasion of a miracle by Dominique Guzman, who was part of Bishop Diego's group and was soon to become founder of the Order of Preachers, at Diego's encouragement. It is a famous incident, but worth recounting in a little detail, as the earliest text differs somewhat from well-known later visual depictions.[12] In Pierre des Vaux-de-Cernay's words:

> One day some of our preachers, men of religion, were debating against heretics. One of our lot, called Dominique, a man of total holiness who had been a companion of the Bishop of Osma, put down in writing certain authorities, which he had brought into the open [*that is, into the debate*]. And he handed the document to a certain heretic, for him to deliberate on the points brought up in opposition. That night, then, the heretics were gathered in a house, sitting by a fire. The one to whom the man of God had given the document brought it out into the open. Then his companions told him to throw it into the midst of the fire. And if that document were to be burnt, the heretics' faith—or rather, perfidy—would be shown to be true.[13]

But of course miraculously the document did not burn, despite being thrown back in three times. (Another account of the same debate, by Guillaume de Puylaurens, completely omits the miracle but relates in greater detail the use of 'written depositions prepared by the two sides and laid before arbiters whom they had chosen', namely two knights and two townsmen).[14] The exchange of written materials is attested in various of these cases, and we have some possible examples still surviving, the earliest from around 1200 in a manuscript now in Albi,

---

[10] C. Compayré, *Études historiques et documents inédits sur l'Albigeois, le Castrais et l'ancien diocèse de Lavaur* (Albi: Imprimerie de Maurice Papailhiau, 1841), pp. 227–28 (doc. 54); translated in full in A&B, pp. 51–52 (doc. 5 appendix A).

[11] Pierre des Vaux-de-Cernay, *Hystoria Albigensis*, ed. P. Guebin and E. Lyon, 3 vols (Paris: Librairie Ancienne Honoré Champion, 1926–29), I, pp. 46–47, 24–26 (caps xxii, liii); trans. A&B, pp. 49, 46 (doc. 5).

[12] Jordan of Saxony's version, written in 1233, sets the action in nearby Fanjeaux and dramatizes the event further: *Libellus de principiis Ordinis Praedicatorum*, Monumenta Ordinis Praedicatorum Historica 16 (Rome: Institutum Historicum FF. Praedicatorum, 1935), pp. 38–39.

[13] Pierre des Vaux-de-Cernay, *Hystoria Albigensis*, pp. 47–49 (cap. liv); trans. A&B, pp. 50–51 (doc. 5).

[14] Guillaume de Puylaurens, *Chronique*, cap. ix, pp. 56–59.

which is filled with biblical quotations glossed as rebuttals to dualist belief and associated matters.[15]

Diego d'Osma debated with heretics at Verfeil (c. 20 km east of Toulouse) around the same time, and with Waldensians at Pamiers, the latter event leading to the conversion of a Waldensian leader, Durand d'Osca (or 'de Huesca').[16] Durand had written a treatise against the other group of heretics in the early 1190s, which reminds us that not only did orthodox bishops debate with Waldensians and heretics, but Waldensians and heretics debated also with each other. (After his conversion, Durand wrote a further treatise in the 1220s in refutation of a written heretical tract, preserving chunks of the heretics' words in his own response).[17] These start to become more visible to us in the early thirteenth century, in part via the recollections from some decades later of those interrogated by inquisitors: in 1245 the notary Pons Amiel, 'an old man' as the inquisitor noted, said that 'he saw Isarn de Castres, heretic, debating with Bernard Prim, Waldensian, in the square at Laurac in the presence of the people of the town'. This was thirty-seven years before, in 1208.[18] From the surviving sentences to penance handed down by another inquisitor, Pierre Cellan, in 1241–42 we find further debates between Waldensians and heretics mentioned, with ordinary lay people in attendance as audience, in Gourdon, Montcuq, Montauban, and Montpezat.[19] Given the terse nature of the sentences it is impossible to date them precisely, but at least some would appear to be from before the start of the Albigensian Crusade in 1209, and a few deponents talked of remembering events from the time before 'the Church condemned the Waldensians' (though when that would be understood to have happened, from the point of view of the laity, is also rather uncertain).[20]

Thus far I have been talking of 'the Waldensians' and 'the heretics', reflecting the language of the sources themselves. Whilst 'the Waldensians' does at least accurately connect that group to their founder, neither term is what the people in

---

[15] F. Šanjek, ed., 'Edizione della Summa auctoritatum contenuta nel MS 47 della Bibliothèque municipale d'Albi', appendix (pp. 355–95) to R. Manselli, 'Una "Summa auctoritatum" antiereticale', *Atti della Accademia Nazionale dei Lincei*, Classe di scienze morali, storiche e filologiche, ser. 8, 28 (1985), 323–95; partial trans. A&B, pp. 92–97 (doc. 11).

[16] Guillaum de Puylaurens, *Chronique*, cap. viii, pp. 52–56.

[17] W. L. Wakefield, 'Notes on Some Anti-heretical Writings of the Thirteenth Century', *Franciscan Studies* 27 (1967), 285–321, at pp. 290–92. On Durand's writings, see also A&B, pp. 20–28 (doc. 2), and W&E, pp. 494–510 (doc. 58).

[18] MS Toulouse 609, fol. 198r; trans. A&B, p. 426.

[19] Gourdon: Doat 21, fols 196v, 203v, 208v. Montcuq: fols 219v, 225v. Montauban: fols 231v, 234v, 250v, 254v, 258v, 263r. Montpezat: fol. 308r. The sentences are edited in J. Duvernoy, ed., *L'Inquisition en Quercy: le registre des pénitences de Pierre Cellan, 1241–1242* (Castelnaud-la-Chapelle: L'Hydre, 2001), and a selection translated in A&B, pp. 310–31 (doc. 42).

[20] Doat 21, fol. 234v: 'Jacobus Carbonel... credidit quod Valdenses erant boni homines usque tempus quo Ecclesia condemnavit eos'; similarly P[ierre] Austorcs, fol. 238r, and Arnaud de la Farge, 289v. Valdes was excommunicated in 1184; the Waldensians were condemned at the synod of Narbonne in 1190 (the precursor to the debate noted above); and they were anathematized as heretics at the Fourth Lateran Council in 1215.

question would have used to designate themselves, and in the case of 'heretics' we must be continually careful not to let the condemnatory vocabulary of ecclesiastical authority skew our understanding. For the Waldensians, it seems reasonably likely from what various later sources tell us that they called themselves 'the Poor of Lyons'; and we can note that after Durand d'Osca was converted at Narbonne in 1207, he was allowed to continue to missionize with a group of followers in northern Catalonia, who called themselves 'the Poor Catholics'.[21] At the same time, various people at the time clearly did call them 'the Waldensians', and as we have seen, for a period of time in the late twelfth century at least, this would not necessarily have had any negative or dangerous connotation to an ordinary layperson.

The issue is very much more complicated for the other southern French 'heretics', as indeed are the wider, and rather fraught, arguments about their core beliefs (dualist or not), organization (formal 'church'-like hierarchy or not), and origins (indigenous to southern France, or linked to similar groups in eastern Europe and Italy). My aim here is to focus on how the ordinary laity in southern France saw and understood them, alongside other spiritual figures, within a wider landscape of faith; and whilst I think it is in fact clear that they did hold, and sometimes expressed, a dualist theology, I do not think that this was a major element in their immediate appeal to most of the laity. Thus, to avoid interrupting this chapter with a tangential discussion of the complex historiography and technical details of various sources, almost entirely focused on the group's elite rather than the broad mass of the laity, I shall leave explicit engagement with the historiographical debate to the Appendix to this book.

But the question of what to call the group cannot be deferred. 'Cathars' commits us to a sense of an international movement, and is a word imposed by hostile commentators; I think it is in fact a defensible term when discussing the group in the wider European setting, but since my aim throughout this book is to keep a localized focus, I shall not use it here.[22] In earlier decades, historians (myself included) tended to talk of 'Perfects', from the Latin *perfecti heretici*. However, the Latin word *perfectus* most commonly means 'completed'; so we might do better to translate *perfecti heretici* as something like 'fully-fledged heretics', perhaps in parallel to another term found intermittently, *heretici vestiti*, 'vested heretics', in both cases meaning those who have adopted the dress and way of life of the sect. In short, 'Perfects', as a stand-alone term, does not reflect the language used in most

---

[21] See generally G. Audisio, *The Waldensian Dissent: Persecution and Survival, c. 1170–c. 1570* (Cambridge: Cambridge University Press, 1999), pp. 6–39; E. Cameron, *Waldenses: Rejections of Holy Church in Medieval Europe* (Oxford: Blackwell, 2000), pp. 11–60; C. Taylor, 'A Presence in Languedoc (12th–13th Centuries)', in M. Benedetti and E. Cameron, eds, *A Companion to the Waldenses in the Middle Ages* (Leiden: Brill, 2022), pp. 35–77.

[22] For rationale, see Appendix, and J. H. Arnold, 'The Cathar Middle Ages as an Historiographical and Methodological Problem', in A. Sennis, ed., *Cathars in Question* (York: York Medieval Press, 2016), pp. 53–78.

contemporary sources. We have then a choice between terms found more commonly: 'Good Men' and 'Good Women' (more occasionally 'Good Christians'), or 'Friends of God'. There is some warrant for the latter term as a self-ascription. For example, in about 1226 a woman called Pagana Torrier came across two men in a field near Maurens (c. 50 k west of Toulouse). She asked them 'what manner of men they were, and they replied that they were friends of God'; she presumably took this to indicate that they had an elevated spiritual status, as she then asked them (perhaps challengingly) 'to say to her why she had lost all her children?' (In response, the men told her that 'all her children were demons', after which she understandably refused to listen to them).[23] A few other later examples can be adduced.[24]

But is 'Friend of God' a formal *title*, or more of a qualitative description of spiritual elevation and access to the divine? One finds it also used by at least one witness in regard to the Waldensians.[25] A similar case can be made regarding 'Good Men/Women', where nothing in the Latin (*boni homines/bonae feminae*) or more occasional Occitan (*bos homes/bonas femnas*) usage necessarily warrants a capital letter; and, as various people have pointed out, 'good man' operates more widely as a term of respect in southern French society, and rather intertwined with the similar 'worthy' or 'trustworthy men' (*probi homines/pros homes*) frequently used as a collective term for the group of men who wielded local political influence in cities, towns, and villages. Nonetheless, 'Good Men' is a term which we can sometimes see similarly self-ascribed in later evidence, and certainly used as a term by many lay people to refer to the group; and, as I have suggested some while ago, the overlap with other resonances of the term may in fact help us to understand the wider way in which those individuals were understood by the laity, combining spiritual and social elevation.[26] Thus, for the purposes of avoiding a further plague of scare quotes if nothing else, I will call them the Good Men (and on occasion Good Women); though will preserve the precise language of any particular source when quoting directly from it.[27]

---

[23] MS Toulouse 609, fol. 117v: '...petivit ab illis hominibus cuiusmodi homines erant et ipsi responderunt quod ipsi erant amici dei, et tunc ipsa testis rogavit eos quod dicerent sibi quare ipsa testis perdiderat omnes filios suos et tunc illi homines dixerunt ipsi testis quod omnes filii sui erant demones, et post ipsa testis noluit eos audire'. Pegg's rather different reading of this passage rests, in part at least, upon a slight misreading of the manuscript (M. G. Pegg, *The Corruption of Angels: The Great Inquisition of 1245-1246* (Princeton: Princeton University Press, 2005), p. 75, 'cuius' for 'cuiusmodi', 'perdiderit' for 'perdiderat').

[24] For example, Doat 22, fol. 51v, Doat 25, fols 46v, 160r.

[25] MS Toulouse 609, fol. 249v, Pierre Marty: 'Item dixit quod credit Valdenses esse bonos homines et veraces et amicos dei, et habere bonam fidem, et posse salvari per ipsos, licet sciret quod Ecclesia persequeretur eos...'

[26] Arnold, *Inquisition and Power*, pp. 138–49 (where I also repeatedly used *perfecti* as an alternative term, which I would now avoid). For a somewhat parallel but slightly different view, see Pegg, *Corruption*, pp. 95–97.

[27] *Pace* Claire Taylor, who sets out at length the issue of this being another qualitative term: 'Looking for the "Good Men" in the Languedoc: An Alternative to "Cathars"?', in Sennis, ed., *Cathars in Question*, pp. 242–56.

That both the Waldensians and the Good Men were condemned as heretics does of course come to matter very much. In the next chapter I shall return to the issues around ecclesiastical authority, the Albigensian crusade and inquisition into heretical wickedness. But to return my focus here to the ordinary laity, the first important thing to note is that in the late twelfth and early thirteenth centuries at least, there is little reason to see the potential 'heretical' or 'dissenting' status of these groups as playing much if any part in why they held a wider appeal. It is true that they criticized the clergy, criticized in particular, that is, the higher clergy's embrace of wealth and status (as with the group from Lombers). The Dominican preacher Étienne de Bourbon wrote, around the middle of the thirteenth century but apparently looking back to the earlier period of debates, that 'I heard from the brothers of Provence that in the land of the Albigensians, when heretics are being overcome by [arguments concerning] the scriptures and reasoning, they have no stronger argument... than the bad examples of Catholics, and above all, of Catholic prelates. So, when other arguments fail... they say "Look at the sorts of people these or those are... look at how they live and how they parade around, not walking as the men of old did, such as Pierre and Paul and the others".'[28] The focus on the higher clergy needs to be set in the context of their close association with lordship and secular power, as we have seen in previous chapters and as we shall explore further below. But the underlying point is the example of the apostles, and from a variety of other evidence it is clear that the predominant frame through which the Waldensians and Good Men and Women were viewed was in relation to the model of piety presented by the New Testament's account of those who followed Christ.

As we have seen in the evidence of some of the debates, the Good Men would only accept the authority of the New Testament. The Waldensians did not adopt that position, but they did take as their fundamental inspiration the New Testament message of leaving family and abandoning wealth to preach the word of God. Both groups were remembered for their preaching, which before the crusade was clearly done publicly: Arnaud Capre 'had many times heard the preaching of the Waldensians in the public square' of Montauban, something similarly attested by several others questioned by Pierre Cellan in 1241 about events from earlier decades.[29] Hélis de Mazerolles, widow to a knight, attested in 1243 that fifty years earlier—that is, some time in the 1190s—she and various other noblewomen had been present at the preaching of Guilabert de Castres in Fanjeaux, where 'he used to maintain his house openly... with many other heretics';

---

[28] A. Lecoy de la Marche, ed., *Anecdotes historiques, legendes et apologues tires du recueil inédit d'Étienne de Bourbon, dominicain du XIIIe siècle* (Paris: Librairie Renouard, 1877), p. 192; trans. A&B, p. 126 (doc.17).

[29] Doat 21, fols 257r; similarly 260v, 265v, 266r, 269r–v, 270r, 273v, 275r, 276v, 282r, 301v, all references to 'in the public square' or, in the final case, 'in the street'. There are many further references to hearing their preaching without a location specified.

Pons Carbonel du Faget recalled that around 1204 he saw in a certain field outside Auriac the Good Man Bernard Fresel preaching to all the people and knights of the *castrum*; a knight called Raimond Aiffre recalled hearing the Good Men preach publicly in the town of Aragon (c. 12 km north of Carcassonne) with 'almost all the people of the said *castrum* present', in the time 'before the crusaders came'.[30] Various further examples could be cited from the inquisition records.

With our focus on the laity rather than the Waldensians or Good Men themselves, the second important point is to think about the emergence of both groups as part of a wider shift in the landscape of faith, and consequently the choices available to the laity; and in particular, the landscape of faith visible in cities and towns. We have already noted in Chapter 3 the emergence of Cistercian monasteries, the spread of Templar and Hospitaller foundations across the south, and by the end of the twelfth century the growth of hospitals, all of which can be seen in the context of changes in elite charitable giving, following the 'crisis of friendship' caused by the Gregorian reform. But whilst all of these do largely emerge initially via elite support, there are some important differences regarding locale, and subsequent engagement. Cistercian monasteries were, perforce, rural. The spread of Templar and Hospitaller commanderies encompassed both urban and rural locations; the essential support given by noble families to the knightly orders meant that they frequently took over some or all of the lordship of various rural locations, and Damien Carraz has pointed to the key role played by reform-minded bishops—often themselves Cistercians—in establishing the military orders in Provence.[31] In that sense, whilst they increasingly gained an urban presence, the dynamic of their appeal and support was quite similar to, and indeed often quite closely linked with, that of the Cistercians (though we should remember that, in the south of France, it was the knightly orders who arrived first).[32] In all cases, one clear and key attraction to some lay donors was gaining a privileged place of burial with one of these new foundations.[33]

In partial contrast, the growing number of hospitals in this period is predominantly an urban phenomenon, found in cities, towns, and larger *castra*; and this would appear similarly to be the case with where we find pre-crusade Waldensians and Good Men. Commenting on the debates we met above, the chronicler Guillaume de Puylaurens commented: 'Grief! To think that amongst Christian people the standing of the Church and the Catholic faith had sunk so low that

---

[30] Doat 23, fol. 162v; trans. A&B, p. 337 (doc. 44); Doat 24, fol.37r-v; Doat 23, fol. 80r.

[31] D. Carraz, *L'Ordre du Temple dans la basse vallée du Rhône (1124-1312): ordres militaires, croisades et sociétés méridionales* (Lyon: Presses universitaires du Lyon, 2005).

[32] J. Schenk, *Templar Families: Landowning Families and the Order of the Temple in France, c. 1120-1307* (Cambridge: Cambridge University Press, 2012), chapter 2.

[33] D. Carraz, 'Templars and Hospitallers in the Cities of the West and the Latin East (Twelfth to Thirteenth Centuries)', *Crusades* 12 (2013), 103-20, at p. 113.

such abuse had to be submitted to the judgment of laymen!'[34] Beyond the ecclesiastical disapproval, he highlights perhaps their most interesting feature: that these were 'public' not in the way that the earlier Peace of God assemblies or relic translations had been, but public in a *civic* sense. It was not just 'laymen', nor just regional rulers, who bore witness to the debates, but rather, as we have seen, townsfolk. One of the ways in which the landscape had further changed, by the late twelfth century, was therefore the greater presence of, and thus lay access to, what we might broadly call 'the holy' in the urban environment, supported directly by townspeople.

Of course, in the great and long-established cities, aspects of the holy were already present in the cathedrals, particularly in the form of certain famous relics—though as we saw in Chapter 2, the holiness of the relics was most often broadcast and resonant when brought *out* of the city, into the countryside, under the orchestration of the bishop. By the late twelfth century, Waldensians and Good Men could be found in several of the large cities: Toulouse, Narbonne, Cahors, Carcassonne. But the shift we are seeing in the later twelfth century also encompasses newly created towns (such as Montauban, founded by Alphonse-Jourdain, count of Toulouse, in 1144), larger rural *castra* such as Castelnaudary, Moissac, Gourdon, and Fanjeaux, and more lowly urban locales, such as Montcuq and Lautrec, all of which saw a strong Waldensian presence. The Good Men were found in those places and elsewhere, as a public presence in the pre-crusade era: the knight Guilabert del Bosquet, confessing in 1246, said that he had seen 'at Toulouse and at Fanjeaux and Montréal and in many other places, heretics [that is, Good Men] living publicly', this being 'forty years ago or thereabouts'; another knight, Pons Magrefort, told inquisitors that he had seen Good Men living 'publicly' in their houses at Mas-Saintes-Puelles, Laurac, and other towns and *castra* 'such that nobody had to guard themselves, before the first arrival of the crusaders'.[35] Again, there is copious evidence from other inquisition depositions of witnesses who remembered seeing the Good Men and the Waldensians 'living publicly', in a variety of other locales.

In the same period, we also see the growth of civic pious foundations. Hospitals existed in a variety of places by the mid-twelfth century, as we have seen in Chapter 3, and more continued to be founded in later decades and well into the thirteenth century, often creating multiple institutions in the same city or town.[36]

---

[34] Guillaume de Puylaurens, *Chronique*, cap. ix, pp. 56–59.

[35] MS Toulouse 609, fol. 213r: 'dixit quod vidit apud Tholosam et apud Fanumjovis et Montemregalem et in pluribus aliis locis heretici publice commorantes'; Doat 23, fol. 86v: 'Dixit se vidisse multos hereticos et hereticas stantes publice in castris de Manso Sanctarum Puellarum et de Lauraco et in aliis castris et villis indifferenter, ita quod a nemine sibi cavebant ante primum adventum cruce signatorum...'

[36] For the east part of the region, see D. Le Blévec, *La part du pauvre: l'assistance dans les pay bas-rhône du XIIe siècle au milieu du Xve siècle* (Rome: École française du Rome, 2000), 2 vols, chapters 7–11. Some form of hospitals—often termed *xenodochia*, and probably focused on providing shelter

By the first decade of the thirteenth century Narbonne, for example, had at least six hospitals, Arles had two leprosaria and eleven different hospitals of various kinds (as well as a 'hospital' of the Knights of St John), and Toulouse had a notable seven leprosaria and twelve other foundations.[37] In Aix, a record of tithing receipts compiled by an archpriest in 1251 lists, among other churches, the hospital of Saint-Jean (that is, the Hospitallers), the house of the Templars, the hospital of Saint-Jacques, the hospital of Saint-Lazar, the hospital of the Madeleine, the 'alms house', and the 'hospital of the poor', all located within the city itself.[38] It is important to remember that 'hospital' primarily meant a place of respite rather than necessarily a centre for medical treatment, and institutions could vary wildly as to their size and activities.[39] The sick poor would be looked after at a hospital, but an establishment might also be a place providing for pilgrims or the desperately indigent. Those in residence would receive 'care', in the form of food and lodging but, most importantly, in the form of spiritual comfort; as a founding charter for the hospital of Saint-Raimond in Toulouse says, 'And in this hospital there will always be an altar to St John, in honour of God, where the poor—and all other Christians—can hear the ministry of God'.[40] The point for the founders and donors was not to provide a welfare or healthcare system, but to perform some of the forms of loving Christian care (*caritas*, 'charity') particularly associated with Christ in the New Testament, namely caring for the poor and the sick and the needy traveller (elements within what later pastoral texts called the 'seven works of mercy').[41] Scattered references in twelfth-century wills make it clear that hospitals existed not only in the cities, but in quite small *castra* also. For example,

for pilgrims—did exist in the early middle ages; see S. Watson, *On Hospitals: Welfare, Law and Christianity in Western Europe, 400–1320* (Oxford: Oxford University Press, 2020). But I have not come across specific evidence for southern France prior to the eleventh century (though this does not mean that none existed); the earliest noted by Le Blévec is Notre-Dame de Nîmes founded in 1090 (see map and list of places in *La part du pauvre*, II, pp. 600–07). Potentially one of the earliest is the hospital of Saint-Raimond in Toulouse, for which we have a small set of undated charters which look to be from around 1080, stating in one that the hospital was 'made and held' by a man called Raimond Gairard, the foundation receiving material support from a *sauveté* created at Matepezoul by the cathedral canons, and further support from the count; see *Cart. Saint-Sernin*, p. 382 (no. 548) and also 379–80 (no. 546), 380–82 (no. 547). However, Gérard Pradalié has argued—persuasively, though not conclusively—that these are later forgeries, produced for a mixture of wider political purposes, and that we should assume a twelfth-century foundation: G. Pradalié, 'La fondation de l'hôpital Saint-Raimond de Toulouse: une remise en question', *Annales du Midi* 119 (2007), 227–36.

[37] J. Caille, 'Hospices et assistance a Narbonne (XIIIe–XIVe siècles)', *CdF* 8 (1978), 261–80; G. Giordanengo, 'Les hopitaux arlésiens du XIIe au XIVe siècle', *CdF* 8 (1978), 189–212, see tabulation pp. 205–08; J. H. Mundy, 'Hospitals and Leprosaries in Twelfth and Early Thirteenth-Century Toulouse', in J. H. Mundy, R. W. Emery, and B. N. Nelson, eds, *Essays in Medieval Life and Thought, Presented in Honor of Austin Patterson Evans* (New York: Biblo and Tanen, 1965), pp. 181–206.

[38] M. Prou and E. Clouzot, eds, *Pouillés des provinces d'Aix, d'Arles, d'Embrun* (Paris: Imprimerie nationale, 1923), pp. 1–8.

[39] See Watson, *On Hospitals*, introduction; Le Blévec, *La part du pauvre*, II, chapters 9, 10, 11.

[40] *Cart. Saint-Sernin*, pp. 380–82 (no. 547). As noted above, possibly a later forgery, though clearly expressing an expected sentiment.

[41] M. H. Vicaire, 'La place des oeuvres de miséricorde dans la pastorale en Pays d'oc', *CdF* 13 (1978), 21–44; Le Blévec, *La part du pauvre*, I, pp. 170–86.

from several wills recorded in the cartulary of the cathedral of Agde, we find mention of hospitals not only in the city of Agde itself (in a will from 1141), but also in Garrigues (1187), Bassan (1176), and Montagnac (1173), all much smaller local towns.[42]

Some hospitals—or perhaps we might sometimes say 'hostels'—also existed in very rural areas, to provide for those on long-distance pilgrimage. For one such rural foundation, the hospital of Sainte-Marie-d'Aubrac (about 50 km north east of Rodez), we have surviving records which give a good sense of the spiritual associations centred on such foundations. From a document in the hospital's own archive, we learn that it was founded by 'Adalard, viscount of Flanders', when he was on pilgrimage to Saint-Jacques-de-Compostelle. Whilst heading through a certain forest 'where pilgrims were attacked by thieves and murderers', there appeared before him 'Our Lord Jesus Christ, in the public road, where there was a dark cave of those thieves' (*Dominus noster Jesus Christus in itinere publico ubi erat ipsorum latronum tenebrosa spelunca*). Christ entreated him that 'there, in honour of Him and the most holy Trinity and the Glorious Virgin His mother, he should construct a house of hospitality for the charitable reception of the poor and pilgrims' (*domus hospitalis construeret pauperibus et peregrinis caritative recipiendis*).[43] The hospital was thus founded for the benefit of pilgrims to Rocamadour, Le Puy, Compostelle, 'and many other saints', and would receive 'the poor of Christ, the infirm, the blind, the weak, the deaf, the mute, the lame, the hungry, and all pilgrims and all who travel through there', all of whom would be received 'in charity by the brothers and sisters of the same hospital'.[44] This narrative is probably a later invention: one of the places listed as a site of eventual pilgrimage is the shrine of St Antoine in Padua, not in existence until some decades into the thirteenth century, whilst other charters make it clear that the hospital existed from the 1160s at least, and probably some decades before that.[45] In this

---

[42] *Cart. S. Étienne d'Agde*, pp. 339 (no. 298), 169–70 (no. 83), 174–75 (no. 87); see also 132 (no. 36), 167–68 (no. 82). This suggests that Brodman underplays the importance of independent secular efforts in founding hospitals (overemphasizing episcopal direction instead): J. W. Brodman, *Charity and Religion in Medieval Europe* (Washington DC: Catholic University of America Press, 2009), pp. 46–47.

[43] Doat 134, fol. 1r–v. This document, undated, was copied by the Doat scribes from a 'livre' in the hospital's own archive. The narrative is repeated, using the same language, in a *vidimus* of a bull of Innocent III from 1216, later in the same archive (fols 33r–39r).

[44] Doat 134, fol. 2v.

[45] Doat 134, fols 10r–14v (1162 'rule' for the hospital, based on Augustinian rule, given by Pierre, bishop of Rodez); 16r–17r (1165 donation by same bishop, of rights of benefice in five villages of Bilhac). There are several other apparently early donation charters from various minor nobles, relating to nearby land and pasturage rights, several undated, the earliest dated one being 1173 (22r–23v). A charter in the cartulary of Conques (undated, but undoubtedly from the first half of the twelfth century from the witness names) records that Adalard gave 'to St Saveur and Ste Foi of Conques that hospital of Aubrac with all its appurtenances...so that after my death, that hospital...will be retained by the abbot and monks of Ste Foi to serve God and the poor', also giving, in recognition of this eventual surrender, a pound of wax to the altar of Ste Foi annually; G. Desjardins, ed., *Cartulaire de l'Abbaye de Conques en Rouergue* (Paris: Picard, 1879), p. 360 (no. 498). Jacques Bousquet dates this to

particular case, the hospital was clearly more of a quasi-monastic foundation, receiving a 'rule' from the bishop of Rodez in 1162, attracting support from some major regional nobles (including the king of Aragon and, in the thirteenth century, the count of Toulouse), and subsequently becoming a major landholder exercising lordship within the region; a reminder again that 'hospital' can describe a very wide variety of institutions.[46] But the ideals and imagery of the foundation narrative do tell us something more generally about how this form of charitable piety was conceptualized.

Leprosaria grew similarly. We might understand leper houses as essentially a specialized subset of hospitals, specialized not 'medically' but in their focus on one particular kind of charitable act. Some are glimpsed before the mid-twelfth century—a donation to 'the poor of the leprosarium' in 1143 in or near Montpellier, for example, mentioned already in Chapter 3, and references to a *domus leprosorum* in Narbonne even earlier—and we again find many more in later decades.[47] Again they existed in quite small locations as well as major cities: there is a passing reference in a charter from late in the twelfth century, for example, to 'the house of the lepers' next to the church of Saint-Martin in Arlos, a small village in the Bavart valley in the foothills of the Pyrenees, and similarly mention of 'the old *del Brugal* leper house' in a charter describing rural lands somewhere north of Nîmes. The late twelfth-century civic statutes of Aucamville, a small town just north of Toulouse, forbid butchers selling the meat of any animals raised 'in the leper house' there.[48] As John Hine Mundy pointed out in an important article many decades ago, by the end of the twelfth century we also find—in Toulouse at any rate—houses of 'recluses', also recipients of pious donations, their precise identity very hard to discern initially, but later in the thirteenth century probably transforming into 'beguins', in the sense of lay people who

---

the early twelfth century, on the basis that 'Adalard' was Adalard d'Eyne, who disappears from Flemish documents after 1119: J. Bousquet, 'Les débuts du monastère-hôpital d'Aubrac', *Revue du Rouergue* 2 (1985), 97–116, at p. 100.

[46] On its subsequent development and lordship, see G. Pradalié et E. Hamon, 'L'Aubrac au l'époque de la Domerie', in L. Fau, ed., *Les monts d'Aubrac au moyen âge: genèse d'un monde agropastoral* (Paris: Éditions de la Maison des sciences de l'homme, 2006), pp. 50–88, new on-line edition 2021 <https://books.openedition.org/editionsmsh/19288>.

[47] A. Germain, ed., *Liber instrumentorum memorialium: cartulaire des Guillems de Montpellier* (Montpellier: J. Martel, 1884–86), pp. 282–3 (no. 150); J. Caille, *Hopitaux et charité publique à Narbonne au Moyen Age de la fin du XIe à la fin du XVe siècle* (Toulouse: Privat, 1978), pp. 32–33; more generally Le Blévec, *La part du pauvre*, II, chapter 11.

[48] *Cart. Lézat*, II, pp. 503–04 (no. 1729). BnF MS Lat. 9994 (Cart. Grandselve), fol. 217r: 'qui honor est inter domum antiquam leprosorum delbrugal et...'. The donation appears to be c. 1190, and the donor Ato *de Garag* (probably Garrigues, c. 6 km north of Nîmes) also mentions lands he holds in Sainte-Anastasia, a village on the Gardon river, further to the north. Customs of Aucamville, c. 39, edited in M. L'Abbé Galabert, 'La charte des coutumes d'Aucamville', *Bulletin archéologique et historique de la Société archéologique de Tarn-et-Garonne* (1886), 97–110.

attached themselves particularly to the Franciscan order, emphatically embracing personal poverty.[49]

To allow ourselves for a moment to look forward over the coming decades, across and after the Albigensian crusade, it is of course also in the cities that the mendicant orders established themselves in the early thirteenth century. As Bernard Gui, the later inquisitor and historian of the Dominican order, tells us, around the time of the 'Great Council' (that is, Fourth Lateran, 1215), 'there came to St Dominique two good and suitable men of Toulouse, one of whom was Brother Pierre Cellan, who was later the first prior of Limoges, the other in truth Brother Thomas, a most gracious man and eloquent in sermons.... [Cellan], who owned houses around the Château Narbonnais in Toulouse, offered and gave these to St Dominique and his companions.'[50] This was the first foundation of the Order of Preachers (following the female convent founded at Prouille by Dominique himself in 1207). In 1222, they were joined in Toulouse by the Brothers Minor, who by then already had convents established in Arles (1219), Montpellier, and Mirepoix (both 1220). In fact it is the Order of the Brothers Minor (the Franciscans) who spread more swiftly through the region, setting up not only in the great cities but in some smaller places also: Le Puy (1223), Lavaur (1226), Castres (1227), Narbonne (1228), Agde (1236), Lodève (1238), Béziers (1238), Largentière (1239), Carcassonne (1240), Alès (1241), Albi (1242), Perpignan (1243), Beaucaire (1248), Nîmes (1248), and Montauban (c. 1250), to list just those from the first half of the thirteenth century.[51] In contrast, despite their strong association with southern France, the Order of Preachers located themselves initially in the larger cities, and were slightly slower to spread regionally, probably because their mission was very quickly made international through the papal support they received. We find them established in Narbonne and Montpellier by 1220, Cahors, Arles, and Marseille in 1225, Valence (1230), Avignon (1241), Perpignan, Nice, and Béziers in 1242, Carcassonne (1247), and Agen (1249). Some other large towns then follow soon after: Tarascon (1250), Alès (1251), Montauban (1252), Figeac (1254), Nîmes (1256).[52] For both orders, additional foundations followed later in the thirteenth century, and it is in this

---

[49] J. H. Mundy, 'Charity and Social Work in Toulouse, 1100–1250', *Traditio* 22 (1966), 203–87, at pp. 230–31. Such figures rather inevitably appear only marginally in the archive; for example, the will of a wealthy man called Carbonel (see further below) made in 1215 mentions, among many other small pious bequests, provision of a sixteenth of wheat to 'a recluse', presumably within Agde; *Cart. S. Étienne d'Agde*, p. 394 (no. 359).

[50] Bernardus Guidonis, *De fundatione et prioribus conventuum provinciarum Tolosanae et provinciae Ordinis Praedicatorum*, ed. P. A. Amargier, Monumenta Ordinis Fratrum Praedicatorum Historica XXIV (Rome: Institutum historicum fratrum praedicatorum, 1961), p. 43. Some extracts from this work are translated in A&B, doc. 9.

[51] F.-R. Durieux, 'Approches de l'histoire franciscaine du Languedoc au XIIIe siècle', *CdF* 8 (1973), 79–100.

[52] Gui, *De fundatione, passim*; and M.-H. Vicaire, 'Le développement de la province Dominicaine de Provence (1215–1295)', *CdF* 8 (1973), 35–77.

period that we find also foundations among the other mendicant orders such as the Sack Friars, the Augustinians, and the Carmelites.[53]

Thus as we enter the thirteenth century, the presence of holy men, and occasionally holy women, had become much enriched in the cities and the towns of the south. Whilst they were very strongly divided theologically, in their manner of life and approach to the laity they were very similar, and designedly so. 'Use a nail to drive out a nail,' Diego d'Osma is said to have counselled:[54] having observed the outward piety ('feigned piety', as he saw it of course) of the Good Men, their attentiveness to local communities, and their good example, he saw that the Church would have to do the same but better, and thus inspired Dominique to start his order. The early similarity between the Waldensians and Franciscans—both Valdes and Francis coming from an urban mercantile background, experiencing a conversion experience which inspired each man to renounce their wealth in order to go and preach—is even more obvious. A number of the people sentenced by Pierre Cellan had contact with both the Waldensians and the Good Men, and seem to have treated them as similar holy men, despite their fierce differences.[55] This does not mean they saw *no* differences between the groups, but that they were viewed as different figures in the same field, as it were. Pierre Roger Boca 'said that he saw Waldensians many times in diverse places...he believed they were good men. Item, he often went to the heretics and heard their preaching...Item, he believed initially that the Waldensians were good men, and he then believed the same thing afterwards of the heretics' (the punctuation by 'Item' reminding us that these are the words distilled by the inquisitor, in order to sentence him).[56] In partial contrast, Bernard Remon 'saw Waldensians and heard their preaching and believed they were good men. Item, he went to the heretics, wishing to test who were better, the Waldensians or the heretics...Item, he disputed with someone regarding the faith of the heretics and the Waldensians, and approved the faith of the heretics.'[57]

As we go on through the thirteenth century, there is a shift—primarily around the end of the crusade—from the public presence of the Good Men and the

---

[53] C. Ribaucourt, 'Les mendiants du Midi d'après la cartographie de l'"enquête"', *CdF* 8 (1973), 25–33.

[54] Jordan of Saxony, *Libellus*, p. 36: 'Clavum clavo retundite', that is, in practical terms, drive a nail out of wood by hammering another one into it head on; symbolically, use like to defeat like.

[55] Contact with both groups attested in Doat 21, fols 187r–v, 188r, 189r, 196r, 196v–197r, 197r–v, 198r, 200v, 201r, 201v, 202r, 203r, 204r, 208r, 210v, 232r, 232v–233r, 233v, 235v, 236v, 242v, 243r, 243v–244r, 245r–v, 245v, 246v, 250r, 251v–252r, 253v, 256r, 258v, 262r, 269v, 271v, 278r.

[56] Doat 21, 231v–232r: 'P. R. Boca dixit quod vidit multotiens Valdenses et in diversis locis...Item credebat quod essent boni homines. Item pluries venit ad hereticos et audivit predicationem eorum...Item credidit a principio quod Valdenses erat boni homines, idem credidit postea de hereticis.'

[57] Doat 21, fol. 242r–243r: 'B. Remon vidit Valdenses et audivit predicationem eorum et credebat quod essent boni homines. Item ivit ad hereticos volens temptare qui essent meliores [ms: '*mulieres*'], Valdenses vel heretici, et ibi audivit predicationem hereticorum...Item disputavit cum quodam de fide hereticorum et Valdensium et approbavit fidem hereticorum.'

Waldensians to the increased public presence of the Franciscans and Dominicans; though we should note that it is likely that the numbers of Good Men in particular probably continued to be much higher than the numbers of mendicant friars until 1244. That was the year in which the mountain fortress of Montségur, which in about 1232 the Good Men had requested for use as their 'headquarters' from its lord, Raimond de Péreille,[58] fell to royal forces after a long siege, leading to the mass execution of 200 of their number. By that year, as we have seen above, there were eleven Dominican and sixteen Franciscan foundations, spread across the entire region. It is impossible to give a precise figure for how many friars would be found in each convent, but one might guess at between 350 and 500 in total, though that figure could be higher.[59] And sat more quietly alongside that struggle over mendicancy there was, as we have seen, the steady growth of charitable urban institutions across the region.

Much of what I have discussed thus far in this chapter falls within a set of overlapping developments which previous historians have identified. One is the growth of the *vita apostolica*, as a spiritual path gaining increased attraction for those who wished to embrace a spiritual life, seen as an outcome from the wider currents of the Gregorian reform movement.[60] The second is the 'charitable revolution', a development grounded in the twelfth-century urbanization and mercantilization of western Europe, but dependent on an awakening of lay piety, particularly intensified in the thirteenth century (as argued by André Vauchez and others) by the salutary effect of mendicant preaching and the good example of newly canonized saints, whose embrace of poverty and personal sanctity were promoted particularly by Innocent III.[61] So the broad outlines of change here depicted will not surprise. But, as in other areas addressed by this book, a regional

---

[58] Doat 24, fols 43v–44r: 'Item dixit we vidisse quod Guilabertus de Castris, episcopus hereticorum, et Bernardus de motta, filius maior, et Johannes Cambiario, filius Hugonis de la Bacona, filius maior hereticorum Agenensium, et Poncius Guilaberti, diachonus hereticorum de Vilamur, et Tento, episcopus hereticorum Agennensium, et multi alii heretici, venerunt in castrum Montis Securi et postulaverunt et suplicaverunt Ramundo de Perella domino olim dicti castri, quod receptaret dictos hereticos infra castrum Montis Securi ad hoc ut in ipso castro posset ecclesia hereticorum habere domicilius et capite, et inde posset transmittere et deffendere predicatores suos...'.

[59] I am estimating on the basis of 'about twelve men' per new Dominican foundation, as set out in the Primitive Constitutions 2.23 (S. Tugwell, 'The Evolution of Dominican Structures of Government', *Archivum Fratrum Praedicatorum* 71 (2010), 164) and guessing at a similar size for Franciscan houses, then adding on somewhat in recognition of the fact that some longer-standing houses might be much larger. I am very grateful to Steve Watts for discussion and advice; the guesstimates, and their obvious potential inaccuracy, remain my own responsibility.

[60] Among various founding discussions, see Grundmann, *Religious Movements*; E. W. McDonnell, 'The "Vita Apostolica": Diversity or Dissent', *Church History* 24 (1955), 15–31; M.-D. Chenu, *La théologie au douzième siècle* (Paris: J. Vrin, 1957).

[61] A. Vauchez, *La spiritualité du Moyen Age occidental, VIIIe–XIIIe siècle* (Paris: Seuil, 1994), pp. 118–24; A. J. Davis, 'The Social and Religious Meaning of Charity in Medieval Europe', *History Compass* 12/12 (2014), 935–50; A. J. Davis, *The Medieval Economy of Salvation: Charity, Commerce and the Rise of the Hospital* (Ithaca, NY: Cornell University Press, 2019), chapters 1 and 2. Arguing for a more episcopal focus and downplaying the mendicants: Brodman, *Charity and Religion*.

focus allows us to examine aspects of these dynamics more closely.[62] In southern France in particular we have not only a highly mercantilized society in towns and cities at least, but also the complicating presence of the Good Men and Waldensians, both seen as embodying particular interpretations of 'apostolicity'.

We must moreover remember that *vita apostolica* is a phrase deployed rather more readily in modern scholarship than medieval texts, and that the modern usage tends to collapse a variety of potential interpretations into one channel. There was in reality not one singular interpretation of the 'apostolic life' in the medieval period, but various different modes of heightened piety that embraced different aspects of the life depicted and enjoined in the New Testament, and different ways of interpreting specific elements. An obvious example is the embrace of 'poverty', which could itself follow various biblical injunctions with differing emphases. To pick just a few passages that might inspire a new way of life: 'If any man will come after me, let him deny himself, and take up his cross, and follow me' (Matt. 16: 24; similarly Luke 9: 23) being in part an injunction to divest oneself of wealth (though in this period adopted particularly in regard to crusade to the Holy Lands); 'It is easier for a camel to pass through the eye of a needle, than for a rich man to enter into the kingdom of heaven' (Matt. 19: 24, Mark 10: 25) similarly addressing one's own salvation. One might read 'Blessed are the poor in spirit: for theirs is the kingdom of heaven' (Matt. 5: 3) in a similar fashion, or might equally interpret it as saying that the prayers of the poor were more efficacious, given their privileged spiritual position. 'Take heed and beware of all covetousness: for a man's life does not consist in the abundance of things which he possesses' (Luke 12: 15) rather less emphatically relegates the distractions of wealth against spiritual knowledge. 'If thou wilt be perfect, go sell what thou hast, and give to the poor, and thou shalt have treasure in heaven' (Matt. 19: 21, Mark 10: 21) emphasizes the act of charity and its rewards; 'if I should distribute all my goods to feed the poor, and if I should deliver my body to be burned, and have not charity, it profiteth me nothing' (1 Cor. 13: 3) warning however that the act is insufficient without the inner motivation of love (*caritas*). These are not in any sense conflicting injunctions, but they proffer different potential emphases over what a focus on 'poverty' might entail.

Jochen Schenk has suggested that in the south of France, noble families who supported the establishment of the Templars and the Cistercians were attracted to them by the wider dynamics of a reform piety that focused particularly on poverty, and that this was already apparent in the region by the very early twelfth century, as seen in the inspiration of Pons de Léras and the founding of various small hermitage communities.[63] In further support of that general suggestion,

---

[62] See similarly Davis, *Medieval Economy of Salvation*, p. 79 regarding hospital foundations.
[63] Schenk, *Templar Families*, pp. 104–08. Schenk points also to Géraud de Sales (d. 1120) as another influential figure in the early twelfth century; however, with the exception of Grandselve, the locations of Géraud's various foundations (generally hermitages that then became Cistercian monasteries) lie

one can note a letter written by Bishop Amiel of Toulouse (d. 1139) to King Henry I of England in perhaps the second decade of the twelfth century, calling for him to bestow patronage on the recently founded monastery of Grandselve (Cistercian by the 1140s, but at this point following the Benedictine rule). The letter places considerable emphasis upon poverty, including the notion of the Lord having 'made Himself a pauper for us' (2 Cor. 8: 9), and the importance of giving to the poor, quoting various passages from the New Testament.[64] Although there is no evidence that Henry responded to Amiel's request (nor indeed that the letter was ever sent), it does clearly demonstrate how such an intervention was framed. From the point of actual donors, Schenk cites a resonant, though in fact extremely unusual, early example of the association between pious donation, poverty, and the Templars, that uses very similar language to Amiel's letter. This is a charter recording the gift made to the commandery of Mas-Deu, near Perpignan, in 1133 by a woman called Acalaidis. As she begins by giving over her body and soul, it was probably made on her deathbed. The gift was made, the charter states:

> because my Lord deigned to be a pauper for me: just as He was a pauper for me, thus I wish to be a little pauper for Him, so that He might make me come to true penance and true confession and make me come to His holy paradise; and that He might have mercy on the souls of my father and my mother and to all my forebears, and might make all my children work to His holy service, so that they should come to a good end.[65]

The apostolic language is striking—and unusual in its detail—but more familiar is the sense of hoped-for reciprocity, for herself and her kin. Acalaidis's emphasis

---

rather further north than the geography I have adopted for this book. On Géraud, including the important point that his connection to Robert d'Abrissel is a confusion introduced by a later biographer, see M.-O. Lenglet, 'Géraud de Salles, ses fondations monastiques, leur évolution vers l'ordre cistercien à la fin du XIIème siècle', *Bulletin de la Société historique et archéologique du Périgord* 114 (1987), 33–50.

[64] N. Vincent, 'A Letter to King Henry I from Toulouse', *Journal of Ecclesiastical History* 63 (2012), 331–45.

[65] *Cartulaire général de l'ordre du Temple, 1119?–1150*, ed. le Marquis d'Albon (Paris: Librairie ancienne d'Honoré Champion, 1913), p. 51 (no. 68): 'Et hoc donum facio propter quod Dominus meus fuit dignatus esse pauper per me: sicuti illo fuit pauper per me, sic volo esse paupercula per illum; et ut ille faciat me pervenire ad veram penitenciam et ad veram confessionem et faciat me pervenire ad suum sanctum paradisum; et habeat mercedem ad animam patris et matris mee et ad omnium parentum meorum et ad omnes infantes meos faciat facere suum sanctum servicium, per quod veniant ad bonam finem.' See Schenk, *Templar Families*, p. 106. Whilst most charters refer primarily to their knighthood and their defence of Christendom, a few other charters from southern France from the 1130s and 1140s describe the Templars as 'poor knights' (*Cartulaire général*, p. 13 [no. 20] 1128 × 32, appended by a long list of people giving small annual sums, and a larger provision upon death; pp. 90 [no. 129], 91 [no. 130], 92 [no. 131], 129–30 [no. 189], 145 [no. 209]). On rare occasion, when the donor was also joining the order, a passage from Matt. 16 ('take up your cross...') is quoted (*Cartulaire général*, p. 87 [no. 125], 1136 × 39), or other biblical quotes regarding apostolic service (for example, *Cartulaire général*, p. 237 [no. 371], quoting Luke 14: 33), and there is one reference to the convert 'leaving the world' to become 'a pauper for God' (for example, *Cartulaire général*, p. 144 [no. 207], 1140).

upon poverty and her claim 'to be a pauper for Him' is particularly interesting given the details of her gift: alongside an allod she held in a place called *Cisano*, she gave other land in the region which the Templars were to 'get from Oliba de Candel...because he [*or possibly* she] has it in mortgage for 4 *livres* of silver'.[66] The emphasis upon 'poverty' thus comes from someone who is really quite rich, divesting themselves of wealth in a testamentary context; as with the passage from 2 Corinthians alluded to in her opening line, the dynamic here is a form of liminal reversal.

If we are thinking about poverty and the *vita apostolica* as chosen and embodied by those spiritual few—Pons de Léras and other converts to Cistercianism, Valdes and Francis and their respective followers—then some sense of a shared path and common spirit must be noted, though the precise interpretation of that apostolic inspiration clearly varies. But if we are looking at them and others from the perspective of the general laity, differences in the visible performance of apostolicism would be apparent: Cistercianism's rural withdrawal, or the ultimate focus on the Holy Lands associated with the Templars and Hospitallers, in contrast to the civic mendicancy of the later orders; the collective wealth dedicated to God gained quite swiftly by the Cistercians set against the display of personal poverty embraced by Francis and Valdes and their immediate followers, and the explicit comparison which the Good Men drew between their own humble status and the ostentatious wealth of the higher clergy. When one then considers the wider dynamics of living in imitation of the apostles, further choices in emphasis become apparent: the Hospitallers' care for pilgrims compared with the mendicant preaching of the Good Men and the friars, and so forth.

What did all of this mean for ordinary lay people? Again, I want to set aside for a moment the more fraught question of 'heresy', and instead focus on the roles played by all these holy men and women and pious institutions, within their communities. For the various mendicants, 'heretical' and orthodox, one of the central features, and presumably the context in which many first encountered them, is preaching. We have noted already the fact of preaching by the Good Men and Waldensians before the crusade, and anti-heresy preaching by Dominique Guzman and others. Whilst some of the sermons delivered by each group undoubtedly had the primary purpose of denouncing the others, it seems likely that much of what they preached would have addressed the form of a good Christian life and the path to eventual salvation. The fundamental point is that, in contrast to earlier centuries, the rise of all these groups meant that there was a substantial increase in the amount of preaching addressed to a lay audience,

---

[66] *Cartulaire général*, p. 51 (no. 68): 'ut milites prescripti Templi traxerunt de Oliba de Candel prescriptum alodem, quia ille habebat in pignus per IIIIor libras argenti'. It is unclear to me from the laconic phrasing whether Oliba lent Acalaidis money and he now holds the land, or whether she lent him the money with the land held by her as surety; perhaps the former? (My thanks to Sethina Watson in discussion on this point.) But in either case, we are dealing with someone of wealth.

particularly an urban lay audience, beyond whatever provision the local priest was able to make in the local church. It is notable that the places mentioned for delivery of such sermons are often outdoors, in the market places and civic squares: larger venues than the local churches, and ones where an audience could come and go more or less at will. Going *to* the audience was very clearly another element which the Franciscans and Dominicans learned from the Good Men and Waldensians, as the impression given in the early histories of the order is of a sustainedly peripatetic life of preaching, going out from the cities where, as we have seen, they had their foundations.

In terms of providing a greater availability of pious services, another element was hearing confession. Domina de Coutes 'saw the Waldensians preaching publicly and gave them alms... Item on Good Friday she twice went to Waldensians and heard their preaching and she confessed her sins to a certain Waldensian, and accepted penance from the Waldensians.' Easter was when the laity were expected to confess their sins. As already noted, it has been very hard to glean much evidence from earlier centuries on how frequently this was done, and in how 'personalized' a manner, a topic to which we shall return again in a later chapter; but that it was an understood expectation is made clear by the fact that the Waldensians could step into the role. We frustratingly cannot date these events precisely, but it seems likely that they happened some long while before her trial in 1241, as she also noted that she had met a couple of Good Men with whom she had sat and eaten cherries, 'and it is said that they were reconciled [to the Church]', which could perhaps indicate the period leading up to the crusade, though this cannot be certain.[67] At what is clearly a point after the mendicants were established in the region, Garcias de Bonafous, who had heard the Good Men preaching and thought that nobody could be saved except by them, confessed to Cellan that 'when someone said to him that they wished to confess their sins to the Brothers Preacher or Minor, if they could find them, he would respond to them that if they were to speak with one of the Good Men, they could be saved'.[68] This did not imply that the Good Men actually 'heard confession of sins' in the same way as the Waldensians, since other evidence strongly suggests that they saw no merit in it (given the fallen nature of the corporeal world) but rather that, in line with Garcias's already stated beliefs, only they could proffer salvation. But it is of course a rather interesting piece of relatively early evidence for some lay people's desire to have a mendicant friar, rather than a parish priest, provide confession and penance; and at the same time, the logistical difficulties of managing this, given the relative sparsity of the mendicants at this time.

---

[67] Doat 21, fol. 241v.

[68] Doat 21, fols 305v–306r: 'Item cum quidam diceret ei quod libenter confiteretur peccata sua Fratribus Predicatoribus et Minoribus si inveniret eos, respondit ei quod si loqueretur cum aliquo de bonis hominibus posset salvari.' This is also quite strong evidence for seeing 'Good Men' as a title.

Of a piece with confession and preaching, the various mendicant holy men could also provide a wider sense of religious instruction. There is more which I shall say on all of these topics in a later chapter, taking evidence from the whole period up to the Black Death in order to draw upon later Dominican and Franciscan materials, among other things. It is however worth noting at this point that this too was an area in which the Waldensians and Good Men were active, potentially prior to the mendicants. Here, as above, I will focus primarily on events before or during the Albigensian Crusade (and will try to stray no later than the early 1240s in this chapter). From Cellan's sentences in 1241: 'Na Sauriz, wife of Bertrand de Montcuq, saw Waldensians and heard their preaching, and they taught her certain prayers, as she said'; 'Bernard de Caraves...heard expositions on the Passion by the Waldensians on Good Friday'; 'Guillaume de Catus...heard an exposition of the Gospels from a certain Waldensian'; 'Pierre Salinier twice saw heretics and heard their preaching, and the heretics...gave him the *Pater noster* of the heretics in writing'; 'Na Fauressa de Jouvengues ate with Waldensians and believed they were good men. Item another time she saw Waldensians on Good Friday and she went to them so that she could hear the exposition of the Passion, which she did'; Guillaume de Barbe went to see the Good Men, 'and he saw there someone reading the Apocalypse'.[69] There are of course some moments at which both groups also instructed lay people in more controversial matters, the Waldensians telling people that one should not swear an oath and that it was forbidden to kill (meaning, even if it was a legal execution),[70] the Good Men reported by a few people in these particular records as saying that one could *only* be saved through 'their Church' and that 'God would not neglect or destroy that which He had made' (potentially an indication of dualist belief, the implication being that God did not make the visible world).[71] But these are fairly rare occasions, and the point is that, whilst the beliefs of the Good Men and Waldensians diverge at points from orthodoxy, a good portion of Christian language, imagery, and practice is shared—which is of course why they were treated as *Christian* heretics.

We can also see more social functions played by certain holy men, some of which are initially more visible (because of the rich nature of the inquisition registers) for those accused of heresy than their orthodox counterparts.[72] We find

---

[69] Doat 21, fols 222v, 234v–235r, 236r–v, 257v, 274v, 300r–v.

[70] For example, Doat 21, fol. 201r: 'B. Bonaldi vidit P[etrum] de Vallibus valdensem et audivit predicationem eius, et credidit aliquando quod non debet homo iurare...'; fol. 214v: 'Blancha vidit Valdenses multotiens et in multis locis...et credebat aliquando quod nemo debebat iurare vel occidere'.

[71] Doat 21, fol. 217r–v, Petrus de Penna: 'Item...credebat quod Ecclesia heretica erat tantummodo Ecclesia, et quod nullus salvabatur in Ecclesia romana, sed omnes salvabuntur in Ecclesia heretica. Item dixit quod Deus non destruet quod fecit, nec praeteribit.'

[72] For interesting parallels in Italy for some of the roles discussed below, as performed by the mendicant orders, see F. Andrews, ed., *Churchmen and Urban Government in Medieval Italy, c. 1200–c. 1450* (Cambridge: Cambridge University Press, 2013), particularly the chapters in Part I, 'Urban Case Studies'.

certain Waldensians, for example, consulted for medical knowledge and advice, as is quite frequently attested in Cellan's sentences: 'Bertrand de Braulès received Pierre del Vals, Waldensian, into his house one time, so that he could have care of his children, who were ill'; 'Bernard de Caraves said that he had an ointment from the Waldensians when he was ill.'[73] Slightly later evidence shows us also at least one Good Man—Guillaume Bernard d'Airoux—who acted as a *medicus* for various people in the 1220s and perhaps later.[74] On a variety of occasions in the 1220s, 1230s, and early 1240s we find a Good Man acting as a peacemaker between disputing parties.[75] Sometimes this was clearly a formal 'arbitration' of the kind we met at the start of this chapter, with arguments from both sides being heard and a decision made by the Good Man. A witness in 1244 reported that the previous year, when the men of Laroque-d'Olmes were in dispute with Pierre Roger de Mirepoix (the co-lord of nearby Montségur), the two parties 'agreed upon [as arbitrator] Bertrand Marty, bishop of the heretics. And then the said Bertrand Marty, heretic, hearing the words and understanding the reasoned arguments (*rationibus*) of each party in the said quarrel or controversy, made amicable agreement between them'.[76] Bertrand Marty was in this instance performing a role which we would frequently find done elsewhere by bishops, judges, legal experts, or other 'worthy men'; and we similarly find some other instances where the dispute settled by a Good Man was regarding some financial issue.[77] This was also the case with orthodox mendicant friars: for example, in 1235 Brother Benoît of the Order of Preachers acted as an arbitrator in a complex commercial dispute between two merchants in Marseille.[78] (In his treatise on preaching, written in the 1260s, the Dominican Humbert de Romans noted that 'Some of the faithful seek counsel on matters of temporal interests, and we should not refuse them when charity demands it').[79] On other occasions though, the process was more explicitly tinged with the principle of Christian *caritas*: Bernard del Mas, knight

---

[73] Doat 21, fol. 189r; 234v–235r.
[74] For example, Doat 23, fol. 103v. Most of the evidence is gathered up in W. L. Wakefield, 'Heretics as Physicians in the Thirteenth Century', *Speculum* 57 (1982), 328–31.
[75] See P. Biller, 'Cathar Peace-making', in S. Ditchfield, ed., *Christianity and Community in the West: Essays for John Bossy* (Aldershot: Ashgate, 2001), pp. 1–23, with all relevant source extracts edited pp. 14–23; brief analysis in Arnold, *Inquisition and Power*, pp. 136–38.
[76] Doat 22, fols. 167r–167v, deposition of Galhard del Congost. The agreement took place in Montségur, which is about 15 km south of Laroque-d'Olmes, with at least eleven men from that village representing their interests. Also reported by Arnaud Roger, knight of Mirepoix, in his evidence, in which he makes clear that those of Laroque-d'Olmes paid Pierre Roger 20 *sous* as part of the settlement (Doat 22, fol. 121r–v).
[77] For example, when the Good Man Raimund Bernard agreed a settlement over a debt between the witness (Bernard Mir) and two knights to whom he seems to have been related, around 1225 (MS Toulouse 609, fol. 30r). For a slightly different reading of this event, cf. Pegg, *Corruption*, p. 120.
[78] Blanchard, *Documents... commerce de Marseille*, I, pp. 95–99 (no. 69).
[79] Humbert de Romans, *De eruditione praedicatorum* in M. de la Bigne, *Maxima Bibliotheca Veterum Patrum*, 27 vols (Lyon : Anissonios, 1677), vol. 25, p. 454 (cap. 42). See also cap. 41 on various ways in which the Dominicans found themselves involved in worldly matters. On the treatise see further C. Carozzi, 'Humbert de Romans et la prédication, *CdF* 36 (2001), 249–61.

of Mas-Saintes-Puelles, in his confession in 1245 recalled an event around 1230, when he had gone to the house of Pierre Cap de Porc. There he found Jean de Sainte-Foi, a Good Man, and his unnamed companion (the Good Men usually travelled in pairs). 'And the said heretic asked him, the witness, to make peace with the said Cap de Porc, as at that time the witness had hatred [for him]; which he did'. The Good Men then preached to an audience of 'many others, up to forty people' who had gathered for the event.[80]

But to ask again what these various holy men provided to the ordinary laity, the overwhelmingly clear role was that, through their closeness to the apostolic life and as 'friends of God', they were suitable recipients for gifts and almsgiving, and presented a potential route to future salvation. Deponents before Pierre Cellan admitted giving unspecified alms to the Waldensians and the Good Men, but sometimes we get more particular detail, in these and other trials. Guillelma de Roquefort admitted to seeing Good Men on one occasion only, but gave them a shirt and shoes and a dish of grain. Raimunda, wife of Guillaume d'Engolema, saw the Waldensians many times, and sent them 10 *sous* and 8d. Pons de la Lonquière saw Waldensians and heard their preaching many times, 'and gave them alms, and believed that they were good men and that a person could be saved in their faith'. Alazais Blancha stayed with some Good Women, and 'gave alms' to Waldensians.[81] Austorga, wife of Pierre de Rosengua, confessed among other things that when she was in Toulouse at 'the time of the war', in about 1227, two Good Women, Asalmurs and Alaicia de Cucurou, were neighbours of hers, and she made them woollen things to wear, and gave them some grain and 6d. Arnaud Pons admitted that when the Waldensians were 'living publicly' at Lordat, he once 'gave alms to a certain Waldensian', this being around 1226.[82]

By far and away the most recurrent gifts to the Good Men (and often also to the Waldensians) were however symbolically rather important: bread and wine and fish, all heavily resonant with the example of Christ.[83] Why were these figures suitable recipients of such gifts? For the most part, running along the rails set by inquisitorial formulae but not necessarily distorting the deponents' own perceptions greatly, because 'they were good men and had a good faith' and could lead one 'to a good end'; that is, could provide salvation. But occasionally we get a little

---

[80] MS Toulouse 609, fol. 16v: 'Et dictus heretics rogavit tunc ipsum testem quod pacificaret se cum dicto Cap de Porc, quem tunc ipse testis habebat hodio, quod et fecit. Et dicti heretici predicaverunt ibi, et vidit ibi in illa predicatione W. del Mas et Jordanum, fratres ipsius testis, et Garnerium del Mas et Jordanum et Petrum Gauta et W. Vital ; et plures alios, usque ad XL personas, sed non recolit de nominibus eorum'. Another similar case involving two identically named relatives, fol. 200v : '...et omnes audierunt predicantes eorum et dicti heretici fecerunt pacem inter Raymundum Unaut et Raymundum Unaut predictos consanguineos qui habebant se odio, et sunt xv anni vel circa'. This was in Toulouse, around 1231; the Good Men named were Guilabert de Castres, Bernard de Mota, and Guillaume del Soler.

[81] Doat 21, fols. 190v, 206v, 243v, 243v–244r.

[82] Doat 24, fols. 1v, 281r: 'et ipse testis dedit cuidam Valdensi semel elemosinam'.

[83] See Arnold, *Inquisition and Power*, 199 and references given there.

more specific nuance: Guillaume de *Catus* sought medical aid for his children from the Waldensians, 'heard an exposition of the Gospels from a certain Waldensian' and when on one occasion 'he wished to give them alms...they refused to accept them'. Overall, 'he believed that they were good men, and that which they said and did pleased him'.[84] Boneta, wife of Guillaume Geral senior, saw heretics a few times, and 'saw Waldensians and twice gave them bread and wine, and believed that they did good'.[85] Guillelma, wife of Pons Guillaume, 'saw heretics and heard their preaching...Item she gave a certain heretic a shirt and some pears, and she believed that the heretics were good men, because they fasted', emphasizing a different aspect of holiness and apostolicity.[86] Rather more intensely, a woman called Pana often received Waldensians, gave them bread and wine, held a disputation in her house between 'believers of the heretics' and the Waldensians, 'and she loved Pierre de Vals [Waldensian] like an angel of God'.[87] It is very hard to find any potential orthodox parallel in this period due to the nature of surviving documents, but very occasionally something becomes visible: in the far south-east of the region, a witness in a case heard by the bishop of Antibes in 1222 reported that in the preceding years, although the priory of Villebruc (a village just outside Valbonne) made use of a certain garden without any formal permission, the owner of the land, Raimond de La Faye, had allowed this 'because [he said] they were good men'. The men of the priory had sent Raimond some of the produce of the garden, though the witness did not know if this was 'through service or through love'; and Raimond sent them bread and wine, and said that they should use things from the garden 'to improve your church'. We get to hear of this only because the relationship had subsequently broken down, leading to a formal legal dispute and episcopal arbitration.[88] It is not hard to imagine that other such relationships existed elsewhere.

In *The Corruption of Angels* Mark Pegg evocatively discusses almsgiving to the Good Men in terms of anthropological theories of 'the Gift', arguing that they were constitutive in forming the social relationship of 'believer' and 'Good Man', a relationship that he sees as being dramatically re-coded by inquisitors—and perhaps thus also in the memory of deponents—in the later interrogations, to present (Pegg argues) something misleadingly structured and sect-like for that particular group.[89] It is true that the act of gifting forged a relationship, implying a spiritual countergift, and perhaps thus hoping for eventual intercession for one's own soul and those of one's family; in other words, a similar dynamic to that which various scholars have suggested for the donations made to monasteries in the preceding centuries. Seen in this way, a point to emphasize is how the spread

---

[84] Doat 21, fol. 236r–v.   [85] Doat 21, fol. 282r–v.
[86] Doat 21, fols 292v–293r.   [87] Doat 21, fol. 203v.
[88] G. Doublet, ed., *Recueil des actes concernant les évêques d'Antibes* (Paris : Picard, 1915), 219–20 (no. 164).
[89] Pegg, *Corruption*, chapter 15. On gifting to monasteries, see this volume, Chapter 1.

of the Good Men and Waldensians—and to some extent the knightly orders, as we saw in Chapter 3, and then subsequently the mendicant orders—made such a relationship more possible below the ranks of the nobility (though both major and minor nobles were undoubtedly still a major source of financial support for the new orders, and sometimes for the heretical groups also).

This kind of dynamic clearly continues into the thirteenth century and beyond. As we have already seen, the first Dominican foundation in Toulouse rested upon the gift of houses by Pierre Cellan, at that point a major citizen. A similar social stratum—that is, the mercantile civic elite, rather than the regional nobility—can be seen in the following extract from Bernard Gui's history of the foundation of the Order of Preachers in Cahors:

> In the year of Our Lord 1226, the brothers of the Order of Preachers, Pierre Cellan of Toulouse (then prior of the convent of Limoges) and Pons de Mons, were called by the venerable fathers and lords Guillaume, bishop of Cahors, and Pons, then his sacrist... to receive a place in the town of Cahors, where the Brother Preachers could be installed, from which to serve God. Raimond Benoît, bourgeois of Cahors, infirm in body and seeing the approach of death, on the counsel of his medic, Master Arnaud de Ségus, had called at night for the said Brothers, who were then staying in the house of the Lady of Concort... They, acceding within the hour to the request of the sacrist, then came to the said ill man... and received the donation of the garden which he possessed near the church of Saint Didier, in the street called La Fordane in the vernacular.
>
> ...After a long time, there was there the convent of the Brothers, with a tile-covered church, a chapel for the sick, the cloister, the dormitory, the infirmary and all the other annexes. They stayed there until the time of Lord Arnaud Béraud, who, because of the particular affection that he had for the Order, and seeing them living in solitude beyond the walls of the town—for at that time there were few houses outside the walls—he invited the Brothers to move themselves to a more fitting place nearer to the town... He then gave them some land which he had beyond the river, near Saint-Pierre de la Hortes, and 100 *livres* of Tours to start upon the building works. Later, the same Lord Arnaud Béraud was buried there, in the year of Our Lord 1261...[90]

The gift for the initial foundation is prompted by the imminent demise of the townsman Raimond Benoît, who probably gained subsequent burial and memorial masses through tying himself to the Brother Preachers. The second gift by Arnaud Béraud, a major merchant involved in the international wine trade (the 'lord' appears to be honorific rather than an indication of noble status), binds him

---

[90] Gui, *De fundatione*, pp. 75–76.

to the order and their spiritual intercession in both life and death.[91] We have in fact slightly more detail on the latter, from a later obituary roll: 'Lady Sebelia, wife of the late Lord Arnaud Béraud, first founder of this convent, who is buried in the chapter, in the tomb of her said husband, that is at the feet of the prior; and she willed 100 *sous* of Cahors annually for the anniversary [mass] for herself, her father and mother and daughter, and in addition two pounds of wax [paid for] by the houses which she possessed at the time of her death…'.[92] Both husband and then widow achieve a continued relationship with the order after death, bound by gifting, obtaining a highly preferential place of burial, and a long-continued obituary mass.[93]

In potential contrast to this kind of act, as we move later in time do we start to see the laity drawing a qualitative distinction between the reciprocal dynamic of 'the gift' and the act of 'almsgiving' as something more disinterested? That is, as the opportunities for pious and particularly apostolic engagement multiply across the turn of the thirteenth century, do we see any sense of the act of donation having meaning *purely* in itself, as an act of piety, 'giving' as a means of engaging in an apostolically enjoined role rather than gifting as a means of binding oneself to a favoured group? This is admittedly by no means a clear binary distinction: one can give to holy men to share jointly in a sense of apostolic performance, and hope that in the process one gains additional spiritual favour from their friendship with God; that is surely what Acalaidis was doing. One can also give to the poor in the hope of them praying for one's soul; a meritorious act, understood in a vaguely transactional way. But it is nonetheless worth asking whether we can see examples of almsgiving which look to be done primarily for the act itself rather than the specific connection it forges or outcome it engineers.

The point in asking this is not because it is a 'better' or 'more authentic' act, but because it speaks to a potential shift in the spiritual dynamic of the role available to the lay donor. For the non-elite, such acts are hard to see in our sources, as what is most visible (and even then, for those lower down the social scale, only occasionally visible even by the early thirteenth century) are pious bequests in wills, where issues of imminent salvation tend to come to the fore. Some elements within these do suggest a general culture of almsgiving in its own right, such as

---

[91] Arnaud Béraud sold 8 barrels of wine to the English king for a payment of over £9 in 1252; see P. Wolff, 'Le problème des Cahorsins', *Annales du Midi* 62 (1950), 229–38, at p. 232 n. 16.

[92] Doat 121, fol. 211r: 'Domina Sebelia uxor quondam Domini Arnaldi Beraldi primi fundatoris istius conventus que sepulta est in capitulo in sepulcro dicti viri sui, quod est ad pedes ad prioris et legavit centum solidos caturceneses annuales pro anniversario suo patris, et matris, et filie, et ultra hoc duas libras cere super domos quas habebat tempore mortis sue…'

[93] The majority of obits recorded in the roll (surviving now only in the seventeenth-century copy in the Collection Doat) are from the fifteenth century, suggesting that as its period of compilation. To give a sense of how 'special' the relationship being forged here was, there are only two other thirteenth-century obits listed in addition to Sebelia's (fols 201v, 203r), and only another eight within the period up to the Black Death.

bequests simply to 'the poor' and to dowries for poor women, with no specific mention of reciprocal prayers. The 1195 will of one Guillaume d'Agde, recorded in the cartulary of the cathedral (where he gained burial), is a fairly rare example from this period left by someone who does not seem to be tremendously rich (he left just over 20 *sous* and various amounts of grain) and who embraced a fair degree of pious giving. Having given larger sums to the priory of Bessan and to various monks, he gave a very small amount of wheat ('unam [h]eminam', a small liquid measure) to the hospital of the poor, the leper house, the 'charity', the lights of a certain church, the upkeep of the city's bridge, the hospital of Garrigue, and similarly to some other foundations. Symbolic rather than useful, given the size of the bequests; but nonetheless embracing a mode of general almsgiving that we might see as 'apostolic' in its inspiration.[94] The habit of spreading bequests around various religious institutions, existing to some extent already from the later twelfth century (as discussed in Chapter 3), can be part of this, though it also sometimes looks to be a means of extending one's pious network and thus hedging one's spiritual bets in terms of post-mortem memorialization.

Greater wealth of course allowed one greater options: another will from the Agde cartulary records one Pons Carbonel in 1234 who, alongside various gifts of around 20 *sous* to particular churches, bequeathed 5,000 *sous* of Melgueil 'to distribute to the poor for redemption of my soul'.[95] There is a sense of a familial shared mode of piety here: we have the wills also of his brother (1233), father (1215), and mother (1225), all of whom also gave to 'the poor' in various different ways, albeit not quite as extravagantly.[96] These were gifts from a wealthy, landowning family. But from moments within the inquisition registers we very occasionally glimpse a wider culture of pious giving, undertaken by less elite people, not when contemplating death in a testamentary mode, but within life. Pierre de Les Barthes said in his confession in 1246 that at some earlier unspecified point 'Gaillarde Brune de Castres asked him... to give her half a quarter of corn for the work of two poor women, which he did, and afterwards he heard it said that these two women were Waldensians'.[97] In the same inquisition, Raimond Biac said that 'at the urging of Pierre Marty, his lord, for three years he gave the Waldensians a quarter of grain annually' (this perhaps around a decade earlier than his interrogation).[98] As with the other cases of almsgiving to heretics noted further above, these all speak to a wider culture of charity, propelled by neighbourly

---

[94] *Cart. S. Étienne d'Agde*, p. 164 (no. 79); see similarly will of Pons de Fenouillet, 1187, pp. 169-70 (no. 83), already mentioned in Chapter 3.
[95] *Cart. S. Étienne d'Agde*, pp. 403-06 (no. 364).
[96] *Cart. S. Étienne d'Agde*, pp. 393-94 (no. 358), 394 (no. 359), 403 (no. 363).
[97] MS Toulouse 609, fol. 248v: 'dixit tamen quod Galharda Bruna de Castris rogavit eum ipsum testis quod daret sibi quod daret [sic] mediam carteria bladi ad opus duarum mulierum pauperum, quod et fecit. Et postea audivit dici quod ille mulieres erant Valdenses.'
[98] MS Toulouse 609, fol. 249r: 'Dixit etiam quod ad instanciam Petri Martini domini sui dedit per tres annos dictis Valdensibus quolibet anno unam carteriam bladi.'

expectation and encouragement.[99] That the recipients were 'heretics' is simply what now makes these specific acts *visible* to us.

One general point to make, in line with other existing work, is essentially a further elaboration of a fundamental change discussed in Chapter 3: that the growth of these various apostolically inspired spiritual specialists provided greater opportunities for people lower down the social scale, and often in a civic setting, to engage in pious giving and invest in their future salvation. Some immediate qualifications are however needed to that statement. Those *founding* hospitals, Templar or Hospitaller foundations, and many of the later mendicant convents, were often still members of the regional nobility; and this would also in fact be the case with many subsequent donors. There is, in other words, some continuity with the social dynamics around Cistercian monasteries, even if more foundations are in civic locations (a point to which I shall return further below). But the foundations discussed in this chapter, in part by dint of their predominantly civic locations, became more permeable to wider donation, as was very clearly the case also with both the Waldensians and the Good Men (both groups sometimes benefiting from elite patronage but for the most part not requiring the expensive architectural investment of the other orders).[100]

Part of what I therefore want to argue is that these developments—the wider lay engagement with those practising a form of *vita apostolica* and the efflorescence of charity—are intimately connected with the growth of towns and cities. The point has been made by others before, primarily in two senses: that cities attract those in poverty, whose needs thus become more apparent to a growing bourgeoisie who had the wherewithal to give charitably; and that the growth of mercantile activity and wealth prompted a spiritual need among the merchant class, eager to find an outlet for their own piety that would offset the clear demerit of personal riches ('Easier for a camel...' etc).[101] As André Vauchez and others have argued, it is the subsequent rise of the mendicant preachers that further amplifies this message and engenders further lay engagement.[102] There is nothing in that picture with which I disagree. But it is worth noting additionally that, as we have seen, there are apostolic models of piety that found some favour in the

---

[99] The claim that these things were given at the urging of someone else could, of course, be read as an attempt to protect oneself from the inquisitor, and this might be the case with Pierre de Les Barthes, who admitted to no other contact; Raimond Biac, however, admitted to believing in the Waldensians, which makes such an interpretation less likely.

[100] One notable exception would be the request by the Good Men to Raimond de Péreille, co-lord of Montségur, to repair the fortress of Montségur, which he said they made to him in about 1204: Doat 22, fol. 217v: 'Item dicit quod ipse testis ad instantiam et preces Raimundi de Mirapisce et Raimundi Blasquo et aliorum hereticorum rehedificavit castrum montis securi quod antea destructum extiterat et postmodum ipse testis tenuit et receptavit in dicto castro prefatos hereticos et alios multos...De tempore quod sunt quadraginte anni et amplius' (the deposition given in late April 1244).

[101] J. Le Goff, *Your Money or Your Life: Economy and Religion in the Middle Ages* (New York: Zone, 1988).

[102] Vauchez, *La spiritualité*, chapter 4 ; Le Blévec, *La part du pauvre*, I, pp. 167–68, 187.

south of France from fairly early on in the twelfth century, and holy men and hospitals—associated strongly, albeit not exclusively, with towns—became widely visible rather earlier than the arrival of mendicant establishments. It is also worth emphasizing again the most basic implication of civic location: it makes any holy person or group or foundation visible and potentially available to a larger number of ordinary people than is the case for any rural foundation, visible not only to those resident within the particular town or city but to a flow of others who would visit a town or city for reasons of commerce. Moreover I would suggest, in partial contrast to an established line of analysis in earlier historiography, that the difference that urbanization made to prompt these developments was not the increased visibility of the actual poor, but the increased civic visibility of apostolic holy men and women.

It is not remotely original for me to note that the growth of towns thus matters to developments in lay piety. But it is still useful to explore the particular features of this growth as it pertains to the south of France, not least because there are aspects to it which matter considerably in negotiations between civic and ecclesiastical authorities in later decades (as we shall see in Chapters 5 and 9). In the region, as across much of western Europe, the twelfth and thirteenth centuries saw considerable population growth, an accompanying expansion in the size of existing urban settlements and the creation of new ones, and an associated growth in artisanal and mercantile economic activity. The causative factors are not fully understood, but recent research tends to point generally to climate change and a 'medieval warm period' that stretched from roughly 950 to 1250, albeit with considerable regional and temporal deviation; a warmer climate, it is thought, increased crop yield and farmable land, depressed infant mortality, and increased protein and nutrients within ordinary people's diets.[103] The wider argument is far beyond the remit of this book; suffice to say that it is clear that population grew, and towns and cities along with it.

A particularly notable feature to increased urbanization in southern France is that it was accompanied by a fairly swift and widespread sense of what, for want of a precise contemporary word, one might call 'self-conscious civicness'. By this I mean, firstly, that from fairly early on—as in northern Italy and Catalonia—we find a number of urban settlements that were run by an elected consulate. 'Election' does not imply a broad democracy, but that the consuls (that title consciously echoing ancient Roman terminology) were chosen by a larger body of adult males—often referred to as the *universitas* of the town or city—and usually then 'approved' by whichever lord or bishop or monarch had ultimate dominion there. The numbers of consuls varied—in small places perhaps only four, in larger cities maybe twelve or more—and the office-holders were to be renewed annually.

---

[103] J. H. Arnold, *What is Medieval History?* 2nd edn (Cambridge: Polity, 2020), pp. 84–85.

Accompanying this, secondly, we have a variety of agreed 'customs' that granted certain rights and liberties to 'all the men and women' of the place (a number of such documents emphasizing that they applied to both sexes). These frequently set out how justice would operate within the town, usually reserving the punishment of homicide and major theft to the lord whilst delegating judicial process for lesser crimes to the consuls or wider community of *prud'hommes*.[104] They often also bestowed rights related to the inhabitants' ability to trade (including, for example, to lend and to borrow against pledged property without interference by the lord), to be freed from various lordly exactions on land or the movement of goods, and affirming the right of all men and women to make wills, to dispose of their own property. And third, probably running alongside these developments and clearly widespread by the turn of the thirteenth century, there were notaries who facilitated, recorded, and archived a variety of transactions, agreements, and arbitrations between people, and also often people's wills. The presence of the notaries meant, in theory at least, that ordinary people had potential access to documentation and law (as it pertained to property, debt, and trade at least), in both the vernacular and Latin.[105] By the early thirteenth century, and probably before then, southern French legal processes clearly treated the written word as providing an authoritative form of proof, and the production of a written notarial 'instrument' was constitutive of commercial and other agreements rather than simply providing a record of them.

It is important to note that by the later twelfth century, we find civic 'customs' not only for the great cities and large towns (the date of the earliest extant customs given in brackets)—Albi (1188), Arles (c. 1162), Avignon (before 1126), Béziers (1185), Cahors (late twelfth century), Castres (1160), Moissac (before 1130), Montauban (1144), Nîmes (1145), Perpignan (1162), Toulouse (1152)— but also for some smaller locales. Thus Aucamville, a small town just north of Toulouse, received a fairly detailed set of customs from the lord of Isle-Jourdain at some point in the late twelfth century; Codalet, a small *castrum* in the far south, in the foothills of the Canigou mountains, gained a charter from the count of

---

[104] Thus, for example, Arles, customs of 1162 (I follow here Carbasse's re-dating), where the consuls play a major role in judgments for assault and other crimes: C. Giraud, *Essai sur l'histoire du droit français au Moyen Âge*, 2 vols (Paris: Videcoq Père et Fils, 1846), II, pp. 1–4, at 2. A formal statement of this role becomes more common in the thirteenth century. The earliest surviving record of consular proceedings of which I am aware is from Nîmes in 1217–18, edited in L. Ménard, *Histoire civile, ecclésiastique et littéraire de la ville de Nismes*, 7 vols (Paris: Hugues-Daniel Chaubert, 1750–58), I, *preuves*, pp. 55–63 (no. 44).

[105] F. Bréchon, 'Autour du notariat: des nouvelles pratiques de l'écrit dans les régions méridionales aux XII et XIIIe siècles', in P. Guichard and D. Alexandre-Bidon, eds, *Comprendre le XIII siècle: études offerts à Marie-Therese Lorcin* (Lyon: Presses universitaires de Lyon, 1995), pp. 161–72; S. Desachy, 'Le XIIIe siècle, ou la révolution du notariat', *Revue du Tarn* 217 (2010), 115–26; S. Desachy, ed., *De la Ligurie au Languedoc: le notaire à l'étude* (Albi: Un Autre Reg'Art, 2012). An important but unpublished study for the notariate in later decades is Jamie Corner, 'Literacy and Lay Society in the Sénéchaussé of Carcassonne, c. 1270–1330', unpublished DPhil., Oxford, 2005.

Barcelona in 1142; Montech (c. 13 km south-west of Montauban) was granted a charter of customs by the count of Toulouse in 1136; and Verlhac-Tescou, a really small settlement (c. 20 km south-east of Montauban), gained one from the duke of Perigord at some point in the late twelfth century.[106] We can see now only those written customs which have survived, sometimes in very local archives; it seems highly likely that many more originally existed in smaller settlements. There are extant customs from the twelfth century for at least thirty different cities, towns, and *castra* falling within the lands covered by this book, nearly a third of which originate before 1150. Between 1200 and 1240 (to take a terminal date for other evidence used in this particular chapter), we find an additional forty-three settlements with customs. Across the whole period to 1240, some of those seventy-three locales generated additional documents, setting out further customs and liberties.[107] Many more are extant for other towns, and fresh customs created for the original group, as we move across the thirteenth and into the fourteenth century.[108]

All of this is interesting in terms of the history of urbanization, and despite good existing work on particular cities and some towns, and on the spread of Roman law via the notariate, there is much which could yet be done, particularly in terms of setting a southern French picture within a wider comparative landscape. But for my present purposes, certain things can be gleaned. We are reminded that trade, both over long distances and more locally, was a key feature of this landscape, particularly but not only for settlements situated near the larger rivers or the Mediterranean coast. The lengthy statutes for Moissac, given by the secular-abbot of the monastery to the town some time before 1130, set out detailed rules regarding debt, mortgages, and a lengthy set of *leudes* (tolls) imposed on goods, the latter providing a fair sense of what incoming and resident merchants traded through the town, which sat at the confluence of the Tarn and Garonne rivers: animal skins, horses, sheep, donkeys, cows, glass vessels, cups, bowls, combs, needles, knives, scissors, and other metal tools, salt, wine, wheat, meat, fish, cumin, and sumac. A few presumably local and low-value items attracted no additional charges: reeds, feathers, stones, 'foliage', grindstones, and

---

[106] There is an invaluable list of published customs compiled by J.-M. Carbasse, 'Bibliographie des coutumes méridionales', *Recueil de mémoires et travaux de la Société d'histoire du droit et des institutions des anciens pays de droit écrit* 10 (1979), 7–89; I am most grateful to Leah Otis for bringing this to my attention, and for general advice. I will give publication references to specific customs below when discussing them in detail.

[107] These figures generated from Carbasse, 'Bibliographie', but ignoring customs listed there which are regional rather than attached to specific towns (and very occasionally re-dating some customs on the basis of their internal evidence).

[108] Demonstrating among other things the profusion of additional customs created by many towns from the thirteenth century onward, see M. Berthe, 'Les coutumes de la France méridionale: programme de recherche et premiers résultats', in M. Mousnier and J. Poumarède, eds, *La coutume au village dans l'Europe médiévale et moderne* (Toulouse: Presses universitaires du Midi, 2001), pp. 121–37. For important recent interpretive work, D. Lett, ed., *La confection des statuts dans les sociétés méditerranéennes de l'Occident (XIIe–XIVe siècles)* (Paris: Éditions de la Sorbonne, 2017).

other sharpening stones.[109] Statutes from nearby Montauban, from the late twelfth century, show us yet more items, including oil, nuts, almonds, lard, flax, pepper, horn, wool, and honey.[110] The variety of goods is suggestive of both the volume of activity and the considerable stratification of trade—and presumably therefore also lay society—ranging from merchants importing goods and livestock over long distances to local traders dealing with low-value items. Nor was concern with trade visible only in larger towns like Moissac. Fendeille, a very small *castrum* just south of Castelnaudary, has customs from 1202 which, whilst much briefer, nonetheless speak to small-scale local economic activity:

> And he who sells oats shall give a penny in grain tax (*in cesterio*); and if he sells a lot, he shall justly give 4d. And he who sells his wine, he shall declare it publicly (*faciat eum clamare*), and if he sells a lot, he shall justly give 12d.... And he who sells grain, of whatever kind, if it is not done via the established measures, buyer and seller will justly give 2 *sous*.... He who sells meat, [shall give] 1d and the offal for each *sous* of profit; and if he sells a lot, he shall justly give 12d.[111]

The mention of the local trade in wine is important, as vast numbers of charters from across the region make it clear that many people had small vineyards, or part shares in vineyards; it must have been a long-standing and perennial feature of local economic activity, as well as some long-distance trade. And of course, at the other end of the economic spectrum, if we were to head to the Mediterranean coast, to Narbonne or Marseille or Montpellier, we would find a huge amount of longer-distance trade, high in value and high in commercial (and human) risk, connecting the region to Italy, Spain, north Africa, and the Levant. Later in the thirteenth century, and continuing through the first half of the fourteenth century, southern France also saw a growing textile industry, connecting major towns and smaller centres of production to international markets.[112]

What all this means, among other things, is that when we come to think about 'apostolic example' and poverty in southern France, we are dealing with a society

---

[109] A. Lagrèze-Fossat, *Études historiques sur Moissac, t. 1* (Paris: J.-B. Dumoulin, 1870), pp. 67–96 (customs), 97–111 (*leudes*). These customs, written in Occitan, survive in a later thirteenth-century *vidimus*; a much shorter version in Latin, possibly pre-dating them, has been edited also: M. Brissaud, 'Les coutumes de Moissac', *Bulletin archéologique et historique de la Société archéologique de Tarn-et-Garonne* (1895), 333–43. As noted in Chapter 3 (p. 88), the monastery of Moissac rather problematically had both a religious-abbot and a secular-abbot at this time.

[110] Customs of Montauban 1194–95: D. Ainé, *Histoire de Montauban* (Montauban: Imprimerie de Forestié Neveau et Compagnie, 1855), pp. 415–26, at p. 423.

[111] A. Sabarthès, 'Charte communale de Fendeille (Aude), 1202', *Bulletin du Comité des travaux historiques et scientifiques: section d'histoire et de philologies* (1901), 579–84.

[112] M. Bourin, 'De nouveaux chemins de développement dans le Languedoc d'avant la peste', in J. Drendel, ed., *Crisis in the Later Middle Ages: Beyond the Postan-Duby Paradigm* (Turnhout: Brepols, 2015), pp. 251–72; J. Drendel, 'The Modern State and the Economy in Provence and Southern France in the Early Fourteenth Century', *Memini: travaux et documents* 19–20 (2016), 213–25.

which by the end of the twelfth century already had growing and widespread experience of commerce and market production, was used to conceptualizing profit and loss in general terms at least, made much use of credit and debt across many strata of society, and which probably had a fair amount of small coin in circulation.[113] At a very basic but nonetheless fundamentally important level, the point about coinage in particular affects both the breadth and the potential nature of charitable engagement: if you are not wealthy but you have pennies, you can give pennies, which may often be a more practical and certainly a more fungible offering than, say, fresh fruit or bread. And as in commerce, coinage permits the *possibility* at least of what we might call an 'impersonalization' of alms, gently dislocating the kind of close bonds imagined in the anthropological model of the gift. The other points about profit, credit, and so forth suggest that one might explore, for an earlier chronology, the powerful analysis presented by Jacques Chiffoleau's study of Avignonnais wills, of how salvation becomes 'accountable' in the later middle ages, that is, cognitively structured in continuum with ideas of profit, loss, and investment.[114]

I shall return to some of these issues in later chapters, but as we consider these early civic customs, it is worth looking to see how much those documents are inflected by explicit or implicit Christian ideas, images, or precepts. The customs are, in every case, 'given' by the relevant lord—whether abbot, bishop, local lord, or distant monarch—to the town or city, occasionally arising through a process of dispute between the lord and the community, but often bestowed by the lord because of the income generated by the town's activities (and on occasion, its direct payment for its privileges). Across the corpus, the repetition of certain phrasing and many general items strongly suggest that the customs emerge from a shared legal culture, and perhaps from circulated textual models (something which becomes more strongly apparent in the second half of the thirteenth century, when particular sets of customs were circulated widely and appeared to become quite influential, such as the so-called 'établissements de Saint Louis').[115] But they assert in most cases the importance of specifically *local* customs, in some early examples not actually listed in detail but simply taken as already being in existence. It is clear that the contents of at least some of these derive not solely

---

[113] Coinage: M. Castaing-Sicard, *Monnaies féodales et circulation monétaire en Languedoc, Xe–XIIIe siècles* (Toulouse: Association Marc Bloch, 1961); I have not been able to consult M. Bompaire, 'La circulation monétaire en Languedoc: Xe–XIIIe siècle', unpublished doctoral dissertation, Université de Paris IV, 2002. On credit and debt as commonplace by the late twelfth century, M. Castaing, 'Le prêt à intérêt à Toulouse aux XIIe et XIIIe siècles', *Bulletin philologique et historique* 1953/54 (1955), 273–78.

[114] J. Chiffoleau, *La comptabilité de l'Au-Delà: les hommes, la mort et la religion dans la région d'Avignon à la fin du Moyen Age (vers 1320–vers 1480)* (Rome: École française de Rome, 1980). See somewhat similarly also T. Ruiz, *From Heaven to Earth: The Reordering of Castilian Society, 1150–1350* (Princeton University Press, 2004), though I do not think one need view such developments as indicating 'insincerity' (see p. 128).

[115] F. R. P. Akehurst, ed., *The Etablissements de Saint Louis: Thirteenth-Century Law Texts from Tours, Orleans and Paris* (Philadelphia: University of Pennsylvania Press, 1996).

from top-down imposition, but also from the desires of the inhabitants—or of those *prud'hommes* who would be likely to be consuls, at any rate. There is a possibility, therefore, that we can see refracted through them some sense of the choices and emphases made by the laity when setting out some fundamental structures for a functioning society, and in the case of some of the small towns and *castra*, a not-very-elite lay society (though it should also be noted that in some towns the consulate includes a balance of local knights and local *prud'hommes*).

The picture we then get regarding Christian ideology is mixed. Some customs are strongly framed by reference to God: 'In the name of the holy and individual Trinity and our mother church and the Catholic faith' as the 1187 customs of Millau begin, for example; or, more impressively from Moissac in the early twelfth century, '...the said inhabitants hold the customs from unchanging law, unchanging for all time, in honour of God and of the blessed Saint Mary mother of our Lord Jesus Christ, and of the blessed apostles St Peter and St Paul, under the power and under the patronage of which the aforesaid bourg of Moissac and all the inhabitants of the said bourg exist'.[116] Quite a few (though by this stage not all) specify that consuls must make an oath to uphold their office whilst touching the Gospels, and in the customs of Arles (1162 × 64), given by the local archbishop, this ends with the injunction 'thus may God aid me and these holy gospels of God', and goes on to say that through this process 'Thus it is confirmed for peace, renewal and reform; and by him [the consul], as best he is able, the church of God, monasteries and religious places, routes and streets, on water and land, will be ruled and governed'.[117] In contrast, other customs make no mention of any Christian elements, such as those for Aucamville in the late twelfth century or for Gaillac in 1221.[118]

The most common mark that Christianity leaves on the customs—of course reflecting the most long-standing and deeply rooted sense of a widespread Christian culture—is in terms of the temporal rhythm to the year. As one would expect, a variety of major Christian feasts and saints' days are used to signal the time at which various events would occur; if one browses any monastic cartulary, a similar pattern would swiftly be visible, principally in regard to when various tithes and other lordly dues are to be rendered. The same basic mechanism persists in an urban setting, sometimes in much the same fashion: for example, the customs of Isle-Jourdain (late twelfth century) include provision that on the feast

---

[116] Customs of Millau, 1187, bestowed by Alphonse, king of Aragon (M. A. F. de Gaujal, *Études historiques sur Rouergue*, 4 vols (Paris: Imprimerie administrative de Paul Dupont, 1858–59), I, pp. 283–84; Customs of Moissac, before 1130, c. 1 (Lagrèze-Fossat, *Études historiques*, pp. 67–68).

[117] Giraud, *Essai sur l'histoire du droit français*, II, pp. 3–4.

[118] Aucamville mentions the feast of St John the Baptist as the date for electing new consuls, but is otherwise devoid of any Christian reference, including in its oath (Galabert, 'La charte des coutumes d'Aucamville'); Gaillac's customs, written in the vernacular, lack even this (M. Greslé-Bouignol, 'La charte de Gaillac de 1221', *Annales du Midi* 86 (1974), 93–97).

of St Martin (11 November), the 'house' of Saint-Martin (a priory at that point) should have all the loins and breasts of animals slaughtered or sold on that day.[119] Similarly those for Cordes (1222) specify that for each pig slaughtered on a Saturday or Sunday, or on the annual feasts of the Blessed Virgin or the apostles 'and all other feasts having fasts' (that is, where there was a day of fasting on the eve of the feast), all the hindlegs were to be rendered to the lord of the town; the butchers also had to pay the lord 2d on Christmas Day.[120] Particular towns had other activities or privileges connected to the ritual year, most frequently the day for choosing the following year's consuls, but also such things as the three periods of the year in which a lord could demand military service (this at Bagnères-de-Bigorre, 1171, a town very far to the west, near Lourdes), or the injunction at Meyrueis (1229) that for the fortnight following the feast of St Michel (29 September) all householders had to clean the street in front of their house or pay a 6d fine.[121]

But the most important aspect was probably the way that mercantile activity and sacred dates combined, as we find in a variety of locales. Bagnères (c. 15) permitted 'any men and women' to sell wine or cider between Easter and Pentecost, so long as they paid the lord 1d for each cask they sold. In Toulouse (customs of 1152) all people both from the city and from elsewhere had safe passage in Toulouse and its suburbs for four days before and four days after the feasts of St Étienne (26 December), St Mary's Assumption (15 August), and St Sernin (29 November), and between Christmas Day and the feast of Circumcision (1 January) and throughout Lent, so long as they were not evildoers.[122] At Saint-Antonin-Noble-Val, customs from 1144 give the same pattern of four days safety either side of the feast of St Antonin (2 September). In Puigcerdà, a town in the Pyrenees (now in Spain), customs from 1181 specify the right to a fair on the feast of the Assumption. Customs for Montcuq give eight days' safe passage, for the

---

[119] Customs of Isle-Jourdain, c. 38; E. Cabié, 'Coutumes de la ville de l'Isle-Jourdain XIIe siècle', *Nouvelle revue historique de droit français et étranger* (1881), 643–53.
[120] Customs of Cordes, 1222, c. 7: C. Portal, *Histoire de la ville de Cordes, Tarn (1222–1799)* (Cordes: Bosquet, 1902), pp. 216–22 at 220–1.
[121] Customs of Bagnères-de-Bigorre, c. 18: F. Soutras-Dejeanne, 'Fors et coutumes de Bagnères-de-Bigorre', *Bulletin de la Société Ramond (Bagnères-de-Bigorre)* (1882), 155–70. Customs of Meyrueis, c. 39: F. Cazalis, 'Haec sunt statuta et consuetudines antique de Mayrosio in tempore Dominorum Contorum', *Bulletin Société d'agriculture, industrie, sciences et arts département de la Lozere* 13 (1862), 270–80.
[122] AM Toulouse, MS AA 1, fols 6r–7r (no. V), at 6v: 'Omnes homines de Tolosano sive extra tolosanum sint securi in Tolosa et in suburbio ad festum Sancti Stephani quod est in estate x' ad festum Sancte Marie augusti et ad festum Sancti Saturnini IIIIor dies ante unamquamque festivitatem et alios IIII dies post unamquamque festivitatem supra scriptam et a prima die ad ventus domini usque ad festum circumcisionis domini et in tota quadragesima id est a capite iuniorum usque ad octavas pasce, nisi sit debitor vel fideiussor vel malefactor.' There are two complementary charters of rights given to the city by Count Raimond V in February 1152, as recorded in this civic cartulary, the other preceding this one on fols 4r–5v. For broader context, see G. Poisson, 'Le comte, le consul et les notaires: l'écriture statutaire à Toulouse au XIIIe siècle', in Lett, ed., *La confection des statuts*, pp. 81–101.

two fairs held on the feasts of St Mark (25 April) and St Luke (18 October).[123] One could continue to multiply the examples. There is no surprise in finding that saints' days mark important points in a secular calendar, but it is perhaps useful to reflect on the multiplication of associations and activities connected with these various different days across the region, as commercial economic activity grew over the course of the twelfth century and thereafter. Just as there was a long-standing rhythm to the agricultural year, entwined with the Christian feasts, so there was a mercantile rhythm (with all its antecedent activities) elaborating itself regionally also.

Some topics that we might associate with more spiritual contemporary ecclesiastical concerns are found in certain customs. Several place restrictions on the use of the ordeal, for example, which was to be banned (though not with complete success) at the Fourth Lateran Council of 1215; in most cases in the customs, the ban is not outright, but forbids using the ordeal to settle disputes unless both parties agree to it.[124] Some customs discuss marriage at certain points, though not necessarily quite in line with the canon law injunction regarding mutual consent. The early thirteenth-century customs of Saint-Antonin-Noble-Val state that the local lord cannot compel 'a widow or other woman of the town' to marry, and those of Carcassonne from around the same date say something similar.[125] On the other hand, the customs of Alès from 1217 warn that a young noblewoman ('donzela') cannot marry without the consent of her parents.[126] A few customs provide an offer to marry by the guilty party as an acceptable recompense for having raped a young woman.[127] Quite a few, from the twelfth century

---

[123] Customs of Saint-Antonin-Noble-Val, 1144: R. Latouche, 'La coutume originale de Saint-Antonin', *Bulletin philologique et historique jusqu'à 1715 du Comité des travaux historiques et scientifiques* (1920), 260–62. Customs of Puigcerdà, 1181: B. Alart, *Priviléges et titres relatifs aux franchises, institutions et propriétés communales de Roussillon et de Cerdagne depuis le XI siècle jusqu'à l'an 1660, 1er partie* (Perpignan: Charles Latrobe, 1878), pp. 66–67. Customs of Montcuq, around 1224, c. 21: E. Dufour, 'Anciennes coutumes de Montcuq', *Revue historique de droit français et étranger* (1855), 98–131 at pp. 114–15.

[124] Thus Perpignan 1162 (Alart, *Priviléges...Roussillon*, p. 45), Carcassonne c. 1205 c. 48 (A. Teulet et al., *Layettes du trésor des chartes*, 5 vols (Paris: Henri Plon, 1863-1909), I, pp. 272–81 at 277), Montpellier 1204 c. 62 (Teulet, *Layettes*, I, pp. 255–66, at p. 261), Pamiers 1238 (*HGL*, VIII, cols 870–76), Saint-Antonin-Noble-Val, early thirteenth century (Teulet, *Layettes*, I, pp. 55–60; I follow Carbasse's redating of the Latin customs edited here). See in general R. Bartlett, *Trial by Fire and Water: The Medieval Judicial Ordeal* (Oxford: Clarendon Press, 1986).

[125] Teulet, *Layettes*, I, pp. 59, 278.

[126] Customs of Alès, 1217, c. 21 (J.-M. Maurette, *Recherches historiques sur la ville d'Alais* (Alès: J. Martin, 1860), pp. 466–97, at pp. 484–5). Customs of Narbonne, 1232, c. 4 notes that a woman under 25 years of age who gets married without parental permission cannot seek to gain any of her father's goods: H. Tarde, 'La rédaction des coutumes de Narbonne', *Annales du Midi* 85 (1973), 371–402 at p. 397.

[127] Thus customs of Moissac, c. 1130, c. 50 (Lagrèze-Fossat, *Études historiques*, pp. 90–91); similarly customs of Toulouse, 1152, though here specifying rape of a virgin only, and if the rapist is of higher social rank, giving him the option of marriage or arranging a marriage for the woman: 'Item, siquis vi devirginabit feminam si magis probus est quam illa, vel ducat eam in uxorem vel donec ei maritum dignum illam.' (AM Toulouse, MS AA 1, fols 4–5v, at 5r). Also customs of Pamiers 1238 (*HGL*, VIII,

onward, include a punishment for adultery, namely forcing both guilty parties to run naked through town, or else pay a hefty fine; though, as I have argued elsewhere, this is as much about arrogating a traditional feature of lordship to civic governance as a concern with sexual morality (and it is important to note that no customs have any injunction against unmarried fornication).[128] One set of customs from 1229 for the small town of Meyrueis (c. 50 km south of Mende) display some wider concern with moral governance, but are very unusual for this period. They include a statute against those blaspheming ('not in jest but against God or the saints') when playing at dice, those who are guilty to be thrown 'into the mud or the water' unless they pay 12d to the lord. They also make provision that on Sundays nobody should sell meat outside the religious house where major mass was being sung; that prostitutes must stay outside the town; and that if any married woman should leave her husband and 'lives badly' and, having been warned by a priest, does not make satisfaction within eight days, she will be expelled and her goods confiscated.[129]

Overall, whilst customs from both the twelfth and the thirteenth century frequently deal with justice and commerce, their engagement with what we might see as Christian principles is rather more patchy. In addition to the examples cited above, there are a very few moments when, amidst the common discussion of wills, issues regarding pious giving are passingly addressed. The customs of Béziers from 1185 state that if someone dies without testament, and no heirs present themselves, 'their goods shall be given to religious places' or shall be left with faithful sequestrators for a year and a day, after which they will become property of the town.[130] But the only other example of something similar is from Salses (near Perpignan) in 1237, which simply states that for those dying intestate, 'if there are no relatives, the *prud'hommes* of the town of Salses should divide and distribute all his things for the good of the dead person's soul, just as seems best to them'.[131] The customs of Carcassonne, probably from around 1205, provide that if someone makes a will orally, for any bequests to 'the church or to pious places or to miserable persons' two witnesses suffice for proof, in contrast to the three needed for any other legacies. 'Miserable persons' is not glossed, but likely

---

cols 870–76, at col. 873). See generally K. Gravdal, *Ravishing Maidens: Writing Rape in Medieval French Literature and Law* (Philadelphia: University of Pennsylvania Press, 1991).

[128] J. H. Arnold, 'Sexualité et déshonneur dans le Midi (XIIIe–XIVe siècles): les péchés de la chair et l'opinion collective', *CdF* 52 (2019), 261–95. The fundamental study of the phenomenon is J.-M. Carbasse, 'Currant nudi: la répression de l'adultère dans le Midi médiéval', in J. Poumarède and J.-P. Royer, eds, *Droit, histoire et sexualité* (Toulouse: Publications de l'Espace juridique, 1987), pp. 83–102.

[129] Customs of Meyrueis, 1229, cc. 22, 29, 40, 41.

[130] Customs of Béziers 1185: J. Azais, 'De Roger II, vicomte de Béziers, et d'un acte portant reconnaissance des droits du vicomte, de l'évêque et des habitantes de Béziers', *Bulletin de la Société archéologique de Béziers* 1 (1836), 45–65 (edition 58–65), at 64.

[131] J. M. Font Rius, *Cartas de poblacion y franquicia de Cataluña*, Escuela de Estudios Medievales, Textos 26, 2 vols (Barcelona: Ferrán-Bot, 1969), I, pp. 330–33 (no. 237).

indicates those normally in receipt of almsgiving—the poor, widows, lepers—and thus this seems to bespeak a positive concern for charity.[132] On the other hand, the same customs order that a married daughter cannot make her own will without counsel from her father (presumably to protect the inheritance of family property), though if she is a mother 'she can [without counsel] relinquish a fourth part of her goods, and no more, to pious places and to miserable persons or her husband'—but exceeding that quarter will result in the whole will being declared null and void, other than the alms she bequeaths.[133]

To return to the general themes explored within this chapter, whilst the growth of towns and cities was accompanied by a growth in charitable foundations and a greater visibility for holy men associated with apostolic piety, the civic customs suggest that we may wish to be cautious over assuming that a 'charitable revolution' or a wider sense of apostolic piety was picked up full-throatedly by lay society in the twelfth and early thirteenth centuries. The few examples of concern with pious giving or moral behaviour given above constitute almost the entirety of the extant evidence up to 1240 from this corpus; interesting, but hardly overwhelming. One might of course put this down to a question of documentary genre and argue that civic statutes are not the place to find such concerns. But I did give one example above—Meyrueis, 1229—where they did seem to have some presence, and I want to finish with one final set of civic customs which throw the others into rather stark relief (though point, to some extent, to things we will find more frequently—though far from universally—in civic customs of the later thirteenth century and thereafter). These are the very lengthy customs for Arles, which have previously been dated to the mid-12th century, but which must in fact come from the thirteenth century as they mention *en passant* 'the house of the Brothers Minor', who arrived in Arles in 1217 or 1218. The latest they can be is 1240, as they also mention Hugh (III) de Baux who was viscount of Marseille up

---

[132] For the phrase in twelfth-century theology, see Brodman, *Charity and Religion*, p. 15.
[133] Customs of Carcassonne c. 1205, cc. 38, 40; Teulet, *Layettes*, I, pp. 276–77. André Gouron argues that the customs should be re-dated to after 1209, in the context of the crusaders' capture of Carcassonne: A. Gouron, 'Libertas hominum Montispessulani: rédaction et diffusion des coutumes de Montpellier', *Annales du Midi* 90 (1978), 289–318, at pp. 52–54. However, this is essentially based on (1) identifying any mention of 'heresy' (Carcassonne cc. 20 and 84) as necessarily post-dating the coming of the French crusaders, and (2) seeing the provision in c. 26 regarding any 'catholicus' coming 'sive de terra pacis, sive de terra guerre' as only making sense within the crusade period. The first point is a weak hypothesis, given other pre-1209 evidence relating to heresy, labelled as such, in the region (see also n. 140 below). The latter is also questionable, given that various comital regions of southern France, and their cities, were also intermittently 'at war' (in the sense in which conflict was understood in the period)—mention of the same found in some twelfth-century customs (for example, for Moissac)—and that 'Catholicus' was as likely used in distinction to 'Judeus'. That the Carcassonne statutes *fail* to prohibit testimony by 'usurers' (also noted by Gouron) to me more strongly suggests a pre-crusade context; see more generally the discussion of usury as part of the wider crusade programme in Chapter 5, below. I note that Maïté Lesné-Ferret more cautiously suggests the statutes 'apparaissent marqués par la lutte contre l'hérésie' (M. Lesné-Ferret, 'L'écriture des statuts languedociens au XIIIe siècle: le modèle des coutumes de Montpellier', in Lett, ed., *La confection des statuts*, pp. 153–71).

until his death in that year—though I suspect that they are from somewhat earlier, as his actual political role in Marseille and thus the region had much diminished by the 1230s.[134] So let us provisionally assume they are roughly of the same date as those of Meyrueis.

The Arles customs are notably concerned with quotidian civic governance. They authorized three 'good men' of the town to patrol the streets to identify any obstructions that required removal, forbade people leaving unhealthy or dangerous waste or defecating in the street (those under 7 years were exempt regarding the latter), and they imposed a nightly curfew announced by the ringing of the bells, anyone caught outside thereafter to have their name recorded and passed on to the consulate. Dice games (*tricharia*) were not to be played at night-time, and no games of chance were allowed in taverns once the curfew had sounded. 'No public whore or panderer should dare to stay in Arles in the streets of the *prud'hommes*', and if a married man left his wife and held 'a public whore', they should both be expelled from the city. Prostitutes were moreover not to dress like respectable women, by wearing a cloak or a veil; if they did, any 'good woman' had the right to snatch it off them.[135] Like Meyrueis, the Arles customs contain a blasphemy statute, this in fact being the earliest appearance of legal condemnation of blasphemy in the region: 'Since we are unwilling to leave unpunished blasphemous deeds against people, so we must act much more against those who blaspheme God or His mother Mary, we will subject them to the most religious financial or scourging penalties'; and thus when people blasphemed when playing some game, they had to pay 20 *sous* for each occasion, the sum divided equally between the commune and the accuser (who must however have witnesses to support their accusation). If they could not pay the sum, they were to be beaten all through Arles 'like a thief and infamous person'.[136] We have no records to tell us whether these provisions were regularly enacted, but the intent is clearly serious; and here, as in the concern with the cleanliness and obstruction of civic roads, the customs are an early foretaste of what would become much more common in later medieval cities.[137]

What of poverty, charity, and apostolic example? The Hospitallers had a house in Arles by this stage, and as already noted, so did the Brothers Minor, though each is mentioned only in the context of practical matters.[138] The Brother

---

[134] M. Zarb, *Les privileges de la ville de Marseille, du Xe siècle a la Révolution* (Paris: Picard, 1961), pp. 61–69.

[135] Customs of Arles (before 1240), cc. 40, 41, 21, 51, 52, 49, 50; Giraud, *Essai sur l'histoire du droit français*, II, pp. 185–235.

[136] Customs of Arles, c. 25.

[137] See generally C. Leveleux, *La parole interdite: le blasphème dans la France médiévale (XIIIe–XVIe siècles). Du péché au crime* (Paris: De Boccard, 2001). Expert analysis re civic 'flow', albeit for a different region: J. Coomans, *Community, Urban Health and Environment in the Late Medieval Low Countries* (Cambridge: Cambridge University Press, 2021).

[138] Customs of Arles, c. 145 (describing the location of common lands in relation to the house and church of the Franciscans), c. 164 (restrictions on where animals belonging to the Hospitallers and other religious houses could be pastured).

Preachers arrived in 1225, perhaps also by the time of the statutes. So we know that at least some examples of apostolic holiness were visible in the city, and might fairly assume some pastoral preaching also. We find some potential reflection of this in the customs. Each month the civic court was to have loaves weighed, to check that the bakers were baking fairly; any found to be illegitimate were 'to be broken up and immediately given to the poor, as alms'. When people made contracts with each other it was commonly the case, as in other southern French towns and cities, that a single coin—'the penny of God'—was given over to the city, as both a symbolic surety (marking the fact of the deal) and a form of transaction tax; these were to be 'distributed in honour of God', probably meaning as alms for the poor, 'and to the candles of St Trophime' (the cathedral church in the city). If anyone had anything 'unjustly' from the commune, as with 'pure usury' (probably meaning 'financial interest') 'or anything else that one cannot retain without damnation to their soul', they could pay it toward the costs of the city's bridge, in recompense.[139] These are the first occasions in this genre of evidence that such things can be found, and are important indicators of a form of apostolically informed piety being placed centrally within civic governance. At the same time, that civic piety had a darker side. No lepers were allowed within the walls of the city at any point, and any found there would be expelled. No Jews were to work openly on Sundays or saints' days, and any who did so were fined 20 *sous* for each offence. Nobody suspected of heresy could be in the consulate or hold public office, and 'nobody should knowingly give hospitality in their house to any thieves or robbers or men who labour badly, nor to heretics or Waldensians'; again those breaking this injunction were to be fined 20 *sous*, to be divided (as with the blasphemy statute) between the accuser and the city.[140]

The presence of almsgiving, the wider moral concerns as a part of good civic governance (within which we may place the concern with heresy), are all arrows pointing ahead into the later thirteenth century. It is not at all the case that all later civic customs have such provisions, but these concerns do start to become more visible in other locales in subsequent decades, and of course in a variety of other evidence, some of which we shall meet in later chapters. Looking back across this chapter as a whole, the concatenation of holy groups and pious activities in Arles is good evidence for the spread of apostolic piety to lay society. It is however also a reminder that we do not see a swift and universal move to the lay embrace of the *vita apostolica*, but something more sporadic and probably rather

---

[139] Customs of Arles, cc. 130, 191, 114.
[140] Customs of Arles, cc. 96, 146, 126, 24. The relative leniency of the penalty for harbouring heretics again suggests a date prior to 1230. Similar injunctions are found in the customs of Carcassonne c. 1205, cc. 84 and 105, and we may wish to remember that, as we saw much earlier in this chapter, Peire II of Aragon had held a disputation in that city in 1203. The editor of the Carcassonne customs suggests that c. 105, expelling heretics from within the city, mistakenly has 'heretices publice' for what should be 'meretrices publice', i.e public prostitutes; this could well be the case, though 'public heretics' does make some sense, as we have seen earlier in this chapter.

slower than the development of new religious orders might suggest; and, as discussed further above, that there could be a range of different forms of piety and pious activity inspired by the example of the apostles. The Good Men and the Waldensians had been present in much of southern French civic society for some decades, the particular style of apostolic holiness they represented providing one kind of outlet for lay enthusiasm and almsgiving. They undoubtedly enjoyed support from some within the higher echelons of lay society, but were also, to put it bluntly, much cheaper to establish and sustain than most other pious foundations, such as Templar commanderies or hospitals. In a purely practical sense, support for heretics could therefore come from a wider tranche of society. Their presence within towns and cities—along with some Templars and Hospitallers, many hospitals, and then later all the mendicant foundations—is part of a continuing and evolving dynamic between urban society and apostolic modes of piety. And, as I have argued above, 'urban' society in southern France stretches far into the countryside, at least in terms of the self-image and aspirations of smaller towns and *castra*. Thus the social landscape and the spiritual landscape for lay piety were still evolving, some strands of these new forms of apostolicity stretching back to the early twelfth century at least, others only quickening some decades into the thirteenth century.

At the same time, to return to a point made very briefly earlier in this chapter, we must remain aware that some aspects of the older connection between lordship, patronage, and piety remained. In the *archives départementales* in Carcassonne, there is a small bundle of documents in which later archivists or historians transcribed several medieval charters, now lost, relating to a new foundation. The earliest dates to 4 October 1219, a charter issued by Alix de Montmorency, Lady de Montfort, widow of the recently deceased Simon de Montfort, who had been killed in the siege of Toulouse in June the previous year. Alix had made and confirmed, in that same year, several pious gifts to existing churches in her late husband's memory, in Carcassonne and elsewhere.[141] This document however created a new foundation, made 'for the remedy of the soul of our dearest lord and husband', to be placed in a house in the town of Limoux, given 'in perpetual alms to God and to the Brothers of the order of the most holy Trinity and of Captives'. These recipients were known generally as the Trinitarians, founded some time before 1198 (when Innocent III approved their rule), an order in some ways similar to the Templars and Hospitallers but dedicated to ransoming back those Christians taken captive by Muslim rulers—another adaptation and interpretation of one aspect of the *vita apostolica*.[142] In the charter, Alix de

---

[141] M. Roquebert, *L'épopée cathare, III: le lys et la croix, 1216–1219* (Toulouse: Privat, 1986), pp. 184, 230.

[142] See J. Flannery, 'The Trinitarian Order and the Ransom of Christian Captives', *Al-Masāq* 23 (2011), 135–44. The order had foundations elsewhere in France and Italy in particular; in southern France it was established in several cities on the Mediterranean coast in the thirteenth century: F. Tiran,

Montmorency states that she thus gives 'that house in Limoux which was of Bon Mancip and his children, which was formerly the school of the Jews (*scola Judeorum*)...which same house my said husband previously promised to make into a hospital'.[143] We may note the particular emphasis on a previously Jewish establishment turned to Christian purposes; as we shall see in the next chapter, among many other things the arrival of the northern French crusaders led by de Montfort altered interfaith relations in the south. But note also the sense of disposition from on high: what was to have been a hospital is now a foundation for this order, and is for the salvation of the dead lord's soul. Acts of foundation and major patronage continue to frame a privileged relationship between wealthy donor and the holy, essentially in continuity with earlier monastic foundations.

The civic location of the new foundations does, as I have argued above, make the holy more permeable and accessible to a wider lay audience; I am not suggesting that the Trinitarians at Limoux or any of the other newly founded religious houses were simply the personal pious property of the wealthy. But the dynamic of patronage, and in various cases its reliance on the underlying continuance of the economics of lordship, reminds us that a differentiated landscape continued, through which dynamics of status were articulated. Possibly by the early thirteenth century, and more strongly thereafter, the newly wealthy merchant classes could elevate themselves, individually or collectively, to some of this role, acting as founding donors in a way previously reserved for wealthy lords. Thus, for example, in 1268 Guillaume Amiel, a wealthy consul of Montauban (and possibly another fortunate merchant engaged in the wine trade to England), founded a hospital and church for the Brothers Minor in the town. For the latter we have not just a textual record in the *Livre rouge* of the town, but a surviving stone fragment on which the fact of his foundation of the church is recorded, 'from his own' goods—something which very clearly proclaimed publicly his status as donor.[144] In that sense, what the presence of the holy within the cities came to provide to the emerging mercantile class was not only an outlet for restitutive almsgiving or

---

'Trinitaires et Mercédaires à Marseille et le rachat des captifs de Barbarie', *Cahiers de la Méditerranée* 87 (2013), 173–86.

[143] AD Aude 4E206 GG233. The *laisse* contains seventeenth- and eighteenth-century copies of various documents relating to the foundation, three of which are from the thirteenth century (two of them copied twice over by different archivists). In 1221 Alix and her son gave the Trinitarians income from the ovens, certain tolls, and the fruit of the orchards she held in Limoux.

[144] *Livre rouge*: AD Tarn-et-Garonne 3E121 AA1, fol. 29r. Stone: M. Méras, 'Un bourgeois de Montauban sous Alphonse de Poitiers: Guillaume Amiel', *Bulletin philologique et historique jusqu'à 1610 du Comité des travaux historiques et scientifiques* (1960), 693–702. See also J. Feuchter, *Ketzer, Konzul und Büsser: Die städtischen Eliten von Montauban dem Inquisitor Petrus Cellani (1236/1241)* (Tübingen: Mohr Siebeck, 2007), pp. 410–11. The stone has only fragmentary text, but 'propriis' is very clearly legible. Mundy noted a possible shift from 'individualism' to 'corporatism' in the founding of hospitals in Toulouse, though perhaps as a cycling between such states rather than a clear binary switch: Mundy, 'Charity and Social Work', pp. 238–39, 278 and n. 238.

a theology that could address the challenges of wealth, but a means by which they themselves could demonstrate the prowess of patronage.

What I have been arguing across the course of this chapter is, firstly, that whilst the twelfth century certainly did see the profoundly important development of new models of apostolic piety, we must recognize that these apostolicities varied in their focus and wider dynamics with regard to society, rather than collapsing all forms into a general and unified model of the *vita apostolica*. Secondly, we must also recognize that wider lay engagement with modes of piety modelled on apostolic *example*—particularly in almsgiving and care for the poor—was a somewhat hesitant and certainly very lengthy process, still elaborating itself in the thirteenth century. And, thirdly, these undoubtedly new developments did not magically displace the preceding dynamic of lordship, but to some degree continued to sustain it via the new opportunities for pious patronage—albeit a patronage which became more available to the higher echelons of the urban elite by the turn of the thirteenth century.

This last point, regarding continuity, begs a codicil. In focusing on what newly arrived in towns and cities, as they grew across the twelfth century, we should not forget aspects of the holy and of pious practice that had long been in place, and remained fundamental to what historians sometimes call 'civic religion'. I am thinking here, as I mentioned at the start of this chapter, of the long-standing presence of saints' relics in cathedral shrines, the acts of worship they facilitated, and the aura of holy protection that the inhabitants of those cities frequently sought from them.[145] A list of 'the names of saints whose bodies rest in the church of St Sernin, Toulouse' is found inscribed in a fifteenth-century breviary, now in the Bibliothèque municipale in the city; twenty-six are named 'and many other bodies are in the said church, whose names we do not know because of their great antiquity'. Some arrived there later in the middle ages, but some would have been (or at least, thought to have been) present for many centuries, including early Christian martyrs and various apostles, including St Jude, St Simon, and St Barnabé, and of course St Sernin himself, first bishop of Toulouse, one of the 'apostles to the Gauls' of the early Church.[146] Particularly where such figures were associated with altars, there would be a very long-standing possibility of them attracting almsgiving for the provision of lights.

The dynamic here is not apostolic example however, but quasi-lordly protection, as we see from one explicit moment in Toulouse's civic cartulary. This records a charter from 11 April 1226 in which the city's consuls, for 'all of the Capitoul', as they named the ruling body of the city, 'and for all of the *universitas*

---

[145] On the general dynamic, albeit for Italy, see D. Webb, *Patrons and Defenders: The Saints in the Italian City States* (London: Tauris, 1996).
[146] BM Toulouse MS 75, fol. Av (the archivist has used letters to designate folios prior to the start of the breviary proper). There is a transcription in Douais, *Documents sur...Languedoc*, II, appendix.

of Toulouse', arranged that 10 *sous* in alms would be given each year 'for all time' to keep burning the lights set before the altar of St Exupéry (an early fifth-century bishop) in the cathedral church. This was done 'so that God and the Lord Jesus Christ, at the intercession of the Blessed Virgin Mary and St Exupéry the bishop, together with all the saints, would guard, protect and defend the city and suburbs of Toulouse and all the male and female inhabitants in it, from all evil and danger from the harassment or incursion of its enemies'.[147] (An ornate thirteenth-century reliquary casket for St Exupéry also survives from Toulouse, depicting his death, along with the crucified Christ and other apostolic figures.)[148] Here is a very clear moment of early thirteenth-century civic piety. But it is directed not to apostolic example, but rather in the hope of divine intervention when the city was under threat—a model more familiar to us from the eleventh- and twelfth-century saints discussed in Chapter 2. As we shall see in the next chapter, in this particular instance, the call for divine intervention ultimately was unsuccessful.

---

[147] BM Toulouse AA1, pp. 226–28 (no. 96): 'habeat in unoquoque anno per omnia tempora de communi urbi tolose et suburbii x sol tol. pro helemosina ut deus et dominus ihesus xperis intercedente beata virgine maria et beato exuperio pontifice cum omnibus sanctis tolosam urbem et suburbium et omnis habitantes et habitantas in ea ab omni malo et periculo et ab inimicorum infestacione sive incursione custodiat protegat et deffendat…'.

[148] See <https://commons.wikimedia.org/wiki/File:Le_Mus%C3%A9e_Paul_Dupuy_-_Ch%C3%A2sse_de_saint-Exup%C3%A8re.jpg> (accessed 2 Dec. 2020), from the trésor of the cathedral, now held apparently in the musée Paul Dupuy in Toulouse.

5
Papal Interventions, c. 1200–c. 1320

In March 1208, Innocent III wrote to the archbishops of Narbonne, Arles, Embrun, Aix-en-Provence, and Vienne, decrying the murder of his legate Pierre de Castelnau, anathematizing the count of Toulouse, whom he blamed for this crime, and effectively launching the call to crusade against the south, by instructing the prelates that they 'may unambiguously promise an indulgence of the remission of sins' for those who 'kindled with the zeal of orthodox faith to avenge just blood' fought against the enemies of the Church.[1] Further letters circulated to all of France in October of that same year made clear that those who took up crosses to 'exterminate the supporters of heretical wickedness' would receive papal protection for their goods and lands, and an indulgence of remission of sin.[2] By July 1209 a crusading army, led by Count Simon de Montfort and the papal legate Arnaud Amaury (abbot of Clairvaux), had reached the south; the infamous massacre of the inhabitants of Béziers followed, setting in motion a number of years of vicious fighting, the confiscation of land from various southern lords, the suppression, rebellion, and re-suppression of cities, until the eventual involvement of the Capetian monarchs brought the conflict more or less to an end in 1229.

There are several good modern narrative histories of the crusade and its events, and I shall not rehearse those details here, though I shall reflect a little further below on its effects on the understanding of religious identity within the region.[3] As is well recognized, the most profound effect of the crusade was to reconfigure the political landscape, ultimately bringing southern France under the control of the Capetian monarchy (though not de facto until Count Raimond VII's death in 1249, and not fully or *de jure* until after Alphonse dede Poitiers's death in 1271).[4]

---

[1] Innocent III, *Ne nos ejus* (10 Mar 1208), PL 215, cols 1353–58 at col. 1356; translation by Rebecca Rist in C. Léglu, R. Rist, and C. Taylor, eds, *The Cathars and the Albigensian Crusade: A Sourcebook* (Abingdon: Routledge, 2014), pp. 38–40. Setting events here within a wider history of papal policy, see R. Rist, *The Papacy and Crusading in Europe, 1198-1245* (London: Continuum, 2011).

[2] PL 215, col. 1469, see letters of 9 Oct and 11 Oct in particular, addressed to 'all prelates in the kingdom of France'.

[3] The most detailed is M. Roquebert, *L'épopée cathare*, 4 vols (Toulouse: Privat, 1970–89), and the most useful recent discussion J.-L. Biget, 'Tenir la pays: Montfort entre villes et châteaux d'Occitanie', in M. Aurell, G. Lippiatt, and L. Macé, eds, *Simon de Montfort (c. 1170–1218): le croisé, son lignage et son temps* (Turnhout: Brepols, 2020).

[4] At the Peace of Paris in 1229, Raimond VII agreed that on his death, his lands would pass to Louis IX's younger brother Alphonse de Poitiers, and this—perhaps rather surprisingly—came to pass. Alphonse ruled as count of Toulouse, but on his death and that of his wife Joanne de Toulouse,

But for the purposes of this book, what matters more are a number of other changes and interventions brought about both around the crusade and in its aftermath, as the Church intervened more decisively in the structures of faith and its governance. As with the wider politics of the region, the control exercised by the Church was not immediate, stable, or complete; for example, as we shall see in a later chapter, various towns periodically pushed back hard against various impositions, a situation which continued into the fourteenth century. As we shall see, some of what the crusade brought with it was of a piece with changes being wrought in the landscape of faith across western Europe, following the pastoral impetus of Innocent III in particular. Those more universal features nonetheless had particular regional variations in terms of their chronology and local implementation, and thus, as with issues around the Gregorian reform movement, the specifics of place and time are worth exploring in regard to their wider effect on the experiences of the laity. And, as is also explored further below and in Chapter 8, some particular aspects of pastoral reform, as enunciated in the 'Great Council' (as contemporary sources called it) of Lateran IV in 1215, gained a very particular inflection when elaborated in a southern French setting.

If we think of the crusade as a period of inflexion, we need to return to two strongly interlinked themes which can help us to understand the wider changes experienced across the decades, and their implications for the ordinary laity. Both long precede the crusade itself, whilst also helping to explain its impetus, and were also themselves reconfigured by its course. They are peace and reform.

The Peace of Crusade

We have of course already met 'peace' as a concept in Chapter 2, in the Peace of God movement, and know already that we are dealing with an ideology that could have very sharp edges to it, closely bound up with issues of authority and dominion. In the eleventh and early twelfth centuries, as we have seen, the nature of the 'peace' was orchestrated largely by bishops and abbots, in collaboration with major secular lords, and often had a particular focus on the protection of monastic and ecclesial lordship, with various local saints as participatory figures within its dynamic. The need for the enforced imposition of an ecclesiastically directed 'peace' continued intermittently in the twelfth century. Marking both some continuities with the past, but also some key shifts pointing toward the future, Archbishop Guillaume of Auch, in the immediate aftermath of the Second Lateran Council (1139), issued a letter to 'all bishops, prelates, counts, viscounts,

---

whilst they both were travelling back from crusade in 1271, the lands were seized by the crown, a move later ratified by a royal *parlement*. See E. H. Hallam and C. West, *Capetian France, 987–1328*, 3rd edn (London: Routledge, 2019), p. 357.

barons and all the clergy and people of the province of Auch'. In it, he declared a 'good peace and truce of God', to run 'from sunset on Wednesdays to sunrise on Mondays' and within certain periods of the year, namely from Advent to the Octave of the Epiphany (that is, from some time in November until some time in January), and from Septuagesima Sunday to Easter (that is, from some time in January through to whenever Easter fell), along with various other major feast days that year; not, in other words, a total and universal truce, but some periods of restraint.[5] Within these periods, there would be protection for all 'canons, monks, priests, clergy and all religious people, converts, pilgrims, merchants, peasants, those coming and going [about their business], and those engaged in agricultural tasks, and pasturing animals and carrying seed to fields. [And] Ladies with their unarmed companions, and all women, and all things belonging to clergy and monks, and mills'. Churches would have a sanctuary declared around them, stretching out thirty paces, and the same for monasteries, but with twice the radius. To enforce this peace, everyone over the age of 7 years was to make an oath to a clergyman, saying that 'they swear themselves to the peace and truth of God following and heeding the tenor of what is afore-written, and to persecute violators of the peace and truce of God, and that they will not knowingly buy any stolen goods'. If someone did not swear, or did not act against violators of the peace, or made use of 'mercenaries or thieves', they and their lands were subject to excommunication, such that no services would be performed except for the baptism of children and the bestowal of final penance. Secular lords and others of the faithful who did observe the peace and fight against mercenaries 'and pestilential men', if they did this 'in true penitence', by the authority of God, the pope, and the universal Church 'they shall not doubt that they will have indulgence from all sin and the fruit of eternal reward'; the letter then instructing bishops who granted any indulgences to those who subsequently joined in to give two years' remission from imposed penances.[6]

Limiting the use to specific periods of the year, the idea of a sanctuary around churches, and of course the phrase 'peace and truce of God', link us back to the early eleventh century. The slightly vague gesture—perhaps more rhetorical than theological—toward full indulgence for sin resonates with the contemporary crusading movement to the Holy Land.[7] But what is particularly interesting, in the

---

[5] These time periods largely follow Lateran II (1139), c. 12, though with the addition of the major feast days. The archbishop expands hugely however on the details of the 'truce' and the relaxation from penance.

[6] *Gallia Christiana*, I, *Instrumenta* (Paris: Ex typographia regia, 1716), p. 162. There is a translation of some of the final passages in R. Rist, *The Papacy and Crusading in Europe, 1198-1245* (London: Continuum, 2009), p. 26, and I am indebted to Professor Rist for discussion. On the broader issues see also R. Rist, 'Salvation and the Albigensian Crusade: Pope Innocent III and the Plenary Indulgence', *Reading Medieval Studies* 36 (2010), 95–112.

[7] See now A. Bysted, *The Crusade Indulgence: Spiritual Rewards and the Theology of Crusade* (Leiden: Brill, 2014).

context of the future Albigensian Crusade, is the focus on mercenaries and the idea of a universal oath to be taken by all. What was the crusade about? 'Heresy', obviously. But in fact, not *entirely* obviously, for how does one fight with armed knights and siege weapons against a divergent set of ideas? A better sense of the dynamic of the crusade against the south might be to see it as a call to fight for a particular idea of 'peace' in which ecclesial *auctoritas* sought to gain its proper influence (as the papacy would see it) over secular *potestas*, in order to assert and enforce a proper Christian order to society.[8] As the anonymous poet continuator of the *Canso de la crozada* has various figures at the papal court declare, in defence of the efforts of Simon de Montfort in the midst of the crusade:

> The count de Montfort stays in the Carcassès | to destroy the wicked and bring in the good | he eliminated the heretics, the mercenaries and the Waldensians | and established the Catholics, the Normans and the French. | And from this, with the cross he conquered the whole | of Agen and Quercy, the Toulousain and Albigeois, | and strong Foix and Toulouse and Montauban; all these he put | into the hands of Holy Church and the Church accepted them.[9]

The primary focus was on removing any lay political support for those deemed heretics, including Waldensian heretics, so that they could be 'driven out'. But it also involved—before, during and after the crusade—a wider set of demands regarding other aspects of 'peace'.

Within all of this a particularly notable place, alongside heresy, was held by the condemnation of the unruly violence of mercenaries and other bandits (*rotiers* in medieval Occitan, *routiers* in modern French scholarship), most probably because, as we see in the archbishop of Auch's letter from c. 1139, they threatened ecclesiastical property and mercantile activity. The two topics—the heresy of 'the Cathars' (thus named) 'and other heretics' in the region of Gascony, Albi, and the Toulousain, and the threat of the 'Brabanters, Navarrese, Basques, Aragonese, Cotarelli and Triaverdini' who were hired as mercenaries—were condemned sequentially in canon 27 of the Third Lateran Council of 1179: the heretics and their supporters were anathematized, and those who took up arms against mercenaries were granted two years' remission of penance, as in the earlier Auch decree. Danica Summerlin argues that the two topics should not be read as seamlessly conjoined, and points to a very early manuscript from Limoges in which they are much more clearly separate topics, possibly representing what was originally intended at the council. (Interestingly, in that manuscript *only* 'the Cathars'

---

[8] For the distinction made here, I find very useful J. Canning, *Ideas of Power in the Late Middle Ages, 1296–1417* (Cambridge: Cambridge University Press, 2011), particularly chapter 1.
[9] *Canso*, liasse 149: E. Martin-Chabot, *La chanson de la croisade Albigeoise*, 3 vols (Paris: Société d'Édition Les Belles Lettres, 1957–61), II, p. 70.

are named, rather than 'those who some call Cathars, some call Publicans, some call Patarenes' as is found in other texts and the standard editions.)[10] Canons from Lateran III were cited explicitly in the council of Montpellier in (it is said) 1195, when another papal legate implicitly confronted Raimond VI of Toulouse with his failure to preserve 'the peace' in the diocese of Narbonne. That council went on to anathematize 'once again all heretics, Aragonese, those retainers who are called mercenaries (*mainatae*), and pirates, and those who carry arms or armaments or wood for ships to the Saracen navy', repeating the injunction that all who had dealings with mercenaries were to be excommunicated each Sunday in every church.[11] Somewhat to the north of the region studied here, a popular movement known as the Caputiati sought to combat mercenary violence in the early 1180s, initially with strong episcopal support (until the movement proclaimed a more socially radical gospel).[12] Although later historians—perhaps particularly those whose gaze defaults to the Angevin and Capetian realms—have sometimes assumed that it was a specifically southern French problem, due to multiple lordships and a lack of central authority, this is not really the case: mercenaries were repeatedly used across much of Europe and the Mediterranean, and papal concern with mercenaries was demonstrably not limited to the south.[13] The issue was in fact perennial and widespread, as medieval lords, counts, and kings bolstered their forces with paid professionals. But as we look to the period of the Albigensian Crusade, it gained a particular urgency, and was combined with 'heresy' into a wider sense of threat, a conjoined challenge to Christian peace.[14] Whilst that concept of peace continued, unsurprisingly, to embrace protection of

[10] D. Summerlin, *The Canons of the Third Lateran Council of 1179: Their Origins and Reception* (Cambridge: Cambridge University Press, 2019), pp. 173–80.

[11] Council of Montpellier, 1195: Mansi, XXII, cols 667–72. On this council and that of Montpellier 1215, discussed below, see D. Carraz, '*Celeberrimum et generalissimum concilium*: Montpellier 1215 et le *negotium pacis et fidei*', *CdF* 54 (2019), 339–76. The council's preface frames its canons in the context of 'the peace' in the province of Narbonne 'just as was previously sworn at the will of the Lord Count of Toulouse and afterwards in the presence of the same legate at Saint Gilles, to the venerable bishops of Uzès and Nîmes and the abbot of Saint Gilles'. As Raimond VI of Toulouse gave a peace oath at Saint-Gilles in June 1209 (discussed further below), at the bidding of the papal legate Milo, in the presence of various bishops including those from Uzès and Nîmes, one cannot help but wonder whether the name of the legate Michael (active in this period in the Iberian peninsula) was confused with 'Milo', and that the 1195 council should be re-dated to around the same time, that is, mid-1209. The text appears only now to be preserved in Baluze and in Mansi, 'from a manuscript codex' belonging to François du Bosquet, bishop of Montpellier (d. 1676). My thanks to Ben Wiedemann for discussion regarding Michael.

[12] See J. France, 'Capuchins as Crusaders: Southern Gaul in the Late Twelfth Century', *Reading Medieval Studies* 36 (2010), 77–94; J. France, 'People against Mercenaries: The Capuchins in Southern Gaul', *Journal of Medieval Military History* 8 (2010), 1–22; D. Barthélemy, 'Les communes diocésaines en Occitanie', *CdF* 54 (2019), at 37–41.

[13] See Summerlin, *Canons of the Third Lateran Council*, pp. 58–62; H. Géraud, 'Les routiers', *Bibliothèque d'École des Chartes* 3 (1841–42), 125–47, 417–47. On their use in the south, see Macé, *Les comtes*, pp. 355–59.

[14] See also useful discussion in the Siblys' appendix D to their translation: Peter of Les-Vaux-de-Cernay, *History of the Albigensian Crusade*, trans. W. A. Sibly and M. D. Sibly (Woodbridge: Boydell, 1998), pp. 299–301.

ecclesiastical property and rights, it also now extended its reach rather more profoundly into politics and society.

This becomes notably clear if one looks closely at the oath of peace which Raimond VI swore in June 1209 at Saint-Gilles, under the direction of the papal legate Milo, in an attempt to ward off the coming crusade. The performance of this oath was itself a piece of religio-political theatre, designed to communicate publicly the fact of the count's submission to ecclesiastical *auctoritas* as much as the detail of his promise: he was led 'naked' (*nudus*, according to Pierre des Vaux-de-Cernay) to the doors of the church, and in the presence of the legate and many bishops, swore an oath on the crucifix, the Eucharist, 'and on numerous relics' which had been brought into public for the occasion; then clothed in a simple robe by the legate, he was ritually beaten, and led into the church. The crowd of spectators was so great, the chronicler says with some glee, that he then had to be led out through the crypt, passing the tomb of the martyred Pierre de Castelnau on his way.[15] For what was Raimond performing such penance? That, in the interestingly conditional grammar of the text, he recognized he was held excommunicate because:

> ...that the peace to which others have sworn I am said to have refused to swear; item, that I am said not to have carried out the oaths which I made regarding the expulsion of heretics or those believing in them; item that I am said always to have maintained and to maintain heretics; item that I am held suspect of faith; item that I have supported bandits (*ruptarii*) and mercenaries (*mainadas*); item that I have violated the days of Lent, feasts, and times that ought to enjoy security; that I am said to have refused to display justice to my adversaries, who have offered themselves to justice and have sworn peace; item that I have entrusted public offices to Jews; item that I hold unjustly ecclesiastical possessions and churches of the monastery of Saint Guillaume; item that I have fortified churches and hold them thus fortified; item that I collect, or have others collect, tolls or [payment for] safe passage that are not owed; item that I have banished the bishop of Carpentras from his own see; item that I am held suspect of the killing of Pierre de Castelnau of sacred memory, most of all that I received his killer in great familiarity; item that I have captured or have had captured the bishop of Vaison and his clerks, and I have destroyed the palace of the same bishop and the houses of the canons, and took the *castrum* of Vaison with violence; item that I am said to have laid violent hands on religious persons and to have committed much pillaging.[16]

---

[15] *Processus negotii Raymundi comitis Tolosani*, cap. ii (PL 216, cols 89–97, at col. 89); Pierre des Vaux-de-Cernay, *Hystoria Albigensis*, I, pp. 77–78 (cap. lxxvii).
[16] *Processus*, cap. ii; PL 216, col. 90.

There were specific contexts for various of these items, in particular an ongoing war between Raimond and 'his barons' in the region, led by Guillaume de Baux, duke of Orange.[17] (These barons were also forced to swear an oath to the peace, repeating some of the wider injunctions we have just seen; and, like Raimond, to hand over various castles as sureties to the legate).[18] The conflict with the bishops of Vaison and Carpentras was also essentially a political struggle for control of specific parts of the region—though this did not make the papacy any happier regarding the challenge to ecclesiastical authority it entailed.[19] It is these matters, plus the issue of giving public office to Jews, that the legate Milo enjoined upon Raimond VI prior to him doing penance and gaining absolution. After absolution, the instructions turned to the other topics, the primary injunction being to cease support for heresy, but also to amend the wider issues outlined above.[20] Importantly both Raimond, and the consuls of Avignon in a separate oath required at the same time, were made to promise that if a bishop named someone as a heretic, that label and its consequences were to be accepted by them—implicitly suggesting that they had previously been unwilling to accept such an interpretation of the holiness of the Good Men or the Waldensians.[21]

So wider issues of ecclesiastical order and 'peace' preceded the crusade, and were strongly present in its immediate launch. They continued to provide a broad ideological frame thereafter, also. The council of Montpellier (1215) set out various statutes regarding keeping the peace, including provision for imposing peace oaths, and appointing officials to enforce the peace.[22] The anonymous poet of the second part of the *Canso de la crozada* has Bishop Foulques of Toulouse declare, in his appeal to Pope Innocent III not to undermine Simon de Montfort's efforts in 1215, that de Montfort was 'truly obedient and a son of Holy Church...driving out heresy, mercenaries and soldiers', and saying of the southern French lords (to whom at that point Innocent was considering restoring lands previously granted to de Montfort), 'not one of them is Catholic nor keeps his oath'—referring back to Raimond VI's promises at Saint-Gilles.[23] Slightly later in the poem, Innocent gives advice to the young Raimond VII: 'If you keep the commands that I shall set

---

[17] Guillaume de Puylaurens, *Chronique*, cap. xii, pp. 64–65. I have not been able to access E. Smyrl, 'La famille des Baux (Xe–XIIe siècle)', *Cahiers de Centre d'études des sociétés méditerranéennes* 2 (1968), 2–108.

[18] *Processus*, caps vii, x, xi, xii, xiii (PL 216, cols 94–97).   [19] Macé, *Les comtes*, p. 342.

[20] The texts are usefully discussed in J. Paul, 'La paix de Saint-Gilles (1209) et l'exercice du pouvoir', in C. Carozzi and H. Taviani-Carozzi, eds, *Le pouvoir au moyen âge: idéologies, pratiques, représentations* (Aix: Presses universitaires de Provence, 2007), pp. 147–68, who suggests that the injunctions before absolution were those requiring reparation by a penitent, those after being 'a long list of obligations which are essential to a Christian prince regarding order and peace'. See also *Canso*, laisse 60 (Martin-Chabot, *Chanson*, I, pp. 148–50).

[21] Oath of the consuls of Avignon, the day after Raimond's public penance: *Processus*, cap. v, cols 92–93.

[22] Council of Montpellier, 1215, caps 32–42 (Mansi XXII, cols 939–50, at 947–49).

[23] *Canso*, liasse 148 (Martin-Chabot, *Chanson*, II, pp. 62–64).

out for you, | you will not fail in this world or in the other. | Be advised to love and honour and give thanks to God, | to obey the commands of the Church and its saints | to hear masses and matins and vespers, | to honour and make offerings to the body of Jesus Christ | to drive out heresy and to keep a good peace', going on to spell out that this involved not attacking monastic houses or allowing banditry.[24] General statutes for Provence issued by Raimond Berengar V, count of Provence, in 1222 and renewed in 1226 required all above the age of 14 to swear to the peace, and in the latter statutes established an annual payment required of ordinary lay people to be part 'of' the Peace.[25] The council of Montpellier in 1224 had Raimond VI renew his oath, including the issues regarding mercenaries and peace, along with other major barons; and at the treaty of Paris (1229) that concluded the crusade, Raimond VII promised to 'keep the peace' in his lands, to expel mercenaries, to defend the Church and its property.[26] Among various statutes regarding heresy, and some other issues to which we shall turn below, the council of Toulouse in 1229 repeated the instruction that all above the age of 14 should swear an oath to keep the peace (though without the monetary payment demanded in Provence), that any who broke the peace were excommunicate, and that nobody should receive thieves, bandits, or mercenaries. The councils of Béziers (1233) and Arles (1234) renewed this call. In statutes which Raimond VII himself obediently issued in 1233 he included, following a large number of instructions regarding the pursuit and detection of heretics, the injunction that in order that 'the tranquillity of peace in our land shall be fully and inviolably observed, we ordain that rebels, fugitives, robbers, little thieves and mercenaries (*latrunculi et statores*) shall be expelled from all the land', then further promising to confiscate the lands and property of those who broke the peace, and to launch formal inquiry (*inquisitio*) against those who bore public bad rumour (*publica fama*) that they received or supported 'thieves or plunderers, or other evil doers'.[27]

One could continue to pursue how the ideas and practices around 'peace' further developed, both within southern France and elsewhere, across the longer period.[28] But what matters with regard to the themes of this book are three

---

[24] *Canso*, liasse 152 (Martin-Chabot, *Chanson*, II, p. 84).

[25] F. Benoît, *Recueil des actes des comtes de Provence, II: Textes et analyses* (Paris: Picard, 1925), pp. 153–57 (no. 57), 207–14 (no. 102). For the schedule of payments, according to goods and personal status (knights were exempt), see statutes of 1226, c. 27, at p. 213.

[26] Council of Montpellier, 1224 (Mansi XXII, col. 1207). Peace of Paris, 1229 (*HGL*, VIII, 883–93), translated as appendix C to Sibly and Sibly, *Chronicle of William of Puylaurens*, pp. 138–44.

[27] Council of Toulouse, 1229, cc. 28, 29, 36 (Mansi XXIII, cols 194–204, at 201–02). Council of Béziers, 1233, c. 26 (Mansi XXIII, cols 269–78, at 278). Council of Arles, 1234, cc. 7, 8 (Mansi XXIII, cols 335–42, at 338). *Statuta Raimundi comitis Tolosani* (Mansi XXIII, cols 265–68, at 267–68). The parts of the council of Toulouse and Raimond VII's statutes relating to heresy are translated in A&B, pp. 190–201 (docs 29, 30). The context of 'peace' in the repression of heresy is discussed in Arnold, *Inquisition and Power*, pp. 33–37; more broadly see also T. N. Bisson, 'The Organised Peace in Southern France and Catalonia, c. 1140–1233', *American Historical Review* 82 (1977), 290–311.

[28] See J. Y. Malegam, *The Sleep of Behemoth: Disputing Peace and Violence in Medieval Europe, 1000–1200* (Ithaca, NY: Cornell University Press, 2013).

elements; I shall outline these across the remainder of this section. The first is that it shows us an important aspect of how the Church was attempting to reconfigure lordship across this period, and doing so in part *through* its intervention in southern France. The elaboration of what constituted 'peace', and the further association of additional issues—usury, the Jews, clerical and lay identity, clothing, and moral behaviour (all of which we shall further explore below and in subsequent chapters)—were a way in which ecclesiastical *auctoritas* sought to extend its practical dominion.[29] Forms of more traditional ecclesiastical lordship continued in this region, as elsewhere, into the thirteenth century, via the continued rural powers that the larger monasteries enjoyed, and the political power that many bishops wielded in the ancient cities. But that latter role was becoming more fraught in this period, with the growing political power of the newer 'bourgs' tending to challenge or conflict with the older episcopal 'cités'.[30] Thus a new dispensation was arising: whilst the notional separation of secular and religious power, rooted in the Gregorian reform, continued to be proclaimed, the Church was increasingly seeking to elaborate an ecclesial-moral frame to the 'justice' and 'peace' that good 'Catholic princes' were supposed to impose and sustain within their lands.[31] This combination of good lordship and governance with moral reform is extremely important to the developments we are tracking, as we shall see further below.[32]

The second element as to why 'peace' is an important theme for us is that its prominence around the crusade is a reminder to think carefully about how 'heresy' was being conceived across this key period. A swift overview of the Albigensian Crusade, where the perspective of the anti-heresy narrative histories and the moments of blunt, horrific violence may tend to loom largest, might lead us to conclude that the Church and the crusaders viewed the heretics and their supporters as utterly, abjectly 'Other', and that they could thus be dealt with only through violent eradication.[33] However, whilst there are undoubtedly events within the violent conflict that played out thus—Béziers in 1209 most famously, but massacres and mass executions at Lavaur, Moissac, and elsewhere also—this tends to lose the rather more complex dynamic that pertained much of the time,

---

[29] See also conclusion to Carraz, '*Celeberrimum et generalissimum concilium*'.

[30] An overview of civic struggles in Provence is provided within J. Chiffoleau, 'Les Gibelins du royaume d'Arles: notes sur les réalités impériales en Provence dans les deux premiers tiers du XIIIe siècle', in P. Guichard et al., eds, *Papauté, monachisme et théories politiques: II, les églises locales* (Lyon: Presses universitaires de Lyon, 1994).

[31] Within one of the documents of Raimond VI's penance, he is to promise 'just as is fitting for a Catholic prince' to defend and protect religious houses and the Church, whilst staying out of its dominion; *Processus*, cap. vi (PL 216, cols 93–94).

[32] See similarly comments in the conclusion to G. Lippiatt, 'Reform and Custom: The Statutes of Pamiers in Early Thirteenth-Century Christendom', in Aurell, Lippiatt, and Macé, eds, *Simon de Montfort (c. 1170–1218)*, pp. 39–67.

[33] This seems to be the ultimate perspective of Pegg, *A Most Holy War*, particularly in its rather controversial depiction of the crusade as an act of 'genocide' in its final chapter.

in the run up to the start of the crusade and in its immediate aftermath also. Heresy was always conceived as an issue about submission to *auctoritas*, as much as, or perhaps even more than, it was about wrong belief. One gets a rather clear example of this in 1217, when Honorius III wrote to the people of Marseille, who had been rebelling in some fashion against the political civic control of the bishop and cathedral canons, and had allegedly committed violent assault against clergy who were carrying crosses and the Eucharist in the church of Saint-Laurent. They were told that they had thus raised 'manifest suspicion of heretical wickedness' against themselves, and must make recompense or else fall under interdict—the demand for 'recompense' rather than relinquishing any beliefs or support for heretical figures clearly indicating that the hovering label of 'heresy' was on this occasion *entirely* about ecclesiastical authority.[34] Before the crusade, as we saw, there was orthodox preaching against heresy and occasions of formal public disputation. Both were attempts to persuade a wider audience that those holding certain beliefs were deservedly labelled 'heretics' (a point emphasized, as we have seen, in the documents surrounding Raimond VI's penance in 1209). These were therefore, moreover, attempts to persuade individuals that they should relinquish these beliefs and thus accept the authority of the Church. On occasion this worked: most obviously with Durand d'Osca, the converted Waldensian, but also sometimes with others. Interrogated by inquisitors in 1245, Ermengaut, wife of Pierre Boer, admitted that forty years before or thereabouts she had been 'hereticated'—that is, made into a Good Woman—by Isarn de Castres, this being when 'the heretics lived publicly in the land'. But she was then 'reconciled by the Blessed Dominic'.[35] Many others who were less centrally involved than Ermengaut did the same, before the crusaders came.

The crusade undoubtedly sought to impose a clear distinction between 'heretic' and 'orthodox' by making the question of *allegiance* paramount, as we have seen in Raimond VI's penance and oath. Resistance often brought ruthless and violent suppression, overriding any complexity regarding how to discern where the boundaries of faith diverged and ignoring any sense that the defence of local liberty might blur into other issues of allegiance. Whilst the famous injunction 'Kill them all, God will know his own' at Béziers was ascribed to the papal legate Arnaud Amaury only some decades later, it undoubtedly captures the way in which crusade was a blunt instrument, unsuited to and uninterested in nuances of faith. Simon de Montfort 'destroys the Catholics just as much as [he destroys]

---

[34] *Gallia christiana novissima II: Marseille* (Valence: Impr. Valentinoise, 1899), cols 105–07 (no. 217), 27 Feb 1217. Whilst the clear conjunction of heresy and politics here might be seen as in line with R. I. Moore's concept of a politically motivated 'war on (fictive) heresy', we may wish to note that on this clearly political occasion there is *no* invocation of a dualist heretical counter-Church; and thus to reflect on the fact that such charges were not alleged in all circumstances, even in the midst of the crusade period.

[35] MS Toulouse 609, fol. 20v. She admitted then to having received another female heretic, Rixende, and her companion in her house after her reconciliation.

the heretics', the anonymous poet has Innocent III say concernedly at one point of debate in the *Canso de la crozada*.[36]

However, even this does not mean that the Church's only response to heresy was destruction, even during the crusade years. If one surrendered to *auctoritas*, repented of the past sin of 'heresy', reconciliation was still possible. The statutes of Pamiers, issued by Simon de Montfort in 1212, made provision for resettling outside of a town any 'clothed heretic' (*hereticus vestitus*) who had reconciled themselves to the Church; the council of Toulouse in 1229 made a similar provision.[37] Another Ermengaut, daughter of Bernard de Saint-Félix, interrogated in 1246 admitted that she had believed in the Good Men since 1216 or so, and had in fact been 'hereticated' by a Good Man called Bon Fil in a certain wood, thus becoming a 'clothed heretic' (*heretica induta*) for three years from around 1228. However, 'she was later reconciled by Lord Foulques, the late bishop of Toulouse, and this was fifteen years ago or thereabouts', namely in 1231 (the year of his death).[38] Another witness in the same trials, Raimond Ademar, a knight of Lantars, said among many other things that he had heard the Good Men saying that God did not make the visible world, that the sacred host was not the body of Christ, that marriage and baptism did not aid salvation, and that the bodies of the dead would not be resurrected; but he left this belief in the Good Men 'on a certain day in which he heard Lord Bishop Foulques preaching', and later made confession to Brother Guillaume Arnaud, a Dominican who worked as an inquisitor from around 1238.[39]

I mention these moments of conversion and submission to authority not in order to defend or attempt to exculpate the Church from its harsh deeds. What I want rather to emphasize is that even amidst the violence, and even more in its aftermath, what was most frequently sought was conversion. But conversion was primarily understood as submission to authority—and this tells us something important regarding how the intervention of crusade and subsequent inquisition sought to reshape the operation of organized religion and lay piety. The Latin word *heresis* famously derives from the Greek word for 'choice' (*hairesis*); and this was what crusade and inquisition worked to impose, the sense that there were

---

[36] *Canso*, liasse 149 (Martin-Chabot, *Chanson*, II, p. 68).

[37] Statutes of Pamiers, 1212, c. 13 (Mansi XXII, cols 856–64, at 858); Council of Toulouse, 1229, c. 10.

[38] MS Toulouse 609, fol. 198v: 'Dixit quod fuit heretica induta per III annos et hereticavit eam Bonus Filius hereticus in quodam nemore prope Fonterz, et sunt [x]viii anni vel circa, sed postmodum fuit reconciliata per dominum Fulconem quondam episcopum Tholosanum, et sunt xv anni vel circa… Dixit etiam quod XXX annis quod primo habuit credulitatem heretici et dimisit illam credulitatem ultimo xvi anni sunt vel circa.'

[39] MS Toulouse 609, fols 200v–201r, at 201r: 'et dimisit illam credulitatem quodam die in qua audivit dominum episcopum fulcone predicantem. Et audivit hereticos dicentes quod deus non fecit visibilia, quod hostia sacrata non est corpus xpisti, quod matrimonium vel baptismus non valebant ad salutem, et quod mortuorum corpora non resurgent. Et ipse testis credit sicut ipsi dicebant et fuit confessus fratri Willelmo Arnaldi cui dixit omnia predicate et forte plura alia de quibus non recolit…'. On Guillaume Arnaud, see Dossat, *Crises*, pp. 217–26 and *passim*.

different belief commitments within which one could choose, and that one *must* choose Catholic orthodoxy or else suffer the consequences. The bedrock of that 'choice' was thus submission to *auctoritas*.

'Inquisition into heretical wickedness' changed in various important ways across the period studied by this book (a topic I have discussed at length elsewhere), and I shall return to some aspects of it in more detail in a later chapter.[40] Here, keeping our focus on the various 'interventions' made into the landscape of faith by the Church and the French crown in the first half of the thirteenth century, it is necessary to note a few particular features and implications of its early operation. Inquisition is, in this early period, not a centralized institution but a legal task carried out under papal authority within specific geographical limits, adapting an existing legal process of inquiry (*inquisitio*) to the task of discovering 'heretics'. It was not specific to southern France: the earliest inquisitors into heretical wickedness were commissioned by Gregory IX in northern France, the Rhineland, and Italy in 1231.[41] Those first commissioned in Languedoc were Dominicans, and they retained a long association with the office, though we also find Franciscans called to serve similarly in Provence in later decades,[42] and at various points around the middle of the century in particular, bishops also took on the task in the region.

It is important to note that in the early years this process of inquiry was largely envisaged as 'seeking out' heretics, identifying the latter primarily via public knowledge and rumour (*fama*). In this it looked back to a diocesan procedure first enjoined in the bull *Ad abolendam* in 1184 which had called on bishops to investigate their dioceses once or twice a year, in places where there was *fama* that heretics were living, making use of the testimony of three or more 'good men' from the locality who should be compelled under oath to reveal the presence of any who were heretics. A version of this process was enjoined specifically in southern France at the council of Avignon in 1209 and in identical language at that of Montpellier in 1215, ordering that the bishop:

> should bind by religious oath one priest and two or three laymen of good opinion (or more if it seems necessary to the work), that if there are any there who are reputed heretics, believers, supporters, or receivers or defenders of them, they will dutifully and with all speed report this to the archbishop or bishop and consuls of the city and lords of the place, or their bailli.[43]

---

[40] See Arnold, *Inquisition and Power*, chapters 1 and 3 in particular.
[41] H. Maisonneuve, *Études sur les origines de l'inquisition* (Paris: J. Vrin, 1960), pp. 250–70.
[42] J. Chiffoleau, 'L'inquisition franciscaine en Provence et dans l'ancien royaume d'Arles (vers 1260–vers 1330)', in *Frati minori e inquisizione: atti del XXXIII Convegno internazionale: Assisi, 6–8 ottobre 2005* (Spoleto: Fondazione Centro italiano di studi sull'alto medioevo, 2006), pp. 151–284.
[43] Council of Avignon, 1209, c. 2 (Mansi XXII, col. 785); council of Montpellier, 1215, c. 46 (Mansi XXII, col. 950).

The council of Toulouse in 1229 repeated and elaborated these instructions, making it very clear that the process envisaged was a physical search: the priest and his lay helpers were to search 'carefully, thoroughly, faithfully and frequently, inspecting every single house and underground room that gives rise to some suspicion, and searching buildings appended or attached under these roofs and other hiding places'.[44] Thus as inquisitors into heretical wickedness took up their task, their 'inquisition' was initially of a similar kind: looking physically to locate those 'vested heretics' and sandal-shod Waldensians, assumed to be visible via their mode of dress as much as anything else.

But it did not, of course, remain that simple (if indeed it was ever thus). The issue was not so much who was a 'heretic', in the fully-fledged sense, as everyone else who might be understood to support them, in the various possible different ways that could include; and what that support was understood to *mean*, in terms of their belief and thus their moral status. Those who were not themselves fully-fledged heretics—were not Good Men or Good Women, nor Waldensians Brothers or Sisters—were themselves to be physically 'marked out' by the process of inquisition, required to wear distinguishing yellow crosses on their outer clothes, 'to correct the guilty life, or at least, to show who walks in darkness and who in light', as the council of Narbonne put it in 1243.[45] We shall turn to such issues again in Chapter 8, but for now the point to take is that the logic of crusade, the logic that required obedient secular *potestas* to submit to ecclesiastical *auctoritas* in order to prove its orthodoxy and sustain 'the peace', continued on, after the conclusion to the crusade itself. And here is the third important strand, most essential to this book, and one explored further in Part II also: such submission came to imply a number of further aspects beyond the apparent binary of 'heresy' and 'orthodoxy'. The 'peace' that the Church wished to impose started with such matters but did not end there. It embraced—or perhaps we might better say, it proffered and demanded—a 'reform' of behaviour, beliefs, and morals as well.

What further complicated all of this was, of course, that for most in the south, the experience of 'the French' besieging, massacring, and dispossessing those in the region created a regional crisis of *potestas* and the destabilizing of its legitimacy in the immediate decades around the crusade. In the midst of its account events, the *Canso* puts the following rather optimistic words into the mouths of the townspeople of Toulouse, when in 1217 the count of Toulouse re-entered the city, ready to fight off the besieging crusaders:

And they said one to the other 'Now we have Jesus Christ! | Now we have the morning star, the star that shines upon us. | This is our lord who was lost, who

---

[44] Council of Toulouse, 1229, c. 1 (Mansi XXIII, col. 194); trans. A&B, p. 191.
[45] Council of Narbonne, 1243, c. 5 (Mansi XXIII, col. 357). See Arnold, *Inquisition and Power*, pp. 57–73 for wider discussion.

was thought to have perished. | Through him worth and *paratge*, which were buried, | now live, and are restored and healthy and healed, | and our whole lineage will be enriched for all time!'[46]

The poet thus presents us with Raimond VI as a Christ-like figure, performing the miracle of resurrecting the 'dead' values of worth and the combination of knightly honour, land, and lineage bound up in the idiomatic Occitan word *paratge*; values that the crusaders had, as the poet saw it, shamed and cast down.[47] But Toulouse's partial victory was not to last, and the anonymous continuation of the *Canso* cannot help but be read ultimately as an elegy for a particular, idealized, southern French notion of order. By its conclusion, the crusade had imposed a new structure of political order, binding the south more tightly both to the Capetian court and to the papacy. With this came a re-formation of Christian piety.

The Reform of Christian Society

Let us return for a moment to the council at Montpellier in (it is said) 1195, convened by the papal legate Michael.[48] The main business of the council was to strengthen 'the peace' in the region, suppressing heretics and mercenaries, and extending protection to ecclesiastical property and beyond.[49] But beyond these measures, the legate had other concerns also, in several instances repeating or amplifying other commands of the Third Lateran Council of 1179. Jews and 'Saracens' were not to have power over Christians, and thus should not have any Christian servants in their houses. 'Manifest usurers' were not to be allowed to take communion, no oblations would be accepted from them, and they were not to be given Christian burial, until they resile from their sin (and in the case of any clergy or religious who were involved in such activities, they were suspended from ecclesiastical office). All clergy were to have the tonsure, and were to dress appropriately, without silver or metal ornamentation on their clothing, and to avoid playing at dice or similar games of chance. Both clergy and laity were enjoined not to wear fancy clothes (*incisas vestes sive linguatas ab inferiori parte*, that which in English would later be called 'dagged', that is, fashionably 'slashed' at the ends) and women should not wear 'sumptuous' dresses with lengthy trains,

---

[46] *Canso*, liasse 182 (Martin-Chabot, *Chanson*, II, 276). 'Morning star', cf. Apoc. 22: 16.
[47] Cf. *Canso*, liasse 154 (Martin-Chabot, *Chanson*, I, 94). See C. P. Bagley, '*Paratge* in the Anonymous *Chanson de la Croisade Albigeoise*', French Studies 21 (1967), 195–204; Débax, *Seigneurie collective*, chapter 5.
[48] Regarding date, see n. 11 above.
[49] The council repeats some of the same language as that of the archbishop of Auch in 1139, regarding protection of 'priests, clergy, monks, scholars, converts, pilgrims, merchants, peasants, those coming and going [about their business], and those engaged in agricultural tasks, and pasturing animals and carrying seed to fields'. Council of Montpellier, 1195 (Mansi XXII, cols 667–72, at 669).

'but should go about in honest and moderate clothing, which should not denote lasciviousness nor display the arrogance of vanity'.[50] And these sumptuary measures were prompted by the Lord's decision to allow the loss of Jerusalem (to Saladin in 1187) and 'the invasion of certain parts of Spain', which should drive all Christians to contrition and to 'amend' their lives. As Jessalynn Bird has made clear across a wide range of articles drawing on the copious preaching materials produced around the university of Paris, by the later twelfth century 'crusade'— whether to the Holy Lands or elsewhere—had become, for theologians and preachers at least, a moral movement, promising not only the defence of Christian sites from 'Saracen' incursion, but the reform of Christian selves across Europe.[51]

The general developments I shall trace here are therefore not only found in southern France. But the circumstances of their implementation amidst crusade and inquisition, and in an increasingly urbanized landscape saturated with mercantile activity, does mean that they had a particular inflection, chronology, and intensity specific to the region. As I have argued above, the crusade can be seen as pursuing a notion of Christian 'peace' which stretched beyond the eradication of heresy. Within this we have seen the suppression of mercenaries, the control of lordly exactions, along with mention of several other important areas to which I shall attend below. Two recurrent and important themes were the desire to circumscribe the role that Jews could play within a Christian society, and, partly but not wholly connected to this, the cessation of usury. Both are key examples of how reforms that were being enjoined across all Christendom had rather particular implications and nuances in a southern French context. Let us look at them in turn.

Marking the Jews

As with other Mediterranean societies, southern France had a large and long-standing Jewish community; and, as Joseph Shatzmiller has wonderfully demonstrated, Jews were not only a part of the population in cities but were found across society, including in more rural *castra*, engaged in a whole variety of labours. Whilst there were Jewish financiers and merchants (alongside many other Christian merchants and, as we shall see below, much use of moneylending between Christians), it was absolutely not the case that these were the only

---

[50] Council of Montpellier, 1195, col. 670: 'sed in habitu honesto et moderato incedant, qui nec lasciviam notet, nec jactantiam vanitatis ostendat'.
[51] Among various pieces, see J. Bird, 'Paris Masters and the Justification of the Albigensian Crusade', *Crusades* 6 (2007), 117–55; J. Bird, 'Innocent III, Peter the Chanter's Circle, and the Crusade Indulgence: Theory, Implementation, and Aftermath', in A. Sommerlechner, ed., *Innocenzo III: Urbs et Orbis, Atti del Congresso Internazionale*, 2 vols (Rome: Istituto storico italiano per il Medio Evo, 2003), I, pp. 503–24.

economic activities in which they were involved.[52] Prior to the council of Montpellier's echoing, in 1195, of the Third Lateran Council's injunctions against Jews having Christian servants, there seems to be no ecclesiastical or secular legislation limiting Jewish activity in the south of France.[53]

That does not necessarily mean that interfaith relations were always amicable. In 1160, the bishop of Béziers, with the agreement of the clergy and consuls of the city, wrote a charter addressing the Trencavel lords and the Jews regarding the 'custom' in that city in which 'between the first hour of the Sunday before Palm Sunday until the last hour of the second day following Easter' Christians would hurl insults and throw stones at Jews. Henceforth, the bishop declared, any cleric who threw a stone at a Jew or threw it into his house, during this symbolically important period, would be excommunicated; and any layperson who did similarly would not be defended by the bishop (against punishment by the count, by implication). One can obviously read this as evidence of existing social tensions, though the document conveys a strong sense that it was a clerically directed activity, a sort of hateful liturgical embellishment to Easter: the clergy were forbidden from stone-throwing 'from whence a major conflict (*bellum*) might arise', which rather suggests that they were usually the ones initiating the activity; and the main point of the bishop's charter is to note that 'because of this remission and surrender'—surrender, that is *guirpitio*, a word familiar in various transfers of property or rights—'you [Jews] give to me, Bishop Guillaume, 600 *sous* of Melgueil, to the work of the church of St Nazaire...and you give to the church of St Nazaire...in perpetuity each year 4 *livres* of Melgueil on Palm Sunday, to the decoration of the said church'.[54] So this symbolic violence was in some sense a 'right' to be relinquished by the bishop. Something broadly similar is found in Arles, where an agreement made in 1178 had the Jewish community of the city paying 50 *sous* up front and a further 20 *sous* annually, until the bridge was built; the agreement was to be announced by the archbishop on Palm Sunday and to be repeated by priests in local churches, warning people not to molest the Jews. And if any 'youths or people' did molest them, the Jewish community could forgo their 20 *sous* annual payment.[55]

There are very occasional other, less violent, early indications that Jews might be treated somewhat differently from Christians. For example, in the lengthy

---

[52] J. Shatzmiller, *Shylock Reconsidered: Jews, Moneylending and Medieval Society* (Berkeley: University of California Press, 1990).

[53] C. P. Hershon, *Faith and Controversy: The Jews of Mediaeval Languedoc* (Birmingham: A.E.I.O, 1999), pp. 48–49.

[54] *Cart. Béziers*, pp. 266–67 (no. 197, 2 May 1160). The charter further notes that this annual sum cannot be redirected to other purposes by the bishop or any clergy, strongly suggesting that this was imposed by Raimond I Trencavel; who, ironically enough, was murdered in that same cathedral church by the citizens in 1167. On the latter, see E. Graham-Leigh, *The Southern French Nobility and the Albigensian Crusade* (Woodbridge: Boydell, 2005), pp. 147–48.

[55] Blanchard, *Documents...commerce de Marseille*, I, pp. 240–41 (no. 140).

customs of Moissac, issued by the abbot-monk and abbot-knight for the town in the first half of the twelfth century, the lordly exaction placed on those who used the services of a butcher specify that anyone having a pig slaughtered should pay 'une maille'—a small coin—to the abbot-knight, and 1d for a cow to both abbots; but Jews had to pay 4d, and 'Saracens' 12d.[56] So they were not treated equally; but on the other hand, they still had access to an important shared service, and these were the only differentiation for Jews noted in those customs—and in fact the only time 'Jews' are mentioned as a separate group in *any* of the surviving pre-1200 urban customs.

What intervention in Jewish–Christian relations did a 'reforming' Church attempt to bring about? The obvious and infamous key development was the requirement of the Fourth Lateran Council of 1215 that all Jews wear a 'distinguishing sign' so that Christians could shun them. This seems to have been picked up for the first time in southern France at the council of Narbonne in 1227, which in its second canon condemns Jewish 'usury' and repeats Lateran III's injunctions against Christian women serving as maids or wet-nurses in Jewish households. In canon 3 it then states:

> To this, so that Jews can be discerned from others, we strictly order that in the middle of their chest they should carry a circular sign, the thickness of which circle should be one digit, the height in truth one half palm. And nonetheless we forbid them to work publicly on Sundays and feast days. And so that they do not scandalize Christians, or be scandalized by them, we wish and order that in Holy Week none of them, except for necessary cause, should leave their houses; and prelates shall guard them from the vexation of Christians, most of all in the aforesaid week.[57]

Canon 4 goes on to note that the Jews must pay 'as oblations' to their parish church 6d of Melgueil for this protection, for each family, on the feast of the Resurrection—suggesting that the hostile 'liturgical' dynamic we saw in the Béziers charter from 1160 still pertained. The requirement regarding clothing was repeated in other southern French councils later in the century, as one would find elsewhere in Europe, sometimes with further elaboration: for example, the council of Arles in 1234 specified that the circular badge applied to Jews over the age of 13 and that Jewish girls and women over the age of 12 were to wear a veil; that of Albi in 1254 forbade Jewish men from wearing round hats similar to those worn

---

[56] Customs of Moissac, early 12th century, market rights c. 23; Lagrèze-Fossat, *Études historiques sur Moissac*, I, pp. 106–07.

[57] Council of Narbonne, 1227, c. 3 (Mansi XXIII, cols 19–26, at 22). On the broader spread of legislation regarding the distinguishing sign, see D. Sansy, 'Marquer la différance: l'imposition de la rouelle aux XIIIe et XIV siècles', *Médiévales* 41 (2001), 15–26.

by priests.⁵⁸ A parallel theme perhaps more particular to the south—and suggestive of how much of a role Jews could play in their wider communities—was an injunction made by the papal legate Milo at the council of Avignon in 1209, that Jews should be deprived of any public office or private administrative role, accompanied soon after by a similar injunction in de Montfort's statutes of Pamiers (1212), that no 'heretical believer *or Jew*' could be made a provost or *bailli* or judge or given other legal office (although Jews could still give evidence against other Jews).⁵⁹ The council of Albi (1254) further ordered that Jews could not sell meat in Christian markets, nor work publicly on Christian feast days, and that, under threat of excommunication, Christians should not consult Jewish doctors.⁶⁰

These injunctions very clearly issue from papal policy, driven by papal legates from the late twelfth century onward, elaborated and repeated as we have seen in various regional ecclesiastical councils. But they started to be picked up in some civic statutes also. The customs of Montpellier from 1204, given by Peire, king of Aragon, ordered that no lord of Montpellier could have a Jew as his *bailli*.⁶¹ Those for the city of Alès (undated, but 1232 at the latest) ordered that whilst Jews were tolerated through the 'common humanity' they shared with Christians, they were to be visibly distinguished through their mode of dress, warned them that they should not carry out work publicly on Sundays where Christians could see them (though closed workshops were permitted), and strictly ordered them not to show themselves in public on the Easter weekend.⁶² Perhaps most tellingly, the customs of Carcassonne from around 1205, within a statute dealing with verbal insult, declared that if any Christian of Jewish or Muslim descent, or indeed any other Christian, was called 'a Saracen or a Jew... this is truly a dispute, equal to being hit or attacked', and thus subject to legal arbitration.⁶³

At the same time, Jews clearly did continue to play a considerable role in southern French society; and, as the detail in the Carcassonne custom just cited indicates, there had been long-standing integration at some points at least. Several civic customs included a specific form of oath that could be taken by Jews (since the Gospels were not appropriate), necessary for them to form business contracts and engage in other dealings.⁶⁴ A number also make it clear that disputes between

---

⁵⁸ Council of Arles, 1234, c. 16 (Mansi XXIII, cols 335–42, at 340); Council of Albi, 1254, c. 64 (Mansi XXIII, cols 829–52, at 851). Albi (1254), c. 65 repeats the requirement to wear the circular badge, as does council of Béziers, 1246, c. 39 (Mansi XXIII, cols 689–704, at 701). Council of Arles, 1260, c. 8 repeats the injunction against wearing round hats like priests (Mansi XXIII, cols 1001–12, at 1007).

⁵⁹ Council of Avignon, c. 2 (Mansi XXII, col. 785); statutes of Pamiers, 1212, c. 14 (Mansi XXII, col. 858).

⁶⁰ Council of Albi, 1254, cc. 66, 68, 69 (Mansi XXIII, cols 851–52).

⁶¹ Customs of Montpellier, 1204, c. 6 (Teulet, *Layettes*, I, p. 256).

⁶² Customs of Alès, before 1232, c. 55 (Maurette, *Recherches historiques... d'Alais*, pp. 461–63).

⁶³ Customs of Carcassonne, c. 1205, c. 20 (Teulet, *Layettes*, I, p. 274).

⁶⁴ For example, customs of Alès, 1217, c. 35 (Maurette, *Recherches historiques... ville d'Alais*, p. 492); customs of Arles, early thirteenth century, c. 193 (Giraud, *Droit français au Moyen* Age, II, p. 244).

Jews and Christians could be heard in civic courts.[65] Thus whilst the thirteenth-century papacy and parts of the Church continued to amplify the sense that Jews were innate enemies of Christ, and whilst antisemitic stories of child murder and Host desecration began to circulate in other parts of Europe, in this region the mercantile cities at least were not readily swayed from continued interaction.[66]

The Crusade against Usury

> Greatly it pleases me when I see, suffering,
> The wicked rich men
> Who fight against *paratge*;
> It pleases me when I see them destroyed,
> Day by day, twenty or thirty,
> When I find them naked, without clothes,
> And begging for their bread.

This is the first *cobla*, or verse, of a poem written at some point in the later twelfth century, sometimes attributed to the Occitan nobleman and troubadour Bertran de Born (d. before 1215), though possibly in fact by a more lowly poet called Guillem Magret (fl. 1195–1210).[67] The poem goes on to rail further against those *vilani*—peasants—who, 'full of trickery and usury' (*plena d'enjan et d'uzura*), had managed to rise up the social ladder.[68] The poet's outpouring of ire can remind us of several important things. One is that the growth in urban landscapes and accompanying mercantile activity, and the rise of non-noble elites, was visible to medieval contemporaries. Another is that, very clearly, such a change to the social landscape could be far from pleasing to contemporaries: the poet ends the poem with a heartfelt negative prayer, *Dieus lur don mal'aventura, Amen*, 'God give them bad luck, Amen'. But what particularly interests me is that the troubadour (whether Bertran—a major lord—or the more lowly Guillem)—sings here of 'trickery and usury'.

---

[65] For example, customs of Carcassonne, c. 1205, c. 54.
[66] See G. I. Langmuir, 'L'absence d'accusation de meutre rituel à l'ouest du Rhône', *CdF* 12 (1977), 235–49, and other essays in the same volume on southern French Jewish communities.
[67] My thanks to Stefano Milonia for alerting me to the contested authorship. Guillem Magret came from somewhat further north, near Vienne, but wrote works in courts in both Provence and Aragon. See Bibliographia Elettronica dei Trovatori (<www.bedt.it>) 223.005a. On Bertran, see note below.
[68] *Mout mi plai quan vey dolenta | la malvada gent manenta/qu'ab paratge mou contenta; | e.m plai quan los vey desfar | de jorn en jorn, vint o trenta, | e.ls trop nutz, ses vestimenta | e van lur pan acaptar.* W. D. Paden Jr, T. Sankovitch, and P. H. Stäblein, eds, *The Poems of the Troubadour Bertran de Born* (Berkeley: University of California Press, 1986), p. 321 (I have given a more literal translation than the one provided there).

Quite a lot of modern scholarship on medieval usury, focused on scholastic intellectual debate around the topic, has sought to try to specify what is meant by it; or, at least, to track how ecclesiastical condemnation of usury developed, and to what degree it was intellectually coherent and defined.[69] This comes to matter, somewhat, in later centuries in some parts of Europe, when the Church reaches an accommodation in practice, if not always in theory, with the apparently unstoppable rise of civic early capitalism.[70] The troubadour poet was not a medieval scholastic thinker, and that he can use the word not only shows its wider circulation but that we are probably best served as seeing it operate as a rather loose label, applied when someone claiming authority felt that they beheld something of which they disapproved. The fact was that various forms of loan, most producing some degree of income, were present in medieval society by the later twelfth century and long thereafter. Cash loans, and a level of interest owed, could be agreed under contract, but most were made against something given in surety, a *pignus* in Latin, often land but also various forms of income-producing rights. With something held *in pignus* the lender might specifically request a level of repayment interest, but would most commonly gain what was in effect a form of interest through taking the income of the land or rights during the course of the loan; and in fact might hope that the loan remain unpaid, thus coming to possess the property directly, or at least to hold it profitably over a sustained period of time.[71] In southern French society, various forms of such activity were extremely common, and the latter example, of gaining ownership of property through taking them as sureties against loans, was, for example, done rather effectively and repeatedly by the Cistercian monastery of Berdoues (c. 26 km south-west of Auch) in the late twelfth and early thirteenth centuries, as Connie Berman has demonstrated.[72]

But 'usury' was a sin, condemned with different degrees of specificity by papal authority across the twelfth century. In 1166, Alexander III permitted the bishop of Cahors to confiscate money from 'usurers, robbers, and goods badly acquired' that could not be restituted, along with other income, in order to construct a bridge over the river Lot.[73] The Third Lateran Council (1179) had excluded

---

[69] Among others, see J. T. Noonan, *The Scholastic Analysis of Usury* (Cambridge, Mass.: Harvard University Press, 1957); D. Wood, *Medieval Economic Thought* (Cambridge: Cambridge University Press, 2002), chapters 7 and 8; J. Kaye, *A History of Balance, 1250-1375* (Cambridge: Cambridge University Press, 2014), chapter 1; and now R. Dorin, *No Return: Jews, Christian Usurers, and the Spread of Mass Expulsion in Medieval Europe* (Princeton: Princeton University Press, 2023).

[70] For example, J. M. Murray, *Bruges, Cradle of Capitalism, 1280-1390* (Cambridge: Cambridge University Press, 2005), particularly pp. 138-65; E. S. Hunt and J. M. Murray, *A History of Business in Medieval Europe, 1200-1550* (Cambridge: Cambridge University Press, 1999), pp. 70-73.

[71] For a clear discussion see C. Bouchard, *Holy Entrepreneurs: Cistercians, Knights and Economic Exchange in Twelfth-Century Burgundy* (Ithaca, NY: Cornell University Press, 2009), chapter 1.

[72] C. H. Berman, 'Land Acquisition and the Use of the Mortgage Contract by the Cistercians of Berdoues', *Speculum* 57 (1982), 250-66.

[73] Doat 120, fols 1r-2r: 'ut de usuris, rapinis et aliis male aquisitis...'.

'manifest usurers' (possibly meaning, as Jacques Le Goff has suggested, those against whom there was public *fama*) from Christian burial; and Urban III, in the decretal *Consuluit nos* (issued 1185–87), emphasized that usury was ultimately a sin of intention, that anything gained in exchange for a loan beyond the initial value constituted usury, and that the sin could only receive absolution if total restitution had been made.[74] As said, this was an issue for all of western Christendom, and it was one which reverberated on through later centuries. But it gained a particular urgency in southern France, as part of the wider issues of reform and order, around the period of the Albigensian Crusade.

One particular figure looms large, as he made the combat of 'usury' a key element in his drive to reform—Bishop Foulques of Toulouse—though in fact his were not the first efforts to combine heresy, usury, peace, and reform, nor indeed the last. Foulques was the son of a Genoese merchant, but clearly underwent some form of conversion, disavowing wealth in a way not dissimilar to Waldes of Lyon. He entered a Cistercian monastery in the 1190s, and became bishop of Toulouse in 1206. He may have been present at the council of Avignon in 1209, which, among the other anti-heresy and anti-Jewish measures already mentioned, ordered that every feast day there should be a blanket excommunication of anyone who committed usury, and that Jews were to repay any usury they had exacted.[75] According to Guillaume de Tudela (the pro-crusader poet of the first portion of the *Canso de la crozada*), in the Spring of 1210 Foulques and Arnaud Amaury had preached against usury (*renou*) in the Agenais, though without notable success.[76] Foulques subsequently travelled to Paris, to help drum up support for the Albigensian Crusade, meeting there the influential Dominican preacher Jacques de Vitry, a key figure in the wider 'reform' movement around crusade. Perhaps fired up by that encounter, later that same year on his return to Toulouse, the bishop founded a great confraternity (*magna confratria*) in the city, later known as the 'White Confraternity' after another 'Black Confraternity' arose to oppose it. Foulques signed the members of the White Confraternity with a cross so that 'his flock, the citizens of Toulouse, should not be deprived of the indulgences granted to strangers', that is, the northern French crusaders, aiming to use the confraternity as a political/judicial weapon to 'drive out heretical wickedness and extinguish the fervour of usurers'. It was, in a sense, another form of sworn 'peace association', forcing usurers to 'answer complaints... and give

[74] J. Le Goff, *Your Money or Your Life: Economy and Religion in the Middle Ages*, trans. P. Ranum (New York: Zone, 1988); expanding upon J. Le Goff, 'The Usurer and Purgatory', in R. S. Lopez, ed., *The Dawn of Modern Banking* (New Haven: Yale University Press, 1979), pp. 25–52. The council of Montpellier in 1195 repeats the Lateran III injunction against 'manifest usurers' gaining Christian burial (Mansi XXII, col. 670).

[75] Council of Avignon, 1209, cc. 3, 4 (Mansi, XXII, col. 786). The preamble to the council states that, in addition to the named archbishops, there were present 'twenty bishops, and moreover many abbots and other rectors of churches'.

[76] *Canso*, laisse 46 (Martin-Chabot, *Chanson*, I, p. 110).

satisfaction', and sending armed men to seize goods from the houses of those who refused to appear before its officers.[77]

Ecclesiastical condemnation of usury was repeated at the council of Narbonne in 1227, which reiterated the Avignon statute to issue blanket excommunication on feast days (alongside those committing incest, concubines, adulterers, and thieves (*raptores*)), as well as a more specific injunction against Jewish usurers taking 'immoderate usury', which one might interpret as meaning those who levied an *excessive* rate of interest. The issue was raised again at Albi in 1230, that council adjusting the Lateran III phraseology to warn 'manifest *or hidden* usurers' that 'if a complaint is brought against them' they would not receive burial, nor would priests say prayers for them, nor receive their oblations, unless they or their heirs made restitution for their gains.[78] Later in the century, Bernard de Combret, bishop of Albi (1254–71), included a briefer injunction in synodal statutes he issued, forbidding burial to usurers against whom there was complaint, and the injunction was periodically repeated thereafter.[79]

The fine detail of these injunctions suggests that, as one would rather expect and indeed as later evidence demonstrates, the Church was not in any sense successful in stamping out 'usury', either in southern France or indeed elsewhere. Despite moments of strong, and frankly unrealistic, ambition when the Church tried to prohibit *any* level of interest on loans, what tended to pertain was a negotiated set of local accommodations, where the focus on 'manifest' usury or specific complaint effectively circumscribed what was legitimate from what might occasion prosecution. Even in Toulouse under Bishop Foulques, the only surviving document from a judicial process in 1215 against usury ordered by him relates to post-mortem recompense, rather than prosecution of an active moneylender; in that case it was 'the hospital' (possibly the Hospitallers, or else one of the various hospital foundations) who had to pay back a sum of interest that a deceased testator had owed, that testator having otherwise left all his goods to the foundation.[80] An inquiry survives from 1255, ordered by the archbishop of Narbonne into another case in Toulouse, where evidence was given by various witnesses, predominantly public notaries and some priests as well as the central complainant. The case is complex and confusing, but it is notable that witnesses were repeatedly questioned as to whether it was 'public *fama*' that certain key

---

[77] Guillaume de Puylaurens, *Chronique*, cap. xv, pp. 70–73.
[78] Council of Narbonne, 1227, cc. 2, 8 (Mansi XXIII, cols 21, 23); council of Albi, 1230, c. 60 (Pontal, *Statuts synodaux*, II, p. 30).
[79] Statutes of Bernard de Combret, 1255 × 61, c. 14 (O. Pontal, ed., *Les statuts synodaux français du XIIIe siècle*, 2 vols (Paris: CTHS, 1983), II, p. 462). Usurers are also listed among the various groups (heretics, those who die in tournaments, robbers, those under excommunication and interdict, and those who commit suicide) who are denied Christian burial in the widely circulated synodal statutes of Nîmes, 1252, c. 130 (Pontal, *Statuts synodaux*, II, p. 370).
[80] ADHG E 508, 11 Nov 1215, edited as appendix 5, doc. 15 in Mundy, *Liberty and Political Power*, pp. 208–09.

figures were known usurers and practised usury; the details however make it clear that what potentially constituted 'usury' was an *excessively* high rate of interest, which in this particular case had allegedly increased an original debt of 60 *sous* to 260 *sous*.[81] And indeed, where 'usury' was mentioned in civic statutes, it was mostly in terms of putting limits on how high a rate of interest could be levied (where the word 'usury' sometimes seems simply to mean 'interest'), or else limiting what kinds of cases regarding lending could be heard in the civic court.[82] The customs of Arles (1217 × 40, discussed in some detail in Chapter 4), whilst generally quite concerned with moral civic governance, simply note that anyone who has anything 'unjustly' from the commune, such as 'usury or any other thing which one cannot retain without damning one's soul', can make recompense by donating the value to the works on the city's bridge over the Rhône.[83] There is one exception to this continued relative civic acceptance of usury, namely the customs of Saint-Gilles, said to be originally given between 1210 and 1215 but subject to later, highly legalistic, reworking, possibly in the mid-thirteenth century and possibly by Gui Foulques, the future Pope Clement IV. These rather unusual statutes state that 'usurers are an abominable contagion', and forbid all such activities; but this is a tone and blanket ban notable for its absence elsewhere.[84]

We might therefore say that, from the late twelfth century onward, the Church succeeded in having 'usury' recognized as a major sin, endangering one's soul and access to Christian burial; and succeeded periodically in providing a means of framing complaints against those who levied excessive interest. It did not succeed in stamping out 'usury', unsurprising given the considerable amount of credit and debt present in an active mercantile society such as we find in southern France. But it sought to make, and probably for many lay people succeeded in making, such mercantile activity morally *suspect*, where 'usury' figured symbolically as the worst example of a larger realm of financial sin into which one might fall. Given the combined efforts against heresy and usury, we might be tempted to see both as newly invented (or at least, newly reinvigorated) crimes, the identification of which fed into the authority of the Church; an aspect of R. I. Moore's 'Persecuting Society'. There is further nuance here worth pursuing, however. As we shall see in a subsequent chapter, in later decades 'heresy' moved from being imagined as the fairly clear category addressed in this chapter—essentially support for Good Men or Waldensians, thought of as easily identifiable figures, thus failing to obey

---

[81] Single document with no archival reference given, edited as *piece justicatif* 9, in A. Blanc, ed., *Le livre de comptes de Jacme Olivier, marchand Narbonnais*, 2 vols (Paris: Picard, 1899), I, pp. 333–44.

[82] See, for example, customs of Montpellier, 1204, cc. 68, 116 (Teulet, *Layettes*, I, pp. 255–66); customs of Carcassonne, c. 1205, c. 54 (Teulet, *Layettes*, I, pp. 272–81); customs of Alès, 1217, c. 430 (Maurette, *Recherches historiques...d'Alais*, p. 491); customs of Draguignan, 1235 (Giraud, *Droit français*, II, p. 15); customs of Aix, before 1245 (Giraud, *Droit français*, II, pp. 18, 19, 20), mostly specified as 'Jewish usury' but allowed at 5d per *livre* per month (an annual rate of c. 25% interest).

[83] Customs of Arles, 1217 × 40, c. 114 (Giraud, *Droit français*, II, p. 226).

[84] Customs of Saint-Gilles, 1210 x–15?, c. 15 (E. Bligny-Bondurand, *Les coutumes de Saint-Gilles (XIIe–XIVe siècles)* (Paris: Picard, 1915), pp. 73–74).

church authority—into something rather more troubling, more diffuse, a potential state of error into which one might discover one had wandered. This is however the case for 'usury' from the start: a type of business practice, whether bound up with moneylending or the use of mortgages, but one which could become coded as deeply sinful, through a mixture of specific practices, public reputation, and ecclesiastical intervention.

Strengthening the Parish, the Faith, and the Church

As we have seen above, the edicts of the Fourth Lateran Council with regard to heresy, usury, and Jews loom large in the 'reform' imposed forcefully on the south of France. Lateran IV is famous also for its reform of pastoral provision, through strengthening the framework that should support a suitable parish priest. However, to speak of a 'framework' may presuppose too much, too soon. Later practices might lead us to assume that each 'diocese' was subdivided into 'parishes', as if mapped from above, each 'parish' having a clearly defined administrative area, spiritual responsibilities, and resident parishioners. But it is not clear that such a system yet pertained across Europe, nor that it was established in the same fashion universally across western Christendom. So it is worth asking what 'a parish' was in southern France, up to the period immediately after the end of the crusade.[85]

As we saw in Chapter 1, the word *parrochia* (parish) is intermittently present in various charters and letters of the eleventh century, though without any very clearly fixed or precise meaning. By the twelfth century we also start to find *parrochiani* (parishioners), though in fact still fairly rarely. The use of 'parish' as a vague geographical marker occurs frequently across the cartularies of the abbey of Grandselve, particularly for charters made in the second half of the twelfth century, and much of the time is used, as is the case in earlier charters, somewhat interchangeably with 'tithing' (*decimaria*). It sometimes turns up simply to identify where a particular piece of land is held, as in an exchange, probably from the 1180s, between Grandselve and a woman called Ramunda and her husband, the couple giving 'whatever they have... in the whole parish of the church of St Marie de *Lassela*' and the monastery giving 'a piece of land... in the parish of the church of Rogonag'.[86] Quite often what was being given was general rights to lordly

---

[85] I am in part influenced here by very interesting reflections and findings for twelfth-century England, in R. Springer, 'Local Religious Life in England, c. 1160–1210', unpublished PhD thesis, Oxford 2017. For various important francophone reflections, see *Médiévales* 49 (2005), a special issue edited by Dominique Iogna-Prat and Elizabeth Zadora-Rio on 'La paroisse, genèse d'une forme territoriale'.

[86] BnF MS Lat. 9994, fols 83v–84r (undated, but sharing some witnesses with charters from the early 1180s): 'Ego Ramunda soror Willelmi Gizu et ego Bertrandus de Assina maritus eius et nos filii eorum Petrus et Bernardus...totum honorem nostrum et quicquid habemus et habere debemus quocumque modo in tota parrochia ecclesie sancte marie de lassela...Et ego Willelmus abbas

income: 'I, Sibilia, wife of Guillaume Begon...give...all that I have...in the whole tithing and whole parish of the church of *Vetula aqua*';[87] though sometimes something more specifically linked to *ecclesial* rights is specified, alongside other land or income: 'I, Helyas Bonvin...give...whatever I have...in the parish of the church of *Lassela*, namely in tenths and firsts and in all *honores* and in all cultivated and uncultivated lands wherever they might be in the aforesaid parish.'[88]

On the rarer appearance, in this period, of the term 'parishioners': Pope Celestine II wrote to Archbishop Arnaud of Narbonne in 1141, calling on him to assist Lord Guillaume VI of Montpellier against certain 'rebels' against comital authority in the town, ordering the archbishop to warn 'his parishioners' not to support the rebels, and to withdraw ecclesiastical services (except for 'baptism of children and penances for the dying') from any who did so.[89] From the same place and time, a mortgage agreement charter from 1138 mentions things held 'in the town and in the parish and in the limits of Montpellier'.[90] 'Parish' once again appears to be fairly loosely geographical, and in the papal letter 'parishioners' seems to mean something like 'those to whom one provides sacraments'—it being unclear however whether Montpellier was understood to comprise one singular 'parish' or, more likely, whether all those who were ultimately spiritually dependent on the bishop might be termed 'his parishioners'.[91]

We do start to see the bounds of a parish described in some more detail as we move later in time, mostly in the context of determining a dispute over tithing rights between different ecclesiastical entities. Whilst there are of course various conflicts in the eleventh and more often the twelfth centuries, often between bishops and religious houses, over who had possession of a particular church and

grandsilve supradictus et fratris eisudem loci...donamus vobis...unam peciam de terra quam habemus et habere debemus in parrochia ecclesie de Rogonag.'

[87] BnF MS Lat. 11008, fols 29v–30r, 1162: 'Ego Sibilia uxor Willelmi Begoni...dono....in tota decimaria et in tota parrochia ecclesia de vetula aqua...'

[88] BnF MS Lat. 9994, fol. 42v (1172): 'Helyas Bona Vinea per me et successores meos...dono et concedo...quicquid habeo vel habere debeo...in parrochia ecclesie de Lassela scilicet in decimis et primitis et in omnia honoribus et in terris cultis [*suprascript*: et non cultis] ubiqumque sint in predicta parrochia...'

[89] *Liber instrumentorum memorialium: Cartulaire des Guillems de Montpellier* (Montpellier: Jean Martel Aîné, 1884–86), pp. 35–36 (no. 5). Same usage in similar 1158 letter of Pope Adrian IV, pp. 36–37 (no. 6); letter of Innocent II in 1141 and 1142, pp. 40–41 (no. 10), 43–44 (no. 14).

[90] *Liber instrumentorum*, pp. 93–94 (no. 53): Rixende, widow of Pons Foulques of *Popiano*, and her son, mortgage various lands and their annual income (listed in detail) for the following four years, for a payment of 10 silver marks, to Pierre de *Girunda* and his wife and children, and to whomsoever else they subsequently relinquish the mortgaged lands.

[91] A similar usage of 'parishioners' and 'parish' meaning those subject to the bishop seems to pertain in the letter of Clement III in 1189 written to Raimond II, bishop of Antibes, regarding the rights of his church; see G. Doublet, *Recueil des actes concernant les évêques d'Antibes* (Paris: Picard, 1915), pp. 153–56 (no. 120), at 156: 'Statuimus quoque ut nullius ecclesiastice persone liceat parrochianum tuum in morte vel in extremis agentem recipere, nisi salva justitia matris ecclesie. Sancimus preterea ut nulli fas sit intra terminos parrochie tue sine consensu tuo ecclesiam edificare vel edificatam consecrare...'. Florian Mazel notes that what we might think of as the bishop's 'diocese' was frequently called his 'parish' in earlier centuries: Mazel, *L'évêque et le territoire*, p. 19 and *passim*.

its income, as these mostly concerned a single church there was not normally any attempt to describe the geographical extent of 'a parish' or 'tithing' in any detail. One of the earliest detailed disputes dates to an 1155 agreement made by the bishop of Toulouse between the canons of Toulouse and the abbey of Saint-Lézat, the former having endowed a new church in the *castrum* of Muret (c. 20 km south-west of Toulouse), which impinged upon an existing church of Saint-Germier, held by the abbey. The agreement discusses those 'parishioners' of Saint-Germier who, for reasons of 'security', come within the 'parochial bounds' (*parrochianales termini*) of the new church in Muret, but does not attempt to spell out where those boundaries lay; nor in fact did these determine what the 'parishioners' might do, as it was agreed that those who so wished could be buried in the new church, and could receive burial rights from the priest of Muret, so long as he gave half of the burial payment to the other priest of the older church. There is no discussion in the agreement of where parishioners were to attend mass, or any other sacramental provision.[92] A possibly clearer sense of a layperson 'belonging' to their 'own parish' is apparent in a letter written by the archbishop of Narbonne in 1171, regarding a church attached to a leper house, noting that, unless they were a leper, no parishioner of the bourg or *cité* of Narbonne could 'on the occasion of leaving their *own* parish' (*occasione dimittendi parrochia sua*) go there to hear divine office.[93] But one has to wait until disputes from the mid-thirteenth century before finding more precise attempts to describe, in circumnavigational fashion, where 'parish boundaries' lay; though it should be noted that in these cases the local witnesses used were usually quite old, and can therefore be understood to be attesting to the customary knowledge of preceding decades.[94] So perhaps by the later twelfth century something more geographically and administratively precise was coming into effect.[95]

As these notions of 'parish' firmed up, they enter the documentary record primarily in terms of their rights over income. Whilst this is not the first thing one might think about when considering wider pastoral provision, the provision of a

---

[92] *Cart. Lézat*, II, p. 464 (no. 1647).
[93] Edited in G. Mouynès, *Ville de Narbonne: inventaires des archives communales antérieures à 1790. Annexes de série AA* (Narbonne: E. Caillard, 1871), pp. 7–8 (no. 5).
[94] For example, *Cart. Lézat*, I, pp. 466–68 (no. 625), 1 Nov 1245, though in this instance not using the word 'parish' but describing the 'temporal jurisdiction and territorial limits and tithing' of the church of Sainte-Suzanne (a few kilometres south of the monastery in Lézat-sur-Lèze). Similarly *Cart. Lézat*, I, pp. 259–60 (no. 330), 4 Apr 1245 where three priests at Peyrissas were questioned on 'the limits of the parishes and tithings of their churches'; pp. 476–78 (no. 636), 14 June 1247, re 'the tithing limits of the churches of Ste Marie de Bajou and Saint-Médard'. There is also an undated example in *Cart. Saint-Sernin*, pp. 49–50 (no. 68), describing the bounds 'of its parish', which includes mention of a couple of other 'parishes' forming part of its limits.
[95] In accord with geographically broader comments in M. Lauwers, 'Paroisse, paroissiens et territoire: remarques sur *parochia* dans les textes latins du moyen âge', *Médiévales* 49 (2005), 11–32, and the powerful case made in Mazel, *L'évêque et le territoire*, chapter 5. See also F. Hautefeuille, 'La délimitation des territoires paroissiaux dans les pays de moyenne Garonne (Xe–XVe siècles), *Médiévales* 49 (2005), 73–88.

sufficient benefice to support a local priest was, we should remember, one of the key provisions called for by Lateran IV, canon 32. The complexity of such income, beyond the primary oblations, can be seen in an early Occitan charter from 1180, describing 'the honour' of the church of Saint-Pierre in the little village of Curieres (c. 70 km west of Mende). This includes, for example, 'in the village of [*illegible*] the fourth part of the fief and of the allod and of the tithe.... And in the *mas* of La Fabrega, 18d *raimondins* which the mother of Aldebert de la Roc gave.... In the *viguerie* of Combradas, one sheep and one lamb and 8d *raimondins* and 3 sixteenths of oats, and a half of the tithe of the four fields and those others which pertain to the *viguerie*...'. The charter goes on to list over thirty different pieces of land on which tithes were levied, the church sometimes receiving the whole tithe, but often 'the third part', 'a half', and so forth.[96] Did this confused mixture of income-producing land constitute 'the parish' as well as the church's 'honour'? Possibly so; though one can see how the potential accumulation of various rights was likely to complicate the geographical boundaries for many churches in the period.

It was upon this complex patchwork of rights and expectations that the Lateran IV reforms were imposed, most probably with rather variable results, the fundamental aim being to try to ensure that there was a resident priest, sufficiently provided for, in each locality. In a southern French context, this desire was sharpened considerably by the desire to combat heresy, partly—though often rather vaguely—in terms of theological instruction, but perhaps also more practically to enable the means of parochial identification of 'heretics' by the local priest and two or three laymen, as described further above. In fact three years prior to Lateran IV, Simon de Montfort's statutes of Pamiers had ordained that 'in all towns where there are no churches and there are houses of heretics, let the most suitable house be made into a church and another be given to the priest to live in'.[97] The council of Montpellier, held in January 1215, focused considerable attention on the suitability and behaviour of the clergy (in addition to the issues of 'peace' discussed above), enjoining bishops to give benefices to 'suitable people', and forbidding them from giving the care of parish churches (*parochialium ecclesiarum curam*) to adolescents or those who were only in minor orders.[98] Narbonne, 1227, ordered that priests in churches held by monasteries 'and by other people' must be given 'a sufficient portion' of the income to support themselves, explicitly citing Lateran IV canon 32 in support.[99] This requirement

---

[96] Brunel, *Plus anciennes chartes*, pp. 167–68 (no. 181), a survey conducted in 1180 by the abbey of Bonneval in nearby Le Cayrol. *Raimondins* were pennies issued by the counts of Toulouse between the mid-twelfth and mid-thirteenth centuries; see P. Spufford, *Handbook of Medieval Exchange* (London: Royal Historical Society, 1986), p. 117.
[97] Statutes of Pamiers, 1212, c. 10 (Mansi XXII, cols 856–64, at 857).
[98] Council of Montpellier, 1215, cc. 11, 12 (Mansi XXII, cols 939–50 at 942), and more generally cc. 2–28 variously regarding the behaviour and dress of priests, canons, and monks.
[99] Council of Narbonne, 1227, c. 9 (Mansi XXIII, cols 19–26 at 24).

was repeated at the council of Béziers 1232, along with the injunction to ensure that those given the care of souls in parish churches were 'of fitting life and knowledge'.[100]

The papal legate who had presided at Béziers (Gautier, bishop of Tournai) can be found in the same year making explicit reference to these provisions when requiring the monastery of Lézat to check on whether or not the parish church of Saint-Médard had fallen vacant in Le Fossat (13 km south of Lézat, just beyond Sainte-Suzanne, mentioned above), this leading to an inquiry by the archdeacon of Lézat. Evidence was taken from both clergy and lay witnesses and found that there were in Le Fossat 'very many parishioners...who received there all the ecclesiastical sacraments'. It was said that the monastery had agreed to hand the church over to one Bernard Pons, chaplain of *Castellanis*, but on the requirement that he pay them 150 *sous* annually, which he was unwilling to do; thus there was a lack of proper provision. It was further established that this agreement had not been approved by a bishop, but had been granted permission by one of the witnesses, the former chaplain of the same church who was now an archpriest elsewhere.[101] As evidence regarding how much of a parochial 'system' was in effect by 1232, the inquiry at Le Fossat cuts both ways. On the one hand, it shows us a close interconnection between conciliar decree and practice, focused in this particular instance on what was a really quite small local church—Saint-Médard is now remembered in the village as a ruined 'chapel'—with a fair degree of effort expended in trying to ensure there was pastoral provision, the needs of the local parishioners noted as the key issue. On the other hand, it makes clear how easily local provision might falter (providing further evidence for the case I argued in Chapter 3, that the surrender of local churches into monastic hands did not necessarily guarantee 'better' provision), and shows that arrangements could be made, or indeed could fail, between local clergy, without any hint of episcopal oversight.

But there are some signs that the repeated injunctions made by papal legates at ecclesiastical councils were having an effect, judging by what starts to appear in the documentary record.[102] The bishop of Toulouse and the monastery of Saint-Papoul (about 30 km north-west of Carcassonne) appointed arbitrators in a dispute over their respective rights to the tithes of various churches near the monastery, in 1233. Whilst the specific issue was this dispute—prompted by argument over which churches the late Bishop Foulques had or had not earlier

---

[100] Council of Béziers, 1232, cc. 11, 12 (Mansi XXIII, cols 269–78 at 272–73); on the dating of the council, see E. Cabié, 'Date du concile de Béziers', *Annales du Midi* 16 (1904), 349–57.

[101] *Cart. Lézat*, I, pp. 496–97 (no. 661); the inquiry ends by noting that several monks had physically prevented the inquirers from entering the said church to check, and refused to take a sworn oath to aid the investigation.

[102] See also Mazel, *L'évêque et le territoire*, chapter 4 regarding the increased episcopal governance of a diocese in various ways, with more of a twelfth-century focus.

possessed—the subsequent charter of agreement rested upon an underlying process of inquiry and consequent episcopal knowledge of the financial state, at least, of these churches.[103] In 1236 the bishop of Lodève conducted an inquiry into the tithing rights of twenty-six churches subject to the dean and chapter of the city (who received a third of that revenue), summoning the priests of most of the churches to give evidence before him.[104] By the second half of the thirteenth century we can find the archbishop of Auch instituting a grand inquiry into the tithing rights and lands associated with various archdeaconries, producing a surviving record of 278 parish churches. This not only listed the tithing rights (a portion of which was often still in lay hands) but also whether the church was 'vacant' or indeed 'uninhabited'—finding the latter, in the archdeaconry of Astarac-cis-Gers, in nearly half of all cases.[105] In short, whilst the extremely patchy nature of the records does not allow us a clear picture of how much active diocesan oversight there was around the state of parish churches, the fragmentary material that does survive tends to suggest that the interventions around the crusade period did prompt more episcopal attention and centrally archived knowledge. From a different angle, this was almost certainly also the case once larger-scale inquisition into heretical wickedness was undertaken in the mid-1240s, as the largest surviving inquisition register shows us that the inquiries from 1245 to 1246 (details from which were used earlier in this chapter) were undertaken by citing parish communities to attend via their priests.[106]

Beyond a somewhat dry interest in the Church as a financial and documentary institution, these developments also matter considerably with regard to the central theme of this book: the *point* of a well-provisioned parish church and priest, governed to some degree of effectiveness by a bishop, was not only to ensure the long-standing sacraments of baptism and burial, but to disseminate Christian knowledge to, and require orthodox conformity from, the laity in general. De Montfort's statutes at Pamiers ordered that all 'parishioners be made to go to church on Sundays and feast days, on which all work shall cease, and let them hear mass and preaching in its entirety', with any 'master or mistress' of a house who failed to obey to be fined 6d on each occasion (to be divided between the parish church and the local lord, presumably to encourage the latter to enforce it).

---

[103] AD Aude G489. The document is somewhat torn, but lists about thirty-six churches, mostly around Saint-Papoul and Castelnaudary; it is notable however that only eight of these have their dedicatee saint specified, which perhaps also indicates some limit to the diocesan knowledge.
[104] J. Roquette, ed., *Cartulaire de l'église de Lodève: livre vert* (Montpellier: n.p., 1923), pp. 97–107. All tithes were here listed as portions of grain, wine, wheat, or other produce.
[105] Ch-E. Perrin and J. de Font-Réaulx, eds, *Pouillés des provinces d'Auch, de Narbonne et de Toulouse*, 2 vols (Paris: Imprimerie nationale, 1972), I, pp. 267–80 from an eighteenth-century manuscript copy of a now-lost original. The inquiry is believed to have been conducted around 1265, and as the editors point out may originally have been even larger. The archdeaconry of Astarac-cis-Gers lists 132 churches, of which about a third still had a portion of tithing rights in the hands of the local count or other lord; of those, five were 'vacat' and 67 'non inhabitatur'.
[106] BM Toulouse, MS 609; see Pegg, *Corruption*.

The council of Toulouse repeated the injunction to attend, increasing the fine to 12d, and added the requirement that all also come to church on Saturday at vespers 'for reverence of the Blessed Virgin Mary'. Priests were also required to expound the statutes of the council four times a year to their parishioners.[107]

The whole 'pastoral revolution' associated with Lateran IV was, of course, directed toward better addressing the spiritual needs (as the papacy saw it) of the ordinary laity, through parochial provision. That is at the heart of the reforms in southern France, but they took on a particular and more regulated hue in the post-crusade context; they became not just spiritual provision, but an attempted form of governance. The council of Narbonne (1227) ordered that:

> the names of all those who go to confess their sins should be written down by the chaplains who hear their confessions; so that they can present praiseworthy testimony of [the fact of] their confessions. Those of 14 years and above who in truth disdain to confess at least once a year, are forbidden, whilst still living, to enter church until they make fitting satisfaction; those who have [subsequently] died, are forbidden church burial. Those who in truth hear their confessions should do so in a fitting place, which is not hidden away.[108]

Thus annual confession at Easter, as enjoined by canon 21 of Lateran IV, was amplified into an index of orthodox conformity. Whilst explicitly citing that canon, the council of Toulouse in 1229 increased the requirement: people should confess to their 'own priest' and receive communion 'with all reverence' not just once but three times a year, namely at Christmas, Easter, and Pentecost, and 'carry out the penance imposed on them humbly and with all their strength'; or else be suspect of heresy.[109]

Making some form of confession three times a year was not in itself an innovation, and can be found in some dioceses in earlier centuries (though we shall revisit in a later chapter the question of what 'confession' and penance comprised in different periods before and after 1215).[110] But what was innovative—and a fundamentally huge development in attempting to make parishes truly into a 'system' that in some sense managed and monitored the faith (still closely linked to 'the peace')—was an accompanying requirement that the priest record the names of those who were conforming or not conforming to this injunction, as in the passage just cited from Narbonne 1227. The council of Toulouse tackled this

---

[107] Statutes of Pamiers, 1212, c. 9 (Mansi XXII, col. 857); council of Toulouse, 1229, cc. 25, 45 (Mansi XXIII, cols 200, 204). The council of Albi, 1254, c. 30 repeats the injunction to attend church, listening to all preaching and the entire mass, 'nor leaving until the mass is completed', with the same arrangement regarding a 12d fine as Toulouse 1229 (Mansi XXIII, col. 840).
[108] Council of Narbonne, 1227, c. 7 (Mansi XXIII, col. 23).
[109] Council of Toulouse, 1229, c. 13 (Mansi XXIII, col. 197).
[110] See S. Hamilton, *The Practice of Penance, 900–1050* (London: Royal Historical Society, 2001).

slightly differently, by requiring that in each parish all men aged 14 or over, and women aged 12 or over, swear an oath to abjure heresy, to observe the Catholic faith, and to 'persecute heretics with all their strength', their names then to be written down. In the following canon regarding confession, the triannual requirement is supplemented with the following instruction: 'priests are to take care through the inspection of [the list of] names, as was explained above, to ascertain whether any people are secretly avoiding communion'.[111] The council of Albi in 1230 called upon the priest to 'admonish his people to come to confession, most of all at the beginning of Lent', and warned the priest that anyone who did not come to confess at least once a year, and to receive communion at Easter, should be expelled from the church as suspect of heresy, and refused Christian burial if they died. Moreover, 'priests should write down the names of those who have accepted penance and communion from them, and those who have not done so, and those who are excommunicate'.[112] In 1232, the council of Béziers linked the requirement to record parishioners' names to the earlier Toulouse 1229 injunction to attend church regularly, further upping the requirements of orthodox conformity. Priests were to promulgate the relevant statutes 'as if preserving the pupil of the eye'; and priests who were not competent at this aspect of their task were to be deprived of their benefice.[113]

As far as I am aware, no such lists of confessants survive from this period; and indeed rather later, the council of Carcassonne in 1303 ordered that lists of excommunicates should be destroyed by the priest once the excommunicate had been absolved.[114] But the injunctions continued to be repeated later in the century and beyond, with the council of Béziers in 1246 largely reproducing the wording used at Narbonne 1227, and the council of Albi in 1254 renewing the requirement that names be recorded for an oath abjuring heresy, to be repeated twice yearly, and for the priest to use 'inspection' of this list to identify (by their absence) any suspect of heresy. The council of Arles around 1275 called upon the priest to make a list each year of those parishioners who came to do penance at Easter, 'and diligently to hold and guard the said *chartularia*', so that at the

---

[111] Council of Toulouse, 1229, cc. 12, 13 (Mansi XXIII, cols 196-97).
[112] Council of Albi, 1230, cc. 39, 40, 46 (Pontal, *Status synodaux*, II, pp. 22, 24).
[113] Council of Béziers, 1232, c. 5 (Mansi XXIII, col. 271).
[114] Council of Carcassonne, 1303, c. 7: 'Item volumus et ordinamus quod quidem rectores nomina excommunicatorum et interdictorum et annum et diem et cuius mandato et ad cuius instantia scribant in eorum registris et quando fuerint absolute a dictis sententiis scripturi deleant eorumdem' (BnF MS Lat. 1613, fol. 52r). Similarly synodal of Albi, 1340: Poitiers BM MS 125, edited in Ludovico de Amboysia, *Sinodale Diocesis Albiensis* (Lyon: Pierre Mareschal & Barnabe Chaussard, 1499), unpaginated, at pp. 107–08 counting from first page of actual text: 'Statuimus etiam quod sacerdotes parochiales... habeant rotulos quilibet suum in quo scribant omnia nomina excommunicatorum sue parochie et quorum auctoritate et ad quorum instantiam sunt excommunicati et tempus receptionis littere excommunicationis vel interdicti; et eos excommunicatos diebus dominicis in ecclesiis suis publice denunciare procurent.... Et cum fuerint absoluti de illis rotulis abradantur.'

following synod the priest could communicate the names to the bishop.[115] Additions made to the council of Albi, dating from some time after 1255, speak of the 'roll of the excommunicated' (*rotuli excommunicatorum*) that each priest should have, in which they recorded the names of all those who had been excommunicated, the year and day it had been imposed, and who imposed it, those listed to be denounced each Sunday and feast day. This is similarly set out in a synodal book created by Raimond de Calmont d'Olt, bishop of Rodez, in 1289; again by Bérengar Batle, bishop of Elne, in 1326; and at the council of Avignon in 1345.[116] The council of Carcassonne in 1299 made it clear that the names, plus those who had committed sacrilege or public fornication, were then to be shared in each synod, and the council of Avignon in 1341 wished each priest to write 'the name and cognomen' of each person who confessed 'in a paper book', and moreover to keep *two* additional records of those excommunicated, one to remain safely in their church and the other to be brought to synod.[117]

As it happens, I have located one, sole surviving document which appears to be an example of something like this process. This is a torn, deeply faded, and in many places illegible parchment now in the *archives départementales Pyrénées-Orientales* in Perpignan. It has lain previously unnoticed having been used some decades after its compilation as the binding for a paper booklet in which a totally unconnected episcopal inquiry from 1375 was recorded, that booklet then being archived.[118] The list of excommunicates thus survives by pure chance.

Whilst much of the parchment is unreadable, due to fading and damage, its rubric is almost entirely clear:

Thursday [*illeg.*] day of March, AD 1308, lords Rigaud Astorgue, Guillaume Arnaud, Jacques Arnaud existing as representatives for Lord Raimund, by divine

---

[115] Council of Béziers, 1246, c. 46 (Mansi XXIII, cols 689–704, at 704); council of Albi, 1254, cc. 11–13 (Mansi XXIII, cols 829–53 at 835); council of Arles, c. 1275, c. 19 (Mansi XXIV, cols 147–54 at 152–53). Cf. brief earlier discussion in Arnold, *Inquisition and Power*, p. 37; P. Biller, 'Applying Number to Men and Women in the Thirteenth and Early Fourteenth Centuries: An Enquiry into the Idea of "Sex-Ratio"', in M. Rubin, ed., *The Work of Jacques Le Goff and the Challenges of Medieval History* (Woodbridge: Boydell, 1997), pp. 27–54 at pp. 49–50.

[116] Additions to council of Albi, 1254, c. 28 (Pontal, *Statuts synodaux*, II, p. 468). Statutes of Rodez, 1289, XVIII.2 (Avril, *Statuts synodaux*, VI, p. 193). Batle's constitutions: Perpignan, BM MS 79 fols 74r–87v, at 75r: '...in eorum cartulariis quod pro hiis ipsi rectores spiritualiter in qualibet ecclesia habeant nomen excommunicatoris et excommunicati et quod de causa et ad cuius id sit instanciam scribatur per eos...'. Council of Avignon, 1345, c. 5 (Martene, *Thesaurus*, IV, col. 570).

[117] Council of Carcassonne, 1299, c. 11 (Avril, *Statuts synodaux*, VI, p. 460); council of Avignon, 1341, c. 2 (Martene, *Thesaurus*, IV, col. 566). Similar are synodal instructions issued by Bernard Gui once he was bishop of Lodève: synod of Lodève 1325, c. 12 (C. Douais, ed., *Un nouvel écrit de Bernard Gui: le synodal de Lodève, 1325–26* (Paris: Picard, 1894), pp. 7–8 and cf. Artonne, 'Livre synodal de Lodève', *Bibliothèque de l'École des Chartes* 108 (1949–50), 36–74). In 1315, the bishop of Carcassonne, Pierre de Rochefort, enjoined priests to send him the names of those who frequently failed to come to church on Sundays and feast days, 'so that we can correct them' ('ut eos corrigamus'); synod of Carcassonne, 1315, c. 9 (BnF Lat. 1613, fol. 64r).

[118] The inquiry conducted in 1375 was into whether or not a certain church of Saint-Jean in the city of Perpignan possessed parochial rights.

providence Bishop of Elne. These are the excommunicated to be denounced on feast days and other days, with the extinguishing of candles and the tolling of bells.[119]

In the three columns which follow it is very hard now to make out much of the writing, but the middle column contains at least fourteen sets of details, where one or more people are listed, followed by a statement of who excommunicated them, though not the reason why. Similar numbers probably appeared in the other two columns, the third of which has however been sliced vertically when the parchment was made into a binding; thus a list of perhaps 40–50 people in total. Among those named a few are more easily legible, albeit lacking much accompanying detail. For example: 'Of those to be denounced as excommunicate, Saurina, daughter of Pierre Guardiola, at the order of Pierre André of *Padaliarto*', 'From those excommunicated, Raimund Asemar, at the order of the consuls of the said place', 'Of those excommunicated François Jaudert notary, at the entreaty of the procurators of St Jean's'.[120] The document thus appears to have been compiled and issued by the bishop's representatives, from sentences of excommunication generated and listed locally.

This particular system of parochial regulation, enjoined by various councils from the conclusion to the Albigensian Crusade onward, thus does appear to have been put into practice. The list is very clearly a working record, speaking to something that reached low down the social scale and spread across a wide array of participants. It speaks to the more bureaucratic end of the 'pastoral revolution', and the extent of regularized episcopal power into the parish.[121] The one surviving document is thus the tiniest surviving trace of what was once a very much larger machinery of governance, a machine which expanded swiftly in the thirteenth century and within which the parish priest had become a key component. In some aspects relations between priest and parishioners at a local level were

---

[119] AD P-O, G245, binding: 'Die jovis V[*illeg*] die mensis marcii. Anno domini MCCCVIII existentibus vicariis dominis Rigaudo Astorgii, G[uillelmo] Ar[naldi], Jacobi Ar[naldi] pro domino R[amundi] di[vin]a providencia ep[iscopi] Eln[ensis]. Isti excommunicati debent denunciati diebus feriatis et non feriatis et candelis stinctis et pulsantis campanis.' Raimond Costa was bishop of Elne 1289–1310.

[120] AD P-O, G245, binding: 'Ex eius utrius denunciarum excommunicatam Saurina filiam P[etr]i Guardiola ad instanciam P[etr]i Andree de Padaliarto…Ex eius parte excommunicatum R[aimundu]m Asamarii instanciam consulum dicti loci…Parte excommunicatus Franciscum Jaudurti notarius ad inita [*illeg.*] procuratorum de Sancti Johannis.'

[121] The list is not an absolutely unique documentary find: there is a curious list of excommunicates 'and those who have been summoned' (*excommunicandi* and *vocandi*) copied in the eleventh century by the canons of Rouen cathedral into an Anglo-Saxon benedictional that had ended up in their possession. As Richard Allen points out, this latter list perhaps relates to an earlier Carolingian injunction to the bishop to keep a written record of who required punishment (R. Allen, 'The Earliest Known List of Excommunicates from Ducal Normandy', *Journal of Medieval History* 39 (2013), 394–415). Those named there were fairly major figures or at least local lords, and the circumstances of its compilation are very unclear.

essentially unchanged from earlier centuries: the bestowal of baptism and burial, the rendering of tithes, and the priest, through the liturgical cycle of prayers and masses, providing the shape of the Christian year. But in other respects, by the mid-thirteenth century things had changed fundamentally. Priests were to be distinguished from their flock in dress and, in theory at least, behaviour. Moreover, they did not just proffer 'care' for the souls of their parishioners, but enacted episcopal power over those souls.

Conclusion

Above all else, Part I of this book has addressed change over time. Those changes did not occur simultaneously nor at a uniform rate. The developments broadly associated with 'Gregorian reform', discussed in Chapter 3, sprawled out unevenly across more than a century, and the shift in possession of local churches and their tithing rights from laity to ecclesiastics was still in process well into the thirteenth century. The effects of urban growth, analysed specifically in Chapter 4, entwined with these developments, and similarly stretched across a 'long twelfth century'; their implications continued to reverberate in the later thirteenth and fourteenth centuries. The changes analysed in *this* chapter are, in contrast, much more temporally focused. They concentrate in the decades around the Albigensian Crusade, and are strongly associated with the intervention from beyond the region of several key papal legates: Arnaud Amaury, Milo, Romanus Bonaventura, Gautier of Tournai, and others. Thus, whilst the implementation and implications of the various injunctions of course rested heavily on local figures and circumstances, the title of this chapter is ultimately justified: these were key interventions, by the papacy, and came to form a fundamental period of inflection. This is not to say that papal *fiat* simply dictated subsequent reality. But as we have seen, there were real effects felt immediately, and attention was paid to the accumulating conciliar injunctions; those of Béziers 1232 and Narbonne 1227 were re-copied, along with Riymond VII's statutes of 1233, into one of the civic cartularies of Toulouse for example, clearly remembered there as statutes decreed by papal legates.[122]

---

[122] AM Toulouse MS 5, fols 47r–59r, headed with the rubric: 'Comitis Ramundi Tholose et legati pape statuta facta post eorum tractum pacis contra hereticos super ordinatione clericorum, super simoniciis, super levitis ordinibus et beneficiis, super canonicis et religosis, super excommunicatis, super Judeis et usurariis, super testamentis, super iuratis, super confitentibus in ecclesia, super excommunicandis, super talhiis et pedagiis, super excommunicatione, super ordinandis clericis, super anno bis sextili, super hereticis et aliis capitibus contra excommunicationes malefactores, pedagia et aliis capitibus.' The statutes in all three cases are nearly identical to those edited in Mansi, though with an interesting variance in Béziers 1233, c. 11, namely that episcopal failure to institute suitable parish priests would be 'gravely punished' by the legate: 'a nobis in presenti et a domino in futuro de gravi inobedientia puniantur'.

Other changes and developments accompanied these interventions, their effects however felt over a longer subsequent time scale. For example, the establishment of the university of Toulouse in 1229 was an explicit attempt to further shore up theological orthodoxy in the region. A number of Parisian intellectuals were briefly present in the city at its foundation—Helinand de Froidment, Roland de Cremona—and whilst it is hard to discern any profound immediate impact of their fleeting presence, the underlying connection to the learning of Paris and its reform enthusiasms perhaps did have a longer effect on the production of pastoral texts in the region.[123] We have already noted, in Chapter 4, the arrival of the mendicant friars in the south; their further establishment, and particularly their focus on preaching, took up another strand of aspirational 'reform' found in the councils discussed here (where preaching was often assumed to be something particularly incumbent on the bishops, who were also called upon—in line with Lateran IV—to crack down on unlicensed wandering preachers).[124]

As noted at the outset of this chapter, the most profound change wrought by the crusade was the ultimate shift of political control to the Capetian crown. But the attempts to develop a parochial system of governance, visibly to define Jews as a clear 'out-group', to reform lay society (in particular, bringing a range of financial and mercantile activity within a moral frame), are all fundamentally important elements to the central theme of this book. They attempted to extend, to the laity as a whole, a system of spiritual governance that made 'being a Christian' more clearly demarcated, demanding, and literally 'regulated'. It can be seen as the sharpest and swiftest example of the wider process which André Vauchez described, some decades ago, as 'the monasticization of the laity' in the later middle ages.[125]

It is useful, however, to re-examine that metaphor and add some additional nuance. Christian monasticism itself was never simply *one* mode of being, and was of course subject to repeated waves of 'reform', each an attempt to produce subtly different kinds of spiritual Christian selves. Something similar can be said for lay 'monasticization'. As argued in this chapter, across the crusade and into the 1230s the most immediate and pressing frame for the regulation of the laity was an ecclesiastical notion of 'peace'. Obedience to ecclesiastical authority, conformity in practice, and the repeated universal oath to abjure support for 'heresy' outlined the fundamental requirements. 'Heretics' were mostly assumed to be part of visible groups, identifiable by dress and behaviour, and subsequent to conversion,

---

[123] See, for example, discussion of Benoit d'Alignan's *Tractatus fidei* in Chapter 7, below. On the university generally, see C. E. Smith, *The University of Toulouse in the Middle Ages* (Milwaukee: Marquette University Press, 1958), particularly chapter 2.

[124] Against *questores*, that is, wandering preachers seeking alms for various causes, see discussion in Chapter 7.

[125] A. Vauchez, *The Laity in the Middle Ages: Religious Beliefs and Devotional Practices*, trans. M. J. Schneider (Notre Dame, IN: University of Notre Dame Press, 1993), p. 72.

still identifiable by the yellow crosses imposed by the council of Toulouse. Jews were similarly to be rendered legible, and Christians were to avoid both groups, and further demonstrate their obedience through regular attendance at mass and confession. So elements of lay 'monasticization', in this particular dynamic, were fundamentally governed by the logic of obedience, in parallel to the monk's obedience to his abbot, and were made manifest through regulated behaviour, lay attendance at the parochial church being roughly similar to monastic attendance at the liturgical cycle of prayers. But as we shall see in subsequent chapters, 'regulation' contained further possibilities and elaborations, both practical and spiritual, and as these played out across a varied and changing social landscape, they invited interpretation, resistance, and independent elaboration. Lay 'monasticization' was thus not really the imposition of one model, but the arrival of a capacious new discursive frame within which various demands and opportunities existed *in potentia*. Accordingly, whilst Part II of this book takes a more thematic than chronological approach, it also seeks to demonstrate the further unfolding of lay Christianity, across the twelfth to fourteenth centuries.

We can see what was to develop in the post-crusade period adumbrated in the precise wording used by the council of Toulouse of 1229 when it echoed the Fourth Lateran Council and enjoined confession on all Christians. For the first time, in a southern French context at least, in its address to lay pious behaviour the council did not simply say *what* the laity should do—make confession three times a year, obey the priest's command to do penance, and receive communion—but *how* they should do it: 'They are to carry out the penance imposed on them *humbly* and *with all their strength*, and three times a year they shall receive the sacrament of the Eucharist *with all reverence...*'.[126] The logic of the mandate is still fundamentally 'obedience to clerical authority', but contains the roots of something more complex: the making of an interiorized Christian self for all lay people, obedient not only in action but inner disposition.

To be clear: I am not suggesting that these specific words simply effected such a change, nor that no layperson prior to 1229 could have had an inner, affective or emotional, response to the sacraments. What changes here however is the *requirement*, and the sense that 'regulation' might reach beyond exterior behaviour to try to govern the emotional and affective dynamics inside each Christian. As we shall see, specifically in regard to confession (both sacerdotal and in the more extraordinary case of confession to inquisitors), such issues would receive much further elaboration. But also more broadly, the wider landscape of faith—both the literal physical landscape of worship, and the figurative cultural landscape of Christian

---

[126] Council of Toulouse 1229, c. 13 (Mansi XXIII, col. 197): '...injunctam poenitentiam et humiliter et pro viribus impleturi, et ter in anno...sacramentum Eucharistiae cum omni reverential suscepturi'; translation in A&B, p. 194.

culture—would increasingly attempt to speak to the spiritual experiences of all lay people. The Church increasingly sought to provide the opportunities, imagery, enticements, and demands for every Christian to develop their own Christian self more fully, and to engage in the necessary work to their own individual salvation; in that sense, to make lay Christianity into 'lay religion'.

PART II

6
Space and Materiality

A man called Guillaume Boyer lived in the *castrum* of Auribeau, about 40 km north of Aix, in perhaps the eleventh or early twelfth century. He was a peasant: a man who 'worked the land' and sustained his family through his labours. When he went blind, it thus caused not only personal suffering, but was a disaster for his wife and young children. Despairing of their situation and in extreme need, his wife had an idea: she had heard from many people of the miracles that God performed through the Virgin Mary of Rocamadour. 'Why should we be the only ones to go without God's favours? Why should it be harder for us than for others, when He said "Seek and you shall find, ask and it shall be given, knock and the door will be opened to you" [Matt. 7: 7]?' In prayer and petition they sought Mary's aid, and made as an offering a wax candle the length of her husband. 'With this candle, o mildest of mild ones, we will honour your house in Rocamadour if... you take pity on our misery and, removing the fog from his eyes, you allow my husband to see.'[1]

There are, as is ever the case when one looks closely at a medieval narrative, a number of different intriguing elements in this tale: the precarity of a peasant household, the dynamic between husband and wife, the words of the Gospel repeated by that wife (still of interest, even if one suspects that they were put there by the monastic compiler of the miracle story). But for the purposes of this chapter, there are three particular interlinked topics which the story of Guillaume Boyer can helpfully frame for us. One is that saints are spatially located—knowledge of the shrine at Rocamadour being as important as knowledge of the Virgin Mary herself. Another is the production of material artefacts associated with holiness and saintliness, here the quite common practice of producing a candle the length of the petitioning person. Third and most importantly is the key role of the laity themselves in making and sustaining saints: the 'many people' from whom Guillaume's wife had heard of Rocamadour, the material production of the candle, the narrative production of the tale itself.

In this chapter we will explore how Christianity was experienced in more local spaces, the cemetery and the church building, spaces which were 'made holy' in various ways, both through ecclesiastical ritual but also through the embodied behaviour of the laity; and we will think further about the embodied and material

---

[1] Albe, *Miracles*, pp. 209–11 (II.18); translation in Bull, *Miracles*, pp. 154–55.

experiences of lay worship within such spaces. But we will begin with the extraordinary spaces that housed saints.

Saintly Spaces and Holy Objects

The shrine of a saint was part of a larger holy space, most often incorporated into a monastery or cathedral church, their body not infrequently brought there from elsewhere in a formal 'translation' reburial service. Successful shrines—successful in that they brought a flow of pilgrims and income—could result in a more lavish rebuilding process, as was apparently the case at the monastic shrine of St Gilles (Saint-Gilles-du-Gard, c. 50 km east of Montpellier): the twelfth-century record of miracles tells that in 1116 the decision was taken to build a new and larger church, as the crowds coming to the shrine were too great for the original foundation. The narrative rather touchingly goes on to record how the saint provided on-site protection for the building workers, preventing any major accidents: one builder slipped and fell, hanging by his hands from a ledge, but was then saved; another who fell had his life saved—for a while at least—by landing on wooden boards used as part of the construction process.[2] The resting place of St Gilles is described in the widely circulated twelfth-century pilgrims' guide to Compostelle: his relics were contained in 'a great golden casket, which is behind his altar, above his venerable body', decorated with three bands of images, one showing the apostles, the Virgin Mary, and the virtues, another the twelve signs of the zodiac, the third depicting twelve of the twenty-four Elders (as described in Apoc. 4: 4). A variety of further visual material also adorned the shrine, framing the specific power and piety of Gilles within the wider frame of the kingdom of Heaven.[3]

The shrine was thus fashioned to be visually impressive. As many past historians have noted, there is a recurrent tension within medieval Christianity over the worship given to the saints themselves, as specific individual figures of power, and the theologically correct understanding of them as conduits to divine power emanating from God. This slightly complex relationship between the specific holy person and the wider edifice was potentially echoed by the experience of the physical space of the shrine: framed by the wider consecrated and authoritative space of the monastic or cathedral church, by the twelfth century an increasingly regulated space, and yet also a specific and physical location more accessible or permeable to lay engagement than the heaven in which the saints were understood ultimately to reside. The church was consecrated, made holy by the ritual administrations of the bishop; and yet the shrine was even *more* holy, and imbued

---

[2] *Livre...Saint Gilles*, pp. 134–37 (no. 19).
[3] *Le guide du pèlerin de Saint-Jacques de Compostelle: texte latin du XII siècle*, ed. J. Vielliard, 5th edn (Paris: J. Vrin, 2004), pp. 40–42.

thus by the innate power of the saint her- or himself. This specifically spatial power could itself assist in supernatural intervention. A woman from Lombardy, possessed by a demon 'for her sins and for those of others', was brought by her husband to the shrine of St Gilles; the demon strongly resisted even entering the tomb, and was eventually driven out of the woman as those present read aloud the Gospels, and spoke the names of Christ, the Virgin Mary, and St Gilles himself.[4]

Thus what made a shrine a shrine was not simply the presence of the saint's remains, nor the religious guardians of their memory, but the lay practices of worship associated with it. Most spectacular among these was pilgrimage. Southern France did not lack for pilgrims; it held the main routes by which those from northern Europe could reach the shrine of St Jacques in Compostelle, and the various holy places in Rome, not to mention travel further overseas to the holy lands.[5] The pilgrims were themselves an important part of the landscape of faith, a visible embodiment for all who saw them of a further performance of apostolic piety. As we saw in Chapter 5, one function of at least some of the many 'hospitals' founded in the twelfth century was to give shelter to pilgrims, something made explicit in the foundation narrative for Sainte-Marie-d'Aubrac. Pious work was thus performed by those giving shelter as well as by those doing the spiritual journeying. Pilgrims were a familiar part of that landscape. In some parts of the region, civic customs noted particular circumstances applying to pilgrims, regarding contracts, for example: those for Montpellier in 1204, in a statute relating to the control of people entering the town, note that 'if, simply in order to pray, a pilgrim comes to the shrine of the Blessed Mary, they can stay securely in town for two days and two nights, and securely leave on the third day'.[6] Ordinary lay people might choose to give hospitality to pilgrims: an inquisition witness, Fabrissa, reported in 1274 that a couple of years earlier she had given bed for the night to three people from Lombardy who said that they were going on pilgrimage to the shrine of St Jacques in Compostelle, something that 'pleased her said husband and... her son in law... and her daughter'. (The inquisitor suspected that the pilgrims were connected to the heretical Good Men.)[7]

These examples speak particularly to pilgrims arriving from elsewhere into southern France but, of course, people from the region could themselves also go on pilgrimage. An archaeological survey of medieval burials in south-west France has found numerous cockle-shell pilgrimage badges interred with the deceased,

---

[4] *Livre... Saint Gilles*, pp. 202–07.
[5] There is a useful map in *CdF* 15 (1980), 64–65, setting out the main routes and shrines through the region; the whole volume is dedicated to pilgrimage.
[6] Customs of Saint-Gilles, 1210–15, c. 17 (E. Bligny-Bondurand, ed., *Les coutumes de Saint-Gilles (XIIe–XIVe siècles)* (Paris: Picard, 1915), pp. 80–81); customs of Montpellier, 1204, c. 29 (Teulet, ed. *Layettes*, I, p. 258).
[7] Doat 25, fol. 44v (ed. *Inquisitors and Heretics*, p. 276).

strongly suggesting participation in pilgrimage from the region to the shrine at Compostelle.[8] As we saw in Chapter 3, with Pons de Léras and others, pilgrimage could also be a form of penance. A man called Pierre d'Auc had various encounters with the Good Men in the 1220s, alongside other things his mother having received the *consolamentum* (a purification ritual) from the heretics on her deathbed. He told the inquisitors in 1247 that he had confessed all of this to his own chaplain some time before, and the priest had, by way of penance, sent him on a barefoot pilgrimage to Rocamadour, which he had duly completed.[9] Pierre was active in the region around Puylaurens, and the journey to the shrine would thus have been over 170 km. By the mid-thirteenth century, inquisitors could impose both local and long-distance pilgrimages as penances upon those who had been found guilty of supporting heretics, and Bernard Gui was still doing this, for a small proportion of those he sentenced, in the early fourteenth century.[10] At a slightly later point, secular authorities in some parts of northern Europe could similarly require pilgrimage as a punishment for other transgressions, bringing various people to southern France as a destination or en route to Compostelle.[11] In these latter contexts, the meaning of pilgrimage was thus as much attrition for sin as hopeful journeying toward the holy.

Pilgrimage is thus a key experience of space, both the holy shrine eventually reached, but also the spiritual journey through the intermediate places on the way there. It is important to note that it was predominantly a *collective* experience, in practical terms—pilgrims travelled in groups—but also sometimes in terms of its spiritual purposes. An Occitan song, the *Canso dels pelegrins de San Jac*, dating to perhaps the early fourteenth century, presents itself as being composed and sung by pilgrims from Aurillac (on the edge of the Massif Central, about 80 km north of Rodez), and emphasizes throughout that they were a group: 'travelling in a great band | toward Saint Jacques de Compostelle' (*per anar en may clientela | veyre San Jac de campestela*).[12] The miracles of the Virgin at Rocamadour mention that a priest from Quercy, Bernard de Lasvaux, would visit with his parishioners each year, on the feast of the Nativity of the Virgin. He would there celebrate mass for those who had accompanied him. (Quercy is about 70 km south, Lasvaux about 26 km north, of Rocamadour.) Another tale from the same

---

[8] S. Vallet, 'La coquille du pèlerin dans les sépultures médiévales du sud-ouest de la France: nouveaux résultats et perspectives de recherches', *Archéologie du Midi médiéval* 26 (2008), 238–47.

[9] Doat 22, fol. 77v: 'Item dixit quod omnia ista confesuss fuit capellano suo, qui iniuxit ipse testi pro predictis quod ires apud Rupemamatoris nudus pedibus quod et fecit.'

[10] See Given, *Inquisition and Medieval Society*, pp. 69–70.

[11] U. Berlière, 'Les pèlerinages judiciaires au moyen âge', *Revue benedictine* 7 (1890), 520–26; X. Rousseaux, 'Religion, économie et société: le pèlerinage judiciaire dans les Pays-Bas (Nivelles, du XVe au XVIIe siècle)', in M.-A. Bourguignon, B. Dauven, and X. Rousseaux, eds, *Amender, sanctionner et punir: histoire de la peine du Moyen Âge au XXe siècle* (Louvain-la-Neuve: Presses universitaires de Louvain, 2012), pp. 61–85.

[12] R. Nelli, 'Trois poèmes autor d'un pèlerinage', *CdF* 15 (1980), 79–92, of which the third is this poem (pp. 88–90).

collection mentions a man from the Toulousain who came with other pilgrims, placed his monetary alms on the altar and then left, but however 'kept back some of the offerings which had been sent for the Blessed Virgin'—thus in that sense performing the pilgrimage on behalf of some wider group of others from, presumably, his home town.[13] The miracles of St Gilles tell of a group of thirty men who came together on pilgrimage from Poitou; aided by the saint in crossing a dangerous river on their way home, some of them returned the following year to give thanks.[14] Chaucer has given us the image of a motley band of medieval pilgrims thrown into fellowship by the happenstance of their journey, but these examples suggest practices of pilgrimage rooted in existing communities, the collective act of piety a choice made by a lay community of neighbours.

Long distance pilgrimage also engaged with shrines as a far-flung skein of holy power, each particular location visited forming one spiritual node within a wider network. The pilgrim's guide to Compostelle illustrates this very clearly, in its account of the various saints one could visit whilst en route to the eventual destination. The *vita* of Pons de Léras and the poem about the unnamed penitent in the *vita* of St Enimie, both of which we met in Chapter 3, relate lengthy journeys between multiple shrines. An occasional miracle story further affirms this particular sense: in those connected to St Bertrand de Comminges (another twelfth-century collection), a crippled man was initially carried by his mother to the shrine of St Thomas of Canterbury, Thomas restoring to him the use of his limbs but also telling him, 'I cannot do any more for you, but the very great and glorious confessor of Christ, Bertrand, is found in Gascony near the Spanish mountains, and if you go there to him, you will be healed and will have perfect health restored as before.' The man and his mother thus took to the road, heading first to Rocamadour, then to the shrines in Toulouse, and then further on to the tomb of St Bertrand (in the Pyrenees, about 100 km south-west of Toulouse).[15] One suspects that behind this story was the habit of sick lay people trying out various different shrines in the hope of finally obtaining the blessing of healing, their peregrinations a mixture of penitential piety and, more practically, the sequential petitioning of potential supernatural patrons. 'In the area around Agen, a little old woman was crippled in all her limbs, who having been carried to many places of the saints, could not gain the gift of salvation. Eventually, in truth, made visible to the holy confessor [St Vivian], her long sought after bodily restoration was miraculously accomplished.'[16] One finds similar tales in other collections across Europe.

---

[13] Albe, *Miracles*, pp. 72–75 (I.2), 82 (I.6); trans. Bull, *Miracles*, pp. 101–02, 105.
[14] *Miracles...Saint Gilles*, pp. 48–50.
[15] J. Contrasty and Mlle Fournie, 'Vie et miracles de saint Bertrand, évêque de Comminges', *Revue du Toulouse* 28 (1941), 173–243, at pp. 241–42. Saint-Bertrand-de-Comminges is a bit further west than most material from my corpus, but I have allowed myself to include him given the links to the Toulousain. Bertrand was born into a high noble family in the Isle-Jourdain, adjacent to Toulouse.
[16] 'Translatio et miraculi Sancti Viviani', p. 275.

Like this woman, pilgrims might come to a shrine in the hope of receiving a healing miracle, or to accomplish a notably demanding pilgrimage, visiting the saint, through their remains, at that site. But saints also brought sacred space with them, their conduit to heavenly power bestowing holiness (either temporarily or permanently) upon other locales, both before and after their death. In various post-mortem miracles, saints appear in person to those in need, distant from the shrine yet bringing with them an aura of holiness. A sleeping couple, parents to a blind son, were visited simultaneously by a miraculous vision of a man dressed all in white; who are you, they asked? 'You shall be safe, and there is nothing to fear. I am called Gilles. Set your only son to learn letters, and promise to render him to me, and soon he shall see.' The parents obeyed, and the miracle came to pass—and the testimony of these events, written by the son in the first person, was subsequently deposited at the altar of the shrine of St Gilles, itself a kind of material proof of the miracle.[17] In life, holy people who would later become saints passed through the human landscape intermittently bestowing a spiritual charge upon certain features. St Bertrand (d. 1126), when alive and in his role as bishop, was petitioned by someone who had given him lunch to bless not only the repast but the walnut tree that had shaded them from the sun. Thereafter, it was said, the tree always produced a huge crop, and in a year when the other trees were affected by blight, it remained unharmed. Similarly, when he was walking past a field in which peasant women were cutting down weeds, they said to him:

> 'Lord, listen to the voice of your maidservants: a very bad weed that is called rye grass prospers in these places, and it smothers much of the harvest, stopping the fields from producing or grain from returning to the sower. Can you in your sanctity deign to bless these fields and in punishment curse that noxious weed, such that the sterility of the land ceases and that by your merits there may follow furthermore a not ungratifying abundance of crops?' The curse of the bishop fell upon the grass, and thereafter that blight never reappeared in the fields, freed from its growth.[18]

The inclusion of such agriculturally practical tales is somewhat particular to Bertrand's *vita*, but they give a good sense of the wider kind of protection that communities might hope to gain from episcopal blessing, in a continuum with the more unusual interventions sought from the saints. And they remind us again of the importance of lay voices in proposing and circulating such testimony (such peasant speech however then considerably reworked by the demands of Latin rhetoric, as we see in this passage).

---

[17] *Miracles...Saint Gilles*, pp. 56–58.   [18] Contrasty and Fournie, 'Vie et miracles', p. 230.

As well as places, particular objects could become imbued with holy power. Bertrand was again notably active in this regard. A crippled and indigent woman called Marie was restored to partial health by the saint, who gave her a staff to help her walk—and if she ever lost it, her affliction immediately returned. As it happened, at one point a wicked man stole the staff, running off with it to somewhere in Spain, 'preaching its miraculous power, showing the staff to people; to which, from regard for the holy bishop, all gave great reverence'. Thus the man received great alms. 'He rejoiced in his gain, but the woman was in tears, lying with her limbs contracted before [the saint's] tomb. Finally, after many tears and sighs, her protector [St Bertrand] returned the staff to her' and she was restored. Betraying a further touch of concern over misdirected worship, the recorder of the miracles makes a point to note: 'not that the force of the miracle was in it [*the staff*]—it resided in the holy bishop'.[19] And yet objects could retain a trace of holiness. When still living, Bertrand had been given hospitality at Villeneuve, and had enquired over how productive their hunting had been. Hearing that they had caught little, he blessed their snares, leading them ever after to be notably good at catching game.[20] There is another continuum beyond the strictly saintly here, to other occasions on which lay people seem to have kept objects which were thought to have some holy, protective power. (In the final chapter we will see that some Pyrenean villagers kept a morsel of the bread blessed by the Good Men in a possibly similar fashion).

The holy object reaches its apotheosis in the medieval reliquary. As mentioned already in Chapter 2, southern France was notable for producing not just reliquary caskets (further north one would note the various famous Becket caskets produced in Limoges in the late twelfth/early thirteenth century) or reproductions of limbs housing the relevant saintly bone, but the fully representational bust known as a *maiestas*, by which the saint was literally re-embodied. That for Ste Foy is perhaps the most famous, encrusted in precious stones, and startlingly visually powerful, still preserved today at Conques.[21] As the miracles associated with Ste Foy relate, when a general fast was declared because of 'some suffering' (*afflictio*) in the town, the *maiestas* was paraded in procession with a huge crowd following it; all who saw it as it passed prostrated themselves. On another occasion the statue was paraded to Molompize (c. 80 km west-north-west of Le Puy), accompanied by cymbals and trumpets, performing various miracles en route.[22] There were other such images also. The miracles of St Vivian relate that on various

---

[19] Contrasty and Fournie, 'Vie et miracles', pp. 237–38.
[20] Contrasty and Fournie, 'Vie et miracles', p. 228.
[21] The image is easily locatable on the internet. One may also note similar extant busts, produced in the late twelfth century, from areas somewhat north of the region studied here: those of St Yrieix (from Limoges, now in the Metropolitan Museum of Art, New York), St Baudime (held by the Mairie of Saint-Nectime, in the Auvergne) and—perhaps made a century earlier—St Theofrid (church of Saint-Chaffre, Le Monastier-sur-Gazeille, near Le Puy).
[22] *Liber miraculorum*, pp. 51 (I.15), 100–04 (II.4); Sheingorn, *Book*, pp. 80, 120–22.

sacred days, such as at Easter, the monks of the shrine would make a procession with the effigy of the saint to the chapel of the Virgin Mary, then returning to the monastery.[23] The laity were not only shown such impressive objects, but could on occasion interact with them directly. At the shrine of St Privat in Mende there was 'a precious image, brightly ornamented on the exterior with silver and gems... into whose hand, it was the habit for those who came to pray there, to place their offerings'. Moreover the same image functioned as a kind of holy arbitrator, akin to the role played by various holy men that we met in Chapter 4: at a certain place in the suburbs of Mende, 'where it is customary for the clergy and people of Javols to gather' the clergy would bring the icon of St Privat and stand it on a certain stone, set there for that purpose, and the people and the clergy, 'gathered equally in the name of the Lord', would adjudicate certain issues relating to peace and good conduct.[24]

Various collections of miracle stories, produced in the twelfth century to promote particular shrines, attest to how the power and holiness of the saint could manifest itself as a particular experience of space. The power of the holy reached out from the central locus of the shrine, extending itself to protect or to respond to petition; as noted in an earlier chapter when discussing saints and the Peace of God, the structure is essentially parallel to that of lordship, albeit embedded in place as much as embodied in person. The dynamic is very clear with the miraculous cures performed by saints, many occurring at the shrine as those in need tried to get as close as possible to the source of power, but also on occasion—as with the cure of Guillaume Boyer's blindness—dispensed at a distance in response to a particular petition.

Beyond the ubiquitous cures and specific interventions, the space of the shrine could also be experienced as suffused with numinous power, its effects not always curative or beneficial. To take another example from Rocamadour, a young man who had perhaps been part of a mercenary band, and who had appropriated church tithes, entered the Marian shrine having failed to first cleanse himself by receiving penance and absolution. 'But the Virgin, the Queen of all the kingdoms, whose temple he had profaned and whose sanctuary he had violated, would not tolerate such impropriety and handed the man's body over to Satan to make him an example to others'; he was possessed by a devil, and much tormented.[25] The collection of miracles attested for St Privat at the cathedral of Mende relate that at the shrine 'nobody would dare to celebrate mass except for a chaste priest', but that one time a priest who was not chaste did thus dare, and began 'irreverently to fulfil the divine office'. And as he continued 'and greater and greater his fetid

---

[23] 'Translatio et miraculi Sancti Viviani', pp. 276–77.
[24] Brunel, ed., *Miracles de Saint Privat*, pp. 9, 105. This thus seems to be a very local 'peace assembly' but appears to be more customary than extraordinary.
[25] Albe, *Miracles*, pp. 80–81; Bull, *Miracles*, pp. 104–05. As I noted in Chapter 1, when he restored the tithes and received absolution from his own priest, he was healed.

pollution profaned the sacred space', he was then struck by a putridity in his loins, 'made totally fetid and full of worms' such that no friend or medic could aid him; and thus died.[26] This particular tale hammers home for an ecclesiastical audience the newly arrived requirement of clerical chastity, but speaks also to a wider sense of the heightened power—and thus behavioural demands—of the space itself. A somewhat gentler parallel to the St Privat tale occurs in the monk Bernard's account of the shrine of Ste Foy at Conques: 'An inhabitant of that village told me that if at any time after having sex, even if it was legitimate sex, he passed beyond the first grills [at the entrance to Ste Foy's shrine] without having washed, he would never complete that day unpunished.'[27]

In that last example we may note how loose a sense of chastity the unnamed local layman had, in comparison to the clerical model. But more importantly, this very short tale reminds us of something fundamentally important about saints, shrines, and holiness: that whilst they were proposed or proffered by ecclesiastical authorities, they were more truly *made* by lay people, made both by what the laity said and what they did. That is, a particular saintly figure can be presented by a bishop or abbot as potentially holy and suitable for worship (one remembers the theft of St Vivian's bones and their transportation to Figeac, as noted in Chapter 2). But only if there is a sustained lay response does a shrine become established. Holiness is thus, among other things, an experience of space that is itself created and sustained *through* that experience; a feedback loop that moves from a frame of storytelling and expectation, to one's bodily comportment at a shrine, to the stories one then recounts to others thereafter.[28] Some of those stories are then actively gathered up, recorded, and promoted by the relevant monks or other ecclesiastics. But there is a strong sense of stories circulating between lay people as well as promoted by the clergy, not only dramatic stories of major cures or other interventions of the kind familiar to us from any miracle collection, but as likely some smaller tales, such as that which the unnamed villager told to the monk Bernard. Such a tale speaks to an individual interpretation of holiness in what was a relatively familiar space, and the interpretation of its power in a personal way by a particular layman; 'personal' in the self-reporting of sexual sin and its consequences, 'lay' in its understanding of what counted as sexual sin, and in the literalization of the idea of washing away sin, not through penance but by the physical application of water.

Thus whilst the actions in life of a holy man or woman contribute to their holiness, saints are made by those still living, in their stories, their acts of memorialization, their petitions, their thanks. Another anonymous writer recording the

---

[26] Brunel, *Miracles de Saint Privat*, pp. 21–22. [27] *Liber miraculorum*, p. 71 (I.27).
[28] I am influenced here by Thomas Csordas's work on charismatic healing in modern Christianities. See T. J. Csordas, 'Embodiment as a Paradigm for Anthropology', *Ethos* 18 (1990), 5–47; T. J. Csordas, 'Somatic Modes of Attention', *Cultural Anthropology* 8 (1993), 135–56.

miracles of Ste Foy noted rather acerbically that she was revered by people 'not from religious worship' (*non enim ob religionis cultum*) but because of her miracles.[29] He perhaps takes too reductive a line, as we have noted already in earlier chapters that the shrines seemed sometimes to be a place people simply came to pray; but the point about a focus for popular devotion still stands. The practices of the laity sustain the saints as saints, but to some extent then *remake* them into the figures they desire.

Important amongst these practices is the habit, attested across Europe, of bringing votive offerings to the shrines, not only money—the coins placed into the hand of the *maiestas* of St Privat, as we have just seen—but objects. These were given both in thanks and to attest to the fact of miracles. Just as the crippled woman Marie, given the miraculous staff by St Bertrand, came to the shrine and 'related the miracles, kissed the tomb, and visited very often to relate what had happened to her', so the objects left by others bore witness to the miracles that had occurred, in the absence of the grateful recipient. Two separate men, among various different people freed from imprisonment by St Bertrand, travelled to the shrine to give thanks, and hung up their chains there in memory of the miracle.[30] A Danish nobleman who had travelled previously to the shrine of St Gilles told a crippled man in his service that, among the fetters and iron manacles hanging up there, he had also seen many votive offerings indicating that health had been restored to the lame.[31] That shrine also contained a small silver bell, given to bear witness to another miraculous deliverance.[32]

But as we know from elsewhere in Europe, what people most frequently gave was wax, sometimes as a candle (as with our opening tale) but sometimes fashioned into something more figurative. The shrine to the Virgin at Rocamadour contained a wax image of a dove, given by a man from Toulouse who owed thanks to the Virgin for having prevented 'wild animals' eating the inhabitants of his dovecote. It also held some wax hands which an artisan was commissioned to make; these were actually presented to the shrine in order to effect the cure of disfigured hands belonging to a young man from Montpellier.[33] The early fourteenth-century evidence relating to St Louis of Toulouse provides several more examples: Gaufrideta, a 2-year-old girl, was brought back to life by St Louis after a fever, and her young mother Jacqueta, 22 years old, gave thanks via an image made from 4 lbs of wax; another witness told a very similar story, again giving wax to the tomb; a brother of another young girl attested that she too was brought back to life, Louis having been promised a candle of the same length as the

---

[29] *Liber miraculorum*, p. 231.　[30] Contrasty and Fournie, 'Vie et miracles', pp. 234–35, 236.
[31] *Miracles...Saint Gilles*, pp. 68–71.　[32] *Miracles...Saint Gilles*, p. 120.
[33] Albe, *Miracles*, pp. 195–96, 238–39; trans. Bull, *Miracles*, p. 149.

child if she lived.[34] One witness, Guillaume de Moissac, a 60-year-old stonemason from Marseille, recounted the breadth of things on display at Louis's shrine:

> ...a certain Sunday he came to the church of the Brothers Minor of Marseille in the morning, at the time when the Brothers would customarily say mass; and having heard mass, he left. And it happened that a multitude of people were coming into the middle of the church; and some were carrying candles, and others entire images, others heads, others diverse kinds of figures of wax in honour of St Louis. Seeing this, he the witness said the following derisive words: 'And now the other saints in paradise can hardly have anything, because St Louis carries the lot!'

He was punished immediately for his impious words, his mouth and lips twisting up and his left eye deformed; only after he himself had made a gift to St Louis was he cured—and thus was his evidence recorded.[35]

All of those gifts were witness to lay agency, to lay saint-making we might say. They are visible to us because of their association with shrines and the record-keeping which successful shrines initiated. But they perhaps also sit in wider continuum with other elements of lay action, not all focused on the major shrines. As we know from various kinds of evidence, as well as donating money for lamp oil in churches lay people, particularly from the later twelfth century onward, might of their own volition give candles to a shrine in their local church. For example, an inquisition witness, Beatrice de Planissoles, questioned in 1320 recalled making a 're-dyed' candle for the church of Saint-Marie-de-Carnesses in Montaillou some twenty-five years earlier, not long after she had given birth to one of her daughters; possibly a gift in thanks.[36] Others might treat a local church as a space for prayer and reflection, whether in thanks or in petition for divine clemency. Another inquisition witness from 1273, providing context for a conversation regarding heresy, reported that a fortnight or so after she had recovered from an illness, she and a female friend 'went to keep vigil at the church of Saint-Jean-de-Mordagne near Cordes'.[37] The same inquisition heard evidence of a man called Guillaume Aribaud, who had earlier been imprisoned and then marked with the yellow crosses for his involvement with the Good Men. On his deathbed, he sent his wife and son to keep vigil at the church of the Carmelites in Toulouse. This was perhaps to get them out of the way whilst the Good Men came to perform the *consolamentum* upon him (which in fact they failed to do, because he had lost the

---

[34] A. Bughetti, ed., *Processus Canonizationis et legendae variae Sancti Ludovici O.F.M.*, Analecta Franciscana 7 (Florence: Ex Typographia Collegii S. Bonaventurae, 1951), pp. 126–27, 136, 144.
[35] Bughetti, ed., *Processus*, p. 233.   [36] *Fournier* I, p. 223.
[37] Doat 25, fol. 56r (*Inquisitors and Heretics*, p. 300).

power of speech), but even if he himself had not given real spiritual import to praying in the church, his obedient family presumably had done so.[38] Thus in a broader sense 'holy spaces' existed where the laity made them, as they fashioned their own ways and places in which to petition and to thank God.

The Places of the Dead

Shrines were rare, albeit famous, holy spaces. But as the previous examples remind us, there were places of at least potential holiness closer to most people's homes: cemeteries and the church. We shall start with the former. There are two main overlapping themes to consider with regard to cemeteries: the relationship between burial practices and the living community; and how and when the space of the cemetery becomes formalized and then sanctified. Let us think a bit about the latter issue first. In the tenth, eleventh, and possibly even the early twelfth centuries we have to bear in mind with regard to the documentary record that the Latin word for cemetery—*cimiterium*—can indicate not a specifically defined space, but rather the 'rights' of a church over burial.[39] For example, in a charter from 1043, Pons the son of Rainaud gave 'every part he holds' of the church of Saint-Pierre in Brignoles to the monastery of Saint-Victor in Marseille, 'namely in the church and in the tenths and firsts or in the cemetery rights (*vel in cimiterio*) and in all other things pertaining to the same church'. Even more clearly, in 1073 Guillaume Calce and his wife Domidia gave the church of Saint-Étienne 'with all burial rights (*omni cimiterio*) and oblations'. Also in the same cartulary, in a charter that mainly records a gift of four churches by Guillaume Rainulf and his mother Aimerude, it is noted that Pons Oeil gave the land that he held in regard to one of them, 'which is in the *cimiterio* of Ste Marie'—possibly meaning 'within the area over which it has burial rights' rather than land used for graves attached to the church.[40] In a few examples given in Chapter 1 it is clear when a specific place is being indicated. But it is sometimes quite hard to decide what exactly is meant: in a charter from 1164, Bertran the priest and his nephew Guiraud, 'procurators' of the church of Saint-Michel-de-la-Bruguière, agreed that Pierre Boer and his wife and children could have a dwelling in the *cimiterium* of the church— possibly still meaning 'within the area over which it has burial rights', but perhaps in fact in this case meaning land which had been used for burials. A miracle story

---

[38] Doat 25, fol. 40v (*Inquisitors and Heretics*, p. 269). [39] Lauwers, *Naissance*, p. 240.
[40] *Cart. Saint-Victor*, I, pp. 375–76 (no. 369); II, pp. 22–23 (no. 683), 31–32 (no. 690, dated 1064–79). Various similar examples found here, for example I, pp. 445–46 (no. 441), 1048, gift of church 'cum ipsa oblatione et cimiterio et decimo'; II, pp. 40–41 (no. 698), 1066, the bishop of Embrun donates various churches and their oblations and tithes, and 'cum omnibus mortuorum donationibus, cimiteriis atque baptisteriis, cartis et judiciis, penitentiis et infirmorum visitationibus'. One can find other similarly examples in *Cart. Moissac*.

in the life of St Bertrand de Comminges, from around the same date, tells of a man who, despite the bishop's warnings, built a house in the cemetery of the church of Saint-Gaudens and was divinely punished. The synodal of Sisteron (1225 × 35), echoing the Synod of the West, includes the injunction that no *new* houses should be built in cemeteries, nor any derelict house rebuilt without specific permission of the bishop. In 1270, the *enquêteurs* sent out by Alphonse de Poitiers to gather any complaints regarding royal government heard from the priest of Montcuq that parishioners had built 'houses' in the cemetery there, which he wished removed—this however clearly part of a wider dispute the priest was having with his parishioners, and the nature of the 'houses' not entirely clear.[41]

It is clear that anywhere that possessed burial rights must regularly have buried people, and most likely did so in a particular plot customarily used for that purpose. Archaeological evidence allows us to see the potential variations in the locations of cemeteries, in the context of the development of rural villages and *castra* in the eleventh and early twelfth centuries. As we saw in Chapter 1, they were mainly either adjacent to churches or were in a separate location outside the *castrum*, the latter choice probably arising from entirely practical issues of available space, though just possibly demonstrating some continuity with more antique practices of burying the dead beyond the boundaries of the living community. In the subsequent centuries there is strong continuity, as unsurprisingly these same basic arrangements continue in rural areas.

But if we look at the larger towns and cities, we find greater changes, intimately connected to the wider urban developments addressed in Chapter 4. Cities, particularly ancient cities such as Toulouse or Narbonne, would originally have buried their dead beyond the settlement—part of a clear 'separation between the living and the dead', as Gregor Wild puts it in his very useful analysis of changes in Toulouse from late antiquity to the later middle ages.[42] At the start of our period, there would often be one key religious institution in a city that laid claim to burial rights, at least as they pertained to the more wealthy; in the case of Toulouse this was the monastery of Saint-Sernin, which provided space around and within its precincts for this purpose. But by the late eleventh century the cathedral church, Saint-Étienne, was in competition for that role, leading to an agreement in 1093 that Saint-Sernin had the right to bury the bishops, counts, and knights, whilst Saint-Étienne could bury all the other inhabitants of the city.[43] Also in the city was the priory of Sainte-Marie-de-la-Daurade, and at some point

---

[41] *Cart. Saint-Victor*, II, pp. 581–82 (no. 1107); Contrasty and Fournie, 'Vie et miracles', p. 233; synodal of Sisteron, 1225 × 35, c. 88 (Pontal, *Statuts synodaux*, II, p. 223); P.-F. Fournier and P. Guébin, eds, *Enquêtes administratives d'Alfonse de Poitiers, arrêts de son parlement tenu à Toulouse, et textes annexes, 1249–1271* (Paris: Imprimerie nationale, 1959), p. 333 (no. 359). See Lauwers, *Naissance*, p. 259.

[42] G. Wild, 'La genèse de cimetière médiéval urbain: l'exemple de la topographie funéraire de Toulouse (vers 250 vers 1350)', *Archéologie du Midi médiéval* 17 (1999), 1–24, at p. 5.

[43] Wild, 'La genèse', p. 13; *Cart. Saint-Sernin*, p. 4 (no. 2).

in the late eleventh century Guillaume IV, count of Toulouse, petitioned Urban II for permission to allow him and his family to 'construct' a cemetery there; the pope agreed, and ordered the bishop of Toulouse to consecrate the cemetery (the earliest mention of the consecration of a cemetery in the city).[44] So by the end of the eleventh century, there was a potential three-way split or competition over burial possibilities within Toulouse—a situation which swiftly further multiplied, as by 1130 the physical expansion of the city brought a further eight or nine existing churches within its walls, and yet more cemeteries associated with various newly founded hospitals. In the thirteenth century the mendicants arrived, and more hospitals and leprosaria were founded. By 1350, there were, Wild calculates, sixty-seven potential places of Christian burial associated with the city, thirty-one of which were attached to hospitals or leprosaria, as well as two Jewish cemeteries (one older, one newer).[45]

There are a number of issues arising here regarding possible urban/rural contrasts, social status, identity, and the choices which lay people could make over burial; to these we shall turn further below. But the first thing to note is simply this: in a civic context, it becomes abundantly clear that 'the cemetery' must be a clearly defined area, for practical purposes if no other. Some become bold statements within the architecture of the city, a prime example being the civic cemetery known as 'Campo Santo' ('the holy field') in Perpignan, which forms a kind of vast cloister, adjacent to the cathedral church of Saint-Jean (see Figure 6.1). It was built in the first decades of the fourteenth century, formed by four vaulted galleries (each side about 56 m) enclosing a large central square, the latter excavated for burials also in 1321. Each vaulted recess in the galleries (originally covered by a roof) formed a burial place, and many are still marked today by inscribed stone tablets bearing the arms of rich families. Also still extant—though possibly not in their original locations—are some bas relief sculptures of religious scenes, such as the Virgin and Christ child attended by angels.[46] Here, not only are the community of the dead located centrally within the community of the living, but given a surprisingly impressive expanse of open space in which to reside, contrasting with the monumentality of the adjacent church.

What in more rural areas? As noted already in Chapter 1, there is evidence by the later eleventh century of some rural cemeteries being marked out by freestanding crosses. Synodal and conciliar decrees suggest that there is increased episcopal concern in the thirteenth century to have cemeteries enclosed by short

---

[44] Wild, 'La genèse', p. 14; bull of Urban II, undated, *Gallia Christiana*, t. 1, *Instrumenta*, p. 40 (no. 24): 'Sane quia te sanctae Mariae apud Tholosam omnino ecclesiam diligere et honorare accepimus...quatenus tibi, tueque progeniei illic cimiterium construas et benedici facias...Episcopo autem civitatis ut illud consecret ex nostra parte mandabimus.'

[45] Wild, 'La genèse', pp. 14–20, and map and list pp. 22–23.

[46] Personal observation. For archaeological descriptions and context of the site, see G. Mallet 'Le cloître-cimetière Saint-Jean de Perpignan: observations', *Archéologie du Midi médiéval* 7 (1989), 125–36; G. Mallet, 'Les cloîtres-cimetières du Roussillon', *CdF* 33 (1998), 417–34.

Figure 6.1 Campo Santo, urban burial ground, Perpignan

walls or fences, to keep out animals and to demarcate the area clearly. The synodal of Sisteron (1225 × 35) called for cemeteries to be 'kept closed up, where it is possible, and kept clean', and the council of Nîmes noted that stones from church buildings should not be put to any profane uses but could be used to repair other churches, hospitals, 'or in closing up cemeteries'.[47] The most common sense of 'demarcation' indicated by such councils is, from the mid-thirteenth century onward, the injunction (discussed in more detail further below) to bury various categories of people—typically unbaptized infants—'next to' the cemetery, which takes for granted a sense of its having reasonably clear bounds.

Alongside the demarcation of the space of the cemetery there was, as importantly, its development as a *sacred* space. As Michel Lauwers explains, in his indispensable analysis of the development of the cemetery in western Europe, this comes about formally via episcopal consecration for the first time in the tenth century, though he suggests that in southern France, the cemetery itself was mostly not formally consecrated until some time in the twelfth century.[48] An early example (in addition to the papal letter regarding Toulouse, above) may be found in a pontifical from Valence dating from 1100 × 25. This sets it out clearly as an adjunct to the consecration of a church: 'After the consecration of the church

---

[47] Synodal of Sisteron, c. 89; council of Nîmes, c. 91. The latter injunction repeated in the synodal constitutions of Carcassonne from around 1270, c. XI.1, and those of Guillaume Durand for Mende in 1292–95, c. XI.2 (Avril, *Statuts synodaux*, VI, p. 273).

[48] Lauwers, *Naissance*, pp. 143–58; regarding southern France, p. 151.

there follows the blessing of the cemetery. Whilst the bishop blesses the church the clergy and priests should circumnavigate the whole cemetery blessing it with water, whilst saying the litany. The bishop moreover is to bless the cemetery in this manner, turning himself to the east and saying "The Lord be with you; let us pray...".'[49] A prayer follows, and the bishop then turns to each of the other compass points, similarly reciting a further prayer each time. Cumulatively the prayers set out the congregation's hopes of eventual entry to paradise, ask for protection of the cemetery from any attack or pollution, and invoke various figures from the Old Testament with regard to burial and future salvation. A thirteenth-century pontifical of Arles, preserved in a Spanish manuscript, elaborates a little further on the same template.[50] It directs the bishop to circumnavigate the cemetery, asperging it with holy water, and then heading to each corner of the plot, saying in each part a prayer, the text of which is very similar to those from the earlier Valence pontifical (which might suggest that both share an earlier, now lost, exemplar).

A much richer ritual is set out by Guillaume Durand, bishop of Mende (d. 1295), in a pontifical he compiled in the 1290s which exists in a fourteenth-century manuscript held in Toulouse. He does say initially that it is usually sufficient simply to go around the circuit of the exterior of the church and cemetery, asperging it with holy water when the church is dedicated; however, he then notes, cemeteries are not always adjacent to the church, nor are all cemeteries consecrated at the same moment as the church. Thus he provides a more detailed ceremony: five wooden crosses, higher than a man, are to be erected in the cemetery the night before, one in each corner and the highest one in the middle. In the morning the bishop, dressed in liturgical clothes, should give the people 'a brief collocation on the sanctity and liberties of the cemetery, and so forth'. Then fifteen candles are to be lit, three placed before each cross, and the bishop should go to each cross (starting with the large one in the middle) blessing it with holy water whilst reciting a simple prayer, moving similarly to the others in turn. The bishop then reclines on the earth, whilst the cantor begins to sing a litany, and as the choir responds the bishop rises up again, holding his staff in his left hand, and makes the sign of the cross three times, saying as he does so that he purges, blesses, sanctifies, and consecrates the cemetery. They then perform a circuit of

---

[49] Vatican Library, MS Ottobon lat. 256, fols 76r-78r: 'Post consecrationem ecclesie sequitur benedictio cymiterii. Interim dum episcopus benedicit ecclesiam clericis et sacerdotes circumdent totum cymiterium cum aqua benedicta facientes letaniam. Pontifex autem benedicat cymiterium hoc modo. Vertat se ad orientem et dicat Dominus vobiscum, oremus...'. I am most grateful to Dr Miklós Földváry and the Usuarium website (<https://usuarium.elte.hu>) for access to a digital scan of the manuscript.

[50] Royal Library, Monastery of El Escorial, MS J.III.24, fols 52v-55r (again accessed via Usuarium). I believe that another copy may exist as BnF MS Lat. 1220, there associated with either Bishop Bernard II (1273-81) or Bertrand III Amalric (1281-86)—see Richard Kay, *Pontificalia: A Repertory of Latin Manuscript Pontificals and Benedictionals* (Kansas: n.p., 2007), p. 128, no. 669.

the cemetery, asperging it with holy water. More prayers are said, and then at each of the crosses in turn the three candles are raised up, placed on the arms and head of each cross, more holy water is sprinkled, and yet more prayers are said; having thus attended to each of the five crosses, the bishop finally blesses the people and leads them in to mass.[51] One may ask how often such a ritual could have been enacted fully—keeping the various candles alight whilst outside would presumably have been a little demanding on windy days—but it clearly imagines a highly ritualized and impressive 'sanctification' of the space, in the presence of the local people, the ritual elements making the point strongly to them, even if the details of the Latin would mostly not be accessible to a lay audience.

So, perhaps as early at the beginning of the twelfth century, and certainly by the later thirteenth century, cemeteries were literally 'blessed', given a publicly ritualized spiritual charge in a similar way to churches. By the early fourteenth century, at least one synodal (for Auch) called upon the priest to recite the *Pater noster* or a 'special prayer for the dead' whenever he walked through the churchyard, giving it a similar sense of formality as approaching the altar, though this is perhaps an unusually high point of ritual respect.[52] But it is clear that the cemetery was intended more generally to become a special place over which care should be taken, in mundane ways as well as more spiritual ones. We noted above the conciliar and synodal injunctions to keep the area 'clean', and indeed a set of confraternity records from Fendeille (near Castelnaudary) record for 1341 the expense of 3d for someone cutting the grass in the cemetery.[53] But 'cleanliness' was moral as much as practical. Bishops enjoined priests to ensure that various unsuitable activities did not occur within the graveyard. From the early thirteenth century, echoing language found in much earlier northern European canon law, no dances or singing of secular songs were to be allowed there, or any judicial cases whether ecclesiastical or secular.[54] The synodal of Lodève, issued by Bernard Gui in 1325, noted that anyone who fornicated in a church or cemetery was

---

[51] BM Toulouse MS 118, fols 104v-108r; discussed in Lauwers, *Naissance*, p. 157. The manuscript also contains Bernard Gui's *Libellus*, a book of synodal instruction discussed further in Chapter 7. Durand's pontifical is edited in M. Andrieu, ed., *Le pontifical romain au moyen-age, III: le pontifical de Guillaume Durand* (Vatican: Bibliotheca Apostolica Vaticana, 1939).

[52] Synodal of Auch, c. 1310, c. 7 (J. Duffour, ed., *Livre rouge du chapitre métropolitain de Sainte-Marie d'Auch*, 2 vols (Paris: Honoré Champion, 1907-8), I, p. 85).

[53] AD Aude G268, fol. 13v: 'pro preconizaronibus erbe scimiterii, iiid tol.' These confraternity records are are to all practical purposes churchwardens' accounts for the local church, and are discussed further in Chapter 9.

[54] Synodal of Sisteron, 1225 × 35, c. 87, versus dances (*choree*), preceded by the council of Paris, 1200 × 08, c. 88 (Pontal, *Statuts synodaux*, II, pp. 52–93), but otherwise I think one of the earliest such injunctions; council of Nîmes, 1252, c. 96 (dances, songs, court cases); synodal of Carcassonne, c. 1270, c. XI.10 (dances, songs, court cases, 'theatrical plays' (*vel ludos facere theatrales*)); synodal of Rodez, 1289, c. XIII.9, XIII.10 (court cases, dances); synodal of Mende, 1292–95, c. II.7 (court cases). The council of Avignon, 1209, c. 17, banned dances and songs 'or the recitation of love poems or little songs' in churches on the occasion of holy vigils. For northern Europe, see Regino of Prüm, *Libri duo de synodalibus causis et disciplinis ecclesiasticis*, ed. G. A. Wasserschleben (Leipzig: Engelmann, 1840), p. 180 (1.398); I am grateful to an anonymous reader for pointing this out.

automatically excommunicate—part of a wider concern over such things, but in this case possibly also influenced by the fact that in 1321 one woman, Beatrice de Planissoles, had confessed to the bishop and inquisitor Jacques Fournier (whom Gui knew well) that she had once had sex with her lover, the priest Pierre Clergue, in church.[55]

Whilst the initial ritual of consecration would be seen by, at best, only one particular generation of parishioners, the cemetery thus became a place which could be 'polluted' by various actions, some of which might then require reconsecration; this was the case if someone had a fight spilling blood there, for example, or if someone was murdered in it.[56] Indeed, we catch sight of the former, in passing evidence given before the inquisitor Fournier in the early fourteenth century, noting an occasion three years earlier when the bishop himself had to reconsecrate the church of Ax-les-Thermes 'because it had been polluted by blood'.[57] So despite episcopal injunctions, some lay people did get into fights in cemeteries. Therefore they probably also did sometimes gather to sing songs, have dances, settle legal disputes, and so forth. On earlier occasions they certainly made formal agreements there, as one can find in a few charters from the eleventh century. This could on occasion continue much later also: a dispute over tithing was settled in the presence of a notary between a priest and his parishioners in 1330 in the cemetery of Saint-Martin-de-Caïssac, for example.[58] On the other hand, by the early fourteenth century a further witness who gave evidence to Bishop Fournier admitted to having had a conversation with another man about which of the young women they'd just seen at mass they most fancied—the witness curtailing the conversation however, as something which was not fitting to discuss whilst still in the cemetery.[59] Another man (one who also voiced a number of rather odd beliefs) called Gausbert d'Aula of Bénas, among various other things, admitted to an inquisitor in 1273 that he had urinated in cemeteries on various occasions—he claimed however not to know that he was not supposed to do it, and that he did it only from an 'infirmity'.[60]

These examples of forbidden activities are primarily about constraining the laity, in an attempt to keep the secular world clearly separate from a now sacred space. But at the same time, the laity were of course eventually going to make up the majority of the inhabitants of the cemetery, and they had some collective and individual investment in it as a place of eventual repose, where their bodies would await the final resurrection at the Apocalypse. As many archaeologists and

---

[55] Synodal of Lodève, c. 20 (Douais, *Synodal de Lodève*, p. 12); *Fournier*, I, p. 243.
[56] For example, council of Nîmes, 1252, c. 96.   [57] *Fournier* II, p. 108.
[58] *Cart. Moissac* no. 149, charter 1090 × 97, 'Facta sunt Moysiaco in cimiterio…'; AD T-et-G, G 801, fol. 1r: 'de cayssaco diocesis caturcensis in cimiterio ecclesie predicte ante foram ecclesiae predicte…' This latter document, and others of a similar kind, are discussed in more detail in Chapter 9.
[59] *Fournier* III, p. 26.
[60] Doat 25, fols 25r–26r (*Inquisitors and Heretics*, pp. 230–33). On Gausbert, see Arnold, *Belief and Unbelief*, p. 226.

historians have emphasized for a variety of locales and times, the cemetery is thus in some ways a mirror of the still-living society around them, and it has sometimes been suggested that the medieval dead could be thought of as continuing members of the local community. There is clearly something to this, and one extraordinary individual, Arnaud Gélis, was reported to Bishop Fournier for telling various people that he could see and talk with their dead relatives, the messages being a mixture of expected piety (the dead asking for more prayers to be said for them) to the highly personal and domestic (a dead daughter unhappy that her still-living mother had hung on to the shawl in which she was supposed to have been buried, among various other examples). When interviewed by the inquisitor, Gélis himself claimed that the souls of the dead walked from local church to local church, doing penance. The heterodoxy of this belief aside, it displays a curious sense of the dead being tethered locally and yet not specifically to their own cemetery.[61]

We may take this as a reminder that whilst the dead may mirror the living, they may not do so in an absolutely straightforward manner. The living community is not homogeneous or static but riven by various shifting distinctions and tensions, status being the most obvious. In death, identity can become fixed and more firmly marked. I noted above, via Gregor Wild's analysis of the development of cemeteries in Toulouse, that at an early stage there was a separation between those who could be buried at Saint-Sernin and those who went to the cathedral cemetery. It was a distinction very explicitly based on status: the monastery got the bishops, counts, and knights, along with their wives and children ('both sons and daughters'). We saw in Chapter 1 the importance placed by various elite lay donors to monastic houses on being buried 'honourably', and being interred within the land of the monastery rather than the local church; some of that eleventh- and twelfth-century picture continued into the later period. It seems very likely that the ability to gain burial, and a familial burial marker, in Perpignan's Campo Santo would similarly have been restricted to an elite, albeit by this stage an elite who were as often mercantile as noble, as evidenced by various guild symbols carved in stone adorning the site. The desire to be buried close to, or even inside, a notable church or monastery continued into the later middle ages— burial 'within' a religious building being forbidden by some conciliar statutes, unless episcopal special permission was granted.[62]

Distinctions of living status were thus long interwoven into burial practices. But, in theory at least, other moral distinctions were also to be made manifest by burial, fixing in place and publicly proclaiming (at the point of burial at least)

---

[61] *Fournier* I, pp. 128–43, 533–52. On Arnaud, see Ladurie, *Montaillou*, pp. 345–51; J.-C. Schmitt, *Ghosts in the Middle Ages*, trans. T. L. Fagan (Chicago: University of Chicago Press, 1998), pp. 140–42; J. H. Arnold, 'Talking with Ghosts: Rancière, Derrida and the Archive', *Journal of Medieval History* 48 (2022), 235–49.

[62] For example, synodal statutes for Elne, 1326, c. 12 (BM Perpignan, MS 79 fol. 76r).

some other ways in which 'the community' might be riven. These appear in the thirteenth century, apparently for the first time. It is once again conciliar and synodal legislation that provides our main evidence. Burial within any consecrated cemetery required that the dead person be part of the spiritual Christian community, and the ideological boundaries of that community were being more tightly redrawn in this period.[63] We have already noted that unbaptized infants were to be buried 'next to' the cemetery. In fact in an early injunction, at the council of Albi in 1230, it was expressed as 'to be excluded from' the cemetery, this in the case of mothers dying in childbirth, where the child did not live long enough to be baptized—a likely quite common occurrence.[64] Others were also excluded, essentially any who were excommunicate at the time of death (though the statutes from the council of Nîmes allowed that someone who might receive post-mortem absolution could be temporarily buried in a wooden coffin outside the cemetery, to be relocated once absolved).[65] Those permanently excommunicated included those who had been deemed heretics but also, by the later thirteenth century, 'public usurers'.[66] Jews were also of course not supposed to be buried in Christian ground; as we have seen in the case of Toulouse, they would usually have their own cemeteries. Specifying the definition of Christian community potentially even more tightly, the synodal statutes for Elne produced by Bishop Batle in 1326 specified that burial was forbidden to anyone who had not received the sacrament of the Eucharist 'unless prevented by death—though not if they refused to accept it out of contempt for it'.[67] As we know from a variety of early inquisition evidence, the bodies or bones of those who were posthumously condemned as heretics—in the sense either of having belonged to the elite of the Good Men or the Waldensians, or having engaged in sustained support for them—were to be dug up and burned. The shape of the community of the dead, at least at the point of burial and at least as *imagined* by the conciliar and synodal decisions, was thus in large part determined by particular ideological factors, that hypostatized a moral version of the faithful, inscribing them onto these spaces of interment. Those spaces were themselves further re-marked as 'sacred' through their repeated use for Christian burial, in contrast to the more occasional 'profane' inhumations of those deemed to be expelled in death from the community.

[63] See generally Lauwers, *Naissance*, pp. 166ff.
[64] Council of Albi, 1230, c. 49: 'eiciatur [*corr.* eicatur] extra cimiterium'.
[65] Council of Nîmes, 1252, c. 131; cf. Lauwers, *Naissance*, p. 175. The same was repeated in the synodal constitutions for Dax, 1283, c. 75 (Avril, *Statuts synodaux*, V, p. 164).
[66] Usurers: synodal of Rodez, 1289, c. XVII.2. Similarly, synodal of Carcassonne, c. 1270, c. 15; synodal of Mende, 1292 × 95, c. X.2; synodal of Lodève, 1325, c. 2; synodal of Elne, 1326, c. 42 (BM Perpignan MS 79, fol. 84v). Also, the very widely circulated guide for confessors attributed to Bérengar Fredoli (d. 1323), bishop of Béziers and then bishop of Tusculum (BM Toulouse MS 191, fol. 82v).
[67] Synodal of Elne, 1326, c. 22 (BM Perpignan MS 79, fol. 77v): 'Sed nec in cimiterio sepeliant quemque qui sacramentum eucaristie non recepit nisi fuerit morte preventus nec tunc etiam si ex contemptu ipsum renuerat acceptari'.

The requirement to disinter the bones of heretics usefully flags up a particularly interesting issue: whether or not individual graves remained identifiable. We saw, in Chapter 1, that on the one hand archaeological excavations have not thus far identified much reuse of the same spaces, and on the other that there is no evidence for above-ground markers. One of the earliest injunctions to exhume those posthumously condemned comes in the inquisitorial manual known as the *Ordo processus Narbonensis*, most likely written in 1244 by the inquisitors Ferrier and Pierre Durand.[68] The injunction there (a sentence to be given against those who died as heretics) makes clear a possible stumbling block: 'through definitive judgment we pronounce [*so and so*] to have died a heretic, and condemning them and their memory in equal severity, their bones—if they can be distinguished from others—are to be exhumed from the cemetery, and we determine that they are to be burned in detestation of so abominable a crime'.[69] 'If they can be distinguished from others'—this practical consideration, repeated in some subsequent conciliar legislation in regard to anyone who died excommunicate (their bones simply to be placed elsewhere rather than burned), indicates that it would not always be possible to tell one grave from another.[70] There is no large-scale archaeological study of which I am aware for later medieval cemeteries in southern France: the modern framework for launching archaeological investigation has not tended to facilitate such work in the midst of existing French towns, and the kinds of analysis on which I reported in Chapter 1 for earlier centuries rested, in large part, on abandoned rural settlements.[71] So we are a little in the dark with regard to material evidence. Work from elsewhere in Europe would tend to suggest that gravestones, with indicators of identity, tend not to appear until the very late middle ages. For southern France in this period, if we want to know whether people's graves were marked and subsequently remembered, we are largely thrown back then on fragmented textual evidence, and a small number of above-ground material objects.[72]

There were certain expectations about where one might be buried: the default general location was one's own parish church (though as we shall see below, this

---

[68] L. Sackville, 'The *Ordo processus Narbonensis*: The Earliest Inquisitor's Handbook, Lost and Refound', *Aevum: rassegna di scienze storiche, linguistiche, e filologiche* 93/2 (2019), 363–95 which provides a fresh transcription from the original manuscript and important discoveries regarding dating.

[69] Sackville, '*Ordo processus*', p. 379.

[70] Council of Nîmes, 1252, c. 131: 'si ossa excommunicati discerni poterunt ab ossibus fidelium defunctorum'. Copied by synodal of Carcassonne, c. 1270, c. 15; synod of Dax, 1283, c. 76; synodal of Rodez, 1289, c. XV.13.

[71] I am grateful to Professor Elisabeth Zadora-Rio for correspondence on this subject.

[72] There are some surviving, personalized, stone tombs in monasteries such as those for the abbots Bernard de Mèze and Guillaume de Roquefeuil at Saint-Guilhem-le-Désert (the monastery of Aniane and Gellone): J. Lougard, J. Nougaret, and R. Saint-Jean, *Languedoc Roman* (Saint-Léger-Vauban: Zodiaque, 1975), plates 22, 23. A personalized stone cross from the fourteenth century, marking the burial of 'Guillemette, wife of Jean', survives in the Musée des Augustins in Toulouse (numéro d'inventaire RA 685).

was not the only choice) and in the case of widows, there was some expectation that they would be buried with their husbands, unless they had made a specific decision to be interred elsewhere. This was set out in the council of Nîmes, 1252: that whilst women could choose to be buried wherever they wished, if they did not record a choice, they would be buried 'in the cemetery of the parish church, in the grave of their husband, if he had died first and was buried in the same parish'.[73] An *exemplum*—a little story for the use of preachers—from southern France makes passing reference to this practice: a wife died eight days after her husband, and his grave was opened up so that she could be buried next to him (at which point it was discovered that three toads were gnawing on his corpse, an indication of how little attention he had paid to his future salvation when alive).[74]

It would not, of course, be that hard to remember where an earlier body was buried just a week or so later. What of longer periods though? There is a little evidence in a few wills of people requesting burial not only in a particular cemetery but in regard to a specific location therein. A man called Grégoire, part of a wealthy noble family whose uncle was the sacrist at the cathedral church in Agde, requested in his will of 1233 to be buried in the cathedral's cemetery 'with my father', the latter having made his will in 1215 (and certainly dead by 1225, as the will of his widow Belisende dates from then).[75] Some families seem to have had a tradition of burial in particular locations: the will of a noble woman called Ava de Magrens from some time in the 1130s includes the request that the senior monks of Lézat should come on the obit of her death 'to my grave and to the grave of my father and my mother and my brother, and absolve us and all our progeny, for the love of God'—this giving a strong sense of a particular plot for family burials.[76] A civic statute given by the consuls of Toulouse in 1207 ordered among other matters that land containing a family member's tomb or burial could never be sold, mortgaged, or alienated.[77] A very strong sense of a family burial plot is visible in a legal dispute from 1302, where a knight called Hugues de Marquas challenged Guillaume Villaret, rector of the church in *Crosetz* in the diocese of Rodez, over the priest's decision to build a certain tomb in his cemetery—the location chosen being, Hugues claimed, the part where 'there are and were many bodies placed

---

[73] Council of Nîmes, 1252, c. 129.

[74] J.-Th. Welter, 'Un nouveau recueil franciscain d'exempla de la fin du XIIIe siècle', *Études franciscaines* (1930), 432–76, 595–629, at p. 459 (no. 70).

[75] R. Foreville, ed., *Cartulaire du chapitre cathédral Saint-Étienne d'Agde* (Paris: CNRS, 1995), p. 403 (no. 363); his father, simply 'Carbonnel', p. 394 (no. 359), his mother Belisende pp. 393–94 (no. 358). His uncle, Pons Carbonnel the sacrist, made a will in 1234 (pp. 403–06, no. 364) in which, among various other things, he left a staggering 5,000 *sous* of Melgueil 'to be distributed to the poor'; he also specified a particular burial place, not with his secular family but 'next to Lord Pierre de *Laudo*'.

[76] *Cart. Lézat*, II, pp. 120–21 (no. 1166), 1130 × 37. Her brother Guillaume was a monk there already.

[77] AM MS AA3, p. 145: 'quod aliquis homo vel femina hic ville tolose monumentum vel sepulturam alios sui generis, postquam videlicet aliquis vel aliqua ibi tumulatus fuerit, nullatenus possit vendere nec dare nec inpignorare nec a se alienare vel a suo genere alio modo alienare'. It is unclear as to whether this implies burial in a parish church still 'held' by a secular owner, burial in some private chapel, or indeed burial in some other unconsecrated ground.

and buried from the lineage of the same knight; and from antiquity, as he said, in the aforesaid place the same knight and his ancestors are in the custom of burying the bodies of their lineage'.[78] We see something similar in the 1324 will of Pierre de Fenouillet, lord of Coustassa (c. 40 km south of Carcassonne), which includes a request for burial with the Brothers Minor in Limoux, 'in the grave [or possibly tomb] in which it is customary to bury my predecessors'.[79]

It is worth noting that in each case we are dealing with *family* rather than individual graves, and that the examples I have been able to locate are all from people high up the social strata (albeit in the case of Pierre de Fenouillet, the lord of a really very small *castrum*).[80] Wealth continued to allow greater possibilities: in his will of 1337, the viscount of Narbonne elected to be buried in the convent of the Brothers Preacher in Narbonne, specifically in a chapel to St George that he was endowing with 20 *livres* to have built (alongside various other very large donations).[81] One suspects that in such circumstances not only provision for one's soul, but a clear memory of the location of one's grave, would persist for some long while. Whether more lowly people also had what were effectively family burial plots is uncertain, but one suspects usually not; it seems likely that the fact of the local cemetery would be a sufficient, albeit general, marker. At Campo Santo in Perpignan, it also seems very likely that the large central area acted as a general burial site—an ossuary, in effect—even whilst the vaulted recesses bore the stone markers of particular people.[82] A few stone burial plaques survive there, and the inscription on one is fairly legible, dating to '1315, 4th Kalends of August', marking the burial of 'Lady Boneta, wife of Pierre de la Rivière, merchant' (see Figure 6.2). The plaque uses the writing to frame a burial scene depicting a woman being lowered into a sarcophagus by two other, possibly female, mourners, with various priests giving blessings, and other onlookers.[83] It provides us with a little idealized image of burial, recording for posterity the name, date of death, and an image of individual interment in a stone coffin—but it seems likely

---

[78] Doat 135, fol. 26r: '...sunt et fuerunt multa corpora progeniei ipsius militis, posita et sepulta et ab antiquo, ut dicebat idem miles, in loco predicto idem miles et sui antecessores sepelire corpora ipsius progeniei consueverunt'. It is definitely a tomb in this instance, as it is described as being newly built ('novo aedificari'). The disputants used a Brother Preacher as an arbitrator, and the knight got to keep the burial place, which is specified as being 'next to the window' of the church (fol. 29v).

[79] AD Aude, 7 J 51 (family archive of the de Fenouillet family), no. 5: 'in sepulcro in quo predecessores mei consueverunt sepelliri'.

[80] For analysis of burial choices in the fourteenth and fifteenth centuries, emphasizing the differences that social status made, see M.-C. Marandet, *Le souci de l'au-delà: la pratique testamentaire dans la région toulousaine (1300-1450)*, 2 vols (Perpignan: Presses universitaires de Perpignan, 1998), I, chapter 1.

[81] E. Martene and U. Durand, eds, *Thesaurus novus anecdotorum*, 5 vols (Paris: Sumptibus Florentini Delaulne, Hilarii Foucault, Michaelis Clouzier, Joannis-Gaufridi Nyon, Stephani Ganeau, Nicolai Gosselin, 1717; repr. Farnborough: Gregg, 1968), I, pp. 1387–88. He also provided 30 *livres* annually, to have three friars celebrate mass there perpetually; plus another 10 *livres* for anniversary masses.

[82] Mallet, 'Les cloîtres-cimetières', p. 422.

[83] As Mallet points out, it visually echoes quite closely a plaque on the south portal of the cathedral, marking the death in 1291 of a canon and sacrist: 'Les cloîtres-cimetières', pp. 424–25, figures 3 and 4.

Figure 6.2 Lady Boneta burial plaque, Campo Santo

that her body, as with others, was actually interred in the central square, as this is a wall-mounted marker, and could only ever have functioned as such. There is some passing evidence that older burials did become forgotten in some places, as the caveat about identifying bones when disinterring heretics indicates. Another witness before the inquisitor Bishop Fournier explained that his doubts about the eventual resurrection occurred to him, in part, when he was with many other people in the village cemetery in Ornolac (c. 20 km south of Foix), watching a new grave being prepared, and saw many old bones being dug up in the process.[84]

I mentioned above the exclusion of unbaptized infants in the cemetery. This was an area in which a number of confusing and upsetting possibilities could arise: if a mother was dying in childbirth, should one cut out and baptize the baby; if no priest was present at a difficult birth, a layperson could *in extremis* baptize an infant, but the priest would then subsequently be uncertain over whether baptism had been administered correctly (or indeed if the child had in fact been alive at the point when it was administered); if a baby was abandoned at a church, and subsequently died before being discovered, did one assume that it had or had not already been baptized? The fate of the child's eventual soul rested on such matters and, probably as importantly to the lay community and family, this would be made visible by its place of interment, inside or outside the cemetery.[85] The rather hard line taken by the council of Albi in 1230, noted above, softens ever so slightly by that of Nîmes, 1252, which gives the priest some leeway:

---

[84] *Fournier* I, p. 206 (confession of Guillaume Austatz, translated in J. Shinners, ed., *Medieval Popular Religion: A Reader*, 2nd edn (Toronto: Broadview Press, 2007), pp. 485–504).
[85] On the fate of unbaptized babies, it is interesting to note a brief discussion in the synodal statutes for Mirepoix, 1334 × 48, that sets out a fivefold arrangement of afterlife locations: paradise, the limbo in which reside all the faithful except for the saints and ancient church Fathers, another limbo in which unbaptized infants reside, purgatory, and hell. BnF MS 15066, fols 68r–69r, at 68v: 'Tercium receptaculum animarum est limbo puerorum qui absque peccato actuali moriuntur sed sol[i] moriuntur in originali peccato et sine gratia baptismali...'

If a child baptized by a layperson dies before the priest is present, and the priest doubts whether it was baptized in the due form, and if this cannot be made certain, in such doubt the infant should be buried in the cemetery of the church. And we believe the same can be done when an infant has been left exposed next to the church or is otherwise found dead, where there cannot be any certainty regarding their baptism.

However, the council goes on to state, if it is shown that they were not properly baptized, they cannot be buried in the cemetery.[86] The synodal statutes produced by Bishop Bernard de Campendu for Carcassonne around 1270 further emphasize leniency of a certain kind. If the priest doubts whether baptism has occurred, he can subsequently use these words: 'If you are baptized, I do not rebaptize you; but if you are not baptized, I baptize you in the name of the Father and the Son and the Holy Spirit, Amen.' And, the statute goes on, 'if there is such doubt, where many are unable to know, the testimony of one person is to be believed.'[87] (The bishop continued to be clear, however, that where the infant clearly had not been baptized, they could not be buried in the cemetery).

Statutes across this period emphasize that lay people had a right to choose where they wished to be buried (whilst also warning ecclesiastics not to try to entice people to choose one religious locale over another), and a lengthy inquiry in Albi in 1335 rested similarly on whether they also had the right to choose where their young children were buried. This arose from a dispute between the cathedral canons and the Brothers Preacher in the city, the former claiming that all young children were automatically to be interred in their parish church. What were partly at stake were the funeral oblations—though as Jean-Louis Biget points out, a key underlying principle was also about patronal legal rights over prepubescent children.[88] As the witnesses (giving evidence for the mendicants) attest, many of the wealthier citizens chose to have their dead children buried in the cemeteries, chapels, or cloisters of the Brothers Preacher, the Brothers Minor, or the Carmelite friars.[89] Sometimes this was part of a wider family tradition of burial: one witness noted that when the child of Pierre Dionysius, a merchant, died at 5 years of age, the body of the child was 'carried publicly to be buried in a certain chapel in the church of the Brothers Preacher, and was there buried in the

---

[86] Council of Nîmes, 1252, cc. 10, 11.   [87] Synodal of Carcassonne, c. 1270, c. 3.
[88] J.-L. Biget, 'Sépulture des enfants et *patria potestas*: un procès devant l'officialité d'Albi en 1335', *CdF* 33 (1998), 365–91. Bérenger Fredol's guide to confessors, from perhaps the early fourteenth century, tersely clarifies a canon legal perspective: 'Item, nota quod quilibet adultus et discretus potest eligere sepulturam ubicumque voluerit. Item, pater filio impuberi in minori potest eligere sepulturam' (BM Toulouse MS 191, fol. 82v).
[89] For example, AD Tarn G 402, fol. 9v (evidence of Bartolomeu Garrigue, merchant, 50 years old): '...quod patres habentes liberos decedentes infra pupillarem etatem possunt eligere sepultimam pro ipsis infantibus sic descendentibus extra suam parochialem ecclesiam videlicet in aliis cimiteriis dicte civitatis alibensis et specialiter in cimiteriis et claustris et ecclesiis religiosorum scilicet fratrum predicatorum minorum et carmelitarum.'

tomb of the lineage of the said Pierre Dionysius his father'.[90] Another witness recalled that twenty-two years earlier, a lawyer (*iurisperitus*) of Albi called Master François de *Fanava* whose infant boy had died declared, 'I wish that my dead child be buried in my chapel in the house of the Preachers'.[91] But on other occasions it seems to have been a decision to bury the child in a particularly holy place, not previously connected with the family; a choice being made by the parents to separate the dead infant from the other associations of parish community in order to gain increased spiritual benefit for their soul. Petrona Baudoza told the inquiry that about seventeen years earlier she had buried her infant daughter Adzemar (not yet a year old, as another witness Astingua, Petrona's sister, also attested). She could not attest to whether or not the parish priest and canons knew about this burial because she herself had been ill when her daughter was buried; but as soon as she had recovered 'she went to the said church of the Brother Preachers to the place where her said daughter was buried, before the altar of the said church, and there—both then and many other times—she said good things and prayed to God for the soul of her said daughter'.[92] Her sister Astingua confirmed that Petrona had often showed her Adzemar's burial place, so that they could both say prayers for her.

In his study of the development of cemeteries in western Christendom, Michel Lauwers writes:

> Whilst sometimes contested, the institution of the cemetery, in the eleventh and twelfth centuries, manifests a sort of tension: on the one hand, the cemetery transforms itself into a homogeneous *space*, sacralized and bounded, controlled by ecclesiastical authority...but on the other hand, the image given by the acts of practice is often that of a fracturing of burial *rights* and a tangle of possessions, mixing together the interests of the clergy and those of the laity.[93]

---

[90] AD Tarn G 402, fols 14v–15r: 'quod quidam infans minor quinque annorum Petri Dynisii mercatorie Albie qui infans decesserit fuit corpus ipsius infantis publice portatum ad sepeliendum in quadam cappella ecclesie fratrum predicatorem et ibi sepultum in cimiterio tumulo generis dicti Petri Dionisii eius patris'.

[91] AD Tarn G 402, fol. 61r (evidence of Jean Galt, merchant, 60 years old and more): 'Ego volo quod iste infans meus deffunctus sepeliatur in capella mea in domo predicatorum.'

[92] AD Tarn G 402, fol. 80r: 'Item interrogata si dicta filia fuit portatis et sepulta in dicta ecclesia predictorum scientibus et concensientibus capellano et dominis canonicis sancti salvii dixit se nescire quia ipso testis tunc infirmabatur ut dixit et non potuit esse presens in sepultura dicte filie sue; set statim eum convaluit accessit ad dictam ecclesiam fratrum predicatorum ad locum ubi fuerat sepulta dicta eius filie ante altaris ipisus ecclesie et ibi tunc et alia pluries dicebat bonum et rogabat deum pro anima dicte filie sue, pro ut dixit.' Astingua's evidence is on fol. 79r–v: 'et ipsa testis loquens ut dixit pluries fuit in dicta ecclesia fratrum predicatorum antiqua una cum dicta petrona sorore sua et dicta petrona ostendebat eam testi tumulum dicte filie sue in quo erat sepulta...ibi dicebant orationes pro anima dicte filie dicte Petrone.'

[93] Lauwers, *Naissance*, p. 247: 'Parfois contestée, l'institution du cimetière manifeste, aux XIe et XIIe siècles, une sorte de tension: d'un côté, le cimetière se transformait en un espace homogène, sacralisé et borné, contrôlé par l'autorité ecclésiastique...mais d'un autre côté, l'image que donnent les actes de la pratique est souvent celle d'un fractionnnement de droits cimetériaux et d'un enchevêtrement de possessions, mêlant la part des clercs et celles des laïcs.'

This we have seen from the southern French evidence (drawn upon also by Lauwers). What has become additionally clear is the role of the laity, not only in asserting their rights in the landholding sense, but, as with the grieving parents choosing a place for burial for their dead children, in their ability to push ecclesiastical authorities to provide nuance to and interpretation of the more abstract rules regarding membership of a spiritual community. The cemetery became, as we have seen, a space demarcated both literally and liturgically, a space set in some ways outside the secular world; and yet it was a space of and for the laity, as much as for the clergy, a space over which lay people—lay *families*, as much as lay individuals—had a particular claim and investment. Those investments were not uniform: the place of the dead remained sharply marked by social distinction, and post-mortem memory echoed the hierarchies of living status.

The Space of the Local Church

On 27 November 1340, Armand de Narcès, the archbishop of Aix, visited the parish church of La Roquebrussanne (about 56 km east of Marseille, and a similar distance south-east of Aix). Whilst he was pleased with the state of the bells, books, and other accoutrements he found there, he was also gravely concerned with the physical position of the church, located as it was up a hill. At some subsequent point the settlement of La Roquebrussanne had extended itself downhill, to cluster around the Issole river in the valley below, a somewhat steep kilometre and a half away—this being where the heart of the village is still today. Having reflected on the matter following his visitation, Armand wrote to the chaplain there; very unusually, the letter was copied into the visitation record and thus still survives. The letter is quite lengthy, beginning with some general reflections on the importance of protecting one's flock from rapacious wolves, before turning to the main issue: the fact that part of the settlement, and thus the parishioners, had moved downhill meant that they could not access their parish church very easily.

> Some of these parishioners—namely those old and decrepit from personal fragility, others through being busy with their children, homes and the things over which they have custody, others because of sluggishness and indolence—thus shunning the harsh road, are not coming to the said church on Sundays and feast days, but remain in the lower place; thereby they might be called brutes. And indeed it has happened in former times that when women carry children to be reborn at the font of holy baptism in the said church, they were compelled by necessity to baptize those children who were then failing [*that is, nearing death*] in the street, in the river or a well, so that they do not die without baptism, just as is the custom at the point of death. And, when the bodies of the dead had to be carried to the said church to be buried there in the neighbouring cemetery, hardly any people could be found to carry them there and to accompany them as

is usually done from pious duty, but instead, contrary to decency and humanity, many were placed like sacks of grain on the backs of animals.[94]

Moreover, he continued, priests with care of souls do not sometimes descend to care for their parishioners when needed, nor the parishioners come to the priests. Thus 'the greater and healthier part of the aforesaid parishioners, for their own salvation, humbly ask and request' that a new church be built, in a more fitting place.

The letter goes on to note that, at the bishop's direction, the prior and perpetual vicar of the church had held a meeting with certain *prud'hommes* of La Roquebrussanne, in which they had decided upon a fitting place near the river, and that the new church should be dedicated to St Sauveur, to thus become the new parish church for the village. The last surviving section of the letter—its ending frustratingly abbreviated by one or more missing folios from the visitation register—then sets out some details on how the church should be constructed. The 'head' of the church (that is, the choir and apse) should be, Armand specified, four canes long and three canes wide (probably about 9 m × 6.5 m), with a 'suitably' high vault.[95] It should have a stone basin on the left wall in which the priest could wash his hands and the sacred vessels for use in mass, and an aumbry cut into the stone for keeping the consecrated host. Above the church there should be a high stone bell tower 'just as at the church of Tourves', placed so that the cord for the bells was not too close to the altar. There should be a 'wooden grill' (*cleda lignea*) in front of the entry to the head of the church, to distinguish the 'place of ministry' from the rest of the building, of about one cane 'in length' (probably what we would call an 'altar rail', that is, something which symbolically separated the spaces rather than an actual barrier). There should be retables (that is, altarpieces) 'painted with fitting pictures' (*picta cum hystoria congruenti*), and windows 'in suitable places' by which the said head of the church could be illuminated. The body of the church was to be 12 canes by 5 canes (c. 26 m × 11 m) 'so that the total populace of the place can be received within it', and at least 4 canes high (c. 9 m). Within the church there should be two altars, one on the right in honour

---

[94] Visitation d'Aix (see n. 98 below for details), fols 14v–15r: '…nonnulli ex ipsis parrochianis, videlicet senes et decrepiti propter persone fragilitatem, alii propter occupationes quos circa liberorum, domorum et rerum suarum habent custodiam, alii propter segniciem et pigriciam, hujusmodi vie asperitatem aborrentes, ad dictam ecclesiam etiam dominicis diebus et festivis non accedunt sed remanent in ipso inferiori loco ut ita loquamur quasi bruta, atque accidit retroactis temporibus quod dum mulieres pueros regenerandos sacri baptismatis lavacro ad dictam ecclesiam deferebant neccessario compulse sunt ut pueros ipsos qui tunc deficiebant in via ibidem baptizarent in rivo vel fonte ne sine baptismate decederent prout est in mortis articulo fieri consuetum. Et dum defunctorum corpora ad ipsam ecclesiam ibidem in cimiterio propinquo tumulanda defere oportet, vix inveniuntur qui ea deferant et associent prout moris est ex officio pietatis, sed plerumque quasi bladi sacrina, quod honestati et humanitati contrarium est, supra dorsum animalium imponuntur.'
[95] Canes—*canna*—were a classical unit of measurement, and varied by place, but tend to average a bit over 2 m.

of St André and one on the left in honour of Ste Katherine.[96] A second visitation report from February 1345 confirms that it had been built within just a few years.[97] Both the old church—now known as the 'chapel of Our Lady of Inspiration', named after a seventeenth-century statue of Mary gifted to it—and the newer church of Saint-Sauveur still exist (see Figures 6.3 and 6.4).

La Roquebrussanne was just one of many places visited by Armand de Narcès between 1340 and 1345, apparently mostly in person, though undoubtedly assisted by a scribe and other attendants. Across those years Armand saw 172 different churches in the region, forty of which were noted as being 'rural', a designation which seemed to indicate not just the nature of their environs—for various other churches, the one at La Roquebrussanne included, were also pretty rural by both medieval and modern standards—but that they lacked a resident priest.[98] The business of visitation was, in this record at least, entirely focused upon the church fabric and the performance of the liturgy, there being no record

Figure 6.3 La Roquebrussanne old church (chapel Notre-Dame d'Inspiration)

---

[96] Visitation d'Aix, fol. 15r–v.   [97] Visitation d'Aix, fol. 111v.
[98] The visitation record survives in a privately owned manuscript of 132 folios, a complete transcription of which was very generously supplied to me by Professor Noël Coulet; above and hereafter 'Visitation d'Aix'. On the document and visitations, see N. Coulet, 'Paroisse, oeuvre, communauté d'habitants en Provence (1e diocèse d'Aix dans la première moitié du XIVe siècle)', *CdF* 25 (1990), 215–37; N. Coulet, 'Au miroir des visites pastorales: les villages du diocèse d'Aix-en-Provence, XIVe–XVe siècle', *CdF* 40 (2006), 121–39. My count of churches and rural churches (conducted via a spreadsheet) differs somewhat from those suggested by Professor Coulet, whose contextual research remains fundamental however. From my reading, the record lists 180 churches, on a few occasions two existing within the same village or parish. Of those 180, there is no entry for eight; in five cases this is

Figure 6.4 La Roquebrussanne new church (Saint-Saveur)

of the moral behaviour of priest or parishioners as one might find in contemporary visitation records elsewhere in Europe.[99] Whilst this makes the visitation less immediately exciting than some more gossipy examples of the genre, it is extremely useful in giving a sustained view of the material fabric, furnishings, and objects found within a large number of local churches in Provence.

The archbishop's specific intervention at La Roquebrussanne—to build a new church in a new location—was a unique instance in this set of visitations. But the second underlying issue regarding the size of the church did however come up in several other places. At Tourves it was noted that 'as the said church is not sufficient to receive its parishioners' it should be enlarged within the following five years, so that it could hold 'all the parishioners of the church without any crowding'.[100]

---

because they were not formally visited because of jurisdiction (or on one occasion because of a dispute over the procuration fee), and in a further three there is simply a blank in the register after the name of the church. From the 172 visited, in five cases no details were noted as all was found to be in order. In 1344 and 1345 the archbishop began to revisit some churches, adding to the record for sixty-six of the 180 seen a few years earlier.

[99] For very rich examples south of the Pyrenees, see M. Armstrong-Partida, *Defiant Priests: Domestic Unions, Violence, and Clerical Masculinity in Fourteenth-Century Catalunya* (Ithaca, NY: Cornell University Press, 2017).

[100] Visitation d'Aix, fol. 10r: 'cum dicta ecclesia non sufficiat ad recipiendum parrochianos ejusdem propter quod neccessario indiget augmento, ordinavit quod infra quinque annos...dicta ecclesia augeatur et augmentetur in longum sic taliter quod universi ipsius ecclesie parrochiani absque pressura aliqua recipi et stare valeant in eadem prout decet'.

The church of Saint-Trophime at Pourrières was 'not sufficient to receive its parishioners, particularly when they come to it on great feast days to hear divine office', and similarly needed to be extended; and moreover to be better lit around the main altar 'where it is exceedingly dark'.[101] A similar need for enlargement was noted in several other parishes.[102] Nor was this something arising only in the fourteenth century. We lack any extant earlier visitation records for the region, but a document from 1275 records that King Philippe III was petitioned by the parishioners of Montréal (a large village about 18 km west of Carcassonne) that they be allowed to enlarge their church, so that it would be 'less narrow' (*minus arcta*).[103]

At La Roquebrussanne the old church has a nave only about 5 m wide and 13 m long.[104] It was probably originally built in the twelfth century judging by its architecture, namely a plain rectangular nave ending in a semicircular apse. There is a circular window at the west end above the door (an architectural arrangement reproduced in the new church), and a narrow window high up in the north wall near the west end. Two other narrow windows are cut in toward the east end of the nave, but these may well have been put in at a later date, as one would find with various other twelfth-century buildings still in use in the late middle ages and thereafter. In comparison the new church of Saint-Sauveur is not only larger—its nave at least twice as wide, and with a substantial choir and apse—but also has buttresses, side aisles that house chapels, and a bell tower at its east end (albeit one rebuilt in the mid-seventeenth century).[105] It is still quite dark inside by northern European standards, but in addition to the large circular window above the west door has another smaller circular window at the head of the apse, two windows high up in the south wall, and two larger windows cut into the north and south walls toward the east end of the nave, the latter four all with classic gothic arches.[106]

The new church dwarfs the older and provides an interior space that whilst superficially the same—a nave, an apse—is quite different in its qualities: interior

---

[101] Visitation d'Aix, fol. 33r: 'cum dicta ecclesia non sit sufficiens ad receptionem parrochianorum suorum dum ad ipsam presertim in magnis festivitatibus conveniunt pro auditione divinorum [*it should be enlarged*]...taliter quod capax sit prout decet omnium parrochianorum suorum et nichilominus ipsa ecclesia illuminetur circa majus altare ubi est nimis obscura'.

[102] Visitation d'Aix, fols 51r (Saint-Jean-de-*Salis*), 53v (Sainte-Marie-de-Rognes), 54r (Saint-Dalmace-de-*Riancio*), 67r (Sainte-Marie-de-*Laureis*), 73v (Sainte-Marie-de-Grambois), 82v (Sainte-Marie-de-Montfuron). In the latter case, at Montfuron, the bishop suggested that the church be extended 'usque ad viam publicam', and rather pleasingly one can see that, judging by the different shape of the window closest to the road, this is precisely how the nave of the church was extended, albeit by only a couple of metres.

[103] Doat 71, fol. 542; edited in Mahul, *Cartulaire*, III, p. 302.

[104] Archaeological survey information provided on site.

[105] The tourist information board at the church says that the nave and apse are now 30 m long, 14 m wide, 16 m high.

[106] There is also a rather pleasing circular 'light well' style window open in the apse, vertically above the altar—but my assumption is that this must surely be a modern addition, on engineering grounds if no other.

subdivisions, much more natural light, greater height, different acoustics, and so forth. We might simply say that we here witness a new gothic architecture supplanting the older romanesque style. But that condenses to an aesthetic description and implied art-historical chronology something which was in reality rather more complex, both in the dynamics of its historical change and in the consequent human experiences it afforded. The architectural style we call 'gothic', its accompanying technological innovations and in particular its utilization of light, rippled out across western Europe from a northern French epicentre, the first stones dropped in the very late twelfth century and then visible in subsequent waves of building and reconstruction of cathedrals and major churches across the thirteenth and fourteenth centuries. If we imagine squinting at that process from a considerable distance, in order to picture three centuries in a glance, what we would see would truly resemble an unstoppable wave, rushing outward and spreading almost everywhere. Particularly spectacular breakers would catch the eye as the waves spread: within the region studied here, the imposing grandeur of Albi cathedral, the light-dappled double-nave of the Dominican ('Jacobin') church in Toulouse, the stunningly high-windowed apse of Saint-Nazaire in Carcassonne, to give just three among a host of examples.

But zoom back in to consider any portion of that landscape and we will discover that wave encountering myriad local conditions, finding its path at a varied pace across a literally uneven local landscape, and leaving many scattered pockets of older ecclesial architecture untouched. The older church at La Roquebrussanne remained, not swept away but adapted into a separate site of worship. And whilst the shift to a new church only appeared on this one occasion in Armand de Narcès's visitations, it most likely happened in other locales for much the same reasons. For example, among sites I have visited myself in Languedoc, one finds what was likely a similar shift at Laroque-d'Olmes (c. 25 km east of Foix), where a small romanesque church, re-dedicated as a chapel to St Roch in the sixteenth century, sits on a hilltop about half a kilometre away from where the main settlement is now located.[107] The village now possesses a grand gothic church dedicated to the Holy Sacrament, located at the higher end of the settlement. The older church is about 9 m × 17 m in exterior dimensions, built in the familiar rectangular-nave-with-semicircular-apse style (though in fact the apse looks to have perhaps extended an earlier, even smaller, original building), and originally it had just two extremely narrow windows, in the north and south walls (see Figures 6.5 and 6.6).[108] The new church was built in the early fourteenth century (with some later additions, probably including its very imposing bell tower), with

---

[107] The tourist information board at the site claims that the chapel was built in the sixteenth century; this is however nonsense, as the architecture is very clearly twelfth century or earlier.
[108] Personal observations. The original window in the south wall has been filled in but is still visible; the north wall now has five larger windows in faux-romanesque style, and a sixth in the south wall of the apse.

Figure 6.5 Laroque-d'Olmes old church (chapel of Saint-Roch)

multiple side chapels, impressively high walls and buttresses, and a choir and apse filled with light from seven windows.[109] Similarly, at Puivert, some 18 km south-east of Laroque-d'Olmes, there is a large gothic church dedicated to St Marcel in the centre of the village, but a much smaller twelfth-century chapel about half a kilometre away, downhill and across the river.[110] An impressive gothic church of Saint-Jean-Le-Baptiste was built in the later thirteenth century in Pezens (about 10 km north-west of Carcassonne); a small eleventh-century chapel, dedicated to Marie Madeleine, sits outside the modern village about a kilometre to the north-west, along the road to Castelnaudary, perhaps always separate but possibly an earlier parochial site, shared with other settlements.

In many other small villages and *castra* there were extensions to existing romanesque churches: we find this in Durfort (20 km north-east of Castelnaudary), for example, where two side chapels and a short, fat bell tower were added in a rather ungainly fashion to an older church. Something similar

---

[109] There is a detailed description given by M. Durliat, 'L'église de Laroque d'Olmes', *Congrès archéologique de France* 131 (1973), 392–99, though he there mistakenly says that it was built on the site of an earlier church of 'St Martin', based on an 1163 charter of peace between Raimond V of Toulouse and Raimond Trencavel witnessed there. That charter in fact refers to a church of Saint-Étienne (cf. *HGL*, V, col. 1271, no. 653), and if the *Ulmos* of the charter is Laroque-d'Olmes, I would contend that the older church is more likely the chapel still standing (of which Durliat makes no mention).

[110] The chapel has a nineteenth-century frontage, and was dedicated to 'Notre Dame de Bon Secours' in 1810 according to a wall plaque, but the main body of the building is clearly a twelfth-century church.

Figure 6.6 Laroque-d'Olmes new church (Saint-Sacrement)

happened to the church of Saint-Martin at Fraisse-Cabardès (17 km north-west of Carcassonne) which gained two side aisles and another stumpy bell tower. In some places the extensions remain fundamentally 'romanesque', as at L'Aiguillon (c. 28 km east of Foix) where the nave has simply been lengthened in the same direction and style; and, at some point, more and larger windows inserted into the north wall (a filled-in older window just visible to the right of the porch). This is similarly the case at Serres (c. 37 km south of Carcassonne), where an eleventh- or twelfth-century church had some minor extension in the fourteenth century.[111] And in some places the twelfth-century church remained as apparently the only local option, perhaps by some point a 'rural' church with a non-resident priest in the way described for the diocese of Aix by Armand de Narcès. For example, at Peyrolles, a tiny village a few kilometres north of Serres nestling in the valleys below the Pyrenees, there is a charmingly simple church measuring about 17 m × 7 m on the exterior, which has had four 'gothic' windows inserted at some point, but otherwise remains presumably the size it was in the twelfth century, its still-active cemetery witness to continued parochial use.

The physical space of the church mattered considerably for the experience of worship. It is important to note here the beginning of the process of building the new church at La Roquebrussanne: there, as elsewhere, it can only have been the local parishioners who brought the issue of size to the attention of the visiting archbishop, and as he makes clear representatives of the people had a say in the new location (and perhaps the size and dedication) for the new church. The copying of the small circular window above the east door from the old church to the new—not an utterly unknown feature elsewhere, but far from standard—strongly suggests that local people had a hand in some elements of its design. And they very likely played some role in paying for it. As noted, the end of the letter is frustratingly missing, but other occasions of higher expenditure in the visitation record usually spell out that the costs should be spread three ways, between the local lord or lords, the parishioners, and the clergy. Elsewhere one can find lay donors proudly announcing their role in paying for a new church. At Montauban, for example, as Jörg Feuchter has nicely argued, the cost of the impressively large thirteenth-century church of Saint-Jacques might be seen as an alternative 'penance' undergone by the civic elite, in negotiation with the inquisitor Pierre Cellan, who had found them guilty of support for Waldensians and Good Men, the ecclesial construction being a commutation of the lengthy pilgrimages he had originally bestowed upon them.[112] The new church at Laroque-d'Olmes also has a stone founder's plaque, unfortunately mostly illegible, beside its door; though the coat of arms of (presumably) the local lord is fairly clear still, making plain the fact, if not its detail, of lay donation.

The coming of gothic architecture to southern France happens over a sustained period, from perhaps the mid-thirteenth to the early fifteenth century. As I have been arguing, it was never a binary switch from the old to the new: plenty of smaller, older 'romanesque' churches survived, particularly in more rural areas, sometimes extended in various ways, but also sometimes alongside a larger new

---

[111] Notice regarding conservation information from the Prefecture, held within the church itself.
[112] Feuchter, *Ketzer, Konzul und Büsser*, pp. 356–61.

church. If we think about the material and sensory environment of the local church, as the site of liturgy and worship, we can see that new kinds of spatial experience start to become available for the laity (and of course the clergy) across the course of the thirteenth century—larger, brighter spaces, more complex in their physical arrangements—but that, in many locales, these would continue to be experienced as *contrasting* spaces to the older, smaller, darker churches. If we are interested in people's potential embodied responses to liturgy, that possibility of contrast seems to me to be extremely important: 'light' and 'dark' are not abstract absolutes but comparative qualities.

Something similar might be said with regard to the difference between collective worship in the airy, resonant, formally arranged space of a new and larger church and that conducted in the typically small, intimate, nave-and-apse construction of older ones. In the more capacious space of a larger church, various side chapels might be positioned, and there could potentially be some sense of 'procession' in certain liturgical contexts. The division between nave and choir— the space of the laity and the space of the priest—would be more clearly demarcated, and potentially there would be division within the nave itself: on one occasion, at the church of Cadenet, which was in the process of being majorly rebuilt, Archbishop Armand directed that within the nave the place for women and the place for men should be divided by a short wall of 'four palms height', with the men sat closer to the altar and the women closer to the west door, so that 'one does not impede or disturb another in contemplation or prayer'.[113] This was for a church being rebuilt in 1343, and whilst such a division had been recommended by Bishop Guillaume Durand in his widely circulated *Rationale* (written before 1286), it is not clear how universally one would find such a gendered arrangement, nor practically how much difference it would make in a smaller edifice.[114] In an older, smaller church the congregation could never truly be 'apart' from each other, nor very far removed from their priest. Entering such a space, with its one or two tiny slit windows, one would move abruptly from the heat and light of the southern French countryside into the coolness and gloom of the stone nave, where (to borrow an image used by the archaeologist Yannis Hamilakis in his description of worship in medieval Byzantine churches) one's breath and that of one's neighbours would make the candle flames flicker, and where the close proximity of other worshippers might encourage a particularly interpersonal and

---

[113] Visitation d'Aix, fol. 65r: 'et fiat infra ipsam ecclesiam unus paries cum sedibus altitudinis quatuor palmorum dividens stationem mulierum a statione vivorum; ita quod in parte superiori versus altare stent homines et in alia parte versus portale suam habeant stationem mulieres prout honestati congruit et unus alium in contemplatione vel oratione non impediat vel perturbet'.
[114] Guillelmus Duranti, *Rationale divinorum officiorum*, I-IV, CCCM 140 (Turnhout: Brepols, 1995), I.i.46, pp. 26-27; more broadly, see M. Aston, 'Segregation in Church', *Studies in Church History* 27 (1990), 237-94. Reading Guillaume Durand, one does need to remember that whilst he describes and proscribes features in a universal manner, he clearly thinks *first* of the space of a cathedral church, rather than a small parish edifice.

embodied sense of community.[115] This at least for those in attendance, since, as we have seen, not all churches were large enough for their congregations.

The Visual and Material Church

With these and other comparative thoughts in mind, let us think a bit further about the range of interior features of these churches, both the older 'romanesque' and the newer 'gothic' constructions. Firstly, lights. As we saw in Chapter 3, the provision of candles (whether wax or tallow) and oil for lamps was something long associated with the laity, evident in various charters from before 1200, plus a very few wills. Bringing 'light into the darkness' must have been a very resonant metaphor in many of the older churches. At the same time, the more complex spaces of the larger gothic buildings, with their larger choir and apse, and in many cases additional side altars or chapels, meant that one might exercise additional choice over *where* to gift lights within the overall array. The Aix visitation mentions the necessity of providing additional lights on a few occasions, noting for five churches that they must be provided with an oil lamp, and a supply of oil, implying that these particular churches had otherwise been lit by tallow candles or tapers.[116] The relative scarcity of these commands strongly suggests that the other 170-odd churches did already have sufficient provision. At the very few other points at which the archbishop ordered something in regard to lights, it was more specific: the church at Mazaugues was to supply itself with two substantial candles to be used when carrying the consecrated host to people on their deathbeds; the church of Saint-Pierre in Seillons needed two copper candelabra to place before the altar (a few other places were similarly told to get two candelabra, which seem to have been standard altar lights in larger churches); the church of Saint-Laurent in *Gabardello* was to have a 'torch' weighing 4 lbs, to use during the liturgy at the elevation of the host.[117] The set of confraternity records from Fendeille briefly mentioned above provides annual churchwardens' accounts for the local church. In 1332, when the accounts start, they record that they bought wax candles from four different men for a total of 19 *sous* 8d. The following year, the confraternity bought 'four candelabra in which is to be placed the wax of the confraternity when celebrating mass', for the surprisingly cheap price of 6d. By 1341 they record more than 50 *sous* spent annually on oil, and more than 60 *sous*

---

[115] Y. Hamilakis, *Archaeology and the Senses: Human Experience, Memory, and Affect* (Cambridge: Cambridge University Press, 2013), p. 78.
[116] Visitation d'Aix, fols 3v, 12r, 21r, 81r, 81v.
[117] Visitation d'Aix, fols 13r ('dicta ecclesia non haberet cereos ad portandum cum gloriossimo Christi corpore cum defertur infirmis…'), 29v ('et provideatur…duobus candelabris de cupro ad ponendum supra altare'), 59v ('provideat eidem ecclesie de uno torticio ponderis IIIIor librarum pro elevatione corporis Christi').

on wax, giving a good sense of how continuously lighting a church could be quite a commitment.[118]

I found only a few legacies directed towards lights in the pre-1200 wills discussed in Chapter 3, and in fact many of the thirteenth-century wills I have encountered also lack this sort of provision. But there are of course some exceptions. In 1207, on his deathbed, Guillaume Thomas gave his brother Pierre most of his lands and possessions, on the requirement that Pierre hand over each year, on the feast of St Germier, half a pound of wax to the church dedicated to that saint. Rather similarly, in his will from 1216, Guillaume Pons Astro, a wealthy consul of Toulouse with close connections to the monastery of Saint-Sernin, passed on most of his inheritance to his son Pons Guillaume, 'on the condition that he...keep in perpetuity a small lamp in the church of St Sernin before the altar of the Blessed Mary, and once a year gives a feast for a hundred paupers on the day of the Lord's Ascension'.[119] In these cases the light has a rather clear purpose with regard to memorialization. Elsewhere we find a more general practice of charitable giving to lights, as in the will from 1225 of Belissende, widow of Carbonel (member of a wealthy landowning family we met in Chapter 4), who among other pious provisions included a 'measure of grain' to provision lamps in two different churches—a more regular form of giving, perhaps reflective of more usual expectations.[120] Similarly the will of a probably rather less wealthy man called Pons d'Olivet left a couple of shillings to candles in two churches, and gifts of 12d for lights at another two.[121]

By the fourteenth century this kind of gift had become much more standard, and also perhaps displays more clearly some sense of the choices over *which* lights the testator wished to support. In a will from 1312 a citizen of Cahors, Geraud de Caussade, asked to be buried in the cemetery of Saint-Pierre in Cahors 'in the place where my father and mother were buried', giving various sums of money to the clergy of that church, and 2 *sous* to its lights. He added also however that he wanted to leave 12d for the 'torches which are lit for the body of Christ'; a way of associating oneself with the key moment of the mass.[122] Lady Sebelia, member of

---

[118] AD Aude G 268, fols 12r–17r, 85v–86v. On the confraternity and these records, see further Chapter 9.

[119] *Cart. Lézat*, II, pp. 427–28 (no. 1603), 313–35 (no. 1452). On Pons Guillaume and the Astra family more broadly, see Mundy, *Men and Women*, pp. 173–83.

[120] *Cart. S. Etienne d'Agde*, pp. 393–94 (no. 358).

[121] *Cart. S. Etienne d'Agde*, pp. 443–44 (no. 402). He begins his will by reckoning to achieve 100 *sous* through selling his bed and other household goods, though does leave other unspecified goods to his widow, so may in fact have been richer.

[122] Doat 119, fols 32v–35r, at 32r-v: 'Et in primis offero corpus et animam meam omnipotenti Deo, et beatissime gloriose virgini Mariae matri eius et toti curie celesti et eligo mihi sepulturam in cimiterio beati Petri de Caturco in loco in quo sepulti fuerunt Pater meus et mater mea...Item cuilibet clerico dicte Ecclesie duodecim denarios Caturcenses semel, luminarie dicte Ecclesie duos solidos Caturcenses. Item torticiis qui accenduntur corpori Christi in dicta ecclesia duodecim denarios Caturcenses.' He made a number of other pious gifts also, including for memorial masses.

a noble family based near Perpignan, included a similar instruction along with many other pious provisions (she chose to be buried with the Brothers Minor in Perpignan): 'I leave to the works of the church of Saint Jacques of Montner 20 *sous* to mend a cerise canopy to adorn the said church or altar; and a great candle of 3 lbs of wax that can be burnt at the elevation of the body of Christ', repeating the same gift of a candle for the elevation at five other churches.[123] A widow called Guillelma Fort, a member of the confraternity of the Blessed Mary at Fanjeaux, made several pious gifts including a fairly paltry 3d to the works of the newly begun cathedral church at Mirepoix (contrasting somewhat with the 10 *sous* she left to the Brothers Minor in the same town). She finished the list of pious bequests with 5 *sous* to the lights of the Blessed Marie Madeleine.[124] Of the twelve wills made by fairly lowly men and women recorded in a surviving notebook by the notary Geraud Boffati from Saint-Sulpice in 1344–45, almost all include gifts of wax, or oil, or money to the lights—or indeed all three—strongly suggesting that it had become practically de rigueur by that point in most places.[125]

What did these lights illuminate? Let us go back to the evidence of the Aix visitation. Most are set in front of an altar, of which in smaller churches there might just be one (plus often a portable altar, presumably for use when giving sacraments to the sick), though often additional side altars dedicated to different saints are extant.[126] Very occasionally the archbishop directed that the altar needed improvement: 'the prior...must have a new altar made, with a good and fitting stone slab'.[127] At least some of the time, as at La Roquebrussanne's new church, the altar was separated from the nave by a screen, probably an altar rail rather than the kind of 'rood screen' found in late medieval English parish churches: at the church of Sainte-Marie-de-Rognes, Archbishop Armand ordered that 'before the altar there should be a wooden grill (*una cleda lignea*) just as there was of old, so that by it the place of the church services is divided from the station of the laity

---

[123] AD Aude 7 J 1, a liasse of various documents from the archive of the Villar family: 'Item lego operi ecclesie Sancti Jacobi de Monnerio viginti sol. ad emendum unum pali ciricum ad ornandum dictam ecclesiam seu altare. Et magis unum cereum trium libr' cere quod comburat ad helevandum corpus xpi.' Will dated 1326.

[124] AD Aude H 563, document 10 within the *liasse* (preceded by gifts to clergy and to the church that her confraternity supported): 'Item quatuor hospitalibus generalibus cuique tres denar' tur'. Item lego operi ecclesie Kathedralis de Mirapicis tres denar' tur'. Item lego fratribus minoribus de mirapicis decem sol' tur'. Item lego fratribus minoribus de Castronovo de arrio duos sol. tur'. Item lego fratribus predicatoribus de Carcassona duos sol. tur'. Item lego fratribus carmelitanis dicti castrinovo de arrio duos sol. tur'. Item lego fratribus Beati Augustini de Limoso duos sol. tur'. Item lego hospitali pauperum beati Jacobi dicti castri faniiovis quinque sol. tur'. Item lego luminariis beate marie magdelene quinque sol. tur'...'. Will dated 1330.

[125] AD Tarn 3 E 55–253, wills at fols 13v, 14r, 14v, 17v, 18v, 21r, 22v, 43r, 44r, 55r, 73r, 74r. For the fourteenth and fifteenth centuries, see similarly Marandet, *Le souci de l'au-delà*, II, chapter 2.ii.

[126] On portable altars, see E. Palazzo, *L'espace rituel et le sacré dans le christianisme: la liturgie de l'autel portatif dans l'Antiquité et au Moyen Âge* (Turnhout: Brepols, 2008).

[127] Visitation d'Aix, fol. 40v (church of Saint-Julien-de-*Manhanella*): 'prior...fieri faciat altare novum cum lauza lapidea bene et decenter'. Similarly 103v, Saint-Jacques-de-Lésignan-la-Cèbe, where the altar needed to be repaired.

and others'.[128] Dressing the altar was probably a cloth, and for liturgical purposes the church would have a cross, a chalice, a paten, and of course some form of lights, whether single candles, a lamp, or a candelabrum to hold several candles. The chalice was, as the archbishop explicitly enjoined for twenty-four different churches, to be made of silver—potentially the most valuable object in some of the poorer and more rural churches. The priest's robes themselves were likely also quite impressive, the need for repaired, renewed, or more impressive clerical vestments being perhaps the most common injunction issued during these visitations.

All of those altars were to have painted 'retables', often one in front of the altar (what is otherwise known as an antependium, placed in front of and below the altar surface), and the other behind. These usually depicted the saint to whom the altar was dedicated, and instructions from the archbishop to provide or to repaint retables were also extremely common, made for more than fifty churches in these visitations: each altar needed a retable 'well and sufficiently painted with a corresponding picture', as the archbishop admonished the rector of one church.[129] Few examples of such things survive, but we do have both a retable and an antependium associated with the church of Saint-André in Angoustrine, high in the Pyrenees, very close to Puigcerdà, both thought to be late twelfth or early thirteenth century. The retable, understood originally to belong to a different local church, has two side panels which depict, in a very simple style, the Annunciation and Visitation. These surround a central three-dimensional frame (a 'baldaquin') that previously contained a small wooden sculpture of the Virgin Mary, sadly stolen at some point in the late twentieth century but preserved photographically (see Figure 6.7).[130] The antependium (90 cm × 130 cm) centrally displays Christ in glory, surrounded by four scenes from his life (Annunciation, Visitation, Adoration, and what is possibly his arrest in the garden of Gethsemane) (see Figure 6.8).[131] If we want to see a surviving retable depicting a saint, rather than

---

[128] Visitation d'Aix, fol. 53r: 'et ante altare ecclesie fiat una cleda lignea sicut erat ab antiquo ut per eam locus servitorum ecclesie a statione laycorum et aliorum dividatur'.

[129] Visitation d'Aix, fol. 31r (Blessed Mary de *Sesolis*): 'bene et sufficienter picta cum hystoria congruenti'.

[130] See also G. Mallet, *Églises romanes oubliées du Roussillon* (Montpellier: Presses universitaires de Languedoc, 2003), p. 77 and plates; Marc Sureda i Jubany, 'Les lieux de la Vierge: notes de topo-liturgie mariale en Catalogne (XIe–XVe siècles)', in M.-P. Subes and J.-B. Mathon, eds, *Vierges à l'enfant médiévales de Catalogne, Corpus des Vierges à l'enfant (XIIe–XVe s.) des Pyrénées-Orientales* (Perpignan: Presses universitaires de Perpignan, 2013), pp. 39–69. Note also the very late thirteenth-century diptych from Rabastens, now held in the Musée d'art et d'archéologie du Périgord in Perigueux, and presumably originally used as a retable. This depicts scenes from the life of Mary and the passion of Christ in a vibrant fashion, with much use of gold and (originally) bright colour; but like the Thouzon example discussed above, this is an unusually high status piece, associated with a rich confraternity which included among its founding members the abbot of Moissac. See M. A. Bilotta, 'Diptyque de Rabastens', in M. A. Bilotta and M.-P. Chaumet-Sarkissian, eds, *Le Parement d'autel des Cordeliers de Toulouse: anatomie d'un chef d'oeuvre du XIVe siècle* (Paris: Somogy, 2012), pp. 110–11.

[131] See Mallet, *Églises romanes*, pp. 83–84; the church is described generally pp. 247–48. The conservators do not attempt to gloss the top left hand scene, which includes a figure with a sword and, presumably, Christ; my suggestion of the arrest is suppositional.

Figure 6.7 Retable with Virgin and Child, Angoustrine (Saint-André), 12th century

Christ or Mary, we may have to look somewhat later. An example made c. 1410, from Thouzon (17 km east of Avignon), is now held in the Louvre, and depicts scenes from the life of St André. It survives in part because it's a notably high quality artistic piece, produced for a noble *château*, thus unlikely to be what one would find in every parish church. If we can nonetheless project out more broadly from this specific late example, it is interesting to note that its two surviving panels depict, in addition to André, two other saints (Sebastien and, perhaps, Katherine) accompanied simply by their iconographic symbols. André himself was presumably the focus of the now-missing central panel, and the side panels also show dramatic narrative moments within his life (putting out a fire, chasing demons from a town). These suggest some representational choices which might be understood to frame the possibilities for all retables more broadly: the saint depicted as abstracted visual object, the saint as participant in their own specific story, the saint as figure accompanied by others from the celestial court.

So some combination of this late Provençal example and the surviving Pyrenean pieces might perhaps give us a reasonable sense of what people across the region could have encountered in their local churches. And we also need to remember that, at the point that the archbishop of Aix made his visitation in the

Figure 6.8 Antependium, Angoustrine (Saint-André), 12th century

early 1340s, on thirty-four occasions—that is, at nearly a fifth of all the churches visited—he was not instructing that an existing retable be repainted, but that one be supplied in the first place. Thus whilst retables are understood to have existed as objects for devotion since the late twelfth century, they might not have reached every parish for at least another 150 years. Some churches might have three separate altars, each with its own depiction of a saint, and perhaps some depiction of Christ or Mary; others might lack any. Most would sit somewhere in between.

Were there any other visual materials within local churches? On two other occasions in the Aix visitation we catch sight of another item with a painted image within the church: at the church of Sainte-Marie-de-Rognes, that the aumbry should have a picture of Christ painted on it, and at Saint-Jean in Salles, that the reliquary casket held by that church should be repainted.[132] In the latter case, it is worth remembering that 'painted' does not necessarily mean 'figuratively depicted'. A thirteenth-century reliquary casket originally from the fairly modest church of Saint-Anne in Labessière-Candeil, now held in the treasury of Albi cathedral, is beautifully decorated with blue and gold—but in an entirely foliate design (though admittedly there is one section missing which might have contained some figurative illustration).[133] A small number of statues survive from the region as a whole. There are two twelfth-century figures of the Virgin and child at the abbey church in Saint-Savin-en-Lavedun (c. 37 km south-west of Tarbes), both formal, regal, and a little expressionless, albeit in one case covered originally in gold leaf.[134] A similar Marian statue is now held in the treasury of Albi cathedral. It is possible that such objects once existed in less exalted settings, and there is an interesting detail suggesting precisely this in a letter written by Alphonse de Poitiers in 1269, calling on the seneschal of Rouergue to inquire regarding an assault upon the church of 'Marcell' (possibly Marcillac-Vallon, 19 km north-west of Rodez): 'they have sacrilegiously carried off the vestments of the said rector, grain, wine, linen, an easter candle, a torch which is lit for the body of Christ, a veil for the head of the image of the Blessed Mary...'.[135] It would be feasible to cover a retable with a veil, but it seems more likely to be a three-dimensional image. One rather amazing statue survives in the Rouergue at the small, rural church of Estables (c. 37 km west of Mende): another rather severely depicted but

---

[132] Visitation d'Aix, fols 53r ('et in ipsius armarii porta ymago Salvatoris pingatur'), 51r ('et caxa reliquiram [?corr. reliquiarum] repinguatur'). Relics are mentioned on only two other occasions, in both cases the archbishop ordering that a casket should be made to hold them: at Saint-Pierre in Peyrolles (fol. 42v) and at Sainte-Marie-de-*Borzeto* (fol. 81r).

[133] <https://commons.wikimedia.org/wiki/File:(Albi)_Cath%C3%A9drale_Sainte-C%C3%A9cile_-_Tr%C3%A8sor_-_Ch%C3%A2sse_reliquaire_XIIIe_Labessi%C3%A8re-Candeil_PalissyPM81000176.jpg> (accessed 14 Aug 2022).

[134] M. Durliat and V. Allègre, *Pyrénées romanes*, 2nd edn (Saint-Léger-Vauban: Zodiaque, 1976), p. 309 and plates 131, 132. See also Mallet, *Églises romanes*, pp. 75–79.

[135] A. Molinier, ed., *Correspondance administrative d'Alfonse de Poitiers*, 2 vols (Paris: Imprimerie nationale, 1894–1900), II, p. 302 (no. 1661), 19 June 1269.

entirely gilden image of the Virgin and child, seated on a throne, both Mary and Christ wearing crowns.[136] A fourteenth-century statue (rather badly restored by a later artist) extant in the church of Notre-Dame-de-l'Assomption in Fanjeaux shows a rather softer image, the Virgin carrying the Christ child, crowned but standing rather than enthroned and looking a touch more maternal than regnal.[137]

Each church would also of course have one or more crosses, and these could be more or less vibrantly depicted. On several occasions Armand made it clear that a church needed a crucifix (that is, not simply an unadorned plain cross), and that this should be painted, specifying at Bouc, for example, that 'the great cross with the crucifix which is burnt and destroyed should be rebuilt and repainted'.[138] Such a cross could be for the adornment of the altar or, as ordained for the church of Saint-Étienne in Rognes, to be carried in processions.[139] Again, the church of Saint-André in Angoustrine had a surviving example from the twelfth century (also sadly stolen, along with the statue of Mary mentioned above): a wooden crucifix 120 cm high, bearing a robed and bearded Christ nailed plainly to the cross (see Figure 6.9).[140] One might contrast its simplicity with the suffering Christ often found in later crucifixes, such as the fourteenth-century example held in Perpignan's cathedral (see Figure 6.10). The Christ of the Angoustrine cross is sober, clothed, his eyes cast down and the nails clearly visible; yet He retains an air of quiet authority, as if patiently awaiting the next stage of the story. That from Perpignan looks ahead to the suffering Man of Sorrows most famously depicted in the Grünewald altarpiece: naked except for a ragged loincloth, ribs jutting starkly out, arms stretched and contorted as the weight of the body pulls him down, head (the crown of thorns clearly visible) cast down in sorrow and suffering. The wound high up in his side is clearly visible, the nail wounds similarly so; there is blood and pain, and death approaches.

Medievalists are familiar with a general representational shift across the period from Christ-as-king to the Man of Sorrows, and the comparison made here can be related to that larger development.[141] But localized chronologies and variation add nuance to that pattern: just across the Pyrenees into the Val d'Aran, one can find a twelfth-century statue of a suffering Christ, ribs visible and arms stretched

---

[136] J.-C. Fau, *Rougergue Roman*, 3rd edn (Saint-Léger-Vauban: Zodiaque, 1990), pp. 334–35 and plate 113.
[137] S. Caucanas et al., *Au temps de la Croisade: sociétés et pouvoirs en Languedoc au XIIIe siècle*, exhibition catalogue from Carcassonne 2009 (Carcassonne: Archives départementales de l'Aude, 2009), p. 95, image 55.
[138] Visitation d'Aix, fol. 36v: 'magna crux cum crucifixo que exusta est et destructa reficiatur et repingatur'. Similarly fols 12r (Salles), 40v (*Manhanella*), 41r (Villevieille), 57r (Lambesc), 71r (*Placito-Dei*).
[139] Visitation d'Aix, fol. 52v: 'provideatur eidem ecclesie de una cruce cum crucifixo picto ad portandum in processionibus'.
[140] Reproduction here: <https://www.pop.culture.gouv.fr/notice/palissy/PM66000017>.
[141] See R. Fulton, *From Judgment to Passion: Christ and the Virgin Mary, 800–1200* (New York: Columbia University Press, 2002).

SPACE AND MATERIALITY   245

Figure 6.9 Crucifix, Angoustrine (Saint-André), 12th century

Figure 6.10 Crucifix, Perpignan cathedral, 13th century

taut, in the small church at Salardu.[142] A thirteenth-century painted wooden crucifix survives in the Musée Paul Dupuy in Toulouse, crowned, slightly stylized, His body bared to view but as if placed rather than suspended—a representation that sits midway between those of Angoustrine and Perpignan.[143] As with architectural styles in general, representational choices do not spread instantly nor evenly across a landscape.

Such statues and images proffer the opportunity for personal reflection and affect, a focal point for prayer. We catch sight of one woman doing precisely this in about 1270, a widow called Arnaude who worked in the hospital in Saint-Antonin-Noble-Val (c. 50 km north-east of Montauban). She reported that she had been praying in the church of Saint-Michel at Cordes (about five hours' walk from Saint-Antonin), when a certain woman called Raimonde Molinier accosted her and said, 'What are you doing? Pray to the Almighty, and don't believe in images of the cross or in other images, because they are worthless.'[144] Raimonde's opinion was a minority one—although one of those interesting moments at which something 'heretical' partly accords with higher level orthodox theology, which whilst not seeing images as 'worthless', certainly emphasized that God should be the eventual recipient of prayer. We have, in any case, a tiny revealed vignette of a lay woman engaging in her own private act of worship, facilitated by images in a local church.

What further? A point which British medievalists often make to a general audience regarding medieval parish churches in their own country is that, in contrast to their current austere, post-Reformation whiteness, in later medieval times they would have been filled with colour, adorned with impressive carvings and statues, the walls richly painted with instructive religious scenes, usually involving some combination of local and universal saints, depictions of the passion, the Last Judgment, and the seven deadly sins. In contrast, in France the continued visual elaboration associated with early modern Catholicism can on occasion lead to a rather overwhelming extreme, as for example in the current interior to Albi cathedral, its medieval bones somewhat swamped by the gilded ornamentation of later baroque design. But for parish churches in southern France—and probably similarly for elsewhere in Europe—there is a question as to precisely how far back in time, and how universally, one projects such a degree of visual richness.[145]

---

[142] Durliat and Allègre, *Pyrénées romanes*, p. 207 and plate 88.
[143] Musée Paul Dupuy, numéro d'inventaire 18117. Image: <http://2000ans2000images.toulouse.fr/fr/search-notice/detail/a8707bm1li74t9vl73aobgvx9npih5x7k4p0vtzk9w7whk7bvr> (accessed 29 Apr 2021).
[144] Doat 25, fol. 56v (*Inquisitors and Heretics*, p. 302).
[145] See important caveats, for example, in the study of churches in Berry by Marcia Kupfer, *Romanesque Wall Painting in Central France: The Politics of Narrative* (New Haven: Yale University Press, 1993).

To be clear: there are of course some artistic schema found in a variety of southern French churches, dating back to the twelfth century at least. One could point, for example, to the cathedral church of Saint-Trophime in Arles, which has rich bas-relief carvings depicting the nativity, the passion, various saints, and perhaps most notably the extraordinary mixture of Old Testament scenes (including Adam and Eve) and the Last Judgment set above its western portal.[146] A similar richness in carved stone images is found at many of the cathedrals and larger monasteries, often on the tympanum above the main door, thus visually available to all who pass by. Impressive examples adorn the abbey of Saint-Pierre in Moissac, the cathedral church at Oloron-Sainte-Marie, and elsewhere. It is not surprising to find these pinnacles of artistic achievement in such places, given the wealth and regional importance of the foundations. A number of larger local churches, and some smaller ones, have stone carvings also, albeit usually far less extensive. Most commonly we find these located on the capitals (that is, the block of stone at the top) of columns. The physical size of a capital restricts the extent of any representational scheme, but can at the same time imbue it with a powerful sense of dynamism, as the carvings can be made to reach around the three-dimensional shape. In the beautiful and imposing church of Saint-Martin in La Plaisance (c. 40 km east of Albi) whilst the surviving twelfth-century capitals have rather deteriorated, they still capture a surprising suggestion of movement, as figures—often menacing—stretch themselves around the corners of the stone (see Figure 6.11).[147] Such dynamism we may imagine being further heightened when viewed by the mobile flames of candles or lamps. Some churches also have similar pieces of small figurative sculpture on their exterior walls, whether framing the west door or placed elsewhere around the perimeter, on occasions their symbolism perhaps working further to emphasize the demarcated sacred space of the church from the profane world beyond.[148]

We can also find a few surviving wall paintings dating to the twelfth- or thirteenth-century within the wider region, including some in a few quite small churches. Around twenty churches in the Roussillon region contain some survivals, entirely located in apses.[149] For example, in the deserted village of Casenoves, just west of Ille-sur-Têt, the church of Saint-Sauveur contains fragments of earlier paintings in its choir and apse, an apostolic schema culminating in the image of

---

[146] J.-P. Dufoix et al., *Le portail de Saint-Trophime d'Arles: naissance et renaissance d'un chef-d'oeuvre roman* (Arles: Actes Sud, 1999).

[147] Personal observation of site. For the very rich and varied capitals found in the major religious houses in Toulouse—rather more complex and ornate, and certainly more extensive, than those found in most local churches—see the many plates and discussion in M. Durliat, *Haut-Languedoc roman* (Saint-Léger-Vauban: Zodiaque, 1976).

[148] C. Weising, '*Obscenitas*: les répresentations sexuelles dans la sculpture des églises méridionales', *CdF* 52 (2019), 147–73.

[149] Mallet, *Églises romanes*, pp. 73–74 with map.

Figure 6.11 Stone capital, church of Saint-Martin, La Plaisance

Christ in Majesty in the rounded ceiling of the apse.[150] Saint-Martin-de-Fenollar, about 30 km to the south-east, depicts the life of Christ, also culminating with Christ in Majesty.[151] Very nearby, the church of Saint-Nazaire at La Cluse Haute, another twelfth-century Christ in Majesty adorns the roof of the choir, accompanied by angels and the Adoration of the Magi (and originally undoubtedly by other additional images also).[152] There is a further cluster in the high Pyrenees, near Puigcerdà, with some surviving wall paintings dating from the twelfth and thirteenth centuries: Saint-André at Angoustrine (that of the retable and antependium discussed above) (see Figure 6.12), Saint-Romain at Caldegas, Saint-Julien at Estavar. In each case the principle image is in the apse and depicts Christ in Majesty (and, at Angoustrine, simultaneously the Last Supper); at Caldegas, very

---

[150] O. Poisson, '"Rien. Rien." L'église Saint-Sauveur de Casenoves et son décor peint', in V. Fernandez, ed., *De la création à la restauration: travaux d'histoire de l'art offerts à Marcel Durliat* (Toulouse: Atelier d'histoire de l'art méridional, 1992), pp. 261–83.
[151] M. Durliat, *Roussillon roman*, 4th edn (Saint-Léger-Vauban: Zodiaque, 1986), pp. 264–65; Poisson, '"Rien. Rien."', pp. 273–74.
[152] Images reproduced here: <https://sites.google.com/site/modillonsetpeinturesromanes/roussillon/la-cluse-haute-%C3%A9glise-saint-nazaire> (accessed 14 Aug 2022).

Figure 6.12 Christ in Majesty/Last Supper, apse, Angoustrine (Saint-André), 12th century

unusually, there is some painting on the exterior above the entrance to the church, again of Christ in Majesty, though perhaps from a later period.[153] Further west, nearer Foix and Pamiers, we find others: the extraordinary church of Sainte-Marie-du-Vals, built partly into the rock face, which has twelfth-century paintings of several saints and scenes from the life of Christ;[154] and about 50 km west of Foix, Saint-Pierre-d'Ourjout and Saint-Jean-des-Vignes at the village of Saint-Plancard, both of which have wall paintings in their apses, possibly from as early as the late eleventh century. Decoration of course continued to be produced later: in the tiny church of Saint-Martin-des-Puits, about 32 km south-east of Carcassonne, there are vestiges of wall paintings from the twelfth century and, probably, fourteenth century, again in the choir.[155]

All of these examples are from the south-west of the region, mostly in the higher plateaux and mountains, and this may be because more remote regions were spared some of the iconoclasm of the wars of religion in the sixteenth and seventeenth centuries; though it perhaps also reflects those areas best known to the important art historian Marcel Durliat (1917–2006), who worked in Perpignan

---

[153] See Mallet, *Églises romanes*, *passim*.

[154] V. Czerniak and J.-M. Stouffs, 'Les peintures murales romanes de Notre-Dame de Vals: nouvelles lectures à la lumière de la dernière campagne de restauration', *Mémoire de la Société archéologique du Midi de la France* 68 (2008), 153–70.

[155] M. Durliat, 'L'église de Saint-Martin-des-Puits (Aude) et son décor peint', *Comptes rendus des séances de l'Académie des inscriptions et belles-lettres* 115 (1971), 659–82.

and then Toulouse, and whose indefatigable scholarship underpins an extraordinary amount of discussion of ecclesiastical art and architecture in the Midi. If not as predominant, there are undoubtedly other wall paintings still extant in some other parts of the south. At Saint-Michel-d'Aiguilhe near Le Puy, an extraordinary church built on top of a tall pinnacle of rock (d'Aiguilhe = 'the needle'), founded originally by Bishop Godescalc on his return from pilgrimage to Compostelle, contains a wonderfully painted high vault, perhaps thirteenth century, the images dramatically rising up through the angelic court to finish once again with Christ in Majesty.[156] The church of Saint-Pierre-de-Rouillac near Montcuq (c. 25 km south-west of Cahors) contains rich but somewhat crude paintings of Christ and the symbols of the apostles in its apse, plus a fairly primitive depiction of the Last Supper, and, on the reverse of the triumphal arch (that is, facing into the apse rather than the nave), Adam and Eve being tempted by the serpent.[157] At Rabastens, halfway between Toulouse and Albi, the church of Notre-Dame-du-Bourg has seven chapels set within the choir, each of which was painted in the fourteenth century, the images devoted to the particular saint to which each chapel's altar was dedicated.[158]

One could continue to multiply specific examples, but it is perhaps more useful for our purposes to consider the landscape overall. Wall paintings are part of Christian culture in this region, from at least the late twelfth century onward. A medieval theologian like Guillaume Durand, bishop of Mende (d. 1296), in his important *Rationale divinorum officiorum* followed a pronouncement of Pope Gregory I in the sixth century that glossed the purpose of wall paintings as 'instruction for the simple'. But such statements are better understood as *post hoc* legitimation of images rather than a statement of ecclesiastical intent; and it seems fairly clear, as art historians have pointed out for some decades, that the function of images was not primarily didactic.[159] They could not in themselves 'explain' anything very much to a layperson, and whilst we may imagine them sometimes being referred to in the course of a sermon, we must remember that the single church mostly attended by a congregation had only a limited range of visual material. That is, the available corpus in any individual church did not supply the medieval equivalent of powerpoint slides: the particular images in any given

[156] C. Lamy-Lassalle, 'Les peintures de Saint-Michel d'Aiguilhe', *Bulletin de la Société nationale des antiquaires de France* 1958/1 (1959), 86–90. There are some excellent images here: <https://unusual-places.org/the-chapel-of-saint-michel-daiguilhe/> (accessed 27 Apr 2021).
[157] Images available at <https://patrimoines.laregion.fr/le-patrimoine-doccitanie-pyrenees-mediterranee/index.html>, search under 'Rouillac' (accessed 14 Aug 2022).
[158] G. Ahlsell de Toulza, 'Les peintures murales dans les chapelles du choeur de l'église Notre-Dame-du-Bourg de Rabastens-sur-Tarn', *Actes du 96e Congrès national des sociétés savantes, 1971, section d'archéologie* 2 (1976), 239–65.
[159] Guillelmus Duranti, *Rationale*, I.iii.1, pp. 34–35; L. G. Duggan, 'Was Art Really the "Book of the Illiterate"?', *Word and Image* 5 (1989), 227–51; A. Reiss, 'Beyond "Books of the Illiterate": Understanding English Medieval Wall Paintings', *The British Art Journal* 9/1 (2008), 4–14.

church usually depicted the saint or saints to whom the altar(s) were dedicated, and, the surviving examples strongly suggest, illustrated some aspects of the life of Christ, with a cumulative focus on Christ in Majesty. So any one church would have certain images that would potentially be available as reference at certain points in the liturgical year, but not by any means sufficient material to illustrate a whole round of Sunday sermons (if such there were) or wider moral instruction. We thus do *not* find, as we would elsewhere in Europe from later in the thirteenth century at least, depiction of the seven deadly sins, of the venial crimes one could commit against the body of Christ (such as labouring on Sundays), or various warnings about the imminence of death.

Moreover, the surviving paintings in almost all of the churches for this region are located in the choir and apse. This is not universally the case: there are a few instances where images spill out from the choir into the first section of the nave, as at Saint-Aventin, in the high Pyrenees. That church also has some surviving decoration that reminds us of a further possibility for the nave: non-figurative painting of floriate or geometric patterns (as one would also find, for example, in the nave of the church of the Brothers Preacher in Toulouse, where figurative illustration is confined to the various side chapels).[160] But it is striking overall that in most churches the nave seems largely to be unadorned. We cannot know for certain, of course, whether circumstances across the centuries have made it much more likely that images would be preserved in the choir and apse rather than the nave; that is, whether the current predominance is a chance of survival. But I tend to think that what we see now reflects the medieval reality. Across the Aix visitations—conducted by an archbishop who was notably concerned with the details of the material fabric of each church, and who commented in considerable detail on all other aspects—there is not a single reference to wall paintings. Moreover, on one occasion (Saint-Siffrein near Reillane) Archbishop Armand specifically noted that the interior of the church needed whitewashing where smoke from candle flames, perhaps made of tallow, had darkened it.[161] This whiteness, one suspects, was in fact the norm.

Where it did exist, the association of wall painting with the choir might be taken further to emphasize for the laity their symbolic division from the priest, in the performance of his liturgical duties at least. He would present an impressive spectacle in himself, dressed in expensive liturgical robes, wielding silver chalice and paten, surrounded by visual glory. Marcia Kupfer argues for as much, in her study of more northerly French churches; however in the region she studied the spatial arrangement of the choir, more often separated from the nave by an arch which closed off part of the sacral space, is not quite the same as usually found in

---

[160] Saint-Aventin: Durliat and Allègre, *Pyrénées romanes*, pp. 60–61 and plates 27–30. Toulouse: personal observation.
[161] Visitation d'Aix, fol. 81v: '... et ecclesia intus dealbetur ubi est fumo denigrata'.

the south.¹⁶² In southern French churches the nave most often leads straight on to the choir and apse, both remaining at least partly visible to the congregation; thus the decorative focus on choir and apse does not necessarily mean that the laity were completely excluded from these visual materials. Sometimes, indeed, illustration was placed on a wall that framed the apse, facing the congregation, as at the church of Saint-Jean-des-Vignes at Saint-Plancard (c. 50 km west of Tarbes), where on the outward facing wall around a side chapel one can see among other things a rather playful image of Adam and Eve being tempted by the serpent, Adam's clear hand gestures pointing out a 'just say no' message.¹⁶³ In the tiny church of Saint-Laurent in Serres (c. 40 km south of Carcassonne) whilst remnants of some images—Christ and, probably, some of the apostles—appear on the side walls of the extended choir, the overall intimacy of the church would make these perfectly visible within the nave.¹⁶⁴ Various art historians have argued that the representational choices found in the wall paintings reflect particular liturgical traditions, and it seems to me that this is the best context in which we can understand their function: as enhancements to the performance of the liturgy, a further element in what Eric Palazzo powerfully describes as its 'synaesthesic' efficacy.¹⁶⁵

The Performance of Parish Liturgy

The liturgical cycle, the prayers and hymns, the repeated production of the body of the Lord in the form of bread; these are the regular ritual performances of local Christianity, the familiar and repeated drone of worship. It is therefore frustrating how little we can see within the space of the parish church during their actual enactment. Very occasionally we can see a medieval layperson comment on the performance of the liturgy, most often a negative comment captured by the process of inquisition into heresy. Despite this particular framing, these moments can perhaps still reveal something broader. Jean Joufre of Tignac (c. 35 km southeast of Foix) gave evidence in 1322 to Bishop Fournier, primarily informing on his neighbour Arnaud Laufre who, according to Jean, had said a number of things mocking the clergy. One of these was that 'the said Arnaud derided the clergy and chaplains when they sang mass... and three times he heard him say that the clergy said "Ho, ho, ho" [*or possibly* "alas, alas, alas"] and cried out as much as they could; and he added that he did not know the point of the said song of the clergy

---

¹⁶² Kupfer, *Romanesque Wall Painting*.
¹⁶³ Durliat and Allègre, *Pyrénées romans*, pp. 41–43 and plate 5.
¹⁶⁴ Personal observation; I cannot find any publication referring to this church.
¹⁶⁵ E. Palazzo, '*Missarum sollemnia*: Eucharistic Rituals in the Middle Ages', in J. H. Arnold, ed., *The Oxford Handbook of Medieval Christianity* (Oxford: Oxford University Press, 2014), pp. 238–53.

and chaplains'.[166] This reported conversation, whilst disparaging and disengaged from the liturgical performance, nonetheless betrays a familiarity with its general repetition, and that Jean knew that it was not to be disparaged. Another witness before Bishop Fournier, Pierre Sabatier, a weaver from Varilhes (10 km north of Foix), was questioned in 1318 having been accused by his neighbours of saying a couple of things that they thought might be heretical. One of these was that 'whatever is sung and said by the clergy in church is lies and foolishness'. Under questioning across several days, he admitted that he may have said such words (although, he said, he had earlier confessed to a priest that he had said them, the confession made whilst on pilgrimage to Compostelle, and that he had never failed to believe in the sacraments and the articles of faith). What he had meant at the time, he said, was that everything except for the Creed and the consecration of the host was made up by the clergy in order to elicit oblations from the laity. Interestingly he then listed in detail all of the components of the mass that, for a period of time, he had thought 'foolish': the Introit, the Kyrie Eleison, the Gloria, the prayer, the epistles, the responsory, the Alleluia, the tract, the Gospel reading, the offertory, the secret, the preface, the Sanctus, the Agnus Dei, the postcommunion, the final prayers 'and generally whatever was said and sung in the mass except for the *Credo* and the words which made the body and blood of the Lord'.[167] Perhaps the bishop was supplying some of the detail here, but the impression given is of a weaver with a pretty thorough knowledge of the full order of the liturgy, and a discernment regarding what he saw as its most important elements.

The Aix visitation also provides one precious moment in which lay voices and opinions come tantalizingly into view from a much more positive perspective. Armand de Narcès noted on his visit on 19 November 1340 to Trets that:

> Furthermore, at the request of the people of the said place—because they are in favour of things being done as conveniently and in as dignified a manner as possible, especially in things bearing upon the salvation of each of them and the increase in various ways of their devotion—he [*the archbishop*] ordained that the morning mass, that customarily in the church of the Blessed Mary is said by the second priest in a low voice, shall be celebrated henceforth with current notation (*cum nota currenti*), in which all those with ministry of that church shall be present just as in major mass, so that the more solemnly the

---

[166] *Fournier* II, p. 109: 'dixit quod clerici dicunt: Ho, ho, ho, [*for* "heu, heu, heu" *perhaps?*] et clamant quantum possunt, et addebat quod ipse nesciebat ad quid dictus cantus clericorum et capellanorum valebat'. Jean Joufre's deposition is discussed more fully in Arnold, *Inquisition and Power*, pp. 190–97.

[167] *Fournier* I, p. 148. Pierre Sabatier's interrogation discussed more fully in J. H. Arnold, '"A man takes an ox by the horn and a peasant by the tongue": Literacy, Orality and Inquisition in Medieval Languedoc', in S. Rees-Jones, ed., *Literacy and Learning in Medieval England and Abroad* (Turnhout: Brepols, 2003), pp. 31–47.

morning mass is said the larger will be the multitude of people that will come together to hear it.[168]

This is, it must be admitted, a unique request in the visitation record. But it speaks clearly nonetheless to some of the laity, at least, having a substantial investment in the performance of the regular liturgy. It also reminds us that the congregation can feel involved in the mass, not simply a passive audience to its performance. An occasional preaching *exemplum* presents the possibility of a particular hymn providing a moment of specific spiritual contemplation (and subsequent miraculous intervention). For example, a tale in a collection collated by a Brother of Penitence (a 'Sack Friar') in southern France in the later thirteenth century adapts a story from a twelfth-century set of Marian miracles, telling of a noble younger son, due to be wed, who wished to retain his virginity. At mass, when the antiphon *Pulchra es et decora* was sung, a vision of an extraordinarily beautiful woman appeared to him. At this vision, 'the said youth, exulting in ineffable joy, asked her what woman she was; to which she responded "I am she who you have been praising and to whom you have given your virginity."' A further miraculous intervention took place, and he escaped marriage.[169]

As attested by the comments above from the Fournier inquisition, one lay perspective on the Latin liturgy might be rather like the later Protestant slur about incomprehensible 'mumbling in Latin'. Over above the fact of language is the issue of particular performances: two preaching *exempla* collated by the same Sack Friar address the issue of clergy who don't pronounce all the syllables of words, nor indeed say all the right passages for the mass. One is a story also found in various other *exempla* collections, but the second is particular to this manuscript. A Brother of the order, whilst in prayer, was granted a spiritual vision by an angel: in a cathedral church, in the midst of the choir, he saw the choristers burying Christ, leaving only his head and feet visible—this, the angel explained, being the clergy who pronounce the beginning and the end of the words, but mumble the bit in the middle.[170]

---

[168] Visitation d'Aix, fol. 6v: 'Preterea, ad requisitionem populi dicti loci et quia quantum commode fieri potest et honeste favendum est dicto populo in hiis presertim que singulorum salutem concernit et per que ipsius devotio multipliciter augetur, ordinavit quod missa mattutinalis que in dicta ecclesia Beate-Marie per secundarium sacerdotem voce submissa dici consuevit celebretur a modo cum nota currenti in qua omnes ipsius ecclesie ministri sicut in majori missa interesse teneantur ut quanto ipsa missa mattutinalis dicetur solennius tanto [ad] ipsam audiendam major convenerit fidelis populi multitudo.' I am grateful to Sean Curran for wider discussion of this passage; it is possible that *cum nota currenti* alludes to something more specifically musical, for example polyphony.

[169] BL MS Add. 60390, fol. 10r-v: 'dictus iuvenis gaudio ineffabili exultavit querens ab ea que mulier esset. Qui respondit ego sum illa quam tu laudas et cui tuam virginitatem dedisti.' As Welter notes (J.-Th. Welter, 'Un recueil d'exempla du XIIIe siècle', *Revue des études franciscaines* 30 (1913), 646–65, 31 (1914), 194–213, at p. 657), the story exists (in a slightly different form) in an earlier collection (BL Cotton Cleopatra C.10). That collection of Marian miracles also survives in an early fourteenth-century copy, owned formerly by Bernard Gui: BM Toulouse MS 478.

[170] BL MS Add. 60390, fol. 15r; Welter, 'Un recueil d'exempla', p. 660 (no. 34).

But linguistic distance or alienation are clearly not the only possible experiences. The *precise* content of much of the Latin would surely have been beyond the ken of most lay people. However, medieval Latin and medieval Occitan had various points of linguistic similarity (for example, *ecclesia/gleza*, *homines/omes*, *anima/arma*). And the Latinity of the liturgy is only one of its features: as noted above, Eric Palazzo and others have very effectively argued that it must be understood as a multi-sensory experience, where sound, light, smell, and movement are all also tremendously important.[171] Moreover, whilst few could presumably follow every detail of each chant and prayer, some elements of the Latin would, through their repetition, very likely become part of a shared collective knowledge.

For example, let us consider a couple of twelfth-century liturgical books from a very small church perched in the Canigou mountains, which survive today. We met these briefly in Chapter 3; they are from the church now known as Saint-Guillaume-de-Combret, an extremely remote structure, about 3 miles from the nearest village, but which had a small community of priests attached to it. One volume is the church's twelfth-century copy of the ninth-century sacramentary of Arles, a liturgical book which provided the priest with all the words, but not the biblical readings, necessary for mass, and for some other sacramental rites. In it we can glimpse some of the acts and embodied experiences that attendance at mass there might have involved: for example, the blessing, in Latin, of the candles that were essential both spiritually and practically, the priest directed to make the sign of the cross as he spoke the key words *sanctificatum* and *benedictum*; the following stage directions, as it were, that instructed the priest at what point during the mass to light the candles, figuring them as a sacrifice to God.[172] One would not have to follow all the words in order to understand the gist or the gestures—and of course these would be actions one saw, and words which one heard, repeatedly. There is also, quite remarkably, a surviving twelfth-century *mixtum* for the same church, a southern France liturgical book which combined the missal, breviary, and some other materials. Here we find elements that would be sung, and again whilst the precise meaning of much of this would surely be very hard to decipher by a non-Latinate audience, it seems very likely that the 'alleluia', coming around repeatedly and sustainedly, would have caught the ear, and invited a general sense of familiarity, comprehension—and thus involvement.[173]

From the period immediately after the Albigensian Crusade onward, we also find episcopal injunctions about lay behaviour at mass, and in quasi-liturgical

---

[171] Palazzo, '*Missarum sollemnia*'; E. Palazzo, 'Art, Liturgy and the Five Senses in the Early Middle Ages', *Viator* 41 (2010), 25–56.

[172] Perpignan, Médiathèque municipale, MS 4, fol. 2r. The manuscript (described as a 'missal') has been digitized by the library: <https://perpinianum.fr/Perpinianum/digital-viewer/c-339027> (accessed 3 Jan 2024).

[173] Paris, BnF MS n.a.l. 557; 'alleluia', for example, at fols 6r, 8v. The manuscript has been digitized on the Gallica website: <https://gallica.bnf.fr/ark:/12148/btv1b10546776k/f1.image.r=nal%20557> (accessed 1 Oct 2020).

contexts, that remind us that they were not simply a passive audience but were increasingly expected to participate. We see this in a negative sense, with injunctions forbidding people from leaving part way through mass, and small penances for those who talked whilst it was being performed. But it is also visible in a more positive way, as the laity were encouraged to engage actively in worship. The council of Albi in 1230 enjoined lay people to kneel and pray in reverence if they saw the Eucharist being carried to an ill person, and to do similarly during mass. Fifty years later a synod at Albi also called upon the laity to bow simply when they heard the name of Jesus, and to show reverence toward the altar when they entered church.[174] It is possible that such practices pre-dated these particular episcopal commands, but other calls for lay activity were clearly a development of the later thirteenth century and after. In 1297, the synod of Carcassonne called upon all priests with care of souls to encourage their flock to attend church after either vespers or compline, when it was customary to sing the *Salve Regina* in praise of the Virgin Mary, and to listen to it 'with devotion'; those who did would receive a relaxation from any penance imposed upon them by the bishop.[175] Another synod in Carcassonne from some time after 1321 instructed priests to have two bells rung every day between the feasts of the Invention and of the Exaltation of the Holy Cross (4 May and 14 September) to petition for the fruitfulness of the land—and any layperson who heard these ring was to say prayers also at that moment.[176] Bernard Gui, as bishop of Lodève, sought to engage the laity in an almost fully monastic fashion with the regular liturgy: whenever they heard the bells rung to sound the liturgical hours, if they themselves then said prayers ('for good rule for the pope...and peace for the lord king of France and his realm') then he would grant them ten days' indulgence from sin.[177] Thus the possibilities—and rewards—of lay participation multiplied over the course of this period.

With regard to all of this we must however bear in mind that not all liturgical performances are necessarily fully 'successful'; as with any human action, the context can affect how well a ritual engages and persuades, and prescriptive evidence needs to be interpreted within a wider range of potential outcomes. To return once again to the Aix visitation: one of the archbishop's overriding concerns was for the provision of up-to-date and usable liturgical books in each church. During

---

[174] Council of Albi, 1230, c. 38; see similarly synodal of Rodez 1289, c. VIII.52, 53 (Avril, *Statuts synodaux*, VI, pp. 148–49). Synod of Albi, 1280, cc. 7, 17 (Avril, *Statuts synodaux*, VI, pp. 79–80).
[175] Synod of Carcassonne, 1297, c. 5 (Avril, *Statuts synodaux*, VI, pp. 458–59). Similarly, Carcassonne 1342 (BnF MS Lat. 1613, fol. 79v).
[176] Synod of Carcassonne, after 1321, c. 4 (BnF MS Lat. 1613, fol. 70v): 'Quod sacerdotes parochiales faciant seu fieri faciant unam pulsationem cum duabus campanis simul inter meridie et nonam qualibet die a festo inventinois sancte crucis usque ad festum exaltationis sancte crucis pro fructibus terre conservandis et dandis et dicant et dicant [sic] aliquas preces et iungant parrochianis suis quod tunc dicunt semel pater noster et ave maria.'
[177] Synod of Lodeve, 1325, c. 10 (Douais, ed., *Synodal de Lodève*, p. 7).

the visitation, he brought up the subject on 134 occasions when first visiting a church, and a further 28 times on a second visit. Very occasionally the visitation simply noted that a certain church had particularly nice books—*plurimum sumptuosa*, as was noted for the church of Saint-Étienne-de-Cadenet—and the most frequent injunctions were either to re-bind the existing books, or to update the existing books to reflect the liturgical 'use' of Aix.[178] But on a number of occasions the issue appeared to be a more basic lack of liturgical material: at Gréasque he found that there was no silver chalice and insufficient books for the divine office, and the same was lacking at *Soqueriis*; very occasionally, as at Saint-Pierre-d'*Assana*, the church was said to be 'desolate' of all liturgical materials and books.[179] In terms of the practicalities of the liturgy, the overall fabric of the church may sometimes also have caused problems. On thirty-two occasions (nearly a fifth of all the churches) it was necessary to order that some part of the roof be repaired, ten of which specified either that the rain currently got inside the church or that the church was in danger of being 'ruined'. In a further twelve additional cases, the church was said simply to be 'desolate' and lacking in the necessary items—at the church of Saint-Pierre-de-la-Mer, for example, 'he found the interior to be desolate in divine things and moreover destitute'.[180] Elsewhere certain key objects were not in a good state: at Saint-Lambert, it was necessary to repair the chalice and paten, and to put in some posts to hold up the retable; at Saint-Pierre-d'*Assana* doves had started nesting in an area beyond the altar; at Cornillon-Confoux the baptismal font was broken.[181] We should not overplay the extent of dilapidation, and in several cases it is clear that things were subsequently repaired or restored. But it is a reminder that the material fabric and setting of a church would not always match up to the ideal.

This was, of course, connected to wealth. At Châteauneuf-le-Rouge, the archbishop noted that whilst the church lacked various items, 'however, because of the paucity and poverty of the parishioners' he would not ordain anything beyond the bare minimum; this was similarly the case at *Brusa*.[182] In other words, we encounter again a range of possible liturgical contexts, which speak not only to the variety of potential experiences any layperson might have, but also make us aware of how some might contrast. When the widow Arnaude whom we met

---

[178] Visitation d'Aix, fol. 124r (Cadenet).

[179] Visitation d'Aix, fols 2r ('nec libros sufficientes ad officium divinum'), 35r ('cum dicta ecclesia libros sufficientes non habeat ad usum divinorum, ordinavit...provideat de uno bono mixto completo et sufficienti'), 45v ('...que valde desolata erat'). The requirement for a silver chalice was, as noted above in the main text, made on twenty-four occasions, but in most cases probably indicates an upgrade to an existing chalice made of another material.

[180] Visitation d'Aix, fol. 60r: 'invenit desolatam penitus in divinis et etiam destitutam'. Similarly 63r, 178r.

[181] Visitation d'Aix, fols 76r, 45v, 61v.

[182] Visitation d'Aix, fol. 4r: 'tamen propter paucitatem et paupertatem parrochianorum ipsius ecclesie hac fuit quoad presens ordinatione contentus'; fol. 119r: 'nichil ordinatum fuit ista vice propter paupertatem parrochianorum'.

above travelled from Saint-Antonin-Noble-Val to pray in the church of Saint-Michel at Cordes in 1270, she would have been entering a newly built church, possibly in fact still in the final stages of construction at the time.[183] We cannot tell exactly how this might have compared with the church of her home village, as the extant church of Saint-Antonin is a late fifteenth-century building that replaced something older. But there is therefore a strong possibility that she—like many others—knew the feel of worship in both a smaller, older, 'romanesque' church and also a newer, larger, more 'gothic' edifice. The point is not a qualitative evaluation of which was better, but rather that Arnaude, like many others, would have experienced spatial and material *contrast*, that contrast in itself framing to the sensory experience in each particular locale.

Eucharistic Materiality

As we have seen, among the corpus of wall paintings surviving in the smaller, romanesque churches, Christ reigning in heaven is an almost universal theme, the image positioned centrally and higher up the apse, potentially visible to the whole congregation. It would be what the laity would see above and beyond the hands of the priest, as he raised the consecrated host in the culmination of the mass. We might read such images as primarily providing a wider emotional and cognitive frame for the production of the Eucharist, the visual fragility of the material wafer supplemented by—or perhaps we could say coexistent with—the richer promise of Christ in heavenly glory. Let us imagine further the successful performance of the mass in a reasonably well-endowed gothic church, one with some space in the nave and with high windows that cast a reasonable degree of light—something like the church of Saint-Jacques, built by the citizens of Montauban in the later thirteenth century, for example. Here the congregation would lose some of the sense of intimacy that one might find in a smaller church; if incense was used in a small church (as should have been the case) it would likely suffuse one's senses, whilst in a larger church we might imagine more of an olfactory ebb and flow. The greater natural light found in a larger church—though still in fact rather less in somewhere like Saint-Jacques than in a contemporary church in northern Europe—would presumably make the actions of the priest, and the elevation of the wafer, more fully visible. Whether that adds to or subtracts from the experience is not certain, but it remains the case that candles and lights—the wax and oil most likely supplied by the laity—would shine out both practically and symbolically. A larger church is a more resonant space, and that which is said and sung will reverberate and echo. As the mass reaches its

---

[183] <https://albi.catholique.fr/eglises-du-tarn/cordes-eglise-saint-michel/> (accessed 3 Apr 2021) states construction estimated to have taken place between 1263 and 1281.

culmination and the host is elevated, a bell is rung—or perhaps, in a large church, several bells. Christ embodied is thus made present in sensory profusion. Beyond the specific words in Latin, the immersion in sound, action, performance could itself 'speak' to a layperson connotatively: a special moment being carved out in time and place, a transformation unfolding.

The tolling of bells may also remind us that whilst the most common spatial context in which to experience the holiness of Christ incarnate was within the parish church, the church itself was less a boundary and more an epicentre. Sound and holiness resonate outward, projecting both the news and experience of that transformation to a wider landscape. Bells were another feature which the archbishop of Aix commented upon fairly frequently. Most often the issue was about repairing a bell that had cracked or been broken, but sometimes other interesting details arise also. It becomes clear that the size and location of bells could vary quite considerably, probably dependent upon the size of a particular church, and thus what its physical fabric could bear. There could be small hand bells, a bell mounted within the church itself, a bell hung on the exterior of a church, or a bell in a small turret on the roof.[184] As noted in an earlier chapter, the most frequent surviving examples are bells arranged either in what French archaeologists call *un clocher-mur*, that is a wall built on the apex of the roof usually at either the west or east end, with openings within which to suspend the bells; or, for larger churches and, by the fourteenth century, some smaller ones, more substantial bells hung within a classic four-square tower. Larger bells produce a louder and more resonant sound which could reach out across a wider landscape.

The main point is once again variation: one bell or several bells, bells of differing weight and thus contrasting sonority. For the small, isolated church of Saint-Guillaume-de-Combret—the one from which we have early surviving liturgical manuscripts—there is also extant a small bell, made from two sheets of beaten iron, about 30 cm high and dating to the eleventh or twelfth century (see Figure 6.13).[185] It would probably be suspended from a bracket on an exterior wall, and its sound would be akin to a cowbell—that is, it could produce a clear signal, but its voice would not be sustained nor reach all that far. This is the kind of bell that would be most common until the later twelfth century at the earliest, when larger, more expensive, cast bells became more widely available. Their sound could reach out to embrace a larger space.[186] As Archbishop Armand spelled out for the church at Cadanet (c. 26 km north of Aix) which was in the process of being rebuilt, the church should gain a full bell tower 'foursquare and high, in the manner of a

---

[184] For bells mounted within the church, for example Visitation d'Aix, fol. 76r (church of Saint-Lambert): 'et campanam ecclesie parari faciat et appendi infra dictam ecclesiam in loco altiori ut pulsari possit'.
[185] See also: <https://www.pop.culture.gouv.fr/notice/palissy/PM66001362> (accessed 3 May 2021).
[186] See generally J. H. Arnold and C. Goodson, 'Resounding Community: The History and Meaning of Medieval Church Bells', *Viator* 43 (2012), 99–130.

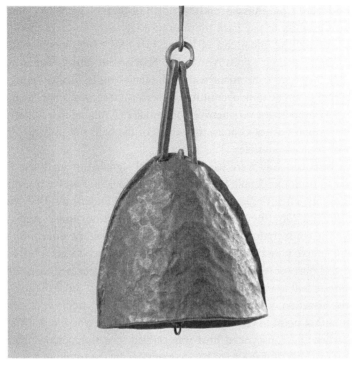

Figure 6.13 Bell, Saint-Guillaume-de-Combret, 11th or 12th century

tower, so that the bells of the church are lifted high up so that they can be heard by the whole of the place of Cadanet'.[187] On various occasions he specified that bells needed to be a particular weight, the size—and thus sound—varying presumably in line with the size of the parish (though perhaps also its wealth). The church of Sainte-Marie-de-Fuveau (c. 14 km south-east of Aix) was said to have bells that were 'insufficient as they are small and have a less good sound', and was thus ordered to get them 'remade and augmented' so that their total weight was about 500 kg.[188] This was at the high end of the spectrum; in Puivert, near Cadanet, the archbishop ordered the church to mend one of its bells and to increase their collective weight to about 150 kg.[189] Large bells were expensive:

---

[187] On one occasion only, it is spelled out that this kind of 'campanile' is intended for the church at Cadanet that was in the process of being rebuilt when the visitation occurred. Visitation d'Aix, fol. 65r: 'et fiat ibidem campanile quadratum et altum ad modum turris, ut campane ipsius ecclesie in altum elevate per totum locum ipsum Cadaneti possint audiri'.

[188] Visitation d'Aix, fol. 1r: 'Item cum campane dicte ecclesie Beate-Marie loci conditione attenta non sint sufficientes cum sint parve et minus sonum bonum habeant ordinavit quod infra unum annum...dicte campane reficiantur et augeantur taliter quod sint ponderis X quintalium in toto.' A 'quintal' was a hundredweight, i.e. 100 lbs, just under 50 kg.

[189] Visitation d'Aix, fol. 124v: 'una campanarum ipsius ecclesie que fracta est reficiatur et augeatur taliter quod facta sit ponderis III quintalium vel circa...'.

we have a record from Puissalicon (just north of Béziers) from 1335 noting that the consuls promise to pay back the sum of 80 *livres* of Tours to the local lord, who had covered the initial cost of having two bells made, weighing a bit over 400 kg.[190] On several occasions Armand de Narcès told churches to amend their bells so that they were 'concordant' with each other—both a further demonstration of the level of detail he took over liturgical performance, and a reminder that the sound experienced might vary between one small bell ringing in a solitary fashion to a more complex set of chimes, the voices of the bells not only amplified but made more sonically complex.[191]

Whilst bells certainly were used as practical signals—to mark the liturgical hours and to summon people to mass, as well as to sound out warnings, deaths, or other events when necessary—it is important to understand that one of the most important jobs they took on, during the period under study, was to announce the consecration of the host. Whilst this could be done with a handbell—on a couple of occasions Armand ordered a church to get a bell weighing 8 lbs for this purpose—it was often also a task for a major bell, suspended in a *clocher-mur* or bell tower. The point was not simply to alert those in the congregation to the elevation of the host, but to bring this to the attention of others who were not at that point in church, so that they too could worship.[192] In a parallel fashion, when the consecrated host was carried to a sick person, for them to receive the last rites, it was also to be accompanied by the sound of a ringing bell, broadcasting the presence of Christ incarnated through the community as it went. The Aix visitation specifies on occasion that the handbell to be used should be about 6 lbs in weight, and several times notes that the host was to be carried through the community in *una columbeta*, which appears to be a kind of pyx either decorated with or shaped as a dove, symbolizing the Holy Spirit.[193] As the council of Albi ordered in 1230:

> ...the laity be frequently admonished that, when they see *and hear* the body of the Lord being carried, immediately they should bend their knees just as they would do to their Lord and, with joined hands, pray whilst it goes by. And, when

---

[190] P. Guibert and H. Barthés, eds, *Le cartulaire municipal de Puissalicon (XIIIe-XVIIe siècles)* (Béziers: Société archéologique, scientifique et littéraire, 2001), p. 9 (no. 5), 3 May 1335.

[191] Thus for example at Trets, the archbishop spelled out that the bells should ideally differ in weight, so as to produce not the same sound but something complementary. Visitation d'Aix, fol. 107r: 'cum due campane majores dicte ecclesie propter nimiam equalitatem ponderis et forme adeo sint unius sonus ut cum ambe pulsantur non videatur esse nisi una ordinavit...una dictarum campanarum videlicet deterior fundatur et reficiatur et augeatur taliter quod inter ipsas sit illa melodia et consonancia que requiritur et esse debet'.

[192] See further Arnold and Goodson, 'Resounding Community', pp. 122–24.

[193] For example Visitation d'Aix, fol. 51v (*Conilho*): 'provideat eidem ecclesie una campana ponderis sex librarum ad portandum ante corpus Dominicum cum defertur egrotis'; 46v (Villelaure): 'et provideatur dicte ecclesie una columbeta ad portandum corpus Christi'.

the Host of salvation is elevated in the parish mass, the major bell shall be rung by three strikes, and the people who hear it shall bend their knees wherever they are.[194]

Rather excellently, we have independent evidence of people doing precisely what was ordered, in an inquisition trial from 1276. Jean Moret, the witness, reported that he and another man called Bernard Fradui had been hired by Bernard de Souillac of Montauban, the latter man being under investigation by the inquisitors for various heterodox views. When Moret and Fradui were working in Bernard de Souillac's vineyard, they 'heard the bell struck at the elevation of the body of Christ and because of this they prayed to God with joined hands'.[195]

All of this was a means of making present to the laity that which their senses otherwise told them was absent: the real, embodied, material presence of Christ their lord. By the later twelfth century, the Eucharist had become both a central focus for worship and a key locus around which re-formed clerical identity and authority cohered. Only the priest could make Christ's body and blood, in the sacrament of the mass; whilst other aspects of clerical authority were practically adjacent to the abilities of the laity—preaching (practically if not lawfully), contracting marriage, contributing to the material needs of worship, baptizing (*in extremis*)—the Church was clear that no unordained person could transmute the substance of bread and wine.

We know, of course, that this central act of faith was not always sustained. Believing that the bread and wine changed into Christ's body was difficult and demanding. In southern France, in addition to a recurrent strand of materialist scepticism found throughout medieval Europe,[196] there was the added challenge of the Good Men, whose rejection not only of clerical authority but of the very idea that physical matter could *ever* be holy, sustained and amplified the issue. 'If Christ's body was as big as a mountain, it would have been eaten up by now', as many different witnesses reported having heard, or indeed said, when questioned by inquisitors. For various lay people such scoffing was voiced in part as a rejection of clerical claims to otherworldly authority, in part because of the evidence of their own senses, and perhaps in part—for a few—because of firmly held belief in the Good Men's theology concerning the evil of material creation.

But such scepticism was only one end of a much broader spectrum. As already described above, the liturgy of the mass orchestrated other sensory cues—light, smell, sound—to help the faithful experience Christ as present. And there were of

---

[194] Council of Albi, 1230, c. 38 (Pontal, *Statuts synodaux*, II, p. 22), my emphasis.
[195] Doat 25, fol. 237r (*Inquisitors and Heretics*, p. 662).
[196] J. H. Arnold 'The Materiality of Unbelief in Late Medieval England', in S. Page, ed., *The Unorthodox Imagination in Late Medieval Britain* (Manchester: Manchester University Press, 2010), pp. 65–95.

course many tales of miraculous events in which those experiencing doubt were amazed and awed by the special revelation of the Eucharist's true nature. The bishop of Marseille, Benoît d'Alignan, in a lengthy treatise on the faith he wrote in the mid-thirteenth century (to which we shall return in more detail in some subsequent chapters), compiled at a certain point a vast array of such miraculous revelations. It is worth quoting at some length, because the combination of volume and brevity gives a clear sense of how widely these circulated in sermons, and perhaps through lay storytelling:

> In confirmation of the Catholic faith, we have many examples for the unbelieving. Many indeed, have sometimes seen with their bodily eyes, in the offering blessed by the priest at the altar, true flesh and true blood. Others have seen the dividing up of an infant in the altar in the hands of the priests. Others, when the Host is broken up, have seen a child sitting on the corporal and do not see there bread or wine; and thereafter the same child transmuted into the figure of bread and wine. Others have seen angels on the surrounds of the altar cloth. Others have seen the splitting of a lamb in the hands of the priest and its blood falling into the chalice. Nothing other than bread and wine, however, was seen by the priests who were handling the sacrament. Others have seen angels giving communion to the priest and certain people, and however the priest did not see this, he was just administering the sacrament to himself and to the people. Others have seen that many people received in their mouths and from the hand of the priest as a sacrament a scorched fragment in the form of a shining star, and many, from unworthiness, received it in the form of burnt charcoal. Others have seen those who took communion worthily as having shining faces, but those who unworthily came to the altar they see as if they were Ethiopians [*that is, with black faces*].[197] Some, when the priest says the canon 'et benediceret oblationem', have seen only the right hand of God in the form of a man's hand, together with the hand of the priest, make the sign of the cross above the offering. Some have seen an angel next to the altar [*illegible word*] writing in golden letters in his book the names of those who have attended mass. Item, to affirm the faith, at the entreaty of St Grégoire, the bread took on the form of a finger and thereafter turned to bleeding flesh.[198] Item, of a peasant...who placed the Eucharist in a certain vessel for bees, and when he returned found in the vessel the Blessed Virgin cradling her son in her arms.[199]

[197] On medieval Christian discourses here, see G. Heng, *The Invention of Race in the European Middle Ages* (Cambridge: Cambridge University Press, 2018), chapter 4.
[198] This refers to a widely circulated exemplum from Gregory the Great; discussed in Arnold, 'Materiality of Unbelief', p. 79.
[199] BnF MS Lat. 4224, fol. 345r-v: 'Ad confirmationem fidei catholice exempla multa habemus propter incredulos. Multi enim corporeis oculis alioquin [*recte* aliquando] viderunt, oblationem sanctificatam a sacerdote super altare, veram carnem et verum sanguinem. Alii viderunt partiri infantem in altari in manibus sacerdotibus. Alii tamquam frangeretur hostia viderunt parvum sedentem in

Aside from the profusion of brief examples, it is interesting to note how firmly Benoît emphasizes that these are things 'seen' only by some, the point being that they are *miraculous* revelations of the true nature of the sacrament; they do not require *all* to experience the same thing, only for others to believe in the attestations listed.[200] Like the wall paintings of Christ in Majesty, such stories provide a hovering cultural frame, above and beyond the specific moment of the ritual.

Unsurprisingly, some preaching *exempla* provide stories of people responding in a model fashion, their great devotion to the Eucharist miraculously rewarded. A blind man, entering a church in Genoa at the point in the mass when the priest was raising the host, begged Christ that he be allowed to see it, promising pilgrimage to the shrine of Marie Madeleine at Saint-Maximin; his wish was granted.[201] Another tale tells of a knight who was much devoted to attending mass, more than to his temporal duties. One day his lord ordered him to come to give military service against a certain castle; he travelled there, but on the way 'he heard four bells rung for mass, and immediately left his companions and hurried to the religious place. Immediately that he entered church... he saw the priest saying *Confiteor Deo etc.*' Outside he began to hear the sounds of battle, but did not want to leave, saying to himself, 'I'm not going to leave for that, I would rather see the body of Christ'. The priest began to say the Gospels, and the knight thought 'it's not mass because of the Gospels, but because of the making of Christ's body; the army outside can do whatever it wants, I am not leaving, I want to stay to see the body of my Lord Saviour'. Finally, the mass complete, he left, knowing that his companions would wonder where he had been, and assume he was absent for fear of battle rather than love of worship. But, miraculously, it turned out that another knight, identical to himself, had fought in the battle and had indeed taken the castle without bloodshed. The Eucharist, so small and fragile, contained great

---

corporali et non videbant ibi panem nec vinum. Et iterum ipsum parvum transmutatum in figura panis et vini. Alii viderunt angelos in circuitu pani altaris. Alii viderunt agnum partiri in manibus sacerdotum et sanguinem eius fundere in calicem. Sacerdotibus autem qui sacramenta tractabant nichil aliud quam panis et vinum videbatur. Alii viderunt angelos communionem tradere sacerdoti et quibusdam hominibus et tamen sacerdos non hoc videbat, sed ipse sibi et populo sacramenta prebebat. Alii viderunt quod multi ex istis particulam sacramentum in specie clare stelle ore accipiebant de manu sacerdotis et multi ex indignis in specie carbonis extincti ipsam accipiebant. Alii eos qui digne communicabant viderunt clara facie eos autem qui indigne ad altare accedebant videbantur ut ethiopes. Quidam viderunt dum sacerdos diceret canonem "et benediceret oblationem" solam dexteram dei in similitudinem manus hominis simul cum dexteram sacerdotis signum crucis super oblationem facere. Quidam viderunt angelum iuxta altare [*illeg.*] scribentem litteris aureis in suo libro, nomina ipsorum qui audiebant missam. Item ad firmandam fidem ad preces beati gregoris panis accepit formam digitis et post versus est in cruentam carnem. Item de rustico qui... posuit eucharistiam in quodam vase apum et rediens invenit in vase illo beatam virginem tenentem filium suum inter ulnas.'

[200] For broader theological context on this point, see C. W. Bynum, 'Seeing and Seeing Beyond: The Mass of St Gregory in the Fifteenth Century', in J. F. Hamburger and A.-M. Bouché, eds, *The Mind's Eye: Art and Theological Argument in the Middle Ages* (Princeton: Princeton University Press, 2006), pp. 208–40, at p. 213.

[201] J. Sclafer, ed., *Jean Gobi l'ancien: miracles de Sainte Marie-Madeleine* (Paris: CNRS, 1996), pp. 88–89 (no. 22).

power. From the same Franciscan collection of *exempla*, there is a tale set during one of the periods of crusade, 'in 1271 [*sic*] when King Louis of France went to Tunis' (the dating is in fact one year out). At Aigues-Mortes a certain young boy on a ship fell ill, made his confession, and received communion; and immediately that he received the host he felt a terrible burning inside himself. His master was asked 'what kind of man he was', and explained that the boy was a Muslim ('*Sarracenus*') who had come to his service as a child, and who had never been baptized. Immediately this was rectified, and the boy was cured.[202]

Whilst inquisition trials give us copious evidence of people rejecting the idea of transubstantiation, they also in fact provide us with some moments in which the worship of the Eucharist is strongly affirmed. Take that final story, about the effect of the host on the Saracen boy. In the inquisition trials conducted by Bishop Fournier, a shepherd called Pierre Maury—who we will meet again in Chapter 10—mentioned having heard that one would rather take a hot coal into one's mouth than the Eucharist, if receiving communion when still in a state of sin; just possibly evidence of having heard some version of precisely that *exemplum*. Some fifty years earlier, Alphonse de Poitiers had had to deal with a case where some parishioners at Montcuq had been excommunicated for failing to pay tithes, and yet had forced their way into church to hear the mass, despite being ordered out by the priest. Their motives are not stated, but a combination of social pride and a desire to see the Eucharist seems not unreasonable to suppose.[203] To return to the Fournier register, another witness, Raimond de Laburat, who had been excluded from church along with some neighbours for non-payment of a new tithe on lambs, explained to the bishop-inquisitor that he had vehemently protested this because of his desire to see the consecration in the mass. He had indeed attempted to attend mass at the church of the Brother Preachers in Pamiers on the vigil of Palm Sunday, but at the door to the church a friar had asked him if he was excommunicated, and hearing that he was, explained that he could not attend, or else 'his sin would be doubled'. And yet he was still very upset, for as he then said in his trial 'he believed that the best thing that there was in the world was the sacrifice of God'.[204]

Conclusion

It is important to understand that the Eucharist was not simply a 'symbol' but a sacrament: something understood by the faithful to be changed in this world by

---

[202] Welter, 'Un nouveau recueil franciscain d'exempla', pp. 453 (no. 39), 615 (no. 193). For historical context on such a convert, see W. C. Jordan, *The Apple of His Eye: Converts from Islam in the Reign of Louis IX* (Princeton: Princeton University Press, 2019), chapter 1.

[203] Molinier, ed., *Correspondance administrative*, II, p. 156 (no. 1443), 5 June 1269.

[204] *Fournier* II, p. 321. Further discussion in Arnold, *Inquisition and Power*, pp. 180–90.

the divine power of God, a piece of bread imbued simultaneously with the past time of the passion, the promise of salvation to come, and the presence of Christ. Its mysterious, internal material transformation promised that things could *become* holy, could be made to shine out spiritually beyond the mundane. All of this of course for those who successfully believed—for others clearly saw and experienced nothing but bread. Such belief was, in its very nature, fragile and effortful. As we have already noted at points above, the Eucharist also reminded one that what was 'holy' need not be static: it could be brought out in processions, to be taken to those on the deathbeds, to be worshipped in the form of sound by those distant from the altar.

Other objects existed within the wider landscape that had something of a similar feel, as things which could become or be treated as particularly holy, though were not perhaps experienced thus at all times. Simple wayside crosses, whether made of stone (and thus static) or wood (and thus potentially portable), could move between symbol—a reminder of the story of Christ's passion—and presence. They could be used in a practical sense to mark out particular areas of land, sometimes explicitly used just temporarily; but, in the very same usage, could also be given a particular spiritual charge, rendering the space therein marked as 'sacred' in some sense (most usually in the sense of promising additional supernatural punishments on any unworthy layperson who misappropriated it).[205] They could be a familiar part of a landscape, invoked in charters simply to describe where something was—lands 'next to the cross of Peyrelade', a field 'which is next to the cross and in front of the lands of Guillaume Mira'[206]—though could also sometimes be placed specifically to mark out an area at the resolution of a dispute.[207]

The point is both the variety of potential implications—more or less spiritually charged—and their simultaneity. All reside in the simple figure of the cross, the cross being both a sign of Christ's sacrifice, and a piece of the landscape, in the colloquial sense of being a familiar object and marker of location. More spiritual meanings are undoubtedly available, 'immanent' we might say; but more mundane interactions are also likely. The point can be extended to most of the spaces and places discussed in this chapter: the parish church and cemetery, the practical

---

[205] Practical temporary useage: *Cart. Moissac*, no. 216, a church being built on an allod, where it states 'Hoc donum vero facio, ut cruces hac de causa in alodio ipso defixe demonstrant et determinant'; on more ritual uses, see P. Ourliac, *Les sauvetés du Comminges: étude et documents sur les villages fondés par les Hospitaliers dans la région des coteaux commingeois* (Toulouse: Boisseau, 1947), p. 47 and *passim*.

[206] *Cart. Lézat*, I, p. 21 (no. 25); BnF MS n.a.l. 1211 (Censier d'Apt), fol. 16v(a): 'R. de Venasca de orto qui est iuxta crucem et confrontatur cum terra W Mira iiii sol.'

[207] Albon, ed., *Cartulaire général de l'Ordre du Temple*, pp. 39–40 (no. 52), 1132: following a dispute resolved by *prudentibus hominibus* at a *placitum* in the town of Puy-Sainte-Marie, regarding the annual payment owed for a certain vineyard: 'Unde etiam...posite sunt cruces in sanciomem ejusdem vinee, quatinus a cunctis nosceretur quod quicumque exnunc et deinceps vineam illam tenuerit, simul etiam servitium illud annuum reddere debebit.'

material objects required by churches, the ongoing financial commitment by the laity to provide oil and wax and so forth. All *could* be given a charged spiritual meaning, and at certain moments were very likely to be. But all also had a certain familiarity and involved the practical demands of material things, in continuum with less exalted locations. Looked at across the whole period addressed by this book, such things witness a balance between long continuities—the core fact of communal worship, the collective investment in the material fabric and sacred space in each locality, the fundamental liturgical rhythms to the year—and fundamental changes: developments in the material environment of the church, an elaboration of the sensory experiences of the liturgy, an increase in visual materials that, we might suspect, provided additional potential for emotional and affective engagement.

Possibly my favourite among all medieval *exempla* is one recorded in the collection compiled by a member of the Brothers Minor in Provence, from which I have already drawn above a few times. It concerns Benoît d'Alignan, bishop of Marseille, author of the treatise containing the list of Marian miracles noted above. The *exemplum* relates that Benoît returned from the holy lands where he had gone on crusade in the 1240s, and brought back with him an extraordinarily precious relic: a piece of the Holy Cross upon which Christ had been crucified. This, he decided, should be divided up into yet smaller fragments, so that it could be distributed between many churches in his diocese, to be given 'great reverence and honour'. To this end, he engaged a 'master' (presumably a master craftsman) to cut it up, this task being done in the bishop's chapel. But as the master attempted to cut into the piece of wood, it shot off 'as if from a crossbow' making a great noise, headed not toward the window that was letting in light, but the other way, becoming lost in some dark corner. The bishop, hearing the noise, asked what was going on. The master threw himself at the bishop's feet, crying out 'I am the cause of this, because how can such a vile and unclean sinner dare to touch such a precious treasure?' The bishop asked if the craftsman would make confession; this he did, and subsequently the piece of wood was found, 'and the wood showed itself to be tractable to the master, such that it was done as the Bishop had ordered'.[208]

For what is quite a brief *exemplum* it is nonetheless rich in details that fascinate. We should note Benoît's desire to provide *many* churches with a sliver of holiness; a contrast perhaps to earlier habits of collating relics into the cathedral or monastic space. There is the narrative emphasis upon the very material nature of the fragment of the cross, perfectly familiar in its behaviour to anyone who has ever done a bit of carpentry and tried to cut up a small, unsecured sliver of wood. We hear the despairing self-accusation of the craftsman, and then the swift and happy resolution of what is, in one sense, a very normal small domestic drama of

---

[208] Welter, 'Un nouveau recueil franciscain d'exempla', p. 608 (no. 167).

a small object lost and then found. But at the same time, at the centre of it all, we witness the potential belief that this fragment connects a worshipper directly back to Christ's suffering, and thus onward to future salvation.

The very fragility of the sliver of the cross speaks to a dynamic that we can find recurrently across the various material and spatial topics explored in this chapter. Between its tiny material presence and the massive spiritual cargo it conveys, it is the quintessence of contrast: an invitation to the *work* required by belief. The point is not that it 'produces' or 'confirms' belief in some mechanical fashion, for in fact of course we do not know if the relic, any more than the Eucharist or the shrines of saints, was accepted by all. The point rather is that its very fragility— the possibility of it splintering, falling apart, shooting off into a dark corner— captures the sense of what is at stake in 'believing' spatially and materially, and the labour which it involved for all Christians, lay as well as clerical.

7
Instruction and Storytelling

Listen: here is a good and instructive tale for our edification. A certain young man never wanted to go to listen to sermons, despite his wife's enthusiasm for doing so. When, on a certain occasion, Brother Pierre de Cendres of the Order of Preachers wished to preach outside town on the other side of a bridge, the people of the same town went there with him. But the young man turned back, and when crossing the bridge once again, met two other youths, who said to him, 'if you promise to us now that you will *never* hear sermons, we will make you rich'. He agreed, and they immediately gave him two pounds of gold. Rejoicing, he hurried back to his house, mocking his wife and others who had gone to hear the word of God. He used the gold first to buy two handsome horses, and then rode around town with his nephew, contemplating which things he intended to buy next. However, on a certain day when they rode near some cliffs, as they crossed over the ridge of the mountain his nephew saw that the young man's horse, with him atop, was being carried by two demons. The nephew toppled to the ground in fear, and in terror the young man rushed to Brother Pierre to tell him what had happened. The preacher dragged the unwilling young man to the church; as he tried to get him actually into the church, the demons tried to hold him back, shrieking wildly all the while. Brother Pierre did eventually succeed, and persuaded the young man to confess what had happened, at which point the demons finally vanished. The friar told the young man, as penance, to give the gold to the poor—but in fact, when he got home, he discovered that it had turned into stinking excrement. And ever after, thanks to the grace of God, he very happily went to listen to sermons.[1]

This is one *exemplum* from over 200 collated by an anonymous friar who was operating in southern France, principally around Montpellier and Béziers, in the later thirteenth century. It is one small example of how Christian culture, particularly as directed toward the laity, was further changing from the late twelfth century onward, as the Church encouraged preachers to inspire the laity to active

---

[1] BnF MS Lat. 3555, fol. 198v; edited in Welter, 'Un nouveau recueil franciscain', p. 606 (no. 161). The manuscript is described in detail in V. Ferval, 'Grégoire et les autres dans le recueil anonyme et sans titre du MS Paris BnF lat. 3555', in M.-A. Polo de Beaulieu, J. Berlioz, and P. Colomb, eds, *Le tonnerre des exemples: exempla et médiation culturelle dans l'Occident médiéval* (Rennes: Presses universitaires de Rennes, 2010), pp. 273–85. The inquisitor Pierre de Cendres is mentioned briefly in at least one mid-thirteenth-century trial: see A&B, p. 379.

participation in their own salvation. For the modern historian, a particular attraction to these sources is that they both reflect something of the world of their production, and are interventions *into* that world, attempting to help reshape—re-form it, we might say—in their telling.

Thus this particular story both makes us aware of some contextual aspects to mendicant preaching—an outdoor setting, beyond the limits of the town, the community heading out together as audience—and also 'performs' that which it narrates, for that audience, as it dramatically frames to them the importance of attendance. As with many such stories, there are other details which present a useful, albeit selective, picture of the contemporary world, one with a varied and perhaps symbolically meaningful landscape (the town, the bridge, the cliffs), that contains wives, relatives, neighbours, but also demons; and yet does not appear to contain a parish priest, narratively banished perhaps by the need to emphasize mendicant intervention. It presents three clear messages: greed is bad, attendance at sermons is good, the act of confession is transformative. It also conveys more complex associated issues, a recognition of human frailty threaded throughout: people like having money, but it is evanescent; it might be fun to ride haughtily around town considering what to buy next, whilst impressing a younger relative, but it is not nice behaviour; whilst it is important to come to sermons, some people do not really want to.

And it is, importantly, a *story*. Good stories are engaging and memorable, with a flow of details that provide various possible points of reference upon which a member of a varied audience may become hooked, and from which the story might later be remembered or reimagined. The story's diegesis operates also to provide narrative distance between elements which might lose some of their pull and power, or be hard to reconcile or sustain, if reduced to simple propositions. Great wealth comes, and then evaporates; but this demonic gold operates in a rather different imagined space from troubled contemporary discussion around the precise nature of usury, or wealth more generally. Whilst the two demons enter the narrative as clearly, visibly present—albeit disguised—their presence becomes more blurred as it progresses, it being (productively) unclear whether they are external or internal to the young man at the point he is dragged into church. Spiritual authority and a guide toward salvation lie ultimately with Brother Pierre (and then, through him, with the preacher currently rehearsing the *exemplum* for a particular audience), but the nephew, seeing the demons and prompting the crisis, also briefly displays the gift of spiritual discernment. And the young man is ultimately responsible, in part at least, for his liberation, through the act of confession. 'Belief' is not reduced to a simple binary of acceptance or non-acceptance, but is narratively distributed across the tale, operating via affective efficacy as much as propositional content; that is, the way the story works is that as it unfolds it encourages the right kind of feelings toward tenets of belief, rather than simply reasserting them to its audience.[2]

There are a number of different issues at play here, to which I shall return later in this chapter and indeed in later chapters, and in particular I shall say more below on the general topic of preaching and its reception. But what interests me most in this tale—and in many other such *exempla* created in the period—is the expectation of lay agency and lay responsibility that it contains, even whilst ultimately bent toward mendicant spiritual authority. A good lay Christian could not simply conform, though conformity (in attending sermons, for example) was still important. The good lay Christian must come to a recognition of the spiritual snares in the world around them, the dangers of greed, pride, and other sins; and to a recognition of their own responsibility in attempting to avoid these pitfalls. The Church would help, by providing guidance and various forms of intercession; but it could not simply be done *for* them by others, it had also to be done *by* them. This, I argue, is the heart of a fundamental shift experienced across the thirteenth century: the making of new Christian selves for all lay people. As we saw in Chapter 5, by the end of the Albigensian Crusade, the Church was consolidating a parochial system that sought to ensure that all Christians were 'good', primarily in the sense of obedient. The *exemplum* discussed above is one tiny element within a much larger subsequent efflorescence, as pastoral care sought to make all Christians not just good, but better.

Lay Knowledge and Pastoral Advice

A fundamental argument of this book is that Christianity was not static nor one simple edifice, and that it always involved much more than simply a set of theological propositions. Nonetheless, there were various tenets of faith and associated ideas that informed the shape of Christian life and behaviour, some of which stayed consistent across many centuries, others developing and changing within the period studied here. Key questions for our enquiry are thus how much of this Christian 'knowledge' were lay people expected to have? And, as importantly, how much did they actually have, and how did they relate to it?

Across the earlier centuries discussed in Part I, there were various things which every Christian had to know, simply in order to participate as a Christian: for example, the fact of at least some key moments within the liturgical cycle of the year (Christmas, Easter, Pentecost) which informed participation in collective worship, the specific knowledge of dates presumably stitched together for most

---

[2] I am influenced here by the insights of J. M. George, 'Religious and Fictional Narratives: An Ontological Comparison with Reference to Max Weber's "Disenchantment of the World"', *International Journal of Philosophy and Social Sciences* 1 (2016), 53–62, adapting his concept of 'aesthetic efficacy' in religious storytelling.

people by some grasp of the narrative of Christ's life and passion; the necessity of paying tithes (though whether this would have sat cognitively within the specific frame of 'Christian worship' or have been part of a wider frame of 'exactions via lordship' is definitely open to question). In a different sense, wider knowledge of the desirability of baptism and Christian burial was, as we saw from details around local churches in Chapter 1, integral to the rights possessed by those churches. These basics—the shape of the year, financial support for the local church, the sacraments that marked the symbolic arrival into and departure from life—might be described also as knowledge gained and sustained via community; that is, we should not necessarily think of them as an abstract 'knowledge of Christianity' separate somehow from the wider practices of life. In part they may be seen as what the anthropologist Pierre Bourdieu called *habitus*: the unreflective knowledge of and shape given to the social world through the repeated actions of living. These basics do however imply a more conscious general knowledge of the fact of 'sin', and the desirability of 'salvation'—though given that these are areas on which vast amounts of later medieval ink would be spilled in theological *summae*, we must surely recognize that 'knowledge of' can cover a vast spectrum, much as my own 'knowledge of' the night sky is minimal in comparison to that of an astrophysicist.

There was undoubtedly also widely held knowledge of the saints, both as the collective heavenly court who had access to certain kinds of intercessory power, and as individual local saints, known for particular deeds. The latter were transmitted particularly via illustrative stories of the miraculous that were often also stories about place and local identity. As discussed in Chapter 1, the pious clauses to eleventh- and twelfth-century charters suggest that at least some of the more elite laity could be familiar with additional ideas about actively seeking salvation, the symbolic importance of Jerusalem, and the imminence of the Apocalypse. And as the developments discussed in Chapters 3 and 4 attest, concepts of apostolic piety, charity, poverty, and so forth also clearly had a wider circulation from the early twelfth century at least. Or perhaps we should say *stories which dramatized* apostolic piety, charity, and poverty had a wider circulation, each specific story once again tending to fold into itself other aspects of local community and interpersonal relations. (As we have seen, some of those contexts were deemed 'heretical' by orthodox authorities, some versions of the stories—such as those addressing the materiality of the Eucharist—challenging head on the perspective of the Church.) But in many areas, how codified and formally 'conceptualized' such issues were in the twelfth century, beyond the intellectual elite and the inspired few, is also very much open to question. And it is quite clear that whilst some of these topics—donations understood as 'charity', for example—may have been promoted as desirable by ecclesiastical authorities, at no point was knowledge of these areas specifically *required* of ordinary Christians, so long as they paid their tithes.

The issue of 'requirement' is important, and points up some key developments across the thirteenth and fourteenth centuries. Throughout western Christendom, at some point after the Fourth Lateran Council it became common to see bishops stating that it was fundamentally required for all Christians to learn and to know three things: the Creed (the short statement of faith that began *Credo in Deum*), the 'Our Father' (*Pater noster*) prayer, and the salutation to the Blessed Virgin (the *Ave Maria*).[3] Requirement of lay knowledge of the first two—the Creed and *Pater noster*—in fact dates back to some Carolingian legislation and episcopal injunctions, but is absent from any surviving council from the eleventh and twelfth centuries in southern France.[4] The conjoined requirement of all three items (*Pater noster*, Creed, *Ave*) does not appear explicitly in the region until the council of Albi in 1254, though knowledge of the Creed might be understood to be implied by the oath required by the council of Toulouse in 1229, in which all were 'to swear to serve the Catholic faith which the Roman church holds and preaches'. The synodal of Sisteron, composed by two Dominicans between 1225 and 1235 at the request of the bishop of that diocese, stated that 'priests should warn their parishioners that children from the age of 7 and above should be taught the *Pater noster* and *Credo*', this presented in conjunction with making confession and receiving communion at Easter.[5]

In thinking about actual lay knowledge, it is important to remember that such injunctions indicate neither a prior total lack, nor an instant and absolute subsequent fulfilment. At least slightly before the Sisteron statutes, we can catch a glimpse, via evidence given to inquisitors, of at least a few lay people having knowledge of the *Pater noster*, as the prayer seemed to be an important part of the rituals used by the Good Men in particular. Thus a woman called Marquesa, giving evidence in 1243 as a spy for the inquisitors, provided a detailed account of a neighbour in Fanjeaux receiving the *consolamentum* on his deathbed some ten years earlier, and related that having made a promise to adhere to their way of life 'he then said the prayer, that is the *Pater noster*, according to the rite of the

---

[3] N. J. Tanner and S. Watson, 'Least of the Laity: The Minimum Requirements for a Medieval Christian', *Journal of Medieval History* 32 (2006), 395–423. A useful overview focused on conciliar and synodal decrees is M. Rubellin, 'Un instrument du contrôle épiscopal au XIIIe siècle: les status synodaux', in M. Rubellin, *Église et société chrétienne d'Agobard à Valdes* (Lyon: Presses universitaires de Lyon, 2003), pp. 513–26.

[4] See C. van Rhijn, 'Manuscripts for Local Priests and the Carolingian Reforms', in C. van Rhijn and S. Patzold, eds, *Men in the Middle: Local Priests in Early Medieval Europe* (Berlin: De Gruyter, 2016), pp. 177–98; S. Patzold, 'Pater noster: Priests and the Religious Instruction of the Laity in the Carolingian *populus Christianus*', ibid., pp. 199–221. We do find it enjoined by Regino of Prüm in the early tenth century, and in the same period in England: S. Hamilton, *Church and People in the Medieval West* (Harlow: Pearson, 2013), pp. 186–87.

[5] Council of Albi, 1254, c. 18; council of Toulouse, 1229, c. 12; synodal of Sisteron, c. 19 (Pontal, *Statuts synodaux*, II, p. 192). In what follows, my research has benefited hugely from the material compiled under Rowan Dorin's direction for the *Corpus Synodalium* database (<https://corpussynodalium.com>), where most of the councils and synods referred to below can be found edited. Professor Dorin also very kindly shared with me digital photographs of some other materials. Here I have however retained citations to print editions and manuscript sources (checked by myself in each case) for the ease of cross-referencing with earlier scholarship.

heretics'.[6] Another witness, Pierre Daide, questioned in 1244, similarly reported details of the *consolamentum* in about 1231 of a woman called Brussende who, 'at the postulations of the heretics, rendered herself to God and to the Gospel and to the order of the heretical sect'. She promised to abstain from sex, not to swear or lie, not to desert their faith 'through fear of death by fire or water', and to abide by their largely vegetarian dietary rules, and that she would not eat anything 'without first saying a prayer, namely the *Pater noster*'.[7] A later thirteenth-century vernacular text setting out various rituals by the Good Men similarly attests to this practice of saying the prayer over food, as well as in various other situations. In this later text, created by those within the faith itself, the Good Men presented multiple repetitions of the *Pater noster* as a key element in their performance of apostolic authority, and consequently forbade lay people from saying it.[8] But as we have just seen, lay people undoubtedly heard it when in the presence of the Good Men—and if they were saying it prior to any consumption of food, lay people would have heard it from them repeatedly, as eating food 'blessed' by the heretics is reported extremely frequently in the inquisition registers.

We noted in Chapter 4 that Pierre Salinier, sentenced by the inquisitor Pierre Cellan, was actually given the *Pater noster* prayer written down by the Good Men, at some point prior to 1241.[9] There is no explanation in this very brief record as to why they did this, though he also mentions that they taught him to 'adore' them—the term used by the inquisitor to re-code the group's ritual of greeting, which they themselves termed the *melioramentum* (which one might translate as 'betterment')—which perhaps suggests some wider frame of instruction. It seems to me unlikely that Salinier, or any of his neighbours, would never previously have met the *Pater noster* prayer. But the presence of a written version, to which one could therefore repeatedly refer, reminds one that 'knowing' something is not a binary state: one might recognize the prayer if it was recited by another, but not be able to repeat it oneself; know the opening, but struggle to remember the whole thing; know how to recite it, but not know what it actually meant, particularly if taught

---

[6] Doat 23, fol. 95r: 'deinde dixit orationem scilicet pater noster secundum usum hereticorum'. 'According to the rite of the heretics' could mean simply 'as they ritually used it', or could indicate a variant version of the prayer, as found in the Latin and Occitan 'Rituals' of the Good Men, surviving from later in the thirteenth century, where the phrase 'supersubstantial bread' (drawn from some versions of the Gospel of Mark) replaces 'daily bread'; see W&E, p. 57 (doc. 57B) and p. 778 n. 8; discussion in B. Hamilton, 'The Cathars and Christian Perfection', in P. Biller and D. Bobson, eds, *The Medieval Church: Universities, Heresy, and the Religious Life*, SCH subsidia 11 (Woodbridge: Boydell, 1999), pp. 5–23 at pp. 17–18.

[7] Doat 23, fols 127v–128r: 'prefata Brunissendis ad postulationem hereticorum reddidit se Deo et Evangelio et ordini secta heretica, et promisit quod ulterius non comedet carnes…nec comederet nisi primo diceret orationem scilicet pater noster'.

[8] See M. R. Harris, 'Cathar Ritual (ms Lyon, Bibl. Mun., PA 36)', edited online: <http://www.rialto.unina.it/prorel/CatharRitual/CathRit.htm> (accessed 15 Aug 2022); translated W&E, doc. 57B, particularly pp. 487, 491, 493, 491.

[9] Doat 21, fol. 275v.

it in Latin (as may often have been the case).¹⁰ It thus raises the question of instruction. *How* were the laity to learn the prayer, the Creed, and the salutation? In some parts of Europe, going back to Carolingian times, it would have been the duty of the godparents to teach the *Pater noster* and Creed to their godchildren. But this does not seem to be the case in southern France, as we shall see.

The synodal of Sisteron simply says that children 'should be taught' these things, but by the mid-thirteenth century we start to see more specific reflection on the process: the council of Béziers, 1246, ordered parish priests to instruct their parishioners in 'the articles of faith' (by implication, the Creed) on Sundays, and to do so 'simply'. The council of Albi, 1254, further elaborated: when bishops visited a parish, people should render the oath set out in Toulouse 1229, the bishops 'first setting forth and explaining those articles to which they must swear'. The same council required moreover that parish priests should expound the articles of faith 'simply and distinctly' to all, on Sundays and feast days, and that parents should bring children aged 7 and over to the church on these days to learn the *Pater noster*, Creed, and *Ave Maria*; whether as part of the one process, or in a separate 'Sunday school' not being entirely clear.¹¹ However, a fourteenth-century synodal book (to which we shall return further below) created for his diocese by Dominique Grenier, bishop of Pamiers, does make the separate instruction of children explicit: each priest, either directly or through someone he appoints to the task, should gather all the boys and girls of his parish during Lent at the end of each day, and on other feast days at whatever hours he prefers, to teach them the Creed in the vernacular.¹² Another set of (probably) fourteenth-century synodal instructions from Lodève orders that teachers (*magistri*) of children 'should not presume to teach anyone more than the alphabet and the psalm *Deus in nomine tuo* [Ps. 53] unless they have taught them the *Pater noster* and *Credo in Deum* and the *Ave Maria*, and how to sign the cross'.¹³ By 1342 Gaucelin de Jean, bishop of Carcassonne, was having to admonish his parish priests that they should not demand payment for doing thus, but should willingly embrace the task of teaching the children, 'particularly the *Credo in Deum, Pater noster*,

---

¹⁰ See Arnold, *Belief and Unbelief*, pp. 38–39 more generally on this point.
¹¹ Council of Béziers, 1246, c. 7 (Mansi XXIII, col. 693); council of Albi, 1254, cc. 12, 17, 18 (Mansi XXIII, cols 835–37).
¹² Synodal of Dominique Grenier, bishop of Pamiers, 1326 × 47 (BM Toulouse, MS 402, fols 1r–137r, at 107r-v): 'Ne autem super ignorancia articulorum fidei parrochiam se valeant excusare, statuimus sub pena excommunicationis quod quilibet curatus nostre dyocesis vel gerens vices eius per se vel per alium ad hoc ydoneum teneantur convocare pueros parochie utriusque sexus ad hoc aptos in quadragesima circa completorium et aliis diebus festivis circa horis per eos parochianis deputandis et docere eos simbolum fidei id est credo minus in vulgari.'
¹³ Douais, *Synodal de Lodève*, p. 43. Artonne pointed out that Douais mis-identified part of the manuscript he edited (the 'synodal of Lodève' actually being that of Nîmes from 1252) and argues that the separate 'ordo' (cited here) may date earlier too, though on rather weaker grounds. See A. Artonne, 'Le livre synodal de Lodève', *Bibliothèque de l'École des Chartes* 108 (1949–50), pp. 36–74.

and other things pertaining to the faith'.[14] Telling priests not to demand payment for something does strongly suggest that they were in any case *doing* it, and indeed we have passing evidence from early fourteenth-century inquisition records that some local priests educated some children.[15]

Other ways of managing these core requirements for lay knowledge come to us from later thirteenth-century evidence (here repeating injunctions found, in part, in early medieval instruction similarly).[16] Bernard de Campendu, bishop of Carcassonne, in a synodal book he compiled around 1270, instructs the priest that when parishioners come to make confession, he should check first whether they know the Creed and the two prayers, and if not, should 'courteously warn them that they should learn them'.[17] This instruction was repeated more peremptorily in a little guide for priests on how to conduct confession, written by Bérengar Frédol (d. 1323), bishop of Béziers (later cardinal-bishop of Frascati), which survives, among other copies, in a fourteenth-century manuscript in Toulouse. It begins:

> First it is necessary that the priest asks the penitent whether he knows the *Pater noster* and *Ave Maria* and *Credo in Deum*. If he does not know, teach or have it instructed to him. And if it is too difficult for him to learn the *Credo in Deum*, advise him to learn the *Pater noster* and teach him the *Ave Maria*.[18]

This caveat regarding the potential difficulty of the Credo—rather implying that it was to be known in Latin—is an interesting recognition of the practicalities of instruction, and feeds into a wider sense that across the later thirteenth century and thereafter, bishops and priests were grappling with the practical experience of lay instruction, refining their attempts as they went.

As already noted, knowing the *Pater noster*, Creed, and *Ave Maria* was generally understood as the minimum requirement, but it was not by any means the

---

[14] Synod of Carcassonne, 1342: BnF MS Lat. 1613, fol. 80r: 'Item precipitur curatis et eorum vicariis ne quid exigant pro docendis pueris suorum parochianorum si gratis teneantur docere specialiter Credo in Deum, Pater Noster, et alia ad fidem pertinencia.'

[15] *Fournier* I, 252.

[16] See, for example, Regino of Prüm, *Libri duo*, pp. 128–29 (I.275); my thanks again to anonymous reader.

[17] Synodal constitutions of Carcassonne, c. 1270, c. IV (Mahul, *Cartulaire*, V, p. 423): 'interroget primo presbiter confitentem utrum sciat "Pater noster etc", "Credo in Deum" et "Ave Maria", et si nesciat, moneat curialiter ut addiscat'. The instruction to check on this knowledge at confession goes back to Raimond de Peñafort's *Summa de paenitentia*.

[18] BM Toulouse MS 191, fols 73r–141r (one part within a miscellany; authorship not known to Molinier when he compiled the manuscript catalogue however) at fol. 73r: 'Incipit summa de foro penitenciali brevis et utilis et valde necessaria sacerdotibus. In primis debet interrogare sacerdos penitentem utrum sciat pater noster et ave maria et credo in deum. Si nescit faciat vel precipiat instrui eum. Et si nimis esset difficile credo in deum precipiat ut addiscat pater noster et ave maria doceat eum.' On the work, see P. Michaud-Quantin, 'La "Summula in foro poenitentiali" attribué à Bérengar Fredol', *Collectanea Stephan Kuttner* (Rome, 1967), pp. 147–67.

entirety of knowledge that it was desirable for the laity to possess. Across the thirteenth and early fourteenth century, bishops enjoined their priests to promote a wider programme of Christian tenets to the laity. These fall broadly into the following categories: knowledge of key sacraments, knowledge of sin and the Ten Commandments, and, on occasion, knowledge of aspects within the wider framework of piety and salvation. Let us look briefly at each of these in turn.

Among the sacraments, those where conciliar and synodal instruction focused particularly on the laity were baptism and marriage. (I shall return to the more complicated case of the Eucharist further below, and save detailed discussion of confession and penance for Chapter 8). With baptism, the important thing was not simply that it be done, but that the laity themselves should be taught how to do it, so that in cases of imminent infant mortality where no priest was immediately available, the child's soul could still be washed clean of the stain of Original Sin. Within the region, it was the council of Albi in 1230 that first set this out:

> Item, we order priests frequently to teach the people—laymen and women or father or mother [of the child]—in cases of necessity, they can and must baptize the child, doing this by proposing a name and then saying 'Pierre or Jean, I baptize you in the name of the Father and Son and Holy Spirit, Amen'. If they do not know how to say this in Latin, they can say it in the vernacular.[19]

The injunction was repeated in some later councils,[20] and given additional gloss and instruction in some of the richer synodal books: that produced by Bernard de Campendu, bishop of Carcassonne, around 1270, for example, addresses various minor errors in performance that the laity might encounter—not saying 'Ego' before 'baptizo' for example, or that the child is not totally immersed in water, or (by implication) if the child is immersed or sprinkled with water but dies before their name can be pronounced—and reassures that in these cases the child is nonetheless considered to be baptized.[21] We should note here that we are again almost certainly seeing a dialectic between advice and practice, where the actions and concerns of lay people and local priests have fed back into episcopal reflections on the topic.

With regard to marriage, the Fourth Lateran Council's reduction of the degrees of consanguinity to four made much simpler one of the long-standing concerns over invalid marriage (albeit a concern which probably only ever really affected

---

[19] Council of Albi, 1230, c. 31 (Pontal, *Statuts synodaux*, II, p. 18).
[20] Council of Arles, 1260, c. 2; synodal of Rodez, 1279, c. V.11 (Avril, *Statuts synodaux*, VI, p. 127); second synodal injunctions produced by Pierre de Rochefort, bishop of Carcassonne, 1300 × 22, c. II.60 (BnF MS Lat. 1613, fol. 62v); council of Albi 1340 (Ludovico de Amboysia, *Sinodale diocesis Albiensis revisum et emendatum* (1499), p. 14), which emphasizes that if no man is present, a woman can perform it.
[21] Synodal of Carcassonne c. 1270, c. 2 (Mahul, *Cartulaire*, V, p. 421).

the noble elite, and even then only when they chose to pay attention to it).[22] What became much more of a feature in the thirteenth-century conciliar legislation was to insist upon the Church's right to publicize contracted marriages, via the banns, and to bless marriages. Thus we find, from the mid-thirteenth century onward, repeated injunctions that priests should strongly instruct their flock not to contract 'clandestine marriage', that is, marriages agreed simply by the pair involved with no formal witnesses and with no prior announcement.[23] In this case, the subsequently repeated conciliar and synodal decrees strongly suggest that ecclesiastical control was far from being totally accepted by all lay people. The council of Arles in 1260 ordered that 'because almost everywhere in the regions of the Province, men and women are presuming to confirm their marriage without ecclesiastical authority', any so doing would be held excommunicate.[24] A decade or so later, Bernard de Campendu's synodal instructions make clear that a potential part of the issue was people getting married outside their own parish, without the banns having been read, rather than necessarily shunning any involvement from a local church.[25] The synodal of Rodez from 1289 provides a detailed gloss on marriage, emphasizing (in a line repeated in several later texts in the region) that marriage was the very first sacrament, instituted by God in Paradise; and given this importance, enjoins its great solemnity, such that it should not be contracted 'with laughter or jokingly, or at night or clandestinely, but celebrated publicly in the sight of the Church', with the banns being read on the three preceding Sundays or feast days 'or other occasion on which the people are present, or the major part of them'.[26] The same injunctions continue to be repeated in the fourteenth century.[27]

What, then, of sin? It is of course the case that lay knowledge of sin as a concept, and knowledge that particular actions were sinful, existed well before the thirteenth century. What changes in this period however is firstly that the laity were increasingly asked to know that sin existed within an overall framework— the seven deadly sins, a wider array of venial sins—and, secondly, to recognize that some perennial aspects of human behaviour were in fact sinful. Beyond this, the thirteenth century also saw much increased discussion over how to address the

---

[22] The synodal of Sisteron, 1225 × 35, c. 48 instructs the priest to teach his parishioners the new degrees of consanguinity, and explains them fairly clearly (Pontal, *Statuts synodaux*, II, p. 206).

[23] This first appears regionally in the council of Isle-sur-Sorgues, 1251, c. 13 (J. H. Albanès, ed., *Gallia christiana novissima*, 7 vols (Montbéliard: Société anonymes des imprimerie Montbéliardaise, 1899–1920), II, col. 444).

[24] Council of Arles, 1260, c. 4 (Mansi XXIII, col. 1005).

[25] Synodal of Carcassonne c. 1270, c. 9 (Mahul, *Cartulaire*, V, p. 427).

[26] Synodal of Rodez, 1289, c.XI.15 (Avril, *Statuts synodaux*, VI, pp. 159–60).

[27] First synodal injunctions of Pierre de Rochefort, bishop of Carcassonne, 1300 × 22, cc. 2, 3, and 8 (BnF Lat 1613, fols 53r–56r); council of Béziers, 1310, c. 8 (Martene, *Thesaurus*, IV, cols 239–40); synod of Lodève, 1325, c. 15 (Douais, *Synodal de Lodève*, pp. 8–9); council of Avignon, 1326, c. 48 (Mansi XXVI, col. 769); council of Albi, 1340 (Ludovico de Amboysia, *Sinodale*, p. 59); synod of Béziers, 1342, c. 25 (Martene, *Thesaurus*, IV, col. 647).

effects of sin through confession and penance. We have already met, in Chapter 5, the ways in which the injunction to confess was legislatively elaborated in southern France in the early conciliar material. There is much more to say, from the lengthy advice created for confessors, on how priests and friars were to elicit and interpret confessions and bestow penances; but as this leads us into further complex aspects regarding how Christian selves were being remade in a disciplinary context, we shall hold that analysis over to Chapter 8. My interest here is simply in knowledge of sin, and the ways in which it was presented to the laity.

Explicit discussion of 'the seven deadly sins' within the conciliar material comes perhaps surprisingly late: we do not find it explicitly enjoined as something about which parish priests should educate their flock until Pierre de Rochefort's synodal statutes for Carcassonne in the first decades of the fourteenth century, which also required priests to 'expound' the fourteen articles of faith, the seven sacraments, 'the precepts of the laws' (that is, the Ten Commandments), the seven works of mercy, and those synodal statutes 'that touch upon the laity such as the form of baptizing in necessity, the manner of confessing their sins, and other similar things'.[28] The council of Albi in 1340 made similar demands.[29] But the framework does appear earlier in some other texts. An undated, but definitely thirteenth-century, pastoral compilation owned and perhaps produced by the Brothers Minor in Toulouse includes them, simply enumerated ('Vitia morttalia [sic]: septem sunt vitia mortalia. Superbia, Individa, Iracundia, Tristitia sive accidia, Avaritia, Luxuria, Gula'), also setting out the Ten Commandments, the articles of faith, the seven sacraments, the gifts of the Holy Spirit, the seven virtues, and 'the nine blessed ones' (that is, the poor, the meek, etc.).[30] Similarly a guide for confessors—argued to have been written by the Brothers Preacher sometime in the 1220s, its earliest manuscript (mid-thirteenth century) held by them in Toulouse—arranges questions that the confessor might use to prompt the penitent via the seven deadly sins and via the Ten Commandments.[31] The seven sins are similarly set out in the synodal of Rodez from 1289, when it turns to advice on administering confession and penance, followed by the seven works of

---

[28] Second synodal injunctions of Pierre de Rochefort, bishop of Carcassonne, 1300 × 22, c. II.60 (BnF Lat 1613, fol. 62v): 'Precipimus et mandamus quod sacerdotes parochiales in ecclesiis suis predicent et exponant parochianes suis articulos fidei, vii sacramenta et ecclesia x precepta legis, vii peccata mortalis, vii opera mercie nec non et statuta synodalia quam tangunt laycos sicut de forma baptizando in nessesitate, de modo confitendi peccata sua et similibus.'
[29] Council of Albi, 1340 (Ludovico de Amboysia, *Sinodale*), pp. 20–21, setting out the seven sins, the seven works of mercy, and the seven virtues, having earlier explained also the articles of faith and the seven gifts of the Holy Spirit (pp. 5–6).
[30] BM Toulouse MS 208, fols 58v–59r. This is a single manuscript compilation, written throughout in the same hand, and includes a lengthy initial section concerning excommunication, some discussion around administering confession, plus a few exempla, as well as these pastoral foundations.
[31] BM Toulouse MS 340, fols 255r–269v; see J. Goering and P. J. Payer, 'The "Summa penitentie Fratrum predicatorum": A Thirteenth-Century Confessional Formulary', *Mediaeval Studies* 55 (1993), 1–50, particularly p. 5 (date of text), pp. 8, 48–49 (date of Toulouse manuscript). As they note, another mid-thirteenth-century copy (BnF MS Lat. 3479, fols 1r–2r) may also have been produced in southern France (p. 48). This work is discussed further in Chapter 8 below.

mercy (that synodal also earlier setting out the articles of faith, the seven gifts of the Holy Spirit, and the Ten Commandments).[32] So we might say that the conceptual framework of sin was potentially available to the wider laity, particularly via mendicant preaching and pastoral activity, in the thirteenth century; and was specifically enjoined by the early fourteenth century.

What also becomes apparent are episcopal orders to instruct the laity that certain specific activities were in fact sinful. We met in Chapter 5 various things which were understood to transgress against ecclesiastical authority, leading to excommunication and endangering the souls of those involved: support for groups declared 'heretical', most obviously, along with other threats to 'the peace'. These elements of course continue, with heresy continuing to be a major concern in most conciliar and synodal statutes throughout the period studied. Something similar pertains with usury, which continues to be denounced, and, by the fourteenth century, occasions episcopal condemnation of consular attempts to manage—and thus legitimate—various forms of debt recovery.[33] At certain points in the thirteenth century, the requirement that the laity pay tithes—always a topic for potential dissent, given that it was fundamentally a form of taxation—is emphatically presented in episcopal statutes, for priests to admonish their parishioners.[34] In 1263, Benoît d'Alignan, bishop of Marseille, held a synod solely devoted to the issue, emphasizing that whilst in previous decades the city had been home to those who heretically and contemptibly 'derided those who pay tithes or firsts or oblations to clerics or to the material needs of churches, and they preached that with impunity one could refuse to hand them over', those dissidents had now been 'extirpated' by orthodox preaching and inquisition, and thus there was no excuse for the laity not to obey; any who failed to do so would indeed be excommunicated.[35] More positively, and presumably around the same time, Benoît wrote a brief exposition of *why* tithes had to be paid, providing brief references to relevant biblical and canon law passages, and explaining, for example, that 'Tenths and firsts are given in sign of universal dominium, whereby through this man recognises God, creator of heaven and earth and all which is in them, and that from Him come forth the fruits and all the goods of the land.'[36]

---

[32] Synodal of Rodez, 1289, cc. VII.5, VII.7 (Avril, *Statuts synodaux*, VI, pp. 130–31). Articles of faith etc: ibid. c. II (discussed further below); Ten Commandments ibid. c. III.

[33] For example, synodal of Elne, 1326, BM Perpignan MS 79 fol. 85r, against consuls who attempt to enforce the payment of usury in their written statutes; similarly, synodal of Pamiers (1326 × 47), BM Toulouse MS 402, fol. 14v regarding consuls who dare to restitute usury.

[34] For example, council of Isle-sur-Sorgues, 1251 c. 5 (Albanès, *Gallia christiana novissima*, II, cols 443–44).

[35] BnF MS Lat. 4224, fol. 476v: 'quia condam errores hereticorum invaluerant in civitate qui contemptibiliter irridebant eos qui decimas vel primitias vel oblationes clericis vel ecclesiis materialibus persolvebant, et impunitatem non prestantibus predicabant…'

[36] BnF MS Lat. 4224, fol. 475r: 'Quare dande. Decime ac primicie dantur in signum universalis dominii, ubi per hoc recognoscat homo deum creatorem celi et terre et omnium que in eis sunt, et quod ab ipso fructus et omnia bona terre proveniunt…'. On Benoît d'Alignan and this topic, see Th. Pécout, 'Dîme et institution épiscopale au XIIIe siècle en Provence', in M. Lauwers, ed., *La dîme, l'église, et la société féodale* (Turnhout: Brepols, 2012), pp. 411–72.

Later in the thirteenth century, concern to educate the laity that sexual relations outside marriage were sinful becomes more apparent: for example, 'manifest concubines' were to be pronounced excommunicate by name every Sunday, and their names to be handed over to the bishop, as ordered by two synods at Albi held in the late 1270s and in 1280, the latter synod also excommunicating 'sodomites and sinners against nature', and those who sin with nuns.[37] Additions to the synodal book of Rodez (1289) include the injunction to 'instruct the people that simple fornication [*that is, between two unmarried people*] is a mortal sin', and broadly instructs priests to preach 'most of all against those sins which are frequently committed in their parishes', which one tends to read partly as a gloss on the former dictat.[38] To be clear, since the early thirteenth century, various sexual sins had been identified as areas in which a confessor might carefully question a layperson, and many of these were among the cases 'reserved' to the bishop for absolution; but only in the later thirteenth century do we start to see bishops enjoining their priests actively to instruct their flock in these dangers through public preaching. More broadly, by 1342 the bishop of Carcassonne told priests that they should explicitly make clear to the laity, in the vernacular, the lengthy list of sins which were 'reserved', to ensure that people did not accidentally attempt to gain absolution for any such from someone not canonically licensed to do so.[39] We shall return to how sexual sins were further disciplined, and how the laity negotiated these issues, in a later chapter; for now, the point is simply that they become part of the programme of public instruction in the second half of the thirteenth century.

This is similarly the case with other activities which were probably fairly common. Statutes imposed by Louis IX, framed by Gui Foulques, and promulgated at the council of Béziers in 1255 attempted to forbid, for the first time, anyone playing games of dice, or indeed making dice; and, in what is probably a connected move given various other occasions on which gambling and swearing were associated, the synodal of Fréjus in 1276 told priests to teach their parishioners that various penalties and penances would be imposed on those who blasphemed the Lord or Mary or the saints.[40] Here in fact the synodal command lags behind

---

[37] Synod of Albi, 1277 × 80, c. 1 (Avril, *Statuts synodaux*, VI, p. 78); synod of Albi, 1280, cc. 12, 20 (ibid. pp. 79–80).

[38] Synodal of Rodez, 1289, cc. XX.7, XX.8.

[39] Synod of Carcassonne, 1342 (Bishop Gaucelin de Jean) unnumbered (BnF MS Lat. 1613, fol. 80v): 'Item in virtute sancte obediencie precipitur curatis ut parochianis suis casus episcopo reservatos in vulgari exponant ne per ignoranciam religiosis vel aliis non habentibus potestatem ad hoc ipsa confiteantur peccata casus aut in synodali plenarie sunt descripti'. The same thing is possibly implied by an injunction by an earlier bishop of Carcassonne (Pierre de Rochefort), instructing priests on the first Sunday after synod to publicize in the vernacular those cases subject to excommunication and interdict: synod of Carcassonne, 1300 × 22, c. 26 (BnF MS Lat. 1613, fol. 56r).

[40] Council of Béziers, 1255, c. 24 (Mansi XXIII, cols 882–83); synodal of Fréjus, 1279, AD Bouche-de-Rhônes H. fonds de St Victor, C 158: 'Praeterea presbiteri omnes insinuent parrochianis suis quod cetera pena et penitencia est inposita illis qui blasfemant dominum vel dominam nostram vel sanctos.' (I am most grateful to Rowan Dorin for providing me with a digital photograph of the surviving fragment of this document.)

things already proposed in certain civic statutes: as we saw in Chapter 4, some town customs had, in the late 1220s, already condemned blaspheming when playing at dice, though the punishment there was to be thrown in the mud—in the case of the town of Meyrueis—or pay a monetary fine, rather than incurring danger to one's immortal soul.[41]

The point about town statutes can remind us once again that the first appearance of a topic in conciliar or synodal legislation does not by any means imply total lay ignorance prior to that point, whether regarding the status of particular sins or the more positive engagements of prayer and the articles of faith. But it is nonetheless a clear indication of something changing across the thirteenth century, as the demands of being a good Christian amplified: in contrast to the engaged orthodox laity of the twelfth century, by the later thirteenth century simply *doing* the right thing was not sufficient, one must also demonstrate that one knew the right things, and indeed *believe* in those things. This produced both demands and opportunities for ordinary lay people. But what did 'knowing' and 'believing' in the articles of faith and so forth actually mean?

The Dynamics of Instruction

We need to remember that almost all the episcopal material considered in this chapter is not addressed directly to the laity but to their parish priests, to then be passed on to their parishioners. The very emergence of synodal books as a textual genre is a key piece of evidence for the development of the parish system as a means of education: the first one extant for the region is that produced for Sisteron in the 1220s, and it is notable how relatively extensive it is, covering the sacraments, including a short guide to confession and another regarding marriage, the duties and way of life of the clergy, on how the laity should make wills, and certain other matters. Thus these synodal books attempt to provide a comprehensive manual for the parish priest, to be referred to on various occasions; they come to overlap with the potentially more dynamic specific statutes issued at particular synods (or issued at councils and then repeated at synod) that we also see mentioned or implied at various points. Explicit requirement for priests to have copies of synodal injunctions is first made in the synodal book that Raimond de Calmont d'Olt, bishop of Rodez, created in 1289—'a synodal book should exist in each parish, which the priest can expound to his parishioners as seems fit'— and something similar is repeated in various fourteenth-century councils.[42]

---

[41] See Chapter 4, pp. 154–55.
[42] Synodal of Rodez, 1289, c. I.5 (Avril, *Statuts synodaux*, VI, p. 116). See similarly synod of Carcassonne, after 1311, c. 11 (BnF MS Lat. 1613 fol. 76r-v), synod of Carcassonne 1315, cc. 4, 18 (ibid. fols 63v, 65r), synod of Carcassonne, 1341 (unnumbered), priests who lack the synodal statutes are placed under interdict, lifted upon payment of a fine of 5 *sous* (ibid., fol. 84r).

A fragment of a copy of episcopal statutes for Elne in 1326 (extant in full in another contemporary manuscript) exists on a sheet of paper in the archives in Perpignan, written with relatively little adornment in a notarial hand of the same century; possibly evidence of precisely the kind of thing with which priests were supposed to supply themselves.[43] Whilst, as we have seen, elements within these materials were supposed to be 'publicized' by priests to their flock, on Sundays and feast days, the larger compilations are clearly designed as works of reference, to which priests could turn for details and models of instruction when they were needed.

This may similarly be the case with other materials which we start to see in circulation in the thirteenth century and thereafter, which sought to gloss aspects of the faith for a wider audience, albeit still written in Latin for an initial readership of priests or mendicant friars. Some of these simply set out in further detail the articles of faith, sins, prayers, works of mercy, and so forth, acting as the most basic *aide mémoire*. We find this included in the thirteenth-century Franciscan compilation mentioned earlier, for example. A short 'booklet on the articles of faith' (*libellus de articulis fidei*) created by the Brother Preacher and former inquisitor Bernard Gui in the 1330s when he was bishop of Lodève, does something similar, albeit providing a little bit of a gloss on each aspect: for example, that the Second Commandment (taking God's name in vain) is against making foolish oaths, and that the commandment against stealing also covers less direct cases such as defrauding people in business deals.[44]

But there are also slightly richer texts, still however clearly designed for pastoral instruction rather than deep theological reflection: short glosses on the Creed or the *Pater noster* prayer in particular, that are best understood as providing additional explanatory authority to the priest when he comes to explain 'clearly and simply' these things to the laity. An early example, an exposition of the *Pater noster*, is another element included in the Franciscan manuscript mentioned above. It provides a simple gloss and explanation of the implications of each phrase of the prayer, for example:

> *Our Father who is in heaven.* Each man who calls out to his Father in heaven, ought to be his son; he ought to show himself and prepare himself as such, so that he may be the son of God. He ought to have the love (*caritas*) of God in himself, and the care (*dilectio*) of his neighbour. If he has this then he is the son

---

[43] AD P-O G9, a *liasse* containing various documents originating from the bishopric in the fourteenth and fifteenth centuries. The paper document in question comprises one sheet folded in half, and uses red and blue ink to mark out distinctions in items on the page, but otherwise looks pragmatically simple.

[44] BM Toulouse MS 208, fols 58v–59r; Bernard Gui, *Libellus de articulis fidei*, in BM Toulouse MS 118, fols 214r–224r, edited in Douais, *Un nouveau écrit de Bernard Gui*, p. 63 (for no very good reason, Douais separates off the final enumeration of the articles of faith from the main treatise; there is no separation in the manuscript).

of God because he does the work of God. And if he is proud or an adulterer or a fornicator or a drunk or a homicide or an avaricious man or a defamer or does other bad deeds, then he is not the son of God because he does not do the work of God. If he does his work he should be called His son.[45]

The commentary is directed very clearly to simple pastoral guidance throughout, the prayer 'explained' in terms of what it instructs all Christians to do, or to recognize in their existing actions. For example (in regard to *blessed be his name*), that we accept our Christian names in baptism from Christ, and ask that his name is sanctified in us; or (*Your will be done on earth just as in heaven*) that, like angels who lack the will to sin and lack any desire for worldly things ('not for possessions or gold or silver'), we humans ask that we should not have a bad will either; or (*give us this day our daily bread*) that 'bread' should be understood to mean all worldly and spiritual victuals, 'but that most of all we must pray, day and night, that he gives us spiritual food from which our soul can live. This is holy scripture and word of eternal life, because just as the body cannot live without food and clothing, so the soul cannot live without preaching and the word of eternal life.'[46] We should note that whilst the *Pater noster* is clearly being glossed as it is phrased in Latin, the glossing depends upon the audience understanding the literal sense of the words, which by implication would also need first to be understood by a lay audience, whether by explaining them initially or by their own memory of earlier instruction.

Benoît d'Alignan, the bishop of Marseille whom we met above in regard to tithes, also wrote short 'expositions' on both the *Pater noster* and the *Ave Maria* at some point before 1261, along with a much lengthier treatise on the faith (from which we met a list of Marian miracles in the previous chapter, and to which we shall return below). These do not offer quite such readily accessible material for lay instruction, but are still designed to guide those with the care of lay souls. His general preliminary framing of the *Pater noster*, for example, adapts (without explicit citation) something Gregory the Great said seven centuries earlier regarding scripture, that the prayer 'is a river in which a lamb may walk and an elephant may swim'; arresting and theologically important words, but one suspects rather likely to lead to a lot of digressive questions if repeated unmediated in a pastoral context. And yet they have considerable importance for lay instruction,

---

[45] BM Toulouse MS 208, fol. 54v: 'Pater noster qui es in celis. Unusquisque homo qui patrem clamat in celis, filius debet esse. Talem se debet exibere et preparare ut filius dei sit. Caritatem dei in se debet habere et dilectionem proximi. Si hoc habet tunc est filius dei quia facit opera dei. Et si est superbus aut adulter aut fornicator aut ebriosus aut homicida aut avarus aut detractor aut cetera mala faciens, tunc non est filius dei quia non facit opera dei. Cuius opera facit eius filius appellatur.'

[46] BM Toulouse MS 208, fol. 55v: 'sed maxime debemus precari die noctuque ut det nobis spiritalem victum unde anima vivere debeat. Hoc est scripturam sanctam et verbum vite eterne quia sicut corpus non po[tes]t vivere sine victu et vestimento ita et anima non potest vivere sine predicatione et verbo vite eterne.'

as Gregory's point, as adapted by Benoît, was that the prayer was simple enough to sustain even children, but had depths which would leave wise people 'suspended in admiration'.[47] His exposition gives some sense of those depths, noting, for example, why 'we' (Latins) disagree with 'the Greeks' (that is, the Eastern Church) over using the different phrase, 'supersubstantial bread', found in the Gospel of Matthew;[48] and throughout (and even more so in the exposition of the *Ave Maria*), he links phrases in the prayer to other biblical passages, setting it in a wider exegetical context.

But amidst this learned approach, he also provides some striking material that a priest might use with his parishioners. For example, commenting on 'our daily bread', he stresses that not only does God provide us with sustenance, but that 'Christ is *ours* in all our necessities. He is our father, our brother, our lord, our master, our priest, our advocate, our judge, our medic, our law-giver, our mediator, our redeemer, our saviour and, in brief, whatever is necessary for us.'[49] On the *Ave Maria*, he rather nicely suggests that the salutation is like a little song (*cantilena*) sung to celebrate the marriage between the son of God and human nature, and goes on to provide the image of a hungry *joglar* at the laden table of a rich man, waiting patiently to begin 'courteously', likening this to how, again in a courtly fashion, we are to ask God to empty us of our vices and sins, as we hunger for his grace. The *Ave Maria* is thus rendered specifically as a courteous petition, something which will have resonance for the more socially elevated laity at least.[50]

Modern historians have sometimes written about lay Christian instruction in the middle ages as if they were time-travelling school inspectors, measuring how 'effectively' bishops and priests had developed their framework for instruction against some idealized whole, or at least, against 'best practice' elsewhere in Europe. This is not totally anachronistic: there is a central push for better lay instruction coming from the thirteenth-century papacy, and it is clearly worth noting regions in which this was embraced with particular zeal (as seems to have

---

[47] BnF Lat. MS 4224, fols 455r–468r, at 455v: 'Hec enim oratio est fluvius in quo agnus peditet et helephas natet. Habet enim in publico unde parvulos nutriat, servat in secreto unde maiores admiracione suspendat.' The passage being adapted here is Gregory's letter to Leander, prefatory to his *Moralia in Job*, Gregory talking about scripture in general, rather than these prayers specifically: 'Habet in publico unde parvulos nutriat, servat in secreto unde mentes sublimium in admiratione suspendat. Quasi quidam quippe est fluvius ut ita dixerim planus et altus, in quo et agnus ambulet et elephas natet' (PL 75, col. 515).
[48] BnF Lat. MS 4224, fol. 461r.
[49] BnF Lat. MS 4224, fol. 462r: 'Christum qui noster est in omnibus necessitatibus nostris. Ipse enim est noster pater, noster frater, noster dominus, noster magister, noster sacerdos, noster advocatus, noster iudex, noster medicus, noster legifer, noster mediator, noster redemptor, noster salvator, et breviter quicquid nobis est necessarium.'
[50] BnF Lat. MS 4224, fol. 473v: 'Salutacio beate Marie est quasi cantilena de nuptiis que celebrate sunt inter filium dei et naturam humanam... Et nota quod sicut si ioculator esuriens ad plenam mensam divitis retinuit sibi placentia non ei cibus negabitur ad inire curiali, sic si nos evacuari volumus a viciis et peccatis esurientes dei gratiam, devoto corde ei diximus *Ave Maria gratiam plenam*.'

been the case in England, for example) or left somewhat in abeyance.[51] But we can miss some important historical dynamics if we view 'lay instruction' as progress against some abstracted ideal. One is that we must remember that educating the laity was not a single task, but a goal to be repeated with each generation. Indeed, in some areas of western Europe the responsibility for instruction was made more clearly intergenerational, as either parents or godparents were required to provide the basic knowledge (*Pater noster*, *Ave*, Creed) to children.[52] But this mode of lay-to-lay education is absent from the southern French evidence. This leads to a second point: 'lay instruction' strongly overlaps with 'clerical instruction', both in the sense that bishops were attempting to ensure that parish priests themselves knew the fundamentals of their faith, but also in terms of further encouraging and supporting them in their parochial pedagogic task. Thus we need to see the synodal material in particular as seeking to immerse the ordinary parish priest within a richer theological landscape, not necessarily to pass on every biblical cross-reference or spiritual inner truth, but to be empowered by *their* knowledge confidently to instruct the laity in theirs.

That deeper theological and spiritual knowledge was thus not bestowed directly upon the laity, but some of it may have become available to them, intermittently at least, as different priests interpreted their task in different ways, and as particular lay people petitioned for deeper instruction beyond the surface knowledge. And here a further and fundamentally important issue arises with regard to lay instruction, to remind us that we should not assume that a medieval pedagogy had quite the same aims as a modern one.[53] The thirteenth-century Church wished all lay people to attain a certain level of core knowledge, in the 'essentials of the faith', in southern France this intertwining with the concern to combat 'heresy' and to ensure 'the peace'. But what the Church did *not* want—and for obvious reasons, particularly in southern France—was lay people ruminating in an unguided way on the faith, and coming to their own, potentially erroneous, conclusions about any of its mysteries. The case of eucharistic unbelief is a very obvious example, one strongly associated with heresy in southern France, given that rejection of Christ's materiality seems to have been central to the beliefs of the Good Men. Thus as the synodal material develops across the thirteenth and early fourteenth century, whilst we see an expansion in the ambitions of the episcopate with regard to lay education, we see also an accompanying concern, firstly over the abilities of the broad mass of lay people to cope with anything beyond the

---

[51] M. Gibbs and J. Lang, *Bishops and Reform, 1215–1272* (Oxford: Oxford University Press, 1924); W. H. Campbell, *The Landscape of Pastoral Care in Thirteenth-Century England* (Cambridge: Cambridge University Press, 2018).
[52] For example, Tanner and Watson, 'Least of the Laity'; Thompson, *Cities of God*, pp. 337–38; Arnold, *Belief and Unbelief*, pp. 67, 137.
[53] Here I depart from the nonetheless important perspective taken in C. M. Waters *Translating Clergie: Status, Education, and Salvation in Thirteenth-Century Vernacular Texts* (Philadelphia: University of Pennsylvania Press, 2016).

basics, and secondly that access to greater knowledge could tempt people into independent exploration and rumination.

Although clergy, and most of all priests with care of souls, must know the articles of faith 'explicitly, namely that they must know the intention of each article to explain it to the people', admonishes the synodal of Rodez (1289), 'it is however sufficient that the laity know them implicitly, that is, simply; namely that they know them coarsely and simply (*rude et simpliciter*), just as they are set down, or they should believe them implicitly in general to be true, as whatever the Church believes; saving the fact that from natural instinct they should believe especially that there is one God, renderer of all good and punisher of all evil.' The synodal goes on to advise that priests should frequently restrain the laity from 'asking reasons how or why something is thus' in regard to the Trinity, the articles of faith, and the sacraments, because these are 'subtleties of faith' that they do not possess the intellect to comprehend.[54] There is a tension at the heart of asking the laity to be engaged more fully with the propositional core of Christian faith: desiring that they know, and thus conform, but worrying that in 'knowing' they may not understand as they ought. And thus there is an attempt to circumscribe the *way* in which they know—simply and implicitly.

A generous interpretation of the synodal instruction is that it simply recognizes the limits of human capacity: not everyone can cope with more abstract thought, the tenets of faith are demanding, and a priest must be reassured that he need not attempt to argue in quasi-scholastic fashion with his uneducated parishioners. Clearly there is something to this. But it is important to note that the concern with wrong belief embraces *all* of the laity—they are *not* to ask questions, but to believe 'implicitly' and 'simply'. And yet this happens even whilst, on the other hand, the Church adds various additional aspects to what they are to believe, and develops additional means by which it checks up on their knowledge. I note the tension not in order to condemn the Church's attempts at proselytizing the faith—its embrace of what André Vauchez once called 'the campaign of interior conversion', in counterpoint to the missionary activities of the Church beyond western Christendom—but to point out the tension that lays at the heart of it; a tension which, elaborated across a number of areas, provides an essential dynamic at the heart of the development of 'lay religion'.

The synod of Rodez was far from the only pastoral text to warn against the laity delving too deeply into the faith. In the early fourteenth century, a succession of bishops of Carcassonne were even more explicit. Bishop Pierre de Rochefort, in two separate synods held some time before 1322, forbade the laity from debate on any such matters, for fear of peril to their souls and error: 'we strictly forbid that any layperson of any status or condition whatsoever, living in our city and

---

[54] Synodal of Rodez, 1289, c. II.10, II.11 (Avril, *Statuts synodaux*, VI, p. 119). This is repeated in the same wording in the synod of Mirepoix, 1334–48, unnumbered (BnF MS Lat. 15066, fol. 6v).

diocese, should presume to begin to dispute the Catholic faith, publicly or privately'.[55] At a synod in 1339, Bishop Gaucelin de Jean made it clear that any such layperson was *ipso facto* excommunicate, an injunction he repeated in 1342.[56] At the synod of Béziers in 1342, in setting out the articles of faith, Bishop Guillaume Fredol gave some indication of what sorts of issues might arise, for example regarding the Trinity: 'And however in the Catholic religion we are prohibited from saying that there are three Gods or Lords.'[57]

The synodal created by Bishop Dominique Grenier for Pamiers in the second quarter of the fourteenth century addresses the issues at greatest and perhaps most sensitive length. This synodal is the longest of the surviving southern French texts, the text running in two columns over 137 folios in a manuscript measuring about 24 cm × 16 cm.[58] It is undoubtedly a manuscript which was used and consulted, containing marginal additions, notes, and manicules from both the fourteenth and fifteenth centuries. Grenier (or Grima, as he is also known) was a Brother Preacher, a Toulousan by birth, who studied theology at Toulouse, Carcassonne, and Paris, assisted Bernard Gui in his work as inquisitor for a short period in 1320, served as a *magister* for a few years at Avignon (writing several exegetical works, at least one of which was presented to Pope John XXII), and became bishop of Pamiers in 1326.[59] His synodal book ranges across much the same areas as preceding and later examples, but with care to set out detail and proffer advice in all areas; for example, taking care to provide the priest with instruction regarding a wide variety of situations relating to where exactly a parishioner has asked to be buried (inside church if given special licence by the bishop, in a different parish, in the cemetery of a religious order) and what is permitted in difficult situations (such as a father choosing the site of burial for their deceased child, or whether someone condemned to death by a secular authority can receive Christian burial).[60]

---

[55] First synod of Carcassonne, 1300 × 22, c. 17 (BnF Lat 1613, fol. 55r): 'districtius inhibemus ne aliqui layci cuiuscumque status vel conditionis existant in nostra civitate et dyocesi plubice [*corr.* publice] vel privatum [*corr.* privatim] presumant intercede [vel] fide catholica disputare'. Similar injunction, second synod of Carcassonne, 1300 × 22, c. II.46 (ibid., fol. 61r) which makes explicit that this is disputing 'between themselves' as much as with the priest.

[56] Synod of Carcassonne, 1339, c. 5 (BnF Lat. 1613, fol. 81v): 'Item quicumque layco [*corr.* laicus] qui de fide catholic publice vel privatim disputat'; synod of Carcassonne, 1342, unnumbered (ibid., fol. 78v).

[57] Synod of Béziers, 1342, c. 4 (Martene, *Thesaurus* IV, col. 640): 'Et tamen tres Deos aut Dominos dicere catholica religione prohibemur.'

[58] BM Toulouse MS 402, fols 1r–137r, followed (137v–144v) by undated synodal statutes in the same hand, the end of which is missing one or more folios. (Two other unconnected works follow, bound into the manuscript at a later date, possibly in the seventeenth century). My profound thanks once again to Rowan Dorin for supplying digital images.

[59] M. Morard, 'Dominique Grima, o.p., un exégète thomiste à Toulouse au début du XIVe siècle', *CdF* 35 (2000), 325–74; the article focuses on his theological writing, and does not mention the synodal book.

[60] BM Toulouse MS 402, fols 33v–36r.

When Grenier comes to discuss the laity's understanding of the Creed, he diverges somewhat from the more minimal line we have previously met. He writes: 'all the faithful, both great and lesser, must believe explicitly [in the articles of faith] just as is contained in the lesser creed, simply and plainly'. And he goes on to emphasize that they must 'have faith', quoting several biblical passages on its importance, and its fundamental basis as hope for future salvation.[61] Thus he appears to set the bar somewhat higher than most previous pastoral advice. But a folio later he takes a more subtle line, prompted one presumes by his own reflection on the wider array of aspects of Catholic faith that his synodal addresses: 'Moreover the aforesaid technical articles, distinctions, and other subtle considerations around them do not have to be known by the simple people, but the better sort (*maiores*) must know these things more or less, or explicitly believe as fits their status and office', going on to say that it is acceptable that the 'simple' believe these more difficult things 'implicitly'. And he continues:

> Moreover, it not only suffices that the simple thus believe the subtleties and difficulties of faith implicitly, but rather, it is not expedient that they should question these things or dispute them. But on the contrary we order, under penalty of excommunication, that no layperson nor moreover cleric, unless they are a theologian, should dare to dispute the articles of faith or difficulties about them, whether publicly or secretly; because on account of the profundity of the matters and the feebleness of the intellect of the simple, these things can easily [lead them to] error. Because of this, moreover, they should not be encouraged to this through other things, nor, further, should there be enquiry or questioning, except of those about whom there is probable suspicion that they were being corrupted by heretics; because heretics are accustomed to corrupting the faith of the simple in those things which relate to the subtleties of faith.[62]

Thus we meet again the essential tension at the heart of the pastoral project, as the making of ordinary Christians into informed religious 'believers' meets the concern with disciplinary control, and the continued spectre of 'heresy'. We should

---

[61] BM Toulouse MS 402, fol. 106r: 'omnes tam maiores quam minores tenentur explicite credere sicut in minori simbolo continentur simpliciter et de plano'; 106v: '...et hac eadem necessitate qua tenentur habere fidem cum ei fides scilicet in apostolum ad Hebre XI "Sic substancia", id est fundamentum sperandanum rerum nichil aliud est fides quam quedam perlibatio istius cogitionis quod nos in futuro beatos faciet quasi iam in nobis res speranda id est futuram beatittudinem...'

[62] BM Toulouse MS 402, fol. 107r: 'Non solum autem sufficit simplicibus subtilitates et difficultates fidei sic implicite credere immo non expedit eis ista perquirere vel de huius disputare immo precipimus eis sub pena excommunicationis quod nullus laycus nec etiam clericus nisi sit theologus audeat disputare de articulis fidei vel difficultatibus circa ea publice vel occulte, quod propter materie altitudinem et intellectus simplicium imbecilitatem possent eadem de facili in errorem, propter quod etiam non sunt ad hoc per alia provocandi nec etiam circa hoc inquirendi seu examinandi nisi quam habeatur suspicio probabiliter quod essent ab hereticis depravati quia in hiis quoad subtilitatem fidei pertinent solent fidem simplicium depravare.'

also note that with Grenier, there is an interesting and important slippage between 'knowing' and 'believing', with further tensions thus arising. Whereas earlier statutes aim that the laity must 'know' the articles of faith and the *Pater noster* in the sense of being able to rehearse them accurately when required, leaving 'belief' to be handled by 'implicit faith' in a broad and fairly undefined way, by the fourteenth century Grenier's synodal wishes to connect knowledge and belief for the laity rather more closely, emphasizing, as we saw, the importance of faith and requiring that the core essentials be held 'explicitly'. More than that, they must be '*firmly* believed', he emphasizes, as he sets out, following the passages above, core tenets relating to the creation, the life and passion of Christ, and Final Judgment.[63]

This echoes, of course, the opening creed of the Fourth Lateran Council (*Firmiter credimus*), a creed that also lay at the core of the huge treatise on faith by Bishop Benoît d'Alignan, which I mentioned briefly above, and to which his much briefer commentaries on the *Pater noster* and *Ave Maria* are essentially appendices. The treatise is his *Tractatus fidei contra diversos errores*, written between about 1240 and 1261, inspired in part by his experience on crusade but also by his pastoral role in Marseille and its environs, which across 450 folios sought to provide a means of affirming every facet of faith contained within that creed, and 'destroying all errors' that could possibly arise in regard to the same.[64] Both works—d'Alignan's at considerable length, Grenier's somewhat more focusedly—further illustrate the *productive* dynamic within the tension over lay instruction: an ambition to 'strengthen' the faith of the ordinary laity leads to the provision of a more elaborated faith, which both proffers and increasingly demands that every Christian apprehend the core tenets of the Christian story; such elaboration however itself providing the possibility of greater divergence and 'error'; such error prompting additional instruction, in an attempt to provide the means of correcting divergences, accompanied by the desire that ordinary people should not simply 'know' but 'believe', not simply 'believe' but 'believe *firmly*', the pastoral guiding hand quivering between further instruction and issuing injunctions against any discussion. These are issues to which we shall return in Chapter 10.

Preaching and Its Reception

As we have seen, the instruction of the laity was in part to be achieved by bringing children to church for some version of Sunday school, and by checking up on the individual knowledge of parishioners when they came to make confession at

---

[63] BM Toulouse MS 402, fols 107v–108r (addressing here also the education of children, as cited further above).
[64] BnF MS Lat. 4224; see J. H. Arnold, 'Benedict of Alignan's *Tractatus fidei contra diversos errores*: A Neglected Anti-heresy Treatise', *Journal of Medieval History* 45 (2019), 20–54.

Easter. But the predominant mode by which the wider understanding of the faith was to be communicated—its moral injunctions and its core narratives of sin and salvation—was by preaching. And at the same time, preaching also sought to do much more than simply 'inform'. It aimed (at its best, at least) to inspire, to move, to *reform* a lay audience. As the thirteenth century wore on, rich resources were developed to help with that task, notably model sermons and collections of *exempla*—such as that from which I drew the story with which this chapter began.

However, preaching to the laity clearly did not begin for the first time in the thirteenth century. At Mende, in an account of one of the early twelfth-century relic councils discussed in Chapter 2, it is clearly stated that the bishops gathered there delivered 'a final sermon' (perhaps implying that others had also been delivered previously) in which they blessed 'the people'. We met several peripatetic preachers in Chapter 3, perhaps including Pons de Léras and his companions in their initial enthusiastic activities at least; and by the later twelfth century we have seen evidence of preaching by the Good Men and the Waldensians, and by Cistercians, bishops, and subsequently by the early mendicant orders. Should we extend the picture given by these various rather extraordinary occasions to suggest a more common, local experience? A famous account of Bernard of Clairvaux preaching at Verfeil in 1145 depicts one such extraordinary occasion of anti-heresy preaching, ending with him 'cursing' the *castrum* for its lack of repentance. The detail does perhaps provide some useful detail (if we can believe what is however a thirteenth-century narrative): Bernard started his preaching in the church 'against those important people (*maiores*) there', who then left 'and the people followed them'; Bernard thus headed outside, preaching then in the street to the ordinary people, though the knights and nobles went into their houses, and subsequently banged on their doors to drown out his words. At that point he gave up, cursed them, and left.[65] Thus, if we can assume that Bernard's orchestration of his performance accorded with existing norms, preaching is something to be delivered in the church, even in a relatively small and rural *castrum*, to an audience that included all social ranks. Preaching outside—which is what we find in most other accounts of twelfth-century sermons (in part given their extraordinary occurrence)—was a feasible tactic, but hard to sustain if one had a hostile audience. Regardless of the unhappy reception of the sermon by some of the audience, its logistical 'framing' was presumably familiar from other, more usual, occasions; though perhaps the degree of direct address and denunciation of the specific audience rather less so.

We simply do not have very much evidence otherwise from the twelfth century, let alone earlier, though there is one extremely precious and tantalizing survival: a set of twenty-two short model sermons written in the southern French vernacular, produced by the Augustinian canons of Saint-Ruf in Avignon, though

---

[65] Guillaume de Puylaurens, *Chronique*, ed. and trans. J. Duvernoy (Paris: CNRS, 1976), cap. 1.

the manuscripts survive only in the collections of other communities of canons in Catalonia, indicating that the texts circulated in the period.[66] Both the sermons and the surviving manuscripts are thought to date to the late twelfth century, and are what later scholarship would call 'homilies', that is brief sermons commenting on a few biblical passages, designed to be delivered within the mass, and thus potentially give us a sense of what regular Sunday preaching *might* provide—albeit Sunday preaching connected to a particularly enthusiastic religious order.

The sermons comprise five Sunday sermons (two specifically for use within Lent), and the remainder are linked to key feasts within the Christian liturgical cycle: Christmas Day, the feast of the Innocents, the Purification of Mary, the Annunciation, Palm Sunday, the Octave of Easter, Pentecost, and the feasts of Jean le Baptiste, Marie Madeleine, Jacques, Pierre, Laurent, the Assumption, the Birth of the Virgin Mary, St Michel, All Saints, and the feast of the Holy Cross. Each begins with a short biblical text in Latin, and some, particularly those on the saints, include further biblical extracts. But there is good reason to think that the sermons probably were directed to a lay audience. They are in the vernacular, each one addressed politely to 'lord' or 'lords' (*sennor, sennors*) and on some (though not all) occasions directly translating a biblical passage after first citing it in Latin: for example, from the first sermon, '*Ego sum pan[is] vivus qui de celo descendit*. Eu son pan vius que dexend del cel' ('I am the living bread which came down from heaven', John 6: 51).[67] Whilst there are some simple classical references in certain sermons, these are very clearly introduced, not as if expecting an audience to have any detailed prior knowledge: 'the mother of an emperor of Rome called Theodosius' founded a church to St Peter-in-chains; 'the Roman histories' telling us of events in Rome in the time of St Boniface; mention of 'Helena, the mother of Constantine'.[68]

None of the sermons is lengthy, each probably taking around five minutes to deliver, if the preacher stuck to the script. Overall, they do a mixture of three things: narrate, in a simple fashion, key elements in the story of Christ or the apostles; provide brief but notable examples or explanations to strengthen the laity in their faith; and enjoin good Christian behaviour, particularly regarding penance and almsgiving. Not every sermon combines all three elements, but they

---

[66] For discussion, see J. Moran, 'La prédication ancienne en Catalogne: l'activité canoniale', *CdF* 32 (1997), 17–35. M. Zink, *La prédication en langue romane avant 1300* (Paris: Champion, 1976), pp. 26–28. There are two surviving copies, one in Tortosa (in Occitan) and another in Organyà (in Catalan). On the canons of Saint-Ruf, see Y. Lebrigand, 'Origines et première diffusion de l'Ordre de Saint-Ruf', *CdF* 24 (1989), 167–79. In addition to this collection, I am also aware of the thirty vernacular sermons, dated palaeographically to the 1120s and 1170s, surviving in BnF MS Lat. 3548a; these however seem to be associated with areas to the north of the region studied here, the manuscript being owned by the abbey of Saint-Martial of Limoges. See C. Chabaneau, 'Sermons et préceptes religieux en langue d'oc du XII siècle', *Revue des langues romanes* 18 (1880), 105–46.

[67] A. Thomas, ed., 'Homélies provençales tirées d'un manuscrit de Tortosa', *Annales du Midi* 9 (1897), 369–418, at p. 374.

[68] Thomas, ed., 'Homélies provençales', pp. 405, 415, 416.

are collectively reinforced across the short cycle—thus if we imagine the same congregation hearing all the sermons, as seems to have been intended, certain repeated themes would recur. The narration of the life of Christ and other biblical episodes is predominantly framed to emphasize the power of Christ's conversion of others, in a fairly basic fashion:

> And by the grand marvels which He did, He was followed by the men of all the lands of Judea, of Samaria, of Palestine, of Persia, and Jews and Saracens, Armenians and Greeks, counts and kings, the poor and the rich. The rich followed Him because when they had illness in their houses, He cured them. The poor followed Him because He gave them things to eat and healed them.[69]

An emphasis upon a general attestation of Christian truth is similarly the focus of the narration of the saints' lives in their sermons, though in a few cases these include details which might provide a more specific point of reference or link for a southern French audience. For example, toward the end of the sermon for the feast of Marie Madeleine, we learn that at God's command she was accompanied by St Maximin on a journey to Provence; they arrived in Marseille, where she made a 'hermitage' (at what is now Saintes-Maries-de-la-Mer, to the west of the city), 'and was there for 30 years, during which time she did not drink nor eat but ate only herbs, and never wore shoes or clothes other than the skin of a goat'.[70] After her death, Maximin then buried her at Aix, where he was archbishop, and subsequently the monks carried her to Vézelay. (All of this is apocryphal, and provides some details which were later popularized by Jacobus de Voragine's *Golden Legend*).[71]

When it comes to strengthening the faith of the laity—in the sense of giving them some deeper understanding of the meaning of the events described—the sermons principally provide simple but potentially memorable glosses upon the biblical passages they cite. For example, following the first sermon's theme of 'the living bread', it goes on to explain that 'Our Lord is called bread for this [reason], because he nourishes all creatures: he nourishes the Christians, the Jews, the Saracens, all the birds and the beasts'.[72] In the sermon for Palm Sunday,

---

[69] Thomas, ed., 'Homélies provençales', pp. 386–87: 'E per las grans meravilas qu'el fazia, sil seguion las gens de totas las terras de Judea, de Samaria, de Palestina, de Persida, e Juzeu e Sarrazin, Ermini e Gregs, e comptes e regs, els paubres els rics. Li ric lo seguion per aiso que quant il avion malautes en lurs maisons, el los sanava. Li paubre lo seguion per aiso que el lur donava a manjar e ssanitat.'

[70] Thomas, ed., 'Homélies provençales', p. 402: 's'en venc en Prohensa, et aribet a Marsela, e fo en ermitage a Sca Maria de la mar, et aqui estet XXX anz, que anc non bec ni non manget mais solas erbas cruzas, et anc sabata ni vestiment non ac, mais de pel de cabra.'

[71] See K. L. Jansen, *The Making of the Magdalene: Preaching and Popular Devotion in the Later Middle Ages* (Princeton: Princeton University Press, 2000), pp. 38–39 and *passim*.

[72] Thomas, ed., 'Homélies provençales', p. 374: 'Pans es apelats Nostre Senhor per aiso car el pai otas creaturas: el paix los Xpians, los Judeus, los Sarrazins, toz los aucels e las bestias.'

which elaborates thematically on trees and foliage, the preacher explains that as the disciples had 'olives placed in their hands; and [so] we must have mercy and charity and other good things, because just as oil gives better light than any other things used, so charity and mercy are higher than all other virtues'.[73] This latter example crosses over into the third main aim of the sermons, enjoining pious activity on the audience, mostly in quite general terms. The Christmas Day sermon concludes with an exhortation 'not to have a bad heart with your neighbours' and to 'do good to the poor', in order to gain the blessings of angels.[74] The Lenten sermons focus particularly on charity toward the poor. As one enjoins, 'And for that [reason], lord, do good to the poor, give them things to eat for the love of God, give them shelter in your houses, bring them things from your clothing and other things which are in your power to do.'[75]

Thus the Saint-Ruf sermons give us a sense of how regular preaching, in a parochial setting, to an ordinary lay audience, *might* have worked. They 'educate' the laity in their faith through an emphasis upon the authority of biblical events (even if on occasion in fact departing from what scripture actually reported), some symbolic links between simple but memorable details (bread, olives, oil) and a deeper moral message, and attestation of the truth of the faith through the invocation of miracles. And they seek to remind the laity that certain things follow on from this: confession, penance, and particularly works of charity— 'because, as Scripture says, *Fides sine operibus mortua est*, faith without works is dead (*Fa senes obra morta es*)', as the sermon for Pentecost emphasizes.[76] Given the transmission of these Provençal sermons (Marseille and Aix are both specifically mentioned within the cycle) to the other houses of canons in the Iberian peninsula, it seems highly likely that they would have had a wider circulation in the late twelfth century. But at the same time, we should probably see them as providing a limit case for what was available and possible for a lay audience prior to the thirteenth century. They are pieces carefully crafted by particularly enthusiastic and educated canons, the sermons undoubtedly accessible to those without Latin and propounding some essentials of Christian faith and behaviour, but in comparison to some of the materials produced for preachers in the following century, comparatively modest in their ambitions. Their general structure also rather suggests the sort of form that a less ambitious Sunday sermon might take: the recitation of the requisite biblical passage from a lectionary,

---

[73] Thomas, ed., 'Homélies provençales', p. 396: 'Il portavon las olivas en lur mans; e nost aiam la misericordia e caritat et altras bonas obras, car aixi con oli va sobre totas altres lugors ab las quals es pausats, aixi caritat e misericordia son sobre totas altras vertuz.'

[74] Thomas, ed., 'Homélies provençales', p. 375: 'e per amor de Deu aquil qui an mal cor vais lurs vezins vengon a concordia et a fin e fason ben als paupres'.

[75] Thomas, ed., 'Homélies provençales', p. 381: 'E per aizo, sennor, faitz ben als paubres, donats lor a manjar per amor de Deu, albergats los en vostras maison, acorrez lor de vostres draps e d'aquo que poiria uns quex segon son poder…'

[76] Thomas, ed., 'Homélies provençales', p. 398.

a brief gloss upon it emphasizing that salvation is found only through Christ, a general injunction to be good.

It is difficult to discuss such issues without once again sounding like a time-travelling school inspector. But the point is not to judge whether such provision was 'good enough' or not, measured against some abstract criteria. We need to try to discern, rather, the role that preaching might have played in the instruction of the laity, and more broadly in terms of their participation in Christian culture. For each period we consider, we are likely to decide that there could be a *range* of possible experiences. In the two centuries before 1200, it does seem probable that preaching by a local priest would usually be somewhat minimal. There are two reasons for this. One is that where we first see strong conciliar injunctions to preach to the laity, they are directed not toward the local clergy but the bishop. The other is that when we can start to see what books were located in parish churches (something not really visible in any detail until the mid-thirteenth century, though the bare fact of at least some books was sometimes the case earlier, as we saw in Chapter 1), we do not find any mention of model sermons or other materials produced specifically for preaching. I shall return to this latter point further below, in a wider discussion of texts, but let us first consider who did preaching, and what array of possible experiences might be covered by that term.

The Carolingian council of Tours in 813 ordered that bishops should have a book of homilies containing the essentials of the Christian faith, and that 'each translate the same homilies clearly into the rustic vernacular language...so that all can more easily understand the things that are said'.[77] There are various other injunctions in Carolingian episcopal *capitula* that instruct local priests to preach to the people, and it may well have been that this did often happen; though as is the case with all elements of Carolingian church reform, how widely this was practised perhaps depended rather a lot on which part of the empire one was in, with how enthused and active an archbishop or monastic leader was in the vicinity.[78] But such matters disappear completely in conciliar evidence for southern France in the eleventh and twelfth centuries.[79] It is then intriguing that even within the later

---

[77] Council of Tours, 813, c. 17 (MGH, *Concilia*, 2.I, p. 288): 'quilibet episcopus habeat omelias continentes necessarias ammonitiones, quibus subiecti erudiantur...Et ut easdem omelias quisque aperte transferre studeat in rusticam Romanam linguam...quo facilius cuncti possint intellegere quae dicuntur'. My thanks to Dr Matthew Hoskin for this reference. On the broader context of Carolingian *correctio* around these and other councils in that year, see R. Kramer, *Rethinking Authority in the Carolingian Empire* (Amsterdam: Amsterdam University Press, 2019), chapter 2.

[78] For an optimistic (but judicious) view, see C. van Rhijn, *Shepherds of the Lord: Priests and Episcopal Statutes in the Carolingian Period* (Turnhout: Brepols, 2007); questions of geographical variation are raised by Geneviève Bührer-Thierry in her review of the same book for *The Medieval Review* (<https://scholarworks.iu.edu/journals/index.php/tmr/article/view/16524>, accessed 12 Feb 2021).

[79] One exception north of the region studied here: council of Limoges, 1031 (Mansi XIX, col. 544), there linking together preaching and indication of fasting days (perhaps implying a fairly basic form of sermon). Moreover the injunction explicitly sets out that which *should* be done 'not only at the episcopal see', that is, is implied to be a reform rather than a reflection of current practice.

wave of ecclesiastical councils and synods in southern France that accompanied the crusade and its immediate aftermath, it is bishops and their immediate subordinates who are enjoined to preach—or perhaps one might more accurately say, enjoined to preach more zealously, in part to ensure that the lower clergy were themselves better informed and inspired. Thus the council of Béziers, 1233: 'that both bishops and others should ensure that archdeacons, who have care of souls, are sufficient to preach the word of God to the clergy and to the people'; and that of Arles, 1234: 'each bishop in his diocese should frequently preach the orthodox faith; and when it is fitting, should have preaching done by other honest and wise people'.[80]

Now, other aspects of these and other councils that we have already noted further above make it clear also that the ordinary clergy were certainly expected to be communicating with their flock, instructing them in the faith; and by the council of Albi, 1254, we meet the conjoined instruction that:

> parish priests, by themselves or through others, should take care frequently to expound to the people the articles of faith, on Sundays and feast days, simply and distinctly, so that nobody can thereafter pretend to be veiled in ignorance. And each bishop should do the same in his diocese frequently and diligently. And, when he cannot do it himself, he should have another honest and wise person preach the Catholic faith and these articles plainly and explicitly.[81]

So what is going on here, where the clergy must 'expound' on Sundays, and the bishop must 'preach'? Perhaps a combination of two things. One is the particular concern over *orthodox* belief in a southern French context, which makes it the bishop's responsibility in particular; so even if the local clergy were in fact regularly preaching, the bishop needed to be leading from the front, as it were. The other, though, is again the point that 'preaching' is not really one standard, interchangeable act but really a range of possible events, in terms of its orchestration, content, style, and who delivered it.

We have in a sense already met this. The Saint-Ruf vernacular sermons are focused on particularly important days within the liturgical cycle, occasions in which some people might perhaps expect something a bit special. On other Sundays, though, the norm; for which in that particular collection, bar two possible examples (both of which probably were related to Lent), there was no elaborated model to follow, and as I suggested above, one might imagine then that 'preaching' on those days consisted of a simple elaboration of the set biblical

---

[80] Council of Béziers, 1233, c. 9 (Mansi XXIII, col. 272); council of Arles, 1234, c. 2 (Mansi XXIII, col. 337). This is repeated at the council of Isle-sur-Sorgues, 1251, c. 1: 'de fide catholica frequenter predicanda, secundum quod in Arelatensi concilio olim noscitur constitutum' (Albanès, *Gallia Christiana Novissima*, II, cols 443).
[81] Council of Albi, 1254, c. 17 (Mansi XXIII, col. 836).

passage. Beyond this, as we know, there could be preaching within the confines of the local church—as we have seen a small, dark, limited space in many villages and *castra*, until some time into the thirteenth century, and in many more rural locations long thereafter—but also, as we have seen with both Bernard of Clairvaux at Verfeil and in the opening *exemplum* to this chapter, preaching outdoors to a presumably larger multitude. Preaching by the Good Men in the first half of the thirteenth century, as reported by witnesses to the inquisitors, displays a similar breadth, from small and intimate occasions in people's houses, to grand outdoor events on key days such as at Christmas.[82] Similarly, on certain liturgical occasions there might be preaching by a bishop in a cathedral which could draw a large lay audience not only from the city but from the wider environs; and on much more intermittent occasions, the bishop might also turn up to preach in a particular locality, when conducting visitation of parishes in his diocese. (We frustratingly lack any detailed records of visitation until the 1340s for southern France, but the command to preach when making visitation is present in the same council of Albi cited just above, and visitation was generally understood to be carried out every three years).[83] Preaching might be in Latin or in the vernacular, depending upon the audience. An interesting and detailed agreement made between the abbeys of Grandselve and Saint-Sernin in 1280, concerning the establishment of a new church dedicated to St Bernard erected within 'the parish' of Saint-Sernin in Toulouse by the Cistercians, included among other things provision that high office could be said there 'and that there they can propound and moreover preach the word of God to the clergy and people, in Latin and in the words or tongue of the laity'. However, on those Sundays and feast days when 'it was the custom' for the monastery of Saint-Sernin to give a sermon to 'the people', the new Cistercian church was 'not to preach to the people in the vernacular' before the canonical hour of prime had been rung in the monastery.[84] It is thus possible—though we lack any other evidence specifically to support it—that both abbeys were providing vernacular sermons for the laity in the twelfth century also; though, again, it is explicit that this is something done on a particular set of special occasions, rather than as a regular Sunday service.

[82] See J. H. Arnold, 'The Preaching of the Cathars', in C. Muessig, ed., *Medieval Monastic Preaching* (Leiden: Brill, 1998), pp. 183–205.
[83] Council of Albi, 1254, c. 57. On visitation, see also c. 12 (receiving oath of peace, and checking that people know the articles of faith), and processes involved, cc. 57–60 (Mansi XXIII, cols 835, 848–50).
[84] M. Fournier, *Les statuts et privileges des universités francaises*, 4 vols (Paris: L. Larose et Fourcel, 1890), I, pp. 454–56: '...ibidem clero et populo latinis verbis et laica verba vel lingua verbum Dei proponere valeant et etiam predicare...Item, quod diebus dominicis et festivitatibus Sancti Saturnini, horis quibus fiet sermo, seu consuetum fieri sermonem populo in dicta ecclesia seu dicto monasterio Sancti Saturnini, dicti monachi qui pro tempore fuerint in dicta domo, dicto loco Grandis Silve, in ea domo seu loco proxime dicto...ante horam pulsationis prime statutam in dicta ecclesia seu monasterio S. Saturnini, dicti monachi vel eorum aliquis non predicent populo in vulgari.'

In addition to all of this, by the thirteenth century—though perhaps not until some decades in, as we saw in Chapter 4—there would be quite a lot of preaching in localities delivered by the Brothers Preacher, the Brothers Minor, and other peripatetic friars; by 1260, this was clearly a sufficiently common provision that the council of Arles went to the trouble of forbidding 'those religious' (presumably meaning such mendicant orders) who preached from doing so at times when the laity were supposed to be gathering in their parish church.[85] And there was also clearly preaching by yet other peripatetic preachers, those called *questores* in various episcopal statutes, who appeared to have no permanent base but roamed the churches to prompt almsgiving, whether for themselves or for a particular pious institution such as a hospital. These figures were clearly an irritation, denounced at the Fourth Lateran Council as deceiving people 'by empty imaginary stories or false documents', and thus only allowed to preach if they could present authentic letters from the pope or the local bishop.[86] This injunction was picked up quite frequently in the southern French material from the council of Narbonne in 1227 onward, the council of Montpellier in 1258 specifically noting that 'because many *questores* passing through from other places gather in this province', bishops should not license them unless they have already seen instruction from the archbishop regarding whatever matter they are pursuing for almsgiving.[87]

The example of the *questores* is useful to us, because it highlights another aspect of how preaching might vary: in its core content. Whilst we have no extant sermons given by such alms-seekers, it seems plain that whilst part of their message would coincide with the prompts to almsgiving we have already seen in the twelfth-century Saint-Ruf sermons, it likely also comprised tales of a particular saint, shrine, institution, or notionally good cause; 'empty imaginary stories', shorn of its condemnation, strongly suggests something narrative, perhaps tales of miraculous cures or the like. In partial contrast, there are a just two *exempla* within the twenty-two Saint-Ruf sermons, one drawn from Gregory the Great, another telling a tale 'from England' in praise of the Virgin; the stories those sermons otherwise tell are tales of Christ and the saints, from (notionally) scriptural sources. One of the ways in which preaching developed in the thirteenth century was the further elaboration of explicit storytelling—in the form of morally instructive *exempla*—in mendicant preaching in particular, often stories purportedly drawn from contemporary life; and by the late thirteenth century we have

---

[85] Council of Arles, 1260, c. 15 (Mansi XXIII, col. 1010). Those who refused to obey were thereafter forbidden to preach, or to hear confessions, which strongly suggests that mendicants were the target.
[86] Lateran IV c. 62.
[87] Council of Narbonne, 1227, c. 19; council of Montpellier, 1258, c. 6 (Mansi XXIII, col. 992). See also council of Albi, 1230, cc. 28 and 29; council of Béziers, 1246, c. 5; synod of Carcassonne, c. 1270, c. 20; synod of Carcassonne, after 1311, c. 10; synod of Lodève, 1325, c. 19 (which specifies *questores* for 'hospitals and religious places' who use false letters); synod of Elne, 1326, c. 24 (BM Perpignan, MS 79, fols 77v–78r).

several rich sets of *exempla* produced within the region itself, and perhaps the circulation of other collections produced elsewhere in northern Europe. We shall return further below to discuss in more detail some of the stories told in the *exempla* collections, but should note here that in addition to these materials, various other sets of sermon manuscripts also survive in Toulouse (to focus on one of the most important regional centres), many originally held by the Dominicans, Franciscans, and Augustinians there. By some point in the fourteenth century, these may have included collected sermons by the Dominicans Jacques de Vitry, Nicholas de Byart, Gui d'Evreux, Gérard de Mailly, and Jacques de Lausanne, as well as several anonymous collections of Sunday sermons.[88] So we can safely assume that the wider European efflorescence of sermon production did embrace southern France—though noting the rough dates of these manuscripts, most of which are late thirteenth-century at the earliest, it is important still to note that model sermon collections did not necessarily arrive in all areas as soon as they were first produced by their authors.

Some of these collections can also remind us that not all preaching aimed to provide storytelling: many of the sermon manuscripts now held in Toulouse are rather drier works which seek to explicate theological points via biblical exegesis. (We should also of course remember that many sermons were designed to be preached to other clergy and the religious, rather than to the laity). For example, MS 318, a very plain and practical manuscript written in perhaps the late thirteenth or early fourteenth century, provides Sunday sermons for the entire year, all of which work to unpack spiritual senses of scripture. They do this almost entirely through cross-referencing biblical exegesis, with no use of *exempla* or non-biblical imagery. That for the fourth Sunday in the year, for example, focuses on salvation, taking as its theme Matt. 8: 25: *Domine salva nos perimus* ('Lord save us, we perish'). The sermon begins by explaining the nature of the 'sea' from which salvation is sought, using other biblical references to do so (for example, 'In this sea, moreover, many are in danger and many perish in it, Eccles. 43[: 26],

---

[88] BM Toulouse MSS 312–16, 337, 389 (for various of those named above); anonymous collections MSS 318–23, 335, 336, 343, 344, 876. (NB Gérard de Mailly previously incorrectly known as Guillaume de Mailly—see D. L. d'Avray, *Medieval Marriage Sermons: Mass Communication in a Culture without Print* [Oxford: Oxford University Press, 2001], p. 7). Ownership by one of the religious houses is attested by the seventeenth century, and sometimes earlier, and it is reasonable to assume that in some cases this indicates holdings contemporary to the production of these thirteenth- or fourteenth-century manuscripts, though this obviously cannot be certain. For example, on the one hand, in at least one case (BM Toulouse MS 316, Jacobus de Voragine's Lenten sermons) ownership is noted within the manuscript to be 'the [Franciscan] convent of Saluzzo', in northern Italy; on the other, a collection of sermons by the northern French Dominican Gui d'Évreux says it was owned by one 'Pierre de Monastruc O.P.' (there are several places called Montastruc in southern France), and contains marginal commentary written in Occitan (BM Toulouse MS 313 fols 218v, 222v, 232v, and *passim*). For descriptions of the manuscripts listed further above, see A. Molinier, *Catalogue générale des manuscrits des bibliothèques publiques des départements, VII: Toulouse—Nîmes* (Paris: Imprimerie nationale, 1885), and pp. iv–xii for an overview of their ownership by religious orders.

Let them that sail on the sea tell the dangers thereof).[89] It proceeds by elaborating carefully enumerated points: 'Item, around this salvation note four other things...', those four things initially listed briefly, then returned to in a more extensive fashion, providing further biblical references in each case. The pattern of discovering that each topic has 'four things' to note is continued through all the sermons in the collection, as a sturdy but perhaps rather repetitious bit of intellectual scaffolding. There *is* spiritual instruction in these sermons: a later one, on the text 'And looking up to Heaven, he groaned' (Mark 7: 34), asks us to 'note that the good groan is fourfold', providing a gloss focused on contrition and devotion: 'the first is the groan of sadness for sin...the second is the groan of compassion for the miseries and sins of others...the third is the groan of devotion, and this rushes forth from devotion of the heart and holy prayers...the fourth is the groan of pious desire and love...', with a further biblical passage to illustrate in each case.[90] So these are not by any means purely 'intellectual' works; they provide a sustained gloss on the spiritual landscape, and could quite possibly have been used with a lay audience. But the kind of sermon they provide clearly has a rather different dynamic than those elaborated via stories drawn from contemporary life, or providing simple metaphors by which to understand the mysteries of the faith.

The Circulation of Texts

Every kind of communication, instruction, and guidance discussed thus far in this chapter has ultimately been about oral communication, aurally received. This is of course the correct focus, as in a pre-modern period, most culture was transmitted orally (or visually and materially, as we explored in Chapter 6). But as we have seen, across the thirteenth century there were more texts being produced to try to assist the clergy in the task of educating the laity—synodal books, model sermons, short guides to confession, glosses on the prayers—and beyond those specialist materials, it is important to ask what other religious texts might have been more widely available. It is also worth asking to what degree the Bible was a real, physical presence in this period, and who might have had access to it; and more particularly the New Testament, as a conduit to the voices of the apostles.

As we saw in Chapter 1, in the eleventh and twelfth centuries various local churches had books associated with them, when being gifted or surrendered in

---

[89] BM Toulouse MS 318, fol. 28v: 'In hoc etiam mari, multa sunt pericula et multi in eo pereunt, Eccl. XLIII[: 26] *Qui navigunt mare enarrent pericula eius*'.
[90] BM Toulouse MS 318, fol. 224v-225r: 'Nota quod quadruplex est gemitus bonus. Primus est gemitus doloris pro peccatis...secundus est gemitus compassionis pro miseriis et peccatis alienis...Tertio est gemitus devocionis, et hic prorumpit ex devocione cordis et orationibus sanctis...Quartus est gemitus pii desiderii et amoris...'

charters, though what these were is never specified. Where we do have surviving evidence, it is for liturgical texts, such as the *mixtum* and sacramentary associated with the rural church of Saint-Guilhem-de-Combret (noted in Chapter 3). We are much better informed by the thirteenth and fourteenth centuries, due to a rich survey of ecclesial possessions made by the monastery of Saint-Sernin in 1246, and to the details provided by the visitation records produced in the diocese of Aix in the 1340s that we met in the last chapter. We thus have two rich snapshots of the texts held in local churches, separated by 100 years. The 1246 document provides, in addition to the holdings with Saint-Sernin itself, a detailed list of all items, including books, within sixty-four churches and priories, five within Toulouse itself but the remainder beyond, stretching from the lowlands north of Toulouse into the highlands of the Ariège.[91] The more rural churches tend to have between three and seven books each, and as one would expect these are almost entirely for the performance of the liturgy, most commonly a missal, a psalter, and a breviary. For example, the church of Saint-Jean of Lissac (c. 40 km south of Toulouse) had a 'complete' breviary, a missal, an *officier* (presumably containing the daily cycle of prayers), an epistolary ('*pistoler*'), a psalter, and an ordinal. That of the very rural Suc-et-Sentenac (c. 30 km south-west of Foix) had just a psalter, a breviary, and a missal (or rather a *mixtum*, a missal with some other liturgical materials added, commonly found in southern France). In contrast, the church in Segura (c. 12 km south-east of Pamiers) possessed not only those same three, but an *officier*, a book of the Epistles (*liber epistolarum*), a book of saints (*liber sanctorum*), and 'a certain part of Hraban[us Maurus]' (perhaps his *De institutione clericorum*, found also elsewhere in the region).[92] Other than just possibly what the 'book of saints' provided (only found in that church and one other, however) none of the churches included in the survey had any books of sermons or materials for more elaborated preaching.[93] Nor did any possess bibles, whether in whole or in part, though various of the materials just mentioned would provide copious biblical passages as part of the liturgical cycle.

If we leap forward a century, the visitations in the diocese of Aix carried out by Archbishop Armand de Narcès that we met in the preceding chapter provide another fairly detailed picture of what parish churches contained in that more eastern region. The main thing to note is continuity. As noted in the previous chapter, the visitations between 1340 and 1344 reached 172 different churches in the region, forty of which were formally designated 'rural', implying no resident priest. We cannot directly compare with the earlier inventory as these are different

---

[91] C. Douais, ed., *Documents sur l'ancienne province de Languedoc*, 2 vols (Toulouse: Privat, 1901–4), II, pp. 8–44 (inventory of moveable and immoveable goods compiled 10 to 14 Sept 1246, under the order of Abbot Bernard de Gentiac).

[92] Douais, ed., *Documents...Languedoc*, II, pp. 24, 38, 39.

[93] The one other example is at *Merglos* (possibly Miglos, south of Foix). Another church had a copy of the *Vitas Patrum*, and a third (a priory church) a '*Vitas sanctorum*'. Douais, ed., *Documents...Languedoc*, II, pp. 23, 28, 40.

geographical areas. Moveover the visitation record tends mostly to note only those things which were in need of correction, though occasionally it does list all objects that exist at a particular site, as at the parish church of Sainte-Marie in La Roquebrussane which had a '"responsory" newly bound in green...with five quite beautiful cords' and a 'portable breviary sufficiently good for the usage of the church of Aix, for readings and psalms and certain other less important things'.[94] More often books become visible because the archbishop was ordering that they be re-bound or renewed, and to be kept under lock and key. He was clearly not happy that liturgical texts could get mauled about by lay people, particularly the young: 'regarding the books of the said church [of Trets], nobody should teach or have people taught or permit in this way that the books be touched or handled by children or others, unless when they are saying divine office'.[95] On occasion there does appear to have been a more total lack of texts, though the record also makes it clear that sometimes a priest would bring books with them, in the case of a dependent chapel, for example.[96]

In general, whilst there are various problems reported concerning books, these are mostly about having them put into newer bindings for their own protection, or calling for very old books to be updated to the liturgical round then followed in the diocese. All of those which become visible are liturgical manuscripts, similar or identical to those noted a century earlier in the Saint-Sernin inventory, and once again we do not encounter any books directed specifically toward preaching, nor the Bible or any substantial part thereof, other than via the various liturgical readings. One particular injunction from 7 December 1340, calling for the renewal of liturgical books for the church of *Brachio*, possibly strengthens the case for 'preaching' in regular parochial mass sometimes taking the form of reciting a simple 'homily' gloss on a biblical text: 'Item, as the said church lacks a historical lectionary [*that is, one with readings from the Old Testament histories*] and the gradual of the church, because of its age, is not sufficient for what is now needed, he orders that...the said church be provided with a lectionary for Sundays and other days, with a full set of homilies and with good readings, following the use of the church of Aix'.[97] In contrast, another church—that of Montfuron (just west of Manosque)—was noted as having amongst its various

---

[94] Visitation d'Aix, fol. 14v: 'unum responserium novum coopertum de viridi de nota galicana cum V cordis satis pulcrum...et unum breviarium portatile satis bonum de usu ecclesie Aquensis pro legendario et psalterio et quedam alia minuta'.

[95] Visitation d'Aix, fol. 7r: 'in libris dicte ecclesie aliquem non doceat nec doceri faciat seu permittat libros hujusmodi per pueros aut alios palpari aut tractari nisi dum dicentur divina officia'.

[96] For example, Visitation d'Aix, fol. 12r: 'Item, quia laboriosum nimis esset si sacerdos cum ibit ad celebrandum ad dictam ecclesiam secum portaret missale, officierium, textum et epistolarium de Gayola, ordinavit quod...provideatur ipsi ecclesie de uno mixto in quo sint officia dominicalia et majorum solennitatum anni, quiquidem liber remaneat in dicta ecclesia Santi-Johannis'.

[97] Visitation d'Aix, fol. 24v: 'Item cum dicta ecclesia legendario hystoriarum careat ac ipsius ecclesie officierium propter sui antiquitatem non sit sufficiens moderno attento tempore, ordinavit quod...provideatur dicte ecclesie de uno legendario dominicali et feriali cum suis omeliis bene completo et cum bonis lectionibus secundum usum ecclesie Aquensis'.

books a *liber omeliarum*, which could mean a copy of Gregory the Great's *Homilies* or else a developed set of model sermons like those from Saint-Ruf.[98]

We saw some of the liturgical activity facilitated by these various books in the previous chapter; the point here is to note that on the one hand many, perhaps even most, local churches had texts which provided for the celebration of the mass and for the cycle of prayers and readings, including biblical readings; but on the other, almost none, even by the mid-fourteenth century, seem to have had texts which might allow a local priest further to elaborate on the instruction of the faith. This does not mean that such texts did not exist in our region—some may have been held personally by various clergy rather than being seen as property of the churches themselves—but it does mean that our understanding of the *range* of lay Christian knowledge must incorporate a local textual base that was primarily liturgical rather than instructional.

However, at the same time the New Testament, and the four Gospels in particular, had a very strong symbolic importance. They were, to state the obvious, the very foundation of the apostolic ideals that inspired various strands of piety in the twelfth century and thereafter, as discussed in Chapters 3 and 4. With those developments in mind, it is very interesting to note that invocation of the four Gospels starts to become much more visible in the second half of the twelfth century in the context of oath-taking. Medieval people had of course been making oaths in a wide variety of contexts for centuries, and they were a fundamental sociolegal mechanism in southern French society as elsewhere. If one looks at the cartulary of the Guilhems family, lords of Montpellier (a rare surviving secular cartulary), we can see various people making oaths across the later eleventh and twelfth century. Many of these are made 'on the altar', sometimes specifying also on relics or on the saints.[99] In a very few examples from the earlier twelfth century, we start to find however the following type of phrasing: 'I, Ildefonse, count [of Toulouse] swear... by God and this holy Gospel'.[100] By the later 1140s, there is more regular evocation of all four Gospels, as in a vernacular formula for the oath which 'his men' should swear to the lord of Montpellier *per Deu et per aquestz sanz quatr' evangelis*. By the later twelfth century here, as elsewhere, swearing on the four Gospels had become very common.[101] In monastic and episcopal cartularies we should perhaps not be surprised to find reference to the Gospels

---

[98] Visitation d'Aix, fol. 82v; the book is mentioned along with others in the context of needing to be re-bound.

[99] For example, *Liber instrumentorum memorialium*, pp. 506–07 (no. 316), 1111, oath of fidelity given by Brémond to Guillaume, lord of Montpellier; pp. 84–85 (no. 46), 1152, Guillaume VII making oath to Bishop Raimond; pp. 512–13 (no. 324), 1140. Many other examples *passim*.

[100] *Liber instrumentorum memorialium*, pp. 154–55 (no. 82), c. 1132, mutual oath between Ildefonse count of Toulouse and Guillaume of Montpellier. Similarly, pp. 148–49 (no. 79), 1164, mutual oath between Count Raimond V of Toulouse, and Guillaume VII of Montpellier.

[101] *Liber instrumentorum memorialium*, p. 292 (no. 153), 1147; similarly pp. 275, 283–84, where the dating might be as earlier as 1130.

appearing somewhat earlier, as oaths taken at monasteries were probably more likely to have the requisite textual objects to hand. For example, in a charter from 1105, the *viguier* of Moissac relinquished an annual payment of 5 *sous* to the monastery there, which the monks owed to his father for lands which they held 'in fief'; the *viguier* did this in the midst of mass, and swore 'on the altar of St Pierre with the book of the holy Gospels'.[102] This is actually the earliest example I have located. Taking the very rich records of the cartulary of Aniane and Gellone, it becomes clear that whilst one can find a few examples in the 1120s where the setting is clearly within the monastery itself, one otherwise has to wait until the 1170s for oaths 'on the four Gospels' to become common.[103] Thereafter it is pretty much ubiquitous.

The presence of 'the four Gospels' in such oaths is suggestive, but does not of course mean that complete copies of the actual texts increased across time proportionately to their invocation. As notarial culture spread, a rather practical adaptation of the need for 'the four Gospels' developed: many official civic registers began to contain just the opening pages of the four evangelists, rather than the entirety of all the Gospels. We find this, for example, in the *Livre rouge* of the town of Montauban, where a few folios in the midst of the civic book are given over to just the first pages of the evangelists John, Matthew, Mark, and Luke (in that order); there are many other similar examples.[104] In a few thirteenth-century notarial 'manuals'—the paper booklets in which notaries recorded copies of the documents they produced—the invocation is minimized even further, simply reciting the names of the apostles along with their iconographic symbol, as in this example from the inside cover of the manual of Pierre Amoros, active in Perpignan 1276-77: 'Luke is a bull, Mark a lion, and John a bird. Matthew is a man; these four, God' (*Est luchas [t]aurus leo marchus avisque johannis | Est homo matheus quatuor ista deus*).[105] Presumably, this allowed oaths to be sworn

---

[102] *Cart. Moissac*, no. 176: 'Et sicut dictum est, super altare beati Petri cum libro sanctorum Evangeliorum sic firmavi et corroboravi tenendum in perpetuum. Actum publice sicut in ecclesia, conventu domni Goderanni memoriam agente, inter missarum solemnia.'

[103] *Cart. Aniane*, pp. 93-96 at 94 (no. 9), 1120, letter of papal privileges, monks taking the oath; pp. 315-16 (no. 179), 1125, sale to a monk, with various monks as witness; p. 193 (no. 52), 1150, in presence of prior with various monks as witness. Two other early examples, both 1155, are pp. 204-05 (no. 65), 363-64 (no. 235). Later examples abound: pp. 209 (no. 70), 1173; 372-73 (no. 246), 1173; 325 (no. 186), 1175; 146 (no. 12), 1176; 205 (no. 66), 1178; 163 (no. 25), 1181; 166 (no. 28), 1183; 324-25 (no. 185), 1183, and so forth.

[104] AD T-et-G, 3E121 AA1 [= AM Montauban AA1], fols 117v-119r (following the modern rather than the seventeenth-century foliation).

[105] AD P-O 3E1-6. Same text on inside cover of manual of Arnaud Miro, 1276-78: AD P-O 3E1-8. This little verse is found in a commentary on the Apocalypse written by the Dominican Hugh of Saint-Cher (d. 1263) (*Opera omnia in universum Vetus et Novus testamentum*, 8 vols (Lyon: Ioannis Antonii Huguetan & Guillelmi Barbier, 1669), 7, fol. 381v) and a similar version is quoted in a sermon by another member of that order, Paio de Coímbra, from Portugal, writing before 1240 (see B. F. da Costa Marques, *Mundividência Cristã no Sermonário de Frei Paio de Coimbra. Edição Crítica da* Summa Sermonum de Festivitatibus *Magistri Fratris Pelagii Parui Ordinis Praedicatorum, A.D. 1250, Cod. Alc.5/CXXX-B.N.Lisboa*, unpublished PhD dissertation, Coimbra 2010, online <https://core.ac.uk/

'touching these four Gospels' in synecdoche, the very little part standing for the much larger whole.

In partial contrast to all of this, the evidence from inquisition trials makes it clear that from the later twelfth century at least, texts of the Gospels (and perhaps the whole New Testament) and other religious books did exist in the region, beyond the few held in monasteries and cathedrals and the extracts contained within liturgical books in local churches. These were books found in the hands of the Waldensians and the Good Men, though they sometimes ended up in the possession of the ordinary laity. For example, Pierre Daide of Pradelles-Cabardès testified in 1245 that some twenty years earlier a Good Man called Matthieu had lived for five years in the house of Bernard Daide, a relative (possibly an uncle) of Pierre's; 'and every day Matthieu...taught in the house of Bernard Daide', and when Matthieu died there, Bernard's sons 'had the books of the said heretic'.[106] A copy of the Gospel of St John was intrinsic to the ritual of the *consolamentum* that the Good Men performed to purify the souls of the dying: the book was held over the head of the dying person and ritually kissed by those present. By this route, its symbolic presence would have been further visible to quite large numbers of people across the late twelfth to mid-thirteenth century, given how frequently such events are recorded in inquisitorial witness statements.

It is these 'heretical' associations—though perhaps particularly the apostolicism of the Waldensians as much as the Good Men's ritual use—that led the council of Toulouse in 1229 to ban lay people from possessing religious texts:

> We also make this prohibition: lay people shall not be permitted to have books of the Old or New Testament, except perhaps for the Psalter or a Breviary for the Divine Office, or Hours of the Blessed Mary, as someone may want to have these out of devotion. But we most strictly forbid them having the aforesaid books in vernacular translation.[107]

Advice given to inquisitors by a council at Béziers convened by the archbishop of Narbonne in 1246 reiterated the point: laity were not to have religious books, and neither laity nor clergy were to have them in the vernacular.[108] Very occasionally

---

download/pdf/144022405.pdf> (accessed Feb 2021), p. 328). Whilst the symbols associated with the evangelists date back to the early Church, neither I nor Costa Marques have found any clear origin for the verse, and one suspects that it must have circulated broadly.

[106] Doat 23, fol. 129v: 'prefatus Matheus hereticus docebat cotidie in domo Bernardi Daide...et post quinque annos expletos prefatus matheus hereticus decessit et prefati filii Bernardi Daide habuerunt libros ipsius heretici, de tempore quod sunt viginti anni'.

[107] Council of Toulouse, 1229, c. 14 (A&B, doc. 29). See similarly the council of Tarragona, 1234, c. 2 (Mansi XXIII, col. 329), which further specifies that any such books must be handed to a priest to be burnt, or else the person will be held suspect of heresy. We should also note council of Albi, 1230, c. 19, which forbade priests from mortgaging any books or church ornaments to lay people (Pontal, *Statuts synodaux*, II, p. 14).

[108] Consultation of Béziers, 1246, c. 36 (Mansi XXIII, col. 724; trans. A&B, doc. 37).

we find examples of people in inquisition registers getting into trouble for book ownership, most often when the books were explicitly understood to have come from the Good Men, but occasionally in other circumstances.[109]

There is one notable deposition given by Bernard Raimond Baranhon, a merchant of Toulouse, in 1274. He denied having any particular contact with Waldensians or Good Men, other than having heard some words by a Waldensian in the city some fifty years earlier ('he said that he heard him speaking about how the Lord went about on earth'). But he was questioned specifically about book ownership. Had he ever had any books of the Old or New Testament, in Latin or in the vernacular? He admitted that he 'had from the late Horombel, citizen of Toulouse, a certain book in a mixture of Romance and Latin, in which he often read. And there were written in the said book the Gospels and the Epistles and the Apocalypse'. He kept the book for about three years, and after Horombel's death, gave it to Raimond de Muret, another citizen. Thereafter, he added, he often asked Raimond de Muret to lend him the book back again, but Raimond did not, because 'Jean de *Grosso* had it, and was having it extracted and transcribed'. He thought that Arnaud Farat had a book, similarly extracted from the original. Bernard Raimond also admitted owning a book in Latin containing 'the life of the Blessed Brendan' (probably the *Voyage of St Brendan*), in which he often read. He was further questioned: did he ever possess or had he ever seen a certain book which is called 'the Bible' (*Biblia*) in the vernacular, which begins 'Deceitful Rome'. No, he replied; but he had often heard a certain song made by the *joglar* Guillaume Figueira, which denounced Rome a number of times.[110] We have a very clear picture of book ownership and book sharing among the lay civic elite here, very similar to things one would find in English and northern French evidence in the fifteenth century, for example, alongside a reminder that a vernacular culture held in memory rather than on the written page could sit comfortably alongside this literacy. And at the same time, as the inquisitors pose such specific questions to Bernard Raimond, it is clear that such book ownership could arouse (or be presented as arousing) suspicion over orthodoxy.

Whilst on the one hand, and in concert with the synodal injunctions against lay 'disputation' of the faith discussed above, the prohibition against lay ownership in Toulouse 1229 speaks to ecclesiastical control, it simultaneously indicates that some vernacular translations of scripture were likely to be in circulation, decades earlier than Bernard Raimond's trial. And the exception made for books that the laity might use themselves during mass is extremely interesting—something

---

[109] See generally P. Biller, 'The Cathars of Languedoc and Written Materials', in P. Biller and A. Hudson, eds, *Heresy and Literacy, 1000–1530* (Cambridge: Cambridge University Press, 1994), pp. 61–82.

[110] Doat 25, fols 196r–199v (*Heretics and Inquisitors*, pp. 578–85). I am indebted to Biller, Bruschi, and Sneddon's additional notes on this deposition; for a wider contextual discussion, see also C. Léglu, 'Vernacular Poems and Inquisitors in Languedoc and Champagne, ca. 1242-1249', *Viator* 33 (2002), 117–32.

which we would expect to find in later centuries, but which perhaps indicates, for a few of the socially elite at any rate, a practice already in place by this period. A century later, there is a sliver of a suggestion that copies of liturgical texts in lay hands might not always be the kind of highly precious object we now associate with surviving books of hours and the like. This comes from an inventory made in 1347 after the death of Gailhard de Fenouillet, lord of Coustaussa (a very small *castrum* c. 17 km south of Limoux), which among other things lists the contents of his private chapel: a small silver chalice 'which he left to the chaplain of Coustaussa in his will', a little bell, a chest, and 'a missal which is said to have no value'.[111] Evidence from the mid-fourteenth century cannot be projected back very securely, but the confident assessment that a liturgical book has 'no value' does suggest that by that time at least some examples were not particularly rare or precious objects, even when owned by the laity, at least in this (minorly) noble milieu. On the other hand, Marie-Claude Marandet's thorough analysis of wills from the region (from 1300 onward) finds few texts being left by lay people until the fifteenth century; though this might indicate that such objects were owned by families as much as by individuals, and thus escape notice unless being left to a separate religious institution.[112]

In thinking about lay ownership of texts, and the possibility of them pursuing their own 'instruction' somewhat independently, the injunction from Toulouse 1229 against vernacular religious literature is intriguing, particularly since it is clearly not simply directed against translations of scripture. Southern France famously had a strong vernacular literary culture exemplified by the troubadour poets (though we should remember this is an oral, sung culture as much as a written one), and the ubiquity of literate notaries by the early thirteenth century meant that many people had potential access to written culture. In northern France, by the second half of the thirteenth century, vernacular manuals of religious instruction are apparent, for the elite at any rate: the famous and influential guide to sin and confession *Somme le Roi*, for example (translated into Occitan as *Libre dels vicis e dels vertutz*, the earliest known version dating to some time after 1343).[113] There is one vast Occitan work which stands proud from the landscape— Matfre Ermengaud's *Breviari d'amor*, written between 1288 and probably 1291— and we shall return to that below; but it is worth asking what may have circulated earlier, and in addition to that monument.[114]

---

[111] AD Aude 7 J 51, item 12 (*liasse* containing the family archive of the de Fenouillet family): 'Item in capella unum calicem argenti ponderis sex oncum vel circa que legavit capello de coustantiano in suo testamento, et unam stillam modicam, unum missale non dici valoris et unam arcam.' For *stilla* as variant of *squilla* ('little bell'), see Du Cange, *Glossarium*, under *skella*.

[112] Marandet, *Le souci de l'au-delà*, I, pp. 317–18.

[113] *Histoire litteraire de France* vol. 19 (Paris: Imprimerie nationale, 1898), p. 400; C. Boser, 'Le remaniement provençal de la Somme le Roi et ses dérivés', *Romania* 24 (1895) 56–85.

[114] My research in this area is indebted to R. A. Taylor, *A Bibliographical Guide to the Study of the Troubadours and Old Occitan Literature* (Kalamazoo, Mich.: Medieval Institute Publications, 2015).

Geneviève Hasenhor, who has worked extensively on French vernacular pastoral writings, suggests that in comparison to northern France, the examples from the south in Occitan are relatively sparse.[115] There are a few vernacular verses on religious subjects in the eleventh and twelfth century, several of which are hagiographic, such as the *canso* of Ste Foy (which situates her in Agen, and in addition to the story of her martyrdom, emphasizes her disdain for worldly wealth, and her charitable acts to the poor and to lepers).[116] Whilst troubadour poetry is most strongly associated with the notion of *fin'amors* and courtly matters which stray quite far from Christian notions of morality, there are also some twelfth-century troubadour poems devoted specifically to spiritual topics (we may recall that Bishop Foulques of Toulouse wrote troubadour poetry prior to his religious conversion), as well as a number which voice critical opinions on the Church and its clergy.[117] Certain Christian tropes and images appeared more generally in other works *en passant*, such as worship of the Virgin Mary and assertions of being a 'good Christian'.

A number of Occitan songs address crusade to the Holy Lands, either specifically or in passing; however, here the emphasis and poetic elaboration is very much focused on knightly valour rather than pious endeavour.[118] This is largely the case also with the few Arthurian tales produced in the region. There are three romances composed in Occitan. One was written in the early thirteenth century (*Jaufré*), another about a century later (*Guilhem de la Barra* by Arnaut Vidal), the third (*Flamenca*) some time between the other two.[119] *Jaufré* touches briefly on some aspects of Christian religious culture—attendance at church, almsgiving—though also notably depicts two lepers as evil, child-murdering rapists, thus departing radically from the charitable emphasis more usually displayed toward lepers in Christian culture of the period. *Guilhem de la Barra* is, in part, more engaged with explicitly Christian themes: the hero Guilhem converts his Muslim captor to Christianity via various miracles. However, as Catherine Léglu notes,

---

[115] G. Hasenhor, 'Modèles de vie féminine dans la littérature morale et religieuse d'Oc', *CdF* 23 (1988), 153–70.

[116] A. Thomas, *La chanson de Sainte Foi d'Agen: poème provençale du XIe siècle* (Paris: Honoré Champion, 1925; reprint 1974); English translation by R. L. A. Clark as an appendix to Sheingorn, ed., *Book of Sainte Foy*. A handful of anonymous poems were written around Limoges in the twelfth century—rather further north than the lands on which I focus, though as with troubadour poetry produced by natives to that region, they could have circulated further south. See P. Meyer, ed., 'Anciennes poésies religieuses en langue d'oc', *Bibliothèque de l'École des Chartes*, 5th ser., 1 (1860), 481–97.

[117] For the latter, see translations and commentary in Léglu, Rist, and Taylor, eds, *Cathars and the Albigensian Crusade*, pp. 107–27.

[118] See L. Paterson, *Singing the Crusades: French and Occitan Lyric Responses to the Crusading Movements, 1137–1336* (Woodbridge: Boydell, 2018), particularly chapter 1.

[119] C. Brunel, *Jaufre: roman arthurien du XIIIe siècle en vers provencaux* (Paris: Société des Anciens Textes Français, 1943); R. G. Arthur, trans., *Jaufre: An Occitan Arthurian Romance* (New York: Garland, 1992). Arnaud Vital, *Guillaume de la Barre: roman d'aventures*, ed. P. Meyer (Paris: Didot, 1895). J.-C. Huchet, ed., *Flamenca: roman occitan du XIIIe siècle* (Paris: Union générale des éditions, 1988); M. J. Hubert, trans., *The Romance of Flamenca* (Princeton: Princeton University Press, 1962).

this is a prefatory episode then left unexplored in the main text, which concerns Guilhem's lengthy wanderings, after having been falsely accused of rape.[120] The third romance appropriates an ecclesiastical setting along with various aspects of worship and religious culture in order however to fashion a highly secular tale: in *Flamenca*, the title character is guarded by a deeply jealous husband who only allows her out of her tower in order to attend mass; and, even then, attending whilst confined within a wooden box! The knightly 'hero', Guillaume de Nevers, feigns a religious conversion so that he can assist the church's priest, and thus exchange a few words with Flamenca during the performance of the mass, eventually thus seducing her. As Giulia Boitani demonstrates, the text is studded with both explicit and implicit biblical and liturgical references, deployed however in the service of profane love rather than spiritual faith.[121] Thus, whilst these romances can provide some interesting moments of insight into the reception and reuse of religious themes, none of them display the kind of sustained spiritual engagement found in the latter parts of the northern French Lancelot-Grail cycle, for example.

A number of other vernacular texts from the thirteenth century are extant, with more produced thereafter. Some are hagiographic, such as Bertran de Marseille's life of St Enimie or an anonymous late thirteenth-century life of Marie Madeleine. Others in this genre were produced also in the first half of the fourteenth century: for example, anonymous works relating apocryphal tales of Christ's infancy, the *vita* of the 'beguine' holy woman Ste Douceline of Digne, and Raimon Feraut's *Vida de Sant Honorat*. In the first half of the fourteenth century there was a further efflorescence of religious poetry by troubadours (including Arnaut Vidal) associated with the 'Consistory of Toulouse', a sort of promotional confraternity for Occitan poetry, founded by seven citizen-poets of the city in 1323 but which, as recent scholarship has demonstrated, in fact operated both sides of the Pyrenees. By that period we would clearly find verses in circulation, influenced by Franciscan spirituality in particular, in civic and courtly settings; though it is important to note that these were also self-consciously 'literary' and elite endeavours.[122]

---

[120] C. Léglu, *Multilingualism and Mother Tongue in Medieval French, Occitan and Catalan Narratives* (University Park, Pa: Pennsylvania State University Press, 2010), chapter 2.
[121] G. Boitani, 'A Note on Liturgical and Mystical Quotations in *Flamenca*', *Medium Aevum* 88 (2019), 93–115.
[122] M. Cabré, S. Martí, and M. Navàs, 'Geografia i història de la poesia occitanocatalana del segle XIV', in L. Badia, L. Cabré, and A. Alberni, eds, *Translatar i transferir: la transmissió dels textos i el saber (1200-1500)* (Santa Coloma de Queralt: Obrador Edèndum, 2010), pp. 349–76; B. Fedi, 'Les *Leys d'Amor* et l'école de Toulouse: théorie et pratique de l'écriture au XIV siècle', *AIEO* 9 (2011), 357–70; S. Martí, 'Joan de Castellnou revisité: notes biographiques', *Revue des langues romanes* 121 (2017), 623–60; M. N. Farré, '*Saber, sen i trobar*: Ramon de Cornet and the Consistory of the Gay Science', *SVMMA* 3 (2014), 176–94. My thanks to Catherine Léglu for advice on the developments in scholarship in this area, and more generally.

In terms of the development of a vernacular literature specifically addressing spiritual themes, there are two works of particular interest, both found in a late thirteenth-century manuscript which otherwise contains an Occitan verse translation of the apocryphal Gospel of Nicodemus, a prose translation of a thirteenth-century Latin text that relates the finding of the Holy Cross, and a poetic adaptation of a widely circulated pseudo-Aristotelian letter to the Emperor Alexander providing medical dietary advice. The two pieces of particular interest are a lengthy poem to the Virgin, which begins 'Dona sancta Maria, flors de virginitat', and the *Doctrinal* of Raimon de Castelnou.[123] Whilst there is a statement of ownership in the manuscript from, probably, the sixteenth century (by one 'Ser Jehan du Pon'), we do not know who commissioned it originally, though its clear, unadorned handwriting and practical size, similar to a modern hardback book, suggests something for personal use rather than for show or collective worship. As it is written in the same plain hand throughout, it must be seen as a compilation that was deliberately chosen, the presence of the dietary poem suggesting something broadly in line with later didactic collections combining medical and spiritual advice.[124]

The poem to Mary is quite lengthy, running to 839 lines across nineteen verses. It begins by imploring Mary—'flower of virginity, queen of the virgins, sun of chastity, font of mercy, mother of charity, door to paradise' (similar praises repeated freshly at the start of each stanza)—to intervene for our sins and faults, which commenced with 'our parent, Adam, the first father'.[125] The poet repeatedly emphasizes Mary's regnal power in Heaven, a greater power than that of the 'lords of Hell'; the poet hopes that his soul might be raised to the celestial court alongside St Sauveur, Ste Marciana, and Ste Catherine, 'to be your parishioner and the friend of God'.[126] Those who are 'traitors and disloyal, if they are not of the faith and good Catholics' cannot enter through the gates (or indeed the 'stairs and windows') of Heaven; thus the poet asks Mary to 'defend his soul from the flames of hell' and to pardon his sins.[127] 'I confess my sins, that which I did through my folly, | from evil and from arrogance, by evil gluttony | both great and small,

---

[123] BL MS Harl. 7403, fols 63r–109v ('Dona sancte Maria'), 111r–132v (Raimon de Castelnou). Edited in H. Suchier, *Denkmäler provenzalischer Literatur und Sprache* (Halle: Niermeyer, 1883), pp. 214–40, 241–55, along with all other materials in this manuscript. Note that, in order to emphasize the rhythmic bifurcation of each line, Suchier lays out the poem to Mary in a fashion not actually found in the manuscript.

[124] It should also be noted that the Latin versions of the Gospel of Nicodemus and the finding of the Holy Cross (incipit *Post peccatum Ade*) are found together in several manuscripts; see J. Crick, *The Historia Regum Britannie of Geoffrey of Monmouth, vol IV: Dissemination and Reception in the Later Middle Ages* (Woodbridge: Brewer, 1991), p. 42.

[125] MS Harl. 7403, fols 63r ('flors de virginitat | Regina de las verges soleils de castitat | Fons de misericordia maire de caritat | Porta de paradis...'), 65v ('Si per las noastra falh del nostre parentat | d'Asam lo nostre primier paire per que fo comensat').

[126] MS Harl. 7403, fol. 73v: 'cui es parochiana | E li amic de dieu'.

[127] MS Harl. 7403, fols 74v ('Porta de paradis escala fenestrals | On non pot intrar hom trachers ni deslials | Si non es de la fe e ben catholicals'), 79r ('defen la mia arma de las flammas ardens').

for which the guilt is mine. | I confess to all the saints, and to the one who has dominion | to the most glorious and highest one who has the power | to pardon sins and is the most powerful.'[128] Salvation is ultimately figured as entry into the heavenly court, the petitions figured throughout in a 'courtly' mode to a powerful benefactor, who through their *'cortezia'* extends tender and gracious care toward others.[129] Whilst written in the vernacular, and presenting throughout a sort of elaborate amplification of the *Ave Maria* prayer, the poet also draws upon learned culture, mentioning various biblical and indeed classical figures: David and Solomon, Hippocrates, Virgil, Ovid, and Cato.[130] By the end, it is clear also that the poet is performing, perhaps somewhat strenuously, a very self-conscious orthodoxy. In the final stanza, he rails against those 'who say that the devil made all that You have created' (*Que dis c'a fait dyable tot cant tu as format*), that is against those who believe that the Devil, rather than God, created the world; and he goes on:

> To You are given praises and thanks because You have kept me | from the seed of heresy because I have not been touched by it. | It has been more than forty years since I was warned | by the good sense of my mother and I never departed from it, | never becoming an *ensabbatat* | nor a *berui* nor a *bolgre* nor an *encrivelhat*.[131]

Ensabbatat is a term for a Waldensian, well attested elsewhere (it appears, for example, in the council of Tarragona, 1242, in advice to inquisitors), and *bolgre* ('bougres') is also fairly clear—a heretic, associated with Bulgaria, but found in other thirteenth-century texts to apply to dualist heretics in France. *Berui* and *encrivelhat* are much less certain, though the latter might possibly be read as one who pokes holes (*cribler*) at theological ideas out of foolish pride. In general though, the sense is clear: the poet asserts his orthodoxy. He goes on to say that he was 'firm in the faith', and that he was found thus by 'Bishop G. P., with whom I lived, | Brother B. de Caux, who was my friend, | And Brother P. Cenres who preached to us'. Brother Bernard de Caux might possibly be the inquisitor of the same name, active in the mid-thirteenth century, and Bishop 'G. P.' perhaps

---

[128] MS Harl. 7403, fol. 96r: 'Comfessi mos peccatz c'ai faitz per ma folia | per mail ni per ergulh, per mala glotonia, | del grant tro al menor don la colpa es mia. | Comfessi a totz sanhs et a la seinoria, | al glorios autisme cui es la majoria | de perdonar peccatz et es la maiestria.'

[129] MS Harl. 7403, fol. 96v: 'Seynher [*here addressing Christ*], donatz m'en part que tota sia mia, | aital coma dones a Marta et a Maria et a la Magdalena que per sa cortesia | uns a los tieus cabelhs ab l'enguent que tenia | e lavet los tieus pes a l'aigua que casia | que plorava dels oils, mais d'ins del cor issia.'

[130] MS Harl. 7403, fol. 101r.

[131] MS Harl. 7403, fol. 109r: 'A tu fas laus e gracias car m'en as estremat | del sement d'eregia, car no m'en as tocat. | Mais a de XL ans que m'en a castiat | lo bos sens de ma maire e m'a entrecelat, | que hanc no m'en parti per nulh essabatat | per berui ni per bolgre ni per encrivelhat.'

Guillaume Pierre, bishop of Albi (1185–1227). We do not have to read this as literal testimony—troubadour poetry has a habit of naming and commenting on people, in a similarly allusive fashion, without this necessarily meaning that the poet has direct knowledge of those of whom he speaks—but the implication of attesting orthodoxy against heresy is extremely clear.[132]

The poem to Mary is anonymous, despite this final bout of name-dropping, but the following work is by a named author, Raimon de Castelnou, who was active in Languedoc, probably in the later thirteenth century, and who also produced a few other poems.[133] His *Doctrinal* exists also in another manuscript (Florence, Bibl. Laurenziana, Ashburnham 40b). He was, he asserts in the conclusion to the piece, 'not a lettered man' but a knight 'of poor heritage', who was instructed in doctrine (*endoutrinatz*) by 'good clergy'. The *Doctrinal* (which he names thus several times) is also presented as a poem in the Harley manuscripts, its 383 lines arranged unequally over fourteen verses.[134] Whilst the 'Dona Sancta Maria' poem can be read as a huge elaboration of the *Ave Maria*, the *Doctrinal* tackles the whole schema of the articles of faith, albeit more briefly: the seven sins, and the seven virtues which can be opposed to them; the precepts of the *Credo in Deum*; the importance of paying tithes; the prayer to the Virgin; the Ten Commandments; the seven sacraments; the seven works of mercy. Raimon not only sets out these precepts but also provides what amounts to spiritual counsel, emphasizing the possibility of making amends for sin, and the hope for future salvation. At the end of the poem, he says that he wishes all Christians might know of it, since there are many men who would benefit from hearing it every day (as he himself would), in pardon for their sins, 'until each was thus affirmed in their faith'.[135] Whilst there is not quite the same strenuous assertion of orthodoxy as in the preceding poem to the Virgin, some sense of it is still present: 'My faith and my belief is in God alone | and in the holy Virgin from whom He was born',[136] and he presents his *Doctrinal*, he says, to make amends for the many 'bad songs' (*crois cantars*) he had previously written. Giannetti thought the work dated to the mid-thirteenth century, though more recently Alessio Collura has suggested sometime between 1280 and 1290.[137] In either case, it is an interestingly early moment for a layperson to address the whole range of the articles of faith. For comparative context, we can

---

[132] On this poem, and on the *Doctrinal*, see Léglu, 'Vernacular Poems and Inquisitors' and C. Léglu, *Between Sequence and Sirventes: Aspects of Parody in Troubadour Lyric* (Oxford: Legenda, 2000), chapter 1, though as noted above and below, some re-dating of *Doctrinal*, at least, may now be necessary.

[133] A. Giannetti, *Raimon de Castelnou: Canzoni e Dottrinale* (Bari: Adriatica Editrice, 1988), edits the *Doctrinal* and translates into Italian.

[134] The Italian manuscript runs to 400 lines, and this is reflected in Giannetti's edition.

[135] MS Harl. 7403, fol. 132v: 'tro que cascus si fos en las fes afermatz'.

[136] MS Harl. 7403, fol. 119r: 'Ma fes e ma crezensa es en Dieu solament | et en la sancta Verge don venc a naissement'.

[137] A. Collura, *Sens e razos d'una escriptura: il Vangelo occitano di Nicodemo* (Rome: Nuova Cultura, 2018), p. 29, though without specifying his grounds.

note, for example, that in England, the archbishop of Canterbury John Pecham issued his influential injunction *Ignorantia sacerdotum* in 1281. That called for (though did not in itself provide) a similarly broad range of instruction, and has often been taken as something of a high and perhaps rather optimistic point regarding lay catechism.[138] Raimon clearly does attempt to allow a lay audience to attempt to know and to believe more than just 'simply' or 'implicitly', if we compare his poem with the synodal materials discussed earlier in this chapter.

As noted above, one other work looms large over this landscape: the *Breviari d'amor* written by Matfre Ermengaud between 1288 and perhaps 1291. Once thought to be a Franciscan author, Ermengaud is now recognized as having been a secular master of law, active in Béziers; he ended his days in the Benedictine abbey of Saint-Aphrodise in Béziers, possibly as a lay member of the community.[139] The *Breviari* is a staggeringly lengthy quasi-encyclopedic poem, running over 34,597 lines of Occitan. It exists in fourteen complete manuscripts (the two earliest thought to date to the 1320s, one produced in Toulouse and the other in Lérida), plus four other incomplete copies, and another fourteen independently surviving fragments. It is 'encyclopedic' in terms of the breadth of its explanations and glosses on the natural world that God had created, from the nature of the stars, planets, and the Zodiac, to the meaning of the weather and the seasons, precious stones, animals, and the effect of the humours on the human body, among various other such matters. Early on Matfre states that it is a didactic work of instruction, for 'lay men who do not have great knowledge' (ll. 538–39, *Laiga gen que non han granda scientia*). It is however very much more than a work of simple instruction, and ultimately embraces a profound philosophical and didactic intent: in the words of the late Peter Ricketts, who produced the modern edition of the text, it is a form of treatise, a *summa*, in which Matfre sought to demonstrate the ultimate centrality and harmony of love in its various forms. 'As the title indicates, it is love which gave rise to the creation of the world. That love manifests itself in diverse forms, distinguished by whether they orient to God or to humanity.'[140] Thus Matfre tries, ultimately, to harmonize the *fin'amors* of the troubadour tradition with the love of God and the charitable love of neighbours. He does this not by attempting to argue that they are all the same, but by arraying

---

[138] F. M. Powicke and C. R. Cheney, eds, *Councils and Synods, 1205–1313*, 2 vols (Oxford: Clarendon Press, 1964), II, pp. 900–05; discussion in Arnold, *Belief and Unbelief*, pp. 35–38.

[139] His status as lay brother is argued by Ricketts (in the book cited below), based on his appearance in a document from 1322 recording those monasteries owing royal taxation. However, there is nothing in the document to clarify his status within the foundation; it certainly lists other monks by their role in this and other abbeys. See E. Carou, 'Compte et répartition des décimes perçues sur le clergé du diocèse de Béziers', *Bulletin de la Société archéologique, scientifique et littéraire du Béziers*, 2nd ser., 4/ii (1867), 113–39 at p. 122.

[140] P. T. Ricketts, *Connaissance de la littérature occitane: Matfre Ermengaud (1246–1322) et le Breviari d'Amor* (Perpignan: Presses universitaires de Perpignan, 2012), p. 43.

them in a balanced structure; homology presented as a revelation of a deeper metaphysical structure.[141]

Within this overarching purpose, the text addresses a wide array of spiritual topics: angels, demons, God's will, predestination, Original Sin, the life and miracles of Christ—too much in fact to discuss in detail here, though I shall return to his extensive discussion of confession in the following chapter. How, then, should we understand the *Breviari d'amor* in terms of wider lay spiritual instruction? It shows us a layman engaging in a sustained and self-directed fashion with ecclesiastical works of edification. In Matfre's discussion of preaching (ll. 12,985–13,212), as Michelle Bolduc has demonstrated, he draws considerably from Gregory the Great's *Cura pastoralis*, and he cites various patristic authorities at different points in the text.[142] Similarly, his lengthy discussion of the practice of confession (ll. 16,783–19,191, itself preceded by a substantial discussion of the origins of sin) very clearly parallels Latin guides to confessors. And Matfre does this without the explicit abasement to clerical authority performed by Raimon de Castelnou or the anonymous author of 'Dona sancta Maria'. The *Breviari*'s overall spiritual/intellectual engagement—to make it possible to discuss God's love and *fin'amors* in the same work—speaks eloquently to a cultural tension which one might otherwise think was simply ignored by writers who stuck resolutely to their own genre.

So on the one hand, the *Breviari* could be seen as a pinnacle in the development of lay spirituality, unthinkable in its reach and grasp a century earlier, prompted, but by no means simply dictated, by the wider encouragement to lay instruction discussed earlier in this chapter. On the other hand it is a *pinnacle* and not the whole edifice. Matfre is unusually learned, and draws upon an enviable range of both vernacular and Latin literature; he is of a piece with the anonymous *Dona sancta Maria* poet, citing Virgil, Ovid, and Cato.[143] Whilst the *Breviari* clearly was a success, we should note that many of the manuscripts are heavily illuminated, in a programme which Federico Botana has convincingly argued was designed by Matfre himself.[144] These are elite manuscripts, in other words, and whilst the *Breviari*'s vernacularity might make it more accessible to a much wider audience, we would need to be very cautious in assuming that it would reach much beyond high social levels.

---

[141] S. Kay, *The Place of Thought: The Complexity of One in Late Medieval French Didactic Poetry* (Philadelphia: University of Pennsylvania Press, 2007), chapter 1. Though see also M. Bolduc, 'Troubadours in Debate: The *Breviari d'Amor*', *Romance Quarterly* 57 (2010), 63–76.

[142] M. Bolduc, 'The *Breviari d'Amor*: Rhetoric and Preaching in Thirteenth-Century Languedoc', *Rhetorica* 24 (2006), 403–26.

[143] On the 'learned' strand within troubadour culture more broadly, see G. Brunel-Lobrichon, 'La formation des troubadours, hommes de savoir', *CdF* 35 (2000), 137–48.

[144] F. Botana, 'Virtuous and Sinful Uses of Temporal Wealth in the "Breviari d'Amor" of Matfre Ermengaud (MS BL Royal 19.C.I)', *Journal of the Warburg and Courtauld Institutes* 67 (2004), 49–80, at pp. 50–52.

Thus, that the *Breviari* came to exist is an extremely important waymarker. It attests to the desire by a highly educated layman to write authoritatively in Occitan about spiritual matters, and, notwithstanding the concerns of various bishops and inquisitors over lay people discussing the Christian faith, similarly attests to his cultural and political ability to do so by the late thirteenth century. However, *that* it existed, and was copied, does not mean that we should assume it actually came to address, directly or indirectly, all the laity who 'lacked knowledge'. Thus it is not an Occitan equivalent of something like the very widely circulated vernacular sermon cycle written by John Mirk in later fourteenth-century England. What the *Breviari* shows, rather, is that by the late thirteenth century lay religiosity was itself further stratified, across a combination of intellectual, social, and spiritual indices. Christianity had long been something to which one could gain differential access through personal material resources, as we have seen in discussion of burial, memorial masses, and charitable foundations in earlier chapters. It had always been differentiated through depth of spiritual commitment: the rare example of a Pons de Léras, Valdes of Lyon, or Francis of Assisi would shine out through the depths of their sacrifice and the heights of their devotion. But by the later thirteenth century it was also something at which certain lay people could become particularly adept intellectually—even against the continued concerns that ecclesiastical authorities held regarding unbridled and independent lay engagements with the faith.

Christianity as Storytelling

Whilst Matfre Ermengaud made use of an intellectual system, his 'tree' of love, much of Christian culture addressed the laity not via a formalized structure, but as a tale unfolding over time. As I have suggested at the start of this chapter, stories allow a greater flexibility to the experience of faith, more easily holding in abeyance the potential disjunctures that might prompt concerned enquiry, and narrating that which might prompt incredulity if presented as a bald proposition.

Core Christian stories—the story of Adam and Eve's fall, the story of Christ's passion, the stories of various specific saints, and their subsequent miraculous doings—were of course a fundamental part of Christianity from its earliest centuries. They were soon joined by stories of Christian martyrs and saints, from the early centuries of the Church. These stories all continue, and indeed multiply, in the period of change addressed here; indeed, many *exempla* collections drew upon the tales found in Gregory the Great's late sixth-century *Dialogues*. But many new stories also appeared, stories like the one about the sermon-avoiding young man and the evanescent gold with which we began. Many of these stories were collated, shared, and preached, particularly by peripatetic mendicants; an element of medieval culture that we can be pretty certain *was* 'broadcast' widely and experienced by many. There are a number of important thirteenth-century *exempla* collections produced (for the most part) in northern Europe—those of Jacques de Vitry, Étienne de Bourbon, and Thomas de Cantimpré most famously—and there was certainly some circulation of these in the south by the late thirteenth century.[145] But there are also some less well-known collections of tales produced *in* the south, all by anonymous compilers, and it is upon these that I will concentrate. They comprise: the Franciscan compilation already mentioned at the outset of the chapter, dating to the later thirteenth century;[146] a collection made by a Sack Friar (another mendicant order, suppressed however in 1274) of a similar date;[147] and another early fourteenth-century Franciscan collection.[148] To these we could also add the narratives of miracles relating to the shrine of Marie Madeleine, founded following the discovery of her relics at Saint-Maximin in 1279, which were collated soon after by the Brother Jean Gobi the elder, of the Order of Preachers.[149]

Whilst I have focused in this chapter particularly on the developments around the core requirements of faith for the medieval laity, it is in these stories for use in sermons that we find another fundamental development in making lay *religion* in the thirteenth century. Collectively, they seek to communicate, and to encourage their lay audience to embrace, wider aspects of Christian culture, comportment, behaviour, and belief. This is notably the case also in stories about saints. As already said, stories of saints long pre-exist the thirteenth century, but in this period they start to include tales not only of the saints' powers (to heal, to punish) but tales also of lay behaviour, spiritual edification, and pious interiority. We will meet details from such stories and *exempla* in subsequent chapters, as they illuminate a variety of themes and facets of Christian life. Here, I will focus on what some of them can show us about lay education in the core aspects of faith, and its

---

[145] There is a previously unnoticed partial copy of Étienne de Bourbon in the Bibliothèque municipale, Albi: MS 28 (145), listed by earlier archivists as an anonymous treatise on the seven sins. Stories from Jacques de Vitry and Étienne de Bourbon appear heavily in the compilation by the anonymous Sack Friar mentioned below.

[146] BnF MS Lat. 3555, edited in Welter, 'Un nouveau recueil franciscain d'exempla'.

[147] BM Arras MS 425 (formerly MS 1019), fols 77r-111v, edited in J. Th. Welter, 'Un recueil d'exempla du XIIIe siècle', *Revue des études franciscains* 30 (1913), 646-65, 31 (1914), 194-213, 312-20. There is another copy, largely identical in terms of content: BL MS Add. 60390, an early fourteenth-century manuscript of 46 folios that contains just this collection, written in very small handwriting; very clearly a *vade mecum* manuscript, measuring 138 mm × 100 mm.

[148] BL MS Add. 33956, fols 2r-90v, described and discussed in J. Th. Welter, *L'exemplum dans la littérature religieuse et didactique du moyen âge* (Paris: Guitard, 1927), pp. 265-72. The compiler appears to have been active across southern France in the early fourteenth century, mentioning various specific ecclesiastical figures there; he then seems to have moved to England, gathering additional stories, principally from East Anglia.

[149] Jean Gobi l'ancien, *Miracles de Sainte Marie-Madeleine*, ed. J. Sclafer (Paris: CNRS, 1996). Gobi was born in Alès, entered the Order of Preachers in 1275 at Sisteron, studied in Paris, and was by 1293 a theologian at Béziers, becoming a prior at Montpellier in 1302 or 1303. He was probably the uncle of the Jean Gobi who compiled the *Scala Coeli* exempla collection in the 1330s—though that collection of tales was not focused on the region, and mostly had success in northern France. See Jean Gobi Jr., *La scala Coeli*, ed. M.-A. Polo de Beaulieu (Paris: CNRS, 1991).

wider dynamics; and also what they demonstrate regarding broader aspects of storytelling, story-sharing, and indeed story-*making* in the middle ages.

In terms of the core tenets of lay instruction, many *exempla* sought to underline the importance of the fundamentals that we have already met, echoing the concerns of the synodal texts. Their narrative form allows them to skirt some of the potential pitfalls and complexities that specific tenets might engender. By the thirteenth century there were, firstly, many tales brought into circulation that seek to demonstrate the truth of the presence of the incarnated Christ in the Eucharist.[150] In one *exemplum* a youth who had joined the Order of Brothers Minor sees angels in the form of white doves appearing in the mass when the priest elevates the host, one having a companion in the form of a very beautiful boy. It is important to note, as in other examples, that the story emphasizes what the youth *sees* rather than making a claim for a universal transformation that might not in fact be experienced by all.[151] (Interestingly, in this period at least, we do not tend to find local origination of the anti-Jewish stories that become common elsewhere in Europe, in which the truth of the Eucharist is emphasized through punishment or conversion of Jews who mistreat it).[152]

Secondly, lay attendance at mass is emphasized bluntly. In one tale, a man 'dedicated to carnal vices' never went to church, 'even on feast days'. Four black and horrible demons seized him, saying that 'a living man who has contempt for all good may be swallowed down to Hell', and began to carry him off. But the words 'of the prophet' were brought to his memory (implicitly despite his prior lack of attention): 'Whatever hour the sinner repents, all his iniquity shall not be recalled', and immediately he began to weep.[153] The demons vanished, and he found himself alone, naked, and terrified in the middle of town. But instead of going to his house, he went straight to church, still naked. The people there, amazed, asked him what he was doing, and with great tears he related what had happened.[154] An accompanying story tells that a 'certain peasant' (*rusticus*), when asked by others to go with him to church on Sundays and feast days, would say 'I shall prepare a meal and take care of those things that will give my body sustenance for a long while.' When on a certain feast day he went down to the seaside before lunch, he was suddenly struck dead, and immediately devils dragged his

---

[150] More generally, see M. Rubin, *Corpus Christi: The Eucharist in Late Medieval Culture* (Cambridge: Cambridge University Press, 1991).

[151] BL MS Add. 33956, fol. 23v: 'ut et angelos adinstar columbarum albarum circa elevacionem corporis christi frequenter videret, ac unum de illis familiarem habuit qui in forma pulcherrima pueri'.

[152] Elsewhere in Europe: M. Rubin, *Gentile Tales: The Narrative Assault on Late Medieval Jews* (London: Yale University Press, 1999).

[153] The precise saying he recalls is not actually scriptural, but other texts of the period similarly have it as a (mis)quotation from Ezek. 33: 12; see, for example, *Gesta Romanorum*, ed. H. Oesterley (Berlin: Weidmannsche Buchhandling, 1872), p. 353 (cap. 55).

[154] Welter, 'Un nouveau recueil franciscain d'exempla', p. 454 (no. 41).

soul to hell.¹⁵⁵ We have already met, at the start of this chapter, a story emphasizing the importance of attending sermons, and others could similarly be attested. The anonymous Sack Friar says that he himself saw a citizen of Montpellier who cared for his son (perhaps by implication, an infant child) 'with a foolish love', and who therefore did not go to church for more than three months, nor heard sermons, nor wished to visit religious houses; his son later decided to become a monk, and thus the man 'lost both himself and his son'.¹⁵⁶ These are, we should remember, stories to be delivered in a sermon to those who *were* actually in attendance—but help then to remind them why they ought to do so, appealing perhaps both to the sense of obedience of those who never missed a Sunday, and nudging the consciences of those who were less diligent. Not all the stories rely on punishment. One tells of a man called Guillaume who lived in Muret and was particularly devoted to getting children to attend church (one remembers the synodal injunctions discussed earlier, about children attending for instruction on Sundays). When, one evening, he died, he was to be buried in the morning without a funeral. But, 'marvellous to tell', all the children of the town, led and inspired by God, spontaneously went to the church and sat vigil.¹⁵⁷

We would struggle to find *exempla* that addressed the complexities of the Trinity, but there are a few which elaborate on the life of Christ. For example, the thirteenth-century Franciscan collection shares a further elaboration on the story of the loaves and the fishes, 'when Jesus preached next to the sea of Tiberias'. There was there 'the sweetest well' around which however the Jewish elders were sitting, such that the lesser people and thirsty minors could not get to it. One of the people petitioned Mary: 'Tell your son that He should give us water to drink, because we lack any, nor can we get to the well.' In response, Christ performed an additional miracle: sending the people to the sea shore, they found that 'the water which first was salty was made sweet; and from that moment, right up to today, the well was made salty'.¹⁵⁸ In a separate short *exemplum* the same collection claims moreover that the well upon which Jesus sat when the Samaritan woman came to use it (John 5: 6-29) could henceforth never be touched or covered by sand, despite the strong winds which blew in that place.¹⁵⁹ In both cases, it is notable that the stories work as additions to the existing biblical tales—implying prior knowledge of the latter by the audience.

What most *exempla* address though is moral behaviour, narrating the punishment of sins and the reward of virtues. I shall save detailed discussion of some of these for later chapters, when dealing with confession and wider spiritual discipline, but it is useful to note here how they address areas of sinful behaviour that

---

[155] Welter, 'Un nouveau recueil franciscain d'exempla', p. 454 (no. 42).
[156] Welter, 'Un recueil d'exempla', p. 313 (no. 212).   [157] BL MS Add. 33956, fol. 35v.
[158] Welter, 'Un nouveau recueil franciscain d'exempla', p. 596 (no. 128).
[159] Welter, 'Un nouveau recueil franciscain d'exempla', p. 596 (no. 129).

had *become* such over the twelfth century: usury and blasphemy. Quite a few stories in the southern French collections address usury, and tend to take what it is for granted, as something the audience would already recognize. 'In the diocese of Béziers there was a usurer, and the lord of the *castrum* tolerated him.' By 'divine justice' he was driven insane, and ran amok, murdering the lord, a certain girl, a man, and then his own brother; the townspeople stoned him to death.[160] 'One of St Antoine's pigs who was fed through begging in Castres in the area of Albi' wandered into the house of a certain usurer and immediately fled 'as if being pursued by a wolf'. The usurer put out various bits of nice food, but the pig fled again just as before.[161] (Pigs of St Antoine are attested elsewhere in medieval Europe: they were unwanted runts that were allowed to forage freely, and were then to be slaughtered to feed the poor, in theory at least.) 'At Saragossa, a city in Spain' some very bright lightning fell into the city square, then circled it, weaving between the feet of many people, until it entered a certain usurer and, leaving the others unharmed, killed him.[162] 'There was in the town of Agen a famous usurer who, through many and diverse usurious contracts, gained many lands, vineyards and possessions.' His vines and grain were destroyed by a magical hail of stones, bringing him to repentance; he sold all his goods and gave the proceeds to widows, orphans, to hospitals, and to the poor, then taking up a religious habit.[163] Regarding blasphemy, the tales recognize the circumstances in which it was likely to occur—though this did not mitigate the spiritual fault. A knight in Port-Sainte-Marie (near Agen) was playing dice with a friend in the porch of a chapel dedicated to the Virgin Mary. As the game went badly, he began 'to blaspheme horrendously about Lord Jesus and his pious mother. And when he piled up and trampled down blasphemies, behold, Our Lord descended on him and began to contort his mouth and lips', stretching them into a horrendous grimace, and making his whole body puffed up. He died soon after.[164] Another noble young man, in the diocese of Lectoure (the city itself is about 30 km south of Agen) became gravely ill, and medics and others had to make it clear to him that he was going to die. And 'seeing that he could not evade it, he began to blaspheme horribly the name of God and of the most high mother of Christ'.[165]

---

[160] Welter, 'Un nouveau recueil franciscain d'exempla', p. 472 (no. 113).
[161] Welter, 'Un nouveau recueil franciscain d'exempla', p. 468 (no. 101).
[162] Welter, 'Un nouveau recueil franciscain d'exempla', p. 471 (no. 111).
[163] BL MS Add. 33956, fol. 19r: 'Fuit quidam in villa ageni usurarius famosus qui multis et diversis contractibus usurariis acquisiverat terras vineas et possessiones multas... Omnia bona sua distraxit et viduis, orphanis, hospitalibus et aliis pauperibus misericordie dispensavit.'
[164] BL MS Add. 33956, fol. 5r: 'Contigit in Portu Ste Mari quod quidam miles coram porta capelle beate virginis ludebat cum taxillis cum quodam compatre suo... Incepit... orrendum blasphemare de domino ihesum et matre pia eius. Et cum exageraret et conculcaret blasphemas, ecce nostra dominum descendit super eum et os et labia contorquere incepit... et inflari in toto corpore...'.
[165] BL MS Add. 33956, fol. 5v: 'videns quod non poterat evadere incepit nomen dei et nomen de ultissime matris christi horribiliter blasphemare'.

Besides the punishment of sin, or the enjoinment of good works, a few tales also address issues of inner spiritual intention. An angel shows a hermit three mills, one powered by wind, another by water, a third driven round by men or animals, and moralizes them. The windmill symbolizes those who do not do any good works 'except when raised up to it by the winds of vainglory'. The watermill indicates those who do good works in times of trouble, but 'in times of peace retreat from the Lord'. The mill driven directly by the labour of men (pushing at it with their chests) 'are those who continually have in their breast memory of the Passion of Our Lord Jesus Christ'.[166] Another story: 'At the time that the king of Castile besieged the city of Seville', there was in that region a certain sinner who, whenever he heard the name of Mary, would immediately genuflect and say the *Ave Maria*. But one night when he slept, he heard the Mother of God say to him 'Miserable sinner, confess, because you will die.' Believing that he had just dreamt it whilst asleep, he paid no heed. But when this was repeated on a second and then a third night, he began to fear, and went to find a Brother Minor to whom he could confess, explaining to the friar that he never actually did any good works, he just bowed and prayed at the name of Mary. (He was hit by a stone from a trebuchet soon after, and died.)[167]

Three mills, a naked man attending church, a peasant falling dead at the seaside, a usurer killed by lightning, a hail of stones—whilst the *exempla* do their work as stories partly through narrative (a situation, a transformation, an outcome), they also deploy striking images likely to stick in the minds of their audience, proffering a store of moral mnemonics. Stories told against 'advocates' in the Franciscan collection, for example, take the primary sin associated with lawyers—tricky speech—and hammer it home via shocking tableaux. A supercilious advocate, who had sniggered at a poor widow when she beseeched aid from the crucifix during her court case against his client, falls to the ground beset by demons, 'continually frothing at the mouth' until his death. The son of an advocate waits three days after his father's death, then goes to view the corpse, to see if he paid any penalty for his lawyerly ways: he discovers a hideous toad gnawing on his father's tongue (the son abandons his inheritance). An advocate from Montpellier, on his deathbed, finally attempts to make confession and come to penitence. But rather than speaking, he 'chews' most horribly, as if a dog with a bone, and then extends a horribly long, fat tongue, so large he can hardly get it back into his mouth.[168]

Other stories use a different tactic, deploying familiar patterns to make them memorable, the same thing happening three times over, for example, as in the *exemplum* already noted about the man saying the *Ave Maria*, or the image of the

---

[166] Welter, 'Un recueil d'exempla', pp. 208–9 (no. 185).
[167] Welter, 'Un nouveau recueil franciscain d'exempla', pp. 618–19 (no. 203).
[168] Welter, 'Un nouveau recueil franciscain d'exempla', pp. 597–98 (nos 133–35).

contrasting mills. Another such tale tells of a remote valley where the inhabitants built a beautiful church which fell down unexpectedly; was restored, and again fell down; rebuilt, again collapsed. Eventually an angel appeared to 'a certain good man' there and explained that this kept happening because they did not give any alms to the poor.[169] The repetition *is* the story, and delivers the moral message; and the very fact of repetition might strike an implicit chime for those who hear the same moral messages time and again in different sermons.

Some stories sought to horrify or to scare; others used humour. A priest was performing the mass in a nobleman's private chapel, and a mime (the nobleman's entertainer) mimicked him, making those present laugh. The mime began jokingly to climb onto the priest's shoulders—at which point he was seized by a demon, who dragged him out onto the roof via a small window, and then, through a small opening 'through which flowers were thrown during Pentecost', threw him back down onto the floor of the chapel. At which point the mime said, 'Alas, Lord God, it is very hard to play with you!' The devil dragged him off, and he was never seen again.[170] The story both invites laughter and narrates its punishment; a neat trick. From the Sack Friar collection: 'I heard that a certain young man asked his father to give him two wives.' The father says, 'Son, wait and see a bit, first I'll give you one wife, and at the end of the year, if you want to marry another, I'll arrange it.' After a year, the question is posed—and the son says that he doesn't even want the one wife. Another tale follows, in which people debate how to punish someone who committed a terrible crime. 'Make him marry my wife,' says one.[171] Misogyny threads through various other tales—the focus often being the vanity of women, as a moralized point—but in these cases, it seems likely that the humour engages with stereotypes that entwine with wider lay culture.

Thus there are a variety of different ways in which the *exempla* attempt to work, to reshape and reinforce Christian culture (and we shall further explore various aspects of this in subsequent chapters). In addition to the tactics already noted, we could add occasions when the framing of the story—its claim to veracity strengthened by specificity of time and place—cites details with a further implicit message. For example (as above), when 'the king of Castille besieged the city of Seville': this being 1247–48, and an occasion of major Muslim defeat by Christian forces in the Iberian peninsula. 'When Raimond, count of Toulouse was, with his followers, excommunicated' begins one tale about excommunication more generally. 'When the noble man Richard de L'Isle, at the time of Raimond count of

---

[169] Welter, 'Un nouveau recueil franciscain d'exempla', p. 605 (no. 156).

[170] Welter, 'Un nouveau recueil franciscain d'exempla', pp. 600–01 (no. 144). The practice of dropping rose petals from the ceiling of cathedrals at Pentecost is attested in Rome, and indeed still practised today at the Pantheon; and apparently in France also, symbolizing the descent of the Holy Spirit: C. Joret, *La rose dans l'antiquité et au moyen âge: histoire, légendes et symbolisme* (Paris: Émile Bouillon, 1892), p. 393. The *exemplum* here suggests private chapels could also have adopted the custom.

[171] Welter, 'Un nouveau recueil franciscain d'exempla', p. 209 (nos 189, 190).

Toulouse, for reason of war came to these parts with others knights' introduces a story about an Aragonese knight encountering a snake inside an egg during Lent. In another collection, a tale is set in Muret, 'at the time of heretical wickedness', during the Albigensian Crusade; another at Pujols 'when heretical perversity reigned in the land'; another 'at the time of heretical wickedness when heresy had corrupted the whole land like strong drink'.[172] This final example introduces a tale that does actually address heresy (in order to demonstrate the power of excommunication): a bishop, interrupted by a 'heresiarch' when trying to preach in church, tells him 'to be quiet, once, twice, three times'. The heretic refuses, is excommunicated and immediately falls down dead, 'dry and black just like a stick that is snatched, burnt and smoking, from the fire'.[173] But with the others it is simply a framing device—and yet a reminder of a shared and troubled history in the region, bearing its own implied message alongside the specific moral points of the *exemplum*.

As will be abundantly clear by now, the intent of the *exempla* is fundamentally didactic. They seek to teach lay people how to be good Christians, 'good' in the sense of being obedient—attending church, respecting the clergy, remembering the articles of faith—but also, on occasion, in the sense of developing their inner moral and spiritual engagement. Stories are a powerful tool, able as we have seen to deploy a panoply of tactics—humour, horror, fear, irony, memory—in order to engage. Their framing as *story* frees them from some burden of explanation. One does not need to explain exactly 'how' the stubborn heretic spontaneously combusts, nor address whether all usurers will have toads gnawing their tongues after death, nor claim that everyone who fails to attend church on Sundays will be struck dead. Discussing religious narratives in general, Jibu Mathew George argues: 'Narratives draw into the vortex of their internal vital dynamics the distinction between the real and the unreal, and transmutes them into another binary—what is aesthetically efficacious and what is not'. They can be 'ontologically ambivalent'; that is, not resting their authority on a simple (but therefore potentially brittle) claim to correspond with reality as usually experienced. Thus '[r]eligious ideation belongs to a realm of narration where the state of affairs described, or the plot narrated, is so vivid, internally so systematized, or rendered so desirable that their relation to reality is no longer the criterion of their validity, but paradoxically have had the greatest claims over reality.'[174] Stories flex and

---

[172] Welter, 'Un nouveau recueil franciscain d'exempla', pp. 618–19 (no. 203), 467 (no. 95), 473 (no. 119); BL MS 33956, fols 24r, 24v, 42v.

[173] BL MS 33956, fol. 42v: 'tempore heretice pravitatis quo heresis totam terram corrumpat ut fermentum... [episcopus] monuit ipsum heresiarcham ut taceret, semel, bis, tercio. Et cum desistere nollet, auctoritate ultissime trinitatis, excommunicavit. Et quod dictu est mirabile, statim cecidit mortuus hereticus maledictus et factus est aridatus et niger sicut lignum quod eripitur de incendis fumigans et combustum.'

[174] George, 'Religious and Fictional Narratives', p. 60.

persuade; and, we might add, braid collectively together, in the kind of oral culture addressed by preaching.

But stories are not programmatic conduits. Precisely because they make *some* ontological claims—some calls upon familiarity, specificity, and so forth—they also bring complex aspects of life into view. Many of the *exempla* outlined above 'work' by addressing occasions of spiritual lack, failure, or even challenge; they acknowledge a wider realm of experience even whilst attempting to direct things to the good. It is important to see the *exempla* and other miracle stories circulating in this period as not simply products of a reformed clerical culture. The development of preaching tools, particularly by and for mendicant friars, does matter hugely in terms of a more uniform dissemination of messages (though, in keeping with my attempted regional focus, we may not want to assume a total uniformity within western Christendom at too early a period). But the *exempla* themselves both address and depend upon a wider culture of storytelling, in which the laity were also active participants. Various of the tales include the suggestion that they arise originally from lay people themselves: the man who rushes to church whilst still naked (as related further above), and tells everyone what had happened to him; the man who said the *Ave Maria* prayer, explaining his supernatural warning of impending death to his confessor. In some stories it is made more explicit. A man experienced a disturbing miracle that reformed his moral behaviour, connected to the shrine of Marie Madeleine, and related this to his confessor, a Brother Minor. He made a point of allowing the friar to tell other people about what he had experienced (that is, to break the seal of confession).[175] Two men, whilst playing at dice by a certain wayside stone cross near (perhaps) Largentière, swore horribly on God, Mary, and the saints. Having angered God they were very badly beaten supernaturally, bashed up against the stone cross by some invisible force, and afterwards were beset by continuous tremors and could not sit still. They went to Arles and confessed to Archbishop Umbert (1190–1202), and subsequently roamed the streets of Montpellier telling their tale and warning people to 'beware of blaspheming!'[176] As we would expect—and indeed would find also in earlier centuries—the laity themselves often spread tales about the miraculous powers of particular saints. The husband of a woman who went blind heard 'from his neighbours' in Bédoin (c. 40 km north-east of Avignon) about the 'many and diverse miracles' performed by God through Marie Madeleine at her shrine in Saint-Maximin. Similarly, at Sillans-la-Cascade (c. 66 km east of Aix), a deaf woman was told by her neighbours—'by signs rather than by words'—of the Madeleine's miracles.[177] Several more explicit examples of both kinds—news of miracles, the recounting of moralized tales—can be found within the *exempla*

---

[175] Jean Gobi, *Miracles*, pp. 68–71 (no. 10).
[176] Welter, 'Un nouveau recueil franciscain d'exempla', p. 622 (no. 211).
[177] Jean Gobi, *Miracles*, pp. 94–95 (no. 27), 102–03 (no. 32).

collections, and a lay origin for various tales, or at least parts thereof, is implicit in many others.

In the Sack Friar collection there is a humorous tale that is explicitly directed 'against vainglory' but which might more obliquely be said to be a warning about what is shared between lay people. 'A simple man' came across someone singing songs, and, wanting to acquire them for himself, asked the singer in private if he might sell them to him. The singer, 'wishing to trick him in his simplicity', sold him a sack full of bees, telling him that these are the songs. 'And when on a certain Sunday the peasants were gathered together in congregation, the man with the sack, hearing the bees murmuring within, believed they were emitting the songs. And gathering all the peasants (*rustici*) of the town, he opened the sack and the hungry bees rushed out, and the peasants who had joyfully come along were gravely stung.'[178] There is a faint echo here of Bernard of Angers's initially disapproving comments on peasants at the shrine of Ste Foy, singing rustic songs through the vigil to her feast day, and more broadly of clerical condemnation of the laity paying more attention to secular songs and tales than sermons. What it also dramatizes are moments of independent lay interaction, the sharing of oral culture. And here we may further remind ourselves that whilst sermons and *exempla* undoubtedly were a means by which ecclesiastics propagated a particular version of Christian culture to a large lay audience, that audience was not passive. The tales which fed into sermon *exempla* sometimes began as stories related by lay people themselves. The laity also then shared, discussed, and debated that which they had heard—in the process creating areas of potential danger, of which some of the synodal texts discussed earlier were all too aware.

Some of that lay discussion was with their local clergy. This is not surprising: increased doctrinal instruction (as strongly encouraged and to some degree demanded by various conciliar and synodal statutes) was always likely to generate a subsequent array of follow-up questions of various kinds. One can glimpse something of this process in Benoît d'Alignan's *Tractatus fidei contra diversos errores*, mentioned earlier in this chapter. We met other short works by Benoît, bishop of Marseille 1229-67, early in this chapter. He was a native of southern France, and in 1226 had persuaded Carcassonne and Béziers to surrender to Louis VIII during the Albigensian Crusade (he was at that point abbot of Lagrasse), twice went on crusade to the Holy Lands, and was present at the council of Lyon in 1245 which excommunicated Frederick II and which brought together representatives of the eastern churches.[179] These experiences all fed into the *Tractatus fidei*, which he based around the lengthy 'Firmiter credimus' creed that formed the first canon of the Fourth Lateran Council. The *Tractatus*,

---

[178] Welter, 'Un recueil d'exempla', pp. 210-11 (no. 195).
[179] M. Segonne, *Moine, prélat, croisé: Benoît d'Alignan, abbé de La Grasse, seigneur-évêque de Marseille 1190-1268* (Marseille: Robert, 1960); Arnold, 'Benedict of Alignan', pp. 27-34.

completed initially in 1261, takes up each element of faith as set out in that creed, attests to its truth through biblical, patristic, and canon law authorities, then notes all 'errors' that might arise in regard to it and provides 'reasons, authorities and examples' in rebuttal. It is actually one of the most widely circulated anti-heresy treatises produced in the thirteenth century, the bulk of its energy directed against 'errors' of every kind, aiming to give bishops, mendicants, and others the tools to defeat any arguments that a multiplicity of real or imagined 'heretics' might put forward at any future moment.

However, within the *Tractatus* Benoît also responds to what we might call 'questions arising'. Some of these are high-level intellectual issues—'If it is asked whether the Divine Essence retains the past and the future', the response proffered drawing explicitly on Augustine's *On Job*—but others less so, and some are clearly more pastoral than theological. What does it mean 'to believe' as a child? 'For infants, however, to believe is to be baptized; not to be baptized is not to believe.' 'If it is asked whether a sinner who is in the Church (in number but not in merit) is lying if he says "I believe in God" (*Credo in Deum*) when he does not hold to Him? Respond "no" because in these locutions, namely the Lord's Prayer and the Creed, it is said not in one's own person but in the person of the Church generally, just as when the priest says "Let us pray".'[180] Why did Christ have to take on human flesh? It is just as an almoner takes his chest to distribute bread to the poor, or a *redemptor* takes a sack of money to redeem captives, or a medic takes a little box of ointment to cure the sick.[181] Regarding the future resurrection, he explains that the body is like clothing for the soul, and we will be returned in clothes fitting for glory, not 'in the old and rent clothing which we have in this life'; going on to explain ('for the common people') that it would be unseemly for a rich person to receive a beloved friend naked or only half dressed.[182]

---

[180] BnF MS Lat. 4224, fol. 43r: 'Quoad infantes tamen credere est baptizari; non credere non baptizari.' 'Si queratur utrum peccator qui est in ecclesia numero non merito mentiatur cum dicit Credo in deum cum non tendat in eum, Responde quod non quia in hiis locutionibus scilicet oratione dominica et Symbolum loquitur non in persona propria sed in persona ecclesie generaliter, sicut sacerdos dicens Oremus.' Being in the Church 'in number but not in merit (*numero non merito*)' comes from Augustine and became part of the Ordinary Gloss on the Bible: see E. Ann Matter, 'The Church Fathers and the *Glossa Ordinaria*', in I. Backus, ed., *The Reception of the Church Fathers in the West, from the Carolingians to the Maurists*, 2 vols (Leiden: Brill, 1997), I, pp. 83–112, at p. 93. (My thanks to Pete Biller regarding this phrase and passage).

[181] BnF MS Lat. 4224, fols 236v–237r: 'Item, si queratur qua ratione assumpsit carnem, responde quod ea ratione qua elemosinarius assumit coferum ad distribuendos panes pauperibus, qua redemptor saccum peccunie ad redimendos captivos, qua medicus pixidem vel alabaustrum unguenti ad sanandos infirmos.'

[182] BnF MS Lat. 4224, fol. 281r: 'Item, cum corpora vestes naturales sint animarum, denudatio earum p[ersoni]s esset miserie propter quod necesse est, ut reddantur eis vestes huius non in vetustate et scissuris in quibus eas habuerunt in vita ista, set in gloria et decore congruenti felicitati future. Item ad satisfacciendum vulgaribus, attende quod indecens esset ut aliquis dives in domum suam recipiat hospitem quem diligit dimidium tantum vel nudum.'

Benoît proffers a number of short images or explanations like these for various aspects of the faith, all of which he likely intended to be used pastorally, for the instruction of priests but potentially thereby for the instruction of all Christians. He tackles some issues which go well beyond the implicit faith required by the synodal texts. How was it that God created all things simultaneously? It is like when the trumpet sounds in an army or city: some take up arms to attack or defend, others go to war machines, others to undermine walls, others to fill up ditches, or others prepare themselves for tasks or works to be attacked; the same sound makes all this happen at once. 'If indeed from the will of a single king or prince there should proceed the works of a multitude, why should we be amazed if from the omnipotent word there proceeded an innumerable variety of works in the world?'[183] (A number of his 'examples' are notably military, and it seems likely that when Benoît thought of 'the laity' it was knights and princes who mostly immediately came to his mind.) Elsewhere he notes a host of questions that people might have about Paradise, what happened to it after the Fall, and so forth. This includes a response to what we might imagine to be a perennial question arising:

> If it is asked for what reason the Creator placed Adam and his wife in paradisical delights, given that such delights are injurious to human souls, respond that temporal delights then were not injurious to them because of the purity and goodness and indeed strength of their natures [*that is, before the corruption of the Fall*]...Just as strong wine is not injurious to certain people because of their good complexion and health, in truth it is injurious to others because of their bad complexion and corruption and infirmity.[184]

He also has a go at explaining the Trinity, through proffering images by which it can be understood: that just as the sun or a coal or fire all emit light or brilliance in proportion but not equally, and similarly heat is generated from them but not equally; so the Son is born of the Father, and the Holy Spirit from both of them,

---

[183] BnF MS Lat. 4224, fol. 127r–v: 'Exemplo ostenditur qualiter deus creavit omnia simul. Item Simul. Sicut eius ad ?sonitum [et] clangorem buccine in exercitu vel civitate alii carunt ad arma protectionis, alii ad arma impugnationis, alii ad machinas, alii ad suffodiendos muros, alii ad fossata implenda vel ad alia impugnandi officia vel artificia se preparant, sic creatore semel tamen loquente et ineffabiliter sonum spiritualem emittente universitas operum naturalium in mundo procedit ac si universitas creaturarum verbum eius audiat. Si enim ex una voluntate regis aut principis unius tanta procedit operum multitudo. Quid miramur si ex omnipotenti verbo procedit innumerabilis varietas operum in mundo.'

[184] BnF MS Lat. 4224, fols 134v–135r: 'Si queratur propter quid creator posuit Adam et uxorem eius in paradyso deliciarum ex quo delicie noxie sunt animabus humanis, Responde quod delicie temporales tunc non poterant eis nocere propter puritatem et bonitatem atque fortitudinem nature eorum...Sicut vinum forte non nocet quibusdam propter bonitatem complexionis et sanitatem ipsorum aliis vero nocet propter malam complexionem et corruptionem et infirmitatem illorum.'

but not equally. Or just as fabric can be made into a tunic and a cloth and a cloak, the common essence is still the same fabric. Or when three candles are placed together and lit, there is one light although there are three candles.[185]

Responding particularly to the 'errors' of 'heretics', who ask how Christ's body can be repeatedly made present in the Eucharist in many different times and places (a common jeer found in various heresy trials), he provides 'similitudes by which this can be further confounded before the common people': that the sun exists, without diminution, in diverse lands; that one and the same light comes from diverse candles; that the same words or sounds can reach diverse ears, and the same light can reach diverse eyes; the same faith can be in diverse faithful people, and the same knowledge in diverse hearts; the same sentence said in diverse voices; the same truth, in diverse believers; the same image in diverse mirrors; the same authority or jurisdiction or lordship or prelacy exercised over diverse subjects; the same paternity in diverse children.[186] The multiplicity of examples appears to try to overwhelm the underlying question, and is clearly directed to a wider audience rather than engaging (as he does elsewhere) in more scholastic debate about 'accidents' and 'substance'.

We do not know if the kinds of images and explanations that Benoît d'Alignan proffered were ever actually used in pastoral instruction. But his attempts to provide them—in a magnum opus that he imagined would 'defeat all error' and 'strengthen the faithful in their faith' across all Christendom—can in themselves tell us two things. One is that a bishop like Benoît—heavily engaged in the defence of Christendom, directly aware of other versions of Christianity (including those deemed 'heretical'), and of Judaism and Islam—thought that such simple explanatory images were important. They were needed for the defence of the faith; simple assertion was insufficient, one had to give people images and tools to understand and hang on to their beliefs. The other is that the images he proffers are almost all imagined as responses to enquiries—to people asking about the tenets of faith, and wanting help in order to believe rightly. His concerns strongly suggest that the pastoral injunction to the laity not to discuss, dispute, or enquire was neither sufficient nor realistic, and that bishops, priests, and friars were likely to encounter a variety of people who 'asked' about a variety of things—and who then needed responses.

---

[185] BnF MS Lat. 4224, fols 177v-178r: 'Item sicut a sole vel carbone vel igne gignuntur radius sive splendor in mediate et non eque et ex illis duobus calor et non equo ita a patre filius et ex illis spiritus sanctus et non eque et sicut splendor et fervor sunt unus sol vel unus ignis...Item idem pannus est simul supertunicale et coopertorium et scapulare ubi communis essentia est idem pannus...Idem in tribus candelis coniunctis et accendis est unum lumen licet tres candele.'

[186] BnF MS Lat. 4224, fol. 352v: 'Item per similitudines quibus coram vulgaribus amplius confutantur. Quod idem sol absque diminucione est in diversis terris, simul in semel idem lumen in diversis candelis. Idem verbum vel sonus in diversis auribus. Eadem lux in diversis oculis. Eadem fides in diversis fidelibus. Eadem sapientia in diversis cordibus. Eadem sentencia in diversis vocibus. Eadem veritas in diversis credentibus. Eadem ymago in diversis speculis. Eadem auctoritas sive iurisdictio sive dominatio sive prelatio in diversis subditis. Eadem paternitas in diversis filiis.'

And indeed one of the things which we can see, via the detail of inquisition registers, particularly from the later thirteenth and early fourteenth century, is lay people talking together about their faith, and asking priests or others about certain difficult questions. Sometimes these are recorded because the conversations themselves were reported to the inquisitors, having been thought potentially heretical, or because they led on to a conversation about support for the Good Men or Waldensians (or, latterly, the Spiritual Franciscans). But on other occasions, they appear contextually in the record, not directly related to the pursuit of heretics. Collectively they give us a sense of many different aspects of Christian faith that would come up for discussion in lay society. In 1273 Durand de Rouffiac, reported to inquisitors for having said various problematic things, recounted a talk he had had with Grimaud de Laumière, a cleric, about the passion of St Laurent. Durand was accused of having said that martyrs had been compelled to their martyrdom; he admitted that Grimaud had said that Laurent willingly endured his martyrdom, and that he had replied, 'But it was rather that he was led forcibly and unwilling, by living men, to his martyrdom.' The conversation took place near the bakehouse in Laumière—that is, not in church or at some formal occasion of worship, but simply a conversation in the streets of a very small village.[187] A man called Pierre Eugrin de Puydaniel, accused by others of a doubtful faith in 1275, reported that his wife, Sicarda, had often told him that she was visited by an apparition of St Jacques in the guise of a pilgrim, and that he said 'that the souls of the dead do not enter Paradise until the Day of Judgment, but go to rest, except for small children and the saints'. Visions of St Jacques were obviously rare—but discussion of where souls go, and what happened to children's souls, perhaps rather less so.[188]

A number of examples can be drawn from the very rich inquisition registers produced by the inquiries of Jacques Fournier, bishop of Pamiers (and later Pope Benedict XII) between 1318 and 1325. Here are just a few. In 1318 or 1319, four men were talking at the entrance to the bridge leading into Tarascon-sur-Ariège. One of the group, Bernard Cordier, had just come back from Pamiers, and the others asked him for any news; he told them that apparently there was a letter circulating from the Hospitallers in the Holy Land, declaring that two cities built on sand would fall into ruin, and that the Antichrist was born. We know about the conversation because one of those present, a stonemason called Arnaud de Savinhan, was dismissive, allegedly saying that 'the world had no beginning and would never end, but always is and will be' and that there was no world but the present one; the others reported him for potential heresy. (Arnaud was sentenced quite harshly for heresy, though he was unconnected to any organized group. Asked who taught him his errors, he said that 'he had taught himself letters,

---

[187] Doat 25, fol. 22r (*Inquisitors and Heretics*, p. 224).
[188] Doat 25, fol. 218r (*Inquisitors and Heretics*, p. 624).

namely the seven psalms, a little of the Psalter, the fifteen signs of Judgment, the *Credo*, the *Pater noster*, the *Ave Maria*', and had come to his beliefs through reflection on these things—in many ways an ideal layman, except for his exercise of additional cognition and reflection on creation.)[189] A man called Raimond de Laburat, excommunicated along with some of his neighbours for refusing to pay a newly instituted tithe on lambs, was out walking with his parish priest, Raimond Frézat. He asked the priest whether there was any scriptural warrant for excommunication, something which Frézat had to go away and think about for a few days.[190] A woman called Galharda Rous reported to the inquisitors things which her neighbour Guillaume Austatz had said to her, when they had been speaking together about the resurrection (Austatz, she alleged, had stated a belief in metempsychosis). That conversation had happened in her house. She also remembered going to see him—he was the *bailli* for the village of Ornolac—because she wanted his help in recovering some stolen money. He wasn't very helpful, which prompted Galharda to say that she would then pray to the Virgin Mary for a miracle, to help her recover her money, and avenge her on the robbers; Austatz responded that Mary would not do this, as she didn't kill people, and did not have that power.[191] Austatz later admitted that he had heard of the transmigration of souls as heretical beliefs propounded by the Good Man Pierre Autier, albeit related to him via his mother; but that, he said, 'he never totally believed this, sometimes staying in the contrary belief, because he had heard this preached in church, and moreover because Guillaume d'Alzinhac, priest of Carbona, who had sometimes stayed in the house of his mother at Lordat, had said to him that there would be a future resurrection of dead men and women, which he had taught to him when he was a young boy and lived with his mother at Lordat'.[192] A weaver called Pierre Sabatier from Varilhès (just north of Foix) admitted, among other things, a conversation that he had had with a neighbour called Bernard Masse. Bernard had asked him why people held a candle over the mouth of a dying person. If the light of the candle was clear, Pierre said, that meant that the dying person had confessed, was free of sin, and their soul would go to heaven. But if they were not repentant 'one might as well put the candle in their arse as in their mouth'.[193] In each case, whilst it is the stain of heresy that inscribes the words of

---

[189] *Fournier* I, pp. 160–61, 164; cf. lengthier discussion in Arnold, *Inquisition and Power*, pp. 167–73.
[190] *Fournier* II, pp. 318–19; cf. Arnold, *Inquisition and Power*, pp. 180–90.
[191] *Fournier* I, pp. 191–93; cf. discussion in J. H. Arnold, 'Inquisition, Texts and Discourse', in C. Bruschi and P. Biller, eds, *Texts and the Repression of Medieval Heresy* (York: York Medieval Press, 2003), pp. 63–80.
[192] *Fournier* I, p. 206.
[193] *Fournier* I, p. 147. Sabatier was in trouble for saying various disparaging things about church services, as well as this ambiguous statement; and yet also went on pilgrimage to Compostelle. On his deposition, see further in J. H. Arnold, '"A man takes an ox by the horn and a peasant by the tongue": Literacy, Orality and Inquisition in Medieval Languedoc', in S. Rees-Jones, ed., *Literacy and Learning in Medieval England and Abroad* (Turnhout: Brepols, 2003), pp. 31–47.

Sabatier, Austatz, and others into the written record, the detail points to other less problematic conversations, between priests and laity, and between the laity themselves.

Conclusion

Another source from the early fourteenth century in which we can hear the voices of a variety of witnesses is the canonization trial of Louis de Toulouse. Louis was the son of Charles d'Anjou. Born in 1274, he spent most of his teenage years as a royal hostage in Catalonia, a prisoner of Peire III of Aragon. He gained his freedom aged 20, and immediately renounced his title. Two years later he became a Brother Minor, and was, at the very young age of 23, appointed bishop of Toulouse, but died a year later. He was buried in the Franciscan church in Marseille, which subsequently became the focus of various post-mortem miracles. These were gathered up as part of the case for canonization, but the inquiry focused also on his personal piety and life, particularly during his long period of captivity (when he was attended to by other Brothers Minor). Here we need to remember that whilst he was by birth a royal, and whilst he ended his life as a bishop and mendicant, for most of that period those things can be stripped away: for many years he was a young layperson, and one trapped in quite sad circumstances.

The reports made of him—prior to his becoming a priest, mendicant, and bishop—show us, undoubtedly with a good deal of retrospective honing, a sort of idealized image of a well-instructed layperson. Bermund de Roca, a squire (*domicellus*) in Louis's service, reported to the inquiry that from the age of 6 or 7, Louis and his brother were taught by another lord how to behave, namely 'to live with humility, to love God, and to receive decently and to honour any good men who came to him'. (And, he added, he taught him to ride.) From an early age, there were two priests who attended Louis and his brother, who celebrated mass for him on alternate days, 'during which mass, the same boys behaved quietly and decently, according to their estate' (the latter comment being interpretable either as meaning 'as they should' or 'as much as you could expect of someone that age'). 'And those priests taught Lord Louis the alphabet and the *Pater noster* and *Ave Maria* and *Credo in Deum* and the seven psalms'—the programme of core lay knowledge, with the addition of the seven penitential psalms (which, as we saw above, were also known to the self-taught humble stonemason Arnaud de Savinhan). Louis, Bermund said, would always upbraid Bermund and his companions if they sang worldly songs, but 'when they sang of God and the blessed Virgin Mary and the saints, he would willingly listen to them' (a passing detail that suggests a wider circulation of vernacular religious culture than is now visible to us, and in continuum with more secular entertainment). And he had a great devotion to lepers, washing their feet and kissing them, without fear of the consequences—this last detail clearly a form of Christ-like sanctity, framing his potential post-mortem beatification, but corresponding nonetheless to the broader strand of lay piety that was encouraged to the works of mercy, as we have seen in earlier chapters and in this one.

As the evidence (from Bermund and others) continued, we are then shown a transition, from a young layman taught 'the first rudiments of the faith' (as another witness, Brother Fort, an aged Brother Minor and former inquisitor, put it) to someone who gained great literacy and wisdom. During his period of imprisonment, he was taught further by the Brothers Minor: after morning mass they would stay with Louis and instruct him, 'and (said Bermund) in that first year [of imprisonment] he hardly heard him speak Latin; in the second year he sometimes heard him talking in Latin; in the third and fourth years he heard the said Lord Louis disputing with the said Brothers Minor, his masters'. But, said Bermund, he could not himself tell the inquiry what they disputed about, 'as he did not know, as he was a layperson'. But, returning to the theme later in his deposition, he often saw Louis disputing with Brothers Minor and Brothers Preacher and Augustinians, 'and he said that Lord Louis would get very worked up and become red in disputation'. Later in life, he had many books, such that 'six or seven sacks were needed' to transport them, Bermund said. Brother Fort attested that when Louis went to Catalonia, he was not a learned man, but when he returned, he could debate difficult theological and philosophical questions— and this was a sign of divine inspiration, because his tutors, although good men, were not themselves of that intellectual calibre.[194]

At the point that Louis was first heatedly debating with his tutors he was, we should remember, still a young layman. As we have seen, dispute and debate by the laity were explicitly forbidden by the conciliar and synodal decrees of the period, though it is perhaps not surprising in such circumstances to see this set aside. Louis is, of course, extraordinary—he was heading toward a career in the Church (albeit one cut tragically short) and to future sanctity. But these memories of that trajectory show us the possibility of continuity between lay instruction and charitable works, Latin learning, and higher spiritual attainment. This is a particularly fine but important point. Obviously most people never attained sainthood, and for that matter most lay people never gained the kind of Latin literacy that facilitated and legitimized theological disputation. Nor did they take the works of mercy and charity as far as kissing lepers. But by the later thirteenth century there was a *potential* path that could be taken from the one to the other,

---

[194] Bughetti, ed., *Processus*, pp. 32–35, 38, 59–60, 95. There are various studies of Louis, the canonization process, and his miracles, notably M. R. Toynbee, *S. Louis of Toulouse and the Process of Canonisation in the Fourteenth Century* (Manchester: Manchester University Press, 1929); J. Paul, 'Evangelisme et Franciscanisme chez Louis d'Anjou', *CdF* 8 (1973), 375–401; J. Paul, 'Miracles et mentalité religieuse populaire à Marseille au debut du XIV siecle', *CdF* 11 (1976), 61–90; J. Paul, 'Le rayonnement géographique du pelerinage au tombeau de Louis d'Anjou', *CdF* 15 (1980), 137–58.

such that witnesses to a canonization inquiry would not think it peculiar to mention instruction in 'the first rudiments' of faith as a beginning step on a much longer journey.

We may see that primarily in positive terms, the opening up of an enriched sense of Christian culture and future salvation to all Christians, not just the extraordinary few. But it carried a potential burden with it also. When the thirteenth-century councils outlined the core essentials that all *should* know, as we have seen they tended to rely on the notion of 'implicit faith' to address what knowledge of those essentials meant for most people: 'knowledge' in the sense of rehearsal and repetition, but not for deeper enquiry or reflection. Belief was obedience, a displacement of deeper knowledge onto those few better suited to the task. And yet, however, if knowing the 'first rudiments' could be a step on a longer journey, at what point precisely was it required that one have 'explicit' understanding and belief? It obviously applied toward the other end of the spectrum, if one were a bishop or theologian. But where was the cut between implicit and explicit, at what point did 'belief' require more than obedience and repetition? And was it always to be trusted, when it moved beyond the implicit? As I argued at the start of this chapter, conformity was essential, and in the thirteenth century the detail of conformity had become that bit more elaborated and demanding; but conformity was also always potentially insufficient for salvation. Beyond conformity lay various virtuous things, most notably charitable acts and spiritual contemplation; but 'heresy' could lurk also, error sometimes indistinguishable from virtue in its appearance.

We shall return to various of these issues in the following chapter, when looking at confession, inquisition, and, in the final chapter, 'belief' itself. In this chapter I have focused on the rudiments of faith and lay knowledge, and have largely discussed what was *required*, rather than the range of inner responses that might have been experienced by any particular lay Christian. We should in that context recall—with perhaps a glance back to Chapter 6—that however we conceive 'belief', for people in the period it was always experienced, embodied, and situated materially. In the late twelfth-century vernacular sermons discussed much earlier in this chapter, one for the Octave of Easter takes 'peace be with you' as its main theme, and mentions St Thomas. 'And he said that "I would not have believed if I had not seen the wounds in his feet and his hands, and if my hand had not touched the wound in his side".'[195] Seeing, touching, experiencing: the material and physical encounter, and the spaces within which it occurred, were also a fundamental part of faith—and perhaps often, from a lay perspective, a much larger part than the abstract propositions contained in the Creed, even when these were dutifully learned and recited.

---

[195] Thomas, ed., 'Homélies provençales', p. 397: 'e dix que ja non o creiria si non vezia las plagas dels pes e de las mans e si sa man non metia en la plaga del costat'.

8
The Discipline of Belief

In 1317 Robert de Mauvoisin, archbishop of Aix, was subjected to an inquisitorial trial at the behest of Pope John XXII. As far as we can tell the reasons for this, rather unusually, were not that he had fallen foul of the fraught papal/imperial politics of the period, but simply that he had become massively unpopular with a range of people in the city and region, vociferous complaints from whom had prompted the pope to order an inquiry.[1] He was accused of a range of bad behaviour. One accusation is particularly interesting, for what it shows about wider behaviour and how it was treated: the charge, levelled against Robert by various people, that he constantly blasphemed.

The nature of the trial evidence, recording the words of many witnesses as they gave evidence against the archbishop, means that rather than vague allusions to blasphemy, we can actually 'hear' it in some detail. 'By the head of God', 'by the body of God', 'curse God', 'I renounce God', 'I renounce the mother of God', 'I curse the mother of God', 'I despise God', 'By the filthy whore mother of God' and other such variations, mostly recounted in the vernacular (*Malgrat de Dio! Jo renec la mayre de Dio! Despich naia Dio! Per la putana merdoza mayre de Dio!* etc.).[2] 'And thereby the said witness heard the same archbishop blaspheme frequently and often, publicly and with many people present, and thereby violently just as a bad, ribald person swears and blasphemes God in a tavern,' one lay witness attested. Another, a priest, reported that lots of people had heard the archbishop blaspheme in this way, and that it caused great scandal, because lay people who swore and blasphemed in the city and diocese were 'gravely punished, and moreover the tongue of a layperson who thus blasphemed could eventually be perforated' (that is, judicially mutilated).[3] Robert de Mauvoisin initially denied having blasphemed, but when pressed harder on the matter, admitted that he might have said some things, but that 'if it was found that he ever said any blasphemy, he did this from the wicked habits of the Gascons and a slippery tongue, and in the heat of wrath, not with deliberation or bad intention'.[4]

---

[1] Edited and discussed in J. Shatzmiller, *Justice et injustice au début du XIVe siècle: l'enquête sur l'archevêque d'Aix et sa renonciation en 1318* (Rome: École française de Rome, 1999), who persuasively argues (pp. 151–52) that the case is interesting precisely because it is 'marginal' to the big political and theological arguments of the period.

[2] Shatzmiller, *Justice et injustice*, pp. 186, 197, 235, 248.

[3] Shatzmiller, *Justice et injustice*, pp. 197, 186.   [4] Shatzmiller, *Justice et injustice*, p. 183.

This seems clearly to be one instance in which evidence about an archbishop provides us with evidence about the behaviour of ordinary lay people: swearing on God and the Virgin, as a 'low' person might do in a tavern. As we saw in Chapters 4 and 7, such behaviour had been condemned and censured for at least a century, from a few early civic statutes and some synodal instructions in the later thirteenth century; preaching exempla recounted various supernatural punishments meted out to blasphemers. We would also find mention of 'blasphemy', alongside other faults, in the stories of supernatural vengeance meted out by saints in the eleventh and twelfth centuries, to those who had wronged them (as discussed in Chapter 2).

So there is continuity here. But there is also change, and the nature of that change is doubly interesting.[5] One aspect is that whilst blasphemy had always been wrong, as I argued in Chapter 7 it became part of the wider realm of lay instruction regarding 'sin' only in the later twelfth century; and, moreover, it became indisputably a *crime* only by the later thirteenth century. That is, that which the Church had long condemned moved from being the subject of warnings and perhaps some penance, to being something which could—as the witness above outlines—result in extreme bodily mutilation. The second aspect is that what constituted 'blasphemy', or perhaps at least that what constituted blasphemy worth recounting as scandalous, had shifted somewhat. The examples from the twelfth century and earlier are all occasions when someone specifically scorned the power of a saint: a challenge to supernatural authority. 'It's probably just the bones of some dead person or other, which are gathered together to be venerated by the foolish beliefs of the people,' as the sceptical peasant who we met in Chapter 2 said in regard to St Vivian. The response was supernatural punishment, bringing the miscreant into line. But the 'blasphemy' found in preaching *exempla* (as we have seen) and as spoken by the archbishop of Aix, like any 'ribald' person in a tavern, was something different: swearing, in something like the modern sense of 'foul language'. It sometimes took the form of an oath—'by the belly of God' (structurally similar, that is, to swearing an oath 'by these four Gospels')—and sometimes a curse (*Despich naia la mayre de Dyo!*), but in both inflections we see blasphemy no longer simply as a challenge to specific spiritual authority, or related to the usurpation of church property, but as a moral and mental crime in itself; the thinking and saying of bad thoughts.

Such behaviour undoubtedly occurred long before this period, but only in the thirteenth century and after did it become potentially subject to discipline. It is thus one part of a wider shift in how lay people were subject to a more complex set of spiritual requirements. It is also a useful illustration of what I intend when I invoke the term 'discipline'. The underlying Latin word *disciplina* most often

---

[5] More broadly see C. Leveleux-Teixeira, *La parole interdite: le blasphème dans la France médiévale, XIIIe–XVIe siècles. Du péché au crime* (Paris: De Boccard, 2001).

means something like 'learning'—this lives on in the sense in which we might talk of the study of history as 'a discipline', like English literature, Theoretical Physics, or the like. But it does of course also have the harsher edge of regulation and enforced behaviour: that one may 'discipline and punish' (to echo the title of a still fundamentally important study of the complex dynamics around punishment and law).[6] Both are at play here. Secular authorities—most influentially Louis IX in 1268 and Charles d'Anjou in 1294—issued legislation imposing fines on those who blasphemed against God, Mary, or the saints, and there are records of such punishments being imposed in southern France in the early fourteenth century.[7] As we saw in Chapter 4, a very few southern French towns had anti-blasphemy statutes in the thirteenth century; in the fourteenth century more were adopted, and by the later fourteenth century one can find local court cases pursuing malefactors.[8] The Provençal nobleman Elzéar de Sabran—destined for post-mortem sanctity—imposed a quasi-monastic 'rule' on his *castrum* of Puimichel around the beginning of the fourteenth century, banning among other things blasphemy and gambling.[9] But that was a rare degree of lay-imposed control. Such behaviour clearly did not *always* lead to judicial intervention; it was simply too common. And yet it was also always potentially available as a sign of someone's poor character—one of the things one might invoke judicially to indicate that someone was 'low' or 'vile' (*vilis*) and thus in a general sense less law-worthy. Thus, for example, in a case of insult and assault heard before the bishop of Béziers in 1353, a hostile witness said in regard to one of the litigants that 'it was spoken and public knowledge in Aspiran that the said Jean is a drunken frequenter of taverns... and a blasphemer of God and His saints'.[10]

In this sense 'disciplining' blasphemy involved a spectrum of responses, at the harshest end of which was secular judicial intervention—particularly severe in the case of Aix, if the witness regarding the mutilation of tongues can be believed—but which largely encompassed moral injunctions and reminders from priests and others regarding 'good Christian' behaviour. Thus whilst such discipline partly rested upon outside authority, it increasingly asked ordinary Christians

---

[6] M. Foucault, *Discipline and Punish: The Birth of the Prison*, trans. A. Sheridan (London: Penguin, 1977).

[7] E. de Lauriere et al., eds, *Ordonnances des rois de France*, 21 vols (Paris: Impriere royale, 1723), I, pp. 99–102; C. Giraud, *Essai sur l'histoire de droit français au Moyen Âge*, 2 vols (Paris: Videcoq, 1846), II, pp. 87–88: 16 Sept 1294, letters from Charles II to Hugh de Vicinis, seneschal of Provence and Forcalquier. On southern French judicial cases from Manosque, see Shatzmiller, *Justice et injustice*, pp. 77–78 and L. Otis, 'Une contribution à l'étude du blasphème au bas moyen âge', in *Diritto comune e diritti locali nella storia dell'Europa* (Milan: A. Guiffrè, 1980), pp. 211–23.

[8] For example, customs of Castelnaudary, 1331: AM Castelnaudary, AA1, fol. 29v, with various cases arising in the post-plague period discussed in Otis, 'Une contribution'; see also Leveleux, *Parole interdite*, pp. 294–95.

[9] F. Mazel, 'Aristocratie, église et religion au village en Provence (XIe–XIVe siècle)', *CdF* 40 (2006), 163–210, at pp. 179–80.

[10] BL MS Add. 11464, fol. 6r: 'dixit quod vox et fama publica est in loco de aspirano, quod dictus Johannes est hebriosus frequens tabernas... et blasphemator dei et sanctorum eius'.

to regulate their own behaviour: to police themselves, in line with the wider rules of Christian society. It is the interplay between imposed punishment and self-regulation that this chapter addresses more broadly. As the thirteenth century progressed, we can see the development of disciplines, plural, where the dynamic between exterior demand and internal volition could differ considerably. As discussed in the Introduction, here we might describe the process as the unfolding of 'religion' in one of its modern senses, as a disciplinary discourse with internalizing effects.

Confessing Subjects

I want to return us briefly once again to Pons de Léras and his act of very public penitence on Palm Sunday in Lodève, probably around 1130. There is Pons at the centre of this very public, very ritual act, about to head off on long-distance pilgrimages in his own spiritual journey. His actions both point back to a much longer tradition of public penance, and point forward to an emphasis upon restitution for sin; this we have already discussed in Chapter 3. But let us look off to one side, to those watching Pons as he reads out his crimes and sins in the market square:

> This confession was useful and necessary, not only for the one who confessed but also for the many others who, timid from embarrassment at their shame, had hidden their sins for a long time. Now moved by his example, seeing him confessing this way they rushed to the bath of penance and confession.[11]

We thus have evidence from the earlier twelfth century, not only that a wider group of people than the spectacular reformed sinner might be moved to make confession, but that a usual bar to doing so was one's own personal comportment and emotional management: people needed to overcome embarrassment and shame in order to purge their sins, and to be washed clean through penitential acts. There is a lingering question however over what exactly this really meant and involved, how much earlier it might have also been happening, and what, if anything, then changed in the management of confession and penance in the coming centuries.

I have touched on such issues at various points in the first half of this book: the few examples we have from the later eleventh century of local churches having the right to provide 'penitences' of some kind; some particularly notable occasions when people engaged in public penitential acts, as with Pons; some twelfth-century heretics decrying the need for confession to a priest; the requirement in

---

[11] Dijon, BM MS 611, fol. 9r; Kienzle, 'Tract on the Conversion of Pons de Léras', p. 231.

southern France, following the Fourth Lateran Council and the end of the crusade, that all lay people make confession not just once but three times a year. In this section I shall focus particularly on the dynamics around confession in the thirteenth and fourteenth centuries, aided by the richer textual sources for these periods. But we must first address once again the issue of what practice pertained prior to 1215.

Historiographical opinion on this question, as it applies generally to western Christendom, has been divided. There is an influential scholarly tradition that has seen canon 21 of the Fourth Lateran Council as a new and radical departure, moving the issue of 'penance' from being a public act, often focused on reparation for wrongs done to others, to something private, interiorized, and individualizing. The prescribed penances of the early medieval Irish penitential tradition are similarly contrasted with the considerable discretion bestowed on later medieval priests to impose penances tailored to the individual penitent.[12] On the other hand, in the last couple of decades historians such as Sarah Hamilton and Rob Meens have demonstrated that some texts for parish priests, providing them with advice on how to administer private penance to individuals, existed from at least the ninth century onward, and argue that the distinctions seen between the practice of penance in early and late medieval Europe are much less than previously assumed.[13] It may be useful to note that the discussion encompasses a number of different elements: how various acts are understood to be 'penitential', the bestowal of a prescribed penance by a bishop or priest, the public visibility or otherwise of such acts, the wider framework and understanding of sin, and various acts labelled 'confession' that might be more or less focused on the specific deeds committed by a particular individual, and might occur regularly or only on particular occasions such as part of the last rites performed at the deathbed, or following a specific crisis. Part of the historiographical debate may in fact rest on a subtle differing of emphasis between what historians are attempting to pursue. In general, for example, the early medievalists are focused on the dynamics of 'penance', whereas later historians are more concerned with 'confession' and its complexities.

For southern France, for the centuries before 1200, it is abundantly clear not only that public acts of penance existed, but that there was a widely understood

---

[12] For the most astute recent discussion, see A. Murray, *Conscience and Authority in the Medieval Church* (Oxford: Oxford University Press, 2015).

[13] S. Hamilton, *The Practice of Penance, 900–1050* (London: Royal Historical Society, 2001); R. Meens, 'The Frequency and Nature of Early Medieval Penance', in P. Biller and A. J. Minnis, eds, *Handling Sin: Confession in the Middle Ages* (Woodbridge: York Medieval Press, 1998), pp. 35–61; R. Meens, 'The Historiography of Early Medieval Penance', in A. Firey, ed., *A New History of Penance* (Leiden: Brill, 2008), pp. 73–95. Most recently, Meens stresses the innate variability of penance across the centuries: R. Meens, 'Penitential Varieties', in J. H. Arnold, ed., *The Oxford Handbook of Medieval Christianity* (Oxford: Oxford University Press, 2014), pp. 254–70; R. Meens, *Penance in Medieval Europe, c. 600–1200* (Cambridge: Cambridge University Press, 2014).

concept of making penitential amends for one's faults, including acts which were rather less public and flamboyant than the Pons de Léras example. We can see this in the recognition of sin found in preambles to some charters, as noted in earlier chapters; and by the twelfth century this may very occasionally include specific mention of confession and a sense of truthful self-conversion. For example, to return to a charter I previously quoted in Chapter 4, a woman called Aladaicis, making a gift to the Templars in 1133 (very probably on her deathbed), included in her pious preamble the desire that God 'might make me come to true penance and true confession and make me come to His holy paradise'.[14] We have one extraordinary text from 1125, mentioned previously in Chapter 1, that purports to be a first-person record of the confession made by a man called Bernard Pierre, also on his deathbed, to a priest from Carcassonne. It is a very curious document, surviving only as a copy in the cartulary of Saint-Sernin. In the text the priest, Pons, explains that Bernard Pierre turned up in the house of Sans, one of his parishioners, and that being very ill, Pons was called to give the last rites. 'Diligently and with humility he [Bernard] was confessed, saying: "I, guilty sinner, confess to omnipotent God and to the blessed Virgin Mary, and to all the saints, and to you brother, all my sins, whatever I have done through pride, thought, speech, desire (*delectatio*), agreement and deeds"', then going on to specify the particular wrongs he and his brother had done to the church of the Virgin Mary in Peyrepertuse, mainly having carried off various of its goods. As he could not make direct recompense—his brother having possession of these things—the actual point of the document was to relinquish any claim over that church's lands by himself or his heirs. The document concludes with Bernard Pierre attesting to the truth of his words and the presence of Pons and Sans as witnesses; and Pons and Sans then relating all of this to various of the cathedral canons in Toulouse, who wrote up the actual text.[15]

Even if the document is a forgery—obviously possible, though a bizarrely baroque way of protecting the rights of the church of Peyrepertuse—as with other charters it must surely present details that were *thought* to be believable. So we can perhaps take this as a reasonably revealing piece of evidence for what an actual lay confession might be like, albeit one made, as noted, on a deathbed. It is particularly interesting in its mixture of the general and the specific: the precise sins committed against Peyrepertuse are listed—the illicit removal of books, clerical vestments, altar cloths—but as we have seen Bernard Pierre begins also with a much broader sense of 'confession', simply acknowledging that he was guilty of 'whatever I have done' in thought and deed. This 'general' confession is important: it is of a piece with the *Confiteor* prayer which was said by the priest on behalf of

---

[14] *Cartulaire général*, p. 51 (no. 68); see Chapter 4 above.
[15] *Cart. Saint-Sernin*, pp. 351 (no. 502), 14 Dec 1125.

all the congregation at the opening of the mass, and which might be said by particular penitents in a Lenten rite prior to engaging in public penance.[16]

So 'confession' might, in the period before 1215, be taken to mean both the admission of particular faults—perhaps most likely to enter the documentary record when they were crimes committed against church property or rights—and the general admission of the guilt of sin, shared to some extent by all Christians. Something of the latter seems still to remain in some injunctions against making too general a 'confession' in texts from the thirteenth and fourteenth centuries: for example, the synodal of Nîmes from 1252 tells priests to ensure that when their parishioners come to make confession, they do not simply speak the names of the sins, but must give all the actual details. Something adjacent is stated in Bishop Bernard de Campendu's synodal for Carcassonne from around 1270, where the sense is in part that a penitent might attempt simply to indicate that some sin was committed, rather than what they themselves had done: 'When confessing one should not use covert words or names for the sins or crimes. Rather, however shameful the sin, one should take pains to use its proper name when revealing it and its circumstances, so that all the pus of sin can be expelled.'[17]

That bishops are still explaining the insufficiency of such rather vague practices in the later thirteenth century itself cuts two ways: it does rather suggest that this might be one of the forms of earlier 'confession', then changed by the pastoral practices developed after 1215; but it also seems likely that it persisted, continuing as a mode of confession that even diligent bishops did not immediately manage to reform. Alexander Murray has argued that the picture of early medieval confession presented by Meens, Hamilton, and others may tell us mostly about practices provided by bishops rather than parish priests, and perhaps particularly in areas where there was a notable centre for reform such as Cluny or Fulda.[18] The nature of the manuscript evidence may not quite fit to his model—Hamilton, Meens, and van Rhijn are persuasive on the fact that some manuscripts were for local use by the lower clergy—but Murray makes also what I think is a fundamentally important point: that practices probably varied considerably by region. This is not least because the kinds of materials that would help a parish priest with the fairly demanding task of hearing confessions and assigning individualized penances were very much the product of *particular* bishops and, later, mendicants. There are very few early medieval penitential texts that survive for southern France;[19] and, as the brief sketch above suggests, the evidence for lay confession

---

[16] On the latter, see D. Iogna-Prat, 'Topographies of Penance in the Latin West, c. 800–c.1200', in Firey, ed., *New History of Penance*, pp. 149–72 at 170–71.

[17] Synodal of Nîmes, 1252, c. 22 (Pontal, *Statuts synodaux*, II, p. 288); synodal of Carcassonne, c. 1270, c. IV.5 (Mahul, *Cartulaire*, V, p. 423).

[18] A. Murray, 'Confession before 1215', *Transactions of the Royal Historical Society*, 6th ser., 3 (1993), 51–81; reprinted in Murray, *Conscience and Authority*.

[19] See Chapter 1, n. 98 re work by Meens.

and penance that exists in this region prior to the later twelfth century tends to make visible occasions of public penance and deathbed confession, neither of which may tell us all that we would like to know about more regular practice, if such existed.

To be clear: it seems indisputable that, certainly from the early twelfth century and probably earlier, on occasion lay people made confession and received penance. But whilst this seems in some form to have been a regular aspect of what happened at someone's deathbed, whether it otherwise happened regularly, on an annual basis, is not certain. Moreover 'made confession' might imply something more like a general statement of being in sin, or the simple naming of the 'kind' of sin one had committed, rather than the detailed, personalized narrative of self-accusation imagined by later texts.

It is also indisputably the case that in southern France, as elsewhere in Europe, the period after 1215 saw a flurry of production of new penitentially directed material. These include a more complex set of stories educating the laity about sin, as found in the preaching *exempla*, and detailed and particular injunctions arising from papal legates and regional bishops over the necessity of regular lay confession—and indeed, as we have seen in Chapter 7, the necessity of making written record that it had been performed. Most usefully and importantly, we also find a number of thirteenth- and early fourteenth-century treatises produced within the region, specifically advising priests and mendicants on how to hear confessions and how to award penances. As elsewhere in Europe, these range from very substantial works which were in large part glosses on canon law, to much shorter pieces which could be consulted more swiftly and practically. The new appearance and subsequent expansion of such materials does still tend to suggest that 1215 formed something of a watershed, in this region at least.

As most of what follows will be arranged thematically, tracking the practicalities and implications of confession and penance, it may be useful first to give a brief overview of the main texts I have drawn upon. It is very likely—as Pierre Michaud-Quantin pointed out, in an early survey of such materials—that southern French bishops and mendicants had access to Raymond de Peñafort's very influential *Summa de poenitentie* (c. 1226), and similarly to Humbert de Romans's *De officiis ordinis*, chapter 46 of which was often produced as a stand-alone guide to confession for mendicants to use, given their importance to the Brothers Preacher generally—though in fact it does not appear that any southern French manuscript copy survives.[20] It is also the case, as Michaud-Quantin notes, that no manuscript evidence survives to suggest that various other of the early manuals produced in northern Europe circulated in southern France in this period; though we can perhaps point to one important exception, John of Freiburg's

---

[20] P. Michaud-Quantin, 'Textes pénitentials languedociens au XIIIe siècle', *CdF* 6 (1971), 151–72.

Summa confessorum which is extant in a fourteenth-century manuscript in Toulouse, and which we know informed at least one specifically southern French text (as we shall see further below).[21] But we do have one very interesting and brief treatise, known by its opening words as *Cum ad sacerdotum*, probably written by a Brother Preacher in the 1220s. The earliest manuscript in which this survives is also in Toulouse (albeit dating to some time later in the thirteenth century) and the text may itself be a southern French composition.[22] The aforementioned synodal booklets produced for Nîmes in 1252 and Carcassonne around 1270 both provide similarly brief guides for priests (the Carcassonne synodal drawing extensively on the former), as does the synodal produced by Dominique Grenier, bishop of Pamiers, in the fourteenth century. There is also a copy of the relatively short *Summa de foro penitenciali* produced by Bérenger Frédol (canon of Béziers, and later bishop of Frascati) in an early fourteenth-century Toulouse manuscript that also contains Bernard Gui's short guide to the tenets of faith.[23] Raymond de Peñafort's *Summa* is very much a work of canon law rather than pastoral advice, and John of Freiburg's *Summa* is a massive treatise; but the other texts just mentioned are all quite brief, practical, and perhaps therefore more likely to guide us to actual parochial practice. finally, there is the one vernacular work: the extensive discussion of sin and penance found in Matfre Ermengaud's *Breviari d'amor* (1288–c. 1291), which we met in the last chapter.

With the aid of all these materials let us think, then, of what the experience of confession was like from the perspective of an ordinary layperson. They would come to their parish priest to confess—when? Most likely in the lead-up to Easter, though in the aftermath of the crusade and the injunctions to make thrice-annual confession, also at Christmas and Pentecost. How long did this thrice-annual practice last? The impression one gets from most of the later thirteenth-century advice texts is that, perhaps after a few decades, normal practice had reverted to making confession only in the period just before Easter; the synodal for Carcassonne says one should confess 'at least once a year', for example.[24] In the fourteenth century, Dominique Grenier warned penitents that they should not

---

[21] BM Toulouse MS 381.

[22] BM Toulouse MS 340, fols 255r–269v, an incomplete copy accompanied by substantial glosses (a few elements from which are discussed below); a full edition drawing on other manuscripts is provided by J. Goering and P. J. Payer, 'The "Summa penitentie Fratrum predicatorum": A Thirteenth-Century Confessional Formulary', *Mediaeval Studies* 55 (1993), 1–50, using a title found in other exemplars. Goering and Payer convincingly argue for its early date due to its slightly curious position on what constitutes marriage. The Toulouse manuscript as a whole contains some material of a north Italian origin; a southern French place of composition for the treatise is nonetheless suggested by the fact that at one point it mentions, notably gratuitously, 'the French and certain other awful people (*Gallici et quidam alii pessimi*)' who swear all the time (Goering and Payer, p. 35). We might imagine that the sentiment being voiced by someone from Languedoc or Provence in the period of the crusade; and certainly many texts from the region talk of 'the French'.

[23] BM Toulouse MS 191, fols 73r–113v; followed immediately by a tiny extract from Raymond de Peñafort's *Summa*, regarding 'reserved' sins.

[24] Synodal of Carcassonne, c. 1270, c. IV.1 (Mahul, *Cartulaire*, V, p. 422).

delay confessing into Easter week itself, as the priest might by that point be too busy with his liturgical duties to find sufficient time for them, rather suggesting that everybody was trying to do it around the same time.[25] However, we do find inquisitors in the early fourteenth century enjoining thrice-annual confession on some of those involved in heresy, as with one cleric, thirteen men and nine women, released from prison in 1318 by the inquisitors Henri de Chamayou and Pierre Brun, who were sentenced also to wear double-crosses, undergo public penance every Sunday at church, and undertake a variety of long-distance pilgrimages.[26] Presumably therefore thrice-annual practice remained an option for others, and Easter certainly wasn't the only moment at which someone might confess. The synodal of Carcassonne told priests to encourage their parishioners to confess sins whenever they had committed them, since death might strike them down before they otherwise got around to it.

But let us assume that the most common experience was a Lenten confession, undertaken in the expectation that one is duly cleansed to receive communion in Easter week. This liturgical context is of course rather important, as it brings into focus a number of key aspects of Christian community, not least the fact that confessing certain sins and making restitution might be a key requirement for being 'in charity' with one's neighbours.[27] Receiving communion whilst still in a state of sin was dangerous for one's soul. More prosaically, we should also remember the southern French injunction to record the names of those who confessed, to inform the bishop of those who had not; a context of explicit monitoring of faith thus also pertained.

Confession would take place in church, in a 'place suitable for hearing confessions', namely somewhere both private—in the sense of being apart from any other worshippers there present, to avoid anyone overhearing—but also not somewhere 'hidden', in that the priest should be seen to be ministering to his flock, and should be careful not to engender any scandal by discussing sinful matters behind closed doors, particularly with women.[28] Thus the details of one's sins were, for the most part, private matters, as would usually also be the case with penance; but the *fact* of having confessed one's sins would be known to all, and commonly experienced by most. The confessant's physical comportment with regard to the priest might vary across the decades: in the early texts, there is a suggestion that the priest should keep himself seated lower down than his

---

[25] BM Toulouse MS 402, fol. 62r: 'moneant etiam parochianos suos in principio quadragesime quod non differant venire ad confessionem quia forte non audirentur in ebdomadas tam propter occupationem sacerdotem circa divinum officium'.

[26] Doat 27, fols 3r–7r, particularly at 3v: 'confiteantur etiam ter in anno peccata sua proprio sacerdoti curato videlicet ante Pascham, Pentecostem, et nativitatem domini'.

[27] J. Bossy, 'The Social History of Confession in the Age of the Reformation', *Transactions of the Royal Historical Society*, 5th ser., 25 (1975), 21–38.

[28] For example, synodal of Carcassonne c. 1270, c.IV, p. 423: 'quod presbyteri confessiones audientes in loco patenti confessiones audiant, non in occulto, et praecipue si confitentes fuerint mulieres'.

parishioner, but by Bérenger Frédol's time, the injunction was for the penitent to be seated at the feet of the priest.[29] The priest, as we saw in Chapter 7, was encouraged to use the opportunity first to check if the confessant knew the Creed, the *Pater noster*, and the *Ave*. He might then begin the actual process of confession with some prompting words, perhaps a mixture of encouragement and stern warning. From *Cum ad sacerdotum*:

> Brother, God does not wish the death of a sinner, but that they might be converted and live... See therefore that you are not stupidly led to hide any sin from foolish shame or fear or honour. Indeed I, miserable sinner, have done or indeed heard many more than you.... I warn you, God is not to be fooled; He knows the way men think. Know without doubt that if you work to conceal one of your sins, you will come to realize that you cannot do so with others. Nor because of the magnitude or enormity of sins is anything hidden in confession, because however great the sins are, God's mercy in confession will wash them away. Therefore, in the name of the Lord, say whatever you wish.[30]

In all of this, the priest is warned not to look straight at the confessant, but with head bowed (and if with a woman, quite probably hiding further away with a hood over his head).

Thus, hopefully, the penitent began to speak, to recount the things done of which they were now ashamed, for which they felt the real sorrow of repentance, and for which they wished to make amends. It might not be easy, and the confessant was probably particularly aware of the priest's potential reaction. (He is warned not to laugh or smile or spit at what he hears, or to turn his face away or make any swift retorts.)[31] 'Priest, if you see the penitent stumbling and doubting and going along as if feeling the way', advises *Cum ad sacerdotem*, 'say to them "Brother, you can safely say whatever you wish, because God is with you".' Further advice on the emotional management of the penitent follows, warning the priest that if they are made to feel great shame, they may cease to confess.[32] In partial contrast, Bérenger Frédol also advises that one may need to frighten the sinner:

---

[29] BM Toulouse MS 191, fol. 73r: 'et quod sedeat humiliter ex transverso ad pedes sacerdotis, si femina sic sedeat ex transverso et ex latere...'

[30] 'Cum ad sacerdotem': BM Toulouse MS 340, fols 257r–258r; Goering and Payer, 'Summa penitentie', pp. 26–27. The synodals of Nîmes and Carcassonne, and Frédol's *Summa*, advise the priest to emphasize that he too is a sinner, and to remind the penitent that God forgave Pierre, Paul, and Marie Madeleine: Nîmes, 1252, c. 28 (Pontal, *Statuts synodaux*, II p. 292); Carcassonne, c. 1270, c. IV (Mahul, *Cartulaire*, V, p. 423); *Summa de foro penitenciali*, BM Toulouse MS 191, fol. 73r.

[31] 'Cum ad sacerdotem': BM Toulouse MS 340, fol. 259r, Goering and Payer, 'Summa penitentie', p. 27; synodal of Carcassonne, c. IV (Mahul, *Cartulaire*, V, p. 423).

[32] 'Cum ad sacerdotem': BM Toulouse MS 340, fol. 259r–260r; Goering and Payer, 'Summa penitentie', pp. 27–28.

'If in truth he does not wish to confess, set forth the terrors of the punishments of future judgment.'[33]

At a certain point, the penitent presumably runs out of things to say; the priest will then probably start to ask some questions. The manuals differ a little on this: Raymond de Peñafort noted that 'some say' that you ought not to do so, though he thought this dangerous, given the 'simplicity' and 'shamefacedness' of people. *Cum ad sacerdotem* advises the priest to do it if 'it seems to the priest that [the penitent] has said things imperfectly and insufficiently'. Most of the later texts simply take it for granted that the confessor will move on to questioning.[34] In asking questions, the priest has to be careful: whilst the circumstances of one's sins are extremely important, as they should inform his understanding of the degree of guilt and thus his enjoined penance, at the same time one was not supposed to reveal any wrongdoing by any other person. It might be that in smaller parishes, such discretion would be honoured more in theory than in reality; it would sometimes have been hard to conceal the fact or likely identity of any collaborators in misdeeds. The priest must also try to be careful not to ask questions which put ideas into the confessant's head, particularly regarding sexual sins (to which we shall return further below). As the fourteenth-century glossator to *Cum ad sacerdotem* noted, 'It is suitable to exercise discretion in all these things, but most of all with simple people and children, because they can swiftly learn to sin.'[35]

Presumably many questions asked by priests were simply for further elucidation of what one had already said. But the manuals also present an array of different questions a priest might ask, to try to uncover anything that the penitent had forgotten or hidden. These could be arranged in several different ways—by the seven deadly sins, by the Ten Commandments, by the five senses, all of which are used in *Cum ad sacerdotem*—but perhaps most commonly they appear as what we might call questions '*ad status*', that is, questions directed toward the kind of person you were, running vaguely in parallel to the *ad status* sermons that addressed suitable moral questions for different groups. The logic here was, firstly, that different stations in life provided the opportunity for different kinds of sins: one could only impose 'bad new customs' if one was a lord who wielded that kind of power, one could only use false weights or give short measure if one was engaged in trade, and so forth. The synodals of Nîmes and Carcassonne provided a fairly simple list of such questions. Various related to other members of the

---

[33] BM Toulouse MS 191, fol. 73v: 'Si vero non vult confiteri terrores futuri iudicii pene inferni terribiliter proponantur.'

[34] Raymond de Peñafort, *Summa de poenitentia* (Avignon, 1715), III.27 (p. 675); Goering and Payer, 'Summa penitentie', p. 28. Later examples: Nîmes, 1252, c. 29 (Pontal, *Statuts synodaux*, p. 294); Carcassonne, c. 1270, c. IV (Mahul, *Cartulaire*, V, p. 423).

[35] BM Toulouse MS 340, fol. 263v: 'Discretionem debet habere in omnibus set maxime circa simplices et pueros quia cito peccare addiscunt.'

clergy, who of course also had to make confession, namely whether they had committed simony, if they had looked after their benefice, attended to divine offices. But most questions were focused on different groups of lay people. For example, regarding princes, castellans, knights, and *baillis*, whether they had impinged on ecclesiastical liberties, had given full justice where they exercised it, had extorted things from those subject to them. Bourgeois, merchants, and others should be asked about 'lying, fraud, usury, sureties and bartering, or regarding unjust weights and measures'. For agricultural workers, 'regarding theft, most of all of tithes, tributes, rents'; moving boundary markers and illegitimately occupying the land of someone else; and burning things and suchlike. Shepherds, servants, and so forth: 'whether they have faithfully guarded the things of their lords, and conducted themselves faithfully in the works and services they carry out'.[36]

The earlier synodals provide just these brief examples. But in lengthier and later texts, the *ad status* questions suggest a deeper sense of the sinner belonging to a particular group, different sins being associated with different kinds of people, in a sort of pathological fashion. Bishop Grenier's synodal for Pamiers, for example, adds to the things one might ask merchants and bourgeois: 'of lying, perjury, and indeed fraud; and of many other almost endless things'.[37] In this sense, whilst the discourse of sin and confession in part sought to individuate people—you must tell of *your* own sins, and work on your own moral behaviour—it simultaneously worked to typologize people, relating them to different categories. This reaches a pinnacle in the *Breviari d'amor*, where Matfre Ermengaud addresses a lay readership to educate them in their own sinful position in the world: 'among lay men, there are diverse estates, with particular ways of falling into mortal sin, each of them, according to their condition, to their better instruction, showing those they must guard themselves against and those they must confess'.[38] He goes on to address, in separate categories, princes, castellans, knights and soldiers, lawyers, medics, bourgeois, merchants, consuls and administrators, servants, labourers, hostellers, gamblers, entertainers (*joglars*) and—at considerably greater length than any other group—women. Each are told of ways in which they are most likely to fall into sin. Lawyers, for example, are warned against drawing up 'false documents' or suborning witnesses; consuls are reminded that when they take office, they make an oath on the Four Gospels, and if they then administer badly they are breaking that oath; labourers are told not to work on Sundays or feast days, nor to conceal their goods to avoid paying tithes or other tolls; *joglars* are chastised for singing songs about worldly vanity, foolishness, and sin.

---

[36] Synodal of Nîmes, 1252, cc. 34, 35, 36 (Pontal, *Statuts synodaux*, II, p. 298); synodal of Carcassonne, c. 1270, c. IV (Mahul, *Cartulaire*, V, p. 424).
[37] BM Toulouse MS 402, fol. 63r: 'de mendaciis periurio atque dolo et de multis aliis quasi infinitis'.
[38] *Breviari d'amor*, ll. 17258–65: 'E quar entre las laiguas gens | ha mans diverses estamens, | qu'an manieiras especials | de cazer en peccatz mortals, | quex, seguon sa condicio, | a major lur estructio, | mostran de que·s devon guardar | e de que·s devon confessar...'

In the previous chapter I discussed some aspects of how the laity were to be instructed in the fact of sin, arguing that over the course of the thirteenth century this increasingly meant making clear that various transgressions were to be understood as *sins*, not simply as social misbehaviour. To amplify that argument a little further here: the texts providing advice on confession show a number of additional ways in which the concept of sin and its entailments was further expanding in this period. One is via the various schematic frames through which sins might be 'recalled', as the priest questioned the penitent. As noted above, *Cum ad sacerdotem* briefly proffers several different schema for the confessor. The seven deadly sins are addressed primarily via bad external behaviour, often directed toward others: wrath leading to angry words or physical assault, sloth making one fail to carry out an enjoined penance or not coming to church on Sundays, avarice leading to theft, lust resulting in adultery or incest, and so forth. Sins committed against the Ten Commandments are for the most part crimes: magic working, blasphemy, murder, theft.[39] But the text then turns to sins associated with the five senses, and here things become a little more diffuse and bound up with intentions and inner disposition. Sight: 'whether one had looked at a woman with desire... or gone to ogle women' (*literally* 'gone to look at remarkable examples of beauty in women'). Smell: whether one had worn perfume to entice people. Hearing: 'whether one had willingly gone to listen to little songs, and in this way when listening to mass had quickly become bored'. Taste: whether one had eaten or drunk unnecessarily seasoned things, or had broken a fast (as at Lent or other times in the year). Touch: 'whether one had touched a woman shamefully, namely touching her breasts or chest or her shameful places'.[40]

The sense that 'sin' included things which might not directly affect another person (or, at least, less directly than assaulting them or stealing their goods), or indeed which might have no clear external manifestation, becomes increasingly apparent in some of the later texts. Bérenger Frédol, proffering questions to do with the sin of pride, for example, says, 'when one believes oneself to be better than one is, and is contemptuous of others, and does not recognize the grace one has from God, as when they say that all that they have they believe came from their own labour and industry; and they wish to dominate their neighbours'.[41]

---

[39] John Bossy argued that there was a general shift, in the transition from the medieval to the early modern period, from a focus on the seven sins—which generally speak to intercommunal relations—to the Ten Commandments—addressing a more hierarchical 'law'. In fact the Ten Commandments seem quite often to sit alongside the sins in various medieval pastoral works; but his analysis of the differing dynamics of the 'sin' they address is nonetheless useful, both aspects being present *in potentia* in medieval society. J. Bossy, 'Moral Arithmetic: Seven Sins into Ten Commandments', in E. Leites, ed., *Conscience and Casuistry in Early Modern Europe* (Cambridge: Cambridge University Press, 1988), pp. 213–34.
[40] Goering and Payer, 'Summa penitentie', pp. 37–38.
[41] BM Toulouse MS 191, fol. 76r: 'Item cum credit se meliorem quam sit et alios contempnit, et gratias quas a deo habet se habere non cognoscit ab eo ut quidam dicunt quod omnia que habunt credunt ex suo labore et industria habere, et volunt vicinis suis dominari'.

With regard to sloth, he counsels asking not only if they come to church on feast days, and abstained from talking during the service, but whether they have regarded the consecrated host with due reverence.[42] Thus increasingly the conception of sin includes faults of omission as well as commission: failing to honour the dead by attending funerals, for example, included by Frédol under the heading of those who break the fourth commandment to honour one's father and mother.[43] The *Breviari d'amor* again amplifies such matters through its more extended discussion, and its conception of sin includes quite subtle faults. For example, in the section on lawyers, alongside the more obvious cases of clear corruption noted above, Matfre Ermengaud chides those who have caused 'great delays' in cases, and those who, from love of money, have taken on many different cases but have consequently neglected the needs of too great a number of clients. Medics sin if, when treating someone who is suffering from gout or leprosy or other such things, they lack compassion and are interested only in their fee. Bourgeois—that is, city dwellers—sin in various prideful ways, concerned with their own honour and status, eating unnecessarily fine foods and showing off; and, if they should fall into poverty, they sin when through pride they will not take on a different and more menial job. Consuls and administrators can sin not only through obvious crookedness or misadministration but, when they stand down from their office, through voting for friends or relatives as their replacement.[44] Women sin when they chatter in church rather than listen to the sermon, they sin when their desire for worldly things leads their husbands into usury or theft or other misadventures, and they sin when they wear revealing clothes.[45]

If the priest's questions include such matters, it becomes clear that the point is not simply to help the penitent 'remember' sins that they may have forgotten, but to *realize* that things they have done are in fact sinful. A preaching *exemplum* gives another illustration of the process, albeit one somewhat more externalized than some of the *Breviari*'s examples: a knight had his castle guarded by a fierce dog, so fierce that pilgrims and paupers never dared to beg hospitality there. Realizing this, he considered getting rid of it, but his wife—who loved the hound, and cared nothing for the poor—stopped him from doing so. When she went on pilgrimage to Compostelle, she went to enter a church whilst en route, but found that she was supernaturally prevented from so doing. 'Whence she confessed her sins, but even then could not enter', and was filled with shame. Others said to her that she must confess completely, the implication being that she had concealed

---

[42] BM Toulouse MS 191, fol. 76v: 'Item si laicus est queratur si bene venit ad ecclesiam in festis et si loquitur in ecclesia cum aliis vel non audit divinum officium libenter vel non videt corpus christi cum reverentia qua decet.'

[43] BM Toulouse MS 191, fol. 74v: 'Si ad ecclesiam in solempnitatibus non bene ivit vel ad mortuos sepeliendo.'

[44] *Breviari d'amor*, pp. 46, 50, 58, 62–64, 80.   [45] *Breviari d'amor*, pp. 110, 106, 114.

something. She protested that 'she didn't know of anything that she had not confessed', but after more discussion and questioning, worked out that the problem was the dog and its uncharitable behaviour. She promised to get rid of the dog on her return, and having done this, was able to enter the church. But in fact, when she got back from her pilgrimage, she forgot her promise—and a few days later the dog attacked her 'and cruelly and totally tore her to pieces'.[46] Punishment for the failure to carry out a promised pious task is a familiar trope in other *exempla*, but what is particularly interesting here is the way in which an insufficiently proactive form of spirituality—the failure actively to care for pilgrims and the poor—is understood as something to which one might confess, the spiritual failings of a privileged layperson thus becoming understood as *sin* rather than insufficiency or hard-heartedness.

Let us return to our imagined scene of confession. The priest has questioned, more or less gently, subtly, and comprehensively, and both the confessant and confessor decide that all sins have been laid bare. The priest may yet have a few more questions however, to try to discern the confessant's disposition and future intention: are you truly sorry for what you have done? Are you really going to try never to do it again; or, like the noblewoman with the dog, are you going to get lax and forget? The synodal of Nîmes reminded priests that they must clearly instruct the penitent to give up any future return to sin if they are to be absolved; at the same time, it warns, one must try not to plunge the penitent into despair.[47] The synodal of Carcassonne advises that if the penitent refuses to promise to abstain from all their sins in the future, or to give up only some of them, the priest must counsel them carefully, warning them that 'if one were to pay for all the paupers in the whole world, and to fast on bread and water for all the time of one's life, nothing will aid your salvation whilst you remain in sin'.[48] The emotional management of the sinner is important, and potentially quite complicated. They must not allow shame to lead them to conceal anything, they must feel true contrition for their sin, and the priest must decide if he can discern this. Frédol sets these out clearly and forcefully: 'First [proper confession] is that which is indeed contrite and sorry for all sins. Second it is that each and every sin is confessed ... Third, that he [*the penitent*] should set out and have firmly declared in his heart that thereafter he will not revert to the former sin'.[49] In this sense, confession is not only a recounting of one's individual past experience, but a promise for the future, an attempt at positive self-(re)making as a better Christian.

---

[46] Welter, 'Un nouveau recueil franciscain d'exempla', p. 602 (no. 147).
[47] Synodal of Nîmes, 1252, cc. 38, 39 (Pontal, *Statuts synodaux*, II, pp. 300–02).
[48] Synodal of Carcassonne, c. 1270, c. IV (Mahul, *Cartulaire*, V, p. 424). Repeated in the same words in synodal of Pamiers (BM Toulouse MS 402, fol. 64r).
[49] BM Toulouse MS 191, fol. 73r: 'Primum est quod sic bene contritus et dolens de peccatis omnibus. Secundum est quod omnia et singula peccata sua confitetur ut supradictum est. Tercium quod proponat et propositum firmum habeat in corde deinceps non revertendi ad pristina peccata'.

That emotional management reaches some kind of climax with the bestowal of penance. The priest will say some formal words—'by the authority of God I absolve you of the sins you have confessed and those you have forgotten, in the name of the Father, the Son, and the Holy Spirit'—and whilst doing this will probably make the sign of the cross and place his hand upon the penitent's head (by the mid-fourteenth century Bishop Grenier had pointed out that these actions were not a necessary part of the sacrament, although they are found in the earlier synodal texts).[50] Confession thus most likely finishes with a small ritual moment, visible to others, and with the promise, in Latin, of redemption. But the penitent must make restitution for anyone hurt by their sinful actions, and must perform penance, the latter in itself a kind of recompense to God. We may note that 'restitution' becomes more complex in a society that is clearly conscious of mercantile contracts: Matfre Ermengaud argues that one must not just pay back something taken from another, but also any subsequent profit made from the goods; and, as Bishop Grenier notes, any wives, children, or household members who have lived off the profits of a husband's usury are implicated, unless they did not consent to the sin.[51] The details of restitution thus might require some discussion; and the priest must also decide what penance to impose, this being very much his discretion, and ideally calibrated to the sinner's emotional state, status in life, and the nature of the sins committed.

The point about penance is that it is, for the most part, voluntary (there are important exceptions to which I shall turn further below). The priest needs to calibrate the right kind of penance, acting as a medic does when prescribing the right kind of medicine; but also needs to persuade the confessant then to undertake the penance. He is thus counselled not to impose something that the individual cannot actually manage to do.[52] Bérenger Frédol also reminds the priest of some other impediments: one should not send young women on pilgrimage, because of the danger this might pose to them; nor should a man make a vow to go on pilgrimage without his wife's permission (unless it is to go to Jerusalem).[53] For the most part, whilst the manuals emphasize the priest's arbitrary judgment in deciding on a suitable penance, they emphasize prayer, fasting, and almsgiving.

---

[50] BM Toulouse MS 402, fol. 65r: 'auctoritate dei absolute a peccatis tuis confessis et oblitis in nomine patris etc [sic], faciendo signum crucis et inponendo manum suum super caput confitentis si voluit quia non sunt de necessitate sacramenti'.

[51] *Breviari d'amor*, p. 138; BM Toulouse MS 402, fol. 70v: 'uxor, filii et familiares usurarii de talibus lucris viventes et unde vivant alium de non habentes excusari videntur, si tamen peccato non consentiunt'.

[52] BM Toulouse MS 402, fol. 64v: 'In multis casibus totum remanent in arbitrio confessoris sicut quamvis actores medicine taxent certas medicinas pro diversis infirmitatibus totum tamen remanet in arbitrio medici ut considerata virtute infirmi et aliis circumstanciis...Caveat etiam confessor ne imponat honus importabile penitenti...'.

[53] BM Toulouse MS 191, fols 78r-v: 'Item caveat sacerdos ne iniungat peregrinationem mulieri iuveni quia pericul[osa] est'; 'Item non potest vir facere votum peregrinationis sine uxoris sue consensu voto ierosolumtano [sic] excepto'. (The latter point is in a section on vows, but does clearly relate to penance more broadly.)

From the synodal of Carcassonne:

Since opposites cure each other, the priest should enjoin a penance on the sinner that is the contrary response: if he sins by pride, impose prayers, so that he can be persuaded to humility. If he has sinned by avarice, he should supply liberal alms. If by greed and drunkenness, he should be given fasting in penance. If by lust, [impose] fasts, prayers, pilgrimages, mortification of the flesh and other disciplines (*carnis macerationes et alias disciplinas*). If he is old, rich, and self-indulgent and says that he cannot fast, the priest should burden him with prayers and almsgiving, relieving him of fasts. If the sinner claims bodily debility, asserting that he cannot manage a harsh penance, or if he cannot be persuaded to complete a chosen penance, the priest should impose a penance agreed with the sinner that he can and will in truth tolerate, so that he does not sin further by infringing penance. In this manner, caution should be taken that married women and virgins do not have a penance imposed which gives rise to negative suspicion.[54]

Thus the sense of negotiation is very strong—though perhaps strongest when the penitent is a person of power and wealth. Various preaching *exempla* provide further evidence of this dynamic, where a penitent bargains the priest down to what they believe will be a lighter penance, only miraculously to discover that it turns out much harsher than they had imagined. For example, a holy man heard the confession of the lord of a castle, and asked him to undertake seven years of penance (the story does not explain what this would comprise, but one imagines a mixture of prayers, fasts, and almsgiving); the lord refuses. Three years? No. One year? No. Seven months? No. Eventually the lord agrees to spend one night in the local church, where he places himself by the altar and prays. As it then happens, various demons come and try to tempt him out through adopting a variety of illusions: in the guise of his sister, telling him that enemies are coming, and that his vigil is stupid; as his wife and children, telling him that an army has captured their castle; an illusion of fire surrounding the church; and finally a demon who appears in the form of a priest, who sets about preparing the church for mass and tells the knight that since he is excommunicate, he cannot stay put. In each case, he refuses, and eventually completes the penance.[55] To be clear, there is no indication that the knight sees through the guise of the demons. He is, rather, keeping to his word in performing the penance, come what may.

The point made by such a story is twofold: true penance is hard, and has to be hard in order to do its job; but if done with commitment, it is a protection from sin and the snares of demons. Priests thus needed to persuade the penitent to

---

[54] Synodal of Carcassonne, c. 1270, c. IV (Mahul, *Cartulaire*, V, pp. 424–25).
[55] Welter, 'Un nouveau recueil franciscain d'exempla', pp. 449–50 (no. 32).

undertake that which was demanding, for their own good. Frédol advises reminding the penitent that the penance they avoid in this life will be visited upon them, but much more harshly, in purgatory.[56] The synodal of Carcassonne suggests that if someone will not truly undertake penance, the priest should nonetheless encourage them to fast, pray, and give alms 'and do whatever other good they can', as whilst this will not be sufficient to give them salvation, it may help God illumine their heart with true penitence, or at least keep them out of the clutches of demons who will lead them further astray.[57] Stories told by preachers warned of the dangers of not making confession and undertaking penance, typically of someone who put off doing it and then died unexpectedly.[58] But they could also tell of its wonderous benefits, even for those who took a while to reform themselves. An *exemplum* recorded by a Brother Preacher tells of a man at Capestang (near Béziers) who went for fourteen years without penance, but who finally decided to go to his parish priest to confess. The following night he was visited by a demon who bewailed the fact that after fourteen years of sinning he had turned away from vice, promising all kinds of things if he will only revert to his old ways. This failing, the demon threatened him with financial ruin. 'I fear nothing', the man said in response; 'God will restore me'.[59]

Confession, penance, and absolution thus made a theological promise about future salvation, but also, at their best, provided present benefits. The inner conversion and peace experienced by the man from Capestang—the freedom from fear—was an idealized individual response to confession, and perhaps speaks to the experience of some, at least in the immediate aftermath of confession, absolution, and Easter communion. (As an *exemplum* recorded by a Sack Friar notes, just as some substances are flexible when in water but hard as a stone when dry, so 'many men, when they have heard the word of God, their heart is softened; but having heard it, they harden').[60] As Nicole Archambeau has demonstrated, using the canonization witness statements for the southern French nobleman Delphine de Puimichel (wife to Elzéar de Sabran, mentioned above), by the mid-fourteenth century the act of confession and the successful completion of penance could themselves be understood as moments of 'danger' by lay people, worried about how well and how thoroughly they had performed them.[61] In part it is indeed thus an individualizing discourse. And yet, the lengthy discussion of confession and sin in Matfre Ermengaud's *Breviari d'amor*, concluding with the subject of

---

[56] BM Toulouse MS 191, fol. 77v: 'et quod qui non facit penitentiam in hoc mundo faciet in purgatorio, ubi est tanta pena quod minor pena qui ibi est maior est quam aliqua huius vite…'
[57] Synodal of Carcassonne, c. 1270, c. IV (Mahul, *Cartulaire*, V, p. 424).
[58] For example, Welter, 'Un nouveau recueil franciscain d'exempla', p. 612 (nos 177, 178, 179), all quite brief and prosaic.
[59] Welter, 'Un nouveau recueil franciscain d'exempla', pp. 609–10 (no. 171).
[60] Welter, 'Un recueil d'exempla', p. 212 (no. 202).
[61] N. Archambeau, *Souls Under Siege: Stories of War, Plague and Confession in Fourteenth-Century Provence* (Ithaca, NY: Cornell University Press, 2021), chapter 5.

restitution, then moves seamlessly into an extended treatment of the love owed to one's neighbours, making it part of his overarching theme of collective Christian love and charity. Sin, confession, restitution, and penance could always be, and perhaps often were, simultaneously personal and private *and* communal and public. And certain kinds of sins—and penances—were very definitely the latter, producing a more visible kind of 'discipline' with much wider implications beyond the individual.

The Inquisitorial Care of Souls

On 3 March 1308, in the cathedral church of Saint-Étienne in Toulouse, the inquisitor and Brother Preacher Bernard Gui presided over a large gathering. Present were the bishop, several canons, the consuls of the city, royal officers, and representatives of the clergy and people 'in a great multitude'. They were there to witness the sentencing of seven people (two of them deceased) for various crimes of heresy. Gui would have begun by addressing the congregation—such events were known as 'General Sermons'—undoubtedly decrying the evils of heresy and warning people what happened if they gave support or aid to heretics, perhaps reminding them of their sworn duty to help inquisitors capture heretics and drive out heresy.[62] Each person was brought forth in turn, and a brief statement of their crimes read out, probably first in Latin and then in the vernacular. First came two people released from prior imprisonment, Pierre de Saint-Laurent from Garrigues and Tholosana, widow of Bernard Hugou, from Roquevidal. They were sentenced to wear single yellow crosses on their clothes, and ordered to visit the churches of Saint-Sernin and Saint-Étienne in Toulouse annually. Tholosana was ordered to undertake 'minor pilgrimages' (probably meaning within the region rather than to Compostelle or Canterbury, for example), whilst Pierre was let off these 'because of infirmity and age'.

Then Pons Amiel of La Garde, near Verfeil, was sentenced for deeds which he had previously admitted. These were briefly set out: in 1290, he had confessed to the late inquisitor Pierre de Mulceone that when he was 7 years old he had associated with the heretic (that is, the Good Man) Aymeri Barrot; had subsequently received other heretics in his house; had commended the sect of the heretics to others; and had believed that they were 'good men and true, and had a good faith and that one could be saved in their faith'. Sixteen years later, in 1306, he had made another confession to a different inquisitor, expanding on what he had previously said, and was imprisoned for two periods of time whilst waiting for people to give sureties that he would serve the Catholic faith; after which he had abjured

---

[62] On Gui's general sermons, see D. Hill, *Inquisition in the Fourteenth Century: The Manuals of Bernard Gui and Nicholas Eymerich* (York: York Medieval Press, 2019), pp. 145–56.

all heresy. In 1307, he had confessed once more before Bernard Gui, who found that after his abjuration Pons had again associated with heretics, namely with Pierre Autier and his son Jacques, hearing their preaching and doctrine and 'adoring' them by bending his knees three times before them and saying ' "Bless you", following the manner of the heretics'.

Next came Philippa de Tounis. She had first confessed in 1274 to two inquisitors, Renou de Plassac and Pons de Parnac, and had crosses imposed on her. Two later inquisitors, Hugues Amiel and Jean Galand, had relieved her of the crosses, and she had abjured heresy before them ('just as is stated in the acts and books of inquisition, and as she herself recognized to be true'). In 1292 she had confessed again before Pierre de Mulceone, initially concealing the fact that she had had contact with a friend of the heretics; and in 1306 and 1307 (probably imprisoned in between) she admitted before Gui that she also had had contact with the Autiers more recently.

At this point, the inquisitor formally intoned: 'having God before our eyes and the purity of the orthodox faith, the holy Gospels of God placed before us, the aforesaid Pons Amiel and Philippa de Tounis on this day being present to hear the decisive sentence assigned, we say and by the sentence in these writings declare you to be relapsed in the abjuration of heresy, relinquishing the same Pons and Philippa to the secular court'. Relinquished: that is, to be burned to death at the stake by the secular authorities.

Gui was not yet finished. Two people who had died some time ago were declared to have been believers of heretics, and to have received 'heretication' (that is, the *consolamentum*) on their deathbeds; their bones were to be dug up ('if they can be discerned from the bones of the faithful') and burned. Moreover the houses in which they had lived were to be knocked down and destroyed, to make them permanently uninhabitable. Finally, there was Étiennette de *Proaudo*, who had said various 'intolerable errors' against the faith, including that Christ could not have been incarnated via a woman, that there would be no resurrection in human form, that the visible world was created by the devil, rejecting the sacraments, and 'speaking and blaspheming against our sacred orders, preferring the condemned and wicked order of the heretics'. She had had contact with seven different fully-fledged heretics in Toulouse, again including the Autiers. And:

> [despite being frequently admonished about all these errors] by me, the aforesaid inquisitor, and by many representatives of the Preachers and Minors and other orders, and by many other worthy men, clergy and laity of the town of Toulouse, and indeed by your parents, that you should abandon the aforesaid errors and with a good and pure heart return to the Holy Mother Church of Rome...you will not agree, nor convert to the Catholic faith...but moreover, with a hardened heart, persevere in this obstinacy.

Thus, Gui pronounced, she was judged to be a heretic, and would also be relinquished to the secular court to be burned.[63]

This is just one of many General Sermons carried out by Gui for which we have a surviving record; all told he sentenced 636 people, of whom 41 were sent to the stake.[64] There are a number of details here to which we shall return below, regarding issues of intention, sincerity, belief, and interiority; and we have not in fact heard the last of Étiennette de *Proaudo*. But where we should begin, and the reason for giving such detail of this one event, is to recognize that whatever else it was, inquisition into heretical wickedness was a public spectacle. What Gui was doing in a General Sermon, and through the sentences he bestowed, was in part akin to what preachers did in other sermons: he was instructing, exhorting, and seeking to move the wider Christian community, to help them in their faith.[65] The 'disciplinary' work of inquisition, in other words, did not end with the particular people subject to questioning; it sought in various ways to reach out to the rest of the laity also.

The General Sermon, as a specific event, was indeed only one part of this wider dynamic. Given that there is already an ample literature on inquisition as a legal process and medieval institution, I shall here only briefly describe some aspects, and shall focus particularly on the implications that go beyond the specific pursuit of heretical groups. Firstly, we need to note that the Sermon was not the only occasion on which people's sins of heresy were made explicitly public. Many of those sentenced for their involvement—as 'believers' or supporters or so forth—were given public penances, which involved presenting themselves at their local church on various days, to be disciplined by the priest. Earlier in this chapter I mentioned twenty-three people sentenced by the inquisitors Henri de Chamayou and Pierre Brun in 1318; among other things, each of them was to be ritually beaten by their parish priest on every Sunday, feast day, and other major event, and on the first Sunday of each month was to present letters to the priest so that he could explain in the vernacular what they had done and why they were undergoing penance.[66] Similar practices went back to the middle of the thirteenth century at least, and were in large part modelled on the much older practice of 'solemn penance' which made a person's faults explicitly public, in contrast, as we

---

[63] A. Pales-Gobilliard, ed., *Le livre des sentences de l'inquisiteur Bernard Gui, 1318–23*, 2 vols (Paris: CNRS, 2002), I, pp. 176–98.
[64] Pales-Gobilliard, *Livre des sentences*, I, pp. 28–34; Given, *Inquisition and Medieval Society*, pp. 67–71.
[65] See D. Hill, *Inquisition in the Fourteenth Century: The Manuals of Bernard Gui and Nicholas Eymerich* (York: York Medieval Press, 2019), chapter 5.
[66] Doat 27, fol. 6v: 'et prima dominica cuiuslibet mensis presentes litteras proprio Capellano presentent, et eas sibi legi, et exponi vulgariter faciat ut per quid facere et quibus abstinere debeant fieri valeant certiores'. See for earlier detail the Consultation of Béziers, 1246, c. 26 (Mansi XXIII, col. 720; trans. A&B, doc. 37).

have seen, to what regular confession and penance aimed to do.[67] In fact, by the later thirteenth century, some advice given to confessors makes it clear that in certain other situations a public penance might also be imposed, for example where a person had committed a publicly manifest sin (where their penitence thus also needed to be made clear to others) or where someone persisted in committing sin; in these cases, as with other 'reserved' sins (such as heresy, murder, incest, and other major faults) the priest had to involve the bishop.[68]

The nature of one of the most common sentences—the imposition of the yellow crosses—was also of course a form of making public one's misdeeds but, as importantly, reminded others of the fact and dangers of this kind of sin. There is good evidence, from various instances mentioned in trial evidence, that people did not like to wear the crosses and sometimes hid them. Indeed the council of Béziers, in 1246, ordered that penitents wearing crosses were not to be 'mocked' by others, nor excluded from their normal homes or business, as 'it is right to rejoice if they receive and undergo the penance willingly'.[69] Thus in a different sense—at least as imagined by the bishops at the council—the cross-wearers were also advertising the salutary fact of penance, and acting as good examples to other Christians in a more general fashion. To give this a little further context: the many people Bernard Gui either sentenced to wear crosses, or relieved from an earlier imposition of crosses, were spread across at least ninety-one separate villages, towns, and cities in southern France.[70] He was only one inquisitor, working over a period of about fifteen years; others came before and indeed after. We must therefore consider the wider 'work' done by those crosses, beyond their effects on the particular penitent. They broadcast widely something important about 'heresy', and about the power of inquisitors; but they also spoke of penitence as an ongoing act, those bearing the crosses embodying penance in every public moment of their lives.

It is also important to note that all penances could later be commuted. If, over a period of time, the person upon whom they had been enjoined displayed true penitence, the inquisitor might give clemency, allowing someone to leave prison and take up the crosses (as with Pierre and Tholosana above), or reduce the number of years for which they were to wear the crosses, lessen the burden of long-distance pilgrimages, and so forth. This could even happen in the most extreme case, for those sentenced to death at the stake—reform of a sinner was always possible, even at the point of death. This indeed was what happened with Étiennette de *Proaudo*. Following the sentence recounted above for her stubborn

[67] See Arnold, *Inquisition and Power*, pp. 58–63; M. Mansfield, *The Humiliation of Sinners: Public Penance in Thirteenth-Century France* (Ithaca, NY: Cornell University Press, 2005).
[68] Synodal of Carcassonne, c. 1270, c. IV (Mahul, *Cartulaire*, V, p. 426).
[69] Council of Béziers, 1246, c. 6 (Mansi XXIII, col. 717).
[70] Following the tabulation in Pales-Gobilliard, *Livre des sentences*, II, pp. 1648–97 (table 2). Some people cannot be clearly located to a particular town, and thus the number may be higher.

adherence to heresy, the next day, 'following wiser counsel, seeing then the preparation of the fire for her punishment to be imminent, she said that she wished to convert to the Catholic faith and to return to ecclesiastical unity— whether feignedly or from her heart, as in truth she may have said this from fear of death, human judgment cannot resolve'.[71] Consequently, she abjured her errors, promised to reveal all she knew of heresy, and was sentenced to imprisonment, where she would 'prove whether her conversion was true or false', whilst being watched closely to ensure she did not 'infect or corrupt' any others with her errors. She was in fact released, along with various other people, on 12 September 1322 and ordered to wear double crosses as penance.[72] It would seem that fourteen years in prison had finally been sufficient to prove 'the truth' of her conversion.

It may be useful to think briefly about inquisitorial confession and penance in relationship to wider pastoral practices.[73] Was confession to an inquisitor in any sense like confession to a priest? When investigating a particular locale, inquisitors first announced to the inhabitants a 'Period of Grace' of two weeks, during which any who had committed faults in regard to heresy could turn up and confess 'spontaneously', in expectation of receiving a lighter penance. After that, those giving evidence were cited to appear, or indeed hunted down and captured. The latter process for the most part has no parallel with pastoral confession (though we might remember that bishops could impose penance on egregious sinners even if they had not come to make confession), but the former notion of spontaneity has some parallels—priests, as we have seen, being instructed to encourage their parishioners to come forward and confess their sins whenever they had committed them, and not only at Easter. The outcomes were of course different: those confessing to inquisitors were not absolved, but rather were made to abjure, and they were not expecting to receive communion from the man to whom they had told their secrets. The penances imposed by inquisitors were, as noted, essentially 'public', and in the case of execution, imprisonment, and the crosses, without pastoral parallel. And yet pilgrimage and almsgiving were, of course, part of a wider penitential array.

If we think about the mode and content of confession, there were obvious further clear differences. The priest had various tools to induce the penitent to speak truly, but these did not include coercive imprisonment.[74] Priests enjoined

---

[71] Pales-Gobilliard, *Livre des sentences*, I, p. 198.

[72] Pales-Gobilliard, *Livre des sentences*, II, p. 1440.

[73] For an earlier consideration, see A. Casenave, 'Aveu et contrition: manuels des confesseurs et interrogatoires d'inquisitions en Languedoc et en Catalogne (XIIIe–XIVe siècles)', *Actes du 99e congrès national des sociétés savantes*, 2 vols (Paris: CTHS, 1977), I, pp. 333–52; and a more sustained analysis in C. Caldwell Ames, *Righteous Persecution: Inquisition, Dominicans and Christianity in the Middle Ages* (Philadelphia: University of Pennsylvania Press, 2009), particularly chapter 4.

[74] On coercion, see Given, *Inquisition and Medieval Society*, chapter 2. Torture seems to have been used very rarely by southern French inquisitors. There are two occasions extant from trials conducted in the 1240s (MS Toulouse 609, fol. 134r; Doat 22, fols 6v–7r—see A&B, p. 414 n. 163). There were

penitents not to name or implicate anyone else in their accounts of wrongdoing; for inquisitors it was quite the reverse. Inquisitors recorded the details of confessions—reminding us also that whereas one confessed solely to a priest, with an inquisitor there would probably also be witnesses and certainly a notarial scribe—and these records were kept as an active archive for decades. In contrast priests, as we have seen, were to record the *fact* that someone had confessed, but they were not to reveal any details of anything they had heard (unless, on rare occasion, they had to inform the bishop of someone who had committed reserved sins, the penitent refusing to go to the bishop him or herself). Both priests and inquisitors were provided with question lists to use when hearing confessions, and there is some overlap here: like the inquisitor, the priest was advised to ask 'what, where, why, how greatly, in what manner, when, and how often?' misdeeds had been committed.[75] However, whilst a good confessor would take 'why' as an opportunity to talk about feelings, intentions, inner disposition, and so forth, the inquisitor asked simply about those who had encouraged one into certain actions, and his task was to try to relate those actions (attending preaching, giving hospitality, 'adoring', and so forth) to a sequence of canon-legal categories that would inform the outcome of the trial: 'heretic', 'believer', 'supporter', 'receiver', 'defender', 'relapsed', and 'suspect'.[76]

For the most part then, particularly in the thirteenth century, it seems likely that those confessing to inquisitors would not have seen any great overlap with their experience of confessing to a priest (assuming of course that they had engaged in pastoral confession, rather than shunning it as a rejected sacrament). But there are some fourteenth-century trial registers which, at points, make one wonder if the person subject to interrogation had fallen into a more general confessional mode, akin to how they might have talked to their confessor. I have discussed at length elsewhere one such deposition, given by a minor noble lady Beatrice de Lagleize (or de Planissoles) before the inquisitor and bishop Jacques Fournier in 1320, who spoke not only of her—in fact relatively marginal—contact with heresy, but of sexual sins, inner feelings, beliefs about salvation, and worries about her gendered identity and piety.[77] A few other deponents interrogated at

fierce allegations made against the inquisitor Jean Galand in the 1280s, and others voiced against Foulques de St George in the early fourteenth century. On two occasions Gui ordered someone to be tortured, in the specific context of trying to extract information on the whereabouts of fugitive heretics. But there is very little sense in most trial registers of torture being threatened or applied, perhaps in contrast to secular justice where it was a common feature for serious crimes. However, practice would change in the second half of the fourteenth century, when inquisitors such as Nicolas Aymeric adopted it more freely.

[75] *Cum ad sacerdotem*, Goering and Payer, 'Summa penitentie', pp. 33–34.
[76] See the widely circulated council of Tarragona, 1242, overseen by Raymond de Peñafort, trans. A&B, doc. 34, discussion in Arnold, *Inquisition and Power*, pp. 42–44.
[77] Arnold, *Inquisition and Power*, pp. 197–214; her deposition is edited in *Fournier* I, pp. 216–50, and she appears frequently in Ladurie, *Montaillou*, particularly pp. 159–68 and 172–74.

length by Fournier—who clearly did not feel constrained by a formal inquisitorial interrogatory, but on occasion asked more wide-ranging questions—might similarly be seen to experience some slippage, as it were, the process of interrogation sliding into a more general kind of 'confession'. The same might be said of a few rare instances within certain depositions when someone was challenged to explain why they had done something or, equally, failed to do something. For example, in 1324 Pierre Astruc, a citizen of Albi, was interrogated about events some thirty years earlier when Good Men had come to the city and preached to some people about the Gospels. When, at the end of his brief deposition, he was asked why he had been so slow to come and confess to these things, 'he said that because the devil kept him from that path, and enchanting his tongue, he concealed the aforesaid for the aforesaid time, until he was cited; and then he confessed what was above. He said however that he had confessed the aforesaid things to a certain monk/friar (*religiosus*), but he had refused to absolve him'.[78] In 1327, a widow called Guillemette Maza of Calvayrac (c. 25 km east of Castres) confessed to inquisitors that, about twenty-five years earlier, she had heard the sermon of a Waldensian preacher called Bartholomeu. She explained that it was in the aftermath of her husband's death, about which she was very sad; someone comforting her had said, '"My daughter, you should take courage and be consoled, and confide in my Lord God, and maintain yourself in your widowhood, and live as a good lady" and many other good words', and had then asked if she would like to see and hear the 'good words' of a 'very good and true man, who knew much good and held a good and holy life'. And although this had to be in secret, as he was a man persecuted by the Church, 'hearing this immediately she was inflamed and burning in her heart for love of the said man and desired to see him'.[79] Do we here perhaps catch some sense of how people in confession might contextualize things they had done, proffering an emotional as well as a practical context for their sins?

One other area in which inquisition was similar to regular penance was in the emphasis placed upon adjusting the nature and severity of the penance to fit not just the specific sin and its context but the status and 'quality' of the sinner. The canonist Gui Foulques—later Pope Clement IV—was consulted on various aspects regarding the conduct of inquisition into heresy in, probably, the early

---

[78] Doat 27, fols 34v–35r: 'Interrogatus quatinus tardavit tantum venire ad confitendum predicta, dixit quod quia diabolus tenebat sibi carreriam, et linguam cantatam committens predicta celavit ea per tempora supradicta, donec citatus fuit, et tunc confessus fuit supradicta, dixit tamen quod cuidam religioso confessus fuerat de praedicta, sed ipsum absoluere noluit.'

[79] Doat 27, fols 82r–83v: '"filia mea confortamini et consolamini, et confide in domino Deo meo, et manutenere in viduitate tua, et vive sicut bona domina" et multa alia bona verba...respondit quod erat unus homo valde bonus, et probus et qui multa bona sciebat et bonam vitam et sanctam tenebat...Quo audito statim ipsa loquens fuit inflammata et accensa in corde suo ad amorem dicti hominis et desideravit ipsum videre...'.

1240s, and addressed this along with other issues.[80] As with other texts advising inquisitors, he stressed the importance of exercising their personal judgment with each person who confessed to them, and when coming to consider a suitable penance: 'And what is to be done is different with simple people than with the wise, different with clergy than with laity, different with the powerful than with those subject to them, and all circumstances are to be noted...Because, however, many fall into this crime through simplicity, I believe that many can be excused through their simplicity, that is, not excused totally but somewhat'.[81] We are reminded that, as in a parochial pastoral context, the purpose of penance is to bring the sinner to redemption, and that that involves the demanding task of discerning their inner disposition. As Bernard Gui noted, before sentencing Étiennette to prison, it was extremely difficult to decide whether someone was truly repentant, or simply feigning it. One might be tempted to add that on occasion it is perhaps difficult even for the sinner him- or herself to know this for certain.

Gui Foulques addressed the associated issues in some detail. The key question was whether to judge someone to be 'a believer' in the heretics, on the basis of various actions—the point being that 'a believer' (*credens*) was, according to canon law, to be sentenced as harshly as one would a fully-fledged heretic. How did actions relate to 'belief'? Foulques makes, firstly, a finely tuned legal distinction which has some interesting, albeit tacit, implications. The canon law on heresy, he notes, condemns 'not simply *believers* but *believers in their errors*' (here citing Gregory IX's *Excommunicamus*); therefore if the actions they have undertaken relate to the heretics' 'rites'—showing them reverence 'according to their custom', receiving confession or communion from them, or so forth—they are clearly to be judged *believers*. If however they have undertaken actions that are more practical—visiting them, giving them alms, escorting them—this does not automatically indicate that status, as these things can occur for other reasons, such as payment, friendship, the encouragement of others. The first set of acts, in contrast, 'cannot be twisted to mean something good' and thus can act as proofs. And one must necessarily interpret external actions in some such fashion, as otherwise 'one cannot establish anything about the mind for "deep is the heart of man and inscrutable"'.[82]

---

[80] Bivolarov argues, contrary to earlier scholarship, that it must have been composed by 1243: V. Bivolarov, *Inquisitoren-Handbücher: Papsturkunden un juristische Gutachten aus dem 13. Jahrhundert mit Edition des* Consilium von Guido Fulcodii (Wiesbaden: MGH, 2014), pp. 214–17. My thanks to Pete Biller on this detail.

[81] Gui Foulques, *Consilium*, c. 14 (Bivolarov, *Inquisitoren-Handbücher*, p. 249): 'Et aliter cum simplicibus est agendum quam cum prudentibus, aliter cum clericis quam cum laicis, aliter cum prelatis quam cum subditis et omnes circumstantie sunt notande...Quia tamen multi ex simplicitate in hoc crimen incidunt, credo multorum simplicitati parcendum, ut non excuset a tota sed a tanto.'

[82] Gui Foulques, *Consilium*, c. 9 (Bivolarov, *Inquisitoren-Handbücher*, pp. 239–41, trans. A&B, pp. 230–32). 'Deep is the heart of man...' is a variant on Jer. 17: 9 (*Pravum est cor omnium et inscrutabile quis cognoscet illud*); the passage is discussed and analysed in detail in P. Biller, '"Deep is the Heart of Man and

Foulques does not return to his distinction between 'believers' and 'believers in errors', but it does perhaps suggest a dynamic that we may already recognize from earlier chapters, that is, belief that the apostolic self-presentation of the Good Men and Waldensians makes them holy, rather than any additional theological propositions they present. The essential issue though, as Foulques recognizes, is that one cannot be sure of what another person thinks or believes. The implications of this, with regard to imposing fitting punishment, were one of the things which particularly troubled inquisitors. The first decade and a half of inquisition into heresy saw a number of such consultative texts, produced either by individual experts like Foulques or by bishops convening councils, and whilst much of their advice was in regard to complexities and difficulties regarding procedure, the issue of how to assess 'belief' was recurrent. Raymond de Peñafort's advice—delivered via the council of Tarragona in 1242, but circulated to inquisitors in southern France and beyond—suggested, similarly to Foulques, that one should not be too swift to ascribe the status of 'believer' to those who had engaged in practical support, 'unless he is so educated or discerning (*litteratus vel discretus*) that he cannot claim ignorance', this being something which the individual judge would have to assess.[83] As with the earlier passage from Foulques, regarding 'simple people' in contrast with the 'wise' or 'discerning' (*discreti*), there is an attempt to divide the many people subjected to inquisition into a larger, gullible flock and a smaller, more educated and thus more culpable subgroup. The mass of the laity were imagined to fall into the former; they were easily led astray, and whilst they had thus still sinned, they were not—it was imagined—engaged in 'believing' in the more theological, interiorized, active fashion.

This is how influential canonists—Foulques, Peñafort, and others—saw the issue in the abstract. The complication was however that the process of actually questioning lay people, particularly when questioning them at length, tended to demonstrate that even the simple and uneducated could on occasion have ideas about faith, and could express a complicated relationship between their actions and their beliefs. They might in fact have 'adored' some Good Men—perhaps, as Mark Pegg would argue, essentially out of social respect, or perhaps because they thought that they would benefit spiritually from the ritual—but might still assert that they did not believe in some of the 'errors' that the Good Men had preached. One deponent questioned in the 1240s, a knight called Matfre de Paulhac, received the *consolamentum* and was a fully-fledged heretic for four years, often hearing a lot of preaching by the Good Men. But, he claimed, he did not actually believe the things they said. Moreover 'he did not believe they were good men or

---

Inscrutable"': Signs of Heresy in Medieval Languedoc', in H. Barr and A. M. Hutchison, eds, *Text and Controversy from Wyclif to Bale: Essays in Honour of Anne Hudson* (Turnhout: Brepols, 2005), pp. 267–80.
[83] Council of Tarragona, 1242, c. 4; see earlier discussion in Arnold, *Inquisition and Power*, p. 44.

had a good *or a bad* faith' (my emphasis), though he often 'adored' them.[84] The inquisitor may well have felt that Matfre was dissembling; we do not know, as we lack any record of his sentence. But simply giving voice to such a confusing position made the task of the inquisitor rather more complicated, and their collective sense of how lay people set about 'believing' perhaps that bit more troubled.[85] Just as historians have previously argued that the actual experience of administering pastoral confession may have fed back into the advice and materials produced by mendicant and episcopal authors across the thirteenth century, so we may also remind ourselves that the inquisitors who experienced the complexities of interrogating lay believers were also mendicants and bishops. Their encounters may also have fed into their understanding of the wider *cura animarum*.

More importantly, however, we must return to the layperson's experience of inquisition, for those who were subject directly to it. As said, it may at a few points have prompted some parallels for them with ordinary Easter confession—though if they had ever been asked to give evidence to a secular legal trial, it would probably have reminded them rather more of that, given the wider apparatus of oaths, witnesses, and notarial scribe. As we have seen, much of what they were required to confess was prosaic: what they had seen, where, with whom, and so forth. But even in the earliest trials, there was a question of belief: 'Did you believe in the heretics or Waldensians, or in their errors?'[86] As noted just above, various people might answer positively to the former but negatively to the latter, forging in the process their own understanding of what 'belief' in this sense might be taken to mean. (We shall return further in Chapter 10 to the innate complexities of 'belief'.) But for most it would be clear that they were being presented with a binary choice, in which 'heresy' was clearly opposed to 'orthodoxy'—clearly opposed *by the inquisitor* that is, as he presented a black-and-white moral universe within which the layperson had to locate themselves. Some, in parallel to Matfre de Poalhac above, averred that they 'neither believed nor disbelieved', attempting to find a sort of third path, beyond the inquisitor's binary. But most acquiesced to the terms set before them, and indeed to the association between belief and action.

In that sense, in addition to the obedience to authority that being subject to inquisition demanded (as per my discussion in Chapter 5), there is a sense that the experience of being questioned taught an additional kind of discipline: subjecting oneself to a particular conception of 'belief', and one's own moral reform. In that sense, being questioned by the inquisitor was indeed a further part of the *cura animarum*, a means by which one was taught how one should understand one's own actions, thoughts, and feelings. And, of course, if one did not take the

[84] Doat 22, fols 60v–61v.
[85] This argument is pursued more fully in *Inquisition and Power*, particularly chapters 3 and 4.
[86] Sackville, 'Ordo processus', p. 376.

stubborn route which Étiennette de *Proaudo* initially adopted, the process was also one of learning humility and surrender, remaking one's self in the fashion which the inquisitor required on behalf of the Church. There is a very interesting deposition given in 1308 by a notary called Pierre de Gaillac from Tarascon (in the Ariège), extremely unusual in that it was largely written by himself, using the first person, though otherwise very largely adopting the form and rhetoric of other trials. He was questioned by the inquisitor Geoffroi d'Ablis; other deponents who appeared before that inquisitor were asked to confirm at the end of their evidence that they had not been suborned or bribed or had said things out of love or hatred for others and so forth. Their usual, formulaic, response was to say 'no' and to affirm that everything they had attested they had done 'from unburdening their conscience and for the salvation of their soul'.[87] In Pierre's case, bearing in mind the slightly greater degree of rhetorical agency he could bring to the text, we are given a little more:

> I also say and declare and confess that I confessed and said those things [in his preceding evidence, not through being tortured or suborned etc, but]...freely, from certain knowledge, and out of pure freedom of mind, with divine prompting and driven by divine grace, not wanting to persist further or any longer in the aforesaid sin or error but wanting to come to a good state and to confession of the aforesaid things.[88]

We perhaps again catch an echo of a layperson's conceptualization of pastoral confession, but at the very least gain a clear sense of how the imposition of inquisition was, among other things, a *self*-discipline. Pierre, an educated man, familiar no doubt with other dealings in law, was here making himself—on paper at least—into the kind of reformed subject most ideally desired by the process. He was not simply obedient to authority: he was an independent subject, of free mind, inspired by divine grace. He was reformed.

There is of course one further important difference between inquisitorial and pastoral confession: most people experienced confession to their priest, or to a friar, once a year or possibly more, whereas inquisitions into heretical wickedness were periodic affairs, not experienced universally. Expanding on this point in a general European context, Alexander Murray once nicely put it that medieval inquisition was not like a 'lawnmower', reducing everyone to the same size. Both Henry Ansgar Kelly and Richard Kieckhefer pointed out some decades ago that there was no formal permanent tribunal of inquisition into heresy (unlike in the post-Tridentine period), but rather a sequence of individually appointed

---

[87] For example, A. Pales-Gobilliard, ed., *L'inquisiteur Geoffrey d'Ablis et les cathares du comté du Foix (1308–1309)* (Paris: CNRS, 1984), pp. 238, 310.
[88] Pales-Gobilliard, *Geoffrey d'Ablis*, p. 344; his deposition trans. A&B, doc. 54.

inquisitors who were required to pursue a particular task for a certain region.[89] If we were thinking in general terms about how 'powerful' inquisitors were or not, we would probably want to recall the fact that in the 1230s they, along with the other Brothers Preacher, were temporarily thrown out of Toulouse by the consuls, that in 1242 the inquisitor Brother Guillaume Arnaud and his colleagues were ambushed and massacred by various knights at Avignonet, and that for a period in the 1250s the bishops of the region were required to take up the task for a few years as the Brothers Preacher were refusing to continue.[90] It is thus true that we are not dealing with an all-powerful or implacable machinery of repression, despite the popular image.

On the other hand, recent studies have convincingly argued that 'inquisition into heretical wickedness' does become 'institutional', in its bureaucratic processes, officers, and shared collective knowledge, perhaps earlier than Kieckhefer had thought.[91] What inquisitors might pursue also expanded in scope across the thirteenth century. Whereas the initial focus was entirely on Good Men and Waldensians, in the mid-thirteenth century we start to find surviving interrogatories for use against those using magic or divinations (one such likely produced by Benoît d'Alignan, bishop of Marseille, probably in the period when bishops temporarily took over the task of inquisition), and at least a couple of trials regarding necromancy and love-magic (the perpetrators in each case clerics) survive from the early fourteenth century.[92] In the early fourteenth century inquisitors in southern France were pursuing not only the last remnants of the Good Men, but also Spiritual Franciscans and 'beguins', and Bishop Jacques Fournier's investigations encompassed a Jew who had been forcibly converted to Christianity and several individuals whose beliefs were deeply idiosyncratic rather than connected to the main 'sects'.

So how large did inquisition into heretical wickedness loom within the lives of the southern French laity in general? How many people did it directly affect? The answer is going to vary depending on when we are looking. From the late 1230s to the mid-1240s at least, the answer is probably 'really quite a lot'. It was in this period that two inquisitors, Jean de Saint-Pierre and Bernard de Caux, summoned people from a huge number of villages and towns from across the diocese of Toulouse, requiring them to come as a group to Saint-Sernin in Toulouse to be questioned. They were not the only inquisitors active in this period, and the

---

[89] A. Murray, 'The Epicureans', in P. Boitani and A. Torti, eds, *Intellectuals and Writers in Fourteenth-Century Europe* (Cambridge: Brewer, 1986), pp. 138–63, at 147. H. A. Kelly, 'Inquisition and the Prosecution of Heresy: Misconceptions and Abuses', *Church History* 58 (1989), 439–51; R. Kieckhefer, 'The Office of Inquisition and Medieval Heresy: The Transition from Personal to Institutional Jurisdiction', *Journal of Ecclesiastical History* 46 (1995), 36–61.

[90] See generally Dossat, *Crises*.

[91] Hill, *Inquisition in the Fourteenth Century*; J. C. Moore, *Inquisition and its Organisation in Italy, 1250–1350* (York: York Medieval Press, 2019).

[92] Doat 27, fols 42r–50r.

surviving records collectively name something like 7,000 people who were directly questioned in inquisition between the mid-1230s and the mid-1250s. But this, it must be emphasized, is only what we can see from the registers that survive—and we know that in fact many more once existed. The largest register, MS Toulouse 609, which contains the names of over 5,500 people cited to appear, was a thirteenth-century fair copy compiled from just two of an original ten volumes. A reasonably conservative estimate, for everyone who was subject to inquisition in south-western France in the mid-thirteenth century, might therefore be around 30,000 people. We have almost no surviving trial records from Provence, and yet we know that inquisitors were active there in the same period.[93] That would push the conservative estimate still higher; and, if we imagined the Provençal inquisitors to have been as active as their colleagues to the west, could conceivably double it. The volume of people questioned drops off markedly in subsequent decades, though it continues to be the case that more once existed than is now extant, with records (either trials or sentences) surviving for perhaps about 1,000 people from the later 1280s to the 1330s.

Some of the earlier encounters, particularly those recorded in MS Toulouse 609, could be extremely brief, nothing more than a statement that one had never seen or had dealings with 'heretics', and an abjuration. But even this involved submission to the authority of the inquisitors and the Church, and placed a textual marker against one's future behaviour. And demonstrably for some the experience was not a 'one-off' event but something which pursued them and their family over decades. Even by the mid-1240s, some deponents report having confessed to other inquisitors before: in 1245 Arnaud Faure of Laurac, giving evidence to Bernard de Caux and Jean de Saint-Pierre, noted that he had previously also confessed to Brother Guillaume Arnaud, and separately to the inquisitor Brother Ferrier (the latter active across a similar period to the first two inquisitors).[94] As we have seen, Bernard Gui's surviving inquisitorial sentences from the early fourteenth century include a number of people questioned about much earlier interrogations, in one case Gui specifically referencing, by book and folio number, an interrogation from forty-nine years previously.[95]

Thus, whilst we should not project a 'Black Legend' of monolithic inquisitorial terror back into this period, we should recognize that in southern France it was far from being a minor strand within the lay experience of faith in the

---

[93] J. Chiffoleau, 'L'inquisition franciscaine en Provence et dans l'ancien royaume d'Arles (vers 1260–vers 1330)', in *Frati minori e inquisizione: atti del XXXIII Convegno internazionale: Assisi, 6–8 ottobre 2005* (Spoleto: Fondazione Centro italiano di studi sull'alto medioevo, 2006), pp. 151–284.

[94] MS Toulouse 609 fol. 195r: 'dixit quod postquam fecit confessionem suam de heresi dicti fratri willelmo arnaldi et socio suo scilicet olim inquisitoribus non vidit hereticos nisi captos...et fuit confessus fratri ferreri apud Saxiacum quam confessionem concedit esse veram'.

[95] For example, Pierre Tardiu of Cabanial who recounted a confession made to the inquisitor Jean de Vigouroux in 1288 (Pales-Gobilliard, *Sentences*, I, p. 266); citation of specific document 49 years ago, confession of Guillaume Sicre the elder (ibid., I, pp. 735–38; trans. A&B, doc. 55D; see similarly doc. 50).

post-crusade period. The actions of inquisitors reverberated well beyond those they directly questioned, as we have noted above with regard to the visibility of those 'signed' with the crosses. One might add the various other family members and suretors for those sentenced to a period of imprisonment who became more widely implicated in the process. Moreover the authority, spiritual and otherwise, of inquisitors could extend beyond their direct role in conducting trials. A document from 1329 records a *vidimus* of an earlier agreement made in 1278 between the consuls of Limoux and the monastery of Notre-Dame de Prouille near Fanjeaux, regarding financial agreements over various properties and the rights held by the monastery to the clothing of those coming there to be buried. One of the witnesses to the *vidimus* was 'Brother of the Order of Preachers Pierre Brun, inquisitor of Toulouse', and subsequently, in November 1329, a large number of named women were summoned to listen to the details of the agreement (presumably because they had previously disputed issues around the clothing).[96] In 1349 the consuls of Albi successfully petitioned the inquisitor Herbert de Sens to be allowed to rebuild the city defences, filling in a gap where a house formerly belonging to Guillaume Adémar had been knocked down for his involvement in heresy on the orders of earlier inquisitors; Herbert allowed the petition because of 'the time of war'.[97] Most interestingly regarding wider religious practices, a dispute heard before the bishop of Albi in 1323 into whether or not a priest had acted badly in celebrating mass in a newly built chapel in Albi (that is, against the parochial rights of another nearby church), the consuls defended the practice by saying that those things that had been done within the said chapel, they had done on the order of the inquisitors Bernard Gui and Jean de Beaune.[98] Both the original order, and the sense of invoking it in defence of the consulate, suggest the wider authority they exercised, by the fourteenth century at least.

One final example gives an additional sense of how the 'disciplinary' effect of inquisition might stretch well beyond those specifically questioned. It is drawn from Jean Gobi's collection of miracles relating to Marie Madeleine, compiled in the 1320s, most of which are akin to preaching *exempla*. Whilst it is just a single example, what it takes for granted seems notably revealing. The story is this: a man called Raimond de Uzès visited the shrine of the Madeleine then went to Marseille, there mentioning to a man called Étienne that he'd seen the shrine, and that he'd kissed the relic arm kept there. Étienne, in contemptuous words spoken irreverently against the saint, 'asserted that the Madeleine did not lie there in St Maximin', and that what he had kissed there was not the arm of the Madeleine 'but of some ass or other animal'. Thus far, thus familiar; in the twelfth century

---

[96] AD Aude 4E206/AA14; see further discussion in Chapter 9.   [97] AD Tarn, 6 J 19.
[98] AD Tarn, 69 EDT FF 59: 'dixerunt quod etiam quod ea que in dicta capella...fecerant de mandato et precepto dominorum fratrum bernardi guidonis et johannis de belna de ordine predicatorum inquisitorum heretice pravitatis...'.

Étienne would have been struck down by the saint with some miraculous affliction. On this occasion however Raimond reprimanded Étienne, saying to him, 'If the inquisitors knew of this, they would have you punished, as what you are saying can be seen as expressing a certain lack of faith!' Étienne was prompted to more 'blasphemy', and Raimond ended up attacking him mortally with a sword—then fled to Saint-Gilles where he was captured and hanged for the assault, but miraculously left unharmed (his account thus entering Jean Gobi's record).[99] The point is not whether or not any of this actually happened, but rather the expression of piety: 'if the inquisitors knew of this', here invoked against someone else's lack of faith with regard to a specific shrine. Even if we view this as nothing more than over-heated rhetoric, it is revealing. The work of inquisition thus reaches out into Christian society, and the laity discipline themselves and others.

Sin and Self-regulation

At some point early in the fourteenth century a Brother Preacher named Gui, a certain 'poor *religiosus* of Toulouse' as he described himself, sat down with a copy of John of Freiburg's massive *Summa confessorum* and extracted a number of topics concerning mercantile practices.[100] These he compiled into a short treatise, adding his own clearly marked additional comments; 'which compilation', he wrote in the introductory lines, 'I wish to call the Rule of Merchants'. The book would serve them well, he promised—whether they read it or heard it read aloud—rather better than 'the useless fables and romances that are accustomed to be read [aloud] in workshops and listened to by those standing around'. It would help save them from falling into sin, by advising them on what in fact constituted

---

[99] Jean Gobi, *Miracles*, p. 56 (no. 5).
[100] The work survives in four manuscripts: Paris, BnF MS Lat. 10689, fols 27–36; Cambridge, Gonville & Caius, MS 122/59, fols 1–19; Oxford, Lincoln College MS 81, fols 33–41; Berlin, Staatsbibliothek MS Theol. lat. qu. 370, fols 115–22. An explicit identifying the author as 'Frater Gwydonis de ordine Fratrum Predicatorum' is found in the Cambridge and Oxford manuscripts cited below, but not in the Paris manuscript (I have not consulted the Berlin manuscript). As various other historians have previously noted, 'Brother Gui of Toulouse' is neither Bernard Gui nor Gui d'Évreux, despite optimistic ascriptions by earlier scholars. Sylvain Piron has suggested that it might be Gui Guidonis, nephew of Bernard Gui: S. Piron, 'Les *studia* franciscains de Provence et d'Aquitaine (1275–1335)', in K. Emery Jr, W. J. Courtenay, and S. M. Metzger, eds, *Philosophy and Theology in the Studia of the Religious Orders and at Papal and Royal Courts* (Turnhout: Brepols, 2012), pp. 1–55, at p. 53 n. 213. A detailed discussion of Gui of Toulouse's use of John of Freiburg is given in J. A. Lorenc, 'John of Freiburg and the Usury Prohibition in the Late Middle Ages: A Study in the Popularization of Medieval Canon Law' (University of Toronto, unpublished PhD dissertation, 2013), particularly pp. 142–53. I am indebted to some of Dr Lorenc's transcriptions from the Oxford manuscript for assistance in deciphering the Paris and Cambridge manuscripts I have consulted. As noted earlier in this chapter, a fourteenth-century copy of John of Freiburg's treatise survives in Toulouse—BM Toulouse MS 381—albeit apparently arriving at the *Bibliothèque* via the Augustinians rather than the Dominicans. There is, intriguingly, a small marginal flag 'de usuris', in what might be a different early fourteenth-century hand, added repeatedly to some of the sections on usury in that manuscript (fols 157v–159r).

a sinful practice (principally, but not by any means only, practices which could be interpreted as usurious). Some of the issues were extremely subtle, and readers should not marvel at the strictness of some of the injunctions, warned the author, since 'just as Christ said, narrow is the road which leads to life' (Matt. 7: 14); some things which earthly laws allow are not allowed by God.[101]

The treatise is not principally concerned with general moral exhortation, but with the technical details that arise around the conduct of various kinds of business. It seeks to warn merchants and others that practices they might think normal or trifling could in fact imperil their souls. Some of this is already present in John of Freiburg's text, but Gui of Toulouse's additions—flagged up explicitly as such throughout—work to illumine and illustrate such issues further.[102] For example, in Gui's additions to a discussion of the sinful selling of false measure of goods, he notes those merchants of wool or pepper or other things who place their goods in a 'damp or humid place', thereby surreptitiously increasing their weight.[103] Those who sell their goods in dark workshops or other obscure places, thus concealing the defects of their wares, 'sin gravely' and cannot excuse themselves by claiming that they bought the goods under similar conditions. And if they further try to excuse themselves by saying that everybody else does similarly, this will not wash, because there are bad things also done 'customarily', and knowing that it is thus done does not excuse prostitutes, usurers, blasphemers, or other evildoers.[104] Cloth-makers or similar, who put the best and most beautiful piece on display, when all the rest of their goods are of lower quality and value,

---

[101] Paris, BnF MS Lat. 10689, fol. 27v(a); Cambridge, Gonville & Caius, MS 122/59, fol. 1r: 'ut in ipsis mercacionibus a via equitatis et iusticie vos deviare et in peccatis vos ipsos involvere non contingat. Quam compilationem volo mercatorum regularum appellari. Quam legere vel saltem audire cuicumque vestrum consulo loco fabularum et romanciorum inutilium que consueverunt legi in operatoriis et ab assistentibus ascultari.... Sunt an alique subtilitates et rationes subtiles posite in primis tribus vel quatuor questionibus propter subtiles et intelligentes homines[?] quibus placent subtilia et quia in eis fundantur fere omnia quod sequuntur. Nec miretur aliquis si aliquarum questionum stricte sunt determinaciones quia ar[c]ta est via que ducit ad vitam sicut dicit Christus in Evangelio, et quod multa per leges sunt concessa que secundum deum nunquam licent.'

[102] As Sylvain Piron demonstrates, it can be seen in the context of a wider set of canon-legal and moral discussions around contracts and business dealings, including other intellectual treatises produced in southern France in the period: S. Piron, 'Marchands et confesseurs: le "Traité des contrats" d'Olivi dans son contexte (Narbonne, fin XIIIe–début XIVe siècle)', L'argent au Moyen Âge: actes des congrès de la Société des historiens médiévistes de l'enseignement supérieur public 28, Clermont-Ferrand 1997 (Paris: Publications de la Sorbonne, 1998), pp. 289–308; S. Piron, 'Contexte, situation, conjuncture', in F. Brayard, ed., Des contextes en histoire (Paris: Centre de recherches historiques, 2013), pp. 27–65.

[103] Paris, BnF MS Lat. 10689, fol. 28v(b): 'Et sic de similibus idem est iuditium de illis qui in loco aquoso vel humido lanam ponunt vel crotum vel piper vel similia ut plus ponderent ita.'

[104] Paris, BnF MS Lat. 10689, fol. 29r(a-b) 'Et quia aliqui mercatores et mercerii et alii multi allegant pro se quidam specialem rationem videlicet quod illa quo vendunt ipsi emerunt modo omnino consimili videlicet in locis obscuris, dico quod secundum deum et secundum veritatem non possunt propter hec excusari... Non etiam excusat eos consuetudo, quia consuetudo mala maius est in consuetudine peccatum nec excusat eos... quia meretrices et usurarii ubique sunt et blasphemi et alii multi malefici nec tum sunt propter hoc excusati...'

sin mortally if they intend to deceive when so doing.[105] In his additions to more explicit cases of usury, Gui of Toulouse discusses those carpenters who undertake a complex contract with someone who owns land and wants to build a house, the landowner not however having sufficient funds to pay for the materials up front. If, Gui says, the carpenter builds the house, and then rents it to the landowner until his expenses are met, plus some more for the favour of having advanced the necessary capital expenditure—thus gaining say 1,200 *livres* for a house that is worth 1,000 *livres*—he is in fact committing usury.[106] The recurrent principle throughout is 'justice' (of which the notion of a 'just price' is a subsidiary concept).[107] Thus, for example, if someone buys something at a good price because the vendor is under external pressure to sell—for example, if they are an orphan and in need of funds—this is a sin.[108] Anyone who knowingly sells against the just price commits a mortal sin, and thus Gui counsels merchants always to have this 'rule' before their eyes (meaning, I think, both that central concept and the *regula* he had produced).[109]

One of the features of ecclesiastical *summae* on sin and penance in the later middle ages was an ever-greater elaboration of the 'branches' of sin, spurring out from the main trunk (pride) and the other deadly sins. This can sometimes seem like the most scholastic form of abstraction, an intellectual game of codification rather than a practical guide. But Gui of Toulouse's little work is a detailed interrogation of one portion of the whole, which takes the bifurcating branches and twigs of usury and fashions it into something *applicable*, addressing merchants and others as people responsible not only for their own actions but also for their own moral education ('ignorance of the law excuses no one', as he notes early on).[110] Its very title—a *regula*, like a monastic rule—proclaims the disciplinary embrace it extends to the laity.

---

[105] Paris, BnF MS Lat. 10689, fol. 29r(b): '...Quod autem dicitur de aliquibus factoribus pannorum et reparatoribus si unius sit videlicet quod unum tapetum panni faciunt melius et pulchrius ad ostendendum emptoribus et totum ad pannum faciunt minoris valoris dico quod si venderent illud quod melius per se in nullo peccarent si autem quasi ostensione partis melioris vendunt quod deterius vel minoris valoris peccaverint mortaliter si sequatur decepcio vel etiam si eam intendunt hoc.'

[106] Paris, BnF MS Lat. 10689, fol. 31r(b): 'De carpentariis qui operantur domos alicui qui habet locum et non habet peccuniam pro opere faciendo, et mutuant scilicet totam materiam et operas suas tali pacto quod factis domibus teneant eas recipiendo precium locacionis earum tanto tempore qui recuperent operas suas et quicquid ibi posuerant vel expenderant et ultra hoc aliquam quantitatem peccunie ultra sortem pro gratia sibi facta de operacione domorum et sumptibus sic quod si carpentarii constiterit totum opus [M libras] quod recuperent inde MCC, idem [est] de omni contractu simili est cui ibi usura.' I have partially corrected the Paris manuscript against the transcription of this passage from the Oxford manuscript in Lorenc's dissertation (Lorenc, 'John of Freiburg', p. 151, n. 88).

[107] On the 'just price', among much other scholarship see Wood, *Medieval Economic Thought*, chapter 6.

[108] Paris, BnF MS Lat. 10689, fol. 28r(b): 'et sic habent eam multo nunquam iusto precio in dampnum vendentis sive sit pupillus sive aliquis in necessitate constitutus...'.

[109] Paris, BnF MS Lat. 10689, fol. 28v(a): 'propter quod consulo quod omnis mercator hoc habeat semper per occulis quasi pro regula'.

[110] Paris, BnF MS Lat. 10689, fol. 27v(a): 'Quia juris ignorandum neminem excusat'.

How important is this particular work? It sits in curious partial contrast to the somewhat earlier, and much larger, *Breviari d'amor*. Both works chide lay people for the various sins they commit, displaying a detailed authorial knowledge of what lurks and recurs in the human heart. Both aim directly to educate the laity, or at least claim that that is their purpose. The practical applicability of the *Breviari* is put somewhat under question by dint of its great length, and highly ambitious overarching intellectual purposes. In the case of the *Regula mercatorum*—short, clearly set out, aiming to explain practical situations in a focused way—we have a much more manageable translation of scholastic discussion into potential pastoral practice, albeit in Latin, and intermittently referencing other sections of the larger source text by John of Freiburg. The text now survives in only four manuscripts, three of which are from the fifteenth century. In one, at least (that in Gonville and Caius College, Cambridge) the *Regula* has been copied into a larger compilation of material amassed over time. In the Paris manuscript it is accompanied by another short work on usury, and in that manuscript the incipit claims that the work was originally written in the vernacular, then translated into Latin. In addition to the four manuscript exemplars, in the very late fifteenth century the work was translated into French and printed as a discrete woodcut *incunabulum*.[111] To have thus survived over nearly two centuries, and indeed to have provoked sufficient interest for there to be a re-translation into print, might suggest that the short treatise did once have a wider circulation.

One would not want to claim that the *Regula* instituted a new age of lay moral reform: it is too rare and too specific in its interests. Yet its close attention to the vagaries of actual mercantile practice does indicate a fundamental development. Sin was not only that which was named and denounced explicitly by the general categories familiar from earlier treatises and sermons; it was something which lurked, something which required constant labour not only to combat, but to identify in the first place. As noted earlier this chapter, the nature of sin had expanded, its tendrils being something one had to reveal and recognize as such. Doing this was ultimately labour that a layperson was required to undertake themselves, albeit with the guidance of mendicants and priests. One may link its emergence to a wider culture of addressing moral questions arising from mercantile activity, specifically in a southern French context; one to which, Sylvain Piron has demonstrated, other contemporary figures contributed, including the radical Franciscan theologian Pierre Jean Olivi. The issues discussed, Piron further argues, may have arisen from lay merchants actively seeking spiritual advice.[112] As we have seen, in the *Regula* they certainly involved a close and technical knowledge of mercantile practices. The specific example of the *Regula mercato-*

---

[111] *Sensuit la reigle des marchans novellement translatée de latin en francoys* (Provins: G. Tavernier, 1496).
[112] See Piron, 'Contexte, situation, conjuncture', p. 55.

rum thus makes apparent a much wider dynamic, one which grew in strength from the later thirteenth century onward, one in which the laity were both active participants and—potentially—obedient recipients.

Sexual Sin and Society

Let us note two final examples from the *Regula*, on the discernment of not-immediately-apparent sin. The first comes from Gui's 'addition' to John of Freiburg's discussion of whether or not those who make swords or poisons or so forth are morally responsible for how they are subsequently used, or whether goldsmiths and others were similarly responsible if they made vain things (Freiburg thought mostly not, given that these also had legitimate uses; unless the fabricator knew in advance that they would be put to evil ends). Gui adds that regarding goldsmiths, the same is true of those who make short, decorative capes 'which are carried by women at night [*or* of the night?] partly for curiosity and vanity' which might lead to lust and sin; as with Freiburg, the makers are guilty if they knew that these would lead to sin when making them, but otherwise not.[113] In parallel vein, the following 'question' relates to those who make dice—are they guilty for the gambling, discord, and other sins that may then ensue? They are, says Freiburg, if they sell them 'indifferently' to anyone, without thought of consequence. To this, Gui adds the following: those who have taverns in which they permit gaming tables sin mortally, as do those who rent houses to known usurers or prostitutes. 'The same moreover I say of those who give or sell them clothes intended and provocative to evil deeds, or colours or make-up for painting their faces and similarly provoking evil deeds.'[114]

The scope of moral intentionality is thus further widened, to embrace the intentions of not only oneself but also others, where all Christians are, ideally, required to have a knowledge of and perspective on the moral fabric of the wider community. Sin exists not only in deeds done, but in the *potential* that it may be committed, and not only by oneself. As we have seen, this is true regarding money and business, where usury or other forms of injustice may lurk in a variety of ways. But also, as the preceding examples show, it is true regarding the other great human appetite: sex.

In trying to trace how lay Christian subjectivity was being refashioned across the thirteenth and fourteenth centuries, and to gain some sense of how much this

---

[113] BnF MS Lat 10689, fol. 30r(a): 'Quod [*illeg.*] de aurifrisis prout dici de cappellis cordatis quos portavit mulieres de nocte in parte ad curiositatem et vanitatem que, si intendant in luxuriam et peccatum et factores hoc agnoscunt, est peccatum quem factori et emptiori aliter non.'

[114] BnF MS Lat 10689, fol. 30v(a): 'Idem etiam dico de illis qui dant eis vel vendant vestes ordinatas et provocativas ad malum vel ad colores vel figmenta ad pinguendum facies suas et similia provocativa ad malum.'

may have had real effects beyond what specific texts construct and imagine, the topic of sex is particularly useful.[115] This is for two reasons. One is that some aspects of human sexual behaviour had always been of disciplinary concern; what is added to, or altered within, that set of concerns is thus a useful index to change over time. The other is that the possibility of committing sexual sin is pretty much universal. Whereas the kinds of sins involving money and trade discussed by the *Regula mercatorum* require a degree of material resource in the first place, all that is required to fall into sexual sin is possession of a body and an imagination.

Some kinds of sexual transgression had been seen as major sins, and indeed crimes, for centuries. Adultery is the most obvious example. The right of the bishop to punish adultery went back to Carolingian times at least, and by the central middle ages it had often become seen as a key element in lordship (along with murder and other felonies): in 1131, for example, the countess of Béziers and her sons gave to the bishop in mortgage 'all those rights of justice and courts' (*justicia et placita*) that they held in the city and a couple of other places, namely the punishment of homicide, adultery, and robbery.[116] As I noted briefly in Chapter 4, various cities and towns in southern France, from the mid-twelfth century onward, claimed the right to punish adultery by forcing the guilty parties to run naked through the streets, or else pay a hefty fine. Their motives were, I have suggested elsewhere, more to do with arrogating an element of lordship to communal governance than with pure morality, notably because having imposed such a punishment on the malefactors, various statutes explicitly state that nothing else should subsequently happen to them. Moreover, in many cases the burden of evidentiary proof was set so high—requiring the couple to be naked and in the act, and observed thus by at least two 'good men' or consuls—that the concern seems to be more with asserting the *right* than actually wishing to stamp out the misdeed.[117] Nonetheless, the concept that adultery was wrong—at least if one got caught committing it—was undoubtedly well recognized, even within the very region that wrote so lyrically about the joys of adultery. (Among other things we may wish to remind ourselves that the key element of this strand of troubadour

---

[115] There is of course a vast literature on medieval sexuality, and ecclesiastical attitudes toward it. For a broader context to the areas explored here, see particularly P. J. Payer, *The Bridling of Desire: Views of Sex in the Later Middle Ages* (Toronto: University of Toronto Press, 1993); J. W. Baldwin, *The Language of Sex: Fives Voices from Northern France around 1200* (Chicago: University of Chicago Press, 1994); T. N. Tentler, *Sin and Confession on the Eve of the Reformation* (Princeton: Princeton University Press, 1997), pp. 162–232; J. P. Poly, *Le chemin des amours barbares: genèse médiévale de la sexualité européenne* (Paris: Perrin, 2003). Poly provides the richest account of early medieval concerns, focused principally on marriage; on pp. 388–89 he essays a brief discussion of other sins, and how they shift between penitentials of the tenth–twelfth centuries, and later conciliar statutes (though without accounting perhaps for how much the penitentials may be focused on monastic faults in these areas).

[116] *Cart. Béziers*, pp. 190–91 (no. 139). They had 5,000 *sous* of Melgueil in return. On the battle to preserve Carolingian episcopal rights in this area, see S. Hamilton, 'Enquiring into Adultery and Wicked Deeds: Episcopal Justice in Tenth- and Eleventh-Century Italy', *Viator* 41 (2010), 21–43.

[117] Arnold, 'Sexualité et déshonneur'. See Chapter 4.

discourse regarding *fin'amors* was, precisely, that it pertained to those who were 'courtly', that is, the noble elite).

One might say something similarly about rape, particularly the rape of virgins. The middle ages had very far from enlightened attitudes regarding sexual violence, most obviously visible in the fact that arranging marriage to the rapist was seen as an acceptable recompense throughout most of the period.[118] Whilst there are some complications over whether the same term—*raptus*—sometimes covered what was essentially elopement (the man 'carrying off' the daughter of a household, with in fact her consent but not that of her parents) as well as sexual assault, it seems pretty clear from various texts that sex coerced by force was similarly long recognized as a sin and a crime.[119] The medieval Church's rather extended concept of consanguinity—reduced to four degrees of connection, from an earlier standard seven, at the Fourth Lateran Council—has the paradoxical effect of making it slightly harder to discern evidence for a less technical and more moral revulsion against incest, but it seems very likely to be the case, for obvious reasons.

What changes, then, does the discourse on sin and confession bring to the general lay understanding of sexual behaviour? (I am here taking somewhat as read the issue of the sacralization of marriage, which re-configures an existing social fact.) Some sins which had long been denounced as such are, for the first time, demonstrably punished as crimes by secular authorities in the thirteenth century—in southern France this being the case, albeit very rare and only by around 1280, for 'sodomy' and for bestiality.[120] But more importantly perhaps, the questions posed by confessors' manuals brought a range of concerns that had previously only swirled around monastic male chastity into a much wider arena, and elaborated various new ways in which ordinary lay people might sin sexually. This involved sexual misdeeds: simple fornication, for example, where neither party was married, a topic which, in contrast to adultery, was never a concern in civic statutes (though, as I have noted in Chapter 7, by the late thirteenth century, priests were being enjoined to ensure that their flock understood that it was in

---

[118] K. Gravdal, *Ravishing Maidens: Writing Rape in Medieval French Literature and Law* (Philadelphia: University of Pennsylvania Press, 1991).

[119] For example, customs of Arles, 1162 × 64 (Giraud, *Essai*, II, p. 2): 'Furta, rapinas, adulteria, homicidia, sanguinis efusionem, raptus mulierum, et alias diversas injurias et turpitudines, juxta arbitrium suum et bonum consilium illorum qui in consiliis fuerint, tam militum quam aliorum proborum virorum, corrigant et castigent et puniant.' Customs of Moissac, early twelfth century, c. 50: 'Derescaps si alcus corrumpia fenna verge, part sa voluntat, et aquel corrumpeire era de proshomes o de nobles o plus averos que ela la penre per molher olh done marit a so covinen daquela fenna e aquo sia en sa voluntat...' (Lagrèze-Fossat, *Études historiques sur Moissac, t. 1*, pp. 90–91).

[120] See Arnold, 'Sexualité et déshonneur', pp. 329–30; and J. Théry, '"Innommables abominations sodomitiques": les débuts de la répression. Autour de l'une des premières sentences conservées (justice épiscopale d'Albi, 1280)', *CdF* 52 (2019), pp. 297–349. Rodrigue Lavoie makes the point that secular justice throughout the period tends to focus only on particular aspects, rather than being guided by the full range of 'moral' concerns: R. Lavoie, 'La delinquance sexuelle a Manosque (1240-1430): schéma général et singularités juives', *Provence historique* 37 (1987), 571–88.

fact sinful). We also find an increased concern with masturbation, and with heterosexual married sex which was nonetheless carried out in the 'wrong' fashion. Beyond this, it also involved thoughts and desires: wet dreams, lustful thoughts, exciting others to desire.

I have mentioned some of this already above, as the early manual *Cum ad sacerdotem* is notably concerned with sexual sin. As well as addressing the more criminal 'reserved sins' of sodomy and rape, the manual includes questions about wet dreams and 'shameful acts' (meaning masturbation). The confessor is further advised to enquire if the penitent has been having sex in the 'right' way, that is, with the woman below the man (what later ages call the missionary position):[121]

> The priest should proceed with caution on this. Thus indeed he should speak or question as if the confessant, if he has done this thing, would immediately understand. If in truth he has not done it, he will not learn it from this. Indeed, one can question thus: 'The natural mode, when a man clings together with a woman, is always with the man above, the woman lying beneath. Have you done otherwise? If you have, don't be ashamed to say'.[122]

These issues are further elaborated upon in the later marginal glosses to the Toulouse manuscript of the treatise, where it is noted that 'bad practices' include 'if a man has a thing with a wife standing or from the side or from behind, or moreover in between the thighs [*that is, 'interfemoral'*], or moreover if placing himself beneath, or in a member that is not natural', going on to further gloss the fine details (the final point noted to be 'most grave' if involving oral sex, for example).[123] This level of detail is not found in all the manuals for confessors, and some take a slightly more reassuring line; Bérenger Frédol notes, for example, that wet dreams are not innately sinful, unless they were provoked by lustful thoughts one had had during the preceding day.[124] But some level of this discourse was more broadly present. In its discussion of sins of lust, the *Breviari d'amor*, for example, includes 'pollution from bad thoughts' (*pollucios | per mala cogitacios*) brought on by too much good food—an extension of an earlier

---

[121] BM Toulouse MS 340, fol. 263v. Such concern with sexual positions is also found in Guillaume Peraud's influential *summa* from c. 1236–39: Guilelmus Peraldus, *Summa aurea de virtutibus et vitiis* (Brescia, 1494), De Luxuria, iii, fol. 216.

[122] BM Toulouse MS 340, fols 267v–268r; Goering and Payer, 'Summa penitentie', p. 34.

[123] BM Toulouse MS 340, fol. 259v: 'Abusus est malus usus, si habet rem cum uxore stando vel a latere vel retro vel autem inter crura, vel etiam quod se subiciat ei, vel in membro non naturali...Gravis autem si in membro non ad hoc deputato, vel non naturali intromittit; gravissimum etiam valde si in ore.' The manual itself returns briefly in its final paragraphs to the ways in which husbands can sin sexually with their wives, namely if having sex on feast days or when fasting, in holy places, when she is menstruating, and 'birth' (presumably meaning soon after birth): Goering and Payer, 'Summa penitentie', p. 40.

[124] BM Toulouse MS 191, fol. 77v.

monastic discourse to the laity.[125] In its discussion of *ad status* sins, nearly half of the section about women is devoted to sexual sin, focused particularly on their love of dressing up to prompt desire in others, and pursuing a number of other familiarly misogynistic lines: women as disloyal temptresses, who bear bastards which their husbands must then support.[126]

My point in noting this level of detail is not prurience, but rather to emphasize further, as with usury and mercantile practices, what *else* had now fallen under the heading of 'sin' and was widely recognized as such. It thus made new demands upon a good Christian subject, in terms of knowledge and self-governance. Aspects of this expanded sense of transgression are visible also in preaching *exempla*—not the anatomical details of sexual misdeeds, but the wider contexts of lust and sexual misbehaviour. One tells of a husband of a very devout woman from the town of Ganges (c. 45 km north of Montpellier) who came to her one night, seeking to have sex; she thought hard upon Christ's passion, and miraculously he lost his desire for her. In the same town, a young single woman solicited various young men to have sex; she then had a vision of a great pot full of boiling water set on a tripod, with a great fire underneath, in which she herself was being tortured (and thus by implication was reformed). In Portugal, an adulterous knight had a vision of demonic cats, which led him to kill the largest one, at which the others cried out 'our prince is dead!' Recounting the story at the dinner table some time later, the house cat leapt upon his neck and bit his throat, suffocating him.[127] A number of tales recount women who 'painted their faces in various colours'—that is, wore heavy make-up—and were punished one way or another as a result. One is visited by the Virgin Mary, who says that she cannot see the woman's face because of the make-up, and that if she doesn't abstain from wearing it, it will stay there forever, horrifying all who see her.[128] Female beauty was both a source of sinful pride and a temptation to men: a man from Lectoure (c. 30 km south of Agen) called Pierre Guillaume had 'contempt' for his own wife, because of the beauty of a 'whore' with whom he had taken up (the term *meretrix* here probably in fact being used as a moral insult rather than a clear identification of the other woman as a professional sex worker).[129] His wife entreated a Brother Minor to remonstrate with the *meretrix*, warning her that God would punish her. And indeed, three days later, in an argument in the town square, she was attacked and wounded in her left breast (by implication making her less lovely, as well as dangerously injured).

---

[125] *Breviari d'amor*, ll. 17170-71. Monastic discourse: see J. Murray, '"The Law of Sin That Is In My Members": The Problem of Male Embodiment', in S. J. E. Riches and S. Salih, eds, *Gender and Holiness: Men, Women and Saints in Late Medieval Europe* (London: Routledge, 2002), pp. 9-22.
[126] *Breviari d'amor*, ll. 18705-869.
[127] Welter, 'Un nouveau recueil franciscain d'exempla', pp. 468 (no. 98), 609 (no. 170), 611 (no. 174).
[128] Welter, 'Un recueil d'exempla', p. 657 (no. 15). Similar theme in no. 219.
[129] BL MS Add. 33956, fol. 33r: 'Contingit villa lactoreii, quod quidam Petrus Guillelmus nomine contempta propria uxore pulcra satis et discreta adhesit uni meretrici pulchritudine.'

As in many areas touching upon lay spiritual instruction, the discussion above has primarily focused on prescriptive texts, those which told people what they *ought* to think. For some areas of human behaviour, we may suspect that the Church's message had at best only partial take-up; as already discussed, this seems to be the case with the more hardline interpretation of usury, for example. One finds it slightly hard to believe that any medieval lawyer would have internalized much sense of sinfulness, for which Matfre Ermengaud chided him, over deeds regularly done in that line of work (though that may just be prejudice on my part). In at least partial contrast, what is notable with regard to the amplification of sexual sin is that we absolutely can see it having an effect—not, that is, the effect of stopping all such activity, but rather the effect of making at least some lay people *recognize* that such activity could or should be seen as wrong and sinful. We know this from some passing evidence in certain other records, and from one extraordinarily curious civic court case in particular.

Some sample of the passing evidence first. There is much one can glean from various depositions given before Jacques Fournier, particularly from the evidence of Beatrice de Lagleize.[130] I have discussed various of the sexual elements recounted in her deposition at greater length elsewhere, but it is worth recalling here one particular detail: a man called Raimond Roussel told Beatrice a story of two women, Alestra and Serena, who had painted their faces in order to disguise themselves as they fled the region, but who were nonetheless captured and sentenced to be burnt as heretics. Before being led to the stake, they requested water with which to wash their faces, 'saying that they would not go painted before God'.[131] Whilst Beatrice's behaviour—which included having affairs with two priests, and having sex in church—clearly demonstrates that the penitential discourse on sex did not by any means compel conformity of behaviour, the story she here recounts nonetheless very clearly taps into the wider strand of discourse found in the preaching *exempla* noted above. Similarly, when about to enter into one affair, with Pierre Clergue (the notorious priest from Montaillou), Beatrice herself expressed the concern that she had heard it said that any woman who had slept with a priest 'would not see the face of God'. As noted, this concern did not *stop* her; but it is clear that it framed her understanding and worries about her own conduct. That is, she recognized herself to be committing sin, this *recognition* being what the elaboration of penitential discourse sought from the laity.

Incidental detail in a set of civic trial records from the town of Cordes, relating to a particular dispute from 1326, makes it clear that both the fact that adultery was subject to de facto excommunication, and the specific excommunication

---

[130] Ladurie, *Montaillou*, chapters 8, 9, and 10 gathers up a variety of material on sexual matters, though the analysis and broader contextualization could now bear considerable revision.
[131] *Fournier* I, pp. 220–21. Detail and discussion in Arnold, *Inquisition and Power*, pp. 198–205.

of named individuals for this sin, were regular features of episcopal pronouncements, repeated at parish level. We do not actually know what the underlying case was about, other than that the accused was called Pierre Chambut. The evidence comes from various witnesses for his defence, including a priest called Durand de L'Albarède, who set about undermining the reputation of the prosecution witnesses by calling their moral character into question. In many instances, particularly regarding the female witnesses, L'Albarède and others noted that they were guilty of adultery or other sexual misconduct; one Bernarda Chantacleira, for example, was 'a bad woman...a whore' and a married woman, who had had a child with a priest, and was thus automatically excommunicate, as such a punishment for adultery was pronounced on Sundays and feast days by order of the bishop of Albi.[132] Another female witness called Arnauda de *Bostani* was said to have been denounced as a concubine and adulterer on diverse Sundays and feast days by the priest of her local church.[133] So we have very clear evidence that the discourse of sexual sin was, by this stage at least, broadcast back to the wider community through parochial preaching.

To turn now to the extraordinarily curious case. It comes from the same set of civic court material from Cordes, again in 1326. Guiraud de Haut-Mont of Vindrac-Alayrac (just east of Cordes), known as 'Bad Bean' (*Malafava*), had been accused by his mother-in-law, Guillemette Laurenssa, of having had unnatural sexual relations with her daughter, his wife, Alamande. We do not have the details of Guillemette's deposition, but can gather what was alleged by the cross-examination of Alamande herself. 'Asked if the said accused, when the witness was facing the ground, had known the witness carnally by her back or by natural [means], she said by natural [means] and not by her back.' This could be taken as a coy or confused reference to anal sex, but seems more likely to mean simply the use of a particular sexual position, because another witness—a friend of Alamande's, Bertrande de Montagnac—attested that, at harvest time, the mother-in-law had several times complained to her that Bad Beans had 'known' his wife 'in the manner of an animal' (that is, entering her from behind, rather than in the

---

[132] AD Tarn, 69 EDt FF18bis, fol. 12r: 'Dicta Bernarda Chantacleira est vilis mulier...vilis meretrix co[m]mitens adulterium licet sic conjugata et...nefariam prolem suscepit a domino Guillemo Mathei, presbitero, et sic est et esse debet excommunicata a majore excommunicatione...nam in diebus dominicis et festivis, palam et publice, in ecclesiis dyocesis Albiensis tale adulterium com[m]ittentes, de mandato domini officialis Albiensis.'

[133] AD Tarn, 69 EDt FF18bis, fol. 16r: 'tanquam cum pluries ipse loquens, diversis diebus dominicis et festivis, per capellanum ecclesie dicti loci, palam et publice in ecclesie dicti loci, tales concubinar[ios] manifest[os] pro talibus adulteris generaliter pro excommunicatis audivit nunciari [?]...audivit eandem Arnaudam Debostani palam et publice reportari in dicto loco.' Folios 13, 14, and 15 are missing, but in fact Durand d'Albareda's evidence appears to continue across the gap without any glitch, suggesting that the court notary pre-foliated the booklet, but then subsequently took out some pages for other purposes. The material here and below is discussed further in Arnold, 'Sexualité et déshonneur'.

missionary position).[134] We do not know the outcome of the case, though it seems likely that, given his wife's support and that other witnesses alleged that Guillemette Laurenssa hated her son-in-law, he would have been found innocent. What is extraordinary here is not simply that it allows us a glimpse of ordinary lay people getting morally upset about sexual positions used within married life.[135] The really extraordinary element is the very fact of the trial: that the accusation of sex 'in the manner of an animal' was sufficient for the consuls of Cordes to interview several witnesses and deploy the use of a notary, all of this happening in an entirely secular jurisdiction. Even if Bad Beans was not punished, that the case was pursued by the court indicates that, by the early fourteenth century, such issues had come to *matter*, even within an entirely secular sphere. This is of course just one case—but that it happened at all strongly suggests that a more elaborated discourse on sexual sin had entered into lay culture. Being a 'good Christian', rather than a 'bad' or 'low' (*vilis*) person like those other besmirched witnesses, now potentially involved the privacy of the bedroom as well as the public performance of faith.

Conclusion

As I have noted above at various points, a number of aspects around sexual sin are essentially the extension of what were originally concerns regarding monastic male chastity onto a much wider realm. In a parallel fashion, as previously said, the very title of the *Regula mercatorum* suggests it can be seen as an attempt to extend a monastic 'rule' for a subset of lay people. These might then be seen as part of what André Vauchez, as we saw in Chapter 5, called the 'monasticization of the laity', as the Church extended the ambition of its pastoral care.[136] The metaphor continues to be a useful one, in as much as it emphasizes the earlier discursive roots of these concerns: that the spiritual discipline within the cloister was being elaborated out into the world, where, despite the continued existence of

---

[134] AD Tarn, 69 EDt FF18bis, fols 1r-3r, at fol. 2v: 'interrogata si dictus perventus, ipsa loquita tenendo faciem suam ad terram, cognoscebat ipsam loquitam carnaliter per dorsum suum vel naturam, dixit quod per naturam et non per dorsum...'; 3r: 'quod hoc anno presenti tempori messium, pluries diversis diebus temporibus et horis, audivit dici apud dictum locum de montanhaco Guillelme Resseguiera alias Laurenssa, mat[ris] Alamandis uxoris dicti perventi, quod idem perventus cognoscat et cognoscebat dictam suam uxorem ad modum animalium prout continetur in perventam predictam'.

[135] As Tentler points out (*Sin and Confession*, p. 190), Burchard of Worms had mildly condemned such sexual positions in the tenth century, albeit awarding only a very light fixed penance; the point is the change now to a much greater level of concern, both in the pastoral literature and as evidenced in the specific legal proceedings in Cordes. The medical and pastoral discourses on this and other topics are usefully summarized and contextualized in K. Harvey, *The Fires of Lust: Sex in the Middle Ages* (London: Reaktion, 2021), pp. 66-69, 118-19.

[136] Vauchez, *Laity*, p. 72; see also Caldwell Ames, *Righteous Persecution*, pp. 144-47.

demarcated spaces of 'holiness' within which a certain kind of 'purity' was maintained, some proximate relationship to that exalted spiritual position could potentially be made available to at least some of the laity, those who were willing to subject themselves to such discipline and do the necessary 'work' on their inner selves.

However, there are also important limitations to the 'monasticization' image. A monastic rule is explicit in its details, focused as much on the management of collective daily life as the restraint of inner sinful temptation (the two however understood to be operating in concert). The rule's dictates apply largely within a clearly circumscribed space, where obedience to a single figure of authority (the abbot) and the wider expectations of a community (the monastic order) frame the disciplinary context, both conceptually and in its practical application. In contrast, whilst medieval parishes and dioceses did become both literally and conceptually more defined spaces across the thirteenth century, they never transmuted into a truly 'monastic' space, and never aimed at, let alone achieved, the obedience of the monastery for their lay populations. Lay religious subjectivity had to swim in choppier waters, the expectations of spiritual transcendence rather lower than for those who could withdraw from the world, but the interruptions, complications, and temptations of secular life providing a more constant distraction.

At one point in the *Regula mercatorum*, Gui de Toulouse advises merchants to have the 'rule' before their eyes, to help them 'flee' sin; but also, he goes on, to tell whether the various sins that they might commit are 'venial' or 'mortal'.[137] The immediate point is to have some sense of what kind of level of penance the merchant then needs to undertake to cleanse that sin; but the implication—unintended but nonetheless present—is to make the varying degrees of sin associated with mercantile activity into something potentially negotiable. It is a point that has been made before, regarding the mendicant development of a *cura animarum* for an increasingly mercantilized civic society: the discourse does not ultimately seek to eradicate the presence of sin within secular society, but rather provides the means for its assuagement, a system of penitential balances that will help all toward potential salvation, even whilst they pursue the grubby worlds of business.[138]

The specific case relates to the mercantile world, one which was extensive in southern France, particularly if one thinks more broadly of the low-level moneylending, deal-making, and intermittent engagement in trade that seems to be a feature of peasant society. Not everyone was majorly implicated in a

---

[137] Paris, BnF MS Lat. 10689, fol. 28v: '...si dictam regulam habeat per occulis fugiendo [*illeg.*] facto periculum peccati per hoc...et adverte de peccato que proximum utrum veniale sit vel mortale'.
[138] L. K. Little, *Religious Poverty and the Profit Economy in Medieval Europe* (Ithaca, NY: Cornell University Press, 1978); see also Chiffoleau, *La comptabilité de l'Au-Delà*.

market-directed economy, but the wider dynamic was nonetheless generally applicable: whilst the disciplinary framework of sin, penance, and salvation emerged from a monastic setting, as it was elaborated in southern French society (as elsewhere) it became something more diffuse and more complex. It was, in the sense I set out in the Introduction, lay *religion*. That is, not only was the notion of a good life as 'regulated' transmitted from the monastic legacy to the lay world of faith, but by the later thirteenth century, in this region at least, lay people were encouraged and indeed sometimes *required* to develop a certain kind of pious subjectivity. Not only were they required to act in an orthodox fashion (attend church, pay tithes, observe the sabbath, etc.) and on occasion perform an external recitation of certain core statements of 'belief' (at a minimum the Creed, *Ave*, and *Pater noster*, as we saw in Chapter 7), but were increasingly also encouraged to foster an interiorized, devout reflection *on* those beliefs. The laity were thus asked not only to remember general categories of sin, but, as we have seen, to engage with a wider penitential regime in which the fact of sin was *revealed* to be embedded in certain kinds of behaviour and indeed thought.

Some of this disciplinary project was sharp-edged, as we have seen with regard to inquisition into heresy, and we may wish to hang on to a sense of 'power' in regard to how Christianity developed this lay Christian religious discourse. But to be clear: by 'power' I do not mean 'repression'. The point about confessional discourse was that it rewarded as well as punished. The promise of salvation was retained for the many; the road there was hard and narrow but, as the pastoral works repeatedly emphasized, potentially achievable. Thus a sense of pious practice—we may by this point perhaps say *religious* practice—unfolded as a spectrum of possibility for the laity, where being Christian was something which one layperson could do 'better' than another; where all might strive to be a 'good Christian', even if many would often fall short.

9
Negotiations of the Faith

On 10 October 1240 in Limoux (some 20 km south-west of Carcassonne), all of the *prud'hommes* of the town gathered under the auspices of the *bailli* Raimond Sernin. Among the 156 men who came together were various who identified themselves as weavers, skinners, tailors, carters, purse-makers, shoemakers, butchers, and smiths, as well as just one 'merchant'; the town elite, but not particularly 'elite' in any wider social context. They had met to confirm a very important agreement: to appoint Geraud Avril and Pierre Raimond Falcho, both *prud'hommes* of Limoux, plus Brother Raimond, prior of the Dominican monastery at Prouille, as procurators (legal representatives) for the town. The three procurators were to go to the papal curia in Rome, to deal with whatever was needed regarding crimes of heresy allegedly committed by men or women from Limoux, 'to undertake, manage, defend, rescue, refute, appeal; and to petition for restitution where it is necessary, and to swear to the calumny or truth of what is said, and to take any other form of oath'. The agreement survives as a single piece of parchment, originally with the town's seal attached but this now lost. The names of all 156 men are carefully recorded there.[1]

There are various other moments at which townspeople in southern France resisted the attentions of inquisitors into heretical wickedness in a rather more confrontative fashion: riots in Narbonne and Albi in 1234 that freed some people arrested for heresy, something similar happening in Avignon at some point in the later 1240s; the temporary expelling of the inquisitors, along with the rest of the Dominicans, from Toulouse in 1235; a plot in Carcassonne in 1285 to steal various inquisitorial registers; major uprisings in Albi and Carcassonne in the first years of the fourteenth century. In a similar vein, several southern French nobles collectively perpetrated the murder of the inquisitor Guillaume Arnaud and his

---

[1] AD Aude, 4E206 GG220. The document is very faded in the final lines. There is an edition: A. Sabarthès, 'Un episode de l'albigéisme à Limoux', *Bulletin philologique et historique jusqu'à 1715* (1932–33), 193–200. Sabarthès argues there for a date around 1244, against a modern archival note of 1240; however, a more recent archivist, who studied the document under UV light, states that the last line reads 'Acta sunt hec in villa limosi anno Domini M CC XL VI idus octobris' (this noted in handwriting on the finding aids at AD Aude). This could also be read as 15 October 1246, depending on whether one thinks the 'VI' belongs to the year or the day of the month ('idus' is in the nominative rather than genitive, but this is not unusual in date forms). Dossat preferred the latter (*Crises*, p. 172) but without having seen the actual document. I prefer 1240, on the grounds that it would thus precede the episcopal complaints to the papacy in 1245, mentioned further below.

entourage in 1242.[2] What the Limoux document shows us in contrast is something less dramatic but arguably as important: a collective attempt by a lay community to *negotiate*, within the existing ecclesial structures of authority, the imposed demands of the faith. The document is essentially a legal agreement (the *prud'hommes* making their goods collectively liable for any costs arising, toward its end), and one might thus be tempted to separate it from a discussion of lay religion. But we should remember what going to the papal curia likely implied in this kind of context: a trip to supplicate via the papal penitentiary, an office that operated within a canon-legal framework, directed toward questions of penance and salvation.[3] Two letters sent in 1245 by various southern French bishops to the papacy and to the college of cardinals complain that people were going to the penitentiary and obtaining letters of remission for crimes of heresy, 'so that either the inquisitors' jurisdiction or your own seems to be weakened, and in this way Christian faith is mocked and ecclesiastical discipline held in contempt' (as the bishops saw it, at any rate).[4] Inquisition into heretical wickedness and its wider accompanying discipline was often termed, by papal legates and bishops, the *negotium fidei*—the 'business' or 'negotiation of the faith'. The document from Limoux affords us a glimpse of the lay equivalent: a local political community banding together to manage, defend, and appeal matters relating to the Christian faith, from the lay side of the equation.

This is not the first time that towns had acted on their own authority in regard to issues around heresy. Even before the crusade—albeit in the period in which ecclesiastical condemnation of Waldensians and the Good Men was heating up— we find some of the larger cities taking a certain stance. The customs of Carcassonne from around 1205 include in a statute against insults the injunction that 'anyone who calls another a heretic, if he cannot prove [the truth of] it, shall be penalized by the penalty for that crime [of heresy], if it [*that is, the insult*] is

---

[2] See Given, *Inquisition and Medieval Society*, chapter 5; A. Friedlander, *Hammer of the Inquisitors: Brother Bernard Délicieux and the Struggle against the Inquisition in Fourteenth-Century France* (Leiden: Brill, 2000), chapter 1 and *passim*. On Avignon (not noted by Given) see the letter of Innocent IV, 24 May 1249, edited in L.-H. Labande, *Avignon au XIIIe siècle: l'évêque Zoen Tencarari et les Avignonais* (Paris: Alphonse Picard, 1908), pp. 347–54, at pp. 352–53: '...cum quidam heretici per inquisitores essent capti et in domo episcopi adducti ut ibidem custodirentur... Avinionenses occupaverunt domum episcopi et voluerunt illam custodire, relinquentes ibi custodiam, et tunc hereticus quidam qui erat de villa liberatus fuit...'.

[3] On the penitentiary, see K. Salonen and L. Schmugge, eds, *A Sip from the Well of Grace: Medieval Texts from the Apostolic Penitentiary* (Washington DC: Catholic University of America Press, 2009); A. Fossier, *Le bureau des âmes: écritures et pratiques administratives de la Pénitencerie apostolique (XIIIe-XIVe siècle)* (Rome: École française du Rome, 2018).

[4] Doat 31, fols 118r-121v, 122r-125v. At 120v: 'multi etiam eorum litteras a vestris poenitentiariis impetratas ad diversos defferunt iudices, ut sive videatur inquisitorum immo potius vestra iurisdictio enervari, propter quod non modicum illuditur fides Christiana et contempnitur Ecclesiastica disciplina...'. The penitentiary remained a possible recourse much later: a number of those from Montaillou and its environs who feared prosecution for heresy in the early fourteenth century also decided to journey to Rome to gain absolution direct from the papacy: see *Fournier* III, pp. 145–46.

proven'.[5] Those from Toulouse, definitely from 1205, state that the consuls, with 'the common counsel' of the people of the city, have made an agreement that no man or woman can be accused of heresy after their death unless a similar accusation had been made when they were alive, or they had given themselves to the heretics when ill, or died 'in their hands'.[6] Certain aspects of matters of the faith—aspects which intersected with other issues of identity, governance, and the good running of the city—were thus already seen, by some of the laity at least, to be in their own hands. A number of civic seals from the thirteenth century onward start to incorporate religious symbols alongside those of the city: municipal seals for Narbonne from the early thirteenth century onward featured the Virgin and Child on the obverse, whilst that for Castres has a classic simplified fortified town on the obverse, and a seated St Vincent performing a blessing on the reverse; St Vincent also appears on the obverse of the grand seal for Marseille, this time mounted, crushing a monster.[7] We should remember that in many places, until specific consular buildings were erected (often not until a point well after the crusade) important civic business was frequently debated and decided in a suitable church, such as Saint-Sernin for Toulouse. Just as the aristocracy had started to build private chapels in the later twelfth century, the later thirteenth century sees a number of wealthy but non-noble citizens establishing their own chapels (either stand-alone buildings, or incorporated into existing churches).[8] Cities and towns could push back against ecclesial authority in order to sustain Christian worship, as, for example, in Béziers in 1297: the city having been placed under interdict, which forbade church services, the consuls apparently responded by having consecrated hosts taken into the communal hall, possibly for worship, and organized public rituals around burials.[9]

As said, there is excellent work already done on some of these topics in terms of southern French 'resistance' to inquisition. In this chapter, what interests me more is the theme of negotiation, both collective and individual, in which lay people demonstrated some degree of agency in their dealings with the Church and in their approach to the Christian religion. Throughout the preceding chapters I have tried to make lay agency visible, not only in its rather unusual dramatic moments—the enthusiasm of a Pons de Léras, the scepticism voiced by a

---

[5] Customs of Carcassonne, 1205?, c. 20. On dating, see Chapter 4, n. 133.
[6] AM Toulouse, AA1, fol. 66r (no. 52): 'Item, consules Tolose urbis et suburbii cum communi consilio eiusdem urbis et suburbii fecerunt stabilimentum tale quod aliquis vel aliqua non possit accusari post mortem de heresi nisi in vita accusatus esset, aut infirmitate positus dedisset seipsum vel seipsam hereticis, aut nisi moreretur in manibus hereticorum.' The statute rather nicely immediately continues on to separate civic issues, such as the duties of those who have watercourses flowing down narrow shared streets outside their property.
[7] L. Douët-d'Arcq, *Collection de sceaux*, 3 vols (Paris: Plon, 1863–68), II, pp. 360 (no. 5628), 363 (nos 5650–55), 388 (no. 5809).
[8] For example, Doat 118, fol. 172 (founding chapel in Cahors by bourgeois, 1281); Doat 119, fol. 43r (letter of John XXII re all chapels founded in Cahors by citizens).
[9] P. Clarke, *The Interdict in the Thirteenth Century* (Oxford: Oxford University Press, 2007), p. 228.

particular worshipper at a shrine—but also in its quieter moments, such as the people of La Roquebrussanne petitioning for a new church building, the support for hospitals and other pious institutions, the quotidian giving of alms to holy people (Good Men and Waldensians included). In this chapter, the choices that lay people made in their orthodox worship, the solidarities that they forged, step centre stage.

The frame for enquiry is as follows: the elaboration of the Christian faith as lay *religion*—as, that is, a disciplinary framework that made certain demands, encouraged particular interior investments, and distributed a varied sense of achievement with regard to these goals—was played out within a social landscape that contained other additional resources and cultural demands. In a southern French context—in common with some, but not all, other areas of western Europe—this social landscape was marked by a number of important features. These include a widespread 'civic' sensibility which, as I suggested in Chapter 4, extended well beyond the larger settlements; a notarial culture that provided relatively broad access to mechanisms of law and archiving that were authoritative but also somewhat flexible and responsive in their documentary forms (an example being the Limoux document with which we began); and a strong vein of mercantile practice, extending across a range of social strata, that operated through agreements, contracts, and often collective negotiations. As we shall see, in certain areas the laity pushed back against some of the demands of the Church, most often when these conflicted too strongly with other areas of material life; but in others, the nature of the negotiations and collective actions aimed to forge an enlarged space for lay engagement with Christian piety. This too was lay 'religion': not something simply imposed, but something reworked and renegotiated in the thirteenth and fourteenth centuries.

Negotiating with the Priest

At various points, perhaps most particularly in Chapter 8, I have talked of 'the Church' making certain demands upon the laity. The use of a capital to indicate the wider, authoritative institution is justified; indeed it mirrors the language and even on occasion the orthography of various contemporary sources. But of course much of the time, ordinary lay people in their own parishes did not experience 'the Church' as an abstract entity, but its more specific representatives: the local priest, and perhaps beyond him and much more intermittently, the bishop of the diocese. As we saw in Chapter 1, in the eleventh and early twelfth century there is good reason to suspect that the local priest was very much an organic part of the local community, perhaps handing down the role from father to son, possibly even on occasion 'unfree'. In possible contrast, at some point in the thirteenth century parish priests began regularly to have bestowed upon them—in documentary sources at least—the honorific *dominus* ('lord' or *senhor*), something which had earlier usually been reserved for bishops, abbots, and other notables.[10] At the same time, even when gaining an honorific title that indicated higher status, the practical demands of rural life for many priests meant that they were still effectively on a par with their lay neighbours, perhaps most obviously so in terms of their management of the bits of land which they themselves held, and which they farmed in some fashion—keeping livestock, growing grapes, and so forth—presumably identically to the rest of the community.

But priests were supposed to be different from their lay neighbours, although the distinctions emphasized by the Gregorian reformers were still in the process of being more consistently elaborated in actual practice. Even by the late thirteenth century, the Church was having firmly to forbid those who had entered clerical orders (presumably those still in minor orders) from taking on artisanal trades. A letter sent by Boniface VIII in 1295 to the city of Narbonne noted that this was the case, leading the consuls of the bourg, a couple of years later, to prohibit more than forty named men from doing so.[11] Previously, in 1283, at the order of the seneschal (presumably prompted by a similar ecclesiastical concern), the *viguier* of Montolieu had compiled a list of 216 clergy who were warned to desist from conducting business or undertaking artisanal jobs.[12] Something similar was done in Albi in 1294, recording the names of more than 100 men who had three times been warned to 'desist from mechanical works and exercise clerical office', or they would otherwise be reputed as laymen; those listed including some identified as hostellers, butchers, shoemakers, weavers, carpenters, and merchants.[13]

In spiritual terms, the fundamental difference between the parish priest and his flock was the sacrament of the altar—the sacrament which only the priest could effect. But in practical terms, there was another important distinction: the priest was the recipient of the parish tithes. The fact of tithing was extremely longstanding, and can be found throughout the period covered by this book. But in the late thirteenth century we start to find an increased number of disputes between lay communities and their priests over the precise details of tithing,

---

[10] Some later twelfth-century vernacular literature, including material that circulated in the Mediterranean regions, does use the formal *dan* (from *dominus*) to address certain priests, though perhaps particularly to elevate the character of particular figures within the narrative rather than reflecting universal social usage: see L. Foulet, 'Sire, messire', *Romania* 71 (1950), 1–48, particularly p. 15.

[11] Blanc, *Livre de comptes de Jacme Olivier*, pp. 490–92 (no. 40), 492–94 (no. 42).

[12] Doat 69, fol. 263 (ed. in Mahul, *Cartulaire*, I, pp. 130–32).

[13] Doat 103, fols 47r-50v: 'cum diceretur quosdam clericos infrascriptos potius exercere mecanica officia, et saecularibus officiis immiscere quam ea quae pertinent, et pertinere debent ad officium clericatus...ut moneret infrascriptos et illos omnes qui sunt eiusdem conditionis ut a dictis officiis mecanicis desisterent, et clericalia officia exercerent...'. A letter from the bishop of Albi in 1310 indicates that this was still going on, and that part of the motive seemed to be claiming clerical status in order to elude taxation; he ordered that all who were tonsured but carrying out 'mechanical trades' were subject to the civic *taille*. See Compayré, *Études*, p. 273 (no. 74); and Clarke, *Interdict*, pp. 225–26.

among other matters. The new appearance of this may be nothing more than a trick of the evidentiary light—that is, it is possible that earlier disputes occurred but never entered the documentary record—and yet the greater number, and the fine level of detail entered into, do rather suggest novelty. They might be seen as emerging from an increased desire to assert 'rights' on both sides of the equation, bolstered by a notarial legal culture that facilitated an authoritative arbitration of such disputes; it is important to note that in most cases we know of the 'dispute' precisely because there was a subsequent amicable agreement drawn up.

Take, for example, the case of Lodève in 1276. The dispute here was between the Cathedral chapter and the city (represented by the consuls), but with implications for all the parishes in and around that place.[14] The issue was the tithe on hay and animal feed, and on olives or olive oil. To resolve it both sides agreed to appoint a judge and a citizen of Lodève as two formal arbitrators, and the hearing was conducted in the house of the Brothers Minor in the city, several friars acting as witnesses. Having heard evidence, the arbitrators decided that, given the hardships experienced by the territories around the city, which were allegedly causing people to leave their settlements, they should moderate the amount owed: tithing should be made on hay at the rate of one-twentieth (rather than the usual one-tenth), and only on the first cutting of hay; one-twelfth was owed on animal feed, but only on that which was to be sold (presumably meaning that for someone's own use was exempt). The tithe on olive oil was set at one-twenty-fifth, to be reckoned at mills or other places where olives were pressed; those in charge of mills were to make an annual oath to the chapter to render this up faithfully.[15] As these details make clear, we are not here seeing a zero-sum contest of authority, but a detailed negotiation, both clergy and laity gaining something in the process.

Nor is it only in a major civic setting that we can find lay people collectively challenging what was claimed. A tithe dispute between the *universitas* of the village of Vinon[-sur-Verdon], south of Manosque, was resolved in 1261 in the hands of the prior of the church of Carluc (to which the church of Vinon was subject). The surviving charter is rather damaged, but it is clear that whilst the church had various tithing rights, the villagers were able to negotiate the precise amounts levied somewhat to their favour. Pons Botitau, the 'syndic' for the village, successfully argued that the amounts owed should be calculated only after having paid other lordly dues (*pagata*) on certain produce, that herbs and plants grown in their gardens were not subject to the tithe, and that when storms caused flooding in the vineyards, they were not liable to carry grapes to the church.[16]

---

[14] A document from 1236 lists twenty-two parishes which must render tithes to the bishop, the bishop confirming that he then hands over a third to the chapter: Rouquette, *Livre vert*, pp. 97–107.

[15] E. Martin, ed., *Cartulaire de la ville de Lodève* (Montpellier: Serre et Roumégous, 1900), pp. 70–72 (no. 72).

[16] AD Bouche-du-Rhône, 2 H 345 (my thanks to Ryan Low for providing me with digital photographs).

In 1268, the people of the village of Blagnac (north-west of Toulouse) successfully petitioned Alphonse de Poitiers to write to his officers to tell the prior of the parish church to desist in pursuing what the laity claimed were 'uncustomary' tithing rights over a certain field; if the prior refused to obey, Alphonse's representative was to tell the abbot of Saint-Sernin to order the prior to do so (the local church presumably being a dependency of the abbey).[17] The following year, Alphonse was again invoked in sorting out a dispute which had turned rather more heated, at Montcuq (c. 29 km south-west of Cahors): the prior there alleged that some of his parishioners were withholding all their tithes, were attending church even when excommunicated, and that they had physically attacked him and his chaplain. In response, in a separate letter, 'the men of Montcuq' alleged that the rector had invented new and unheard of tithes, and was using armed men to collect them.[18] Other letters in Alphonse's administrative collection make clear that intervening in local tithing disputes on behalf of one bishop or other, particularly where new tithes had been imposed, was a rather familiar bit of business.[19] Slightly less dramatically but in some ways more importantly, a stand-alone notarial document survives for the village of Esparsac (c. 40 km west-south-west of Montauban) from 1280, recording a detailed agreement made between the rector, Raimond de Guillemette, and the village 'consuls', in which the tithes on wine, oil, grain, hemp, and the like were set at one-twelfth of the harvest, and the *carnalage* tithe exacted on most newborn livestock to be given as 4d rather than an actual animal.[20]

It is important to note that we do not find people objecting to tithes in general: in each case, these are disputes over what *precisely* was owed, on what lands or activities. Newly instituted areas of exaction were most likely to prompt complaint, for obvious reasons. A famous example is a newly imposed level of tithe on lambs (known as *carnalages*), which Jacques Fournier introduced in his diocese when bishop of Pamiers. This prompted various complaints, some of which ended up recorded via his inquisitorial activities, most particularly because some of those excommunicated for non-payment had, like the men of Montcuq, nonetheless attempted to go to church to attend mass. One of them, Raimond de Laburat, protested that if one paid the tithe in the same manner as one's father had done,

---

[17] Molinier, *Correspondence administrative*, I, pp. 513–14 (no. 796).

[18] Molinier, *Correspondence administrative*, II, p. 156 (no. 1443); pp. 175–76 (no. 1472).

[19] See, for example, Molinier, *Correspondence administrative*, I, p. 600 (no. 930); II, p. 133–34 (no. 1412); p. 159 (no. 1447).

[20] AD T-et-G, G 691: 'Noveritis quod cum cause seu discordie venissent...inter...dominum B. den Guilhemotam rectorem ecclesiarum de Iuniaco et d'Espsaco ex parte una et consules et universitates de Iuniaco et d'Espsaco ex altera...Et ibidem predicti arbitrii arbitacione sue amicabiles compositiones dixerunt et pronuntiant...videlicet quod quilibet homo et femina de universitate dictorum castrorum...soluat dicto rectori decimam et primitiam bladi vini, linorum et canaborum et decima feni videlicet xii partem...Item, quod habitantes in dictis castris et in pertinenciis eorum soluant [*illeg.*] carnalagiorum videlicet de pullae, equorum, mulorum et asinorum et viculorum de quolibet iiii d. tol.'

and as was customary, it was unjust to excommunicate them. Moreover, it was unjust to demand an Easter candle of a particular weight from a parish community: as he allegedly told a priest, 'we will make a candle if *we* wish to do so', and when questioned by Fournier he continued to hold to the opinion that a community could only be asked to make one 'in the best manner that we can', and not to supply something to a specified weight.[21]

The experience of Raimond de Laburat and others reminds us that the implications of tithing disputes were not purely economic. Excommunication, being disbarred from attendance at church, had important spiritual implications, and the whole issue spoke to a wider sense of the laity's role with regard to Christianity. Raimond, another witness alleged, had proclaimed publicly to others 'the lord bishop [Fournier] ordered that we should make the churches and the bells, and the churches and the bells are ours, but when the chaplains wish, they can expel us from church and make us stay out in the rain!' Raimond himself admitted to saying, 'we made the churches and we buy all that is necessary for the churches, and the churches are ours, and now they expel us from church!'[22]

A further clutch of fascinating documents from the later thirteenth and early fourteenth century record a number of other negotiated settlements between communities and their priests. Tithes are sometimes a part of the issue, but various other duties and obligations are more often the focus. A recurrent issue is about what the priest is allowed to retain when burying somebody: it was customary for him to be able to retain some of the burial clothes or other items of clothing, but what *precisely* he could claim could give rise to further collective debate. In 1268, the rector of the church of Mirepoix, Jean de Burgo, and the consuls of the town were in disagreement over how much free choice he had in this regard when it was a woman who was to be buried. After various witnesses were called, it was agreed that

> the aforesaid rector and all his successors in the aforesaid church shall receive in perpetuity, without any contradiction, in peace, from the heirs or successors or from those who hold the things, from each and every woman who dies in the aforesaid parish, namely the best tunic, if she has two or more tunics. If she does not have a tunic or tunics, and has a *brizaud* [*an undergarment*] and pelisse, he shall have the better one. And if she had neither of those garments and has a *gardacors* [*probably an overcoat*] the aforesaid rector shall have that.

And, the document went on, if the deceased woman did have tunics and *brizauds* but they were worthless and not fit to be worn, the priest could be given either the

---

[21] Fournier II, pp. 325, 313; cf. Arnold, *Inquisition and Power*, p. 184.
[22] Fournier II, pp. 310, 316.

gardacors or 2 *sous*, as the surviving relatives preferred.[23] At Limoux, in 1275, a detailed agreement was drawn up by the notary Guillaume Negre between the priory church of Saint-Martin (owned by the monastery of Prouille) and the consuls; the agreement itself is now unfortunately lost, but the fact of it was recorded in a separate charter, noting that it concerned the 'bed linen, clothing, and shoes of the dead' which customarily went to the church, and also the costs of the meal for the clergy that was customarily given at funerals.[24]

Mirepoix and Limoux are both quite large towns, but such agreements are also extant for much smaller villages, sometimes as the original documents. In 1287, the 'syndics' of Pia (just north of Perpignan) made a lengthy agreement with the chaplain of the church of Saint-Cyr. The parchment is torn in places, obscuring a few details, but overall it describes an arrangement agreed regarding the tithe on grapes (at what looks to be considerably less than 'one-tenth'), provided that the people of the village delivered it direct to the chaplain's cellar without having to be reminded. Beyond that, the document addresses at some length a dispute that had arisen, again regarding what rights the chaplain and his deacon had over the clothing of the dead. It was ultimately agreed that the clergy should not be given anything for children or young adults who died (those under the age of 20), but that when a man died they should have the best tunic or coat, and for a woman, the best tunic, hood or cloak; or else, in either case, 9 *sous* if the heirs preferred. The deacon should receive the dead person's shoes, or 16d. 'And thus always the choice of giving or paying should be for parishioners of the said church to decide: to give only the best garment, as is said, or to pay the said 9 *sous*, as it better pleases them. And they cannot be compelled to any other payment by the chaplain or his successors; and in the same manner regarding payment of the said shoes or said 16d as best pleases the said parishioners.' A further detail arose: what of those who died in the hospital at Pia? It was agreed that whoever died there—whether a 'brother' of the hospital, a warden, a *comeditor* (someone with dining rights?), a pilgrim, a rich man, or a poor man—the chaplain would have their best garment, and the deacon would again gain the shoes. And yet more: what if 'a cleric'—meaning someone in minor orders—died when still under the age of 20, and living with his parents? In that circumstance it was agreed that the chaplain did have rights over the clothing. Finally, the lengthy document was agreed, by the chaplain Lord Guillaume de Clairan; and 'Bernard Olivier and Bernard Ferret and Pierre Docesi and Michel Amarel, syndics or procurators of the men of Pia, in our own names and those of the people of the parish of the said

---

[23] F. Pasquier, ed., *Cartulaire de Mirepoix*, 2 vols (Toulouse: Privat, 1921), II, pp. 11–13.
[24] AD Aude 4^{E}206/GG221; edited in J. Guiraud, ed., *Le cartulaire de Notre Dame de Prouille*, 2 vols (Paris : Picard, 1907), II, pp. 173–74 (no. 428).

church, and the name of our heirs and successors, praise, approve and confirm all this', with a further thirty-one male names following thereafter.[25]

What is going on with this flow of clothing? There were always strong markets for second-hand clothing in the middle ages, so in large part we are simply here seeing another source of income for the priest, as the possibility of rendering a cash payment instead indicates.[26] Regarding the choice over cash or item: the consuls may here have been negotiating a purely economic reckoning—families being loathe to render up a good tunic that they thought worth more than 9 *sous*—but one cannot help but wonder if it was also an emotional choice about burial clothes. (We might recall, from Chapter 6, the shawl which the ghost of a dead daughter told Arnaud Gélis should have been buried with her.) In an agreement made in Lagrasse in 1327 between the consuls and the rector of the parish church, surviving as a rather damaged single parchment, the rector gave up his rights to the clothing of the dead, so long as the parishioners transported their tithes to him at their own expense; clearly the laity in that place preferred not to hand over the garments of the deceased.[27]

But it may not have been that the clothing rendered to the priest was always sold; it could sometimes have been repurposed. This was certainly the case with caps made for children when they were to be baptized (what is called in French *un chrémeau*), which would have been touched by holy oil: an agreement between the priory church of Rieudaure and the inhabitants of the village made in 1303 included the provision that 'the sacrist of the said church... will faithfully conserve all the caps of the children baptized there, and that the same caps be converted and made into supertunics, clothing, and other necessities for the aforesaid church'.[28] This is not stated in the various instances of burial clothing, but is clearly a possibility. Thus, as we have seen elsewhere in other cases of donation by charter and in wills, clothing that once belonged to a family member could become part of the material provision for the church, potentially storing up a complex bundle of personal memory and spiritual implications for the surviving relatives who worshipped there.

---

[25] AD P-O, G838: 'Et semper sit electio dandi et soluendi parrochianis dicte ecclesie, quod solum melius indumentorum, ut dictum, vel dictos ix sol. quod magis eis placuit; et ad alterum solum solvendum non possit compelli per capellanum vel succesores suos... Et nos predicti Bernardus Olivarii et Bernardus Ferreti et Petrus Docesii et Michaelis Amarelli sindici vel procuratores hominum de Apiano nomine proprio et ipsorum hominum parrochianorum dicte ecclesie et nomine heredum et successoribus nostrorum hec omnia predicta laudamus abprobamus et confirmamus.'
[26] See J. V. García Marsilla, 'Avec les vêtements des autres: le marché du textile d'occasion dans la Valence médiévale', in L. Feller and A. Rodríguez, eds, *Objets sous contraintes: circulation des richesses et valeur des choses au Moyen Âge* (Paris: Sorbonne, 2013), pp. 123–43.
[27] AD Aude, H114.
[28] AD Aude, H103: 'quo sacrista dicte ecclesie... fideliter conservare omnes capidas puerorum ibidem baptizandorum et quod ipse capide convertantur et mittantur in superpelliciis vestimentis et aliis necessariis ecclesie supradicte'. The archival notes provide 'Rieudaure' for *Rividano*, which I cannot now locate; just possibly in fact Rieunette, or Rieux-en-Val, both south-west of Carcassonne?

The agreement regarding baptismal caps at Rieudaure was in fact just an addendum to the main point of negotiation: who should pay for repairs and essential provisions for the parish church? The prior of the monastery held that the villagers were responsible for everything, including the provision of 'books, vestments, and other ornaments', as well as internal and external works; the people of the village thought the sacrist of the church was bound to contribute part of these expenses. An 'amicable agreement' was reached through arbitrators: the people were responsible for all such provisions, but the sacrist was to pay annually 30 *sous* of Barcelona toward the costs, and to supply oil at Advent for the parishioners, presumably for use in lighting the church.[29] Another agreement was made in 1330 at (possibly) Vaissac, about 15 km east of Montauban, between twenty-one male and one female parishioners and the priest, agreeing which tithes were customary, with the priest promising not to impose any new ones, the parishioners in turn promising to help repair a house attached to the church (supplying 'forty rafters' and paying the surprisingly large sum of 15 *livres* of Tours), and also to make some kind of ornament in honour of St Martin for the church, at a cost of 100 *sous*.[30]

In each of these cases, we see a local negotiation over resources and responsibilities, based on custom, as attested by various local lay witnesses. Several of the documents just cited are single parchments, the sort of writing that is least likely to survive across the centuries, particularly when originating from quite small towns and villages. It is thus quite possible that the ones I have located are just a small portion of what once existed.[31] Each example shows us the laity collectively bargaining with 'the Church', in its local manifestation, over issues which related primarily to material wealth, but always additionally to spiritual services and the management of worship within the local community. This is demonstrated most clearly by two final examples of the genre. One is a crumpled and somewhat illegible parchment from 1280, recording a detailed agreement between the rector

---

[29] AD Aude, H103: 'quod sacrista...donet inperpetuum...parrochianis...in adjutorium ipsarum operarum triginta sol. Barch....annuales et nichil aliud in aliquibus operibus ipsius ecclesie quos tenentur eis soluere, et tradere quolibet anno in festo natalis domini. Et quod ipse sacrista...donet et dare teneatur ipsis parrochianis oleum in adventum domini quolibet anno prout est antiquitus fieri consuetum.'

[30] AD T-et-G, G 801. A seventeenth-century copy of a now-lost original, with some confusions of transcription possibly arising. The ornament is written as 'unum bonum induzantum', and later 'induzentium' (fol. 5r); I cannot identify either in Latin or Occitan, though they are perhaps connected to vestments (*indusium*, for 'outer tunic' in Latin; my thanks to Pete Biller on this point). The scribe gives 'Cayssaco' for the place name, and a later archivist translating this to 'Cays', which cannot be located. There are various villages called Cayssac in regions to the north; however, there is a church of Saint-Martin in Vaissac.

[31] There are certainly some other likely examples, judging on the basis of archival inventory descriptions: for example, in 1296 an agreement made between priest and people in Confoux (35 km west of Aix), fixing the proportion of tithe on various goods, and another in 1303 between the people of Puyricard (10 km north-west of Aix) and the chapter of Aix (AD Bouches-du-Rhône, 2G56 and 2G66).

of the church of Saint-Étienne in Montescot (c. 7 km north-east of Moissac) and his parishioners, as represented by their 'syndics', all drawn up by a notary as a 'public instrument'. It asserts the priest's right to various tithes and oblations on particular feast days, including that women coming to church after childbirth must give the priest a loaf, some wine, and a candle. The document sets out, *inter alia*, some liturgical celebrations in which the parishioners were to participate, the particular concern being the provision and conservation of suitable candles for processions and the like. It also addressed issues such as how burials were to be conducted, the contracting of marriages, and how much a woman had to pay the priest if she married outside the parish (the last costing 5 *sous* apparently).[32]

The other is another single document on parchment, this time from the town of Cordes (c. 22 km north-west of Albi), dating to 1287. It covers more items than any other agreement, and essentially fixes what payments the parish priest is owed for a variety of spiritual services. It is framed as a dispute between the priest ('Lord Vivian') and the consuls of the town, though in fact the priest's claims appear to be straightforwardly upheld rather than contested. (Note that there is a distinction throughout between what he is owed personally, and what is owed to the parish church; the latter presumably to be dedicated to its maintenance and running.) It is worth citing at some length, given the detail it contains regarding the priest's duties:

> ...for each marriage [he is owed personally] 3 *sous* of Cahors, more or less moreover according to the status of their wealth and persons, namely 4, 5, or 6 *sous*. Item, he aims to prove that in the name of the said church he possesses the right to receive for each marriage 2 *sous* of Tours or 3 *sous* of Cahors, in which <coinage> is current today; and this is for marriages within the *castrum*. Item, he aims to prove that when a woman parishioner wishes to leave her parish in Cordes in order to contract marriage, the said rector receives 3 *sous* of Tours for giving the licence, or granting the letter to go to the other chaplain <in the new parish>, so that the marriage can be solemnized in his church; and this is in due possession in the name of the said church...Item...he receives for each dead body of someone over the age of 12, 3 *sous* less 2d of Tours, or at least 2 *sous* and 4d of Tours. Item...for each baptized child who dies, 12d of Tours. Item...he receives in oblations from each woman who has risen after childbirth when she hears her first mass, one candle or 1d and also one loaf or cake. Item...rectors who came before him used to receive in oblations, from the married couple on the day after the marriage was contracted, a candle and in addition a penny of Tours, and a loaf and a full pitcher of wine. Item...for each baptized child, a little torch or two matching candles, with a penny of Tours and the child's

[32] AD T-et-G, G636.

baptismal cap. Item...all the torches and purple clothes which are carried to the church on behalf of strangers who are not from the *castrum*, for the purpose of honouring the dead and those buried in the cemetery of the aforesaid church of Cordes; or if they are buried elsewhere, provided they can carry the torches and purple clothes into the church or the cemetery. Item...when the chaplains are invited to the marriage feast, all the chaplains and clergy of the church are to eat with the married couple and they should dine in the evening.[33]

To this, a chaplain called as an additional witness added that, regarding marriage dues, 'in this land [*that is, local region*] sometimes [it has been] 18d of Tours from poor people'; and that in addition to the burial dues mentioned above, 'they received 30d for trental masses sometimes and from some people, when they were making a will or bequeathing or wanting to do this, who pay this money; but those who refused or said no were not compelled to pay'.[34]

The detail here is rather precious. We have already met elsewhere the rights to burial clothing and baptismal caps, and it is not a surprise to see that it cost money to conduct a marriage ceremony. But it is very interesting to note the requirement for sending a letter of permission for a woman who married outside the parish (presumably the letter confirming that she was eligible to marry), the lack of such a letter meaning that the marriage could not be solemnized.[35] We see also the requirement for a 'loaf or cake' (or, in the case of

---

[33] AD Tarn, 69 Edt FF32: '...quod ipse...est in possession percipiendi de nupciis singulis iii sol. Caturcensis ad minus et plus, etiam secundum statum diviciarum et personarum scilicet IIIIor, quinque et sex solidos. Item intendit probare quod ipse est in possessione nomine dicte ecclesie sue percipiendi de nupciis singulis ii sol. tur' vel iii sol. carc' qui hodie currunt, et hoc de nubentibus in castro. Item intendit probare quod quando mulier parochiana sua exit parochiam suam de Cordua causa contrahendi matrimonium, pro danda licensia seu pro litteris concedendis alteri capellano ut matrimonium possit sollempnizari in ecclesia sua, percipit dictus rector, et de hoc et in possessione percipiendi nomine dicte ecclesie sue, iii sol. Tur'. Item intendit probare quod est in possessione percipiendi pro corpore mortuo quod excesserit xii annos iii sol. minus duobus denariis Tur' vel ii sol. et iiii denarios Tur's ad minus. Item intendit probare quod est in possessione percipiendi de super Turon' puero baptizato et mortuo xii d. tur'. Item intendit probare quod est in posesione percipiendi de qualibet muliere que surrexerit de partu dum audit primam missam pro oblatione unam candelam vel uno denario et cum uno pane vel uno placenta. Item intendit probare quod rectores qui pro tempore fuerunt ante ipsum percipiebant in crastinum matrimonii contracti a nubentibus pro oblatione unam candelam cum denario desuper et unum panem et unum pecherium plenum vino. Item intendit probare quod est in possessione percipiendi pro quolibet puero baptizato unum torticium parvum vel duas candelas duplicatas cum uno denario de super Turon' cum capulla sua. Item intendit probare quod est in possessione percipiendi torticia et purpuras que aportantur ad ecclesiam pro homines extraneos qui non sunt de castro causa honoras faciende defunctis et sepultis in cimiterio ecclesie predicte de Cordua vel si alibi essent sepulti dummodo in ecclesia vel cimiterio torticia vel purpuras apportarent. Item intendit probare quod quando invitantur capellani ad comestionem pro nupciis comedunt cum nubentibus omnes capellani et clerici ecclesie, et in cero [*recte* sero] cenant'.

[34] AD Tarn, 69 Edt FF32: 'in terra ista aliquociens a pauperibus xviii d. tur'...Item quod aliquociens et aliquibusdam percipiebant triginta d. pro trentariis quando legabantur seu reliquebantur seu volebant hoc soluere set resistentes seu contradicentes non compellebantur.'

[35] This practice is also attested in a marginal comment to the missel from Moussoulens, discussed further below: AD Aude, 1 Mi 30, fol. 31v: 'Si sponsus et sponsa sunt de diversis parrochiis illo qui pro sollempnizando matrimonio ad aliam transit ecclesiam litteras vel [*illeg.*] sui exhibeat sacerdotis; alia

Montescot, bread, wine, and a candle) from a woman who was attending mass after childbirth, the loaf and wine from the happy couple the day after a wedding, and the emphasis placed on the priest and other clergy eating with the married couple. Between these various different points one glimpses something of the complexity of the priest's position in the community, and thus the range of perspectives that the laity might have in return. The priest has a certain power and authority, able to grant permission for marriage, and he levies tithes and requires various other cash payments for his services. But he also asks for perishable goods—loaf, cake, wine—which would thus appear more akin to gifts (indeed 'oblations', even if canonically these cannot be demanded), and he and his colleagues wish to have it recognized that their status requires the married couple to break bread with them.

It is important to note that whilst the opening to both documents—Montescot and Cordes—present the matters as a dispute, in both cases what we are seeing is a negotiated agreement. In fact, in the latter case in particular, the priest's requirements are simply listed and appear to be upheld without counter-claim by the laity, since the consuls of the town sign up to them as witnesses at the end of the document. It thus seems likely that producing the arbitrated agreement was in the service of the parishioners as much as the priest, fixing the customary amounts in a clear fashion. There is a very clear bit of evidence for precisely this sort of process, some years later in nearby Montauban. In 1410, a huge inquiry was launched into the respective rights of the canons of Saint-Étienne-de-Tescou and the rector of the town church of Saint-Jacques, over that church (the main church of the city, built in the thirteenth century by the laity, possibly, as Jörg Feuchter argues, to appease the inquisitor Pierre Cellan, as we saw in Chapter 6). Across 332 paper folios a number of claims are presented as separate numbered 'articles', and then witness statements taken from both sides, the witnesses including both clergy and older members of the laity, their memories stretching back into the period before the Black Death. One 'article' is the claim that in the time of the chaplain Guillaume de Blé, a 'public instrument' was made to agree the levying of tithes with the consuls and community of the town—that is, precisely the kind of notarial document we have met further above.[36] One witness, a fairly wealthy shoemaker called Pierre de *Tulio*, over 65 years old, remembered that many years earlier, he had got into a dispute with a previous rector of the church regarding tithes. He went to the 'house of the commune of Montauban' and asked those who were consuls of the town of Montauban that year whether they could show

---

qui ad sollempnizandum matrimonium nullatenus admittuntur' (this written next to the marriage service in the original missal). The practice had been complained about by the citizens of Toulouse earlier in the thirteenth century: *Layettes*, II, pp. 306–09.

[36] AD Tarn-et-Garonne, G1161, fols I.15v–16r. The foliation is not continuous, but rather starts afresh on folios 111 and 277, creating three separate parts to the manuscript. I have thus given references as a folio number preceded by I, II, or III.

to him 'in the books of the said house, how the said rector should behave and govern when levying and exacting the said tithe'. They duly did so, 'in a certain parchment book commonly called the *Liber Albus*, and in which book the same witness read and saw that there was a controversy or apportionment which was due to the rector of Saint-Jacques of Montauban for tithes, from the inhabitants of Montauban, just as was contained in the said book'.[37]

Such agreements could be recorded—effectively 'archived' in a local sense—in other textual contexts. Within an eleventh-century missal, a fourteenth-century hand—most likely the priest of Moussoulens (14 km north-west of Carcassonne)—wrote the following additions, just after the office of the mass:

> It is the custom in the parish of Moussoulens that for each male child baptized the godfather should offer 2d and a candle worth 2d, and it should have a cap. For a baptized woman [*that is, female child*], 1d and a candle worth 2d should be offered, and it should have a cap. If in truth they receive a cap and candle from the chaplain, they must give 2d for the candle and 3d for the cap, in addition to the aforesaid oblations. All the caps, moreover, are the rector's. A woman getting up after childbirth, moreover, must offer a candle worth 2d and bread and wine, namely 2d for bread and wine. For weddings there should be the payment of 3 *sous* of Tours... moreover each spouse must offer a candle worth 2d, and bread and wine, that is 2d for bread and wine. Moreover, on the morning of the wedding it is custom for the bride to come to mass and to offer [*illeg.*] and a candle worth 2d. Moreover the married couple should pay the priest a hen.[38]

We are now familiar with this sort of list, from the preceding documents; but as we can see, each varies in the precise details. These are truly the customs of *this* parish; just as the second priest, in the document from Cordes above, noted a detail 'in *this* land'. Two things are simultaneously apparent: the Church as an

---

[37] AD Tarn-et-Garonne, G1161, fol. III.12r-v: 'quod sibi ostenderent in libris dicte domus [illeg] quomodo haberet se rector et gubernare in levando et exhigendo dictam primitiam'; '...quendam librum in pergameno scriptum qui vulgariter vocabatur "Liber albus". In quoquid libro idem testis loquens legat et vidit controv[ersiam] quodam seu [?]portionem quam debet habere rector Sancti Jacobi Montisalbani pro primitia ab habitatoribus Montisalbani prout in dicto libro continetur.'

[38] AD Aude, 1 Mi 30, fol. 5v: 'Consuetum est in parrochia de Mossolinchis quod pro puero masculo baptizato debet offerre patrinus II d et candelam II d, et debet habere capidam. Pro muliere autem baptizata debet offerre unum denarium et candelam II d. et debet habere capidam. Si vero recipient capidam et candelam a capellano, debet dare pro candela II d et pro capida III d ultra oblationem predictam. Omnes autem capide sunt rectoris. Mulier autem surgens de partu debet offerre candelam valentem duos denarios et panem et vinum videlicet duos denarios pro pane et vino. De nupciis debent solutio tres solidos t[uronenses]...etiam sponsus et sponsa offerre quamlibet candelam ij d. Et panis et vinum ut duos denarios pane et vino. Etiam in crastinum nupciarum sponsa consuevit venire ad missam et offerre [*illeg.*] et unum candelam valentem ij d. Etiam nuptos soluere presbitero unam gallinam.' Microfilm reproduction of a manuscript held in the seminary in Carcassonne. The additions are probably those of Bernard Amouroux, rector of the church, c. 1330; cf. V. Chomel, 'Droit de patronage et pratique religieuse dans l'archevêché de Narbonne au début du XV siècle', *Bibliothèque de l'Ecole des Chartes* 115 (1957), 58–137, p. 101 n. 3.

overarching structure, dispensing not only sacraments but other particular spiritual services and rituals; and local communities of the laity negotiating the precise costs and details with the local clergy. Beyond the issue of tithes, such negotiations were uncanonical, as priests were not supposed to demand specific oblations for their ministration; and indeed in 1255 Alexander IV had written to the archbishop of Narbonne, forbidding priests from demanding payment for burials, marriage blessings, or other sacraments.[39] Nonetheless, they occurred. The notarial culture of the region, happy to produce an ad hoc document of agreement between different parties (sometimes, though not always, facilitated by an agreed arbitrator), thus creates what is essentially a locally negotiated contract between priest and people.

These specific agreements were not the only kind of 'negotiation' one can find, when looking at how lay priorities might sometimes re-fashion ecclesiastical priorities. We saw, in Chapter 4, how the liturgical cycle of feast days entwined with the growing mercantile activities of towns, with various major markets attached to particular saints' days. Worship and business were there conjoined in a notably civic fashion. In partial contrast, in Chapter 5 we met the Church's attempts to eradicate 'usury', as a growing feature of an economically active lay society; though in practice this also often resulted in some kind of compromise. Here, I want to explore a few other similar areas where the practical needs of life, particularly civic and mercantile activity, butted up against the spiritual aspirations of Christianity, sometimes happily, sometimes rather less so. Unsurprisingly, one again tends to find degrees of negotiation and compromise.

Coming from the same 'crusading' impulse as the war against usury, a major area of potential tension was the fact that Mediterranean trade involved Christians with Jews and Muslims. Scholarship has tended to focus particularly on the Italian port cities, given their predominance; but of course Marseille, Narbonne, Perpignan, and other southern French settlements were also deeply involved as well. From the later twelfth century onward, the papacy had sought to excommunicate any Christian merchant who supplied 'the Saracens' with material that might aid them in their fighting: weapons, iron, shipbuilding timber were all embargoed, and Christian sailors who lent their sailing expertise to Muslim leaders were also excommunicated. At various points, and particularly after the fall of Acre in 1291, these specific prohibitions expanded into a wider attempt to prevent financial or other material support reaching Muslim kingdoms in the Middle East.[40] But of course such commerce did nonetheless exist.[41] By the fourteenth

[39] Blanc, ed., *Livre de comptes de Jacme Olivier*, I, pp. 349–50 (no. 11), letter of Alexander IV, 7 Oct 1255, written in response to petition by the consuls of Narbonne.
[40] S. Menache, 'Papal Attempts at a Commercial Boycott of the Muslims in the Crusade Period', *Journal of Ecclesiastical History* 63 (2012), 236–59; S. K. Stantchev, *Spiritual Rationality: Papal Embargo as Cultural Practice* (Oxford: Oxford University Press, 2014).
[41] For an example of a contract between 'Alfaquim, Saracen of Alexandria' and a Christian merchant in 1227, see Blanchard, *Documents... commerce de Marseille*, I, pp. 18–19 (no. 14).

century, a number of merchants from southern France and elsewhere were gaining short-term 'licences' from the papacy to allow them to trade goods with the Levant.[42]

Less fraught, but undoubtedly more constant, were potential tensions over the general Christian injunction to refrain from labour on Sundays, something which we have met in this region as early as the Peace of God councils of the eleventh century, and in de Montfort's 1212 statutes which attempted to ban any markets held on Sundays.[43] Before the crusade, Sunday markets clearly existed, in quite small places as well as larger cities: an agreement from 1153 between Raimond Trencavel and some local lords shows the latter gaining or retaining the right to a Sunday market in the castle of Cabaret near Lastours.[44] But the continued reiteration of such prohibition tends to suggest that some Sunday trading activities did in fact continue, and the details in some prohibitions indicate an element of compromise and negotiation. In 1249, the archbishop of Narbonne, with the apparent agreement of the consuls, ordered that on Sundays and various major feast days (more than fifteen named, all relating to the life of Christ), nobody should presume to transport goods, using beasts or otherwise; 'unless they are for eating or for clothing' (*sinon eran cauzas manjadoyras o trocelhs*).[45] The spirit of this may mean that the permitted activities related only to the needs of that specific day. This is spelled out more clearly in the council of Narbonne a decade or so later, convened by Gui Foulques, which ordered that priests for three successive Sundays should warn their parishioners that on Sundays and feast days they should abstain from servile work, not transporting wood, grain or wheat, or other venial things, except those which pertain to the day. It was further forbidden to hold markets on Sundays.[46]

These prohibitions are not a dead letter: they are picked up in various statutes issued by trade guilds, which independently bound themselves to this kind of pious obedience. In 1306 the bakers in Narbonne repeated the list of feast days in some detail, saying that they would not allow their ovens to be used to cook bread, meat, or fish for anyone on those days 'no matter what their status'.[47] Statutes for the guild of millers in the same city from 1331 similarly promise collectively to refrain from all activity on a lengthy list of holy days.[48] In Toulouse, in statutes collated in the late thirteenth to early fourteenth century, the guild of

---

[42] M. Carr, 'Crossing Boundaries in the Mediterranean: Papal Trade Licenses from the *Registra supplicationum* of Pope Clement VI (1342-52)', *Journal of Medieval History* 41 (2015), 107-29. Carr (p. 114) notes that some papal licences, notably under John XXII, precede the establishment of this register. Stantchev, *Spiritual Rationality*, p. 56 points out that Innocent III issued a licence to Venice for such trade in 1198, and gives a few other specific examples, relating to cities rather than individuals.

[43] See Chapters 2 and 5.   [44] Mahul, *Cartulaire...Carcassonne*, III, p. 30.

[45] G. Mouynès, ed., *Narbonne: inventaire des archives communales antérieures à 1790: série AA, Annexes* (Narbonne: E. Caillard, 1871), pp. 47-48 (no. 33).

[46] Council of Narbonne, 1259/61, cc. 4, 5 (Avril, *Statuts synodaux*, VI, pp. 394-95).

[47] Blanc, *Livres de comptes de Jacme Olivier*, pp. 548-54 (no. 55).

[48] Mouynès, *Narbonne*, pp. 260-63 (no. 150), at 261.

pelterers promised not to work on Sundays, nor the four feasts of the Blessed Mary, or the feasts of the apostles, St Romain, 'nor on other feast days in which the clergy and people are led to celebrate', nor Christmas, Easter, and Pentecost; and if anyone within the guild contravened, they were to render 3 lbs of oil to the lights of the church of Saint-Romain. The wine-sellers followed a similar practice, albeit with fewer specified days. The guild of *frenerii* ('rein-' or 'bridle-makers' perhaps?) followed suit, specifying that the oil went to 'the lamp of the said *frenerii* which is in the church of St Étienne'—which does however slightly raise the possibility of accepted fines becoming a form of pious donation.[49]

But other documents give a strong sense that the apparent strictness of the prohibition against Sunday working was often leavened. The synodal for the diocese of Carcassonne from 1297 enjoined refraining from labour on Sundays, banning barbers, scribes, and cloth merchants from their trade. But they also noted that one could receive a testament from a dying person, and that 'for human necessity' bakers were not forbidden from selling bread or butchers from selling meat or other mercers from selling foodstuffs on feast days, only that they should not do this whilst mass was being celebrated in their parish churches.[50] The synod of Montauban, 1337, decried the fact that many were *not* observing the prohibition against Sunday working, were failing to come to church to hear mass, were carrying around grain and other goods, 'and moreover on the said Sundays were making markets, buying and selling indiscriminately' as if feast days 'hardly existed', in 'contempt of divine precept and canonical sanctions'. Thus any who continued to do this were excommunicated. A very hard line, it would appear. But the canons following immediately after rather soften the blow: in certain places in the diocese that were 'not very populated', where it was customary for local people and visitors to congregate together on Sundays, they could continue to do so, as long as they still attended mass. Moreover various foodstuffs, such as bread, wine, and meat, could be sold on Sundays. It was also permitted to lead around people, horses, and carts, and to provide anything that was needed for those who were ill. If a funeral happened on a Sunday, it was fine to buy or sell those things necessary for the burial; and similarly, for a baptism, whatever was needed.[51]

The sense of '…except when things are needed' is found in some of the other guild statutes from Toulouse (and it should also be noted that not all the guilds included any prohibition against Sunday work in their statutes). An earlier set of statutes for the wine-sellers forbids trade on Sundays, feast days, and between the

---

[49] M. A. Mulholland, *Early Gild Records of Toulouse* (New York: Columbia University Press, 1941), pp. 26–27, 31–32, 42–43. For a more recent study of the craft aspects of these records, see F. Garnier, '*Statuere et in melius reformare*: écrire la norme pour les métiers à Toulouse (milieu XIIIe siècle-milieu XIVe siècle)', in D. Lett, ed., *La confection des statuts dans les sociétés méditerranéennes de l'Occident (XIIe-XVe siècle)* (Paris: Éditions de la Sorbonne, 2019), pp. 131–52.

[50] Synodal of Carcassonne, 1297, c. 4 (Avril, *Statuts synodaux*, VI, p. 458).

[51] Synod of Montauban, 1337, cc. 1–7 (E. Martene, *Veterum Scriptorum et Monumentorum*, 9 vols (Paris, 1724–33), VIII, cols 1559–63, at 1561–62).

Nativity of Mary (8 September) and the feast of All Saints (1 November)—'except for great necessity or other just and honest cause'. The guild of Cutlers swore to abstain from work on Christmas, Circumcision, Epiphany, Easter, Ascension, Pentecost, All Saints, and on all Sundays and other major feast days, except however for any tasks which might arise related to the feasts themselves. (Transgression in this case was punished by the very light fine of 2d, going to wax for the light they kept in the church of Sainte-Marie-de-la-Dalbade). A second set of statutes for the Pelterers reaffirms not selling on Sundays and so forth, 'unless however a market day should fall thus, in which case it can be done'.[52] A similar exemption is noted in civic statutes from Moissac, agreed with the local abbey (who had lordship there), in 1321: people of the town would not sell any goods on Sundays after midday mass, unless it was a market fair day.[53]

For later periods, in various parts of Europe it can be possible to use diocesan visitation records to gain a rough impression of how often people were absent from church on Sundays, with the demands of trade sometimes cited as the reason.[54] We do not have that kind of evidence for southern France in these centuries. But there are some hints from other documentation, for a few individuals at least. One man questioned by Jacques Fournier in the early fourteenth century, Arnaud de Savignac, tried to excuse his idiosyncratic theological ideas on the grounds that his job as a stonemason kept him very busy, such that he often missed the sermon on Sundays.[55] That he thought this a viable excuse at all suggests that the phenomenon was not unknown elsewhere. Some of the many various surviving notarial registers from southern France can also hint at actual practice. The register of Géraud Boffati, notary of Saint-Sulpice-la-Point, a town on the Tarn about halfway between Toulouse and Albi, gives what appears to be an absolutely complete picture of his work activities between February 1344 and March 1346, listing in rough every bit of business he conducted in that period. He was a busy man, producing documents for people on most days, sometimes three separate items a day. Much of the time he worked on every day except for Sunday. But there were ten exceptions, when for one reason or another he failed to follow this rule, and broke the sabbath.[56] He also worked on various other days that one might have thought sacrosanct: Good Friday and Christmas Eve, for example.[57]

---

[52] Mulholland, *Early Gild Records*, pp. 16, 24–25, 46–47.
[53] AD Aude, G 551 (cartulary of the abbey of Moissac), fols 71r–77r.
[54] See Arnold, 'Materiality of Unbelief'; D. Wood, 'Discipline and Diversity in the Medieval English Sunday', in K. Cooper and J. Gregory, eds, *Discipline and Diversity*, Studies in Church History 43 (Woodbridge: Ecclesiastical History Society, 2007), pp. 202–11.
[55] See Arnold, *Inquisition and Power*, p. 170.
[56] AD Tarn 3 E 55-253, fols 3v, 6v, 14v, 18v, 24v, 26r, 33r-v, 38r, 51v, 67v. I have followed C. R. Cheney and M. Jones, *A Handbook of Dates for Students of British History*, 2nd edn (Cambridge: Cambridge University Press, 2000) in identifying the days of the week, having first translated Boffati's dating (which takes 25 March as marking the change of year) into standard historical dating.
[57] AD Tarn 3 E 55-253, fols 34r, 65v.

On a couple of the occasions of Sunday working Boffati was engaged in taking down somebody's will, perhaps made *in extremis*, thus a forgivable reason for breaking the sabbath; though one of the wills had a codicil added to it some days later, suggesting that it had not perhaps been made quite at the point of death. But for most of the Sundays on which he worked he was engaged in other kinds of business, drawing up documents to do with debts, sales, and the like. On the unusually busy Sunday of 18 April 1344 he made rough notes for six different sets of business, each involving a number of people, reminding us that it was not only the notary who was failing to observe the sabbath.

It seems unlikely that Géraud Boffati was a particularly irreligious man; he did, after all, mostly keep the sabbath. But that 'mostly' is interesting and important, and one suspects would be replicated not only among other notaries but among a large part of the wider lay population. As we would find elsewhere in later medieval Europe, the Church laid down a framework for a good Christian life and suitable pious behaviour, and sought frequently to remind the laity of these strictures. Lay people listened and obeyed—some of the time, but not always.

Confraternities and Collective Enthusiasm

Medieval Christianity, in Languedoc as elsewhere, was experienced by most people most frequently as part of a group, and was often conceived and discussed in collective terms. *Ecclesia* was used not only to designate the stone building within which worship took place or the collective hierarchical institution of 'the Church', but also to mean 'church' in the sense of the 'gathered faithful'. *Caritas*—'charity', but perhaps more accurately translated as something like 'love for one's fellow Christians'—was a fundamental principle of Christian life, a requirement not simply to give alms to the poor, but not to be in conflict with one's community. Christians came to their local church to worship as a group, a congregation; as we have seen, at a certain point, perhaps as early as the mid-twelfth century though possibly not until a few decades later, they would very likely have thought of themselves as members of a 'parish', as a *parrochianus* or *parrochiana*, connected to a local collective identity.

Of course, as noted at various points in earlier chapters, the collective experience of Christian worship was not seamless. Many of the local churches built in or before the eleventh century were almost certainly too small for the whole flock to gather within; it is likely that their specific experience of worship was syncopated at best, and perhaps always much more partial in reality. Even by the mid-fourteenth century, some churches were noted as being too small to fit their community. Whilst an emphasis upon the 'collective' experience is undoubtedly correct, it should not be taken to mean 'uniform'. There are exceptions and nuances that one must note, such as very personal pious bequests (as noted in

Chapter 3 and explored further below), the individuating discourse of confession and penance (as explored in Chapter 8), and the variations that status and wealth had upon one's place within the community. In this section I want to focus on spiritual engagement and lay enthusiasm, as framed and at least partly experienced as collective action, in the form of confraternities. It is in the pious confraternity that the notion of *caritas* takes institutional form; though as we will see, the 'communal' in fact then involves hierarchy and elements of exclusion, as well as inclusion and care for others. *Caritas* in its lived reality had contours and limits, and was another aspect of negotiated faith.

For southern France before the later fourteenth century, the evidence for religious confraternities is relatively sparse, perhaps surprisingly so, and thus poses a particular question, for reasons we shall see below, of whether we glimpse the tip of an iceberg, or whether formalized confraternal arrangements were in fact comparatively rare prior to the Black Death.[58] There are substantial records extant for two confraternities, each dedicated to the Virgin Mary; these are examined in detail further below. Most else of what survives tends to comprise brief statutes, or passing references in wills and other documents, sometimes elusive in their implications; or, as we will see, attempts to *forbid* the laity from forming sworn mutual associations, even for the purposes of charity and worship. Whilst much of what one can say about confraternities is much the same as for other regions of western Europe, this last point may have a particularly southern French inflection, where lay enthusiasm runs up against ecclesial concern and control.[59]

A potential precursor to the confraternity was the practice, found among some of those laity sufficiently rich and connected to make it happen, of becoming a *confrater*—co-brother—to a monastic foundation. This usually meant becoming *confrater* to a long-standing Benedictine house, with no obligation to take a monastic vow or join the order, but hoping to guarantee through such confraternity that the monks would provide burial and prayers for one's soul; not essentially different from other donors who are recorded in monastic obit lists, but presumably raised in visibility within the foundation by the particular claim to status. There are in fact a few rare examples for other orders also: in 1150 Arnaud de Gaure made himself a *confrater* of the Templars at Douzens, providing them with his *honor* in the village of Gaure (with the exception of the local church, which Arnaud explained that he held from another man, and could thus not include in his gift). About a decade later, the Templars at La Selve received an

---

[58] They certainly existed in northern Italy in the twelfth century in some abundance: see N. Şenocak, 'Twelfth-Century Italian Confraternities as Institutions of Pastoral Care', *Journal of Medieval History* 42 (2016), 202–25; Thompson, *Cities of God*, pp. 69–103 and *passim*, though focused specifically on penitential confraternities. It is clear that many exist in southern France by the later fourteenth and fifteenth centuries: C. Vincent, *Les confréries médiévales dans le royaume de France, XIIIe–Ve siècle* (Paris: Albin Michel, 1994), p. 41.

[59] Cf. Vincent, *Les confréries*, p. 111.

annual gift of 3d and a certain amount of flour 'in confraternity' from Imbert Rigal (who also gave them a quarter share in some named local woods, for a generous counter-gift of 50 *sous* that perhaps looks more clearly like a payment).[60] Practices such as these provided the language of confraternity, and perhaps some aspects of its core dynamics: the desire, for a layperson who was planning to remain a layperson, to be connected to a group that would continue and persist in its collective strength, able therefore to provide some guarantee of a decent burial and remembrance after death. This we have of course seen more generally in donations to monasteries, in Chapter 1.

In the earliest examples of collectivities which we might see as being non-monastic 'confraternities'—though often in fact still involving the local bishop or abbot—the fundamental concern with burial and memorial masses is still marked. The first of these dates to around 1130: a 'charter of confraternity' agreed by Bremond, bishop of Béziers, and the canons of the cathedral church. They would make a funeral procession and mass for any who died among their number, the bishop carrying a wax candle of a pound in weight, each canon carrying a half-pound candle similarly. 'If moreover any other clergy or laity wish to participate in this fraternity, with a candle and whatever offering pleases them, they can have themselves written into this charter, and the aforesaid canons will receive the same offering with their candles'. The names of six priests, and eight apparent laymen, follow.[61] The statutes for the confraternity of the Blessed Virgin Mary of Cros, formed by the people of Caunes most likely around 1190, required that when someone within the confraternity had died, one man was to walk through the town ringing a bell (*squilla*), announcing 'O lords, *confratres* and *confratrissae* of the venerable house of the Blessed Mary of Cros, prepare yourselves to honour such-and-such a man or woman who has left this most brief life for eternity'. ('Venerable house'—it is not made entirely clear, but it seems that the confraternity was focused on a kind of hospital; though it is certain that the confraternity members themselves were drawn more generally from the town, and as another statute makes explicit, were the kind of people who might go away on mercantile business from time to time). The death having been announced, the confraternity members were to say prayers—twelve *Pater nosters* and seven *Ave Marias*—'and all the *fratres* who are in the town, of whatever sex or estate, shall come to do honour at the burial', each giving alms of one penny and one candle. Moreover, having gathered collectively to celebrate a great mass on the feast of the Blessed Mary in August, the next day the confraternity members were enjoined to gather again, first at the confraternity house, to 'name and recount all those who have died in the confraternity that year, with friends of the dead, and all together should go to church...and there have celebrated a solemn mass for the dead,

---

[60] *Cart. Templiers de Douzens*, pp. 155–56 (A173); *Cart. de la Selve*, p. 225 (no. 149), c. 1160.
[61] *Cart. Béziers*, pp. 186–87 (no. 136).

for the salvation of the souls of all the dead and their relatives and friends, and the aforesaid confraternity and all the faithful dead.'[62] In 1212, the citizens of Marseille formed a confraternity 'to the honour of the holy and individual Trinity, Father, Son and Holy Spirit, and to the most blessed Virgin Mary, and all the saints, and to the holy Roman Church'. Their statutes promise that if any of the confraternity should die in poverty, the alms of the confraternity would pay for all necessary honours. Moreover they ordained that each year, on a specified day, divine office would be celebrated by all the priests in the city for all those, both living and dead, in the confraternity, and for all the faithful dead; and the poor in the hospital of the Holy Spirit, both healthy and ill, would be fed that day from the alms of the confraternity.[63] As we will see below, these sorts of provisions continued in later confraternities.

Ensuring an 'honourable' burial and some element of memorial is in continuity with the pious donations made to monasteries by certain lords, as discussed in Chapter 1; the difference is the mechanism by which this is to be achieved—a sworn lay collective rather than a religious foundation—and, perhaps, the social scale that it embraced. Both the Caunes and the Marseille confraternities seem to indicate some range of social scale within their association: 'of whatever sex or estate', as I quoted above from the statutes of the former, whilst the Marseille statutes include provision for addressing internal dissension between 'the lesser or greater *confratres*', and, as just noted, protection for those who had fallen into poverty. At the same time, both associations operated under high authority: the Marseille confraternity included the bishop and canons of Marseille (the bishop at that time being the lord of the *cité*), and the statutes survive in a notice of approval issued by the archbishop of Narbonne. The Caunes example is not quite so elite, but was also approved by the local abbot and the local lord and lady.

In addition to these civic examples, there are a few tantalizing fragments of evidence that suggest smaller, and possibly more rural, confraternities in the twelfth century. A confraternity of Saint-Saveur and the Holy Cross—apparently dedicated to the altar of St Saveur within the church of Saint-Sernin in Toulouse—appears in a charter from the 1170s, bestowing a piece of land upon a couple and their offspring, to make a vineyard there, and to render one-quarter of the produce annually to the confraternity. The land itself had been donated to the confraternity by one Arnaud Garonz 'for redemption of his sins'.[64] Whilst the confraternity's worship was directed toward the abbey church in Toulouse, its named members

---

[62] Doat 58, fol. 294 (ed. Mahul, *Cart. Carcassonne*, IV, pp. 162–64, cc. VII, XIII). The preamble mentions Pope Clement, which if assumed to be Clement III, dates the statutes to 1187 × 91. A later date under Clement IV or V seems unlikely because the statutes go to the trouble of specifying the nature and initial wording of the *Ave Maria* prayer.

[63] Martene and Durand, *Thesaurus novus anecdotorum*, IV, cols 165–68, at 167–68.

[64] *Cart Saint-Sernin*, p. 296 (no. 413), undated but one witness—W. Gras—appears in another charter from the 1170s and nowhere else in the cartulary.

were all laymen, and its area of operation was rural (the land being 'at Mont Vincent'). A possibly similar confraternity was founded in support of the monastery of Saint-Martin-du-Canigou, in the foothills of the Pyrenees, in 1195, directed toward supporting the lighting of the altar and as a burial confraternity.[65]

Even more fleeting, yet intriguing, are occasional mentions, in a survey of dues owed by the rural holdings of the cathedral church of Apt, of land 'of the charity' (*de la caritat*). These pop up in two different locales, as something for which particular people owe an annual payment: 'Rai[mond] Durant [pays] 2 *sous* for his house, and 6d for the land of the charity', 'Jean de Saint-Christoph [pays] for his house and the land of the charity, 9d', 'Sansa, sister of [Ricard Asalman] and wife of P[ierre] Grimaud, for the land of the charity, 12d.'[66] This is slender evidence, but suggests the presence of some collective entity holding land in the area, directing some of its income toward the cathedral, as with the Saint-Saveur example. There is another similar example from a will made by a woman called Belisinde in 1225, who left, among other small pious bequests, a measure of wheat to the 'charity of Pouzolles' (*karitati de Podolis*).[67] Much clearer (in one sense at least) is a short charter from 1206, surviving for no very clear reason in the cartulary of Lézat, in which Pierre de Saint-Béat and three other men establish that whosoever should come to the confraternity of the church of Saint-Béat, they would receive four days sanctuary (with the exception of murderers and those who had wounded their own lord).[68] This was a very small rural church in the high Pyrenees, about 100 km west of Foix; the purpose of the rather curious 'four days' might have been to assist pilgrims—'sanctuary' as a place to rest, rather than as legal protection as such—but the key thing here is the undoubted existence of something announcing itself as a confraternity in a very small, very rural location. As historians have found for later periods elsewhere, it is possible that the framework of a 'confraternity', meaning here perhaps no more than a sworn association capable of collective ownership, existed in many places as the means by which almsgiving to the local church could be channelled effectively.

Prompting the giving of alms was also a fundamental element for the larger confraternities. The Marseille association required all members to give a coin (*obolus*) every Sunday to the confraternity. The Caunes confraternity of the Blessed Virgin Mary of Cros only required members to give 2d each year on the feast of the Virgin in August, the money going toward making a candle for the altar, with 'what is left over... given to the poor and infirm of the confraternity, and to the

---

[65] L. Blancard, 'Role de la confrérie de Saint-Martin-du-Canigou', *Bibliothèque de l'École des Chartes* 42 (1881), 5–7. My thanks to Paul Fouracre for pointing me to this example; see his discussion in Fouracre, *Eternal Light and Earthly Concerns*, pp. 143–45.

[66] BnF, MS NAL 1211, fols 4v(b), 5r(a), 16r(a). MS described as '12th or 13th century', but mention of land owned by the Brothers Minor—fol. 13v(a)—means definitely the latter; though the hand would suggest not very far into that century.

[67] *Cart. S. Etienne d'Agde*, pp. 393–94 (no. 358).   [68] *Cart. Lézat*, I, p. 329 (no. 429).

indigent and other poor people lying in the said house'. The confraternity expected to have other income however, from other almsgiving including legacies in wills, and it required financial officers to make report of receipts and expenses annually, suggesting that it perhaps also held land which generated income.[69] In addition to funeral provision, the alms would help support confraternity members in times of crisis, as the Marseille statutes set out: 'If a *confrater* should fall into poverty, or sustain injury, the *confratres* who have been elected [to this task] shall give him support'. The Caunes confraternity had a similar clause.

Through giving relief in the event of injury or sudden poverty, and protecting against having a pauper's funeral, confraternities could be seen as associations for the protection of status. Their ability to facilitate collective patronage, even on occasion an element of lordship (as with the land bestowed on the couple by the confraternity of Saint-Saveur and Saint-Croix), could further be seen as a way of raising the collective status of their members. As noted above, that they facilitated something—the guarantee of an honourable funeral—previously engineered between nobles and monasteries does lend something to this line of argument. The confraternity allows more lowly people access to some of the same mechanisms previously open to the elites, through pooling resources and authority. However, that precise point also suggests that we should not think of social status and Christian piety as two clearly separate spheres. A funeral with all honours, and remembrance and prayers thereafter, were a way of signalling social rank but were also for the good of one's soul. They were facilitated by the higher social status that permitted one to bestow, rather than receive, alms; but the activities undertaken were from a shared script of Christian piety.

The entwining of Christian identity and social position permeates the Caunes confraternity statutes in particular. The confraternity was to elect twelve trustworthy men (*probi viri*) each year, who governed it. They could admit men or women to the confraternity from within or beyond the town, but those admitted must be 'of honest life and conduct…men or women who are not *foveratores, foveratrices* [*from* fodio, stirrers-up, goaders of others?], nor fornicators or breakers of contracts…'. Officials of the confraternity were to let the twelve governors know if any *confratres* or *confratrissiae* were living shamefully or carrying rancour or ill-will for another person; any thus identified were to be warned three times to correct themselves 'in the name of the holy and individual Trinity', and if they did not abstain from turpitude and vice 'immediately the names of those erring will be removed from the book of the aforesaid confraternity'.[70] There is a strong concern with good conduct and collective honour here, intimately bound up with Christian precepts—the concept of *caritas* surely underlies the concern with anyone carrying 'rancor or ill-will' for another—and nascent mercantile,

---

[69] Doat 58, fol. 294 (Mahul, *Cart. Carcassonne*, IV, p. 163, cc. IX, X, XII).
[70] Doat 58, fol. 294 (Mahul, *Cart. Carcassonne*, IV, p. 162, cc. II, VI).

civic virtue (no 'breakers of any contracts', *tractatores alicuius negotii*). In their final statute—which has the feel of something added at a later point, perhaps as the confraternity became more successful—the confraternity promised to try to provide two priests who would 'perpetually celebrate for the salvation of souls and remission of sins of the male and female confraternity members, in the church of the Blessed Mary of Cros', providing for them from the goods of the confraternity.[71] Thus a pooling of collective wealth permitted simultaneously the patronage usually associated with lordship in this period, and the privileged salvation of the souls of the members.

It is important to remember that the Caunes example is just one form of confraternity, a particularly elaborated and spiritually ambitious form. At its simplest, a confraternity was formed by the collective swearing of an oath to some agreed purpose. In the examples we have met thus far, the common thread of purpose was burial (something which we might see as helpfully distinguishing confraternities from the craft and trade guilds of the thirteenth century which, whilst sometimes engaged in pious acts such as supporting lights at a particular altar, did not make provision for burial for their members).[72] But other aims were also possible, some of which we might see as both spiritual and political. This may in fact have been the underlying case with the Marseille confraternity statutes from 1212, which the archbishop of Narbonne rather curiously approved in terms of how the confraternity would help 'defend the innocent and repress the wicked violence of men' (*ad deffensionem quoque innocentium et ad violentias iniquas hominum reprimendas*). Just five years later the city was threatened with interdict by Honorius III, the cathedral canons having reported the deeply impious behaviour of the citizens to him, which had apparently involved violence against the clergy, 'manifest suspicion of heretical wickedness', the violation of sacred spaces, and 'blasphemy against Christ's ministry'.[73] The charge of 'heresy' might conceivably have had some reality behind it, in terms of the presence of Waldensian preachers or even dualist Good Men; but the history of the city across the first half of the thirteenth century was one of sustained political conflict between the episcopal *cité* and the mercantile *bourg*.[74] In this light, and given the archbishop's framing of the statutes, the confraternity looks like an attempt at building a political vehicle within the city, no less 'spiritual' for being nonetheless tied up in the power politics of that particular time and place.

---

[71] Doat 58, fol. 294 (Mahul, *Cart. Carcassonne*, IV, p. 163, c. XVI).
[72] This is the case at least with those statutes edited in Mulholland, *Early Gild Records*.
[73] J. H. Albanès, ed., *Gallia christiana novissima*, 7 vols (Montbéliard: Société anonymes des imprimerie Montbéliardaise, 1899-1920), II, cols 105-07 (no. 217), 27 Feb 1217; this incident also discussed briefly in Chapter 5 above.
[74] On the politics, see V.-L. Bourrilly, *Essai sur l'histoire politique de la commune de Marseille, des origines à la victoire de Charles d'Anjou (1264)* (Aix-en-Provence: Libraire d'histoire de la Provence, 1926), pp. 46-124; M. Zarb, *Les privilèges de la ville de Marseille, du X siècle à la Révolution* (Paris: Picard, 1961), pp. 53-69.

This was very certainly the case with the 'White' and 'Black' confraternities formed in Toulouse during the years of the crusade. The 'White' confraternity was started by Bishop Foulques (as we saw in Chapter 5) to attack judicially those accused of usury (and subsequently joining in with de Montfort's crusade forces), the 'Black' confraternity springing up in opposition to its efforts. The 'White' and 'Black' labels recall the political confraternity factions in Florence, and suggest ultimately a similar sense of supporting or opposing papal political power, though we know nothing more of these confraternities beyond what the chroniclers tell us; they were perhaps more like a form of sworn militia. That is similarly the case with the confraternity of the Holy Spirit, apparently founded by over 200 men in Carcassonne at Louis IX's urging, with statutes dating to around 1242 (recorded in a fifteenth-century royal *vidimus*). They had a chapel in Saint-Sernin, and each member paid one *sous* to join; but the statutes suggest a civic militia with the duties of a night watch, rather than purely pious focus.[75] There are other examples in this vein, such as the sworn association made in 1219 by the citizens of Narbonne in defence of their rights and the 'confederation' of peace formed at Rocamadour in 1233 (the latter focused against mercenaries, echoing the Caputiati from fifty years earlier).[76] Perhaps more spiritual in activity, albeit also political in purpose, were the 'Grey Penitents' confraternity founded in Avignon by Louis VIII in 1226, in thanks for his initial victories in the reinvigorated crusade against the south.[77]

So confraternities could be formed specifically for political purposes, albeit with pious activities embedded therein. But we should note that the swearing of an oath to form a collectivity always had political potential. In Chapter 5 I mentioned the late twelfth-century movement of the Caputiati, which had involved such an oath, and which, in its very public devotion to the Virgin Mary and requirement of dues from its members, looks much like another form of confraternity. The statutes of the confraternity of the Blessed Mary of Cros emphasize, in their penultimate chapter, that the *confratres* did not intend to make any congregation or '*parlamentum*' in prejudice or damage to the king or the local abbot, but had been formed only to the honour and praise of the Trinity and the Virgin, 'and of all the popes, and of our lord King of France, and for the emendation of the life of the aforesaid *confratres* and in remission of their sins'.[78] These self-conscious provisions, produced in Caunes around 1190, perhaps bear the imprint of the recently suppressed Caputiati uprising to the north.

---

[75] Mahul, *Cart. Carcassonne*, V, pp. 701–03.
[76] *HGL*, VI, p. 2; C. Taylor, *Heresy, Crusade and Inquisition in Medieval Quercy* (York: York Medieval Press, 2011), pp. 103–04.
[77] My thanks to Jean Dunbabin for pointing me to *les pénitents gris*; see Anon., *Notice historique sur la confrérie et la procession jubilaire des pénitents gris d'Avignon, par un confrère* (Avignon: L. Aubanel, 1851).
[78] Doat 58, fol. 294 (Mahul, *Cart. Carcassonne*, IV, p. 163, c. XV).

Of course the political potential in, and consequent concern about, confraternities is not limited to southern France: there is quite a lot of Carolingian and other early medieval legislation against groups who swore oaths to each other, in each case reflecting the concern that rulers had over collectivities that might challenge their power.[79] But the Albigensian Crusade and its aftermath may have created a particular climate of concern. Simon de Montfort's statutes of Pamiers from 1212 included the injunction that 'no barons, knights, townspeople or peasants are to dare to bind themselves together through means of faith or oath or co-swearing, even if on the pretext of confraternity or any other good cause', unless with the consent of their lord.[80] Canon 38 of the council of Toulouse (1229) ordered 'that all barons, castellans, knights, burghers of the cities, or moreover rural dwellers, should not presume to make any co-sworn associations, assemblies, confraternities (*coniurationes, colligationes, confratrias*) or any other forms of obligation of faith or oath, or other kind of mutual support', imposing heavy fines for those who dared go against this, and declaring all previously formed associations null.[81] A set of town privileges granted to Montolieu in 1231 by the local abbot echoes the ban on collective oath taking, forbidding any 'co-sworn associations, confraternities, assemblies or illicit conventions' (*coniurationes, confratrias, colligationes seu conventiones illicitas*) without the abbot's consent.[82] Pope Gregory IX, writing to his papal legate the archbishop of Vienne on 28 April 1236 in the context of re-establishing the Brother Preachers, the inquisitors, and the university in Toulouse, ordered him to suppress all confraternities in the city.[83] The royal seneschal, reacting in 1237 to a recent uprising in Narbonne, similarly banned 'all confraternities and all forms of confraternity' in the city.[84] In 1249 Innocent IV wrote to the abbot of Psalmodi to carry out sentences of excommunication against the citizens of Avignon for a variety of reasons, but including the fact that despite having both witnesses and documents proving that all Avignonnais over the age of 14 had promised under oath 'that they would not make any confraternity nor permit there to be any assembly or confraternity in the town', they had now done so, despite excommunication by the local bishop.[85] The similarity to the Montolieu example suggests that this kind of civic restriction was common, and had not immediately faded away after the conclusion to the crusade.

[79] R. Naismith, 'Gilds, States and Societies in the Early Middle Ages', *Early Medieval Europe* 28 (2020), 627–62.

[80] Statutes of Pamiers c. 33 (Mansi XXII, col. 861).

[81] Mansi XXIII, col. 203. NB also the 'statutes of peace' promulgated in 1226 by count of Provence, including (c. 14) against 'conjurations and conspiracies, which are called confraternities' (Benoit, *Recueil des actes des comtés de Provence*, II, p. 210).

[82] Mahul, *Cart. Carcassonne*, I, pp. 127–28.

[83] L. Auvray, ed., *Les registres de Grégoire IX*, 4 vols (Paris: A. Fontemoing, 1896–1955), II, cols. 378–79 (no. 3127).

[84] *HGL*, VI, *preuves*, pp. 410–11 (no. vii).

[85] Bull of Innocent IV, 24 May 1249, edited in L.-H. Labande, *Avignon au XIIIe siecle: l'évêque Zoen Tencarari et les Avignonais* (Paris; Alphonse Picard, 1908), pp. 347–54, at p. 351.

Some similar concerns continued even when Capetian control of the south was fully implemented. Between 1267 and 1269, Alphonse de Poitiers, brother of Louis IX and, since Raimond VII's death in 1249, count of Toulouse, wrote several letters concerning problems with a confraternity that had recently formed, apparently connected to the Carmelite friars in Toulouse. The confraternity had been created 'under the pretext of goodness' (*sub specie boni*) but there were concerns that it was a threat to the political order.[86] In November 1270, as a part of his response to local *enquêtes*, Alphonse reproved the formation of 'illicit meetings…and especially confraternities in the region of Toulouse prohibited by the legate of the apostolic see'. Any confraternities that had been made were to be dissolved and prohibited, and not to be re-formed, particularly those made by 'illicit pacts'.[87] In addition to the concerns over the Carmelite confraternity, this may have been prompted by the nervousness with which other local lords viewed such associations. Just slightly earlier that year Alphonse's *enquêteurs* had responded to a complaint from the townspeople (the *universitas*) of Lavaur that when many people from the town had formed a confraternity in honour of St Elanus, Lord Pierre de Landreville had unjustly forbidden it. (On that occasion their wish to be allowed to continue the confraternity was granted, 'so long as they should not in any way presume to hold illicit meetings'.)[88] In the same period, he had written to the seneschal of Agen and Cahors on behalf of a knight, *bayle* of Castelnau-de-Montratier (north of Montauban). The *bayle* had attempted to suppress a confraternity formed by many people from the said *castrum*, who had reacted violently in response.[89] What looks to be a similar case appears in several documents from 1277, a knight and lord of a *castrum* called Feraud de Brunet complaining to the local bishop that the people of Brunet (north-east of Manosque) had formed an 'illicit conventicle' against him. A brief document somewhat inexplicably bound into the back of the survey of rural dues owed to the cathedral of Apt (mentioned earlier in this chapter), relates that one Guillaume Lautier was sent as a judge in the matter, and found in the knight's favour, subjecting the people of Brunet to a fine and making them swear never to do it again.[90]

---

[86] A. Molinier, ed., *Correspondance administrative d'Alfonse de Poitiers*, 2 vols (Paris: Imprimerie Nationale, 1894–1900), I, pp. 250–51 (no. 405), 21 Mar 1268, calling upon the vicar of Toulouse to investigate. See also p. 169 (no. 270), p. 622 (no. 968), II, pp. 110–11 (no. 1377)—the final letter indicating that the confraternity was interfering in a dispute settlement between the cathedral canons and the Carmelite friars, on the side of the latter.

[87] P.-Fr. Fournier and P. Guébin, eds, *Enquêtes administratives d'Alfonse de Poitiers, arrêts de son parlement tenu a Toulouse, et textes annexes, 1249–1271* (Paris: Imprimerie nationale, 1959), p. 362 (no. 35).

[88] Fournier and Guébin, eds, *Enquêtes administratives*, p. 345 (no. 459).

[89] Molinier, ed., *Correspondance administrative*, II, pp. 197–98 (no. 1504), 29 June 1269; see also p. 260 (no. 1602), 2 Feb 1270 which mentions ongoing investigation into the confraternity.

[90] BnF MS NAL 1211, fol. 23r, dated 1 kalends February 1277, followed by two other documents relating to the same; one of which is transcribed, from a different manuscript copy, in *Gallia Christiana Novissima* I, instrumenta, cols 381–82.

Similar concerns continued under Philip IV of France, who in 1289, in response to various questions from his seneschal, noted that the 'confraternities...forbidden by the peace of Paris' were now clandestinely reappearing in various towns and other places, and caused 'homicides' and other evil deeds; thus they were to be suppressed. We can then see one specific suppression subsequently occurring, in Limoux in 1293–94.[91]

These examples may all start to look more like episodes from a history of popular politics than popular piety. In some cases noted above, the political clearly does predominate massively. But the examples from Lavaur and the Carmelite confraternity in Toulouse show something much more intertwined, and suggest—along with the various edicts suppressing sworn associations cited above—that in southern France religious confraternities were always *liable*, at least, to being perceived in a political manner, as a potential source of threat to orthodox authority. This does not by any means imply that all confraternities were self-consciously rebellious, and we must keep in mind the fact that the associations just discussed enter the documentary record only because of dissension. Others almost certainly existed, even if for the most part we can glimpse them only very rarely, such as a passing reference to 'the confraternity of Palaja', to which a woman called Raymunda Porca de Puigcerdà left 10 *sous* and her best item of clothing in her will of 1294, among a variety of other pious and personal bequests;[92] or the very faded, badly damaged, and highly fragmentary accounts book for the early 1320s, produced by two officials of a confraternity to the Blessed Mary attached to the church of Saint-Sauveur in Castelsarrasin;[93] or, as in a letter of 1345 from the vicar-general of the bishop of Carcassonne to the 'jurats' of the confraternity of the Conception of the Blessed Mary of Mont Carmel focused on the confraternity's funeral practices, a brief mention of the processions similarly made 'by other confraternities of the city', otherwise now invisible to us.[94]

As we look across the late thirteenth and fourteenth centuries, there are however two richer sources of evidence, for two particular confraternities, both dedicated to the Virgin Mary, both from the same region. One is the confraternity of

---

[91] Archives Municipale, Toulouse, AA4, fol. 11r: 'De confratria et coniurationibus que olim in pace Parisiensis et aliis statutis prohibite fuerunt nunc de novo clandestine et aliis sustinentur et fuerint in villis et locis magnis et alibi et ex hoc omicidia et alia facinora aliquociens perpetrantur.' On Limoux, see Guiraud, *Cartulaire de Notre-Dame de Prouille*, II, pp. 274–75 (nos 535–39).

[92] AD P-O, 7 J 40 (*Liber testamentorum Puigcerdà*, 1294), fol. 4r.

[93] AD T-et-G, 4 E 11. I am very grateful to the archivist Dr Emmanuel Moureau for a digital copy of this source, originally mis-identified by a nineteenth-century archivist as a confraternity of 'notaries' (rather than 'of Notre Dame'). It is, somewhat curiously, a long, thin 'saddle-bag'-shaped paper manuscript written in a mixture of Latin and Occitan, torn in many places and missing many of its original pages, the ink frequently too pale to read. A few folios (34r–36v, modern foliation) are fairly legible, and record for the year 1324 donations and other income from 100 men and 21 women; this however includes legacies made in wills, so is not a straightforward indication of actual confraternity membership; more work would be needed to produce additional usable information. It has been digitally photographed by the archive (CD-ROM 2 NUM 171).

[94] Doat 64, fol. 326r (ed. Mahul, *Cart. Carcassonne*, V, pp. 442–43).

the Blessed Mary of Fanjeaux, for which we have detailed statutes, written in Occitan in 1266, close to its foundation date, and a large number of other documents, mostly land transactions and wills, at least some collated by the confraternity itself in the first half of the fourteenth century. The other is the confraternity of the Blessed Mary of Fendeille, a small *castrum* a few kilometres south of Castelnaudary, for which we have a detailed accounts book beginning in 1332, possibly as the confraternity itself was founded. There are things in common to the two confraternities, beyond their devotion to the Virgin: both were based in rural *castra* rather than large cities (albeit, in the case of Fanjeaux, quite a regionally important *castrum*); both were governed by four *baillis*, elected annually by the confraternity members; they contained male and female members, though women held office in neither; both foundations became financially successful in the space of a few decades, and survived into the fifteenth century. There were also however some differences, interesting in themselves but also further illuminating as to how there could continue to be more than one function to a 'confraternity' even by the fourteenth century.

In the case of Fanjeaux, the material fact of the statutes is in itself informative.[95] They are written in a very clear hand, on good-quality parchment, with no ornamentation beyond highlighting in red ink the very first letter on the very first page; an important document designed to last, but for an internal readership, one might suggest, not going to lengths to impress an external eye. Unlike the other examples we have met above, the statutes are not here confirmed by, nor contain any reference to, a higher authority, other than beginning 'In the name of our Lord God Jesus Christ and of the blessed Virgin Mary his mother, Amen'. The document describes itself as a 'cartulary' (*cartolari*) in which can be written *las causas*, the business transactions of the confraternity and its receipts (although in fact it does not now contain any such matters); 'and men began to write in it in the year of our Lord 1266, the *baillis* existing in that year being T[homas] Message, notary of the said *castel*, Pons Vidal, B[ernard] Brus and P[ierre] Sarrauta...and to begin...are written the statutes (*les establimens*) of the confraternity...'. So the confraternity already existed in 1266, and declared its rules and procedures with confident and self-generated collective authority.

The *establimens* set out the governance of the confraternity—as said, four trustworthy men (*prosomes*) are elected annually as *baillis* (*balles*); there is mention further on of an 'almoner' also—and then turn to its core purposes: to raise money to pay for lights and for alms, the basic source being membership fees (1d for lights, 3d for alms annually); to visit sick members of the confraternity; to arrange burial and subsequent masses, with confraternity members to be present at the funeral, and to pay a fine if absent; to provide financial assistance for

---

[95] AD Aude H558-1 (ed. A. Ramière de Fortanier, 'La confrérie Notre-Dame de Fanjeaux et son développement au moyen âge', *CdF* 11 (1976), 321–56, at pp. 352–56).

members who fall ill; and to hold an elaborate procession at the feast of the Purification of the Blessed Virgin Mary in February.

The document's sense of the confraternity's collective authority underwrites a similar self-confidence in lay involvement in spiritual and liturgical activity. As we have seen in earlier chapters, making provision for lights before an altar had long been a channel for lay pious giving; confraternities collectivized that impulse, allowing some of those lower down the social scale to be involved other than at the moment they drew up their will, and by consequence ensured that lights would burn longer, perhaps constantly.[96] Perdurance of a kind thus became available, beyond the liturgical round of the monasteries; lay people could gain collective access to one of the benefits previously limited to those of higher social status. Every month, when the mass of the Holy Spirit was sung in the local church in Fanjeaux, the *baillis* would make an offering on behalf of the whole confraternity. Pious giving was thus magnified. Each Lent an anniversary mass would be sung for all the dead of the confraternity, and again the *baillis* would give on behalf of the collective. The confraternity members were to involve themselves in the actual funeral ritual also, bringing with them a coin (*una mesalha*) for the soul of the dead man or woman. Members were to carry the body, from their house to the church and from the church to the cemetery. 'And in the cemetery, those who brought bread should distribute it to those in need and to poor people (*mercenables... et a personas pauras*) as seems best and most profitable to the soul of the dead person; and everyone there should each say fifty Pater nosters for the soul of the dead person.' And on the feast of the Purification, each member of the confraternity 'shall come to the church of St Mary in the said *castel* in Her honour on the vespers of the Purification of St Mary, with lit candles in the manner and form ordained by the said *balles*, two-by-two, rightly and orderly,... and the *balles* shall gather up the candles' which were then kept burning from vespers to matins and to the mass, remaining especially at the altar.

So this confraternity, and surely some others like it, opened up aspects of pious worship to lay activity, not simply allowing lay people to provide materially for worship, but giving—indeed, demanding—an active role in spiritually meaningful activity for its members. At the same time, however, other elements within the statutes, and other of the surviving evidence, caution us against assuming that the confraternity was the sole route for the expression of its members' piety, or indeed that their activities were purely focused on salvation. The burial provisions, and a statute promising some financial assistance for members who fell ill, were also about mutual protection. Soon after the statutes were first recorded, there is a strong indication that the confraternity felt the need to protect itself from being swamped by those who were less fortunate: an addition made in 1271, as decided

---

[96] See Fouracre, *Eternal Light*, passim.

by the *baillis* and on 'the counsel of the major part of the confraternity', established that those who were already ill could not join, that when someone did join, they must pay 20 *sous* of Toulouse 'at the will of the *baillis*', and that anyone who joined part way through the year had to pay up the previous year's dues.

The various wills surviving in the archives of the confraternity (some certainly archived by the confraternity in the period, though others may have been collated by a later archivist) record the final pious donations made by various members. In each case, the confraternity was only one among a number of recipients. Guillaume Arnaud made his will in October 1300 in preparation for a pilgrimage to Rome, presumably for the papal jubilee declared that year by Boniface VIII. He gave to the confraternity—'of which, by grace of God, I am a *confrater*'—5 *sous* of Tours, in addition to 12d for works on the church of Fanjeaux and another 21d to its clergy (these latter gifts almost certainly a local requirement for all wills). Five *sous* was a larger amount than his legacies to the ten other churches and hospitals he mentioned, most of which just got 3d; but not so much in comparison to the 100 *sous* he left to his heirs.[97] Another example: Paula, wife of Arnaud Faure, in her will of December 1324, gave 5 *sous* of Tours to the works of the church of Fanjeaux, where she wished to be buried, and 2 *sous*, 12d, and 6d respectively to the chaplain, sub-chaplain, and clergy of the church. Part way through the will she granted a *sextus* of grain to the confraternity ('of which by grace of God I am a *confratrissa*'); but donated various amounts of either 12d or 6d to four other churches, a monastery, and two hospitals, gave 16 *sexti* of grain and two casks of good wine to 'the poor of Fanjeaux', and left a favoured god-daughter 10 *sous* of Tours (various other apparently less favoured god-daughters each getting 5 *sous*). She also made provision for a *dotal* of 25 *livres* of Tours.[98] Here, as elsewhere, despite pride in being a *confratrissa*, the confraternity was not the prime focus of testamentary bequests.

By the early fourteenth century this may have been because the members— keeping out the hoi-polloi since 1271—were aware of how wealthy the confraternity had become via its ownership of land. A document from 1324 records seventy people confirming that they held land or other property *in emphitressem* from the confraternity; that is, owing an annual payment each Christmas. The dues ranged from 1d to 13d, but as each landholder was made to confirm, other dues could be levied when desired.[99] By this point in the fourteenth century, the confraternity's records show it surveying the extent of inherited estates, having the contents of relevant wills copied into its own documents, and generally producing an active archive of lordship, not much dissimilar to some of the content of monastic cartularies.[100] A kind of 'lordship', collective in nature, went along with faith.

---

[97] AD Aude H558-3.   [98] AD Aude H562-2.
[99] AD Aude H561-1 and H561-2 (one document split into two pieces).
[100] See analysis in Ramière de Fortanier, 'La confrérie Notre-Dame de Fanjeaux'.

The confraternity of the Virgin Mary at Fendeille also did well for itself: the accounts for 1332 announce that they spent slightly over 52 *sous* of Toulouse, whilst those for 1341 indicate expenditure on lights (both oil and wax candles), church fabric and furnishings, and other expenses of over 220 *sous*, plus an extraordinary one-off purchase of priestly vestments for the very large sum of £27 23s 7d (this included a few *sous* in associated costs, but mostly went on the clothing).[101] But there are some apparent differences between this confraternity and the one in Fanjeaux, not explained simply by the difference in the surviving record. At Fendeille, the accounts book spells out in its opening folio that the village asked permission from the local lord to found the confraternity, and indeed got him to provide a letter with his seal to confirm that permission (the brief contents of which are copied into the book). There is no apparent focus on burial, as far as one can tell from this preamble and from the content of the expenditure, or on helping members of the confraternity who fall into poverty. And whilst the confraternity has four *baillis*, they are at various points described more clearly as *operarii ecclesie*—that is, a word that in an English context one would normally translate as 'churchwarden'.[102] In other words, the accounts book could in fact be seen as one of the earliest surviving churchwarden's accounts in western Europe. The responsibility of the *operarii*, and the focus of the confraternity, was the upkeep of the parish church, and indeed—as noted above—that is where its expenditure very largely went. This did still involve the provision of lights: they spent over 50 *sous* on oil in 1341, and over 60 *sous* on wax and associated labour by the candle-makers. So the sense of collective patronage persists; but perhaps in a somewhat less exclusive fashion than at Fanjeaux, if the confraternity was managing all receipts of alms for the church (as seems to have been the case).[103]

A point of comparison in conclusion here is simply the respective focus of the two confraternities from Fanjeaux and Fendeille. Both were devoted to the Virgin. Both undoubtedly brought some prestige and sense of elevated pious identity to their members. Both were the product of lay enthusiasm, self-organization, and engagement in the provision of worship and salvation. But they were not identical: at Fanjeaux, their attention was on burial and mutual support; at Fendeille, on the

---

[101] AD Aude G268, fol. 86r (1332 total), fols 12r-17r (1341 expenditure list), fol. 16v (priestly vestments). In this small paper book, the earliest 1332 accounts are split between the front (income) and, reversed upside down, the back of the book (expenditure). There is a gap of a few years before recording continues, but the scribe then adopted a more linear approach, giving expenditure and then income.

[102] AD Aude G268, fol. 12r: 'operarii ecclesiarum sancti martini de fendelia et de Lauraca'—here, and at some other points, Laurac has been scored through, presumably indicating that at an early stage the two villages shared responsibility for the one church. This is somewhat odd, as Laurac's own church of Saint-Laurent was in existence by 1266 (see <www.pop.culture.gouv.fr/notice/merimee/PA00102731>, accessed 16 Nov 2021).

[103] AD Aude G268, fol. 9v, the *baillis* report, for example, that on a particular feast day they 'found from the town' 2s 3d on the Sundays before and after the feast of St Mark (other examples on same page and elsewhere); an indication of alms generally received in church on those days?

building in which the community worshipped. The latter was in a fairly clear sense in the service of the whole community, in terms of its collective worship; the former was a subgroup that became increasingly select as it accrued land, wealth, and status. All confraternities were exclusive to some degree—and one wonders whether this was in part why some 'heretical' groups objected to the swearing of oaths—but some were more exclusive than others, their dynamic more clearly directed toward marshalling piety in the service of additional strength. In each case, we can see groups of the laity adapting available elements of Christian worship toward the particular choices they had made collectively.

Testamentary Choices

An exemplum recorded by a Sack Friar tells of a wealthy man who sat down to make his will. He had many daughters, and provided richly for each of them, so that they had ample dowries and could marry. A wise man was in attendance: 'Lord, you have another daughter, to whom you have given nothing.' 'Who is she?', asked the rich man. 'Surely I have none other than Berta, Maria, Bertranda...have I more daughters?' Prompted further by the wise man, he was made to realize that he had forgotten one more 'dependant': his own soul, for which he had thus far left nothing.[104]

The story mildly dramatizes the negotiation that inevitably occurred for every lay Christian as they contemplated death and their legacies: whether to focus on their eternal soul, or to prioritize kinship. Additional factors—gender, status, material resources, local and familial expectations—all further complicated the mix. One of the 'customs' claimed and established most often in civic statutes, from the twelfth century onward, was the right that inhabitants of the relevant town or city had to make a will, disposing of their goods as they wished. The primary implication was to protect inheritances from arbitrary seizure or constraint by local lords, but such customs also more generally asserted the right of non-noble people to attempt to provide for a lineage, be it ever so humble. At the same time, as we saw in Chapter 4, some civic customs could also attempt to limit how much of a woman's goods she was allowed to bestow upon pious places in her will (up to a fourth part, according to the customs of Carcassonne, c. 1205), without having permission from her husband or father. Whilst the choices made by testators were, ultimately, individual, the contexts in which they made those choices were almost always quite collective, and heavily inflected by the possibilities or constraints of material resource and, in terms of the pious provisions they made, the particular religious institutions or beneficiaries available in a locality. The wise

[104] Welther, 'Un recueil d'exempla', p. 315 (no. 221).

man in the story stands in for the wider weight of ecclesiastical expectations upon testators; but on occasion it seems likely that secular counterparts might also have a voice, shaping the shared expectations of a family or local community over what a good person would do in terms of providing for those who survived them. For all of these reasons, it is in this chapter that I have chosen to focus on wills and the negotiated choices made by testators, thus setting them amongst other more overtly collective negotiations. As Marie-Claude Marandet notes, a medieval will can be seen as a kind of 'negotiated contract' with the community.[105]

We have of course met wills already, at various earlier points in this book. We saw in chapter three how various factors made it more likely, in the latter part of the twelfth century, that one could distribute pious bequests around a number of different institutions. In Chapter 4 we saw the rise of several avenues of charitable donation found commonly in wills (though not only in wills), notably bequests to hospitals and to 'the poor'; whilst in Chapter 6, wills provided us with evidence over the choice of burial place made by people, including the occasions in which it seems that a family had established a particular location within a cemetery (or more rarely, within a church) as 'their' plot.

Part of what Christianity promised was that upon death all Christians, no matter their social status, went forth equally, to be judged for their actions and not their material worth. The potential promise of salvation, as we have seen in preceding chapters, became more actively apparent to all lay people across the thirteenth century. What they did during their lifetime had come to matter more clearly, not only in terms of dutiful conformity but active pious engagement. But the moment at which one contemplated death (whether actually on the deathbed or not) was a particularly charged occasion, a final chance to help oneself, before handing over the care of one's soul to the memories and possibly fragile interventions of those who survived you.

Something we should note very clearly is that, the Church's moral condemnation of wealth notwithstanding, greater material resource allowed one more options. Take, for example, the will of Sicard Alaman the younger, made in March 1280. He was a knight, from a family much favoured by Raimond VII of Toulouse, and by the later thirteenth century his family had become extremely rich. In his will, alongside passing on the various lands he owned to his widow, Sicard set out a large number of pious provisions. He wished to be buried in the church of the Brothers Preacher in Toulouse, at the foot of his father in the tomb already established there; however, he specified, should the Preachers refuse permission for this (perhaps because of the increased restrictions against allowing lay people to be buried within major churches) he would prefer the relevant monetary provision to be switched over to the Brothers Minor in Toulouse, and to be buried

---

[105] Marandet, *Le souci de l'au-delà*, I, p. 59, citing an article on fifteenth-century wills by Bernard Saint-Pierre.

with them. He left 1,500 *livres* of Tours 'for the salvation and redemption of my soul and of my forebears and of all the faithful dead', then dedicating various parts of this vast sum to particular recipients: the church of Saint-Étienne in Toulouse, the Brothers Preacher, the Brothers Minor, and the Sisters Minor, all in the same city; the convent at Prouille; the various mendicant foundations in Albi, Lavaur, Castres, Montauban, Agen, and a number of other monasteries. He left further money for the physical upkeep of various bridges, towers, churches, and yet more monasteries; 2,000 *sous* to 'the poor women of my lands' to help them marry; and 100 *sous* each to two hospitals in towns he had founded, and to a leprosarium. Overall, he distributed substantial funds to more than thirty different pious institutions or causes. Toward the end of the will, he additionally instructed his heirs to make a new hospital next to his parish church in Saint-Sulpice, with a chapel to be dedicated to St Grégoire; and to install a chaplain who was to celebrate divine office there perpetually, for Sicard's soul and for those of his father and mother.[106] The point about Sicard's wealth is not just the amounts that he left, but that it allowed him to make pious bequests to such a vast range of places—'allowed' both in the practical sense and in the sense that he was confident in his ability to broadcast his piety across an extended landscape—and indeed attempt to found an entirely new place of worship in his home town. His desire to be buried in the church of the Brothers Preacher, and his negotiation should they refuse, speak similarly to the agency granted by wealth and status.

This is not to say that less exalted and wealthy testators could not spread their piety around; only that they had to do so under greater constraints. Take, in partial contrast, another will from Saint-Sulpice, albeit from some decades later, recorded in Geraud Boffati's notarial register: that of a single woman called Gibellina, 'daughter of the late Pierre Gastar', written in July 1344. It is notably broad in its aspirations. She wished to be buried in the parish church of Saint-Sulpice, 'where she is a parishioner', giving 4d to the main altar, 2d to each of the other altars, and 6d to the 'works of the church' (meaning its upkeep). She gave 2 lbs of wax to the confraternity of the Blessed Mary, the same to that of Saint-Sulpice, and 2 lbs of oil to the church of St Mary in the town in which her father was born. She then made a number of tiny gifts, ranging from 2d to 6d, to some symbolically important religious centres: to the Brothers Preacher, the Carmelites, and the Sisters Minor, all in Toulouse, plus 3d to support those who wished to go 'ultra mare' (whether on pilgrimage or crusade is unclear). Her largest pious gift was 5 *sous* for a trental mass, and 8 *sous* to her god-daughter Jeanne, to go toward her dowry. Toward the end of the will, apparently as an additional thought, she also gave wax to two other altars.[107] The sums involved—a tiny, tiny fraction of

---

[106] E. Cabié and L. Mazens, eds, *Un cartulaire et divers actes des Alaman des Lautrec et des de Lévis* (Toulouse: A. Chauvin et fils, 1882), pp. 23–29.
[107] AD Tarn 3E55-253, fols 17v-18r.

the amounts wielded by Sicard Alaman—suggest that Gibellina had limited means. She nonetheless also wished to spread her bequests about; in this case, however, her choices were largely focused on her own parish, that of her late father, and the famous foundations in Toulouse, in contrast to Sicard's wide-ranging pious embrace. Perhaps the most interesting aspect is the fact that the largest single gift she made was not for masses, or to institutions, but to her goddaughter—a pious gift, but one inescapably bound up with personal connections in this world, not focused solely on the next.

Marandet's very thorough and wide-ranging study of testamentary culture in later medieval Languedoc looks at wills across the fourteenth and fifteenth centuries to discern various patterns and complications. Much of what Gibellina chose to do would be very familiar within that wider setting, particularly the focus on lights and local foundations. One point which Marandet emphasizes is that there can be very notable local differences in will-making practices, including in the aspects around pious provision: 'each little isolated community, each village itself produced a type of comportment, a model of piety and charity', she notes.[108] Her aggregate analysis is based on a very large corpus of material, but covers a period that stretches well beyond the Black Death (and indeed mostly starts after 1350). In contrast, in what follows I have focused closely upon one particular community, to explore in more detail what the bounds of 'choice' were for a usefully broad range of laymen and women living in or near the same community, in the very late thirteenth and early fourteenth centuries.

The community in question is Puigcerdà. Located high in the Pyrenees, the town now sits just south of the border into Spain. In the specific period addressed here it was in fact part of the independent kingdom of Mallorca, created by Jaume I of Aragon in the late thirteenth century. As passed on to his son, Jaume II, that kingdom also encompassed the lordship of Montpellier and the county of Roussillon.[109] There is ample evidence of close connections and regular commerce between the town and those ordinary people who lived in and around Foix, Pamiers, the Ariège, and Perpignan, as well as lands to the south in the kingdom of Aragon.

The evidence comes from three 'books of testaments' (*liber testamentorum*, as each is explicitly labelled) produced by local notaries, recording wills from those in the town and from various of the small villages in its environs. The first two books record wills from 1294 and 1297-98, the third and largest from 1309-10. They are written on paper, as is quite usual for notarial records, and are in each case the notary's working draft, from which a separate full and neat version would have been drawn up subsequently. It is clear from the varied handwriting that a

---

[108] Marandet, *Le souci de l'au-delà*, II, p. 553.
[109] For background, and wider-ranging economic analysis, see D. Abulafia, *A Mediterranean Emporium: The Catalan Kingdom of Majorca* (Cambridge: Cambridge University Press, 1994).

number of different notaries all contributed to the same *liber testamentorum* for this purpose; in other towns in this period one would more normally find wills recorded in among other documents in an individual notary's book, as with the example of Gibellina above. The implication is probably that the town of Puigcerdà itself took an interest in archiving the wills, ensuring their probity in the case of subsequent challenge. In most cases the will is neatly scored through, to show that the notary did indeed create the proper copy ('cancelled', as the slightly confusing technical terminology denotes it); in a few cases, we find a more heavily scored-through will, in each case because the testator changed their mind about some details and had the notary start again afresh. Very occasionally a will is not scored through at all, for reasons that are uncertain. (Very, very occasionally a will appears to be incomplete, either because a folio has gone missing, or because the testator—possibly, though by no means definitely, on their deathbed—had failed to finish dictating their wishes). These three books survive now in the Archives départementales Pyrénées-Orientales in Perpignan, and provide an overall corpus of 145 wills, almost half of which (70) are from the fourteenth-century register. The attraction of this source is the extent to which it allows us to focus on a particular place and time whilst also providing a rich social range of testators. (It should be noted that some other wills also survive from Puigcerdà across this same period and also later, located in the municipal archives, but are not included in the following analysis.[110])

A few caveats need to be noted initially. The wills recorded in each *Liber testamentorum* clearly cannot be *all* the wills that were made in this locality in those years—there just aren't enough of them, particularly given that they include those made by people coming from villages somewhat outside Puigcerdà itself. On the other hand, as we shall see, a number of them are from really quite poor and lowly people, so they do provide us with a good range, if not perhaps an absolute cross-section of society. As with all wills, we cannot be certain that what the testator set out as their wishes subsequently transpired; nor can we be certain that what they specified in their will reflected the entirety of their dispositions, and thus their relative wealth and status. On a few occasions, the testator added a codicil to a will, or, as I note above, revised a will. We can sometimes also see what looks like a testator having a sudden afterthought, the notary inserting additional details or cognate bequests interlined above the original text, or crossing out a short passage and rewriting it slightly differently. These instances may simply reflect the testator's thought processes, but could also have been prompted by questions or comments from the notary or other advisers. In almost all cases, the testator appointed between one and three '*manumissores*'—essentially executors—and when these included specific ecclesiastical figures, such as the prior of the

---

[110] On these, see R. I. Burns, *Jews in the Notarial Culture: Latinate Wills in Mediterranean Spain, 1250-1350* (Berkeley: University of California Press, 1996).

Brothers Preacher, this probably inflected the particular choices made (though of course the choice to appoint him in the first place was presumably the testator's). Most importantly, we should not mistake the picture of piety given by a will as a transparent snapshot of an individual's religious feelings throughout their life. Wills are made when contemplating the end of one's life; they undoubtedly reflect aspects of one's living connections and affections, but they may contain new pious aspirations, or equally a retrenchment of one's attentions. Nonetheless, they are important and revealing.

To sketch out some of the overall contours of the corpus a little further: of the 145 wills, 9 were made by priests, and 50 by women, 19 of whom were stated to be widows. The later part of the corpus, the wills from 1309-10, are disproportionately skewed towards male testators: only 17 of the 70 wills from that period were by women. Two of the women were married to Jewish men. It is perhaps useful to try to arrange the apparent wealth of the testators into social strata—'apparent' because, despite the strong propensity of the Puigcerdà wills to focus on monetary amounts, on a few occasions a will mentions land or property without specifying its value. There is no unproblematic way to assign 'social status' to medieval people, but something impressionistic is nonetheless helpful. None of the wills were for people who styled themselves as 'lord' or 'knight', so we may assume that nobody was what we would think of as 'noble'. A few testators stated what we might think of as a fairly lowly occupation—'weaver', 'skinner', 'shepherd'—but some of these were in fact demonstrably wealthy. I have divided the testators into five groups: 'very poor', 'poor', 'comfortable', 'quite rich', and 'very rich'. These assessments are based on the total monetary amount visible in each will, combining the pious provisions and other personal bequests. It is inevitably imprecise, but the rough gradations of wealth (following the five categories just set out) work as follows, the cash amount indicating the total value of bequests mentioned within the will, all amounts equated to *sous*:

'very poor'	120 *sous* or less	30 people (including 15 women[111] and 1 priest)
'poor'	120-400 *sous*	48 people (including 20 women, plus 4 priests)
'comfortable'	400-900 *sous*	34 people (including 13 women, plus 2 priests)
'quite rich'	900-1,500 *sous*	13 people (including 1 woman and 1 priest)
'very rich'	above 1,500 *sous*	20 people (including 1 woman and 1 priest).

To express that another way, half of the corpus were, by my terms, poor or very poor; under a quarter were somewhat or very rich; the final quarter were somewhere in the middle. These terms are relative, as it is likely that there was a further level of poverty that never participated in this testamentary culture, and as we

---

[111] None of this group were named as widows.

have seen above with Sicard Alaman, there could be a level of regionally wealthy people who were even richer. One could slightly alter the size of each group if adopting different divisions for the monetary values given. But the point is to provide some socioeconomic texture for comparative purposes, not to suggest that any of my putative categories constituted some fundamental social fact.[112]

What, then, can we see of pious choices made by these lay people? Firstly, burial: 71 people asked to be buried in their own parish church, half of the total number. In fact this was the choice in the majority of the wills from 1294 to 1298. By 1309-10 it had started to change: the Brothers Preacher arrived in Puigcerdà in about 1288, and in the wills from the 1290s only 15 people asked to be buried in their cemetery or cloister, 3 of whom were priests. By the end of the first decade of the fourteenth century they had however become a more clearly established presence: in the 1309-10 wills, 25 people asked for burial there, 7 of whom were women. And this is a higher proportion of those wills, because in another 25 of the later wills, no place of burial was specified (for reasons we shall see further below). In other words, by 1310 the church of the Brothers Preacher was preferred by slightly over half of all testators who stated a burial location.

Thus, to make a simple point, the establishment and growth of the Brothers Preacher in the locality allowed and indeed encouraged this specific pious choice. It was also however a choice inflected by wealth. Of the 40 who asked to be buried with the friars, 15 (= 38%) were in the wealthiest two groups ('very rich', 'rich'), a disproportionate number if we remember that those two groups only comprised around 22% of the whole corpus. To put it another way, of the 27 'very rich' or 'rich' testators who stated a desire to be buried somewhere, more than half chose the mendicants' church; whereas with the lowest two social groups ('poor', 'very poor'), of the 63 who stated a place of burial, only 13 asked it to be with the Brothers Preacher.

A similar pattern recurs with pious giving: three-quarters of the 'very rich' gave bequests to the Brothers Preacher, the sums ranging wildly from 30 to 1,390 *sous*, and three-quarters of 'the rich' did likewise, gifting between 5 and 115 *sous*. In the middling group (the 'comfortable') about half of the people left them donations, and in the lower groups the numbers fall further: less than half of the fourth group ('the poor'), and less than one-sixth of the 'very poor'. There were two other mendicant establishments in the local region: that of the Brothers of Penitence (the 'Sack Friars') in Puigcerdà, who had managed to hang on in this locality for

---

[112] I am very grateful to Elizabeth Comuzzi for some contextual information at the 'very poor' end: 100 *sous* might be around, or slightly above, the annual salary of an artisanal labourer (one who might receive shoes and meals in their contract, in addition to the cash payment); 100 *sous* was the lowest dowry found by Dr Comuzzi in the region for this period, suggesting that such brides were very poor in comparison to others. As noted above, whilst there would undoubtedly be some poorer people who did not leave wills—perhaps unable to afford the 5 *sous* fee that was normally charged—those with assets of under 120 *sous* clearly were very low down the socioeconomic scale.

some decades after their formal suppression by the papacy;[113] and a community of Brothers Minor in Villefranche-de-Conflent, about 52 km to the north-east. Both of these attracted a few pious donations (but not requests for burial), again primarily from the wealthier testators. Twenty people donated to the Sack Friars, eight of whom were in the richest two groups, and none of the remainder were among the 'very poor'. Donations to Brothers Minor came from fifteen people, eight of whom were again in the richest two groups. One 'very poor' woman, Faure Costarnez from Foix, did donate to them, as part of a wide mix of donations that she made; but she was at the wealthier end of this category, and was travelling from Foix to Granada (on which see further below), so her circumstances were quite particular. One wonders whether, if we had a fuller picture of her background, we might find that she was in fact rather better off.

So one's social economic status made a difference. Wealth in Puigcerdà came primarily through a thriving textile trade, the town acting as a kind of entrepôt between northern European markets and the Iberian peninsula, and this connected it with Villefranche, as well as Perpignan, and the lands to the south.[114] What we may partly be seeing in the pattern of donations to the mendicants is not simply the fact that having more money allowed one to donate to a wider range of recipients, but that the travel associated with trade was more likely to build connections with religious institutions beyond the immediate locality (the Brothers Minor in particular).

It may be useful to tabulate a few other features across the wills, to show the variations in pious choices more clearly. Firstly, something which shows the range of gifting and associated decisions, by the proportion of people in each financial group (Table 9.1)

A few things become immediately apparent. On average, the richer you were, the more places you were likely to spread around your pious donations. Such distributed largesse was not impossible for the poor, just less likely. If you were rich, you were more likely to be able to pay for memorial masses—though it is interesting that this provision was still only present in a minority of cases, namely 47 out of 144 wills, roughly one-third. Some other kinds of pious giving were present fairly equally across the social range: gifting for lights, for example, which in a testamentary context did not seem to be a priority in Puigcerdà (possibly because confraternities supporting particular lights received donations or income through other routes). You were a bit more likely to give 'to the poor' if you were rich, though the nature of those donations could vary wildly: a few people gave measures of wheat to make bread to be distributed 'to the poor',[115] whereas others

---

[113] R. I. Burns, 'The Friars of the Sack in Puigcerdà: A Lost Chapter of Thirteenth-Century Religious History', *Anuario de estudios medievales* 18 (1988), 217–27.
[114] See Abulafia, *Mediterranean Emporium*.
[115] For example, AD P-O 7J40, fol. 22r, will of Andreas Traper of Llo.

Table 9.1 Distribution of pious legacies

Wealth	Avg. no. pious gifts (and range)	% testators wanting memorial masses	% leaving gifts to hospitals	% leaving gifts to lights	% leaving gifts to 'the poor'	% asking debts be paid	% leaving gifts to godchildren	% leaving pious decisions to *manumissores*
V. rich	6 (0–19)	45	45	15	20	40	10	40
Rich	5 (0–22)	54	38	15	30	23	23	23
Comfortable	4 (0–14)	26	15	15	24	21	26	32
Poor	4 (0–21)	33	19	19	13	25	8	25
V. poor	2 (0–38) *or* 1 (0–11)[a]	20	3	10	13	13	0	13

[a] The 38 gifts are made by the aforementioned Faure Costarnez, mostly of 4d on each occasion, as she was en route to Granada. The second set of figures here exclude her anomalous contribution.

might bequeath huge sums, such as Jean Casther of Puigcerdà who left 4,000 *sous* in alms.[116] The idea of leaving specific sums to pay any debts 'or injuries' (meaning financial complaints), or at least asking your *manumissores* to deal with any such from your estate, was more common the richer you were. The same appears to be true of making provision for godchildren, and it is particularly notable that of the thirty wills written by people in the poorest group, not a single one contains this kind of bequest. This could suggest that if you were very poor, you might leave some small personal token, outwith the written testament, to godchildren; but it might also suggest that the very poorest did not have access to the social and spiritual networks provided by godparenthood. Finally, what to make of the propensity of testators to leave precise pious provisions up to their *manumissores*? This is quite a marked feature among the richest group, who also however display the largest number of specified pious donations. The point here really is variation: the richest group contains the widest set of variants, where any particular testator might choose to write a complex list of places to which he or she wished to donate, or might hand all of that over to their spiritual advisers and executors. The poorest group was much less likely to do either; their choices were more constrained in this sense as well.

It is also possible to attempt to re-address some of this pious giving in terms of relative monetary value. There are three particular markers I have examined here: (1) the total value of all *specified* pious provisions, including the amounts given to have priests present at one's funeral; (2) the value of any sum stated initially as being dedicated 'pro anima' (this occurring in 84 of the 144 wills, sometimes as a sum from which other specific provisions should be drawn, sometimes just for the costs of funeral provision); and (3) the largest single pious donation stated (not counting any 'pro anima' provision), which one might read as having particular symbolic importance to a testator. The categories are not perfect, and in a few cases overlap, but they nonetheless provide us with some useful reference points. The values of all three markers can then be compared with the total value of the bequests in the will, and in the case of (3), against the largest bequest made to a person for familial or personal reasons, rather than as a pious act (Table 9.2).

We should of course be unsurprised to see the monetary values decline as one moves down the table, since this reflects the wealth of the testators. But it is worth noting just how extreme the variance is from richest to poorest, the total amount of pious giving and the largest single personal bequests of the poorest being only 2% of the value of the richest. Two other features are particularly interesting. One is that, as one moves down the social scale, the proportion of pious giving and/or 'pro anima' provision grows markedly: the very richest dedicated between 20% and 25% of their total testamentary resources to these areas, whereas the poor

---

[116] AD P-O 7J42, fol. 17v.

Table 9.2 Proportion of pious and non-pious legacies

Wealth	Avg. total pious gifts (in *sous*)	Avg. 'pro anima' provision (in *sous*)	All pious/all bequests	'Pro anima'/ all bequests	Avg. largest single pious bequest (in *sous*)	Avg. largest single personal bequest (in *sous*)
V. rich	850	830	20%	25%	1581	990
Rich	127	488	15%	36%	184 (*or* 83)[a]	570
Comfortable	111	103	25%	32%	74	175
Poor	52	47	36%	52%	23	65
V. poor	17	19	36%	72%	13	15

[a] There is one very large pious bequest of 1,400 *sous*; without this, the average drops markedly.

and the very poor committed between 36% and 72%.[117] This does not make the poor 'more pious' than the rich. It speaks, rather, to constraints and demands. If one wishes to have a funeral, priests must be paid; if one wishes to make any form of pious donation, it cuts into meagre resources rather more swiftly than for those with plenty. For the richest two groups, the single largest sum mentioned in any particular will was almost always a personal bequest; for the 'comfortable' and 'poor', this was the case roughly half of the time, but for the 'very poor', in only a third of all wills was the largest mentioned sum a personal bequest—more usually it was for pious provision.

This leads us to the second interesting feature, seen by comparing the two columns furthest to the right: largest pious sum and largest personal bequest. Only in the case of the very richest does the former exceed the latter, and for that group this probably needs to be contextualized by the fact that they tended to have more, and more complex, personal bequests to make, thus bringing down the average value of those. The picture otherwise visible here is that whilst pious bequests were, usually, important to all testators (taking up on average between an eighth and a third of the total value of their estate), personal bequests and the continuation of family kin groups probably mattered even more.

All of this is to look at the averaged values across these wills. These of course conceal within them very considerable variations, which themselves demonstrate a much wider sense of choice and negotiation. Each of the 144 wills is interesting in its own right, and the variation one can find is visible not only between different levels of wealth—the strata I have concentrated on in aggregate above—but between testators who in other respects seem rather similar. For example, the will of Berengaria, 'wife of Pierre Mercier' (the latter presumably deceased, given his absence otherwise in what follows), of Puigcerdà, made on 23 September 1297, displays strong individual choices, tinged with some deference to her three *manumissores*. She wished to be buried in the parish church in Puigcerdà, with 'all the priests' of the church present (to each she would pay 8d, which was the highest value frequently found—other testators might specify 7d or 6d), and she additionally provided 100 *sous* for an anniversary mass. But rather unusually she also gave money to the church of Saint-Martin in nearby Hix for there to be another separate mass 'for my soul and those of my forebears', calling for twenty-four priests to be present, each of whom would receive 7d. Her sister lived in Hix, and perhaps this was where she too had been born? Her pious gifts ranged widely, with a particular focus on the poor: 20 *sous* to the 'shamefaced poor' to be given at the notice of her *manumissores*, 20 *sous* to support poor women's marriages, 20 *sous* to be spent on bread to distribute to the poor on the obit of her death

---

[117] In considering the large variance of the very poor with regard to all pious (36%) and pro anima (72%), one should remember that some wills contained no 'pro anima' provision, whereas in others—particularly at the very poor end—the 'pro anima' provision covered all pious commitments.

(this not being at all a common provision in these particular wills). She set aside 30 *sous* for the 'restitution of my injuries [to others]', specifying however that if no such complaints appeared the sum was to be given also to the poor, in the form of clothing, at the notice of her *manumissores*. She gave 5 *sous* to the Brothers of Penitence, 10 *sous* to the Brothers Preacher, 4 *sous* to the Brothers Minor, sums ranging from 6d to 12d to seven different hospitals and local churches, and 12d to the candle that was carried before the body of Christ during processions in Puigcerdà. Two other notably individual pious bequests followed: 12d to help redeem Christian captives (that is, those captured by Muslim raiders elsewhere in the Mediterranean), and 12d to the money collected in Puigcerdà on the 'day of the Apparition of the Lord' (that is, 6 January, Epiphany). After all of that, she made just two small personal bequests, and otherwise left the residue of her estate to her sister.[118] The collective sums found in her will put her into the second to last category of my schema, as someone who was 'poor'. In Berengaria's case, however, this did not prevent her from donating to all three mendicant orders, and from fashioning her own particular choices regarding pious legacy and memorial masses.

In contrast, we find wills with very limited pious concerns, demonstrating a different kind of testamentary choice. G[uillaume] Mascala from Sant-Martí-d'Aravo (2 km west of Puigcerdà), who appears also to be a very poor testator, in his very brief will of 2 January 1294 simply asked to be buried in the cemetery of the newly arrived Brothers Preacher, giving them 20 *sous*, otherwise leaving 6d to his own parish church, and assigning his son and his wife as his heirs.[119] It is hard to tell whether this indicates a particularly devotional distribution of wealth or not, as we do not know the size of the residue of his estate; it is, at any rate, succinct and focused. At what was probably the other end of the social scale, the will made on 5 February 1298 by Pierre Mabant, a rich merchant with seven daughters, similarly requests that he be buried with the Brothers Preacher, donating 50 *sous* 'to their table' (a standard formulation) and 100 *sous* to the costs of burial, with any residue from the latter amount to be used 'for my soul at the notice of my *manumissores*'. That, however, is the sum total of his pious provision: the rest of his quite lengthy will concerns complex matters of personal bequests and inheritance, particularly around the 700 *sous* dowry that his wife had brought to the marriage, and various gifts to his daughters.[120] One cannot help but wonder whether Pierre Mabant was whom the Sack Friar had in mind when compiling the *exemplum* with which we began.

---

[118] AD P-O 7J41, fol. 14r.
[119] AD P-O 7J40, fol. 21v; the will is not cancelled but does appear to be complete.
[120] AD P-O 7J41, fols 24r-25r. The will of Bernard de Puy of Puigcerdà (same document, fol. 5v) provides an example of a very rich testator who makes absolutely no specific pious provision other than setting aside 500 *sous* 'pro anima', leaving the detail up to his *manumissores*.

There are various further details that we can glean from across the corpus, that speak both to the idiosyncrasies of people's personal circumstances and their individual choices: Marchesia den Ladier of Osséja, who left 'a white ass' in recompense for the priests she hoped would attend her funeral; the widow Elissendis, sister to a Brother Preacher and thus with a good connection to that order, who nonetheless wished to be buried in her own parish church in Saga (just to the south-west of Puigcerdà) and who left money to go toward a chalice for it; Pierre Dugame of Puigcerdà, another very rich merchant, who left books to his son, a cleric (though *what* books he frustratingly does not say), and specified the considerable sum of 500 *sous* 'pro anima' but, like some others, left the details of pious provision up to his *manumissores* to decide; Arnaud Gris of Puigcerdà, who accompanied his bequest to his wife with the requirement that she 'live chastely' after his death; Jean Casther, fantastically rich, who left a silver jug for the priest to use during mass, and 4,000 *sous* in alms, with the instruction, among other things, that the money should be used to save any relative of his from future poverty.[121]

One further external development strongly inflects many of the wills from the final chronological tranche, those made in 1309-10. This was the decision by Pope Clement V to grant a plenary indulgence in support of the siege of Almería in 1309, at the request of Jaume II of Aragon.[122] The possibility of the indulgence swept through the subsequent wills like a sudden wave. In the language of the preamble of one, that of a weaver called G[uillaume] Traper, written on 1 October 1309: 'wishing to go to Granada to profit from the indulgence of punishment and guilt conceded by the Lord Pope…'. Others associated themselves more with the possibility of the fight: 'Wishing to go to the land of Granada against the Saracens, infidels to Our Lord Jesus Christ…'.[123] The vast majority were men, prompted to make their will—and for obvious reasons not specifying a place of burial—by the fact that they were about to head south. Twenty-two wills were produced in this context, as well as two codicils made by men from Foix, en route to Spain, who wanted to add to wills they had already drafted at home (these latter are excluded from my various calculations above). There were also at least two women who also decided to go to Granada to gain the indulgence, and others who included a pious donation to support those who went, hoping that some of the indulgence from sin might thus accrue also to them.[124] For some of those making this choice, their wills include further pious donations, for memorial masses and to various

---

[121] AD P-O 7J40, fol. 19r; 7J41, fols 6r, 25r; 7J42, fols 16v-17r, 17v.

[122] N. J. Housley, 'Pope Clement V and the Crusades of 1309-10', *Journal of Medieval History* 8 (1982), 29-43.

[123] AD P-O 7J42, fols 26v, 22v.

[124] Women going to Granada: AD P-O 7J42, fols 27v, 36v, and possibly 34v (though this testator also specifies that she wishes to be buried in the Brothers Preacher); supporting those going: fols 21r, 21v, 58r.

charitable causes; but in some cases, such as an apparently very poor man from Puigcerdà called P[ierre] Castells, he simply left three personal bequests, and the instruction that any 'residue' should go on 'pro anima' expenditure, as decided by his *manumissores*.[125] For Castells, the decision to go on crusade looks close to an all-or-nothing bid for spiritual redemption; for others, it sits within a wider realm of pious choices.

All of these people and more were making choices, always in some negotiation however with their personal resources, their wider social connections, the expectations of those around them, and, as we have just seen, wider currents of spiritual possibility within the Christianity of their region. And this point can be extended to a whole range of other activities, beyond the rather specific moment of testamentary production: being Christian, in a whole variety of ways—engaging in collective worship, dealing with the local priest, planning for one's future in this life and the next—involved activities common to all, but pursued and experienced in socially differentiated ways. Neither uniformly 'communal' nor purely 'individual', the conduct of one's faith was always in some fashion something negotiated between demands, resources, and one's own spiritual desires.

---

[125] AD P-O 7J42, fol. 32r.

10
Being Christian

On 25 June 1323 Pierre Maury, a shepherd from the small village of Montaillou high in the Pyrenees, was led into the upper chamber of the episcopal house in Pamiers. Touching the four Gospels, he swore an oath to tell the full and simple truth about himself and about others, both living and dead, relating to the crime of heresy and 'all other things touching upon the office and business of inquisition into heretical wickedness'. He was about 41 years old.

You may have heard of Pierre before, as he figures prominently in Emmanuel Le Roy Ladurie's classic work of microhistory, *Montaillou*. Pierre was converted to the dualist faith of the Good Men by the notary Pierre Autier (who had recently returned from Lombardy). He was friend to the somewhat immoral 'Good Man' Guillaume Bélibaste, and was latterly a fugitive from the inquisitors, fleeing through Aragon to Mallorca, before returning to the town of Flix (halfway between Tortosa and Lleida) where he was captured thanks to an inquisitorial spy called Arnaud Sicre. He was questioned briefly by the Aragonese inquisitor before being handed back to the inquisitor of Carcassonne who, together with Jacques Fournier, bishop of Pamiers, conducted a much more lengthy interrogation. His deposition, written in a small, neat script, covers twenty-seven double-columned folios in the fair copy made of Fournier's inquisitorial investigations, now surviving in the Vatican Library; 142 pages in the modern print edition by Jean Duvernoy.[1] It is, I think, the lengthiest of the surviving depositions.

In this final chapter, with the help of Pierre's evidence, alongside that of other witnesses and additional material, I want to explore what it meant to 'be Christian' at an individual level, in the later thirteenth and early fourteenth centuries. What did it mean, that is, in terms of the practices of life, bodily comportment, personal actions? And what did it mean in terms of inner disposition, internal reflection and cognition, 'belief'? These are difficult questions to answer for any period, and any attempt is always necessarily something of a composite picture, indicating a range of possibilities. But it is worth the effort; and the extraordinary detail of the

---

[1] Vat. Lat. MS 4030, fols 247–74. The manuscript is now scanned online: <https://digi.vatlib.it/view/MSS_Vat.lat.4030> (accessed 12 Sept 2021). Edited in *Fournier* III, pp. 110–252. I will cite the Duvernoy edition, but have checked details against the manuscript itself. More narrative episodes from Pierre's life are found in Ladurie, *Montaillou*, particularly chapters 4–7. R. Weiss, *The Yellow Cross: The Story of the Last Cathars, c. 1290–1329* (London: Viking, 2000), whilst fanciful in some of its interpretations, provides a usefully detailed reconstruction of the timeline of particular events.

Fournier inquisition material allows us to shed some light on what would otherwise remain almost totally obscure.[2]

Was Pierre 'Christian', one might immediately ask, given his involvement in heresy? Undoubtedly yes: we must remember firstly that the heresy of the Good Men was still a *Christian* heresy, modelled on apostolic piety, despite its radical doctrinal departure from orthodoxy in various respects. Here, as elsewhere, the evidence generated by 'heresy' tells us much about orthodoxy also, both through what it specifically criticizes, and more subtly, through certain dynamics of faith and worship that are still shared between the opposing interpretations of Christianity. Pierre operated within a world that was, despite the presence of these last few Good Men, predominantly Catholic and orthodox, and his rich testimony also reveals a host of interesting details about that landscape. It is interesting, for example, just how many saints' days he noted in his evidence, largely as markers of time: not only really major dates such as Easter, Pentecost, Michaelmas, the feast of St John the Baptist ('when they say major mass in church') or the nativity of Mary, but the vigil of All Saints, the vigil of St André, and the feast of St Cyrice and St Julitte. Moreover, whilst Pierre himself was reckoned a 'great believer' in the heretics by his brother Jean, as we shall see his own perspective on his faith was rather more complex and fluid. In much of what follows, I shall use Pierre as a guide, elements within his testimony introducing us to a sequence of topics which we can then explore more widely. But at the end of the chapter, when we turn to the individual experience of belief and faith, Pierre himself will come to stand centre stage to have his say.

The Actions of a Lay Christian

The anthropologist Pierre Bourdieu, in his theoretical analysis of the practices of everyday life, proffers the influential concepts of *habitus*, the embodied practices that structure and value the world, and *doxa*, the conceptual regime that frames the world as just that which is, setting the requirements and limits to an embodied regime that is so engrained 'it goes without saying because it comes without saying'.[3] In a time and place where certain core Christian practices *were* in fact criticized by the Good Men, and where the contrasting practices of Jews and Muslims were also visible, we may need to shy back slightly from a very strong theory of *habitus*; a sense of active choice and collective participation may have

---

[2] In this chapter I am inspired in part by Alec Ryrie's *Being Protestant in Reformation England* (Oxford: Oxford University Press, 2013). The source base upon which Ryrie draws is in most respects rather richer than my own, and deals with a cultural subset of early modern Christianity; nonetheless, his focus on the individual human *detail* of religious experience and identity is inspiring.

[3] P. Bourdieu, *Outline of a Theory of Practice*, trans. R. Nice (Cambridge: Cambridge University Press, 1977), chapter 2 and p. 167.

been more present to the southern French laity than we might otherwise assume. Nonetheless, certain elements of 'being Christian' look to be deeply engrained, and almost inseparable from simply participating within one's local community. Other practices or actions may have come 'naturally' to some, but were in a sense how one knew oneself to be a *good* Christian; or, at least, were what one might present as evidence of one's 'good Christian' status if challenged by another. In short, the embodied and repetitive aspects of 'habitus' are undoubtedly useful to us, but probably need to be accompanied by recognition of some additional cognition, whether or not we see that cognitive element as fully present at all times to those undertaking such practices.

Let us think about some common but important deeds that lay people could perform. Take almsgiving, for example. The spiritual benefits of giving alms were something preached and specifically enjoined by priests and mendicants, but in a wider sense the practice of providing for others in a selfless fashion was engrained in society—not that everybody did it, but that everybody understood it when it was done. Pierre Maury gave alms frequently, something which the Good Man Bélibaste teased him about on one occasion, when Pierre gave 12d to a *questor* who was raising money for the hospital of Roncesvalles, suggesting that he would do better to spend his money on some fish for them both to eat.[4] Pierre also gave lambs to his six godchildren, and gave money to the Good Men; though on one occasion, having bought six other lambs, he refused Bélibaste's suggestion that Pierre should give three of them to the Good Man 'for the love of God'.[5] In that particular context, Bélibaste's attempt to garner 'alms' both exceeded the material amount that Pierre felt he could afford (given that it was central to his livelihood), and, perhaps as importantly, transgressed the dynamic of giving *freely*.

Questioned closely by Fournier, in the wider context of what the heretics had said about the power to absolve sins, Pierre had quite a lot to say about the social context of almsgiving, firstly as the Good Men presented it, and, a little later on, as he himself considered it:

> Regarding alms, in truth they [the Good Men] said that when believers gave alms to the said heretics, they gained great mercy [*that is, help toward future salvation*]; any other [non-believers] though, when they gave alms to them, did not receive great mercy from this. And he heard from Jacques Autier, heretic, that a man should give alms and do good to all, because from some men one would have mercy, just as from the heretics, and from others one would have grace. However, the said heretics induced their believers to give alms to all because, as they said, from this they gained a good reputation among neighbours, and because some had given thanks to them, and moreover because

---

[4] *Fournier* III, p. 238. [5] *Fournier* III, pp. 243, 166, 167.

a man does not know if anyone who is not a heretic or believer, to whom one gives alms, might later become a heretic or believer; and because of this one should do good to all men equally.[6]

And then, a little later, returning to the topic apparently by his own choice, Pierre emphasized his own perspective:

He frequently gave alms to anyone, when he could, although he more liberally and willingly gave alms to the said heretics, because he believed that giving alms to the heretics would have more merit than giving them to other people, because the said heretics gave him to understand this. In truth, oblations which were given in church were given no value by the said Guillaume Bélibaste, heretic.[7]

Yet such oblations were of course frequently given, including by Pierre himself.

Whilst the justifications for almsgiving by the Good Men were, clearly, inflected by the position of their heretical sect, both their comments and Pierre's on his own practices tell us something useful about almsgiving in general. It is not that everybody gave alms, not least because it was, for obvious reasons, affected by one's material circumstances (Pierre gave them 'when he could', as he said). But almsgiving had social recognition as a moral good, among 'neighbours'—part of being a good Christian—and 'alms' could involve support which was not specific to a particular pious cause, but could be giving done *for the good of giving*, not necessarily within a specifically ecclesiastical frame, nor with the direct promise of a reciprocal spiritual benefit.

There is a blurring here into a wider sense of charity, *caritas*, love for one's neighbour, as, for example, when Pierre mentioned in passing an occasion when his mother, Guillelme, gave shelter for the night to a passing stranger, a poor man, 'for the love of God'.[8] Similar actions turn up in some preaching *exempla*, presented as good examples but not formalized in the way that some kinds of almsgiving and oblations might be: a rich lady attending mass in wintertime noticed a poor neighbour and, 'seeing the woman afflicted [by the cold], moved by piety' took her quietly outside the church and gave the neighbour her fur coat.[9] Some poor people came to the house of a man from Auriac called Raimond, asking for alms, and he gave them bits of dough that his wife had been mixing up in a bowl to turn into bread. His wife—who was 'impious', and hardly ever gave anything to the poor—was extremely displeased when she found out; but miraculously the bowl refilled itself with dough.[10] To be clear, all of this was 'almsgiving',

---

[6] *Fournier* III, p. 230. [7] *Fournier* III, p. 232. [8] *Fournier* III, p. 189.
[9] BL MS Add. 60390, fols 3v–4r: 'Et videns mulierem multum afflictam pietate mota...pauperculam mulierem loco secrete extra ecclesiam aducebat et expoliavit se ipsa pellicio tradidit ipsum pauperi mulieri.'
[10] BL MS Add. 60390, fol. 42v; edited in Welter, 'Un recueil d'exempla', p. 212 (no. 203).

as the latter example makes explicit. But it was less structured and less transactional than some other forms of giving, for example less of an expectation than symbolic gifts made 'to the poor' that we saw in the wills discussed in the previous chapter. Other deeds—also figurable as 'alms'—were small contributions to collective worship, either materially or practically. One thinks here of a woman who swept and cleaned the parish church every single Sunday, 'for honour of the most Blessed Mother of God', as reported in one *exemplum*.[11] She was from the village of Lavérune, just outside Montpellier, and the local bishop thought her service exceptionally devout; but some degree of similar activity was extremely likely to be found in most if not all other parishes across the whole region. Another tale tells of a devout woman who was inspired by the Virgin Mary to bake bread, just at the point that it was needed in the church of the Sack Friars in Marseille, who had begun a mass without realizing they lacked any bread to distribute as blessed bread at the end of the service.[12] The miraculous element is particular to the story, but the fact of women providing bread probably is not. Pierre, reporting a conversation he had had before the Autiers reappeared in the region, told a friend that he was planning to make lambswool veils for the statues of St Antoine and the Blessed Mary in the church in Montaillou (presumably to veil them for Lent)—another kind of personal act of devotion and giving that also had a wider social recognition.[13] Many of these actions only very rarely enter the written record—and yet must have constituted a fairly common element in what 'being Christian' involved.

Let us think about a few other kinds of activity that, if not exactly 'involuntary', were at least fairly automatic. Some are obvious, but still worth consideration: regular attendance at church, for example. Despite his enthusiasm for the Good Men, Pierre still attended church. In the process of recounting his 'conversion' by Jacques Autier, he talks of the sermons he had heard from priests in church, and of a Brother Minor whose preaching he had just recently heard. On another occasion he mentions in passing that during his travels he and another supporter of the heretics 'went to the church of Arques where they heard mass'.[14] There is no sense that this was done in order to conceal their heretical involvement, as it was not their own parish church but in a village about 20 km south-east of Limoux, more than 50 km from his home in Montaillou. Going to hear mass was just a thing that you did, as a Christian, and it was something you had an expectation of being able to do in places beyond your home parish. As we saw in Chapter 9, it was not necessarily a thing that everyone did on every occasion that they ought— but attendance was, unsurprisingly, part of the normal rhythm of life.

---

[11] Welter, 'Un nouveau recueil franciscain d'exempla', pp. 619–20 (no. 206).
[12] Welter, 'Un recueil d'exempla', p. 658 (no. 21).
[13] *Fournier* III, p. 120.   [14] *Fournier* III, pp. 123, 136.

Sometimes attendance at a particular church could also bespeak a greater enthusiasm: when travelling in Catalonia, Pierre wanted to go and visit 'the church of the Blessed Mary of Montserrat' (namely the Benedictine abbey there, home to a famous image of the Virgin).[15] We can glimpse other people making similar proactive choices in other evidence. For example, when contributing to the evidence for the post-mortem miracles performed by Louis of Toulouse, a widow called Gauffrida Rossa, about 40 years old, explained that she and her relative Beatrice Brune decided to make a 'pilgrimage' to the church of Saint-Michel of Marseille (this 'pilgrimage' being very local, as they both lived close by). And moreover, 'as they entered the city of Marseille, the said Beatrice said that she wanted to visit the church of the Brothers Minor and the tomb of the blessed Louis, who cured her daughter of a certain disease which for a long time and many years she had had in her shins, and to offer a candle'.[16] A mother planned a trip to the shrine of Marie Madeleine in Saint-Maximin, and her son—who was disabled by 'gout'—told her that 'from devotion' he wished to go with her. she was happy for him to come, but they needed an animal to help carry him there and, by implication, could not afford such a thing. The son prayed to Marie Madeleine for help, and was in fact immediately cured; in thanks, he instituted his own annual pilgrimage on foot to her shrine.[17] As with almsgiving, things done 'normally', more or less by rote, could also be done through personal choice and with more pious agency.

There are also some other actions which were, once again, expected of all Christians, but which occurred rather less regularly. One was paying tithes, a topic we have encountered periodically throughout this book. Tithing is most 'visible' to us when it generates conflict, and whilst the fact of that conflict should not be ignored, it is an imperfect guide to what the experience of rendering tithes was like for most Christians in ordinary circumstances. Where conflict broke out, as with the *carnalages* on lambs imposed by Fournier, as we have seen the frames of understanding were the entwined and notionally reciprocal authorities of (ecclesiastical) lordship and custom. Whilst claims of 'custom' should not be read naively as a statement of historical fact, they provide nonetheless a sense of how tithing might normally be understood and experienced, as something performed in a tradition that stretched back through families and communities. The lived experience of this could vary considerably, depending on period and circumstance. Pierre Maury himself asserted that, whilst the Good Men always said that there was no value in paying tithes to clerics or churches, he himself 'always believed that it was good to pay the first and tenths, and moreover to pay to churches, as he said, and he would have it on his conscience (*habuisset*

---

[15] *Fournier* III, p. 234. [16] Bughetti, *Processus*, pp. 236–37.
[17] Jean Gobi, *Miracles*, pp. 120–21 (no. 41bis).

conscienciam) if he retained them'.[18] Given how peripatetic his life as a shepherd was, it is not clear what 'giving' or 'retaining' them would mean in actual practice, but the sense of duty and conscience is clear. (Here, as elsewhere, there is no very strong reason to suppose that Pierre was saying things only to try to please the bishop—he was already in such a huge amount of trouble for his admitted contacts with and support for the heretics that it would have made very little difference). In some of the quasi-contractual 'agreements' drawn up with priests that we saw in Chapter 9, it is clear that having parishioners deliver their tithes—when they were being paid in actual goods rather than in cash—was a boon to the priest, and one can imagine that rendering tithes thus became part of the rhythm of harvest time. But it may sometimes have been experienced in a more 'taxational' way, as something assessed and exacted. In the 1410 inquiry into the previous decades regarding the church of Saint-Jacques in Montauban, one of the witnesses, Master Arnaud du Carla, gave evidence that his father Durand, also a notary, had for many years been the person who 'levied' the tithes for the parish church of Saint-Jacques, on behalf of the priest.[19] Another witness, Jean de *Garerus*, more than 60 years old, attested that at an earlier period, for around a decade, he had been the *decimarius*, deputed to collect tithes by the monks of the cathedral church (Saint-Étienne-de-Tescou) in Montauban, which meant that he saw who 'laboured' in their parish.[20] It therefore seems quite likely that 'tithing' in a civic context was probably experienced rather differently from in a more rural setting.

Attending church, hearing sermons, paying tithes—there is one more regular duty of all Christians, as we have seen from earlier chapters: making confession. Pierre did this also, despite his allegiance to the Good Men. The inquisitorial spy Arnaud Sicre alleged that Pierre had told him that believers in the Good Men simply feigned confession to priests, in order to be reputed good Christians.[21] Pierre's account of his own practices was, characteristically, a bit more complex. He told Fournier that he thought that the orthodox clergy, from the pope to the parish priest, could absolve men from their sins, although he also thought that the Good Men could do this better, because 'they better held the path to God'. And because of this:

> as he said, each year he confessed his other sins, but not those that he committed in heresy, because he did not believe that he sinned in those things. And the

---

[18] *Fournier* III, p. 250.
[19] AD T-et-G, G1161, fol. 31r-v: 'quod magister Durandus de Castellario notarius quondam Montis Albani, eiusdem testis pater, qui decessit ut eidem testi videtur viginti tres anni fuit elapsi seu ultra, quiquidem Magister Durandus pater suis... per plures annos levavit primicias pertinentes parochiali ecclesie sancti Jacobi montisalbani'.
[20] AD T-et-G, G1161, fol. 54r-v: 'ipse testis fuit decimarius deputatus per dominos monachos ecclesie cathedralis Montisalbani, et ex post vidit quod illi qui laborabant et laboraverant ac laborare fecerant in tota parrochia dicti ecclesie sancti Stephani Tesconis Montisalbani... solvebantur primiciam rectori ecclesie sancti Stephani Tesconis Montisalbani seu altari eius'.
[21] *Fournier* II, p. 38.

heretics moreover persuaded the believers that they should go to the Roman Church and confess their sins and do the other things which the Catholic faithful are accustomed to do, so that it would seem that they were faithful Catholics. But however he [Pierre] did not take communion from the time when he began to be a believer in the heretics, even though he had heard from the heretics that believers could take communion, because it was just the same as if they ate a morsel of bread or drank a mouthful of wine... And, as he said, when he confessed to priests... he believed himself to be absolved of those sins of which he had made confession, and he refused to accept the body [of Christ, *that is, to take communion*] because he had heard from priests that if one who was in sin took communion, he would do better to take a burning hot coal into his mouth.[22]

Whether or not we completely believe Pierre on his past actions, he clearly enunciates an interesting betwixt-and-between perspective on the management of sin, and reports the charged power that confession and Easter communion might have for the laity more generally. Making confession was, as we have seen in an earlier chapter, something which southern French priests were required to monitor, precisely to search out heresy; and attendance at confession was something that perhaps further signalled to one's neighbours not only that you were 'orthodox' but that you were part of the community.

This last point applies particularly to one other specifically lay Christian practice, close to Pierre's heart: godparenthood. As one would expect, we saw that this was a feature in the Puigcerdà wills examined in Chapter 9, though not perhaps quite as common as one might expect: out of 144 testators, 18 (7 women, 11 men) mentioned bequests to godchildren in their legacies. Pierre Maury loved the practice of godparenthood, mentioning in his deposition one of his godfathers and, as noted above, his own godchildren. It was a point of some contention between him and the Good Men. Bélibaste chided him:

'You make many godfathers and godmothers and baptize children, and expend your goods on such deeds, and however such baptism and godparenthood has no value, except only the degree of friendship it brings about between people; and it's obvious that you do not understand the words that we are saying'; to which he [Pierre] replied that he had saved up his things, and could thus spend them as he wished, and he wasn't going to leave off doing this for him or for anyone else, because he gained great friendship through it.[23]

They had the same argument again at another point, when staying at Flix with his godfather Pons Ortolan, Pierre on that occasion emphasizing that he wanted to benefit both 'the one and the other' (meaning orthodoxy and the heretics) with

[22] *Fournier* III, p. 231. [23] *Fournier* III, p. 185.

what he had saved from his labour, 'because he did not know which faith was more efficacious, although he adhered more to the faith of the heretics, as he conversed more, and more frequently, with heretics than with others'.[24] Kinship connections mattered greatly to him, and could be forged through orthodox ritual. Kinship also ultimately overrode other spiritual considerations: asked by Fournier about the Good Men's rejection of the ties of consanguinity, Pierre asserted that he never believed what they had to say about that, and that 'nor, as he said, did he love strangers who were believers as much as he loved his relatives who were not believers in the heretics'.[25] With godparenthood, as perhaps with almsgiving, social bonds and Christian culture strongly entwine, but—and this is rather crucial—without necessarily requiring a specific doctrinal proposition to be embraced consciously en route. In moments of enforced reflection—as when challenged by a Good Man with his own agenda, or by the inquisitorial questions of a bishop—one might formulate a wider justification that was partly theological and partly social. But outwith those contexts, they were things that you did; not quite 'habitus', but not simply a logical playing out of doctrine either.

Lay Christian Embodiment

There is a well-developed area of analysis around 'the body' and medieval Christianity, focused on the tensions between sinful embodiment and the future salvation of the soul, and reflecting on the ways in which the incarnation of Christ resonated, both spiritually and culturally. The heretical theology of the Good Men presented an even more radical separation between body and soul, as all material matter was associated with evil creation, the process of salvation being an attempt to release the pure soul from its prison; Pierre was told elements of this by Pierre Autier and Guillaume Bélibaste, though it is unclear how prominently it was made present to ordinary lay believers in earlier decades. For Christian orthodoxy and its struggles with body, important work has often focused on the spiritually elite and extreme in these areas: women undertaking extreme fasting, transcendent mystics, holy virgins, and the like. But elements of these issues were woven through all Christian culture, affecting the ordinary laity to some extent also. We met an element of this in Chapter 8, when noting the way in which sins associated with the bodily senses formed one strand of penitential discourse, and in the moral concerns regulating sexual activity.

There is some evidence for the occasional ordinary layperson being beset by some of the charged concerns over the sinfulness of the body: a woman called Aude Fauré fell into disbelief in the presence of Christ in the Eucharist having

[24] *Fournier* III, p. 209.   [25] *Fournier* III, p. 242.

been deeply troubled by thoughts of the 'uncleanliness' that women produce during birth, and how the Lord's body would have been 'infected' by it, as she confessed to Bishop Fournier.[26] But that degree of struggle was unusual. Whilst I shall return further below to some other thoughts which ordinary people had about Christ's incarnation, and ways in which they were confronted by the sinfulness of particular bodies, my initial focus is on a rather less fraught kind of embodiment, namely aspects of bodily comportment and gestures of lay Christians.

Let us think first about bowing and kneeling. These are parts of a repertoire of gesture that is found throughout medieval society, familiar from various courtly and secular ritual contexts, for example.[27] Much modern analysis of these actions focuses on particular moments of petition or ritual performance, the bodily self-abasement used as a means by which another person's superiority is acknowledged, that acknowledgement displayed in the hope of gaining some boon, or in recognition of what has already been granted. There are of course strong parallels for such moments in a spiritual setting also, as when someone falls to their knees to petition God or a particular saint for intervention. For example, Katherina Balasteria, a 40-year-old widow, successfully sought aid from St Louis of Toulouse to resuscitate her 6-year-old niece who had died of a fever: 'the witness cried out, on bended knees invoking and saying "O blessed Louis, return this girl to us, and I promise that I shall carry her to your tomb with a candle of her length!"'[28] According to one *exemplum*, a woman from Fleucher (near Montpellier), beaten by her wayward daughter, dropped to her knees and joined her hands, imploring God and his Mother to give her justice against her child.[29] One might pay reverence to particularly important ecclesiastical figures, where it is perhaps impossible to separate out the spiritual and social aspects of their superiority. Arnaud Gélis, the man who claimed to see ghosts, related to Bishop Fournier how he had gone to morning mass in the cathedral church of Saint-Antonin in Pamiers and then saw, standing where he had been buried, the dead Bishop Bernard, who was (he noted) wearing a white mitre on his head. 'Which, when he saw him, he bent his knees before him, saying to him that the grace of God should be with him,

---

[26] *Fournier* II, pp. 82–105; for an astute close reading, see W. L. Anderson, 'The Real Presence of Mary: Eucharistic Disbelief and the Limits of Orthodoxy in Fourteenth-Century France', *Church History* 75 (2006), 748–67.

[27] See J.-C. Schmitt, *La raison des gestes dans l'Occident médiéval* (Paris: Gallimard, 1990), chapter 8; J. A. Burrow, *Gestures and Looks in Medieval Narrative* (Cambridge: Cambridge University Press, 2002), chapter 2.

[28] Bughetti, *Processus*, p. 133. Her surname there given as Albarestyevia; in correcting to Balasteria, I follow P. A. Sigal, 'L'anthroponymie féminine en Provence d'après Le livre des Miracles et le procès de canonisation de Saint Louis d'Anjou (fin xiiième–début xvième siècle)', in M. Bourin and P. Charelle, eds, *Genèse médiévale de l'anthroponymie modern, II-2: persistances du nom unique* (Tours: Presses universitaires François-Rabelais, 1992), pp. 187–205.

[29] Welther, 'Un nouveau recueil franciscain d'exempla', p. 621 (no. 209). Welther supplies the place name; I cannot locate it myself.

and may God grant him Paradise'.[30] This was not the first apparition that Arnaud had experienced, as he had met a couple of deceased cathedral canons also—but he had not knelt before them, presumably because they did not have quite the same status. As we have seen in earlier chapters, the Good Men themselves taught their believers a ritual that combined reverence and petition, which they called 'betterment' (*melioramentum*) and which inquisitors labelled 'adoration'. Pierre describes being taught it: 'at the mandate and instruction of the aforesaid Pierre Autier, he bent his knees and adored, saying these words, as he had instructed him: "Good Christian, the blessing of God and of you", and the aforesaid Pierre Autier responded "You have it from God and from us". And then the aforesaid Pierre Autier embraced [him].'[31] Here the combination of specific pious petition and kneeling does look rather more formal, as with Gélis's encounter with the dead bishop. The point in any case is that, heretical or otherwise, it draws from the same familiar gestural resources as wider Christian culture.

The preceding examples all involve a conscious moment of petition, even if only a generalized petition for God's blessings for oneself or for another. But there are other regular contexts in which bowing or kneeling was perhaps less of a specific decision, and more part of a familiar flow of embodied worship. I am thinking here particularly about the reverence paid to the altar or the Eucharist or the Virgin Mary. Pierre Maury, questioned by the bishop inquisitor on the topic, said that he had seen Bélibaste feigning the usual reverence to the host, 'bending his knees and bowing his head when the body of Christ was elevated in church'.[32] Here, as elsewhere, what is normal and regular is made visible to us in moments of heretical resistance; as with the example we previously met in Chapter 6, where two men working the fields stopped and prayed 'with joined hands' when they heard the bell rung to announce the consecration of the host, their employer then deriding their 'credulity'.[33] An *exemplum* similarly makes normal conduct visible, this time from the perspective of extreme orthodoxy: a very pious lay woman, who mortified her flesh with a hidden belt and by beating herself with a rod when she could, visited various saints' shrines, and then came to the church of Sainte-Marie in Montpellier. She heard the first mass, and then when staying for the second mass became so piously intent on the body of Christ at the prospect of the elevation of the host that 'all around prostrating themselves, she, ardent with love for the Son, could neither bow nor remain stood appropriately'. Thus frozen, she directed her thoughts to Mary; and 'trying to see therefore if she could genuflect, she bent one leg to free it, and trying the other found she was cured', and was then able to join in with the others.[34]

That is a story of extreme piety temporarily preventing bodily conformity. But other tales make apparent how the same regular gestures and postures could also

---

[30] *Fournier* I, p. 130.   [31] *Fournier* III, p. 111.
[32] *Fournier* III, pp. 235–36.   [33] Doat 25, fol. 237r.
[34] Welther, 'Un nouveau recueil franciscain d'exempla', p. 623 (no. 215).

be used to foster deep pious contemplation. Another *exemplum* from the same collection tells of a knight from Cahors who was being courted by the Brothers Minor to join their order. The knight was 'prostrate before the altar in prayer'.[35] A witness to the personal piety of St Louis of Toulouse tells of how he was often found 'prostrate in the chapel, on the ground with his arms extended in the manner of a cross'.[36] People might adopt a similar posture when imploring aid from a saint, as is related a couple of times in the miracles of Marie Madeleine, including again someone lying in the shape of a cross.[37]

Signing the cross by gesturing, rather than with one's whole body, was of course a common action. It was explicitly *taught* to the laity, as we saw from a fourteenth-century synodal in Chapter 7, and was potentially to be accompanied by the words 'in nomine Patris et Filii et Spiritus sancti', as Pierre recalled, when recounting one of the Good Men's dismissal of how this made out that there were 'three Gods'. He remembered another occasion when he was at a certain spring and wanted to drink the water, so made the sign of the cross over it (implicitly to 'purify it', though he does not make this explicit); Bélibaste teased him for doing so.[38] An *exemplum* tells of another person mocked for signing the cross for protection, a woman who was crossing a river near Narbonne in a boat along with various ill-behaved youths. She made the sign of the cross as she got in, prompting them to deride her: 'You see demons, you see demons, that's why you signed.' (They subsequently drowned, the woman was left unharmed, and a vision of the cross appeared in the air.)[39] Other tales tell of the efficacy of signing the cross: protection from drowning, protection from lascivious desire.[40] These give us a useful way of thinking about the bodily performance of Christian identity: a set of regular gestures and postures that much of the time work passively, undertaken in comfortable familiarity, but which on occasion could be activated with more intensity, to perform greater piety or to petition for greater protection from the Lord.

There are two highly overlapping but nonetheless distinguishable dispositions here. One is gesture as part of Christian *identity*, where its very availability for performance is a form of 'habitus'; gestures of genuflection and signing that are part of a Christian repertoire, a 'natural' mode of acting (even if sometimes mocked or disparaged). The other is gesture as a mode of enacting intensified Christian *piety*, a reaching out to Christ and the saints through a combination of embodied action and inner emotional disposition. This latter is potentially also available to all—though in practice is perhaps experienced only rarely, in

---

[35] Welther, 'Un nouveau recueil franciscain d'exempla', p. 624 (no. 217). The story goes on to tell that a bolt of lightning blew the soles off the knight's shoes, without harming his feet.
[36] Bughetti, ed., *Processus*, p. 34.   [37] Jean Gobi, *Miracles*, pp. 142–43 (nos 58, 59).
[38] *Fournier* III, pp. 217, 226.
[39] Welther, 'Un nouveau recueil franciscain d'exempla', p. 467 (no. 94).
[40] Welther, 'Un nouveau recueil franciscain d'exempla', p. 468 (nos 97, 99).

situations of particular need, or by more unusual individuals like the self-mortifying woman in the church in Montpellier.

Other elements of embodied Christianity have this same dual potential. Consider diet and fasting. Pierre Maury told Bishop Fournier, when setting out the orthodox practices which he did follow despite his heretical friends, that among other things 'he fasted on Fridays and some other days in Lent... he fasted, as he said, believing that by this he made satisfaction for his sins'.[41] 'Fasting' primarily meant avoiding meat and fatty foods, and was in fact extremely similar to the ascetic practices of the Good Men. Pierre noted that around Easter he once met up for a meal with various lay people who supported the Good Men (including, he claimed, a man who was the procurator of the archbishop of Narbonne); and he noted, probably questioned on this specifically by the inquisitor, that 'they ate meat and milk and cheese', by implication in defiance of normal orthodox expectation.[42] However, he also told Fournier that 'he often ate mutton fat and pork fat on Fridays, and, as he said, it was customary to do this in Cerdanya [*the region around Puigcerdà*], and he did not believe that it was sinful to do this'.[43] What 'fasting' implied was thus, perhaps unsurprisingly, something which the laity tended to negotiate to some extent. Nor did the precise requirements of fasting settle down until some point in the fourteenth century: the synodal of Sisteron from the earlier thirteenth century had, for example, enjoined priests to instruct the laity to abstain from meat on Wednesdays and Saturdays, whilst that of Carcassonne from c. 1270 specifies Lent 'and other customary times'.[44]

So some form of fasting, particularly around Lent and particularly in the sense of limiting one's diet, was another familiar aspect of Christian behaviour—not necessarily always obeyed, but recognizably part of what one *ought* to do, and how one knew oneself to 'be Christian'. But it could also be something undertaken more rigorously, as a form of penance and piety, whether enjoined upon one by a confessor or embraced spontaneously. The wicked daughter from Fleucher who had beaten her mother, noted above, was miraculously punished by severe bodily contractions. Carried to church, her sins publicly confessed, the priest there enjoined penance upon her, that she should fast on nothing but bread and water for seven days, and abstain from meat on all Saturdays.[45] Inquisitors could impose sustained periods of fasting on penitents, both for those who had

---

[41] *Fournier* III, p. 231.
[42] *Fournier* III, p. 139. Elsewhere he notes that another man, Arnaud Bailli, 'ate eggs, although it was Lent' (p. 209), and that two men of Limoux 'ate meat... with fried eggs on a certain Friday' (pp. 248–49).
[43] *Fournier* III, p. 249.
[44] Synodal of Sisteron (c. 1225 × 35), c. 85; synodal of Carcassonne (c. 1270), c. XII.3. Injunctions about lay fasting do not occur much in the surviving synodal evidence; it is slightly more frequently the case, in fact, that the clergy were told additionally to avoid meat on Saturdays, unless there were special circumstances (see, for example, Narbonne 1240, c. 32; Carcassonne c. 1270, c. XII.2; Mende 1292-95, c. I.3; Béziers 1351, c.7).
[45] Welther, 'Un nouveau recueil franciscain d'exempla', p. 621 (no. 209).

relatively light penances and in some cases for those sentenced to 'hard' imprisonment. These are imposed penances, but the spiritual benefits of additional fasting could also be embraced more spontaneously. A rather extraordinary man from Saint-Paul-de-Fenouillet (c. 50 km north-west of Perpignan) called Limoux Nègre, who had developed an idiosyncratically personal theology and subsequently found himself in trouble with the inquisitors in 1326, explained how when he was just 11 years old and first made confession to his parish priest, he thought about Christ having fasted for forty days and forty nights in the desert, and consequently took himself off to a lonely place in the Pyrenees to do likewise; though in fact hunger drove him back to find something to eat after just ten days.[46]

We are here approaching practices of more extreme bodily control or bodily negation, undertaken by the few rather than the many. The point is that for most people, most of the time, that kind of attempted somatic transcendence was not what these practices implied. They were, rather, a repertoire of gesture, deportment, and action, the knowledge and performance of which were part of what constituted a lived Christian identity. Knowing how to genuflect, how to sign the cross, how to eat on Fridays and in Lent, were akin to knowing the *Pater noster* and *Ave Maria*, part of the rhythm and fabric of life. Hugues Lambert, another witness to St Louis of Toulouse's sanctity, described how, discovering their young child apparently dead, he and his wife called out to Louis to save him, whilst the child 'stayed dead for such a period that night, as he said, that he could have said the *Pater noster* twenty times, namely the entire Lord's Prayer'.[47] To be clear, Hugues was not using the *Pater noster* as a petition, but taking its performance as a means of measuring time; here we approach something like Bourdieu's sense of *habitus*. Pierre Maury helps us further here once again. Talking with the Good Man Pierre Autier, he cavilled at the heretical injunction that only the Good Men, and not ordinary lay people, could say the prayer to God. 'And if we cannot pray to God, what shall we do?' Pierre asked. 'We should be just like beasts!'[48] At a later point, responding to a question from Bishop Fournier on what the Good Men said about the nature of God, Pierre reiterated their belief that only they could say the *Pater noster* prayer; 'He, however, did not believe the said heretics about the aforesaid, as he said, but rather, as he said, often said the *Pater noster*.'[49] To do otherwise would be to lose one's humanity; saying the Lord's prayer was, in that sense, a natural and essential act, over and above any specific pious meaning or intent it might sometimes be given.

---

[46] Doat 27, fol. 223v; on Nègre, see L. A. Burnham, 'Unusual Choices: The Unique Heresy of Limoux Negre', in M. D. Bailey and S. L. Field, eds, *Late Medieval Heresy: New Perspectives* (York: York Medieval Press, 2018), pp. 96–115 and a larger forthcoming study she is currently completing.
[47] Bughetti, ed., *Processus*, p. 138.   [48] *Fournier* III, p. 126.
[49] *Fournier* III, p. 218. The scribe's double use of 'ut dixit' ('as he said') rather suggests that the inquisitor was doubtful; but Pierre was in any case asserting what he thought it was *normal* for a Christian to do.

The actions and bodily practices discussed thus far applied to all Christians (or at least, all over a certain age, from when they were tutored in the faith). But some aspects of behaviour were notably marked by gender. Pierre attested, in response to another question by Fournier, that the Good Men had told him that the souls of men and women were identical, and 'when the soul of a man or a woman departed from their flesh, they had no difference between them', which he believed also.[50] But he knew all too well that the lives of women and men were different in this life. Pierre's sister was stuck in an abusive marriage, and prompted by the Good Man Philippe d'Alayrac he attempted to help her to escape it by leading her away from her home in Laroque-d'Olmes. The Good Men planned that she could come and serve them 'so that she would not wander through the world like a whore'. 'But if some of her husband's relatives should follow us, what should we do?' asked Pierre. 'Tell them that you and she are going on pilgrimage or to Rome', advised Philippe.[51] These would be legitimate reasons for a woman to go on a journey, to 'wander'; but otherwise not. Even then, it might not be safe: Bérenger Frédol strongly warned priests against enjoining pilgrimages as penances on young women because of the danger involved. Instead, he said, 'enjoin many more prayers on women than on men...and if you cannot induce them to say them every day, at least get them to say them on feast days; and to say them twenty times a day on working days'.[52] A late thirteenth-century Occitan poem of advice to a young woman proscribes her behaviour when out in public and in the church, in a fashion familiar from other later medieval texts elsewhere in Europe: 'Regarding your gaze, I order you, when in church for a service and to hear mass, that you know to keep your eyes from glancing around foolishly, and instead lowered or toward the altar, if you can manage it. And do not strike up conversation or discussion there.'[53] It is notable that a parallel poem by the same author, directed toward men, has no such injunction. There could be expectations around women's behaviour even when giving birth: a woman called Bezersa was reported to the inquisitors in part because during labour she had not cried out to the Virgin Mary as expected, but to the Holy Spirit. She was accused also of failing to fast when expected, and refused the blessed bread distributed in church at the end of mass; whether or not her behaviour came from a personal lack of orthodoxy, the accusations speak to the existence of the norm.[54]

---

[50] *Fournier* III, p. 223.   [51] *Fournier* III, pp. 149, 151.

[52] BM Toulouse MS 191, fol. 78r: 'Item caveat sacerdos ne iniungat peregrinationem mulieri iuveni quia periculum est. Item iniungat mulieribus orationes plures quam viris...et si non possunt induci ad dicendum omni die saltem dicant diebus festivis et quod dicant xx vicibus diebus quibus laborant.'

[53] M. D. Johnston, 'The Occitan *Enssenhamen de l'Escudier* and *Essenhamen de la Donzela* of Amanieu de Sescás', in M. D. Johnston, ed., *Medieval Conduct Literature: An Anthology of Vernacular Guides to Behaviour for Youths with English Translations* (Toronto: Medieval Academy, 2009), pp. 23–60, at p. 46 (ll. 200–09).

[54] Doat 25, fols 60r, 62v, 165v (ed. *Inquisitors and Heretics*, pp. 308, 312, 516). A man was similarly noted for crying out, when ill in bed, 'Holy Spirit, aid me!': Doat 26, fol. 10v (*Inquisitors and Heretics*, p. 856).

All of this is of course about gendered expectations in society generally, rather than simply piety. But it should be noted that expectations about women's bodily deportment and conduct were a feature in the preaching *exempla* of the thirteenth century and thereafter; women's embodiment was a focus for a particular sense of Christian selfhood, notably for the relation between interior essence and exterior appearance. In Chapter 8, I mentioned some stories which focused on female make-up as a sign of potential moral failure. Here is another tale, taken from a Sack Friar collection. It is worth providing in its entirety, as it speaks more generally to the moral policing of women's bodies in a Christian cultural frame:

> Exemplum against the ornamentation of women. I heard that a certain woman, against her husband's will, put makeup on her face. And when on a certain feast day she made herself up in this way, such that she looked like quite another woman, her husband asked her where his wife was. To which Portia said, 'Lord, sign yourself [with the cross] and commend yourself to God, for am I none other than Portia, your wife?' 'Truly you do not seem to be my wife, for my wife is usually brunette, and you are blond, she is usually pallid and you are ruddy-faced'. 'For God', said Portia, 'I am your wife!' Her husband said, 'If you are my wife, I will see if I can shift those adornments that I see on your face'. And using his robe as a scourer, he took her by the hair and began to scrub strongly at her cheeks until the blood ran. She, in truth, cried out 'Lord, I am your wife!' And thus, her being well scrubbed, he said 'Now I can see, because indeed you are Portia my wife!'—and thus he held his wife in check.[55]

Thus both male authority and the particular comportment demanded on a Christian feast day are asserted, and strongly entwined. Other stories emphasize the problems of female vanity and embodiment in relation to particular days: a vain woman from Montpellier who, on the day 'which is given to the bread of charity' (perhaps Lammas, 1 August), went out to church heavily made up, and when returning asked her godmother whether she 'had seen such beautiful hair' as her own. That night in bed, all her hair fell out.[56] Others again simply assert a combination of male authority and Christian 'nature': a man from Spain was much displeased when his wife had herself heavily made up, much preferring that which had been 'given naturally to her by God'; he shaved her skin and hair to remove her adornments, and she never did it again.[57]

---

[55] Welter, 'Un recueil d'exempla', pp. 314–15 (no. 219). Discussed briefly in Arnold, 'Problems of Sensory History', pp. 32–34.
[56] Welter, 'Un nouveau recueil franciscain d'exempla', p. 460 (no. 76); similarly Welter, 'Un recueil d'exempla', p. 211 (no. 196).
[57] Welter, 'Un nouveau recueil franciscain d'exempla', p. 461 (no. 81). See similarly nos 77–80 from the same collection.

Female bodily unruliness just occasionally makes itself, and its policing, visible in another context: demonic possession. As Sari Katajala-Peltomaa notes, in her landmark discussion of the topic, most people possessed by demons were women, at least in terms of the evidence of later European miracle and canonization collections.[58] This is reflected absolutely in the small number of examples found in the southern French evidence before the Black Death. One *exemplum* tells of a woman possessed by a demon encountered in church by Brother Mansuet, chaplain to Pope Gregory IX. Under questioning, the possessed woman said that the things which most vexed demons were the preaching and oblations made during mass.[59] This is a narrative example of the convenient 'truth-telling' demon; more frequent are those people whose uncontrolled, unneighbourly, and potentially un-Christian behaviour is explained as 'possession'. The twelfth-century *vita* of St Bertrand of Comminges tells of two such examples, both women. One was mainly afflicted in her body, rolling on the ground with a distorted face; she fasted and prayed in the church of Saint-Just, and when the bishop came to her aid and asperged her with holy water, she was freed. Another, from after Bertrand's death, was a woman originally from the Val d'Aran who 'terrified' those around her and was rejected by her family. She made her way eventually to the church at Comminges and prostrated herself before his tomb. After inflicting a final terrible torment upon her, the demon ran from the presence of the saint.[60] There is one case of possession reported by the canonization witnesses for St Louis of Toulouse. Jean Olier of Marseille explained that his daughter Guillelmine, then 10 years old, one day 'after vespers became frenzied or possessed by a demon. Asked how he knew this, he said because of the mad and shameful and dishonest words which she said, which she was not otherwise accustomed to say, and moreover because she clawed at her face and clothes, such that they had to bind her with rope'. Guillelmine herself, now 19 years old, also gave evidence. She could not remember what happened, except for the fact that her hands were tied.[61]

These are all stories which to a greater or lesser extent were designed to operate as examples for others—albeit, in the case of the St Louis miracles, stories related by particular named witnesses, all attesting to a real, lived experience. But the notion of demonic possession also floated more freely in southern French culture. Pierre Maury's aunt Mersende had a troubled relationship with her grown-up daughter Jeannette. On one very public occasion the two came to blows, at a meal also attended by Pierre and by Jeannette's husband Bernard: Jeannette called the

---

[58] S. Katajala-Peltomaa, *Demonic Possession and Lived Religion in Later Medieval Europe* (Oxford: Oxford University Press, 2021), p. 46.
[59] Welter, 'Un nouveau recueil franciscain d'exempla', p. 601 (no. 145).
[60] Contrasty and Fournie, 'Vie et miracles', pp. 225, 238.
[61] Bughetti, ed., *Processus*, p. 214. There are other cases in which 'madness' is cured by Louis, but only in this case is it described as possession. Guillelmina's experiences are set into a wider context in Katajala-Peltomaa, *Demonic Possession*, chapter 3, and other cases of madness in chapter 4.

aunt 'an old heretical woman' who would eventually end up burned at the stake, and Mersende ended up throwing Jeannette down the stairs, saying 'Get out, devil!' (*Eat le dyablat!*) Later that same evening Mersende and Bernard, presumably in a state of considerable agitation, said that it would be good if someone threw Jeannette off a cliff 'because she was possessed by a demon'. On another occasion, the same was said of Pierre's brother Jean, because the latter, when ill, steadfastly refused to let the Good Man Bélibaste come to him.[62] In neither case is it clear that those saying this meant it literally and definitively. It seems more like a kind of floating suggestion, both a kind of insult and a potential means of explaining unhappy behaviour, where somebody was not 'fitting in' as others desired. One notes that even in the case of Guillelmina above, her father proffers both the possibility of her being 'frenzied' or mad rather than possessed ('*fuit amens seu demoniata*'). On very rare occasion such a suggestion might become firmed into a social 'reality', hopefully then to be assuaged by holy intervention; but most of the time it functioned as a cultural idea of a limit to bodily comportment, a marker for boundaries of Christian behaviour one would seek not to transgress.

There are further details regarding the normal habits, behaviours, and bodily responses of being Christian—the elements which most truly approach Bourdieu's notion of 'habitus'—which are practically inaccessible to us, though we can guess somewhat in their direction. Pierre's Christian landscape included the local and quotidian—the cross next to the cemetery in Laroque-d'Olmes that he mentions in passing,[63] the shrines in his local church in Montaillou, his knowledge that the priest's mother was buried next to the shrine of the Virgin there, and doubtless other details that he had no cause to mention—and the more distant, such as the church at Montserrat that he'd heard about, and the still more distant sites of pilgrimage, at Compostelle and Rome. Like all Christians, he would have other embodied knowledge also, of the sound of church bells and their particular meanings, the sound of clerical voices singing, whether at regular mass or for funerals (these being things he reports in the context of the Good Men deriding them—and yet present to his ears, nonetheless).[64] He would know what it felt like to stand with one's neighbours in church, attentive or otherwise as the liturgy was performed and the priest gave a sermon, watching the flicker of candles lit before images, perhaps admiring the painted interior of the church or perhaps not even noticing it in its familiarity; the costs of such adornment borne by the community, whether with pride or resentfully, and perhaps amongst them some particular personal additions (candles donated in thanks for healings, veils made for images).[65] And he would know things that he can never tell us, having never been

---

[62] *Fournier* III, pp. 178, 206.   [63] *Fournier* III, p. 154.
[64] *Fournier* III, pp. 234–35.
[65] *Fournier* III, p. 235–36 reporting the Good Men's disparagement of such costs and expenses.

asked by the inquisitor: how the feeling of all these things altered slightly across the passing of the year and the cycle of particular festivals, how the church felt different in the Lenten period, how it felt as Easter—and the need to make confession—drew close, how in winter most households would try to save up something for a suitable feast for Christmas Day, how other kinds of celebration might entwine with the Christian calendar, such as the rather wild Midsummer festivities found in various parts of Europe. (The people of Albi, for example, apparently had the custom of making a great wheel of branches and twigs which they called a 'Johannata', and set alight in order to roll it down a hill—something we only know about because men from a neighbouring *castrum* objected, and set about them, this resulting in a royal inquiry in 1291 into the violence, for what was essentially a territorial dispute.)[66] And the point is that of course these things would also be known and experienced by hundreds of thousands of other ordinary Christians, the broad frame of their experience largely the same, and yet the specific details and variations all going to make up *their* sense of what 'being Christian' felt like in a particular locale.

Lay Religion and 'Belief'

As we have noted at several points in earlier chapters, medieval southern France was a multi-faith society. This meant that 'being Christian' could be understood, in part, as 'not being Jewish or Muslim'. Given the actual, continued presence of and contact with people of different faiths, it's important to note that this could mean that a Christian believer might recognize that alongside their own identity, a Jew or a Muslim also had their own beliefs, accompanied by their own pious practices. That is, rather than imagining a Christian identity as necessarily constructed as possessing spiritual truth in comparison to a lack—'Jewish blindness' or 'Saracen idolatry', both familiar ecclesiastical tropes, perhaps particularly in northern Europe—we may want to consider that the 'belief' elements of Christian identity, the 'propositional content' as it were, could be recognized as one

---

[66] AD Tarn 4 EDt FF4, FF5 (both parchment rolls, the latter rather badly damage). From FF4: 'Item, quod dicti homines dicte civitatis Albie sunt et fuerunt in possessione sua quasi et usu suo quasi quicumque anni x xx xxx xl l sunt elapsi et a tanto tempore citra quod memorata hominum incontrarium non existit [?]ademprandi, custodiendi, deffendendi, manutenendi dictum territorium et Johannatam faciendi.... Item, quod dicti homines dicte civitatis habent de antiqua observatione usum et consuetudinem faciendi Johannatam sue accumulationem lignorum nomine Johannate circa adventum festis nativitatis beati Johannis babtisme quolibet anno in summitate dicti montis in loco covato domoleux constituto in dicto territorio civitatis Albie, in qui loco ubi fuit dicta Johannata facta et combusta est infra limitationem dicte civitatis, et deinde in vespere dicti festi [*illeg.*] Johannatam seu accumulationem lignorum accendendi et cremandi in honorem et obsequium et gratulationem dicti festi et populi dicte civitatis ut moris est in dicta civitate et locis circumvicinis...'. An anonymous reader of this book points out that Midsummer usually coincides with the feast of St Jean le Baptiste, which may have been the root of the 'Johannata' name.

possibility amongst several; and, just possibly, that its acceptance was a choice. People did convert *to* Christianity in these lands: there are a few people in the records who had 'Sarraceni' as their surname, and there were undoubtedly other converts from Judaism.[67] We do not have any clear evidence in southern France for anyone travelling in the other directions, though the fear of illicit 'Judaizing' was certainly visible within inquisitors' handbooks by the time of Bernard Gui. But it is certainly the case that south of the Pyrenees, religious identities could in certain circumstances retain some fluidity.[68]

In any case, people of other faiths were visibly present. I mentioned in Chapter 9 the wills of three women from in or near Puigcerdà who were widows of Jewish men. Their first names—Regina, Simona, and Manchesa—do not clarify whether they themselves were Jewish or Christian by birth, but it is notable that they have Christian as well as Jewish witnesses, and two of the three follow the convention of the other wills in naming a specific 'pro anima' sum (though none of the three specify a place of burial, which may imply that they were automatically going to a Jewish cemetery, as is more explicitly the case with some other Jewish wills from Puigcerdà).[69] For the notary and the witnesses—and in fact most likely for every Christian inhabitant of the region—the fact that Jewish culture had its own choices and beliefs around death and salvation, different from but not utterly dissimilar to Christian practice, would have been abundantly evident. When travelling south of the Pyrenees, Pierre Maury spent time in Flix, a settlement he described to Arnaud Sicre as 'a Saracen town' when they went there together; they had arrived, Pierre explained to Arnaud, during the feast 'which the Saracens call the feast of mutton; that is, the feast of Easter'. In fact it was almost certainly Eid, and it is not clear whether the inaccurate gloss was Pierre's or Arnaud's (this piece of evidence comes from Arnaud's deposition); but in either case, it shows an ability to make a cross-faith comparison. A Muslim friend, a boatman, offered to come along with Pierre when he went to meet someone else, in case he needed any help defending himself.[70] Pierre had other Muslim friends there also, including a fellow shepherd called Moferret (as Pierre remembered it at least), who gave him hospitality.[71]

In noting these encounters and connections, my present purpose is not to pursue the topic of inter-faith relations and the ever-fascinating notion of

---

[67] For example, 'Raimundus Sarraceni' (BnF MS 9994 fol. 79v), 'Gauzberti vocabulo Sarraceni' (*Cart. Moissac*, p. 160 (no. 109)). There were also of course occasions of forced conversion, as we see from the painful testimony of Baruch, a Jewish man forced to accept Christianity by the Pastoureaux rebels, and then made, in a more intellectual frame, to re-accept Christianity following lengthy debate and instruction with Bishop Fournier (*Fournier* I, pp. 177–90).

[68] A. Remensnyder, 'The Boundaries of Latin Christendom and Islam: Iberia and the Levant', in J. H. Arnold, ed., *The Oxford Handbook of Medieval Christianity* (Oxford: Oxford University Press, 2014), pp. 93–113.

[69] See Burns, *Jews in the Notarial Culture*.

[70] *Fournier* II, p. 77.   [71] *Fournier* III, p. 164.

'convivencia', but instead to help us think further about 'belief'. A strand of modern anthropological discussion of religious belief has found it helpful to distinguish between 'belief that' and 'belief in'; between, that is, the presence of particular propositions about the world and the spirit and so forth ('belief that'), and having spiritual trust or allegiance, potentially seen as a mode of interior disposition as well as exterior action, to something or someone ('belief in').[72] What the fact of inter-faith encounters suggests to me is that this distinction might have made some sense to the medieval lay people discussed here. That is, they would have been aware that there were multiple 'beliefs', including, of course, the more heretical beliefs of the Good Men which Pierre relates in some detail. But they would also be aware that not everybody *believed* in these beliefs; indeed Pierre's brother Jean steadfastly refused to adhere to the beliefs of the Good Men. They might further recognize that some people believed *more strongly* than other people, whether this was believing in certain abstract beliefs or 'believing in' the sanctity of particular people. Thus, for example, Pierre told Bishop Fournier that certain particular people were not just 'believers' but '*great* believers' (*magni credentes*) in the heretics, marking them out on the qualitative nature of their adherence.[73]

I have to some extent discussed 'belief' as an abstract category in earlier chapters, particularly in Chapter 7—where we noted the distinction, voiced in synodal advice and elsewhere, between the 'explicit' belief of the ecclesiastical few and the 'implicit' faith that was required of the mass of the laity—and, in Chapter 8, the inquisitorial dynamics of attempting to discern inner belief from external action. The focus there was on what bishops and inquisitors attempted to prescribe and require, albeit whilst also noting the considerable tensions within their discourse, as it was applied to lay people who often turned out to be more heterogeneous and challenging than assumed or desired. In the remainder of this chapter I want to try to get us closer to the dynamics of belief for lay people themselves, by looking at some areas adjacent to orthodox conformity—belief in magic or soothsaying, doubt and apostasy—and grappling with some aspects of interiority, in terms of the emotional and affective 'pull' of orthodox belief. Pierre will continue intermittently to be our informant, and in the final section we will focus particularly on the complexities of his own personal faith, in terms both of what he believed and of *how* he believed. As Rodney Needham pointed out some decades ago, 'belief' is a tremendously slippery concept, the dynamics of which tend to elude us the more closely we look; and, as Ethan Shagan has discussed more recently, it is something which might be seen as having changed over time in the Christian West, not simply in its content but in how it was understood to

---

[72] For example, M. Ruel, 'Christians as Believers', in J. Davis, ed., *Religious Organization and Religious Experience* (London: Academic Press, 1982).
[73] *Fournier* III, pp. 143, 144.

operate (and, perhaps, in its very nature).[74] Responding to such works I have elsewhere explored the idea of 'belief acts' as performative events in which belief is not simply communicated or manifested, but enacted into meaningful existence, such acts depending in part upon varied material resources and cultural/historical contexts.[75] All of which is to say that in what follows, we are necessarily going to find ourselves circling around the topic, to try to generate several tangential glimpses of it from different perspectives.

Magic and Belief

It is useful to look to 'magic', to use a modern catch-all word for a rather blurry area, firstly to note that other, essentially additional, 'beliefs' existed alongside the orthodox tenets of faith ('alongside' because they were not voiced in opposition to orthodoxy, even if they were sometimes condemned by it); and secondly to consider to what extent or in what ways people 'believed in' these areas. In the fourteenth century, magic-working began to be an area of increased ecclesiastical policing, based particularly upon a greater focus on the demonic; this shift being particularly associated with the pontificate of John XXII, as Alain Boureau and others have demonstrated. But prior to that it was only intermittently an ecclesiastical concern, and the line more often taken was that it was superstitious nonsense that did not work.[76] The kind of 'magic' most frequently apparent was what we might call divination: attempts either to locate missing objects or to predict some aspect of the future, through various means. Pierre remembered the Good Man Bélibaste telling him about having consulted a neighbour, a woman called Galia, about whether it was safe for him to make a certain journey; Galia took a shoe off the heretic and simply measured how many fitted between her firepit and the doorway, having told him that if the last shoe extended beyond the threshold, it meant that he wasn't going to return from his journey. This was indeed the case, and he decided not to go.[77] Arnaud Sicre reported that, at Pierre and Bélibaste's urging, they all went to visit a 'Saracen' diviner (*divinus*) who used a combination of a small wooden frame and an arabic text to make some prognostication. (Arnaud was unimpressed by the outcome).[78] Inquisition records from the thirteenth century throw up a few other earlier examples, largely as incidental

---

[74] R. Needman, *Belief, Language and Experience* (Oxford: Blackwell, 1972); E. Shagan, *The Birth of Modern Belief: Faith and Judgment from the Middle Ages to the Enlightenment* (Princeton: Princeton University Press, 2018).
[75] Arnold, 'Believing in Belief'.
[76] A. Boureau, *Satan hérétique: naissance de la démonologie dans l'Occident médiévale (1280–1330)* (Paris: Odile Jacob, 2004); M. Bailey, *Battling Demons: Witchcraft, Heresy and Reform in the Late Middle Ages* (University Park, Pa : Penn State University Press, 2003).
[77] *Fournier* III, p. 207.   [78] *Fournier* II, p. 40.

evidence: an 'augurer' called Raimond de Pouts in Sorèze was consulted by someone worried about whether the inquisitors were on his trail. Raimond himself was subsequently interrogated also, and admitted that he had been told to stop telling auguries by some previous inquisitors; he claimed that his past clients included a number of bishops, including—albeit through an intermediary—Gui Foulques. (This may not be as preposterous as it sounds: the disgraced, blaspheming archbishop we met in Chapter 8, Robert de Mauvoisin, was also accused of having consulted a Jewish 'astrologer' who attempted to predict the future through various learned means.) By 1344, we find an entirely secular court, namely the consular court at Cordes from which I drew some other evidence in Chapter 8, pursuing a case against one of its citizens, a 'weaver and merchant' called Bernard Fort. He was accused of practising some form of predictive magic using ants—how, exactly, is sadly not made clear—and as being a 'mathematician' (this being a label given to a form of 'idolatry' condemned in earlier ecclesiastical texts).[79]

The other main kind of magic people sought out was either for protection or to influence someone else (that is, in some sense the same process reversed). Adémar Galos from Montesquieu admitted among other things that his wife had consulted a female 'diviner' from the region around Carcassonne, because she thought herself cursed (*maleficiata*) because she could not conceive; the inquisitor asked if she worked through invoking demons, but Adémar's somewhat vague response suggested otherwise.[80] Beatrice de Lagleize, when arrested by Bishop Fournier's men having fled with her young lover (a priest), was found to be carrying a number of apparently suspicious items including a blood-stained cloth. The latter was, she explained, for making a love potion for her daughter's eventual use (the blood was the daughter's menses), to ensure that her husband loved her; but, Beatrice explained, they had not yet used it, as it was better to wait until the marriage was already established.[81] In the late 1320s there were also several inquisitorial trials of priests who engaged in rather more dubious forms of 'necromancy', and one Carmelite monk who fashioned five wax figures that apparently allowed him to seduce five different women.[82]

It is clear, from the preceding details, that we should not imagine 'magic' to be something of interest only to the laity; in fact, as Richard Kieckhefer demonstrated some time ago, magic was probably more often associated with learned clerical culture than anything 'folkloric'.[83] It was not the product of a different culture, certainly not a 'pagan survival'. But it is interesting to think about how it

---

[79] AD Tarn 69EDt FF18bis, fols 66r–89v, 102r–111v. The case requires further study; the main charge seems to be that Bernard Fort asked various people to gather ants for him, and then carried them to a place where he was building a house, to get them to 'work' in some sense, possibly to reveal something about the land.

[80] Doat 25, fols 122v–123r, 208r, 272r–274v (*Inquisitors and Heretics*, pp. 430–33, 602–03, 724–31).

[81] *Fournier* I, p. 248.   [82] Doat 27, fols 42r–50r, 149v–155r.

[83] R. Kieckhefer, *Magic in the Middle Ages*, 3rd edn (Cambridge: Cambridge University Press, 2022).

operates alongside Christian orthodoxy. Some divination could be seen as accessing obscure knowledge of how God designed the universe to work, when used to search for missing objects, for example. But any attempt to predict the future, if thought about in the round, is rather hard to square with other ideas about God's grace, human free will, and so forth. In the Cordes case against the ant-wrangling 'mathematician', the witnesses for his defence were clear that what was fundamentally at stake was belief: Vital de Moser, another merchant, attested, for example, that Bernard Fort was a good man of honest life, 'and that he practised just as a good Catholic and faithful Christian should and must do, serving the mandates and precepts of God, just as he the witness firmly believed'.[84]

Given the number of senior clergy who nonetheless clearly drew upon diviners and augurers, what thus seems likely is that 'belief *that*' divination worked was usually something which people framed for themselves in a rather limited way, in the sense that those engaging with it were not likely to relate it to a wider array of beliefs about creation. It suggests that specific 'beliefs that' could be discontinuous, able to operate alongside other 'beliefs' without causing major cognitive dissonance. Moreover, given the extremely specific ends to which divination was put, 'belief *in*' divination was automatically quite circumscribed, resting only upon a particular outcome (whether revealed positively or negatively, or whether self-fulfilling, like Bélibaste's decision not to undertake his journey).

With protective magic, and just possibly with magic that sought to influence others, we may be looking at a slightly different kind of dynamic, more clearly in continuity with some strands of orthodox faith. The saints were of course frequently petitioned for protection and for intervention, and it is clear that people often used Christian symbols for similar reasons: an *exemplum*, reporting something recounted by a bishop of Béziers, tells of a lady from Spain who wore an amulet depicting the Lamb of God, blessed by the pope, because she wanted protection from lightning when there were storms.[85] The twelfth-century sacramentary in use at the rural church of Saint-Guilhem-de-Combret, in the Canigou mountains, includes a mass to be said 'in time of storms', petitioning God for protection.[86] An ordinance from the bishop of Carcassonne in 1303 forbids priests from handing over holy water to lords or their families, only allowing the priest to asperge them rather than give them possession of the sacramental; presumably, prior to this injunction, the water would have been used domestically to bestow some form of purification or protection.[87] When parishioners were

---

[84] AD Tarn 69EDt FF18bis, 'et exer[c]ere ut bonus homo catholicus et fidelis xp[ist]ianus faciens potest et debet servando mandata et precepta dei prout ipse testis firmiter credit'.
[85] Welter, 'Un nouveau recueil franciscain d'exepla', p. 467 (no. 96).
[86] BM Perpignan, MS 4, fol. 124r: 'Per tempestare...'.
[87] Mahul, ed., *Cartulaire...Carcassonne*, V, p. 440. An anonymous reader points out that Carolingian canon law allowed people to take holy water to sprinkle upon houses, fields, livestock, and their own food and drink: see Regino of Prüm, *Libri duo*, p. 107 (I.214).

anointed by oil by their priest at Advent—something for which we have evidence from one of the notarial agreement documents—some might well similarly have experienced it as offering spiritual protection.[88] One wonders about the function of preserving morsels of bread that had been blessed by the Good Men, keeping them in Pierre's own case for more than twenty years (according to Arnaud Sicre); an object for domestic devotion, or also thought to bring some form of protection?[89] Finally, in a sort of clearly overlapping space between 'magic' and 'orthodoxy', we can note a rather extraordinary thirteenth-century parchment, found bundled up in the medieval walls of a private house in Cordes, on which was written, in Occitan, a sort of prayer-cum-invocation which it describes as the 'spells of the apostles'. The text—known also in a Latin example from northern France—combines both spiritual exhortation ('Extend your right hand to the Father, pray to your God and you will obtain peace and good hope') and what look like rather more material promises of aid ('the object of your desires will come to you soon if you pray to God...'; 'He who has thought to harm you will be vanquished by you; pray to God and you will obtain that which you hope for').[90]

Doubt and Unbelief

The magical 'beliefs' we have just met are all essentially mechanistic promises: do this, and the following will follow. Whether one believed 'in' such promises presumably depended upon one's level of desperation at a particular moment, and on how often a positive outcome was obtained. In contrast, the more orthodox prayers for protection or intervention were petitions for God's grace, where disappointment could be interpreted as a failing on one's own part. It is notable however that some occasions of doubt or indeed apostasy came about when such orthodox petitions seem to have failed.

One such example is another witness to the Louis of Toulouse canonization inquiry, a 40-year-old woman called Beatrix from the city of Nice. She explained that her mother had gone to Rome on pilgrimage, but that when the rest of her party returned healthy, her mother, now ill, remained there. Beatrix began to think that her mother had in fact died there, and this threw her into an emotional frenzy: she tried to harm herself and spoke terrible blasphemies against God and

---

[88] AD Aude H103 (Rieudaure, 1303): 'Et quod ipse sacrista vel ille qui tenuerit officium ipsius sacristie precipiat omnia et singula que precipere consuevit sine diminucione tam intus ecclesiam predictam quam extra per parrochiani, et quod donet et dare teneantur ipsis parrochianis oleum in adventum domini quolibet anno prout est antiquitus fieri consuetum.'

[89] *Fournier* II, p. 75, partly confirmed by Pierre in *Fournier* III, p. 134. See similarly Doat 25, fol. 229r–v (*Inquisitors and Heretics*, p. 648).

[90] F. Roquain de Courtemblay, 'Les sorts des saints ou des apôtres', *Bibliothèque de l'École des Chartes* 41 (1880), 457–74. I am very grateful to Florence Journot for bringing this document to my attention.

Mary and the saints, and against religious men, and indeed neighbours.[91] (Louis of course subsequently healed her of this madness.) The implication is a sense of betrayal: despite journeying to one of the holiest sites, her mother was not rewarded with healing but with death. A rather similar dynamic is on show in another *exemplum*: a knight from the region of Agen was devoted to St Francis. After many prayers on his behalf by the Brothers Minor, the knight's wife was able to conceive their first and only child. However, the child then fell gravely ill. The knight's mother-in-law said. 'The faith that you have in St Francis is foolish (*inanis*), and now see that he is dying!'—at which point the child expired. Overcome by paternal feeling, the knight picked up the child's body, strode to the house of the Brothers Minor, and threw the body of the child at the altar, saying 'St Francis, you gave him to me, but he should be yours, as he is—so I return him to you!' Miraculously the child revived—thus occasioning the *exemplum*.[92] But as in various other cases found across other such sources, whilst the happy outcome renders these moments visible to us, miraculously happy outcomes surely did not occur on every such occasion. The sense of a promise broken shows us a further aspect to the spectrum of what 'believing' might involve more generally.

Other doubts or indeed strongly held disbeliefs could occur when one's personal experience of and reflection upon material reality led one to diverge from what orthodoxy presented as a tenet of faith. I have written about this in some detail elsewhere, including a number of southern French examples, and will not repeat them all here. One point to make is that heretical ideas could overlap with more materialistic unbelief, as for example regarding the future bodily resurrection. The Good Men held that this would not happen, because in their theology the purified soul would join with God, whilst everything corporeal was innately corrupt; in their preaching on the topic they might emphasize how bodies rotted and corrupted in the earth, as did Bélibaste (as Pierre remembered it).[93] But others could come to that conclusion somewhat independently also, through having seen bodies dug up when a new grave was being made (as already noted in Chapter 6). The oft-repeated joke of the Good Men against the Eucharist—that if Christ's body was as big as a mountain, it would have been eaten up by now, were it actually present in the host, given how often priests said mass—ran alongside the inevitable possibility that the host was sensorily experienced to be nothing but material bread.

Having questioned Pierre about the resurrection, Bishop Fournier then asked him if the Good Men had ever told him that when the soul left the human body it retained the same shape as the flesh and bone person. Pierre replied that he had never heard this from them, 'but however that he believed that all human souls

---

[91] Bughetti, ed., *Processus*, p. 218.
[92] Welter, 'Un nouveau recueil franciscain d'exempla', p. 624 (no. 218).
[93] *Fournier* III, p. 243.

separated from bodies were just like people; and he had always believed this, from the use of reason'; and yet he had also marvelled at how it was that one could not then see the soul leave the body of a dead person in the form and figure of a person—'although afterwards he attributed this to divine power'.[94] It is important to note that at this particular moment, Pierre was simply sharing his inner musings. Nothing really rested on his conceptualization of what a soul looked like (though it is true that another deponent did end up believing that the soul was nothing but blood or breath, when she watched a dying person very carefully and saw nothing else coming out at the final moments).[95] He was simply explaining to Fournier what he himself had made of what he had been told about the soul, and the way in which he satisfactorily explained it to himself, through the capacious safety net of 'divine power'; a means of assuaging cognitive dissonance, and allowing specific beliefs still to be held, even if in a fairly distanced fashion. At a different point in his deposition, Pierre recounted the story of Doubting Thomas, as told to him by one of the Good Men (unsurprisingly in accordance with how it is given in the Gospel of John, albeit not in the exact words), repeating as its core conclusion: 'Blessed are those who have seen me, and blessed are those who have not seen me and yet believe.'[96] The Good Man then took the argument in an interesting direction, focused on the first half of Christ's statement: Thomas had seen what was really there (the wound in Christ's side); when the Good Men blessed bread, they said what was really there—bread; and this was in contrast to the Catholic priests who said that they could turn bread into Christ's body, when in reality it was just bread. Christ had gone to heaven, and was not coming back. That theological position neatly tipped all non-corporeal and spiritual issues into the unseen world to come, so that almost all the heretics' belief-claims in the present life were material and in accordance with one's sensory experience. Catholic orthodoxy had a somewhat harder hill to climb, resting on the entirety of the message: that those who had *not* seen would still believe.

Addressing the challenge of doubt was, in that sense, an essential element within Catholic belief. From the perspective of the ordinary layperson, the point is that the propositional content of 'belief' came simultaneously in both forms, the seen and the unseen; or at least, in *reports of* the 'seen' (in miracle stories, *exempla*, and the like), alongside the more likely requirement that they themselves believe without direct experience. Gauffrida Rossa, one of the visitors to the tomb of Louis of Toulouse whom we met further above, entered the canonization record because of her experience of doubt. As we previously saw, she had gone there because her friend, Beatrice Brune, wanted to light a candle at the shrine. 'She [Gauffrida] said to the said Beatrice, "O good lady, do you believe

---

[94] *Fournier* III, p. 243.
[95] *Fournier* I, pp. 260–67; similarly, *Fournier* II, pp. 129–30 and Arnold, *Belief and Unbelief*, pp. 225–29.
[96] *Fournier* III, p. 184.

that this son of the lord king is really made into a saint? The Brothers Minor say and preach this, so that they can have money for wax".' They both went into the church nonetheless, Beatrice getting a candle, 'and she the witness saying that she did not have a candle for the Blessed Louis, but she would bless his body just as any other dead person, and she said some of the seven psalms for him'. But at that point she began to feel very ill, which she perceived to be punishment for her lack of belief; she was swiftly contrite, and recovered (and could thus have the 'miracle' recorded).[97] Doubt, crisis, conversion, all in the space of a brief prayer.

Dominique Grenier, successor to Fournier as bishop of Pamiers, in the synodal book he wrote sometime between 1326 and 1347 was concerned, as we saw in Chapter 8, that the laity should believe *firmly*. This was not that hard to achieve, he wrote rather optimistically (albeit interestingly):

> All the aforesaid can easily be believed firmly, because they are proved by miracles; following that which is in the last part of Mark['s Gospel], namely that the apostles 'going forth preached everywhere, the Lord working withal' [Mark 16: 20]...That once upon a time almost the entire world worshipped idols, as is shown in the histories of pagans, and also by the remains of their temples, which one can still see in many places, among us for example in Bordeaux, Perigueux and Narbonne. Moreover, therefore, the world was converted from idolatry to faith by the miracles that they saw. And thus we have the proposition, namely that faith is proved by miracles or without miracles. And this was the greatest miracle, namely that the world should leave off the rite of idolatry, which it had held for many thousands of years, at the words of simple men...[98]

That final idea, that the conversion accomplished by Christ was itself a miracle, is something one can find in Augustine's *City of God*.[99] But Grenier's point about the visible evidence of the pagan past, in Narbonne and elsewhere, appears to be entirely his own. It is a rather neat way of attempting to provide visible, present proof of the earlier passage of the miraculous. And yet, he continues:

> If a man refuses to believe except for that which he can know for certain, he cannot live in this world: in what way can you live unless you believe in something

---

[97] Bughetti, ed., *Processus*, pp. 236–37.
[98] BM Toulouse MS 402, fol. 108r: 'quod omnia predicta possunt de facili firmiter credere quia fuerunt probata miraculis secundum illud Marchi ultimo ipsi scilicet apostoli *Profecti predicaverunt ubique domino cooperante* [Mark 16: 20]...quod olim quasi totus mundus coluit ydola patet per istorias etiam paganorum et per vestigia etiam templorum adhuc in multis locis apparentium ut apud nos in Burdegala, Petragorius et Narbona, autem ergo mundus fuit conversus ab ydolatria ad fidem per miracula que viderunt; et sic habemus propositum, scilicet quod fides est probata miraculis aut absque miraculis. Et hoc fuit maximum miraculum scilicet quod mundus dimittent ritum ydolatrie quem tenuit multis milibus annorum ad verba simplicium hominum...'
[99] Augustine, *De civitate Dei*, CCSL 48 (Turnhout: Brepols, 1955), cap. XXII.5 (pp. 810–12). I am very grateful to David d'Avray for pointing me to this passage.

other than yourself, or unless you believe that so-and-so is your father or so-and-so is your mother or so-and-so is your son or daughter. Whence it is necessary that a man should believe some of those things which he cannot know perfectly.[100]

Thus *not* having proof is reinserted—as it must be—by appeal to a more everyday sense of 'believing' (a sense we in fact met briefly above, spoken by a witness to the trial of the ant-wrangling mathematician, who said that he 'firmly believed' in the evidence he had given).

All of this speaks to how people might come sustain to 'beliefs that': belief that God created the world, belief that Christ was sacrificed and rose again, belief that bishops had apostolic authority. Can we say any more about 'belief *in*'; about, that is, the way in which an interiorized *experience* of belief might be presented to, or inculcated in, ordinary lay people? In Chapter 8 I discussed some kinds of interiority with regard to the discourse on sin and confession; what I am pursuing here is the wider dynamic of an interiorized engagement with the Christian faith, not only in regard to its penitential aspects. For example, something which is found in various later medieval pastoral works addressing the laity is the idea of engaging in prayer or contemplation 'wholeheartedly' or 'in full faith', sometimes with suggestions on how to achieve this state of devotion and sincerity; and, as Jennifer Bryan has wonderfully demonstrated for Middle English texts, there are a variety of ways in which late medieval pastoral writing seeks to help construct 'inner selves'.[101]

Can we find this kind of dynamic before the Black Death, in southern France? There are hints of it, I think. One *exemplum* tells of a sinner whose only pious activity was always to rejoice and recite the *Ave Maria* when he heard Mary's name. She appeared to him, warning him that he must confess because he was going to die. This he did, realizing that the mechanical recitation of the *Ave* meant little in comparison to his other faults.[102] We saw above the tale of a woman who, at mass, was so transfixed by the image of Christ's body that she could not kneel down to worship appropriately. The tale is expressly about devotion to Mary, who implicitly frees her, but also models a kind of extreme interiorized piety, set in relation (not opposition) to external bodily worship. Another tells of a woman from Ganges (c. 45 km north of Montpellier) who 'from reflection on the Passion of the Lord was inflamed with total sanctity, which she thought upon most of all

---

[100] BM Toulouse 402, fol. 108v: 'Item si homo nollet credere nisi ea que pro certo sciret, non posset vivere in hoc mundo; quomodo posset vivere nisi crederet se aliquem vel nisi crederet quod talis est pater suus, vel talis mater sua, vel quod talis est filius suus vel filia. Unde necesse est ut homo credat aliqua de hiis que non potest perfecte scire.'

[101] J. Bryan, *Looking Inward: Devotional Reading and the Private Self in Late Medieval England* (Philadelphia: University of Pennsylvania Press, 2007).

[102] Welter, 'Un nouveau recueil franciscain d'exempla', pp. 618–19 (no. 203).

on Fridays'. On a certain Friday night, her husband 'came to her'; she was horrified by the thought of having sex with him, and instead 'reflected with him on the sadness of Christ's Passion'. Miraculously his desire left him, and similarly her.[103] The story is structurally the same as others in which a wife wards off a husband's unwanted attentions by signing the cross or so forth, but at its core is something rather different: a shared act of pious contemplation, at home, unaccompanied by any other intervention, that allows both wife and husband to reach a higher level of sanctity.

As well as these proffered models of reflection, we can consider the ways in which some *exempla* presumed to work upon their lay audience, their stories of flesh and suffering attempting to evoke an embodied response and subsequent interior reflection: something like the tale of Portia having her make-up scrubbed violently from her face by her husband, for example; or another story of a young man who was given a foretaste of eternal suffering by some demons who breathed into his mouth, the youth then feeling as if his whole body, inside and out, was burning 'such that it seemed to him that he had no flesh, but that whatever was in him was fire'.[104] Such examples remind us that inculcating belief had become not simply a matter of providing instruction on specific tenets of faith, but something also to be pursued by evoking emotion and affect, narratives and images that sought to encourage lay people to strive internally for their own salvation.

The Shepherd's Beliefs

Let us turn again finally to Pierre Maury, to what he believed and to *how* he believed. I have above drawn upon various moments from his very lengthy deposition, for what they can show us about lay Christian society more generally. Here I want to focus on Pierre as an individual, given the extraordinary detail in which we can see something of his experience of religion. As with all inquisition depositions, we do not have a simple window onto his world. Bishop Fournier's questions frame and shape what Pierre had to say, in the several senses that they prompted responses in certain areas but not others, that they set his words within a wider inquisitorial discourse of interpretation, and in that Pierre himself may have attempted to conceal some aspects of his deeds (though, as I said further above, given how heavily he was implicated, this does not seem to be the case with regard to what he has to say about issues of belief). But it is clear that Fournier gave Pierre considerable space and freedom in his responses, and that his interrogation was carried out across various different encounters. We only know the dates for when he first spoke to the Aragonese inquisitor and then when

---

[103] Welter, 'Un nouveau recueil franciscain d'exempla', p. 468 (no. 98).
[104] Welter, 'Un nouveau recueil franciscain d'exempla', p. 620 (no. 207).

he began to speak to Fournier, but other lengthy interrogations elsewhere in the register make clear that they were the product multiple sessions; it is very likely that Pierre was similarly returned to the inquisitorial prison in between each of his encounters with the bishop. The first two-thirds of the written deposition largely form a chronological narrative, prompted by questions (sometimes visible, more often implied) about when he first met a heretic, who was connected, what happened next, and so forth. The final third comprises sixty-two 'articles', numbered as such in the margins of the manuscript, regarding the heresy of the Good Men: Fournier presented these in turn to Pierre, asking him to report in each case on what he had heard from the Good Men, and in most cases what he himself believed. As recorded in a separate manuscript, on 9 August 1324 Pierre and his brother Jean were sentenced to strict and perpetual imprisonment for their involvement in heresy.[105]

As noted at the outset, much of the story of Pierre's shepherding life, reconstructed from this and other depositions, has already been told elsewhere. From the more 'narrative' bulk of his evidence, I shall focus on the trajectory of Pierre's encounters with the faith of the Good Men, his understanding of how this 'church' related to the orthodox one, and what his evidence can show of the dynamics to his own continued engagement with religious belief. We shall then turn to Fournier's sixty-two articles, to see how Pierre addresses a variety of specific beliefs, and what this can further show about his own experience of 'believing'.

The first that Pierre heard of the Good Men, so he said, was around the turn of the fourteenth century, near the feast of Pentecost, when he was tending the sheep of some neighbours near Montaillou. His late brother Guillaume, and another man called Guillaume Belhot, came to him and told him that 'Good Men and Good Christians had come to this land, and were there, men who held the life which St Pierre and St Paul and the other apostles had held, who followed the Lord, who did not lie or deceive'. Nothing more came of it at that point, and for the following two years Pierre left Montaillou and stayed in the valley of Arques, some 50 km away, in love with a woman there (he was in his early twenties at this point). 'And during those two years nobody spoke to him, as he said, about the fact of heresy, because they saw that he was much in love with the said woman'— the implication being that a young man in love would not be very bothered about religious topics, rather than just 'heresy' specifically.[106]

A few years later, in the company of various friends, Pierre found himself at the house of another man, Raimond Pierre, where a large meal was being prepared; and he met there Pierre Autier 'the late heretic', who sat Pierre Maury down next to him, and set about converting him. 'Pierre, I can give you great joy! It has been

---

[105] Doat 28, fols 47v–48r; the public sermon announcing this was on 14 August, Doat 28, fols 55r–76v.
[106] *Fournier* III, pp. 119–21.

said to me that you will be a good believer, if God wishes, and will place you on the path to God's salvation, if you will believe in me, just as Christ placed the apostles, who did not lie or deceive.' Autier went on to explain how they were persecuted for the 'Law' (*legem*) that they held, much like those early Christian martyrs, and that there were 'two Churches', one being their own apostolic Church, the other being the persecuting Church of Rome. Pierre protested that he had heard a Brother Minor preaching 'many good things' just the other day. Forget all that, said Autier, the Roman Church says many false things; 'listen to what I am saying to you, and place it well in your heart'. Autier then gave an example of how the Roman Church 'lied', describing in some detail what happened when, a few days after it was born, parents brought a child to be baptized, how the priest promised that this would make the child a good and faithful Christian—and yet how this often turned out not to be so. And how could it, 'because the child in their own person could not promise that they would be a good and faithful Christian, but it was promised by another for them'.[107] And thus, after this and some other words, Pierre was 'converted', and Autier taught him how to 'adore'.

The dynamics of the dualist heresy in the Pyrenees have already been well explored elsewhere.[108] What I want to pick out here firstly is what Pierre Autier—a well-educated notary, before he went off to become a Good Man—expected of Pierre the shepherd. He expected that the image of the apostles would be familiar and have considerable resonance, not least in the sense of enduring persecution; that he could persuade Pierre by means of a kind of logical, moral case (regarding the non-effects of baptism); that Pierre would recognize the sense in which someone who is 18 years old, rather than 12 years old, 'can now have understanding of good and evil'. And he asked Pierre to place these words 'in his heart', in the sense of reflecting hard upon them—an interiorized process. The point is that this is not peculiar to 'heresy', but that the context of heresy makes visible to us a wider sense of what might be expected of or possible for an ordinary lay believer.

In his turn, in this first encounter and in the various occasions when he recounted words spoken or preached by other Good Men (most often by Bélibaste), Pierre displays a fascinating combination of memory and independent engagement. When I say 'memory', I cannot of course check that what Pierre recounted directly matched what was once originally spoken. But the details that Pierre supplies often contain biblical references and quotations, sometimes explicitly recognized as such, which give us a sense of how much an ordinary layperson might retain from preaching; and presumably thus from orthodox

---

[107] *Fournier* III, pp. 123–24.
[108] In addition to *Montaillou*, see particularly E. Griffe, *Le Languedoc cathare et l'inquisition, 1229–1329* (Paris: Letouzey et Ané, 1980), pp. 270–99; J. Duvernoy, 'Le catharisme en Languedoc au début du XIVe siècle', *CdF* 20 (1985), 27–56.

preaching as much as heretical. I should emphasize that there is no case for seeing these references as being supplied by the inquisitor: Fournier would undoubtedly have been interested to note them, but such details do not turn up in every deposition he received. 'It is not surprising if the world hates us,' Pierre recalls Autier saying, slightly adapting John's first letter (1 John 3: 13). Jacques Autier (Pierre Autier's son) preached at length to Pierre, which the shepherd recounted in detail, including that 'The Son of God ordered that man should not judge another', a clear reference to 'judge not lest ye be judged' (Matt. 7: 1), and that '[God] said and gave to us in scripture that now and henceforth he is within the hands of sinners' (an adaptation of Matt. 26: 45).[109] Bélibaste preached to Pierre and a few other about the example of Saul who formerly persecuted the early Church, but who then converted and took the name Paul; the way in which Pierre relates the sermon suggests that the audience was already familiar with the story, Bélibaste's specific purpose being to relate it to the Church of the Good Men. The same is the case in a sermon of Jacques Autier in which the Song of Songs was mentioned.[110] As already noted further above, Pierre also heard the story of Doubting Thomas from him.

Independent engagement: even if one wonders if some of the instances that Pierre relates were in fact later thoughts than quite what he said at the time, they nonetheless speak to the shepherd's ability to question and enquire around the detail of beliefs. 'If they are good men, as you say, and hold the path of the apostles, why do they not preach publicly just as the apostles did?', he asked those who first told him about the Good Men; and similarly, to Pierre Autier, 'if you therefore hold the path of truth and of the apostles, why don't you preach just like the priests in church?' When Jacques Autier had given a sermon about the spirits who (in their theology) fell from heaven, Pierre asked 'And did the holy Father speak of those who were in the Kingdom, or those who fell, in the aforesaid words?' The latter, Autier said. 'And in what way,' Pierre further enquired, 'were those spirits who fell to earth able to hear the holy Father speaking in heaven, especially since the aforesaid opening [through which they fell] had closed?' He had various further questions on the heretics' theology of creation.[111] We have already seen, further above, occasions when Pierre held a different opinion—for example, regarding godparenthood—from Bélibaste. Pierre was, without doubt, a 'believer' in the Good Men: he admits this from the time of his first arrest, and at various points in his deposition. But being 'a believer' did not mean simply passive or uncomprehending acceptance; and the sense of his existing engagement with Christian culture and biblical stories strongly suggest that this would have been the case even if no 'Good Man' had ever set foot back in Montaillou.

---

[109] *Fournier* III, pp. 131, 133.   [110] *Fournier* III, pp. 175, 132.
[111] *Fournier* III, pp. 120, 123, 131.

As said, at the end of his deposition, having told the chronological story of his involvement in heresy (almost certainly across multiple periods of interrogation), Pierre was confronted by a series of 'articles' regarding the Good Men, and regarding what he himself believed. These allow us the most precious and revealing evidence on his beliefs, and on his processes of believing. In some cases, asked about key tenets of the heretics' faith, Pierre reported what he had heard from them, and then simply confirmed that he had believed it. This was the case regarding the creation of this world by the evil God, for example; and similarly that the souls of those who were not saved by the heretics transmigrated from body to body. In response to a few topics—whether good spirits had been 'seduced' by bad ones, whether the Good Men rejected Sundays and feast days, or spoke against the hierarchical ordering of the clergy—he said he had not heard anything from them.

More commonly he reported in some detail what the Good Men had said about a certain topic, and then said that he had sometimes believed it, but sometimes not; or that he had neither believed nor disbelieved it. This was the case, for example, regarding the question of whether Satan or the Bad God had always existed, or had been created by the Good God (namely 'absolute' or 'mitigated' dualism): he talked about how sometimes the heretics seemed to be saying one thing, and sometimes another, but mostly that he thought they meant to say that the Good God had not created evil. 'And sometimes he believed that they said the truth, other times he doubted it.'[112] Prompted by a question from Fournier about whether the heretics said that the Old Testament was a bad law, given by the Bad God, he said that 'he neither believed nor disbelieved this firmly, but sometimes believed it and sometimes the contrary'.[113] Pierre gave a similar response in various other areas, such as the calumnies the Good Men spoke against ecclesiastics, that excommunication had no value, that eating the flesh of animals was a sin: that he neither believed nor disbelieved.

There is an *exemplum* Étienne de Bourbon recorded that he had heard, he said, from other mendicants in Provence: when 'certain heretics in the land of the Albigensians' were holding forth about their asceticism, a *joglar* there present responded that 'his horse was better than them', because whilst they didn't eat meat, the horse didn't even eat bread or drink wine, and slept in a much worse bed than theirs. Moreover, these austere things would profit his horse more than theirs did them, because they disbelieved in the articles of faith. His horse's deeds would please God more, 'because although he did not believe, he also did not disbelieve in anything, and thus both in actions and in faith, his horse was in a better state than they were'.[114] Neither believing nor disbelieving is thus presented

---

[112] *Fournier* III, p. 222 (article 9).   [113] *Fournier* III, p. 224 (article 13).
[114] J. Berlioz, ed., *Stephani de Borbone, Tractatus de diversis materiis predicabilibus: tertia pars*, CCCM 124.2 (Turnhout: Brepols, 2006), p. 41 (trans. A&B, p. 125).

as a lack of cognition, associated with a more limited mental capacity. But in contrast, Pierre's similar statements did not mean that he did not think about these topics; quite clearly he did, as the many details in his deposition demonstrate. As when voiced similarly by other deponents questioned by inquisitors, it suggests instead two overlapping dispositions: that he had thus far withheld personal judgment on that particular topic, for want of something truly persuasive in either direction; and/or that a certain topic, whilst perhaps important to both the Good Men and the inquisitor, simply did not seem to demand a clear allegiance on his part. The point once again is that whilst it is the fact of 'heretical' belief that brings these issues into our view, it seems likely to apply similarly to some orthodox tenets of faith.

Elsewhere, as we have already seen, Pierre was capable of rejecting aspects of what the Good Men preached, as for example in the case of godparenthood, almsgiving, and tithing. He was also capable of further reflection on his own part, where the issue mattered to him or where he had heard something persuasive to the contrary. For example, had the Good Men ever said that secular lords sinned when they lawfully bestowed the death penalty? He had heard Bélibaste say that nobody should do to another what they themselves would not wish done to them (Pierre does not explicitly flag up the Gospel reference), and thus one should not kill. But Pierre 'did not believe this however, as he said, because he had commonly heard it said that blessed is the land in which justice is done; and that someone who killed another should themselves be killed'.[115] Various of the Psalms address 'justice', and the latter part of Pierre's statement is of course a version of the *lex talionis*. We cannot know if he was intending biblical authority behind his words, but he clearly did see it as quoting an authoritative statement, in the sense of it being common knowledge.

In another area—the incarnation of Christ and the passion—there is a real sense of Pierre struggling to work out his own understanding of the competing things he had been told by the Good Men and by priests, and in light of his own understanding of the world. It is worth quoting at some length from what Fournier asked him, and how he responded:

> Item, asked if he had heard from the heretics or had believed that God the Son descended from heaven and assumed our humanity in the Blessed Mary, namely a true body and a true human soul, or that he carried a body from heaven and did not have a true body but only appeared to do so with an imaginary one, he responded that he had indeed heard from the said heretics that the Son of God had descended from Heaven and come into the world, so that he could show the path of God the Father, and preach words in this world. But he did not hear

[115] *Fournier* III, p. 246 (article 51).

from them if he was conceived and born of the Blessed Virgin Mary, because he did not hear them name the Blessed Mary.

He said however that up until now he had believed that just as God the Father always had, as he said, a human body united with him, so also therefore did God the Son always have a human body in heaven, namely in the same manner as the son of a man, he had a human body just like his father. And when the said body of the Son of God descended from heaven, he carried with him the said body, in the similitude of a body of a child, and entered into the uterus of the Blessed Virgin Mary, where he was not formed into a human body, since he already had one; but that it was only the body that he carried from the sky that was nourished by the blood of the Blessed Mary, whilst the Son of God stayed in her belly. And from therein the Son of God was born. And thus he believed that the Son of God was the son of God the Father and the Blessed Virgin Mary, even though his human body was not formed in the uterus of the Blessed Mary but was carried from heaven.[116]

Further questioned by Fournier as to whether Christ, incarnated, experienced thirst and hunger, Pierre explained that the Good Men had never discussed this; he himself however believed that Christ could eat and drink, but did not need to, as he was sustained by the power of his Father. 'He had however indeed heard from the heretics that he was offered fish and honeycomb by the disciples' (here quoting Luke 24: 42, on their encounter with Christ after he had risen). What of the Passion—had Christ truly experienced pain and suffering? Bélibaste had preached to him on this, that all of what Christ suffered was in appearance only 'to show the will and feelings that Satan had toward him'. Pierre had said to Bélibaste 'that God had indeed had the power to prevent the Jews from harming him, if he had so wished'; the heretic corrected him, telling him that he ought rather to believe that they had not harmed nor indeed killed him.[117]

That final point seems to illustrate how orthodox theology was still part of the mix of beliefs for Pierre, 'translating' parts of what the Good Men told him into a slightly more familiar form (until forcibly corrected by Bélibaste). The lengthier passage above is also witness to this, in Pierre's clear desire to construct a theological picture in which the Virgin Mary still played an essential role, 'nourishing' the body of Christ in her womb, even if that body had been brought with him from heaven. The insistence that God the Father had a body is something that Pierre had already asserted earlier in the interrogation, and appears to be a kind of reversed implication of a specific belief of his that 'man had the face of God'; this perhaps derived from having heard orthodox preaching on God having created man in his own image (Gen. 1: 27), or from other biblical moments when

---

[116] *Fournier* III, pp. 224–25 (article 14).   [117] *Fournier* III, p. 225 (articles 15 and 16).

'the face of God'—inconceivable other than as a human face—was referenced. This can be seen also in what Pierre says above about Christ having a human body in heaven, in the same way that the son of a man has a body just like his father does. The knowably human comes to illuminate the divine.

All of that is to explore some ways in which Pierre's personal 'beliefs that' God's creation and Christ's sacrifice had meaning, as he brought together orthodox preaching, heretical instruction, and his own personal knowledge of and reflections on the world around him. One further final example may help us understand something of how his 'belief in' something also operated—how, that is, that interior affect and adherence operated, above and beyond tenets of faith. It is worth initially reminding ourselves that we have already seen some areas where Pierre had strong feelings about what he ought to do—perhaps less 'beliefs' in an abstract sense, but in terms of affect, that which governed his actions in the world, as for example regarding almsgiving and godparenthood. It is unclear how he would relate these beliefs to abstract propositions: in the case of godparenthood he apparently accepted the Good Men's position that it had no spiritual value. And yet the 'great friendship' it brought between people mattered to him sufficiently to value it; a lived belief of a slightly different order.

The particularly illuminating example is the question of whether Christ was truly present in the host. Here, as in several other instances, Pierre said that he believed what the heretics said when he was with the Good Men, but disbelieved when he was elsewhere.[118] But the precise details are important:

> Asked if he heard from the said heretics, or believed, that after the words of consecration the sacrament of the altar was the body of Christ, or that it was only bread and wine...he replied that he had heard from all the aforesaid heretics that the sacrament of the altar—before or after consecration—was not the body of Christ, but only bread and wine, because, as they said, God the Son, after he had appeared to resurrect from the dead, said to his apostles that henceforth he would not be between the hands of sinners [*cf. Mark* 14: 41] and moreover that from henceforth carnal eyes would never see him [*cf. John* 14: 19, albeit rather allusively]; and because of this, as they said, the body of Christ was not between the hands of the priest nor could be seen by carnal eyes. [*The heretics go on to deride the notion of a material Host, via familiar tropes...*] And he, as he said, when he was with the heretics, believed the aforesaid. But afterwards, when he went to church, and saw the people and important men adoring the consecrated Host, sometimes he believed that it was the body of Christ.[119]

---

[118] For example, that there was no value to clerical singing and prayers, or to marriage, and against the final resurrection (*Fournier* III, pp. 234, 239, 243).

[119] *Fournier* III, pp. 233–34 (article 27).

Pierre's memory of how the heretics challenged orthodox belief shows us a mixture of biblical quotation and an appeal to base materiality (in addition to the usual 'if as big as a mountain…' argument, they emphasized that if the body of Christ was eaten by the priest it would then end up in the 'vile' belly of a man). Thus two routes to 'belief', scriptural authority and quotidian experience. But Pierre's final statement shows us something more, perhaps the most fundamental aspect of the dynamics of belief. It is important to note that, in the various other occasions when he said that he sometimes believed and sometimes did not, or that he neither believed nor disbelieved, this was the entirety of his gloss. But on this topic, we have something more: reference to the experience, with others, of worship. That not just people but 'important men' (*valentes viri*) worshipped; that this happened in church, with the people; and, we may perhaps presume, that this happened in a moment of heightened ritual, where the elevation of the host would be accompanied by ringing bells and candles, quite likely framed by an image of Christ in majesty painted on the wall of the apse—all of this could lead 'belief' in Christ's presence to be felt by Pierre as well.

'Felt' is perhaps the apposite word here, and returns us to the probably irresolvable question of how we should conceptualize 'belief'. The point, once again, is that whilst Pierre's experiences were to some extent idiosyncratic—both in terms of his experience of heresy and, perhaps as importantly, his wide journeying as a shepherd and his knowledge of different lands and peoples—the core *dynamic* to his experience of belief was not. Belief might come through a mixture of authoritative claim, familiar and repeated propositions, socially expected behaviour, personal reflection on material reality, and, perhaps most importantly, moments of heightened engagement alongside others. Belief, when it came, was performed and felt, as much as thought.

Conclusion

The record of Pierre Maury's interrogation by Jacques Fournier runs to about 60,000 words of Latin. Inquisitorial boilerplate constitutes a portion of this, but if we had Pierre's words written out in his Occitan vernacular, the length would increase considerably. It is problematic to describe their encounter as a 'conversation', given the utterly unequal power dynamics. Yet it was to some extent nonetheless a form of exchange, a to-and-fro of detail and reflections, as Fournier's questions and Maury's explanations pursued a wide range of issues, beyond the specifics of the heresy of the Good Men. The deposition is, in a word, extraordinary—as indeed are others from the same register.

But whilst it is extraordinary, its very existence was also the product of profound changes to the framework and compass of Christianity across the period addressed by this book. What could be understood to constitute 'heresy' had broadened in scope from the late twelfth century: by the early fourteenth century, heresy comprised not only active support for a dualist theology but public denial that certain bad behaviour—usury, fornication—was actually sinful. The Church's concern over 'supporters' of heresy was no longer directed primarily toward lords and lordship, but embraced shepherds and artisans; the eradication of heresy had become a responsibility for all Christians. Parish priests, whether or not they lived up to the task, knew themselves to be key components within a wider *system*, within which the care of ordinary souls was managed and to some extent monitored.

As a marker of change let us note, above all else, this: the fact that someone like Jacques Fournier—learned theologian, reforming bishop, and, in just a few years to come, pope—should expend very considerable time and effort talking to someone like Pierre Maury, an itinerant shepherd, a man more familiar with the hills and valleys of the Pyrenees than with an episcopal court. As noted in the previous chapter, we do not know the dates of Pierre's interrogations other than for their initial sessions; but from the parallel evidence of other deponents, we must assume that the encounter between Maury and Fournier was carried out over many days, whether consecutively or spread out across months. They must in some sense have come to know each other through these encounters, even if only through the tense and particular theatre of inquisition. Both men cared for their 'flock', it is true; but for Pierre that meant on occasion bedding down at night in a field next to his sheep, to keep watch. What is most extraordinary is thus the very fact of the encounter, that the man who would be pope spent such time asking the shepherd questions about belief and faith, and listening carefully to the answers. This level of engagement—unequal, ultimately harsh, and yet still part of the *cura animarum*—would have been utterly unthinkable in the eleventh century. The embrace of organized Christianity, of Christianity as a 'religion', had changed.

This does not imply that people in earlier centuries did not have Pierre's inner life. For those earlier periods, the issue in part is that no mechanism of encounter and consequent documentary recording existed to capture it. However, to a large extent the changes in the later medieval source base are themselves a product of the wider shift to lay religion explored in this book: the development of inquisition and other recorded inquiries, the production of preaching *exempla*, parochial records and agreements, non-elite people making wills, and so forth, are all bound up in the processes of change. A change in the evidence is thus not simply making visible that which was always there; in important ways it was itself intimately involved in bringing into being new modes of Christian identity.

Beyond the inescapable difference between earlier and later sources, there were other very real differences. Whilst some practices might have been much the same across the centuries—attendance at mass, pilgrimage to shrines, paying tithes, an expectation of baptism and burial—other aspects would have been rather different. As we have seen, the space of the church in which they worshipped had changed, and with it an increased potential for any individual Christian to experience contrast between different holy spaces. Ordinary Christians from earlier centuries were not confronted by the same sense of 'choice' that Pierre was. Opportunities for almsgiving and the variety of 'holy people' and institutions to whom they might be given had grown hugely. The possibility had arisen of hearing both regular and expert preaching by mendicants and others, such sermons addressing the laity directly with a more developed spiritual discourse which, among other things, proffered to them an active role in their own salvation. By Pierre's time *all* Christians had been made aware of the requirement for annual (or at some points triannual) confession, within a framework of sin that had expanded to incorporate a wider variety of human experiences and indeed thoughts; his earlier predecessors were probably presented with a concept of sin and the possibility of penance, but the dynamics do tend to look rather different.

With these changes, I would argue, a further shift took place also, in the very mode of belief proffered to, and increasingly demanded from, all Christian people. This might be summed up as a shift from an external conformity of practice and adherence to an internalized disposition and degree of self-responsibility for one's salvation. To explore this briefly further, via one key phrase: in a huge number of different documents found throughout the period covered by this book, one can see the statement that something was done 'for the love of God', *pro amore Dei* or *per amor de Deu*. The phrase is found in the pious clauses of eleventh- and twelfth-century donation charters, in twelfth-century papal letters exhorting lords to proper Christian behaviour, as an encouragement to charity in the twelfth-century vernacular sermons we met in Chapter 7, in civic statutes regulating testamentary choices, in trade guild statutes and in wills regarding the disposition of residue goods, in thirteenth-century *exempla* describing states of pious fervour, in a deponent's petition to an inquisitorial court in the early fourteenth century, and framing the hope for successful business transactions in a notary's handbook. As a common and powerful phrase, it indicates and embodies long continuities. But careful attention to its precise use suggests also a profound shift in meaning. Early occurrences are all essentially petitionary, an address to the Lord God, hoping for his favour—his 'love'. This is fairly clear in examples where it is paired with *timor*, 'fear': 'all of this [*agreed in a charter from 1081*] is said from the fear and love of God, and dread of the eternal fires of Gehenna'.[1] So to give something piously 'for the love of God', or rather 'for God's love', has embedded within it the key dynamic of lordship. The Lord God is a *lord*. One gives, in the hope of clemency and favour.

In later uses a different inflection appears: to give alms (in particular) 'for the love of God' comes to mean 'out of love *for* God'—thus, for example, a female donor in 1229 attesting that she gave land to the Templars 'for love of God and of her soul to God and to Our Lady Mary', or a reformed character in an *exemplum* resists demonic temptation, 'exulting with joy in his heart and cleaving to such love of God'.[2] Perhaps we should read other later examples similarly, even when the precise wording differs not at all from earlier charters: that one gives *per amor de Deu*, out of one's own love for God, rather than in hope of gaining God's love?

What we see here, I am suggesting, is a shift from a dominant petitionary mode, structured by the logic of lordship, to a dominant affective mode, structured by the logic of *caritas*, where one acts precisely because one 'loves' Christ and God, as one loves (or at least, should love) one's neighbours. The former meaning never totally disappears, but the latter shines more brightly as we move into the later centuries. As I have argued more fully in Part II, we see a shift to an affective expectation for all of the laity; that is, a shift not only in *what* they were to believe (in the increased elaboration of sin and an increased expectation of what might lie beyond 'implicit belief'), but in *how* they were to believe, in their internal, emotional, embodied response to the demands of the faith. In this sense, a key development in the 'history of belief' that Ethan Shagan explores across the medieval to modern periods might be said to have occurred a couple of centuries earlier than he suggests, as belief itself, believing 'firmly' (to cite the Lateran IV creed) and to believe in an affective mode, became a more universal requirement.[3]

---

[1] *Cart. Mas d'Azil*, pp. 157–58 (no. 1).
[2] *Cart. de la Selve*, p. 145 (no. 36); Welther, ed., 'Un nouveau recueil franciscain d'exempla', p. 610 (no. 171).
[3] Shagan, *Birth of Modern Belief*; this is not to argue however that further profound developments, as identified by Shagan, do not also then occur.

What brought about these and other changes was the combination of a variety of factors. Some were deeply structural, most importantly the growth in European population and its expansion of urbanization, the latter giving rise to both new possibilities and new demands. Urbanization and increased mercantilism went hand in hand, and as various historians have explored (Jacques Le Goff and Lester K. Little perhaps most influentially) these prompted profound developments in the spiritual address provided by the Church. Mercantilism also went hand in hand with an expansion of coinage, and part of what facilitated the increased diversity and complexity of almsgiving was, I have argued, the basic fact of more fungible currency in circulation and a greater array of potential recipients. Other factors were ideological, in the sense of being driven by conscious human reflection upon the world, and consequent attempts to re-form it. Here the diffuse sets of concerns associated with 'the Gregorian reform' are hugely important, both in terms of their discursive effects and the reorganization they prompted in the relations between nobility, ecclesial structures, and spiritual governance. For southern France in particular, the unfolding of the long 'Lateran IV moment' and the brutal intervention of the Albigensian Crusade brought with them further ideological and practical changes.

Both as part of Gregorian reforms, and having its own independent dynamic beyond papally inspired rhetoric and theology, we have noted the demonstrable wave of 'apostolicities' that inspired and engaged a wide lay audience in the twelfth century and thereafter. This wave forms a crucial part of the 'charitable revolution' but gave rise to heterodox variety as well as orthodox renewal. Here we can be reminded that as well as ideas and attempts at governance 'from above'—from the papacy and from reform-minded bishops and abbots—we have seen agency 'from below', in the sense of factors arising within lay society itself: the active embrace of certain apostolic models, various elaborations of the ideal of *caritas*, the practical investment in new religious institutions, the growth of collectivities that could renegotiate their relationship toward Christianity, both in terms of its practical institutional representatives and in regard to its important and affective cultural contours. Thus another key element in the *combination* of factors was a complex dialectic between ecclesial ambition and lay response, between lay enthusiasm and ecclesial concern, and between Christian aspiration and varied material circumstances.

I am far from the first historian to note that Christianity changed considerably between the eleventh and the fourteenth centuries. Others have also previously argued that it is in this period, particularly following the Fourth Lateran Council, that there is a major shift in the way in which the Church treated the ordinary laity. Florian Mazel has argued that this should itself be seen as a part of a longer period of 'la réforme grégorienne', constituting a profound reordering of faith and society across the eleventh to thirteenth centuries. Past scholarship has also suggested that the later middle ages (though perhaps most usually focused on the later fourteenth and fifteenth centuries) bear witness to a more interiorized, individualized form of faith. My work here does not seek to overthrow those past accounts, but to adjust some of the chronology, to give due weight to what *precedes* the pastoral revolution associated with Lateran IV, and to explore and make visible the texture of the underlying dynamics. Through a close focus upon one region, I have thus tried to show in some detail how these developments unfolded and to capture something of their complexity, rather than treating them simply as the consequence of papal fiat, reforming zeal, or the teleological unfolding of some innate and transhistorical essence of Christianity.

For the centuries before 1215, I have presented evidence for a fair degree of liturgical and pastoral engagement with the laity, suggesting that this nonetheless changes in intensity and focus following not only the Lateran Council but as importantly the Albigensian Crusade; and that, as we have seen, the pastoral reforms of Lateran IV take on a particularly disciplinary hue in southern France. It is a mixture of that disciplinary apparatus and the elaboration of cultures of Christian storytelling and story-making that gives rise to what can, *in potentia* at least, produce a more individualized, interiorized, and affective experience of faith. At the same time, I have emphasized that such 'individualized' religion operates always in conjunction with more collective worship, and indeed collective negotiation with the demands of Christianity. In reflecting upon the affective aspects of lay religiosity, we have seen also that the increased likelihood of *contrasting* embodied experiences is an essential part of their dynamic, a fundamental mechanism in how 'belief' works in its sociocultural context and subjective experience. Cumulatively, we might see these changes as being as profound as those experienced across the Reformation of the sixteenth century.

There are of course some important caveats to that statement: most obviously, despite the complexities involving heresy, there was no resulting division in western Christianity, nor the same entwining of faith with political loyalty, as we find in the sixteenth and seventeenth centuries. As importantly, the changes did not take place across as short a period, and thus largely did not prompt contemporary reflection upon their passing; what Christianity was and meant for ordinary people shifted very considerably but without much explicit discussion of that fact (beyond, perhaps, some recognition of how the confession of sin was to be understood).

Nonetheless, there are similarities with the Reformation period, particularly if we note that recent scholarship on the Reformation has stressed medieval continuities as well as 'early modern' change.[4] The spaces of worship changed qualitatively; the opportunities for lay engagement in the propositional content of

---

[4] See, for example, P. Marshall, *Beliefs and the Dead in Reformation England* (Oxford: Oxford University Press, 2002); A. Walsham, *The Reformation of the Landscape: Religion, Identity and Memory in Early Modern Britain and Ireland* (Oxford: Oxford University Press, 2011).

faith increased dramatically, this leading also to an increase in the Church's policing of beliefs; and, as argued above, what 'belief' meant for the many was further defined, refined, and intensified. In the eleventh century, as in previous times, ordinary lay people were Christians, and could dutifully engage with their faith. On specific life occasions—when entering and leaving this world, and perhaps at certain moments of socio-spiritual crisis—that engagement might gain a particular focus and affect. By the fourteenth century, whilst these elements continued, the experience of 'being Christian' for all of the laity involved much more activity and more interiorized demands. And by that period, the laity were aware not only of the requirement to be Christian, but to aspire to be *good* Christians; they were to have not just faith, but religion.

APPENDIX

The New Cathar Wars

Did Cathars exist? Did Catharism exist? These are not questions which historians asked themselves in the twentieth century, but they have become quite vocally present in the first decades of the twenty-first.[1] I have previously published a comment on the historiographical debate, there making the following main points: that the anti-heresy rhetoric of medieval authors was not univocal and monolithic, and could react to specific external real-world stimuli; that the radical changes to the extent and nature of the available documentation, between the twelfth and thirteenth centuries, present varied methodological challenges, noting in particular that problematizing a single document has a larger interpretive effect before c. 1200 than thereafter; and that everybody engaged in the current arguments sees themselves as on the side of the alleged heretics, some wanting to emphasize how people were wrongly repressed by the Catholic Church, others wanting to emphasize that dissident believers nonetheless had individual and collective agency.[2] I will not rehearse those same points again in detail here, and I have not seen the knottier issues as having any major effect on the main aims of this book. However, given the heat of the debate, it might be frustrating for some already engaged in the field, and confusing for those coming newly to it, if I did not proffer a few thoughts on the key issues.[3] Hence this appendix.

We should note that although, for convenience of discussion, the debate has tended to be presented as falling into two camps of 'traditionalists' and 'sceptics', these inevitably oversimply and homogenize different individual perspectives, and roll up a number of distinct critical issues into one package. To unpack the critical issues first, sceptical perspectives on the traditional picture of Catharism have presented the following challenges to past interpretations. Almost nobody in southern France used the term 'Cathar', whether about themselves or others; why, then, should we allow it to suggest a connection with heretics elsewhere, such as in northern France, the Rhineland, and northern Italy?[4] In particular, do we have any solid evidence to link southern French 'heretics' (I'm going to

---

[1] Some key critical interventions: M. Zerner, ed., *L'inventer d'hérésie? Discours polémiques et pouvoirs avant l'Inquisition* (Nice: Centre d'études médiévales, 1998); M. Zerner, ed., *L'histoire du catharisme en discussion: le 'concile' de Saint-Félix (1167)* (Nice: Centre d'études médiévales, 2001); Pegg, *Corruption of Angels*; U. Brunne, *Des contestataires aux "Cathares"* (Paris: Institut d'études augustiniennes, 2006); Pegg, *A Most Holy War*; Moore, *War on Heresy*; J.-L. Biget, S. Caucanas, M. Fournié, and D. Le Blévec, eds, *Le "catharisme" en questions*, CdF 55 (Toulouse: Privat, 2020).

[2] J. H. Arnold, 'The Cathar Middle Ages as a Methodological and Historiographical Problem', in A. Sennis, ed., *Cathars in Question* (York: York Medieval Press, 2016), pp. 53–78.

[3] The heated quality of the debate has most recently been noted with regret in the conclusion to *Le "catharisme" en questions*. Given this, I hope it is not inappropriate to mention that I have enjoyed a convivial bottle of wine and/or pint of beer with almost every single person currently engaged in the discussion, regardless of the position they take; and hope to do so again in the future.

[4] Biget made this point some time ago in his 'Les albigeois: remarques sur une dénomination', in Zerner, ed., *L'inventer*, p. 219 n. 2: 'Les hérétiques méridionaux n'ont jamais pris, ni reçu, au cours du Moyen Âge, le nom de *cathares*.' However, we should in fact note that Alain de Lille, Durand d'Osca, the anonymous author of the Albi *Summa auctoritatem*, and (copying Alain) Benoît d'Alignan did all use the term 'Cathar' on occasion.

assume that the reader can continue to supply their own scare-quotes hereafter) with the dualist Bogomil heretics in eastern Europe? Furthermore, twelfth-century hostile sources that alleged the presence of dualist heresy in southern France may not have been responding to an external phenomenon. Some might be seen as having political motives, particularly but not only when connected to the court of Henry II of England. Others emerge from the intellectual culture associated with the Schools of Paris, where the antique spectre of heretical dualism was (it is argued) a recurrent object of theological fascination, a practice ground for orthodox intellectual gymnastics. Thus 'dualism' might be thought to exist nowhere outside the Ivory Tower of academe. Beyond these issues, various details supplied in the interrogations of thirteenth-century inquisitors (in line with earlier polemic and narratives sources) suggest a structured 'church-like' sect with its own rituals and hierarchy; but are these not the distortions of an inquisitorial mindset, framed by and thus imposing a view of heresy shaped by the aforementioned political rhetoric against the south and the intellectual ivory-tower fascination with dualism? And even if everyone in the debate accepts that 'heresy', thus labelled, is to some extent inescapably the construction of orthodoxy, should we in fact see anyone as intentionally opposing the Church in various periods? Or, particularly in the twelfth and early thirteenth centuries, were those accused of heresy simply reformers or long-standing local holy men who were the victims of unfortunate circumstance?

It is useful to say something briefly about the complexity of modern scholars' perspectives, and to note that individuals' positions have shifted at least slightly across the last couple of decades. On the allegedly 'traditionalist' side, for example, as a minor but nonetheless important point, we may note that some decades ago most historians talked of Cathar 'Perfects', but have now abandoned that terminology, recognizing that it does not reflect the language of the Good Men and Women themselves, or of most of the surviving sources. Those who still find it useful to treat 'Catharism' as a real phenomenon, with links beyond southern France, and dualist in nature, can also adopt a range of specific positions over the detail and the implications of this. An important issue, for example, is whether one thinks that dualism was a key element in the sect's wider attraction to lay people; as indicated in an earlier chapter in this book, and in line with various earlier historians including, for example, Herbert Grundmann, I think probably not.[5] Another issue is whether one thinks that possible Bogomil missionizing is sufficient explanation for the emergence of a dualist heretical sect in southern France and elsewhere; again, one may wish to suggest (as at an earlier point did Jean-Louis Biget) that what arises locally is best explained locally, as an 'autochthonous' reaction to specific needs and conditions, even if one can also admit to international connections (this latter element never being Biget's position, I should clarify). It is important also to note that arguing for the real existence of an organized group does not imply that one 'blames' it for its own repression. In 1987 R. I. Moore, in his *Formation of a Persecuting Society*, made the powerful point that generations of earlier historians *had* effectively 'blamed the victim'; but the dynamic does not automatically continue to follow.[6] Indeed, as noted above, one sympathetic perspective can

---

[5] Grundmann, *Religious Movements*, p. 215. For commentary on some misinterpretation of this earlier scholarship, see J. Feuchter, 'The *Heretici* of Languedoc: Local Holy Men and Women or Organized Religious Group? New Evidence from Inquisitorial, Notarial and Historiographical Sources', in Sennis, ed., *Cathars in Question*, pp. 112–30 at pp. 113–14.

[6] For comments on this seminal work, see J. H. Arnold, 'Persecution and Power in Medieval Europe: *The Formation of a Persecuting Society*, by R. I. Moore', *American Historical Review* 123 (2018), 164–74.

precisely be to give due credit to the organizational and intellectual abilities of a group who refuse to submit to the demands of orthodoxy.

In the more sceptical camp, precise scholarly positions are also not identical nor utterly fixed. Moore's *War on Heresy* (2012) sought to demolish the idea of any twelfth-century dualist group in southern France, arguing that nothing should be projected back from thirteenth-century evidence, particularly Italian evidence. (In one of the final chapters of that book Moore does admit, albeit almost tacitly, to the existence of dualist groups in mid-thirteenth-century Italy, and moreover that these had some connections in that period with southern French Good Men. But overall, as in his other important works, Moore positions himself fundamentally as a historian of the tenth to twelfth centuries, and thus seems to see the thirteenth century as a separate problem, to be addressed by other historians.) Biget, as noted earlier, tended to see the Good Men as a local group who were consciously opposed to the orthodox Church and to some extent dualist; more recently, he has evinced some scepticism about the latter also, suggesting that it might be an inquisitorial imposition.[7] Julien Théry-Astruc is sympathetic to the sceptical stance taken overall, but his own research focus is primarily on the politics around heresy accusations in the later thirteenth century, arguing that we there see a 'dissidence' that is primarily anti-clerical, emerging in a context of increased episcopal and papal power. In *The Corruption of Angels* (2001) Mark Gregory Pegg took a strongly sceptical stance, arguing that any sense of sect hierarchy or ritual were inquisitorial inventions, suggesting that dualist thought might similarly be something imported. He there argued that inquisitors imposed a foreign perspective on a locally rooted form of holiness, the latter founded essentially on a blend of social respect and a transcendent sense of the sacred. More recently Pegg has further emphasized the latter point, arguing that a peculiarly southern French form of *cortezia* was what underpinned the dynamics of a local faith; whilst also however averring that the very pressure of repression—particularly through crusade and perhaps then further through inquisition—itself made the group adopt elements of the image imposed upon it by orthodoxy, as it constructed a hierarchy (and perhaps adopted a more radical theology?), these developments, which he dates to some time after 1220, being however a sad and hollow act of 'nostalgia' for the world they had then lost.[8]

Scepticism is important, in making us question assumptions and check for unnoticed and unwanted legacies lingering on from past historiography. As academia rightly values a sharpness of intellect, scepticism will tend to have a greater appeal, on first sight at least, than what might appear to be the embrace of a long-accepted interpretive orthodoxy. Moreover, the Cathars are probably only second to the Templars, in western medieval history, in terms of attracting intense, wild-eyed nonsense; so for all scholars *some* scepticism is undoubtedly essential. There are moreover three other contextual factors that it may be useful to note. It is just possible that a touch of confessional allegiance, or at the very least an inheritance of the Protestant image of the Catholic Church as powerfully repressive monolith, feeds into some critiques. Perhaps more importantly, as I noted in my previous

---

[7] Compare J.-L. Biget, 'Réflexions sur l'hérésie dans le Midi de la France au Moyen Âge', *Heresis* 36–37 (2002), 29–74, and his more recent contributions to *Le "catharisme" en questions*.

[8] Pegg, *A Most Holy War*, chapter 16. The southern French specificity to *cortezia* (a word which has close equivalents in various other European vernaculars) is presented by Pegg as emerging from the fragmented nature of landholding in Languedoc, the various *honores* (a word he sees as implying 'honour' in the broader sense, as well as a parcel of lands and rights) that are often in shared ownership and non-contiguous locations. This is imaginative, but we may wish to remember that such landholding and language was also the case for institutions such as monasteries and churches, which complicates the issue at the very least.

intervention into the debate, the methodological and epistemological approaches of those who work before c. 1200 can differ profoundly from those whose focus falls later, perhaps more profoundly than either party fully realizes. In particular, for the earlier period scepticism about a single source or single author can produce a more profound change to the overall apparent picture than is the case for later decades. And finally, modern scholars professionally based in southern France are continually confronted by distorted images of 'les Cathares' via modern tourism, popular culture, and a strand of Occitan quasi-nationalism. A parallel would be trying to research the politics of medieval Scotland whilst having Mel Gibson's film *Braveheart* playing outside the window on an endless loop. For some sceptics, it may therefore feel as if giving any ground to 'Catharism' as an edifice will import the whole panoply of nonsense. This is less visible to those working in the anglosphere.

I set all of this out in order to make clear my overall sense of the field (others may of course see it differently); to note that it is a complicated debate, rather than two clear 'sides'; and to flag up that I am in sympathy with various challenges from the more sceptical scholarship. Nonetheless, I remain of the view that the Good Men and Women in southern France were an organized group, were dualist, were conscious of their challenge to orthodox Christianity, and did have meaningful connections beyond the region, fairly directly with northern Italy, and primarily via shared theological and liturgical materials with eastern Europe. In most of these areas, I would further hold that these things were true from at least some point in the second half of the twelfth century and definitely not only in the post-1220 period. As I have already discussed in Chapter 4, these aspects were not necessarily visible or important to the ordinary laity; though I will note below some evidence to suggest that at least *some* lay people did see the Good Men as 'heretics', or at least knew that the Church condemned them as 'heretics'. To make the case briefly for all of this, I will flag up a few pieces of primary evidence and some interpretive rationale, simply in order to make my position legible to others.

The case *against* there being an organized group is in part in regard to the presence or absence of hierarchy and ritual and in part via a different model for how we should see the Good Men, namely as local holy men and women, operating in something like the way in which Peter Brown discussed such figures in late antiquity.[9] To take the 'holy men and women' point first: in part, I agree. This clearly is a role that the Good Men and Women played, most visible in a Peter Brown dynamic when they were involved in dispute settlement, but also visible, as discussed in Chapter 4, when they were the recipients of almsgiving. But that does not in itself obviate organization: we could make similar points about Templars, Hospitallers, Cistercians, and subsequent mendicant orders. People can function as holy men and women within a locality and also be part of a wider organized spiritual entity. Cistercians are a useful parallel here, not least because one strand of sceptical scholarship regarding Cathars is similar in part to the critique of early Cistercianism made by Connie Berman. Berman argued that 'Cistercianism' as an order and organization was a back-projection from the later twelfth century when such things had *become* true, made retrospectively to embrace the early twelfth century before such dynamics clearly existed.[10] Not all have agreed (in part demurring over whether key early documents were, as she

---

[9] P. Brown, 'Arbiters of the Holy: The Christian Holy Man in Late Antiquity', in P. Brown, *Authority and the Sacred: Aspects of the Christianisation of the Roman World* (Cambridge: Cambridge University Press, 1995).

[10] C. Berman, *The Cistercian Evolution: The Invention of a Religious Order in Twelfth-Century Europe* (Philadelphia: University of Pennsylvania Press, 2000).

argued, forgeries from later in the twelfth century), though recent scholarship tends to see merit in her overall point: that early converts to Cistercianism, such as Pons de Léras, initially embraced a mode of piety rather than a formal 'order' with a clear hierarchy and constitution. To return to the Good Men, it is however then useful to think through the example of Pons a little further: the motives for his original conversion were to embrace not 'Cistercianism' but a mode of apostolic holiness; and yet the group he founded *did* undoubtedly become Cistercian. One can imagine a similar dynamic for Catharism: one can be attracted to a mode of apostolic piety, and then embrace, and be embraced by, an organized group holding some unorthodox theological beliefs.

A key document for the twelfth century is the so-called Cathar council of Saint-Félix-de-Caraman, which narrates a great meeting in 1167 at which one Papa Niquinta bestowed the *consolamentum* and preached to representatives of southern French and northern Italian 'churches', those churches choosing bishops for themselves. Niquinta also explained briefly that the divided eastern European 'churches' operated in harmony, thus presenting a clear connection to that geographical locale—though equally clearly speaking to already-existent groups in southern France. The document presents itself as a copy made in 1223 by Pierre Pollan on the orders of Pierre Isarn 'from the old charter that had been made'.[11] As it now survives only in a seventeenth-century edition by Guillaume Besse, some earlier sceptics argued that it was a forgery from that period; recently Biget has cleverly attempted to revive that position.[12] However, the close study of the document by various French specialists in 1999, plus Monique Zerner's discovery of three different handwritten versions by Besse—most obviously interpreted as different attempts at transcription—suggests that a thirteenth-century document did exist.[13] More recently, in response, sceptical attack has changed tack: Pegg, for example, now suggests that the document was a thirteenth-century forgery created by the Good Men themselves, Pollan and Isarn deciding earnestly to back-project a heretical 'church' for their movement, under the pressure of the crusading attacks.[14]

It is a curious document, but there is nothing innately suspicious about a thirteenth-century copy of a twelfth-century document, nor even that such a document survives only via a later seventeenth-century antiquarian; such a trajectory is not that unusual for medieval material. If one takes seriously Pegg's argument for the Good Men in the 1220s forging for themselves a fifty-year-old past that emphasizes bishops, 'churches' (in the sense of dioceses), and international connections, in something like the manner that Berman suggests the Cistercians similarly did, 'scepticism' seems in fact to have given quite a lot of ground. But to argue that nothing but orthodox pressure supplied all of these details in 1223 requires us to believe that under the onslaught of crusade and propaganda, the hitherto local, unorganized, non-hierarchical, and not-dualist local Good Men and Women, over the space of just fourteen years, performed a total volte-face wholly to embrace that which was alleged against them, and to claim 'churches' not only in the southern French

---

[11] Translated A&B, doc. 1.
[12] Biget in CdF 55. Biget, it should be noted, argued in 2001 that it was a thirteenth-century forgery by orthodox enemies of Catharism, in an attempt to promote the crusade.
[13] Zerner, ed., *L'histoire*, pp. 207–13 and plates between pp. 249 and 250. Zerner seeks to suggest that Besse still invented some of its details, though this seems to me to continue to fall foul of a point made some years ago by Bernard Hamilton: that Besse patently did not fully understand the content or import of the document.
[14] Pegg, *A Most Holy War*, p. 171.

region but in northern France, Italy, and eastern Europe.[15] A rather simpler argument would be that these features were already part of the sect's memory and actual past.

The memories of witnesses in inquisitorial trials supply us with details that demonstrate the presence of hierarchy prior to the 1220s. Raimond de Mirepoix, for example, was remembered as being named a 'deacon of heretics' around 1209, and one Bonfils (*possibly* de Cassès) given the same title 'in the time when the count of Montfort held all this land', that is before 1218 and probably somewhat earlier. A witness in 1245 recounted, in the context of evidence apparently from very much earlier, seeing Bernard de Lamothe 'confirmed as bishop of the heretics' following sermons given by the Good Men at Montesquieu (this Bernard is later frequently mentioned as 'bishop' in evidence relating to the besieged castle at Montségur in 1244).[16] It is true that the evidence for such titles becomes stronger as one gets closer to the 1240s—a witness in 1238 recounted a 'general council' (*concilium generale*) of Good Men held in 1226 at which people were made not only 'bishop' but appointed to the lesser roles of 'Elder Son' and 'Younger Son' (idiosyncratic titles which seem very hard to reconcile with any model supplied or imposed by orthodoxy).[17] But that chronological thickening of detail is the case for all aspects regarding the sect, since no interrogations survive from earlier than the late 1230s, and the weight of evidence is thus inevitably skewed toward the more recent period. As it is, polemical orthodox sources name various people as 'bishops' of the heretics earlier than this, and some such figures then indeed appear as 'bishop' in later inquisitorial evidence. We should also note that mention of 'bishops' and other hierarchy declines markedly in the trial evidence from the later thirteenth century, a phenomenon most straightforwardly explained as the objective result of repression diminishing the size and organization of the group.

The evidence for formal 'rites' connected with the sect is also strong. This is very clear with the *consolamentum*, as its elaborated conduct is frequently spelt out in some detail by deponents, and is attested also through the surviving late thirteenth-century Occitan Ritual. With regard to the *melioramentum* it is true—as, in different ways, both Pegg and I have previously argued—that inquisitors' investment in the idea of 'adoring' a heretic as a marker of support could sometimes distort more complex interactions, and might on occasion blur together a formal ritual and more general social rituals of respect. But this does not mean that no formal ritual existed, independently of an inquisitorial perspective. Strong evidence for this is given by the various occasions on which deponents interrogated in the 1240s report in earlier years being *taught* how to perform the ritual (something attested quite frequently), being prodded into performing the ritual by others (such as Pierre d'Aura, who remembers being given a smack around the head to join in, when he was a young boy), and occasionally that they had not fully participated because of incapacity (such as a woman called Berbegueira who 'adored' but without bending her knees, because of infirmity).[18] Others note occasions when they chose not to 'adore' for various reasons, including because they were nervous about others then present, whom they did not know; by implication, because all recognized that it would be interpreted as a sign of allegiance and might get them into trouble.[19] A woman called Austorga on one occasion

---

[15] As Pegg is fond of suggesting that the survival of the Saint-Félix document resembles something out of Borges, it is perhaps worth noting that his current argument has parallels with the plot of Umberto Eco's novel *Foucault's Pendulum* (1988), in which the invention of an occult conspiracy brings about the conspiracy itself.

[16] Doat 22, fols 215r–217r; MS Toulouse 609, fols 216v, 62r.

[17] Doat 23, fols 269v–270r (deposition of Raimond Jean d'Albi; trans. A&B, doc. 41).

[18] Taught the ritual: for example, Doat 23, fols 94v, 96r; Doat 24, fol. 10r. Pierre de Aura: Doat 22, fols 76r–78r. Berbegueira: Doat 24, fol. 136v.

[19] Thus Pierre de Cabanil: Doat 24, fol. 28r.

specified that she 'embraced' (*amplecta fuit*) a female heretic but did not 'adore', apparently signalling a divergence from the more formal and elaborate ritual, whilst clearly not distancing herself from attachment to the particular Good Woman. Similarly, another deponent admitted that he 'bowed toward them' (*inclinavit eis*), by implication again distinguishing this from the kneeling that the ritual proscribes.[20]

Another issue is whether the Good Men and Women themselves, and as importantly the ordinary laity, recognized them to be a specific and separate spiritual 'choice', as a distinct group, and thus potentially—if adopting the label bestowed by the orthodox Church—as 'heretics'. To be clear, there is no question but that this is the case in later decades, as for example when a witness interrogated in 1285 talked of an occasion a couple of years earlier when heretics asked someone on their deathbed if they wished to be received 'into the law and sect (*legem et sectam*) of the Good Men', using terminology that could contemporaneously be applied equally to Judaism or Islam.[21] Something of this is strongly implied too by the large number of witnesses from the 1240s who reported being told that there was no salvation except through the Good Men.[22] Another witness from 1274 heard the Good Men talk of how the count of Foix, despite his political troubles, was 'a friend to the Church of the heretics'. 'Heretics' is obviously an inquisitorial imposition, but 'Church' may not be, and it is worth remembering that to speak of heretics having 'a Church' need not imply a whole ecclesiastical superstructure but the sense of a gathered faithful.[23] One witness in 1237 reported a conversation with Good Men from around 1229 in which they asked him to look after a peasant who had led him to them 'out of love of the Church', apparently meaning their 'Church'.[24]

For the pre-crusade era various hostile polemical sources allege a 'counter-Church' of heresy, on occasion even claiming that the heretics presented their own 'pope' in opposition to orthodoxy. We should not accept polemic as fact; such a degree of organization is highly unlikely. But equally neither should we leap to the opposite interpretive pole: to do so would be methodologically akin to deciding that because western European crusading sources misrepresent Mohammed and Islam, medieval Islam did not exist. Witnesses talk of family members who formerly were Good Men or Good Women and then left 'the sect of the heretics' in the years before the crusade, on one slightly later occasion spelling out that a woman then 'converted to the Catholic faith'.[25] It is clear from various witness statements that before the coming of the crusaders, and perhaps still in some places thereafter, the Good Men and Women lived collectively in gender-segregated houses and wore clothing that marked them out as belonging to the group, operating in a quasi-monastic fashion.[26] As a witness called Aladaicia attested in 1244, she had become a Good Woman at her mother's behest back in the very early thirteenth century, holding to the sect for three and a half years, 'praying with them, fasting, wearing their habit and clothing, performing her *apparellamentum* [*a form of collective confession*] with them from month to

---

[20] Doat 24, fol. 4v; Doat 22, fol. 22r.   [21] Doat 26, fols 277r–278v.
[22] For example, Doat 21, fol. 200r; Doat 22, fol. 81r; Doat 23, fol. 94v.   [23] Doat 25, fol. 77r.
[24] Doat 24, fol. 112r–v (evidence of Guillaume Matfred): '…adduxit eundem ad hereticos rusticus predictus, et rogaverunt ipsum testem predicti heretici ut custodiret amore ecclesie rusticum supradictum, sed non adoravit eas. De tempore ex quo Comes fecit cum Ecclesia et Rege pacem.'
[25] Doat 24, fols 126r, 130r, 136r; Doat 23, fol. 124r '[her sister] tendendo sectam hereticorum, ieiunando ter in septimana in panne et aqua, et orando secundum morem hereticorum, et postea conversa fuit ad fidem Catholicam et accepit virum' (this from around 1218).
[26] For example, Doat 23, fol. 76v, evidence of Guillaume de Conrelian, a knight, that his father was a 'clothed heretic' (*hereticus indutus*), but that when the crusaders came he left the heretics and 'returned to the world' (*rediit ad saeculum*); Doat 24, fol. 240v, regarding a 'hostel' or 'hospital' of 'around 50' heretics in Mirepoix.

month, and otherwise doing that which the heretics prescribed and observed'.[27] Pegg himself notes in passing that the clothing seemed akin to that adopted by the Waldensians and mendicant orders.[28] It is very hard to see how one views this other than as a group—a 'sect'—distinguishable from other groups; as I have emphasized in Chapter 4, we should see the Good Men as a group visible to many alongside other groups, including the Waldensians, the knightly orders, and later the mendicants.

It is also clear that some awareness in southern France that people might be condemned as, or at least alleged to be, 'heretics' also pre-exists the crusade. We have seen this, for example, in some early thirteenth-century civic statutes, discussed in earlier chapters. It is inescapably part of the dynamic to the various pre-crusade 'debates' between bishops and Good Men, and indeed between Waldensians and Good Men. Moreover, as Jörg Feuchter has pointed out, it appears in a charter from 1189 dealing with a land transfer, the stated occasion being when a woman called Ava 'gave herself to those men whom they call heretics'.[29] This contextual detail does not imply that Ava herself counted the men 'as heretics' in a condemnatory sense; but it very clearly does indicate that she and others knew them to be sometimes labelled thus, and knew them to be a group. It seems very likely that a similar dynamic would pertain in regard to the Waldensians in southern France in the pre-crusade period: they had been condemned as heretics at the synod of Narbonne in 1190, and so might well be known sometimes to be labelled as such. But they continued to be present and visible to the laity, a spiritual choice available within that landscape, a clearly separate group—and one which was, moreover, clearly in fierce opposition to the Good Men.[30]

What, then, of geographical connections beyond southern France? Strong connections to northern Italy are unequivocally the case in the later thirteenth and early fourteenth century, attested via abundant statements to inquisitors.[31] These are visible also in mid-thirteenth-century records: in his lengthy deposition, given in 1244 after the fall of Montségur, Imbert de Salles stated that in January that year, 'Jean Reg de St-Paul-Cap-de-Joux entered Montségur with a letter from the bishop of the heretics of Cremona, and gave it to Bertrand Marty, bishop of the heretics of Toulouse. And the letter said that the church of the heretics of Cremona was in tranquillity and peace, and that Bertrand Marty should send two of his brother heretics, through whom he [Bertrand] could inform him [the Cremona bishop] about the state they were in'.[32] Direct evidence for connections to eastern Europe (the Saint-Félix text aside) are more fragmentary, and for earlier periods found particularly in hostile narrative or polemic accounts; though among those we should perhaps note the indigenous southern evidence of Guillaume de Tudela in the *Canso de la crozada* that talks of Diego d'Osma debating at Carcassonne in 1204 with 'those of Bulgaria' (*ab cels de Bolgaria*).[33]

---

[27] Doat 24, fol. 205r: 'orando cum eis, ieiunando, portando habitum et vestes eorum, apparellando se cum eis de mense in mensem, et alia omnia faciendo quae heretici precipiunt et faciunt observari'.

[28] Pegg, *Corruption of Angels*, p. 102.

[29] Feuchter, 'The *Heretici* of Languedoc', pp. 123–27.

[30] Emphasizing the sense of 'choice', see A. Roach, *The Devil's World: Heresy and Society, 1100–1300* (Harlow: Pearson, 2005).

[31] See P. Biller, 'Heretics and Long Journeys', in P. Horden, ed., *Freedom of Movement in the Middle Ages* (Donington: Shaun Tyas, 2007), pp. 86–103.

[32] Doat 24, fols 171v–172r; similarly, re a different messenger and another letter from Cremona, fol. 178r. The deposition is translated in full in A&B, doc. 46.

[33] *Canso* liasse 2; Martin-Chabot, *Chanson*, I, 10. Durand d'Osca also attests to links, in his treatise written c. 1223.

Beyond that material, there are also other very suggestive links: the Bogomils, for example, reserved the right to say the *Pater noster* to those who had formally entered the sect, and such entry was achieved by holding a copy of the Gospel of St John over the head of an initiate; two features that are identical in reports regarding southern French Good Men.[34] If one wishes to avoid the 'intellectualist bias' against which Pegg warns us, here are two rather key examples of shared *practice*, clearly set apart from contemporary orthodox behaviour. If we are allowed to consider ideas, as contained in theological texts, Bernard Hamilton demonstrates that as early as the 1220s (from the evidence of the converted Waldensian Durand d'Osca), and from various bits of later evidence also, we can see southern French reception of a Bogomil adaptation of the early Christian text *The Vision of Isaiah*.[35] From a variety of disparate evidence it is also apparent that southern French Good Men used the phrase 'supersubstantial bread' in their version of the *Pater noster*, in concert with both those of the Greek Orthodox Church and the Bogomils. Were we also to allow ourselves to draw upon orthodox sources hostile to heresy, several key Italian works written by inquisitors would add considerable detail to the filiations suggested here.

Finally, dualist thought itself. Again, later inquisitorial evidence is absolutely explicit on this fact: the early fourteenth-century witnesses to Bishop Fournier's inquisition provide considerable detail of dualist sermons, theological stories, and so forth, for example. There is one extremely detailed account of dualist belief in the witness statements against Pierre Garcias given in 1247 by Franciscan friars.[36] Various witnesses throughout the slightly earlier inquisition trials from the late 1230s and 1240s talk of the Good Men telling them that God had not made 'visible things'. One man called Guillaume de Brouil from Beaucaire confessed in 1241 to Pierre Cellan that he had seen both Waldensians and 'heretics' (that is, Good Men) and with the latter had 'debated with them about the Creation'.[37] As said above, this facet probably was not a major factor in how ordinary lay people perceived the Good Men or interpreted the 'salvation' that they offered; but it was nonetheless present. It is the case that various anti-heresy treatises deal with dualism at length from the later twelfth century onward, and that other hostile sources mention the existence of dualism in southern France in this period. We may rightly be highly cautious over precisely what is presented by such works. However, the claim that 'dualism' was a major feature of Parisian intellectual discussion rests on fairly shaky foundations, prior to the anti-heresy texts under discussion; it really is not, for example, a major feature of Peter Lombard's *Sentences* or commentaries upon the same. In any case, the fact of a hostile agenda does not automatically mean that nothing exists independently, beyond the polemical frame. As a methodological parallel, consider the febrile 'reds under the beds' rhetoric deployed in the 1950s by Senator McCarthy and the House Un-American Activities Committee. Their right-wing polemics undoubtedly conjured up phantasms of people and ideas that were never truly connected. But that does not mean that Communism itself did not exist, nor that there was never a Communist Party in America, nor even that *some* people accused of Communist sympathies did not hold such views.

Those already wedded to a more sceptical position may not be persuaded by all that is set out above. However, if (as seems to be the case with some scholars) the sceptical position has now moved to the point of saying that an organized, dualist, self-consciously

---

[34] See B. Hamilton, 'Cathar Links with the Balkans and Byzantium', in Sennis, ed., *Cathars in Question*, pp. 131–50 at p. 132.
[35] Hamilton, 'Cathar Links', p. 147.
[36] Doat 22, fols 89r–106v; ed. Douais, *Documents... de l'Inquisition*, II, pp. 90–114.
[37] Doat 21, fol. 263r.

dissident group with connections to Italy (at least) did exist by the 1220s, a larger area of agreement with other scholarship can become apparent than one might have previously assumed. Moore's explicit attempt not to read any later evidence 'back' into an earlier period is a perfectly sound heuristic method, a means of avoiding teleology to explore possibilities; but does not in itself provide a sustainable epistemological end point. If one accepts that an organized group is visible after the 1220s, it is then incumbent on sceptical scholars to explain how what now looks a lot like 'Catharism' leaps up like a spring-form easy-erect tent, only after the crusade called against it was ending.[38] To argue that the whole edifice is produced by the almost-defeated Good Men under the pressure of repression is unconvincing. A much easier and more sustainable analysis is to admit to elements of the edifice pre-existing that period. This does not mean that one must accept simply what orthodox sources allege, and it still leaves plenty of room for debate over when precisely we should see dualism and organized heresy emerging in southern France and elsewhere. But it does give due recognition to what the Good Men and Women actually *did*, of their own inspiration and volition, beyond the strictures of Catholic orthodoxy.

Let me finish with three final methodological points. The first is to reiterate that demonstrating a political context for a piece of evidence does not automatically invalidate all that the evidence then claims. If we were to adopt this perspective broadly across a wider landscape, vast areas of medievalist study would become impossible, as most medieval narrative sources can be situated within at least some political context of composition. It does not mean we should simply believe what such evidence presents; but equally it does not require us to take a 'dualist' position ourselves, facing a binary choice of outright acceptance or total rejection.

A second point is in regard to inquisition evidence, much of which is drawn upon above. Some may be tempted to suggest that any details drawn from trial material that attest to organization, hierarchy, ritual, or dualist belief must be inquisitorial impositions. An implied parallel here is presumably the evidence from late medieval witchcraft trials—where witches' sabbaths, night flights, and demonic encounters are often judged to be brought into the frame by the inquisitors or civic authorities—or perhaps Robert Lerner's demolition of the 'organized sect' of the fourteenth-century 'Free Spirit' heresy where, following Grundmann's earlier work, in the 1970s Lerner demonstrated how much detail in the trial evidence was dependent on the inquisitorial frame of questioning. However, the trials we are dealing with in thirteenth-century southern France are very different from these later examples. In contrast with later witchcraft cases, there is the almost total absence of torture, something which demonstrably facilitates such distortions.[39] Nor in fact are they very much like those related to the 'Free Spirit', where Lerner's points relate particularly to the extensive theological detail presented, a feature largely absent in the thirteenth-century material.

If one imagines that inquisitors constructed and projected details at will, one may also ask a basic methodological question: why only sometimes and not always? That is, for example, why did inquisitors not allege dualist thought also against Waldensian heretics? The most obvious answer is because they, like everybody else around them, knew that the Waldensians held to a different theology. Similarly, if one wishes to claim that the hierarchical labels 'bishop', 'Younger Son', 'Older Son', and so forth are inquisitorial impositions,

---

[38] I recycle a line from 'Catharism as a Methodological and Historiographical Problem', p. 72.
[39] For a very clear example of the distorting effects of torture, see R. Comba and A. Nicolini, eds, with introduction by G. G. Merlo, *'Lucea tavolta la luna': i processi alle 'masche' di Rifreddo e Gambasca del 1495* (Cuneo: Società per gli studi storici, archeologici ed artistici della provincia di Cuneo, 2004).

why are they only applied to *some* people in *some* trials? Why not spread them about much more freely, if the (witting or unwitting) point was to conjure up a 'threat'? Why do such terms fade out in the trials of the later thirteenth century? The simplest answer is that they are applied only to those who were identified by deponents as holding such positions. Similarly, whilst it is true that the apparently dualist statement that God did not make visible things is in response to an inquisitorial question, why did only some deponents (a clear minority in fact) affirm that they had heard this from the Good Men and Women? I have written at considerable length elsewhere about the methodological challenges of inquisition records, particularly from southern France in this period, so I am extremely sympathetic to treating such material with considerable care; but this needs to be a sophisticated sceptical stance, not simply ignoring inconvenient details.

The third point is that in the detailed and often very clever critiques that sceptical scholars have presented of specific pieces of documentary evidence—usually twelfth-century material though in some cases later treatises also—the demands of close-reading and contextualization may sometimes fall prey to a degree of 'tunnel vision', causing one to forget what else sits around the Good Men in a southern French context. Some scholarship seems to tend toward a romantic vision of the pre-crusade south as the virgin territory of an indigenous people, sadly destined to be dominated, despoiled, and distorted by northern French colonial powers who imposed a wholly new reality upon them. But in fact the south was strongly connected to a variety of other parts of western Christendom, via trade, via pilgrimage, and—in the demonstrable connections between southern French *trobador* and northern French *trouvère* compositions—via some shared courtly culture. The south was not *terra incognita*. It is moreover very problematic to see the early inquisitors as Catholic 'outsiders' imposing their viewpoint on an indigenous southern French population. This is for the simple reason that they almost all came from the south: Pierre Cellan was a citizen of Toulouse, Guillaume Arnaud came from Montpellier, Brother Ferrier was Catalan. We cannot tell for Jean de Saint-Pierre; but judging from Bernard de Caux's surname, he came from a town about 25 km north-east of Béziers. In terms of personnel, there is a considerable contrast here with the crusaders and papal legates who preceded them. This is not to say that inquisitors did not operate within an ideological discourse. But they were not quasi-colonialist arrivals from the north confronted by a 'foreign' society they did not understand.

The domination of the northern French was important, but did not play out, either politically or culturally, in quite the way that a colonial model might imply. Before the crusade the landscape of holiness included (as we have seen earlier in this book) local priests, some holy hermits, civic and rural hospitals, small communities of quasi-monks located in rural churches, and some major shrines. By the mid-twelfth century, it had already seen the arrival of a fairly considerable number of new 'holy men' via the Templars, the Hospitallers, the Cistercians, and the Trinitarians. At a certain point it also had Waldensians wandering the towns and countryside, preaching an apostolic message—and indeed denouncing and debating with the Good Men. The two apostolically inspired groups, before the coming of the crusaders, recognized that they differed, even when both had been denounced as 'heretics' by the Church. It would be a shame if, focused wholly on the issue of heresy being in the eye of the beholder, we lost sense of that wider, vibrant complexity.

Bibliography

Manuscript and Documentary Sources

Albi
Archives départementales du Tarn
   3 E 55-253 (notarial booklet, Géraud Boffati, 1344-45)
   G 402 (inquiry into burial rights, 1335)
   6 J 19 (petition of consuls of Albi to inquisitor Pierre Brun, 1349)
   4 EDt FF4 (royal inquiry into disturbances at Albi 1291)
   4 EDt FF5 (royal inquiry into disturbances at Albi 1291)
   69 EDt FF18bis (consular court records, Cordes, 1326-44)
   69 EDt FF32 (agreement between people and priest of Cordes, 1287)
   69 EDT FF 59 (episcopal inquiry 1323)
Bibliothèque municipale
   MS 28 (145) (partial copy of Étienne de Bourbon, *Tractatus de diversis materiis predicabilibus*)

Cambridge
Gonville & Caius College
   MS 122/59 (Gui de Toulouse, *Regula mercatorum*)

Carcassonne
Archives départementales de l'Aude
   4E206/AA14 (1329 royal vidimus of consular agreement at Limoux)
   4E206 GG220 (agreement of *prud'hommes* of Limoux, 1240)
   4E206 GG221 (agreement between consuls of Limoux and prior of Saint-Martin, 1275)
   4E206 GG233 (documents relating to Alix de Montomorency and Simon de Montfort)
   G268 (confraternity records, Fendeille, 1340s)
   G489 (episcopal inquiry re various churches)
   G551 (cartulary of the abbey of Moissac)
   H103 (agreement between people and church of Rieudaure, 1303)
   H114 (agreement between consuls and priest of Lagrasse, 1327)
   H558-63 (documents relating to confraternity of Fanjeaux)
   7 J 1 (Villar family archive)
   7 J 51 (de Fenouillet family archive)
   10 J 287 (will of Ugo de Sallela, 1187)
   1 Mi 30 (microfilm of missal of Moussoulens)

Castelnaudary
Archives municipales
   AA1 (customs of Castelnaudary)

Dijon

Bibliothèque municipale
  MS 611 (Hugh of Francigena's *vita* of Pons de Léras)

London

British Library, London
  MS Add. 11464 (episcopal court trial record, Béziers, 1353)
  MS Add. 33956 (preaching exempla)
  MS Add. 60390 (preaching exempla)
  MS Harl. 7403 (Occitan religious poems)

Madrid

Royal Library, Monastery of El Escorial
  MS J.III.24 (Pontifical of Arles, 13th-century copy)

Marseille

Archives départementales des Bouches-du-Rhône
  2G56 (agreement between people and priest of Confoux, 1296)
  2G66 (agreement between people of Puyricard and Chapter of Aix, 1303)
  H. fonds de Saint-Victor, C 158 (synodal of Fréjus, 1279)
  2H345 (agreement between *universitas* of Vinon and prior of Carluc, 1261)

Montauban

Archives départementales du Tarn-et-Garonne
  3E121 AA1 ('Livre rouge')
  4E11 (account book, confraternity of Notre-Dame, Castelsarrasin, 14th century)
  G636 (agreement between people and priest of Montescot, 1280)
  G801 (tithing dispute, 1330)
  G691 (agreement between consuls and rector of Esparsac, 1280)
  G1161 (inquiry into rights over church of Saint-Jacques, Montauban, 1410)

Paris

Bibliothèque nationale de France, Paris
  Collection Doat, MS 21 (inquisition material, incl. sentences of Pierre Cellan)
  Collection Doat, MS 22 (inquisition trials, 1240s)
  Collection Doat, MS 23 (inquisition trials, 1240s)
  Collection Doat, MS 24 (inquisition trials, 1240s)
  Collection Doat, MS 25 (inquisition trials, 1270s–1280s)
  Collection Doat, MS 26 (inquisition trials, 1270s–1280s)
  Collection Doat, MS 27 (inquisition trials, 1290s–1320s)
  Collection Doat, MS 28 (inquisition trials, 1290s–1320s)
  Collection Doat, MS 31 (various relating to conduct of inquisition)
  Collection Doat, MS 58 (materials re monasteries in Narbonne, Limoux, and elsewhere)
  Collection Doat, MS 69 (materials relating to Montolieu)
  Collection Doat, MS 64 (materials relating to Carcassonne)
  Collection Doat, MS 103 (materials relating to Albi)
  Collection Doat, MS 118 (materials relating to Cahors and Quercy)
  Collection Doat, MS 119 (materials relating to Cahors and Quercy)
  Collection Doat, MS 120 (materials relating to Cahors and Quercy)

Collection Doat, MS 134 (materials relating to Rodez)
Collection Doat, MS 135 (materials relating to Rodez)
MS lat. 1220 (Pontifical of Arles, 13th century)
MS lat. 1613 (synodal statutes for Carcassonne)
MS lat. 3479 (manual for confessors and sermon collection, 13th century)
MS lat. 3555 (Franciscan exempla collection)
MS lat. 3860 (Burchard of Worms, decretals; council of Nîmes, 1096)
MS lat. 4224 (Benoît d'Alignan, *Tractatus fidei contra diversos errores*)
MS lat. 9994 (Cartulary of Grandselve)
MS lat. 10402 (various manuscript fragments)
MS lat. 10689 (Gui de Toulouse, *Regula mercatorum*)
MS lat. 11008 (Cartulary of Grandselve)
MS lat. 11009 (Cartulary of Grandselve)
MS lat. 11010 (Cartulary of Grandselve)
MS lat. 11011 (Cartulary of Grandselve)
MS lat. 15066 (Statuts synodaux de Mirepoix, 1327–48)
MS n.a.l. 557 (12th-century liturgical *mixtum*)
MS n.a.l. 1211 (*censier* of Apt)

Perpignan

Archives départementales des Pyrénées-Orientales
    3E1-6 (notarial booklet of Pierre Amoros, 1276–77)
    3E1-8 (notarial booklet of Arnaud Miro, 1276–78)
    G9 (various episcopal documents)
    G245 (episcopal inquiry, 1375; binding, 1308 list of excommunicates)
    G838 (agreement between syndics of Pia and chaplain of Saint-Cyr, 1287)
    G 1007 (will of Pons Aribert, 1173)
    H1 (will of Blancha Fina de Rivesaltes, 1170)
    1J816 (will of Gauzbert de Château Roussillon, 1143)
    7J40 (*Liber testamentorum Puigcerdà*, 1294)
    7J41 (*Liber testamentorum Puigcerdà*, 1297)
    7J42 (*Liber testamentorum Puigcerdà*, 1309–10)
Bibliothèque municipale
    MS 4 (12th-century copy of sacramentary of Arles)
    MS 79 (episcopal statutes)

Toulouse

Archives municipales
    MS AA1 (town charters and customs)
    MS AA3 (town charters and customs)
    MS AA4 (town charters and customs)
    MS AA5 (town charters and customs)
Bibliothèque municipale
    MS 75 (breviary)
    MS 118 (Pontifical of Guillaume Durand and Bernard Gui's *Libellus*, 14th century)
    MS 191 (Miscellany including pastoral works, 14th century)
    MS 208 (Franciscan compilation of pastoral works, 13th century)
    MS 313 (Guy d'Evreux sermons)
    MS 318 (anonymous Sunday sermons)

MS 316 (Jacobus da Voragine Lenten sermons)
MS 340 (compilation of pastoral works, 13th century)
MS 381 (Jean de Freibourg, *Summa confessorum*)
MS 402 (synodal of Bishop Dominique Grenier, 1326 × 47)
MS 478 (collection of Marian miracles)
MS 609 (inquisition register of Bernard de Caux and Jean de Saint-Pierre)

Vatican
MS Ottobon lat. 256 (Pontifical, Valence, 1100 × 25)
MS lat. 4030 (inquisitorial register of Jacques Fournier, 1318–25)

Edited Primary Sources

Ainé, D., *Histoire de Montauban* (Montauban: Imprimerie de Forestié Neveau et Compagnie, 1855)

Akehurst, F. R. P., ed., *The Établissements de Saint Louis: Thirteenth-Century Law Texts from Tours, Orleans and Paris* (Philadelphia: University of Pennsylvania Press, 1996)

Alart, B., *Priviléges et titres relatifs aux franchises, institutions et propriétés communales de Roussillon et de Cerdagne depuis le XI siècle jusqu'à l'an 1660, 1er partie* (Perpignan: Charles Latrobe, 1878)

Albanès, J. H., ed., *Gallia christiana novissima*, 7 vols (Montbéliard: Société anonymes des imprimerie Montbéliardaise, 1899–1920)

Albe, E., ed., *Les miracles de Notre Dame de Rocamadour au XIIe siècle* (Paris: H. Champion, 1907)

Albon, Le Marquis d', ed., *Cartulaire général de l'ordre du Temple, 1119?–1150* (Paris: Librairie ancienne d'Honoré Champion, 1913)

Andrieu, M., ed., *Le pontifical romain au moyen-age, III: le pontifical de Guillaume Durand* (Vatican: Bibliotheca Apostolica Vaticana, 1939)

Anon., 'Translatio et miracula Sancti Viviani Episcopi', *Analecta Bollandiana* 8 (1889), 256–77

Anon., 'Visites pastorales du diocese d'Aix, 1340–1358', typescript transcription of manuscript in private hands, copy kindly supplied to the author by Prof Noël Coulet

Arnold, J. H. and P. Biller, eds and trans., *Heresy and Inquisition in France, 1200–1300* (Manchester: Manchester University Press, 2016)

Arthur, R. G., trans., *Jaufre: An Occitan Arthurian Romance* (New York: Garland, 1992)

Augustine of Hippo, *De civitate Dei*, CCSL 48 (Turnhout: Brepols, 1955)

Auriac, E. d', *Histoires de l'ancienne cathédrale et des évêques d'Alby* (Paris: Imprimerie impériale, 1858)

Auvray, L., ed., *Les registres de Grégoire IX*, 4 vols (Paris: A. Fontemoing, 1896–1955)

Avril, J., ed., *Les statuts synodaux français du XIIIe siècle*, 6 vols (Paris: Bibliothèque nationale, 1971–2011)

Azais, J., 'De Roger II, vicomte de Béziers, et d'un acte portant reconnaissance des droits du vicomte, de l'évêque et des habitants de Béziers', *Bulletin de la Société archéologique de Béziers* 1 (1836), 45–65

Benoît, F., ed., *Recueil des actes des comtes de Provence, II: textes et analyses* (Paris: Picard, 1925)

Bernard de Fontcaude, *Adversus Waldensium sectam liber*, PL 204, cols 793–840

Bernard Gui [Bernardus Guidonis], *De fundatione et prioribus conventuum provinciarum Tolosanae et provinciae Ordinis Praedicatorum*, ed. P. A. Amargier, Monumenta Ordinis

Fratrum Praedicatorum Historica XXIV (Rome: Institutum historicum fratrum praedicatorum, 1961)

Bernard of Clairvaux, *Epistolae*, PL 182

Bertran de Born, *The Poems of the Troubadour Bertran de Born*, ed. and trans. W. D. Paden Jr, T. Sankovitch, and P. H. Stäblein (Berkeley: University of California Press, 1986)

Biller, P., C. Bruschi, and S. Sneddon, eds, *Inquisitors and Heretics in Thirteenth-Century Languedoc: Edition and Translation of Toulouse Inquisition Depositions, 1273–1282* (Leiden: Brill, 2011)

Blanc, A., ed., *Le livre de comptes de Jacme Olivier, marchand Narbonnais*, 2 vols (Paris: Picard, 1899)

Blancard, P., ed., *Documents inédits sur le commerce de Marseille au moyen âge*, 2 vols (Marseille: Barlatier-Fessat, 1884)

Bligny-Bondurand, E., *Les coutumes de Saint-Gilles (XIIe–XIVe siècles)* (Paris: Picard, 1915)

Bolland, J., et al., eds, *Acta sanctorum quotquot toto orbe coluntur, vel à Catholicis scriptoribus celebrantur*, 68 vols (Antwerp: apud Ioannem Meursium, 1643–1940)

Boretius, A., ed., *Capitularia regum Francorum* I, MGH (Hanover: Hahn, 1883)

Bouillet, A., ed., *Liber miraculorum sancte fidis* (Paris: Alphonse Picard, 1897)

Brissaud, M., 'Les coutumes de Moissac', *Bulletin archéologique et historique de la Société archéologique de Tarn-et-Garonne* 23 (1895), 333–43

Brunel, C., ed., *Les Miracles de Saint Privat, suivi des opuscules d'Aldebert III, évêque de Mende* (Paris: Picard, 1912)

Brunel, C., ed., *Les plus anciennes chartes en langue provençale: recueil des pièces originales antérieures au XIIIe siècle* (Paris: Picard, 1926)

Brunel, C., ed., 'Vita, inventio et miracula Sanctae Enimiae', *Analecta Bollandiana* 57 (1939), 236–96

Brunel, C., ed., *Jaufre: roman arthurien du XIIIe siècle en vers provencaux* (Paris: Société des anciens textes français, 1943)

Brunel, C., 'Juges de la paix en Gévaudan: au milieu du XIe siècle', *Bibliothèque de l'École des Chartes* 109 (1951), 32–42

Bughetti, A., ed., *Processus canonizationis et legendae variae Sancti Ludovici O.F.M.*, Analecta Franciscana 7 (Florence: Ex Typographia Collegii S. Bonaventurae, 1951)

Bull, M., ed., *The Miracles of Our Lady of Rocamadour: Analysis and Translation* (Woodbridge: Boydell, 1999)

Cabié, E., 'Coutumes de la ville de l'Isle-Jourdain XIIe siècle', *Nouvelle revue historique de droit français et étranger* 5 (1881), 643–53

Cabié, E. and L. Mazens, eds, *Un cartulaire et divers actes des Alaman des Lautrec et des de Lévis* (Toulouse: A. Chauvin et fils, 1882)

Cadier, L., ed., *Cartulaire de Sainte Foi de Morlaas* (Pau: L. Ribaut, 1884)

Cassan, L. and P. Alaus, eds, *Cartulaires des abbayes d'Aniane et de Gellone* (Montpellier: Jean Martel Ainé, 1900)

Cau-Durban, D., ed., *Abbaye du Mas-d'Azil: monographie et cartulaire, 817–1774* (Foix: Veuve Pomiès, 1897)

Cazalis, F., 'Haec sunt statuta et consuetudines antique de Mayrosio in tempore Dominorum contorum', *Bulletin Société d'agriculture, industrie, sciences et arts département de la Lozere* 13 (1862), 270–80

Chevalier, U. and J. H. Albanès, eds, *Gallia christiana novissima II: Marseille* (Valence: Impr. Valentinoise, 1899)

Comba, R., and A. Nicolini, eds, with introduction by G. G. Merlo, *'Lucea tavolta la luna': i processi alle 'masche' di Rifreddo e Gambasca del 1495* (Cuneo: Società per gli studi storici, archeologici ed artistici della provincia di Cuneo, 2004)

Compayré, C., *Études historiques et documents inédits sur l'Albigeois, le Castrais et l'ancien diocèse de Lavaur* (Albi: Imprimerie de Maurice Papailhiau, 1841)

Contrasty, J. and Mlle Fournie, 'Vie et miracles de saint Bertrand, évêque de Comminges', *Revue du Toulouse* 28 (1941), 173–243

Desjardins, G., ed., *Cartulaire de l'Abbaye de Conques en Rouergue* (Paris: Picard, 1879)

Devic, C., and J. Vaissète, eds, *Histoire générale du Languedoc*, 16 vols (1730–45; re-edition, Toulouse: Privat, 1872–1905)

Didier, N., et al., eds, *Cartulaire de l'église d'Apt* (Paris: Libraire Dalloz, 1967)

Douais, C., *Cartulaire de l'abbaye de Saint-Sernin de Toulouse (844–1200)* (Toulouse: Privat, 1887)

Douais, C., ed., *Un nouvel écrit de Bernard Gui: le synodal de Lodève, 1325–26* (Paris: Picard, 1894)

Douais, C., ed., *Documents sur l'ancienne province de Languedoc*, 2 vols (Toulouse: Privat, 1901–4)

Doublet, G., ed., *Recueil des actes concernant les évêques d'Antibes* (Paris: Picard, 1915)

Douët-d'Arcq, L., *Collection de sceaux*, 3 vols (Paris: Plon, 1863–68)

Duffour, J., ed., *Livre rouge du chapitre métropolitain de Sainte-Marie d'Auch*, 2 vols (Paris: Honoré Champion, 1907–8)

Dufour, E., 'Anciennes coutumes de Montcuq', *Revue historique de droit français et étranger* 7 (1855), 98–131

Durliat, M., *Haut-Languedoc roman* (Saint-Léger-Vauban: Zodiaque, 1976)

Durliat, M., *Roussillon roman*, 4th edn (Saint-Léger-Vauban: Zodiaque, 1986)

Durliat, M. and V. Allègre, *Pyrénées romanes*, 2nd edn (Saint-Léger-Vauban: Zodiaque, 1976)

Duvernoy, J., ed., *Le registre d'inquisition de Jacques Fournier, évêque de Pamiers (1318–1325)*, 3 vols (Toulouse: Privat, 1965)

Duvernoy, J., ed., *L'inquisition en Quercy: le registre des pénitences de Pierre Cellan, 1241–1242* (Castelnaud-la-Chapelle: L'Hydre, 2001)

Étienne de Bourbon, *Stephani de Borbone, Tractatus de diversis materiis predicabilibus: Tertia pars*, ed. J. Berlioz, CCCM 124.2 (Turnhout: Brepols, 2006)

Fau, J.-C., *Rouergue Roman*, 3rd edn (Saint-Léger-Vauban: Zodiaque, 1990)

Font Rius, J. M., *Cartas de poblacion y franquicia de Cataluña*, Esculea de estudios medievales, Textos 26, 2 vols (Barcelona: Ferrán-Bot, 1969)

Foreville, R., ed., *Cartulaire du chapitre cathédrale Saint-Étienne d'Agde* (Paris: CNRS, 1995)

Fournier, M., ed., *Les statuts et privileges des universités francaises*, 4 vols (Paris: L. Larose et Fourcel, 1890)

Fournier, P.-F., and P. Guébin, eds, *Enquêtes administratives d'Alfonse de Poitiers, arrêts de son parlement tenu à Toulouse, et textes annexes, 1249–1271* (Paris: Imprimerie nationale, 1959)

Galabert, L'Abbé, 'La charte des coutumes d'Aucamville', *Bulletin archéologique et historique de la Société archéologique de Tarn-et-Garonne* (1886), 97–110

Gaujal, M. A. F. de, *Études historiques sur Rouergue*, 4 vols (Paris: Imprimerie administrative de Paul Dupont, 1858–59)

Gérard, P. and E. Magnou, eds, *Cartulaires des Templiers de Douzens* (Paris: Bibliothèque nationale, 1965)

Gérard, P. and T. Gérard, eds, *Cartulaire de Saint-Sernin de Toulouse*, 4 vols (Toulouse: Amis des Archives de la Haute-Garonne, 1999)

Germain, A., ed., *Liber instrumentorum memorialium: cartulaire de Guillems de Montpellier* (Montpellier: J. Martel, 1884–86)

Germer-Durand, E., ed., *Cartulaire du chapitre de l'église cathédrale Notre-Dame de Nîmes (834–1156)* (Nîmes: A. Catélan, 1874)
Giraud, C., *Essai sur l'histoire du droit français au Moyen Âge*, 2 vols (Paris: Videcoq Père et Fils, 1846)
Girault, M., P.-G. Girault, G. Duhil, and A. Chupin, eds and trans., *Livre des miracles de Saint Gilles* (Orléans: Paradigme, 2007)
Goering, J. and P. J. Payer, 'The "Summa penitentie Fratrum predicatorum": A Thirteenth-Century Confessional Formulary', *Mediaeval Studies* 55 (1993), 1–50
Greslé-Bouignol, M., 'La charte de Gaillac de 1221', *Annales du Midi* 86 (1974), 93–97
Guérard, M., ed., *Cartulaire de l'abbaye de Saint-Victor de Marseille*, 2 vols (Paris: C. Lahure, 1857)
Guibert, P. and H. Barthés, eds, *Le cartulaire municipal de Puissalicon (XIIIe–XVIIe siècles)* (Béziers: Société archéologique, scientifique et littéraire, 2001)
[Gui de Toulouse] *Sensuit la reigle des marchans novellement translatée de latin en francoys* (Provins: G. Tavernier, 1496)
Guillaume de Puylaurens, *Chronique, 1145–1275*, ed. and trans. J. Duvernoy (Paris: CNRS, 1976)
[Guillaume de Puylaurens] William of Puylaurens, *The Chronicle of William of Puylaurens: The Albigensian Crusade and its Aftermath*, trans. W. A. and M. D. Sibly (Woodbridge: Boydell, 1998)
[Guillaume Durand] Guillelmus Duranti, *Rationale divinorum officiorum, I–IV*, CCCM 140 (Turnhout: Brepols, 1995)
[Guillaume Peraud] Guilelmus Peraldus, *Summa aurea de virtutibus et vitiis* (Brescia, 1494)
Guiraud, J., ed., *Le cartulaire de Notre Dame de Prouille*, 2 vols (Paris: Picard, 1907)
Harris, M. R., 'Cathar Ritual (ms Lyon, Bibl. mun., PA 36)', online edition: <http://www.rialto.unina.it/prorel/CatharRitual/CathRit.htm>
Hubert, M. J., trans., *The Romance of Flamenca* (Princeton: Princeton University Press, 1962)
Huchet, J.-C., ed., *Flamenca: roman occitan du XIIIe siècle* (Paris: Union générale des éditions, 1988)
Hugh of St Cher, *Opera omnia in universum Vetus et Novus Testamentum*, 8 vols (Lyon: Ioannis Antonii Huguetan & Guillelmi Barbier, 1669)
Humbert de Romans, *De eruditione praedicatorum* in M. de la Bigne, *Maxima bibliotheca Veterum Patrum*, 27 vols (Lyon: Anissonios, 1677), vol. 25
Jean Gobi Jr., *La scala Coeli*, ed. M.-A. Polo de Beaulieu (Paris: CNRS, 1991)
Jean Gobi Sr., *Jean Gobi l'ancien: miracles de Sainte Marie-Madeleine*, ed. J. Sclafer (Paris: CNRS, 1996)
Johnston, M. D., 'The Occitan *Enssenhamen de l'Escudier* and *Essenhamen de la Donzela* of Amanieu de Sescás', in M. D. Johnston, ed., *Medieval Conduct Literature: An Anthology of Vernacular Guides to Behaviour for Youths with English Translations* (Toronto: Medieval Academy, 2009), pp. 23–60
Jordan of Saxony, *Libellus de principiis Ordinis praedicatorum*, MOPH 16 (Rome: Institutum historicum FF. Praedicatorum, 1935)
Kienzle, B. M., ed., 'The Works of Hugo Francigena: *Tractatus de conversione Pontii de Laracio et exordii Salvaniensis monasterii vera narratio; epistolae*', *Sacris erudiri* 34 (1994), 273–311
Kienzle, B. M., ed. and trans., 'The Tract on the Conversion of Pons of Léras and the True Account of the Beginning of the Monastery at Silvanès', *Cistercian Studies Quarterly* 30 (1995), 219–43

Labande, L.-H., *Avignon au XIIIe siècle: l'évêque Zoen Tencarari et les Avignonais* (Paris: Alphonse Picard, 1908)
Labbé, Ph., ed., *Sacrosancta concilia* (Paris: Impensis Societatis typographical, 1671)
Lagrèze-Fossat, A., *Études historiques sur Moissac, t. 1* (Paris: J.-B. Dumoulin, 1870)
Latouche, R., 'La coutume originale de Saint-Antonin', *Bulletin philologique et historique jusqu'à 1715 du Comité des travaux historiques et scientifiques* (1920), 260–62
Lauriere, E. de, et al., eds, *Ordonnances des rois de France*, 21 vols (Paris: Imprimerie royale, 1723)
Lecoy de la Marche, A., ed., *Anecdotes historiques, legendes et apologues tires du recueil inédit d'Étienne de Bourbon, dominicain du XIIIe siècle* (Paris: Librairie Renouard, 1877)
Léglu, C., R. Rist, and C. Taylor, eds, *The Cathars and the Albigensian Crusade: A Sourcebook* (Abingdon: Routledge, 2014)
Lougard, J., J. Nougaret, and R. Saint-Jean, *Languedoc roman* (Saint-Léger-Vauban: Zodiaque, 1975)
Ludovico de Amboysia, *Sinodale diocesis Albiensis* (Lyon: Pierre Mareschal & Barnabe Chaussard, 1499)
Mahul, M., ed., *Cartulaire et archives des communes de l'ancien diocese et de l'arrondissement administratif de Carcassonne*, 6 vols (Paris: V. Didron et Dumoulin, 1857–71)
Mansi, G. D., ed. *Sacrorum conciliorum nova et amplissima collectio*, 53 vols (1759–98; repr. Graz: Akademische Druck- und Verlagsanstalt, 1961)
Marca, P. de, *Marca Hispanica sive Limes Hispanicus, hoc est geographica & historica descriptio cataloniae, ruscinonis, & circumiacentium populorum*, ed. É. Baluze (Paris: F. Muguet, 1688; repr. Barcelona: Editorial Base, 1972)
Martene, E., *Veterum Scriptorum et Monumentorum*, 9 vols (Paris, 1724–33)
Martene, E. and U. Durand, eds, *Thesaurus novus anecdotorum*, 5 vols (Paris: Florentini Delaulne, Hilarii Foucault, Michaelis Clouzier, Joannis-Gaufridi Nyon, Stephani Ganeau, Nicolai Gosseli, 1717)
Martene, E., and U. Durand, eds, *Thesaurus novus anecdotorum*, 5 vols (Paris: Sumptibus Florentini Delaulne, Hilarii Foucault, Michaelis Clouzier, Joannis-Gaufridi Nyon, Stephani Ganeau, Nicolai Gosselin, 1717; repr. Farnborough: Gregg, 1968)
Martin, E., ed., *Cartulaire de la ville de Lodève* (Montpellier: Serre et Roumégous, 1900)
Martin-Chabot, E., ed., *La chanson de la croisade Albigeoise*, 3 vols (Paris: Société d'Édition Les Belles Lettres, 1957–61)
Matfre Ermengaud, *Breviari d'amor*, ed. P. T. Ricketts, 5 vols (Leiden: Brill, 1976; London: AIEO, 1989–98; Turnhout: Brepols, 2004)
Maurette, J.-M., *Recherches historiques sur la ville d'Alais* (Alès: J. Martin, 1860)
Ménard, L., *Histoire civile, ecclésiastique et littéraire de la ville de Nismes*, 7 vols (Paris: Hugues-Daniel Chaubert, 1750–58)
Meyer, P., ed., 'Anciennes poésies religieuses en langue d'oc', *Bibliothèque de l'École des Chartes* 5th ser. 1 (1860), 481–97
Molinier, A., ed., *Correspondance administrative d'Alfonse de Poitiers*, 2 vols (Paris: Imprimerie nationale, 1894–1900)
Mouynès, G., *Ville de Narbonne: inventaires des archives communales antérieures à 1790. Annexes de série AA* (Narbonne: E. Caillard, 1871)
Mulholland, M. A., *Early Gild Records of Toulouse* (New York: Columbia University Press, 1941)
Nelli, R., 'Trois poèmes autor d'un pèlerinage', *CdF* 15 (1980), 79–92
Oesterley, H., ed., *Gesta romanorum* (Berlin: Weidmannsche Buchhandling, 1872)
Ourliac, P., *Les sauvetés du Comminges: étude et documents sur les villages fondés par les Hospitaliers dans la région des coteaux commingeois* (Toulouse: Boisseau, 1947)

Ourliac, P., ed., *Le cartulaire de la Selve: la terre, les hommes, et le pouvoir en Rouergue au XIIe siecle* (Paris: CNRS, 1985)
Ourliac, P. and A.-M. Magnou, eds, *Cartulaire de l'abbaye de Lézat*, 2 vols (Paris: CNRS, 1984-87)
Pales-Gobilliard, A., ed., *L'inquisiteur Geoffrey d'Ablis et les cathares du comté du Foix (1308-1309)* (Paris: CNRS, 1984)
Pales-Gobilliard, A., ed., *Le livre des sentences de l'inquisiteur Bernard Gui, 1318-23*, 2 vols (Paris: CNRS, 2002)
Pasquier, F., ed., *Cartulaire de Mirepoix*, 2 vols (Toulouse: Privat, 1921)
Perrin, Ch.-E. and J. de Font-Réaulx, eds, *Pouillés des provinces d'Auch, de Narbonne et de Toulouse*, 2 vols (Paris: Imprimerie nationale, 1972)
Peter the Venerable, *Contra Petrobrusianos hereticos*, ed. J. Fearns, CCCM 10 (Turnhout: Brepols, 1968)
Pierre des Vaux-de-Cernay, *Hystoria Albigensis*, ed. P. Guebin and E. Lyon, 3 vols (Paris: Librairie ancienne Honoré Champion, 1926-29)
[Pierre des Vaux-de-Cernay] Peter of Les Vaux-de-Cernay, *History of the Albigensian Crusade*, trans. W. A. Sibly and M. D. Sibly (Woodbridge: Boydell, 1998)
Pontal, O., ed., *Les statuts synodaux français du XIIIe siècle*, 2 vols (Paris: CTHS, 1983)
Pontal, O., ed., *Conciles de la France capetienne jusqu'en 1215* (Paris: Cerf, 1995)
Portal, C., *Histoire de la ville de Cordes, Tarn (1222-1799)* (Cordes: Bosquet, 1902)
Powicke, F. M. and C. R. Cheney, eds, *Councils and Synods, 1205-1313*, 2 vols (Oxford: Clarendon Press, 1964)
Processus negotii Raymundi comitis Tolosani, in J. P. Migne et al, eds, *Patrologiae cursus completus. Series Latina* (Paris: J.-P. Migne, 1855), 216, cols 89-97
Prou, M. and E. Clouzot, eds, *Pouillés des provinces d'Aix, d'Arles, d'Embrun* (Paris: Imprimerie nationale, 1923)
Raimon de Castelnou, *Raimon de Castelnou: canzoni e dottrinale*, ed. A. Giannetti (Bari: Adriatica editrice, 1988)
Raymond de Peñafort, *Summa de poenitentia* (Avignon, 1715)
Regino of Prüm, *Libri duo de synodalibus causis et disciplinis ecclesiasticis*, ed. G. A. Wasserschleben (Leipzig: Engelmann, 1840)
Roquain de Courtemblay, F., 'Les sorts des saints ou des apôtres', *Bibliothèque de l'Ecole des Chartes* 41 (1880), 457-74
Roquette, J., ed., *Cartulaire de Béziers (livre noire)* (Paris: Picard, 1918)
Roquette, J., ed., *Cartulaire de l'église de Lodève: livre vert* (Montpellier: n.p., 1923)
Sabarthès, A., 'Charte communale de Fendeille (Aude), 1202', *Bulletin du Comité des travaux historiques et scientifiques: section d'histoire et de philologies* (1901), 579-84
Sabarthès, A., 'Un episode de l'albigéisme à Limoux', *Bulletin philologique et historique jusqu'à 1715* (1932-33), 193-200
Sackville, L., 'The *Ordo processus Narbonensis*: The Earliest Inquisitor's Handbook, Lost and Refound', *Aevum: rassegna di scienze storiche, linguistiche, e filologiche* 93/2 (2019), 363-95
Sainte-Marthe, Denis de, ed., *Gallia Christiana*, I, *Instrumenta* (Paris: Ex typographia regia, 1716)
Šanjek, F., ed., 'Edizione della Summa auctoritatum contenuta nel MS 47 della Bibliothèque municipale d'Albi', appendix (pp. 355-95) to R. Manselli, 'Una "Summa auctoritatum" antiereticale', *Atti della Accademia nazionale dei Lincei*, Classe di scienze morali, storiche e filologiche, ser. 8, 28 (1985), 323-95
Shatzmiller, J., ed., *Médicine et justice en Provence médiévale: documents de Manosque, 1262-1348* (Aix: Uni de Provence, 1989)

Shatzmiller, J., *Justice et injustice au début du XIVe siècle: l'enquête sur l'archevêque d'Aix et sa renonciation en 1318* (Rome: École française de Rome, 1999)

Sheingorn, P., trans., *The Book of Sainte Foy* (Philadelphia: University of Pennsylvania Press, 1995)

Soutras-Dejeanne, F., 'Fors et coutumes de Bagnères-de-Bigorre', *Bulletin de la Société Ramond (Bagnères-de-Bigorre)* (1882), 155–70

Tarde, H., 'La rédaction des coutumes de Narbonne', *Annales du Midi* 85 (1973), 371–402

Teulet, A., et al., eds, *Layettes du trésor des chartes*, 5 vols (Paris: Henri Plon, 1863–1909)

Thomas, A., ed., 'Homélies provençales tirées d'un manuscrit de Tortosa', *Annales du Midi* 9 (1897), 369–418

Thomas, A., ed., *La chanson de Sainte Foi d'Agen: poème provençale du XIe siècle* (Paris: Honoré Champion, 1925; repr. 1974)

Tierney, B., ed. and trans., *The Crisis of Church and State, 1050–1300* (1964; Toronto: PIMS, 1988)

Verlaguet, P.-A., ed., *Cartulaire de l'abbaye de Silvanès* (Rodez: Imprimerie Carrère, 1910)

Vielliard, J., *Le guide du pèlerin de Saint-Jacques de Compostelle: texte latin du XII siècle*, 5th edn (Paris: J. Vrin, 2004)

Wakefield, W. L. and A. P. Evans, eds, *Heresies of the High Middle Ages* (New York: Columbia University Press, 1969)

Welter, J.-Th., 'Un recueil d'exempla du XIIIe siècle', *Revue des études franciscaines* 30 (1913), 646–65; 31 (1914), 194–213, 312–20

Welter, J.-Th., *L'exemplum dans la littérature religieuse et didactique du moyen âge* (Paris: Guitard, 1927)

Welter, J.-Th., 'Un nouveau recueil franciscain d'exempla de la fin du XIIIe siècle', *Études franciscaines* (1930), 432–76, 595–629

Zarb, M., *Les privileges de la ville de Marseille, du Xe siècle a la Révolution* (Paris: Picard, 1961)

Zerner, M., ed. and trans., *Guillaume Monachi: contra Henri schismatique et hérétique*, Sources chrétiennes 541 (Paris: Cerf, 2011)

Online Resources

de la Haye, R., 'Recueil des actes de l'abbaye de Moissac, [680]–1175' (2011), unpublished pdf, <https://www.academia.edu/40493765/Recueil_des_actes_de_labbaye_de_Moissac_680_1175>

Dorin, Rowan, *Corpus Synodalium* database: <https://corpus-synodalium.com/>

Secondary Sources

Abulafia, D., *A Mediterranean Emporium: The Catalan Kingdom of Majorca* (Cambridge: Cambridge University Press, 1994)

Adam, P., *La vie paroissiale du XIVe siècle* (Paris: Sirey, 1964)

Ahlsell de Toulza, G., 'Les peintures murales dans les chapelles du choeur de l'église Notre-Dame-du-Bourg de Rabastens-sur-Tarn', *Actes du 96e Congrès national des sociétés savantes, 1971, section d'archéologie* 2 (1976), 239–65

Allen, R., 'The Earliest Known List of Excommunicates from Ducal Normandy', *Journal of Medieval History* 39 (2013), 394–415

Anderson, W. L., 'The Real Presence of Mary: Eucharistic Disbelief and the Limits of Orthodoxy in Fourteenth-Century France', *Church History* 75 (2006), 748–67

Andrews, F., ed., *Churchmen and Urban Government in Medieval Italy, c. 1200–c. 1450* (Cambridge: Cambridge University Press, 2013)

Anon., *Notice historique sur la confrérie et la procession jubilaire des pénitents gris d'Avignon, par un confrère* (Avignon: L. Aubanel, 1851)

Archambeau, N., *Souls Under Siege: Stories of War, Plague and Confession in Fourteenth-Century Provence* (Ithaca, NY: Cornell University Press, 2021)

Ardagna, Y., D. Blanchard, E. Pélaquier, L. Vidal, M. Seguin, 'Aux marges de l'ancienne agglomération antique du Camp de César: Saint-Jean de Todon *alias* Saint-Jean de Rousigue (Laudun-L'Ardoise, Gard)', *Archéologie du Midi médiéval* 28 (2010), 161–80

Armstrong-Partida, M., *Defiant Priests: Domestic Unions, Violence, and Clerical Masculinity in Fourteenth-Century Catalunya* (Ithaca, NY: Cornell University Press, 2017)

Arnold, J. H., 'The Preaching of the Cathars', in C. Muessig, ed., *Medieval Monastic Preaching* (Leiden: Brill, 1998), pp. 183–205

Arnold, J. H., *Inquisition and Power: Catharism and the Confessing Subject in Medieval Languedoc* (Philadelphia: University of Pennsylvania Press, 2001)

Arnold, J. H., '"A man takes an ox by the horn and a peasant by the tongue": Literacy, Orality and Inquisition in Medieval Languedoc', in S. Rees-Jones, ed., *Literacy and Learning in Medieval England and Abroad* (Turnhout: Brepols, 2003), pp. 31–47

Arnold, J. H., *Belief and Unbelief in Medieval Europe* (London: Bloomsbury, 2005)

Arnold, J. H., 'Religion and Popular Rebellion, from the Capuciati to Niklashausen', *Cultural and Social History* 6 (2009), 149–69

Arnold, J. H., 'The Materiality of Unbelief in Late Medieval England', in S. Page, ed., *The Unorthodox Imagination in Late Medieval Britain* (Manchester: Manchester University Press, 2010), pp. 65–95

Arnold, J. H., ed., *The Oxford Handbook of Medieval Christianity* (Oxford: Oxford University Press, 2014)

Arnold, J. H., 'The Cathar Middle Ages as a Methodological and Historiographical Problem', in A. Sennis, ed., *Cathars in Question* (York: York Medieval Press, 2016), pp. 53–78

Arnold, J. H., 'Persecution and Power in Medieval Europe: *The Formation of a Persecuting Society*, by R. I. Moore', *American Historical Review* 123 (2018), 164–74

Arnold, J. H., 'Sexualité et déshonneur dans le Midi (XIIIe–XIVe siècles): les péchés de la chair et l'opinion collective', *CdF* 52 (2019), 261–95

Arnold, J. H., 'Benedict of Alignan's *Tractatus fidei contra diversos errores*: A Neglected Anti-heresy Treatise', *Journal of Medieval History* 45 (2019), 20–54

Arnold, J. H., *What is Medieval History?* 2nd edn (Cambridge: Polity, 2021)

Arnold, J. H., 'Talking with Ghosts: Rancière, Derrida and the Archive', *Journal of Medieval History* 48 (2022), 235–49

Arnold, J. H., 'Believing in Belief: Gibbon, Latour and the Social History of Religion', *Past & Present* 260 (2023)

Arnold, J. H. and C. Goodson, 'Resounding Community: The History and Meaning of Medieval Church Bells', *Viator* 43 (2012), 99–130

Artonne, A., 'Livre synodal de Lodève', *Bibliothèque de l'École des Chartes* 108 (1949–50), 36–74

Asad, T., *Genealogies of Religion: Discipline and Reasons of Power in Christianity and Islam* (Baltimore: Johns Hopkins University Press, 1993)

Aston, M., 'Segregation in Church', *Studies in Church History* 27 (1990), 237–94

Audisio, G., *The Waldensian Dissent: Persecution and Survival, c. 1170–c. 1570* (Cambridge: Cambridge University Press, 1999)
Aurell, M., G. Lippiatt, and L. Macé, eds, *Simon de Montfort (c. 1170–1218): le croisé, son lignage et son temps* (Turnhout: Brepols, 2020)
Bagley, C. P., '*Paratge* in the Anonymous *Chanson de la Croisade Albigeoise*', *French Studies* 21 (1967), 195–204
Balagna, C., 'L'église romane de Croute à Lasserrade (Gers): un édifice inachevé de Gascogne centrale autour de 1125', *Archéologie du Midi médiéval* 26 (2008), 59–91
Baldwin, J. W., *The Language of Sex: Fives Voices from Northern France around 1200* (Chicago: University of Chicago Press, 1994)
Banks, P. J., 'Mensuration in Early Medieval Barcelona', *Medievalia* 7 (1987), 37–56
Barriere, B., 'Les abbayes issues de l'érémitisme', *CdF* 21 (1986), 71–105
Barthélemy, D., *La mutation de l'an mil a-t-elle eu lieu? Servage et chevalerie dans la France des Xe et XIe siècles* (Paris: Fayard, 1997)
Barthélemy, D., *L'an mil et la paix de Dieu: la France chrétienne et féodale 980–1060* (Paris: Fayard, 1999)
Barthélemy, D., *Chevaliers et miracles: la violence et le sacré dans la société féodale* (Paris: Armand Colin, 2004)
Barthélemy, D., 'Les communes diocésaines en Occitanie', *CdF* 54 (2019), 31–61
Bartlett, R., *Trial by Fire and Water: The Medieval Judicial Ordeal* (Oxford: Clarendon Press, 1986)
Baudreu, D., and J. P. Cazes, 'Les villages ecclésiaux dans le bassin de l'Aude', in M. Fixot and E. Zadora-Rio, eds, *L'environnement des églises et la topographie religieuse des campagnes médiévales*, Document d'archéologie francaise 46 (Paris: Éditions de la Maison des sciences de l'homme, 1994), pp. 80–97
Bayrou, L., et al., 'L'église Sainte-Marie de Peyrepertuse', *Archéologie du Midi médiéval* 8–9 (1990–91), 39–98
Belperron, P., *La croisade contre les Albigeois* (Paris: Pion, 1942)
Bergeret, A., 'L'église Saint-Martin-de-Castries (La Vacquerie-et-Saint-Martin-de-Castries, Hérault), dépendance de l'abbaye de Gellone sur le Larzac', *Archéologie du Midi médiéval* 28 (2010), 193–208
Berlière, U., 'Les pèlerinages judiciaires au moyen âge', *Revue benedictine* 7 (1890), 520–26
Berman, C. H., 'Land Acquisition and the Use of the Mortgage Contract by the Cistercians of Berdoues', *Speculum* 57 (1982), 250–66
Berman, C. H., *The Cistercian Evolution: The Invention of a Religious Order in Twelfth-Century Europe* (Philadelphia: University of Pennsylvania Press, 2000)
Bernstein, A. E., 'Esoteric Theology: William of Auvergne on the Fires of Hell and Purgatory', *Speculum* 57 (1982), 509–31
Berthe, M., 'Les coutumes de la France méridionale: programme de recherche et premiers résultats', in M. Mousnier and J. Poumarède, eds, *La coutume au village dans l'Europe médiévale et moderne* (Toulouse: Presses universitaires du Midi, 2001), pp. 121–37
Biget, J.-L., 'Sépulture des enfants et *patria potestas*: un procès devant l'officialité d'Albi en 1335', *CdF* 33 (1998), 365–91
Biget, J.-L., 'Réflexions sur l'hérésie dans le Midi de la France au Moyen Âge', *Heresis* 36–37 (2002), 29–74
Biget, J.-L., S. Caucanas, M. Fournié, D. Le Blévec, eds, *Le "catharisme" en questions*, CdF 55 (Toulouse: Privat, 2020)
Biller, P., 'Words and the Medieval Notion of "Religion"', *Journal of Ecclesiastical History* 36 (1985), 351–69

Biller, P., 'The Cathars of Languedoc and Written Materials', in P. Biller and A. Hudson, eds, *Heresy and Literacy, 1000-1530* (Cambridge: Cambridge University Press, 1994), pp. 61-82

Biller, P., 'Applying Number to Men and Women in the Thirteenth and Early Fourteenth Centuries: An Enquiry into the Idea of "Sex-Ratio"', in M. Rubin, ed., *The Work of Jacques Le Goff and the Challenges of Medieval History* (Woodbridge: Boydell, 1997), pp. 27-54

Biller, P., 'Cathar Peace-making', in S. Ditchfield, ed., *Christianity and Community in the West: Essays for John Bossy* (Aldershot: Ashgate, 2001), pp. 1-23

Biller, P., '"Deep is the Heart of Man and Inscrutable": Signs of Heresy in Medieval Languedoc', in H. Barr and A. M. Hutchison, eds, *Text and Controversy from Wyclif to Bale: Essays in Honour of Anne Hudson* (Turnhout: Brepols, 2005), pp. 267-80

Biller, P., 'Heretics and Long Journeys', in P. Horden, ed., *Freedom of Movement in the Middle Ages* (Donington: Shaun Tyas, 2007), pp. 86-103

Bilotta, M. A., 'Diptyque de Rabastens', in M. A. Bilotta and M.-P. Chaumet-Sarkissian, eds, *Le Parement d'autel des Cordeliers de Toulouse: anatomie d'un chef d'oeuvre du XIVe siècle* (Paris: Somogy, 2012), pp. 110-11

Bird, J., 'Paris Masters and the Justification of the Albigensian Crusade', *Crusades* 6 (2007), 117-55

Bird, J., 'Innocent III, Peter the Chanter's Circle, and the Crusade Indulgence: Theory, Implementation, and Aftermath', in A. Sommerlechner, ed., *Innocenzo III: Urbs et Orbis, Atti del Congresso Internazionale*, 2 vols (Rome: Istituto storico italiano per il Medio Evo, 2003), I, pp. 503-24

Bisson, T. N., 'The Organised Peace in Southern France and Catalonia, c. 1140-1233', *American Historical Review* 82 (1977), 290-311

Bisson, T. N., *The Crisis of the Twelfth Century* (Princeton: Princeton University Press, 2009)

Bivolarov, V., *Inquisitoren-Handbücher: Papsturkunden un juristiche Gutachten aus dem 13. Jahrhundert mit Edition des* Consilium *von Guido Fulcodii* (Wiesbaden: MGH, 2014)

Blancard, L., 'Role de la confrérie de Saint-Martin-du-Canigou', *Bibliothèque de l'École des Chartes* 42 (1881), 5-7

Boitani, G., 'A Note on Liturgical and Mystical Quotations in *Flamenca*', *Medium Aevum* 88 (2019), 93-115

Bolduc, M., 'Troubadours in Debate: The *Breviari d'Amor*', *Romance Quarterly* 57 (2010), 63-76

Bom, M. M., *Constance of France: Womanhood and Agency in Twelfth-Century Europe* (London: Palgrave Macmillan, 2022)

Bonnassie, P., 'L'espace "Toulousain" (Toulousain, Comminges, Quercy, Rouergue, Albigeois)', in M. Zimmermann, ed., *Les sociétés méridionales autour de l'an mil* (Paris: CNRS, 1992), pp. 107-45

Bonnassie, P., 'Les *sagreres* catalanes: la concentration de l'habitat dans le "cercle de paix" des églises (XIe siècle)', in M. Fixot and E. Zadora-Rio, eds, *L'environnement des églises et la topographie religieuse des campagnes médiévales*, Document d'archéologie française 46 (Paris, 1994), pp. 68-79

Bossy, J., 'The Social History of Confession in the Age of the Reformation', *Transactions of the Royal Historical Society* 5th ser., 25 (1975), 21-38

Bossy, J., 'Some Elementary Forms of Durkheim', *Past & Present* 95 (1982), 3-18

Bossy, J., *Christianity in the West: 1400-1700* (Oxford: Oxford University Press, 1985)

Bossy, J., 'Moral Arithmetic: Seven Sins into Ten Commandments', in E. Leites, ed., *Conscience and Casuistry in Early Modern Europe* (Cambridge: Cambridge University Press, 1988), pp. 213-34

Bouchard, C., *Holy Entrepreneurs: Cistercians, Knights and Economic Exchange in Twelfth-Century Burgundy* (Ithaca, NY: Cornell University Press, 2009)
Bougard, F., C. La Rocca, and R. Le Jan, eds, *Sauver son âme et se perpétuer: transmission du patrimoine et mémoire au haut moyen âge* (Rome: École française de Rome, 2005)
Boureau, A., *Satan hérétique: naissance de la démonologie dans l'Occident médiévale (1280–1330)* (Paris: Odile Jacob, 2004)
Bourin-Derruau, M., *Villages médiévaux en Bas-Languedoc*, 2 vols (Paris: L'Harmattan, 1987)
Bourin-Derruau, M., 'Le Bas-Languedoc', in M. Zimmermann, ed., *Les sociétés méridionales autour de l'an mil* (Paris: CNRS, 1992), pp. 55–106
Bourin[-Derruau], M., and A. Durand, 'Église paroissiale, cimetière et castrum en bas Languedoc (Xe–XIIe s.)', in M. Fixot and E. Zadora-Rio, eds, *L'environnement des églises et la topographie religieuse des campagnes médiévales*, Document d'archéologie francaise 46 (Paris: Éditions de la Maison des sciences de l'homme, 1994), pp. 98–106
Bourin[-Derruau], M., 'De nouveaux chemins de développement dans le Languedoc d'avant la peste', in J. Drendel, ed., *Crisis in the Later Middle Ages: Beyond the Postan-Duby Paradigm* (Turnhout: Brepols, 2015), pp. 251–72
Bourrilly, V.-L., *Essai sur l'histoire politique de la commune de Marseille, des origines à la victoire de Charles d'Anjou (1264)* (Aix-en-Provence: Libraire d'histoire de la Provence, 1926)
Bousquet, J., 'Les débuts du monastère-hôpital d'Aubrac', *Revue du Rouergue* 2 (1985), 97–116
Boser, C., 'Le remaniement provençal de la Somme le Roi et ses dérivés', *Romania* 24 (1895), 56–85
Botana, F., 'Virtuous and Sinful Uses of Temporal Wealth in the "Breviari d'Amor" of Matfre Ermengaud (MS BL Royal 19.C.I)', *Journal of the Warburg and Courtauld Institutes* 67 (2004), 49–80
Bourdieu, P., *Outline of a Theory of Practice*, trans. R. Nice (Cambridge: Cambridge University Press, 1977)
Bowman, J. A., 'Do Neo-Romans Curse? Law, Land, and Ritual in the Midi (900–1100)', *Viator* 28 (1997), 1–32
Bowman, J. A., 'Councils, Memory and Mills: The Early Development of the Peace of God in Catalonia', *Early Medieval Europe* 8 (1999), 99–129
Bréchon, F., 'Autour du notariat: des nouvelles pratiques de l'écrit dans les régions méridionales aux XII et XIIIe siècles', in P. Guichard and D. Alexandre-Bidon, eds, *Comprendre le XIII siècle: études offerts à Marie-Therese Lorcin* (Lyon: Presses universitaires de Lyon, 1995), pp. 161–72
Brentano, R., *A New World in a Small Place* (Berkeley: University of California Press, 1994)
Brodman, J. W., *Charity and Religion in Medieval Europe* (Washington DC: Catholic University of America Press, 2009)
Brown, A., *Popular Piety in Late Medieval England* (Oxford: Oxford University Press, 1995)
Brown, P., *Authority and the Sacred: Aspects of the Christianisation of the Roman World* (Cambridge: Cambridge University Press, 1995)
Brown, P., *The Rise of Western Christendom: Triumph and Diversity, A.D. 200–1000* (Oxford: Blackwell, 1996)
Brunel-Lobrichon, G., 'La formation des troubadours, hommes de savoir', *CdF* 35 (2000), 137–48
Brunne, U., *Des contestataires aux "Cathares"* (Paris: Institut d'études augustiniennes, 2006)
Bryan, J., *Looking Inward: Devotional Reading and the Private Self in Late Medieval England* (Philadelphia: University of Pennsylvania Press, 2007)

Bull, M., *Knightly Piety and the Lay Response to the First Crusade: The Limousin and Gascony, c. 970–c. 1130* (Oxford: Clarendon Press, 1993)

Burnham, L. A., 'Unusual Choices: The Unique Heresy of Limoux Negre', in M. D. Bailey and S. L. Field, eds, *Late Medieval Heresy: New Perspectives* (York: York Medieval Press, 2018), pp. 96–115

Burns, R. I., 'The Friars of the Sack in Puigcerdà: A Lost Chapter of Thirteenth-Century Religious History', *Anuario de estudios medievales* 18 (1988), 217–27

Burns, R. I., *Jews in the Notarial Culture: Latinate Wills in Mediterranean Spain, 1250–1350* (Berkeley: University of California Press, 1996)

Burrow, J. A., *Gestures and Looks in Medieval Narrative* (Cambridge: Cambridge University Press, 2002)

Bynum, C. W., *Docere verbo et exemplo: An Aspect of Twelfth-Century Spirituality* (Missoula, Mont.: Scholars Press, 1979)

Bynum, C. W., 'Did the Twelfth-Century Discover the Individual?', *Journal of Ecclesiastical History* 31 (1980), 1–17

Bynum, C. W., 'Seeing and Seeing Beyond: The Mass of St Gregory in the Fifteenth Century', in J. F. Hamburger and A.-M. Bouché, eds, *The Mind's Eye: Art and Theological Argument in the Middle Ages* (Princeton: Princeton University Press, 2006), pp. 208–40

Bysted, A., *The Crusade Indulgence: Spiritual Rewards and the Theology of Crusade* (Leiden: Brill, 2014)

Cabié, E., 'Date du concile de Béziers', *Annales du Midi* 16 (1904), 349–57

Cabré, M., S. Martí, and M. Navàs, 'Geografia i història de la poesia occitanocatalana del segle XIV', in L. Badia, L. Cabré, and A. Alberni, eds, *Translatar i transferir: la transmissió dels textos i el saber (1200–1500)* (Santa Coloma de Queralt: Obrador Edèndum, 2010), pp. 349–76

Caille, J., 'Hospices et assistance a Narbonne (XIIIe–XIVe siècles)', *CdF* 8 (1978), 261–80

Caille, J., *Hôpitaux et charité publique à Narbonne au Moyen Âge de la fin du XIe à la fin du XVe siècle* (Toulouse: Privat, 1978)

Caldwell Ames, C., *Righteous Persecution: Inquisition, Dominicans and Christianity in the Middle Ages* (Philadelphia: University of Pennsylvania Press, 2009)

Caldwell Ames, C., 'Medieval Religious, Religions, Religion', *History Compass* 10 (2012), 334–52

Callahan, D. F., 'The Cult of the Saints and the Peace of God in Aquitaine in the Tenth and Eleventh Centuries', in T. Head and R. Landes, eds, *The Peace of God: Social Violence and Religious Response around the Year 1000* (Ithaca, NY: Cornell University Press, 1992), pp. 165–83

Campbell, W. H., *The Landscape of Pastoral Care in Thirteenth-Century England* (Cambridge: Cambridge University Press, 2018)

Cameron, E., *Waldenses: Rejections of Holy Church in Medieval Europe* (Oxford: Blackwell, 2000)

Canning, J., *Ideas of Power in the Late Middle Ages, 1296–1417* (Cambridge: Cambridge University Press, 2011)

Carbasse, J.-M., 'Bibliographie des coutumes méridionales', *Recueil de mémoires et travaux de la Société d'histoire du droit et des institutions des anciens pays de droit écrit* 10 (1979), pp. 7–89

Carbasse, J.-M., '*Currant nudi*: la répression de l'adultère dans le Midi médiéval', in J. Poumarède and J.-P. Royer, eds, *Droit, histoire et sexualité* (Toulouse: Publications de l'Espace juridique, 1987), pp. 83–102

Carou, E., 'Compte et répartition des décimes perçues sur le clergé du diocèse de Béziers', *Bulletin de la Société archéologique, scientifique et littéraire du Béziers*, 2nd ser., 4/ii (1867), 113–39

Carozzi, C., 'Humbert de Romans et la prédication, *CdF* 36 (2001), pp. 249–61

Carr, M., 'Crossing Boundaries in the Mediterranean: Papal Trade Licenses from the *Registra supplicationum* of Pope Clement VI (1342–52)', *Journal of Medieval History* 41 (2015), 107–29

Carraz, D., *L'Ordre du Temple dans la basse vallée du Rhône (1124–1312): ordres militaires, croisades et sociétés méridionales* (Lyon: Presses universitaires du Lyon, 2005)

Carraz, D., 'Églises et cimetières des ordres militaires: contrôle des lieux sacrés et *dominium* ecclésiastique en Provence (XIIe–XIIIe siècle)', *CdF* 46 (2011), 277–312

Carraz, D., 'Templars and Hospitallers in the Cities of the West and the Latin East (Twelfth to Thirteenth Centuries)', *Crusades* 12 (2013), 103–20

Carraz, D., '*Celeberrimum et generalissimum concilium*: Montpellier 1215 et le *negotium pacis et* fidei', *CdF* 54 (2019), 339–76

Casenave, A., 'Aveu et contrition: manuels des confesseurs et interrogatoires d'inquisitions en Languedoc et en Catalogne (XIIIe–XIVe siècles)', *Actes du 99e congrès national des sociétés savantes*, 2 vols (Paris: CTHS, 1977), I, pp. 333–52

Castaing, M., 'Le prêt à intérêt à Toulouse aux XIIe et XIIIe siècles', *Bulletin philologique et historique* 1953/54 (1955), 273–78

Castaing-Sicard, M., *Monnaies féodales et circulation monétaire en Languedoc, Xe–XIIIe siècles* (Toulouse: Association Marc Bloch, 1961)

Catafau, A., 'Paroisse et *cellera* dans le diocese d'Elne Xe–XIIe siècles', *Les cahiers de Saint-Michel de Cuxa* 30 (1999), 91–100

Catafau, A., 'Les *celleres* du Roussillon, mises au point et discussions', *CdF* 40 (2006), pp. 17–40

Caucanas, S., et al., *Au temps de la Croisade: sociétés et pouvoirs en Languedoc au XIIIe siècle*, exhibition catalogue from Carcassonne 2009 (Carcassonne: Archives départementales de l'Aude, 2009)

Chabaneau, C., 'Sermons et préceptes religieux en langue d'oc du XII siècle', *Revue des langues romanes* 18 (1880), 105–46

Chastang, P., 'Réforme grégorienne et administration par l'écrit des patrimoines ecclésiastiques dans le Midi de la France (Xe–XIIIe siècle)', *CdF* 48 (2013), 495–522

Chenu, M.-D., *La théologie au douzième siècle* (Paris: J. Vrin, 1957)

Chenu, M.-D., 'The Evangelical Awakening' [first publ. 1957], in Chenu, *Nature, Man and Society in the Twelfth Century*, trans. J. Taylor and L. K. Little (Toronto: PIMS, 1997)

Chevalier, P., 'Topographie et hiérarchie au sein de l'édifice ecclésial: l'espace du choeur et l'aménagement de ses limites (XIe–XIIe siècles). Quelques réflexions', *CdF* 46 (2011), 59–78

Cheyette, F. L., *Ermengarde of Narbonne and the World of the Troubadours* (Ithaca, NY: Cornell University Press, 2001)

Chiffoleau, J., *La comptabilité de l'Au-Delà: les hommes, la mort et la religion dans la région d'Avignon à la fin du Moyen Âge (vers 1320–vers 1480)* (Rome: École française de Rome, 1980)

Chiffoleau, J., 'Les Gibelins du royaume d'Arles: notes sur les réalités impériales en Provence dans les deux premiers tiers du XIIIe siècle', in P. Guichard et al., eds, *Papauté, monachisme et théories politiques: II, Les églises locales* (Lyon: Presses universitaires de Lyon, 1994)

Chiffoleau, J., 'L'inquisition franciscaine en Provence et dans l'ancien royaume d'Arles (vers 1260–vers 1330)', in *Frati minori e inquisizione: atti del XXXIII Convegno internazionale:*

Assisi, 6–8 ottobre 2005 (Spoleto: Fondazione Centro italiano di studi sull'alto medioevo, 2006), pp. 151–284

Chomel, V., 'Droit de patronage et pratique religieuse dans l'archevêché de Narbonne au début du XV siècle', *Bibliothèque de l'École des Chartes* 115 (1957), 58–137

Christian, W., *Local Religion in Sixteenth-Century Spain* (Princeton: Princeton University Press, 1981)

Clarke, P., *The Interdict in the Thirteenth Century* (Oxford: Oxford University Press, 2007)

Codou, Y., 'Le paysage religieux et l'habitat rural en Provence de l'antiquité tardive au XIIe siècle', *Archéologie du Midi médiéval* 21 (2003), 33–69

Collinson, P., 'Religion, Society and the Historian', *Journal of Religious Studies* 23 (1999), 149–67

Collura, A., *Sens e razos d'una escriptura: Il Vangelo occitano di Nicodemo* (Rome: Nuova Cultura, 2018)

Constable, G., 'Monasteries, Rural Churches and the *Cura Animarum* in the Early Middle Ages', *Settimane di studio* 28 (1982), 349–89

Constable, G., *The Reformation of the Twelfth Century* (Cambridge: Cambridge University Press, 1996)

Coomans, J., *Community, Urban Health and Environment in the Late Medieval Low Countries* (Cambridge: Cambridge University Press, 2021)

Corner, J., 'Literacy and Lay Society in the *Sénéchaussé* of Carcassonne, c. 1270–1330', unpublished DPhil., Oxford, 2005

Costa Marques, B. F. da, 'Mundividência Cristã no Sermonário de Frei Paio de Coimbra. Edição Crítica da *Summa Sermonum de Festivitatibus Magistri Fratris Pelagii Parui Ordinis Praedicatorum*, A.D. 1250, Cod. Alc.5/CXXX-B.N.Lisboa', unpublished PhD dissertation, Coimbra 2010

Coulet, N., 'Paroisse, oeuvre, communauté d'habitants en Provence (1e diocèse d'Aix dans la première moitié du XIVe siècle)', *CdF* 25 (1990), 215–37

Coulet, N., 'Au miroir des visites pastorales: les villages du diocèse d'Aix-en-Provence, XIVe–XVe siècle', *CdF* 40 (2006), 121–39

Crick, J., *The Historia Regum Britannie of Geoffrey of Monmouth, vol IV: Dissemination and Reception in the Later Middle Ages* (Woodbridge: Brewer, 1991)

Csordas, T. J., 'Embodiment as a Paradigm for Anthropology', *Ethos* 18 (1990), 5–47

Csordas, T. J., 'Somatic Modes of Attention', *Cultural Anthropology* 8 (1993), 135–56

Czerniak, V. and J.-M. Stouffs, 'Les peintures murales romanes de Notre-Dame de Vals: nouvelles lectures à la lumière de la dernière campagne de restauration', *Mémoire de la Société archéologique du Midi de la France* 68 (2008), 153–170

Davies, W., *Acts of Giving: Individual, Community and Church in Tenth-Century Christian Spain* (Oxford: Oxford University Press, 2007)

Davis, A. J., 'The Social and Religious Meaning of Charity in Medieval Europe', *History Compass* 12/12 (2014), 935–50

Davis, A. J., *The Medieval Economy of Salvation: Charity, Commerce and the Rise of the Hospital* (Ithaca, NY: Cornell University Press, 2019)

d'Avray, D. L., *Medieval Marriage Sermons: Mass Communication in a Culture without Print* (Oxford: Oxford University Press, 2001)

Deanesley, M., *The Pre-Conquest Church in England* (London: Oxford University Press, 1961)

Débax, H., *Le féodalité languedocien: serments, hommages et fiefs dans le Languedoc des Trencavel (XIe–XIIe siècles)* (Toulouse: Presses universitaires du Mirail, 2003)

Débax, H., *La seigneurie collective: pairs, pariers, paratge, les coseigneurs du XI au XII siècle* (Rennes: Presses Universitaires de Rennes, 2012)

Débax, H., 'Serments prêtés, serments contestés: pour une mise en perspective du refus du serment chez les hérétiques (Languedoc, XIIe siècle)', published online: <https://halshs.archives-ouvertes.fr/halshs-01981204/document>

Delaplace, C., ed., *Aux origines de la paroisse rurale en Gaule méridionale (IVe–IXe siècles)* (Paris: Errance, 2005)

Delumeau, J., *Le péché et la peur: la culpabilisation en Occident (XIIIe–XVIIIe siècles)* (Paris: Fayard, 1983)

Desachy, S., 'Le XIIIe siècle, ou la révolution du notariat', *Revue du Tarn* 217 (2010), 115–26

Desachy, S., ed., *De la Ligurie au Languedoc: le notaire à l'étude* (Albi: Un Autre Reg'Art, 2012)

Dossat, Y., *Les crises de l'inquisition toulousaine au XIIIe siècle* (Bourdeaux: Bière, 1959)

Drendel, J., 'The Modern State and the Economy in Provence and Southern France in the Early Fourteenth Century', *Memini: travaux et documents* 19–20 (2016), 213–25

Du Cange, C. du Fresne, et al., *Glossarium mediae et infimae latinitatis* (Niort: L. Favre, 1883–87)

Duffy, E., *The Stripping of the Altars: Traditional Religion in England, 1400–1580* (New Haven: Yale University Press, 1992; 2nd edn, 2005)

Dufoix, J.-P., et al., *Le portail de Saint-Trophime d'Arles: naissance et renaissance d'un chef-d'œuvre roman* (Arles: Actes Sud, 1999)

Duggan, L. G., 'Was Art Really the "Book of the Illiterate"?', *Word and Image* 5 (1989), 227–51

Durand, G., 'Les églises rurales du premier âge roman dans le Rouergue méridional', *Archéologie du Midi médiéval* 7 (1989), 3–42

Durieux, F.-R., 'Approches de l'histoire franciscaine du Languedoc au XIIIe siècle', *CdF* 8 (1973), 79–100

Durliat, M., 'L'église de Saint-Martin-des-Puits (Aude) et son décor peint', *Comptes rendus des séances de l'Académie des inscriptions et belles-lettres* 115 (1971), 659–82

Durliat, M., 'L'église de Laroque d'Olmes', *Congrès archéologique de France* 131 (1973), 392–99

Duvernoy, J., 'Le catharisme en Languedoc au début du XIVe siècle', *CdF* 20 (1985), 27–56

Engen, J. van, 'The Christian Middle Ages as an Historiographical Problem', *American Historical Review* 91 (1986), 519–52

Farré, M. N., '*Saber, sen i trobar:* Ramon de Cornet and the consistory of the gay science', *SVMMA* 3 (2014), 176–94

Fedi, B., 'Les *Leys d'amor* et l'école de Toulouse: théorie et pratique de l'écriture au XIV siècle', *AIEO* 9 (2011), 357–70

Ferval, V., 'Grégoire et les autres dans le recueil anonyme et sans titre du MS Paris BnF lat. 3555', in M.-A. Polo de Beaulieu, J. Berlioz, and P. Colomb, eds, *Le tonnerre des exemples: exempla et médiation culturelle dans l'Occident médiéval* (Rennes: Presses universitaires de Rennes, 2010), pp. 273–85

Feuchter, J., *Ketzer, Konzul und Büsser: Die städtischen Eliten von Montauban dem Inquisitor Petrus Cellani (1236/1241)* (Tübingen: Mohr Siebeck, 2007)

Feuchter, J., 'The *Heretici* of Languedoc: Local Holy Men and Women or Organized Religious Group? New Evidence from Inquisitorial, Notarial and Historiographical Sources', in A. Sennis, ed., *Cathars in Question* (York: York Medieval Press, 2016), pp. 112–30

Firnhaber-Baker, J., *Violence and the State in Languedoc, 1250–1400* (Cambridge: Cambridge University Press, 2014)

Flannery, J., 'The Trinitarian Order and the Ransom of Christian Captives', *Al-Masāq* 23 (2011), 135–44

Fliche, A., *La réforme grégorienne et la reconquête chrétienne (1037–1123)*, Histoire de l'Église vol. 8 (Paris: Bloud & Gay, 1944)
Fliche, A., *Du premier concile du Latran à l'avènement d'Innocent III (1123–1198)*, Histoire de l'Église vol. 9 (Paris: Bloud & Gay, 1944)
Fossier, A., *Le bureau des âmes: écritures et pratiques administratives de la Pénitencerie apostolique (XIIIe–XIVe siècle)* (Rome: École française du Rome, 2018)
Foucault, M., *Discipline and Punish: The Birth of the Prison*, trans. A. Sheridan (London: Penguin, 1977)
Foulet, L., 'Sire, messire', *Romania* 71 (1950), 1–48
Foulon, J.-H. and M. Varano, 'Réforme et épiscopat en Provence: étude comparée des cas de Gap et de Sisteron au milieu du XI siècle', *CdF* 48 (2013), 311–42
Fouracre, P., *Eternal Light and Earthly Concerns: Belief and the Shaping of Medieval Society* (Manchester: Manchester University Press, 2021)
France, J., 'Capuchins as Crusaders: Southern Gaul in the Late Twelfth Century', *Reading Medieval Studies* 36 (2010), 77–94
France, J., 'People against Mercenaries: The Capuchins in Southern Gaul', *Journal of Medieval Military History* 8 (2010), 1–22
French, K., *The People of the Parish* (Philadelphia: University of Pennsylvania Press, 2001)
Friedlander, A., *Hammer of the Inquisitors: Brother Bernard Délicieux and the Struggle against the Inquisition in Fourteenth-Century France* (Leiden: Brill, 2000)
García Marsilla, J. V., 'Avec les vêtements des autres: le marché du textile d'occasion dans la Valence médiévale', in L. Feller and A. Rodríguez, eds, *Objets sous contraintes: circulation des richesses et valeur des choses au Moyen Âge* (Paris: Sorbonne, 2013), pp. 123–43
Garnier, F., '*Statuere et in melius reformare*: écrire la norme pour les métiers à Toulouse (milieu XIIIe siècle–milieu XIVe siècle)', in D. Lett, ed., *La confection des statuts dans les sociétés méditerranéennes de l'Occident (XIIe–XVe siècle)* (Paris: Éditions de la Sorbonne, 2019), pp. 131–52
Geary, P., *Furta Sacra: Thefts of Relics in the Central Middle Ages* (Princeton: Princeton University Press, 1978)
George, J. M., 'Religious and Fictional Narratives: An Ontological Comparison with Reference to Max Weber's "Disenchantment of the World"', *International Journal of Philosophy and Social Sciences* 1 (2016), 53–62
Géraud, H., 'Les routiers', *Bibliothèque de l'École des Chartes* 3 (1841–42), 125–47, 417–47
Giallard, A., S. Kacki, C. Puig, J. Bénézet, and A. Corrochano, 'Premiers résultats concernant le site des Jardins de Saint-Benoît (Saint-Laurent-de-la-Cabrerisse, Aude), pôle religieux et funéraire des Corbières', *Archéologie du Midi médiéval* 28 (2010), 209–18
Gibbs, M. and J. Lang, *Bishops and Reform: 1215–1272* (Oxford: Oxford University Press, 1924)
Giordanengo, G., 'Les hôpitaux arlésiens du XIIe au XIVe siècle', *CdF* 8 (1978), 189–212
Given, J. M., *State and Society in Medieval Europe: Gwynedd and Languedoc under Outside Rule* (Ithaca, NY: Cornell University Press, 1990)
Given, J. M., *Inquisition and Medieval Society: Power, Discipline and Resistance in Languedoc* (Ithaca, NY: Cornell University Press, 1997)
Goetz, H.-W., 'Protection of the Church, Defense of the Law, and Reform: On the Purposes and Character of the Peace of God, 989–1038', in T. Head and R. Landes, eds, *The Peace of God: Social Violence and Religious Response around the Year 1000* (Ithaca, NY: Cornell University Press, 1992), pp. 259–79
Gouron, A., '*Libertas hominum Montispessulani*: rédaction et diffusion des coutumes de Montpellier', *Annales du Midi* 90 (1978), 289–318

Graham-Leigh, E., *The Southern French Nobility and the Albigensian Crusade* (Woodbridge: Boydell, 2005)

Gravdal, K., *Ravishing Maidens: Writing Rape in Medieval French Literature and Law* (Philadelphia: University of Pennsylvania Press, 1991)

Griffe, E., *Le Languedoc cathare et l'inquisition, 1229–1329* (Paris: Letouzey et Ané, 1980)

Grundmann, H., *Religious Movements in the Middle Ages*, trans. S. Rowan (Notre Dame, Ind.: University of Notre Dame Press, 1995)

Grundmann, H., *Herbert Grundmann (1902–1970): Essays on Heresy, Inquisition and Literacy*, trans. S. Rowan, ed. J. K. Deane (York: York Medieval Press, 2019)

Hall, D. D., *Worlds of Wonder, Days of Judgement: Popular Religious Belief in Early New England* (Cambridge, Mass.: Harvard University Press, 1989)

Hall, D. D., ed., *Lived Religion in America: Toward a History of Practice* (Princeton: Princeton University Press, 1997)

Hallam, E. H., and C. West, *Capetian France, 987–1328*, 3rd edn (London: Routledge, 2019)

Hamilakis, Y., *Archaeology and the Senses: Human Experience, Memory, and Affect* (Cambridge: Cambridge University Press, 2013)

Hamilton, B., 'The Cathars and Christian Perfection', in P. Biller and B. Dobson, eds, *The Medieval Church: Universities, Heresy, and the Religious Life*, SCH subsidia 11 (Woodbridge: Boydell, 1999), pp. 5–23

Hamilton, B., 'Cathar Links with the Balkans and Byzantium', in A. Sennis, ed., *Cathars in Question* (York: York Medieval Press, 2016), pp. 131–50

Hamilton, S., *The Practice of Penance, 900–1050* (London: Royal Historical Society, 2001)

Hamilton, S., 'Enquiring into Adultery and Wicked Deeds: Episcopal Justice in Tenth- and Eleventh-Century Italy', *Viator* 41 (2010), 21–43

Hamilton, S., *Church and People in the Medieval West, 900–1200* (Harlow: Pearson, 2013)

Hanne, O., 'La genèse médiévale d'une figure de l'épiscopat de Gap: saint Arnoux (c. 1065–c. 1079)', Colloque: *Les évêques de France au XXe siècle*, 2011; online publication 2016: <https://halshs.archives-ouvertes.fr/halshs-00995817/document>

Harvey, K., *The Fires of Lust: Sex in the Middle Ages* (London: Reaktion, 2021)

Hasenhor, G., 'Modèles de vie féminine dans la littérature morale et religieuse d'Oc', *CdF* 23 (1988), 153–70

Hautefeuille, F., 'La délimitation des territoires paroissiaux dans les pays de moyenne Garonne (Xe–XVe siècles), *Médiévales* 49 (2005), 73–88

Head, T. and R. Landes, eds, *The Peace of God: Social Violence and Religious Response around the Year 1000* (Ithaca, NY: Cornell University Press, 1992)

Heng, G., *The Invention of Race in the European Middle Ages* (Cambridge: Cambridge University Press, 2018)

Hershon, C. P., *Faith and Controversy: The Jews of Mediaeval Languedoc* (Birmingham: A.E.I.O, 1999)

Hill, D., *Inquisition in the Fourteenth Century: The Manuals of Bernard Gui and Nicholas Eymerich* (York: York Medieval Press, 2019)

Housley, N. J., 'Pope Clement V and the Crusades of 1309–10', *Journal of Medieval History* 8 (1982), 29–43

Hunt, E. S. and J. M. Murray, *A History of Business in Medieval Europe, 1200–1550* (Cambridge: Cambridge University Press, 1999)

Iogna-Prat, D., *Order and Exclusion: Cluny and Christendom face Heresy, Judaism and Islam (1000–1150)*, trans. G. R. Edwards (Ithaca, NY: Cornell University Press, 2002)

Iogna-Prat, D., and E. Zadora-Rio, eds, *La paroisse, genèse d'une forme territoriale*, special issue of *Médiévales* 49 (2005)

Iogna-Prat, D., 'Topographies of Penance in the Latin West, c. 800–c.1200', in A. Firey, ed., *A New History of Penance* (Leiden: Brill, 2008), pp. 149–72

Jansen, K. L., *The Making of the Magdalene: Preaching and Popular Devotion in the Later Middle Ages* (Princeton: Princeton University Press, 2000)

Jiménez-Sanchez, P., 'Les actes de Lombers (1165): une procédure d'arbitrage?', in H. Débax, ed., *Les sociétés méridionales à l'âge féodal (Espagne, Italie et sud de la France, Xe–XIIIe siècle): hommage à Pierre Bonnassie* (Toulouse: Presses universitaires du Midi, 1999), pp. 311–17

Jiménez[-Sanchez], P., 'Source juridiques pour l'étude du catharisme: les actes du "concile" de Lombers (1165)', *Clio et Crimen* 1 (2004), 365–79

Jiménez-Sanchez, P., *Les catharismes: modèles dissidents du christianisme médiéval (XIIe–XIIIe siècles)* (Rennes: Presses universitaires de Rennes, 2008)

Jong, M. de, *The Penitential State: Authority and Atonement in the Age of Louis the Pious, 814–840* (Cambridge: Cambridge University Press, 2009)

Jordan, W. C., *The Apple of His Eye: Converts from Islam in the Reign of Louis IX* (Princeton: Princeton University Press, 2019)

Joret, C., *La rose dans l'antiquité et au moyen âge: histoire, légendes et symbolisme* (Paris: Émile Bouillon, 1892)

Jurasinski, S., *The Old English Penitentials and Anglo Saxon Law* (Cambridge: Cambridge University Press, 2015)

Kay, S., *The Place of Thought: The Complexity of One in Late Medieval French Didactic Poetry* (Philadelphia: University of Pennsylvania Press, 2007)

Katajala-Peltomaa, S., *Demonic Possession and Lived Religion in Later Medieval Europe* (Oxford: Oxford University Press, 2020)

Katajala-Peltomaa, S. and R. M. Toivo, eds, *Lived Religion and the Long Reformation in Northern Europe, c. 1300–1700* (Leiden: Brill, 2017)

Katajala-Peltomaa, S., and R. M. Toivo, *Lived Religion and Gender in Late Medieval and Early Modern Europe* (Abingdon: Routledge, 2021)

Kay, R., *Pontificalia: A Repertory of Latin Manuscript Pontificals and Benedictionals* (Kansas: n.p., 2007)

Kaye, J., *A History of Balance, 1250–1375* (Cambridge: Cambridge University Press, 2014)

Keefe, S. A., *Water and the Word: Baptism and the Education of the Clergy in the Carolingian Empire*, 2 vols (Notre Dame, Ind.: University of Notre Dame Press, 2002)

Keefe, S. A., *Catalogue of Works Pertaining to the Explanation of the Creed in Carolingian Manuscripts* (Turnhout: Brepols, 2012)

Kelly, H. A., 'Inquisition and the Prosecution of Heresy: Misconceptions and Abuses', *Church History* 58 (1989), 439–51

Kieckhefer, R., 'The Office of Inquisition and Medieval Heresy: The Transition from Personal to Institutional Jurisdiction', *Journal of Ecclesiastical History* 46 (1995), 36–61

Kieckhefer, R., *Magic in the Middle Ages*, 3rd edn (Cambridge: Cambridge University Press, 2022)

Kienzle, B. M., *Cistercians, Heresy and Crusade in Occitania, 1145–1229* (Woodbridge: York Medieval Press, 2001)

Koziol, G., *The Peace of God* (Leeds: ARC Humanities Press, 2018)

Kramer, R., *Rethinking Authority in the Carolingian Empire* (Amsterdam: Amsterdam University Press, 2019)

Kupfer, M., *Romanesque Wall Painting in Central France: The Politics of Narrative* (New Haven: Yale University Press, 1993)

Lamy-Lassalle, C., 'Les peintures de Saint-Michel d'Aiguilhe', *Bulletin de la Société nationale des antiquaires de France* 1958/1 (1959), 86–90

Landes, R., 'Can the Church be Desperate, Warriors be Pacifist, and Commoners Ridiculously Optimistic? On the Historian's Imagination and the Peace of God', in K. L. Jansen, G. Geltner, and A. E. Lester, eds, *Center and Periphery: Studies on Power in the Medieval World in Honor of William Chester Jordan* (Leiden: Brill, 2013), pp. 79–92

Langmuir, G. I., 'L'absence d'accusation de meutre rituel a l'ouest du Rhône', *CdF* 12 (1977), 235–49

Langmuir, G., *History, Religion and Antisemitism* (Berkeley: University of California Press, 1990)

Lassalle, V., 'Le décor sculpté de l'église romane Saint-Michel de la Garde-Guérin à Prévenchères (Lozère)', *Archéologie du Midi médiéval* 22 (2004), 77–102

Lauranson-Rosaz, C., 'Peace from the Mountains: The Auvergnat Origins of the Peace of God', in T. Head and R. Landes, eds, *The Peace of God: Social Violence and Religious Response in France around the Year 1000* (Ithaca, NY: Cornell University Press, 1992), pp. 104–34

Lauranson-Rosaz, C., 'La paix populaire dans les montagnes d'Auvergne au Xe siècle', in P.-R. Gaussin, ed., *Maisons de Dieu et hommes d'église* (Saint-Étienne: Publications de l'Université de Saint-Étienne, 1992), pp. 289–333

Lauwers, M., *Naissance du cimetière: lieux sacrés et terre des morts dans l'Occident médiévale* (Paris: Aubier, 2005)

Lauwers, M., 'Paroisse, paroissiens et territoire: remarques sur *parochia* dans les textes latins du moyen âge', *Médiévales* 49 (2005), 11–32

Lavoie, R., 'La delinquance sexuelle a Manosque (1240–1430): schéma général et singularités juives', *Provence historique* 37 (1987), 571–88

Le Blévec, D., *La part du pauvre: l'assistance dans les pay bas-rhône du XIIe siècle au milieu du Xve siècle*, 2 vols (Rome: École française du Rome, 2000)

Le Bras, G., *Institutions ecclésiastiques de la Chrétienté médiévale: préliminaires et 1ère partie, livre I* (Paris: Bloud & Gay, 1959)

Le Bras, G., *Institutions ecclésiastiques de la Chrétienté médiévale: première partie, livres II à VI* (Paris: Bloud & Gay, 1964)

Lebrigand, Y., 'Origines et première diffusion de l'Ordre de Saint-Ruf', *CdF* 24 (1989), 167–79

Léglu, C., *Between Sequence and Sirventes: Aspects of Parody in Troubadour Lyric* (Oxford: Legenda, 2000)

Léglu, C., 'Vernacular Poems and Inquisitors in Languedoc and Champagne, ca. 1242-1249', *Viator* 33 (2002), 117–32

Léglu, C., *Multilingualism and Mother Tongue in Medieval French, Occitan and Catalan Narratives* (University Park, Pa: Pennsylvania State University Press, 2010)

Le Goff, J., 'The Usurer and Purgatory', in R. S. Lopez, ed., *The Dawn of Modern Banking* (New Haven: Yale University Press, 1979), pp. 25–52

Le Goff, J., *La naissance du purgatoire* (Paris: Gallimard, 1981)

Le Goff, J., *Your Money or Your Life: Economy and Religion in the Middle Ages*, trans. P. Ranum (New York: Zone, 1988)

Lenglet, M.-O., 'Géraud de Salles, ses fondations monastiques, leur évolution vers l'ordre cistercien à la fin de XIIème siècle', *Bulletin de la Société historique et archéologique du Périgord* 114 (1987), 33–50

Le Roy Ladurie, E., *Montaillou* (Paris: Gallimard, 1975)

Lesné-Ferret, M., 'L'écriture des statuts languedociens au XIIIe siècle: le modèle des coutumes de Montpellier', in D. Lett, ed., *La confection des statuts dans les sociétés méditerranéennes de l'Occident (XIIe–XIVe siècles)* (Paris: Éditions de la Sorbonne, 2017), pp. 153–71

Lett, D., ed., *La confection des statuts dans les sociétés méditerranéennes de l'Occident (XIIe–XIVe siècles)* (Paris: Éditions de la Sorbonne, 2017)

Leveleux, C., *La parole interdite: le blaspheme dans la France médiévale (XIIIe–XVIe siècles). Du péché au crime* (Paris: De Boccard, 2001)

Lewis, A. R., *The Development of Southern French and Catalan Society, 718–1050* (Austin: University of Texas Press, 1965)

Leyser, C., 'Review article: Church Reform—Full of Sound and Fury, Signifying Nothing?', *Early Medieval Europe* 24 (2016), 478–99

Leyser, H., *Hermits and the New Monasticism: A Study of Religious Communities in Western Europe, 1000–1150* (Manchester: Manchester University Press, 1984)

Licence, T., *Hermits and Recluses in English Society, 950–1200* (Oxford: Oxford University Press, 2011)

Lippiatt, G., 'Reform and Custom: The Statutes of Pamiers in Early Thirteenth-Century Christendom', in M. Aurell, G. Lippiatt, and L. Macé, eds, *Simon de Montfort (c. 1170–1218): le croisé, son lignage et son temps* (Turnhout: Brepols, 2020), pp. 39–67

Little, L. K., *Religious Poverty and the Profit Economy in Medieval Europe* (Ithaca, NY: Cornell University Press, 1978)

Lorenc, J. A., 'John of Freiburg and the Usury Prohibition in the Late Middle Ages: A Study in the Popularization of Medieval Canon Law' (University of Toronto, unpublished PhD dissertation, 2013)

McDonnell, E. W., 'The "Vita Apostolica": Diversity or Dissent', *Church History* 24 (1955), 15–31

Macé, L., *Les comtes de Toulouse et leur entourage: XIIe–XIIe siècles* (Toulouse: Privat, 2000)

McHaffie, M. W., 'Law and Violence in Eleventh-Century France', *Past & Present* 238 (2018), 3–41

Magnani Soares-Christen, E., *Monastères et aristocratie en Provence milieu Xe–début XIIe siècle* (Münster: Lit, 1999)

Magnou[-Nortier], E., *L'introduction de la réforme grégorienne à Toulouse* (Toulouse: Association Marc Bloch, 1958)

Magnou-Nortier, E., *La société laïque et l'église dans la province ecclésiastique de Narbonne (zone cispyrénéenne) de la fin du VIIIe à la fin du XIe siècle* (Toulouse: Associations des Publications de l'Université de Toulouse-Le Mirail, 1974)

Maisonneuve, H., *Études sur les origines de l'inquisition* (Paris: J. Vrin, 1960)

Malegam, J. Y., *The Sleep of Behemoth: Disputing Peace and Violence in Medieval Europe, 1000–1200* (Ithaca, NY: Cornell University Press, 2013)

Mallet, G., 'Le cloître-cimetière Saint-Jean de Perpignan: observations', *Archéologie du Midi médiéval* 7 (1989), 125–36

Mallet, G., 'Les cloîtres-cimetières du Roussillon', *CdF* 33 (1998), 417–34

Mallet, G., *Églises romanes oubliées du Roussillon* (Montpellier: Presses universitaires du Languedoc, 2003)

Mallet, G., 'Entre traditions et innovations: l'espace liturgique de deux églises romanes du diocèse d'Elne, Saint-Michel de Cuxa et Sainte-Marie d'Arles-sur-Tech', *CdF* 46 (2011), 37–57

Mansfield, M., *The Humiliation of Sinners: Public Penance in Thirteenth-Century France* (Ithaca, NY: Cornell University Press, 2005)

Marandet, M.-C., *Le souci de l'au-delà: la pratique testamentaire dans la région toulousaine (1300–1450)*, 2 vols (Perpignan: Presses universitaires de Perpignan, 1998)

Martí, S., 'Joan de Castellnou revisité: notes biographiques', *Revue des langues romanes* 121 (2017), 623–60

Matter, E. A., 'The Church Fathers and the *Glossa Ordinaria*', in I. Backus, ed., *The Reception of the Church Fathers in the West, from the Carolingians to the Maurists*, 2 vols (Leiden: Brill, 1997)

Mazel, F., 'Amitié et rupture de l'amitié: moines et grands laïcs provençaux au temps de la crise grégorienne (milieu XIe–milieu XIIe siècle)', *Revue historique* 307 (2005), 53–95

Mazel, F., 'Aristocratie, église et religion au village en Provence (XIe–XIVe siècle)', *CdF* 40 (2006), 163–210

Mazel, F., *Féodalités, 888–1180* (Paris: Belin, 2010)

Mazel, F., *L'évêque et le territoire: l'invention médiévale de l'espace* (Paris: Seuil, 2016)

Mazel, F., 'Pour une redéfinition de la "réforme grégorienne"', *CdF* 48 (2013), 9–38

Mazel, F., 'Histoire et religion, entre pratique historiographique, principes épistémologiques et enjeux de sociétés', *Recherches de science religieuse* 109 (2021), 701–16

Meens, R., 'The Frequency and Nature of Early Medieval Penance', in P. Biller and A. J. Minnis, eds, *Handling Sin: Confession in the Middle Ages* (Woodbridge: York Medieval Press, 1998), pp. 35–61

Meens, R., 'The Historiography of Early Medieval Penance', in A. Firey, ed., *A New History of Penance* (Leiden: Brill, 2008), pp. 73–95

Meens, R., 'Penitential Varieties', in J. H. Arnold, ed., *The Oxford Handbook of Medieval Christianity* (Oxford: Oxford University Press, 2014), pp. 254–70

Meens, R., *Penance in Medieval Europe, 600–1200* (Cambridge: Cambridge University Press, 2014)

Melve, L., 'Ecclesiastical Reform in Historiographical Context', *History Compass* 13 (2015), 213–21

Menache, S., 'Papal Attempts at a Commercial Boycott of the Muslims in the Crusade Period', *Journal of Ecclesiastical History* 63 (2012), 236–59

Méras, M., 'Un bourgeois de Montauban sous Alphonse de Poitiers: Guillaume Amiel', *Bulletin philologique et historique jusqu'à 1610 du Comité des travaux historiques et scientifiques* (1960), 693–702

Michaud-Quantin, P., 'La "Summula in foro poenitentiali" attribué à Bérengar Fredol', *Collectanea Stephan Kuttner* (Rome, 1967), pp. 147–67

Michaud-Quantin, P., 'Textes pénitentials languedociens au XIIIe siècle', *CdF* 6 (1971), 151–72

Michelozzi, A., 'L'église romane Saint-Laurent à Jonquières-et-Saint-Vincent (Gard)', *Archéologie du Midi médiéval* 22 (2004), 27–44

Michelozzi, A., 'L'église Saint-Pierre-de-Campublic à Beaucaire', *Archéologie du Midi médiéval* 25 (2007), 19–34

Miller, M. C., *Clothing the Clergy: Virtue and Power in Medieval Europe, c. 800–1200* (Ithaca, NY: Cornell University Press, 2014)

Molinier, A., *Catalogue générale des manuscrits des bibliothèques publiques des départements, VII: Toulouse–Nîmes* (Paris: Imprimerie nationale, 1885)

Moore, J. C., *Inquisition and Its Organisation in Italy, 1250–1350* (York: York Medieval Press, 2019)

Moore, R. I., *The War on Heresy: Faith and Power in Medieval Europe* (London: Profile, 2012)

Moran, J., 'La prédication ancienne en Catalogne: l'activité canoniale', *CdF* 32 (1997), 17–35

Morard, M., 'Dominique Grima, o.p., un exégète thomiste à Toulouse au début du XIVe siècle', *CdF* 35 (2000), 325–74

Morris, C., *The Discovery of the Individual, 1050–1200* (London: SPCK, 1972)

Morris, C., *The Papal Monarchy: The Western Church from 1050 to 1250* (Oxford: Clarendon, 1989)

Mousnier, M., 'Dono unum hominem meum: désignations de la dépendance du XIe au XIIIe siècle en Languedoc occidental', Mélanges de l'École française de Rome: moyen âge 111/1 (1999), 51–60

Mundy, J. H., Liberty and Political Power in Toulouse, 1050–1230 (New York: Columbia University Press, 1954)

Mundy, J. H., 'Hospitals and Leprosaries in Twelfth and Early Thirteenth-Century Toulouse', in J. H. Mundy, R. W. Emery, and B. N. Nelson, eds, Essays in Medieval Life and Thought, Presented in Honor of Austin Patterson Evans (New York: Biblo and Tanen, 1965), pp. 181–206

Mundy, J. H., 'Charity and Social Work in Toulouse, 1100–1250', Traditio 22 (1966), 203–87

Mundy, J. H., Men and Women at Toulouse in the Age of the Cathars (Toronto: PIMS, 1990)

Murray, A., 'The Epicureans', in P. Boitani and A. Torti, eds, Intellectuals and Writers in Fourteenth-Century Europe (Cambridge: Brewer, 1986), pp. 138–63

Murray, A., 'Confession before 1215', Transactions of the Royal Historical Society, 6th ser. 3 (1993), 51–81

Murray, A., Conscience and Authority in the Medieval Church (Oxford: Oxford University Press, 2015)

Murray, J., '"The Law of Sin That Is In My Members": The Problem of Male Embodiment', in S. J. E. Riches and S. Salih, eds, Gender and Holiness: Men, Women and Saints in Late Medieval Europe (London: Routledge, 2002), pp. 9–22

Murray, J. M., Bruges, Cradle of Capitalism, 1280–1390 (Cambridge: Cambridge University Press, 2005)

Naismith, R., 'Gilds, States and Societies in the Early Middle Ages', Early Medieval Europe 28 (2020), 627–62

Nedkvitne, A., Lay Belief in Norse Society, 1000–1350 (Copenhagen: Museum Tusculanum Press, 2009)

Needman, R., Belief, Language and Experience (Oxford: Blackwell, 1972)

Nongbri, B., Before Religion: A History of a Modern Concept (New Haven: Yale University Press, 2015)

Noonan, J. T., The Scholastic Analysis of Usury (Cambridge, Mass.: Harvard University Press, 1957)

Oberste, J., Religiosität und sozialer Aufstieg in der Stadt des hohen Mittelalters, Band 2: Städtische Eliten in Toulouse (Cologne: Böhlau Verlag, 2003)

Orsi, R. A., The Madonna of 115th Street: Faith and Community in Italian Harlem, 1880–1950, 3rd edn (New Haven: Yale University Press, 2010)

Otis, L., 'Une contribution à l'étude du blasphème au bas moyen âge', in Diritto comune e diritti locali nella storia dell'Europa (Milan: A. Guiffrè, 1980), pp. 211–23

Ott, M., 'Saint-Nazaire-de-Marissargues à Aubais (Gard): une église et son cimetière du VIIIe au Xe siècle', Archéologie du Midi médiéval 28 (2010), 147–59

Ourliac, P., Les sauvetés du Comminges: étude et documents sur les villages fondés par les Hospitaliers dans la région des coteaux commingeois (Toulouse: Boisseau, 1947)

Palazzo, E., L'espace rituel et le sacré dans le christianisme: la liturgie de l'autel portatif dans l'Antiquité et au Moyen Âge (Turnhout: Brepols, 2008)

Palazzo, E., 'Art, Liturgy and the Five Senses in the Early Middle Ages', Viator 41 (2010), 25–56

Palazzo, E., 'Missarum sollemnia: Eucharistic Rituals in the Middle Ages', in J. H. Arnold, ed., The Oxford Handbook of Medieval Christianity (Oxford: Oxford University Press, 2014), pp. 238–53

Parodi, A., 'Les églises dans le paysage rural du haut Moyen Âge en Languedoc oriental (IX–XIIe s.)', in M. Fixot and E. Zadora-Rio, eds, L'environnement des églises et la *topographie religieuse des campagnes médiévales*, Document d'archéologie francaise 46 (Paris: Éditions de la Maison des sciences de l'homme, 1994), pp. 107–21

Panfili, D., 'Transferts d'églises, de dimes et recomposition des seigneuries en Languedoc (vers 1050–vers 1200)', *CdF* 48 (2013), 581–602

Passarrius, O., R. Donat, and A. Catafau, 'L'église et le cimetière du village médiéval déserte de Vilarnau à Perpignan', *Archéologie du Midi médiéval* 28 (2010), 219–38

Paterson, L., *Singing the Crusades: French and Occitan Lyric Responses to the Crusading Movements, 1137–1336* (Woodbridge: Boydell, 2018)

Patzold, S., and C. van Rhijn, eds, *Men in the Middle: Local Priests in Early Medieval Europe* (Berlin: De Gruyter, 2016)

Paul, J., 'Evangelisme et Franciscanisme chez Louis d'Anjou', *CdF* 8 (1973), 375–401

Paul, J., 'Miracles et mentalité religieuse populaire à Marseille au début du XIV siècle', *CdF* 11 (1976), 61–90

Paul, J., 'Le rayonnement géographique du pelerinage au tombeau de Louis d'Anjou', *CdF* 15 (1980), 137–58

Paul, J., 'La paix de Saint-Gilles (1209) et l'exercise du pouvoir', in C. Carozzi and H. Taviani-Carozzi, eds, *Le pouvoir au moyen âge: idéologies, pratiques, représentations* (Aix: Presses universitaires de Provence, 2007), pp. 147–68

Pawlowski, K., 'Villes et villages circulaires du Languedoc: un des premiers modèles de l'urbanisme médiévale?', *Annales du Midi* 99 (1987), 407–27

Payer, P. J., *The Bridling of Desire: Views of Sex in the Later Middle Ages* (Toronto: University of Toronto Press, 1993)

Pécout, Th., 'Dîme et institution épiscopale au XIIIe siècle en Provence', in M. Lauwers, ed., *La dîme, l'église, et la société féodale* (Turnhout: Brepols, 2012), pp. 411–72

Pegg, M. G., *The Corruption of Angels: The Great Inquisition of 1245–1246* (Princeton: Princeton University Press, 2005)

Pegg, M. G., *A Most Holy War: The Albigensian Crusade and the Battle for Christendom* (Oxford: Oxford University Press, 2008)

Pellecuer, C., and L. Schneider, 'Premières églises et espace rural en Languedoc méditerranéen (V–Xe S.)', in C. Delaplace, ed., *Aux origines de la paroisse rurale en Gaule méridionale (IVe–IXe siècles)* (Paris: Errance, 2005), pp. 98–119

Peterson, D. R. and D. Walhof, eds, *The Invention of Religion: Rethinking Belief in Politics and History* (New Brunswick, NJ: Rutgers University Press, 2002)

Piron, S., 'Marchands et confesseurs: le "Traité des contrats" d'Olivi dans son contexte (Narbonne, fin XIIIe–début XIVe siècle)', *L'argent au Moyen Âge: actes des congrès de la Société des historiens médiévistes de l'enseignement supérieur public 28, Clermont-Ferrand 1997* (Paris: Publications de la Sorbonne, 1998), pp. 289–308

Poisson, G., 'Le comte, le consul et les notaires: l'écriture statutaire à Toulouse au XIIIe siècle', in D. Lett, ed., *La confection des statuts dans les sociétés méditerranéennes de l'Occident (XIIe–XIVe siècles)* (Paris: Éditions de la Sorbonne, 2017), pp. 81–101

Poisson, O., '"Rien. Rien." L'église Saint-Sauveur de Casenoves et son décor peint', in V. Fernandez, ed., *De la création à la restauration: travaux d'histoire de l'art offerts à Marcel Durliat* (Toulouse: Atelier d'histoire de l'art méridional, 1992), pp. 261–83

Poly, J. P., *Le chemin des amours barbares: genèse médiévale de la sexualité européenne* (Paris: Perrin, 2003)

Postles, D., 'Lamps, Lights and Layfolk: "Popular" Devotion before the Black Death', *Journal of Medieval History* 25 (1999), 97–114

Pradalié, G. and E. Hamon, 'L'Aubrac au l'époque de la Domerie', in L. Fau, ed., *Les monts d'Aubrac au moyen âge: genèse d'un monde agropastoral* (Paris: Éditions de la Maison des sciences de l'homme, 2006)

Pradalié, G., 'La fondation de l'hôpital Saint-Raimond de Toulouse: une remise en question', *Annales du Midi* 119 (2007), 227-36

Pradalié, G., 'Une assemblée de paix à Toulouse en 1144', *Annales du Midi* 122 (2010), 75-82

Ramière de Fortanier, A., 'La confrérie Notre-Dame de Fanjeaux et son développement au moyen âge', *CdF* 11 (1976), 321-56

Reiss, A., 'Beyond "Books of the Illiterate": Understanding English Medieval Wall Paintings', *The British Art Journal* 9/1 (2008), 4-14

Remensnyder, A., 'Un problème de cultures ou de culture? La statue-reliquaire et les *joca* de Sainte Foy de Conques', *Cahiers de civilisation médiévale* 33 (1990), 351-57

Remensnyder, A., 'Pollution, Purity and Peace: An Aspect of Social Reform between the Late Tenth Century and 1076', in T. Head and R. Landes, eds, *The Peace of God: Social Violence and Religious Response around the Year 1000* (Ithaca, NY: Cornell University Press, 1992), pp. 280-307

Remensnyder, A., 'The Boundaries of Latin Christendom and Islam: Iberia and the Levant', in J. H. Arnold, ed., *The Oxford Handbook of Medieval Christianity* (Oxford: Oxford University Press, 2014), pp. 93-113

Reynolds, S., *Fiefs and Vassals* (Oxford: Blackwell, 1994)

Rhijn, C. van, *Shepherds of the Lord: Priests and Episcopal Statutes in the Carolingian Period* (Turnhout: Brepols, 2007)

Rhijn, C. van, 'Manuscripts for Local Priests and the Carolingian Reforms', in C. van Rhijn and S. Patzold, eds, *Men in the Middle: Local Priests in Early Medieval Europe* (Berlin: De Gruyter, 2016), pp. 177-98

Rhijn, C. van, *Leading the Way to Heaven: Pastoral Care and Salvation in the Carolingian Period* (Abingdon: Routledge, 2022)

Ribaucourt, C., 'Les mendiants du Midi d'après la cartographie de l'"enquête"', *CdF* 8 (1973), 25-33

Ricketts, P. T., *Connaissance de la littérature occitane: Matfre Ermengaud (1246-1322) et le Breviari d'amor* (Perpignan: Presses universitaires de Perpignan, 2012)

Rist, R., *The Papacy and Crusading in Europe, 1198-1245* (London: Continuum, 2009)

Rist, R., 'Salvation and the Albigensian Crusade: Pope Innocent III and the Plenary Indulgence', *Reading Medieval Studies* 36 (2010), 95-112

Roach, A., *The Devil's World: Heresy and Society, 1100-1300* (Harlow: Pearson, 2005)

Roche, M., 'La société languedocienne d'après les testaments (813-1270)', unpublished PhD thesis, 2 vols, Toulouse 1986

Roquebert, M., *L'épopée cathare*, 4 vols (Toulouse: Privat, 1970-89)

Rosenwein, B. H., *To Be the Neighbor of St Peter: The Social Meaning of Cluny's Property, 909-1049* (Ithaca, NY: Cornell University Press, 1989)

Rousseaux, X., 'Religion, économie et société: le pèlerinage judiciaire dans les Pays-Bas (Nivelles, du XVe au XVIIe siècle)', in M.-A. Bourguignon, B. Dauven, and X. Rousseaux, eds, *Amender, sanctionner et punir: histoire de la peine du Moyen Âge au XXe siècle* (Louvain-la-Neuve: Presses universitaires de Louvain, 2012), pp. 61-85

Rubellin, M., 'Un instrument du contrôle épiscopal au XIIIe siècle: les status synodaux', in M. Rubellin, *Église et société chrétienne d'Agobard à Valdes* (Lyon: Presses universitaires de Lyon, 2003), pp. 513-26

Rubin, M., *Corpus Christi: The Eucharist in Late Medieval Culture* (Cambridge: Cambridge University Press, 1991)

Rubin, M., *Gentile Tales: The Narrative Assault on Late Medieval Jews* (London: Yale University Press, 1999)

Ruel, M., 'Christians as Believers', in J. Davis, ed., *Religious Organization and Religious Experience* (London: Academic Press, 1982)

Ruiz, T., *From Heaven to Earth: The Reordering of Castilian Society, 1150–1350* (Princeton: Princeton University Press, 2004)
Ryrie, A., *Being Protestant in Reformation England* (Oxford: Oxford University Press, 2013)
Sabean, D., *Power in the Blood: Popular Culture and Village Discourse in Early Modern Germany* (Cambridge: Cambridge University Press, 1984)
Salonen, K.Â. and L. Schmugge, eds, *A Sip from the Well of Grace: Medieval Texts from the Apostolic Penitentiary* (Washington DC: Catholic University of America Press, 2009)
Sansy, D., 'Marquer la différance: l'imposition de la rouelle aux XIIIe et XIV siècles', *Médiévales* 41 (2001), 15–26
Schenk, J., *Templar Families: Landowning Families and the Order of the Temple in France, c. 1120–1307* (Cambridge: Cambridge University Press, 2012)
Schmitt, J.-C., *La raison des gestes dans l'Occident médiéval* (Paris: Gallimard, 1990)
Schmitt, J.-C., *Ghosts in the Middle Ages*, trans. T. L. Fagan (Chicago: University of Chicago Press, 1998)
Schneider, L., 'Le site de Saint-Sébastien-de-Maroiol', *Archéologie médiévale* 25 (1999), 133–81
Schneider, L., 'De l'archéologie du monument chrétien à l'archéologie des lieux de culte: propos d'introduction et repères historiographiques', *Archéologie du Midi médiéval* 28 (2010), 131–45
Segonne, M., *Moine, prélat, croisé: Benoît d'Alignan, abbé de La Grasse, seigneur-évêque de Marseille 1190–1268* (Marseille: Robert, 1960)
Selwood, D., *Knights of the Cloister: Templars and Hospitallers in Central-Southern Occitania, 1100–1300* (Woodbridge: Boydell, 1999)
Sennis, A., ed., *Cathars in Question* (York: York Medieval Press, 2016)
Şenocak, N., 'Twelfth-Century Italian Confraternities as Institutions of Pastoral Care', *Journal of Medieval History* 42 (2016), 202–25
Shagan, E., *The Birth of Modern Belief: Faith and Judgment from the Middle Ages to the Enlightenment* (Princeton: Princeton University Press, 2018)
Shatzmiller, J., *Shylock Reconsidered: Jews, Moneylending and Medieval Society* (Berkeley: University of California Press, 1990)
Sigal, P. A., 'L'anthroponymie féminine en Provence d'après le livre des miracles et le procès de canonisation de Saint Louis d'Anjou (fin xiiième–début xivème siècle)', in M. Bourin and P. Charelle, eds, *Genèse médiévale de l'anthroponymie modern, II-2: persistances du nom unique* (Tours: Presses universitaires François-Rabelais, 1992), pp. 187–205
Smith, C. E., *The University of Toulouse in the Middle Ages* (Milwaukee: Marquette University Press, 1958)
Smith, J. Z., '"Religion" and "Religious Studies": No Difference At All', *Soundings: An Interdisciplinary Journal* 71 (1988)
Smith, J. Z., 'Religion, Religions, Religious', in M. C. Taylor, ed., *Critical Terms for Religious Studies* (Chicago: University of Chicago Press, 1998), pp. 269–84
Somerville, R., *Pope Urban's Council of Piacenza* (Oxford: Oxford University Press, 2011)
Springer, R., 'Local Religious Life in England, c. 1160–1210', unpublished PhD thesis, Oxford, 2017
Spufford, P., *Handbook of Medieval Exchange* (London: Royal Historical Society, 1986)
Stantchev, S. K., *Spiritual Rationality: Papal Embargo as Cultural Practice* (Oxford: Oxford University Press, 2014)
Stroll, M., *Calixtus the Second, 1119–1124: A Pope Born to Rule* (Leiden: Brill, 2004)
Summerlin, D., *The Canons of the Third Lateran Council of 1179: Their Origins and Reception* (Cambridge: Cambridge University Press, 2019)
Sureda i Jubany, M., 'Les lieux de la Vierge: notes de topo-liturgie mariale en Catalogne (XIe–XVe siècles)', in M.-P. Subes and J.-B. Mathon, eds, *Vierges à l'enfant médiévales de*

Catalogne, Corpus des Vierges à l'enfant (XIIe-XVe s.) des Pyrénées-Orientales (Perpignan: Presses universitaires de Perpignan, 2013), pp. 39–69

Tanner, N. J.Â.and S. Watson, 'Least of the Laity: The Minimum Requirements for a Medieval Christian', *Journal of Medieval History* 32 (2006), 395–423

Tannous, J., *The Making of the Medieval Middle East: Religion, Society and Simple Believers* (Princeton: Princeton University Press, 2018)

Taylor, C., *Heresy, Crusade and Inquisition in Medieval Quercy* (York: York Medieval Press, 2011)

Taylor, C., 'Looking for the "Good Men" in the Languedoc: An Alternative to "Cathars"?', in A. Sennis, ed., *Cathars in Question* (York: York Medieval Press, 2016), pp. 242–56

Taylor, C., 'A Presence in Languedoc (12th–13th Centuries)', in M. Benedetti and E. Cameron, eds, *A Companion to the Waldenses in the Middle Ages* (Leiden: Brill, 2022), pp. 35–77

Taylor, N. L., 'The Will and Society in Medieval Catalonia and Languedoc, 800–1200', unpublished PhD (Harvard, 1995)

Taylor, R. A., *A Bibliographical Guide to the Study of the Troubadours and Old Occitan Literature* (Kalamazoo, Mich.: Medieval Institute Publications, 2015)

Tellenbach, G., *The Church in Western Europe from the Tenth to the Early Twelfth Century*, trans. T. Reuter (Cambridge: Cambridge University Press, 1993)

Tentler, T. N., *Sin and Confession on the Eve of the Reformation* (Princeton: Princeton University Press, 1997)

Théry, J., '"Innommables abominations sodomitiques": les débuts de la répression. Autour de l'une des premières sentences conservées (justice épiscopale d'Albi, 1280)', *CdF* 52 (2019), 297–349

Thomas, W., *Der Sonntag im frühen Mittelalter* (Göttingen: Vandenhoeck & Ruprecht, 1929)

Thompson, A., *Cities of God: The Religion of the Italian Communes, 1125–1325* (Philadelphia: University of Pennsylvania Press, 2005)

Tiran, F., 'Trinitaires et mercédaires à Marseille et le rachat des captifs de Barbarie', *Cahiers de la Méditerranée* 87 (2013), 173–86

Töpfer, B., 'The Cult of Relics and Pilgrimage in Burgundy and Aquitaine at the Time of the Monastic Reform', in T. Head and R. Landes, eds, *The Peace of God: Social Violence and Religious Response around the Year 1000* (Ithaca, NY: Cornell University Press, 1992), pp. 41–57

Toussaert, J., *Le sentiment religieux en Flandre à la fin du moyen-âge* (Paris: Plon, 1963)

Toynbee, M. R., *S. Louis of Toulouse and the Process of Canonisation in the Fourteenth Century* (Manchester: Manchester University Press, 1929)

Trivellone, A., 'Le développement du décor monumental et la conquête de l'extérieur des églises: *sagreres* et façades catalanes au cours de la première moitié du XIe siècle', *CdF* 46 (2011), 175–227

Tugwell, S., 'The Evolution of Dominican Structures of Government', *Archivum Fratrum Praedicatorum* 69 (1999), 5–60; 70 (2000), 5–109; 71 (2001), 5–182; 72 (2005), 29–79

Vallet, S., 'La coquille du pèlerin dans les sépultures médiévales du sud-ouest de la France: nouveaux résultats et perspectives de recherches', *Archéologie du Midi médiéval* 26 (2008), 238–47

Vauchez, A., *La spiritualité du Moyen Âge occidental, VIIIe–XIIIe siècle* (Paris: Seuil, 1994)

Vauchez, A., *The Laity in the Middle Ages: Religious Beliefs and Devotional Practices*, trans. M. J. Schneider (Notre Dame, Ind.: University of Notre Dame Press, 1993)

Vicaire, M.-H., 'Le développement de la province Dominicaine de Provence (1215–1295)', *CdF* 8 (1973), 35–77

Vicaire, M. H., 'La place des œuvres de miséricorde dans la pastorale en Pays d'oc', *CdF* 13 (1978), 21–44

Vincent, C., *Les confréries médiévales dans le royaume de France, XIIIe–XVe siècle* (Paris: Albin Michel, 1994)
Vincent, C., *Fiat Lux: lumière et luminaires dans la vie religieuse du XIIe au XVIe siècle* (Paris: Cerf, 2004)
Vincent, N., 'A Letter to King Henry I from Toulouse', *Journal of Ecclesiastical History* 63 (2012), 331–45
Vovelle, M., *Piété baroque et dechristianisation en Provence au XVIIIe siècle* (Paris: Plon, 1973)
Wakefield, W. L., 'Notes on Some Anti-heretical Writings of the Thirteenth Century', *Franciscan Studies* 27 (1967), 285–321
Wakefield, W. L., 'Heretics as Physicians in the Thirteenth Century', *Speculum* 57 (1982), 328–31
Waters, C. M., *Translating Clergie: Status, Education, and Salvation in Thirteenth-Century Vernacular Texts* (Philadelphia: University of Pennsylvania Press, 2016)
Watson, S., *On Hospitals: Welfare, Law and Christianity in Western Europe, 400–1320* (Oxford: Oxford University Press, 2020)
Webb, D., *Patrons and Defenders: The Saints in the Italian City States* (London: Tauris, 1996)
Weinberger, S., 'Les conflits entre clercs et laïcs dans la Provence du XI siècle', *Annales du Midi* 92 (1980), 269–79
Weising, C., '*Obscenitas*: les représentations sexuelles dans la sculpture des églises méridionales', *CdF* 52 (2019), 147–73
Weiss, R., *The Yellow Cross: The Story of the Last Cathars, c. 1290–1329* (London: Viking, 2000)
Werner, K. F., 'Observations sur le role des évêques dans le mouvement de paix aux Xe et XI siècles', in *Mediaevalia christiana XIe–XIIe siècles: hommage à Raymonde Foreville* (Brussels: Éditions universitaires, 1989), pp. 155–95
West, C., *Reframing the Feudal Revolution* (Cambridge: Cambridge University Press, 2014)
Wild, G., 'La genèse de cimetière médiéval urbain: l'exemple de la topographie funéraire de Toulouse (vers 250 vers 1350)', *Archéologie du Midi médiéval* 17 (1999), 1–24
Wildhaber, B., 'Catalogue des établissements cisterciens de Languedoc aux XIII et XIVe siècles', *CdF* 21 (1986), 21–44
Wolff, P., 'Le problème des Cahorsins', *Annales du Midi* 62 (1950), 229–38
Wolff, P., *Commerces et marchands de Toulouse (vers 1350–vers 1450)* (Paris: Plon, 1954)
Wood, D., *Medieval Economic Thought* (Cambridge: Cambridge University Press, 2002)
Wood, D., 'Discipline and Diversity in the Medieval English Sunday', in K. Cooper and J. Gregory, eds, *Discipline and Diversity*, Studies in Church History 43 (Woodbridge: Ecclesiastical History Society, 2007), pp. 202–11
Zadora-Rio, E., 'L'Historiographie des paroisses rurales à l'épreuve de l'archéologie', in C. Delaplace, ed., *Aux origines de la paroisse rurale en Gaule méridionale (IVe–IXe siècles)* (Paris: Errance, 2005), pp. 15–23
Zadora-Rio, E., 'Archéologies des églises et des cimetières ruraux en Languedoc: un point de vue d'"Outre Loire"', *Archéologie du Midi médiéval* 28 (2010), 239–48
Zarb, M., *Les privilèges de la ville de Marseille, du X siècle à la Révolution* (Paris: Picard, 1961)
Zerner, M., ed., *Inventer l'hérésie? Discours polémiques et pouvoirs avant l'Inquisition* (Nice: Centre d'études médiévales de Nice, 1998)
Zerner, M., ed., *L'histoire du catharisme en discussion: le 'concile' de Saint-Félix (1167)* (Nice: Centre d'études médiévales, 2001)
Zink, M., *La prédication en langue romane avant 1300* (Paris: Champion, 1976)

Index

Note that medieval people are indexed by first name

Adrian IV, pope 83, 186n89
Agde 28, 29, 68, 106, 129, 131, 144, 222
Agen 131, 165, 182, 205, 309, 320, 321, 409, 417, 455
Aix 10, 42, 128, 162, 184n82, 227, 294–96, 303, 334, 336, 391n31
 see also Armande de Narcès, archbishop; Robert de Mauvoisin, archbishop
Albi 14, 44n70, 52, 66, 68, 110, 117–19, 120, 121, 131, 147, 165, 225–26, 232, 243, 247, 282, 313, 320, 359, 366, 377, 381, 385, 417, 449
 see also councils of Albi (1230, 1254)
Albigensian crusade 10, 12, 13, 18–19, 81, 122, 125–27, 131, 132, 136, 137, 138, 155n133, 159, 162–85, 190, 194, 195–97, 256, 272, 323, 325, 338, 342, 366, 382, 383, 397, 406–8, 471–72, 477, 479, 481–5
 see also Arnaud Amaury; Simon de Montfort
Alès 131, 153, 179, 180n64, 184n82, 318n149
almsgiving 39n49, 48n86, 66, 71, 100, 107, 128, 137, 140–44, 150, 154, 155, 157–60, 196n124, 205, 207, 294, 299–300, 310, 322, 351, 352, 358, 360, 384, 400–5, 411, 414, 424, 428, 432–34, 435, 438, 465, 467, 469–71, 478
 see also charity/*caritas*; oblations; tithes
Alphonse-Jourdain, count of Toulouse 88, 109, 127
Alphonse de Poitiers 162, 213, 243, 266, 387, 408–9
Amiel, bishop of Toulouse 77, 135
Aniane, monastery 30, 86, 98, 114–15, 305
antependium 240–43, 250
 see also retables
apocalypse/apocalypticism 71, 72, 74, 138, 218, 273, 307
apostolic example/*vita apostolica* 3, 9, 94, 133–36, 140–46, 150, 155–61, 307
 see also books, Gospel books; Christ; poverty
Aragon, king/kingdom 13, 120, 130, 151n116, 157n140, 165, 166, 179, 180n67, 323, 331, 418, 428, 430, 461

Arles 50, 57n6, 58, 68, 109, 111, 116, 128, 131, 147, 151, 155–57, 162, 169, 177, 179, 180n64, 184, 193, 216, 248, 256, 279, 297, 299, 324, 373n119
 see also councils of Arles (1041, 1234, 1260)
Armand de Narcès, archbishop of Aix 227–29, 232, 235, 236, 239, 241, 252, 254, 260, 262, 302
Arnaud Amaury, OCist., papal legate 162, 171, 182, 195
Arnaud Gélis 219, 391, 438–39
Arnaud Sicre 430, 436, 449, 453, 455
Asad, Talal 8–9
Auch 163–64, 165, 175n49, 190, 217
Avignon 131, 147, 168, 289, 292, 381, 407, 408
 see also council of Avignon (1209)

baptism 45n74, 50, 53–54, 76, 83, 76, 83, 86, 110–11, 118–19, 164, 172, 186, 191, 195, 215, 220, 224–25, 227, 258, 263, 273, 278–79, 280, 285, 326, 390, 392, 393, 395, 398, 437, 461, 469
 see also children; women baptizing children
Barthélemy, Dominique 15n26, 56n4, 57n8, 66, 69
Beatrice de Planissoles/de Laglaize 211, 218, 359, 376, 452
bells 31–32, 48–49, 53, 99, 101, 156, 194, 210, 228, 231, 232, 233, 257, 260–63, 265, 308, 388, 402, 440, 448, 467
Benoît d'Alignan, OFM, bishop of Marseille 264–65, 268, 281, 285, 291, 325, 364
Bérengar Frédol, bishop of Béziers 220n66, 225n88, 277, 342, 344, 347–50, 352, 375, 444
Bernard de Campendu, bishop of Carcassonne 225, 277, 278, 279, 340
Bernard de Caux, OP, inquisitor 312, 365, 485
Bernard Gui, OP, inquisitor and bishop 131, 142, 193n117, 204, 217, 255n169, 257, 284, 289, 342, 353, 354, 356, 360, 365, 366, 367n100, 449
Bernard of Angers 63, 66, 325

Bernard of Clairvaux 109–10, 114, 292, 298
Bertrand de Comminges, St 205–7, 212, 447
Béziers 14, 29, 53, 54, 68, 83, 105, 131, 147, 154, 162, 170, 171, 177, 178, 262, 270, 277, 289, 314, 320, 326, 336, 352, 372, 383, 402, 452
  See also councils of Béziers (1233, 1246, 1255); Saint-Nazaire, Béziers, cathedral
Biller, Peter 5–6, 139n75, 193n115, 307n109, 361n82
Bisson, Thomas 15n26, 26–27, 70
blasphemy 154, 156, 283, 320, 324, 334–36, 347, 354, 367, 368, 406, 453, 454
books, liturgical 45n74, 48, 112, 116, 256, 257–58, 296, 301–4, 306–8, 339, 390, 453
  Gospel books 100, 138, 141, 151, 203, 256, 265, 304–6, 307, 311, 335, 346, 354, 359, 430, 483
Bourdieu, Pierre 273, 431–32, 438, 441, 443, 447
Brothers Minor (Franciscans) 131–33, 137, 138, 155, 156, 159, 173, 211, 223, 239, 266, 268–69, 280, 284–85, 299, 300, 310, 314, 317, 318, 319, 321, 324, 329, 331–32, 364, 371, 386, 404n66, 416–17, 422, 427, 435, 441, 455, 456, 461, 483
  see also Benoît d'Alignan; Francis of Assisi
Brothers of the Holy Trinity (Trinitarians) 158–59, 485
Brothers of the Order of Penance (Sack Friars) 132, 255–56, 317, 319, 322, 325, 352, 415, 422, 427, 434, 445
Brothers Preacher (Dominicans) 121, 125, 131, 133, 137, 138, 139, 142, 156, 172, 173, 182, 223, 225, 226, 232, 252, 266, 270, 274, 281, 299, 300, 318, 341, 354–55, 364, 366, 381, 408, 416–17, 420–21, 427
  see also Dominique Guzman; inquisition into heretical wickedness
Brown, Peter 11, 478
burial, *see* cemeteries

Cahors 58, 64, 88, 127, 131, 142, 147, 182, 238, 383n8, 409, 441
candles 48–49, 62, 102–3, 108, 157, 194, 201, 210–11, 216–17, 237–40, 243, 248, 252, 256, 260, 328, 330, 388, 392, 393, 395, 402, 404, 412, 414, 427, 435, 439, 448, 456, 467
Canso de la crozada 165, 168–69, 172, 174–75, 182, 482
Caputiati uprising 166, 407
Carcassonne 14, 29, 44n70, 68, 73, 119n5, 120, 127, 131, 153, 154, 155n133, 157n140, 158, 179, 180n65, 184n82, 193, 225, 257–58, 277, 280, 282, 288, 326, 339, 340, 342, 381, 382, 398, 407, 410, 415, 430, 442, 453, 482
  See also: Bernard de Campendu, bishop; council of Carcassonne (1303); Gaucelin de Jean, bishop; Pierre de Rochefort, bishop; Saint-Nazaire, Carcassonne, cathedral
Carmelite friars 132, 211, 225, 239n124, 408–10, 417, 452
Carolingian period 12, 14, 16, 17, 27, 29, 31, 45, 51, 60n18, 87, 91, 194n121, 274, 276, 296–97, 372, 407, 455n87
Castelnaudary 127, 149, 190n103, 217, 233, 336n8, 411
Castres 131, 144, 147, 320, 383, 417
Cathars *see* Good Men
Catherine of Alexandria, Ste 229, 241, 312
cemeteries 33, 35, 39, 40–44, 49, 50, 53, 57, 61, 69, 115, 212–27, 228, 235, 239, 267, 289, 392–93, 403, 412, 416, 421, 427, 447, 449
chalice 48–49, 240, 252, 258, 264, 308, 428
charity/*caritas* 128, 129, 134, 139, 145, 155, 156, 273, 285, 295, 333, 343, 353, 400–1, 405, 418, 433, 445, 470, 471
Charles d'Anjou, count of Provence 14, 331, 336
children 29, 83, 84, 88, 110, 111, 118, 119, 124, 139, 141, 164, 180, 186, 201, 210–11, 220, 224–27, 228, 266, 274, 276–77, 278, 286, 287, 290, 291n63, 292, 303, 310, 319, 326, 328, 329, 345, 350, 351, 377, 389, 390, 392, 395, 437, 439, 443, 455, 461
  see also baptism; godparenthood; women, baptizing children; women, childbirth
Christ 31n21, 35, 62, 68–69, 76, 110, 111, 117, 125, 128, 129, 140, 151, 161, 169, 172, 175, 180, 203, 205, 215, 239, 240–42, 244–47, 250–52, 253, 255, 260, 263, 264, 265, 266, 267, 268, 285–86, 291, 293, 296, 300, 315, 318, 319–20, 321, 326, 332, 354, 368, 397, 411, 427, 437, 438, 439, 440, 442, 443, 457, 458, 462, 464–67, 470
  See also crosses; Eucharist
Cistercians 93–95, 101, 120, 126, 134–36, 145, 181, 182, 292, 298, 478–79
  see also Grandselve; Silvanès
Clement IV, pope *see* Gui Foulques
Cluny, monastery 77, 82n16, 88, 109, 340
coinage 105–6, 108, 150, 157, 181, 210, 471
  see also oblations; usury
Compostelle (Compostella), shrine of Saint Jacques 92, 93, 107, 129, 202–5, 251, 254, 331n193, 332, 348, 447

confession 20, 52, 71, 72, 73, 90, 91, 113, 118, 119, 135, 137, 191–92, 197, 254, 266, 268, 271, 274, 277, 280, 281, 284, 292, 295, 299n85, 302, 309, 315, 320, 322, 324, 337–53, 357–59, 360, 362, 363, 373, 400, 436–37, 443, 449, 459, 469, 472
   to inquisitors 172, 198, 353–67
   See also penance
confraternities 20, 182–83, 217, 238, 239, 311, 400–15, 417, 422
   see also guilds (trade)
Conques 66, 129n45, 207, 209
Constable, Giles 4, 82n16, 83
Cordes 152, 211, 247, 259, 377–78, 392, 394, 395, 452–54
councils, ecclesiastical
   Albi (1230) 183, 192, 220, 224, 257, 262, 280, 307n107
   Albi (1254) 179, 191n107, 193, 274, 276, 297–98
   Arles (1041) 50, 57n6, 58, 68,
   Arles (1234) 169, 179, 297
   Arles (1260) 179n58, 278n20, 279, 299
   Avignon (1209) 173, 179, 182, 183, 217n54
   Béziers (1232/33) 169, 189, 192, 195, 196n122, 297
   Béziers (1246) 193, 276, 299n87, 307, 356
   Béziers (1255) 283
   Carcassonne (1303) 192, 455
   Narbonne (990) 58, 60
   Narbonne (1043) 58
   Narbonne (1054) 58, 68, 80, 108
   Narbonne (1055) 58
   Narbonne (1227) 178, 183, 189, 191–93, 195, 299
   Narbonne (1243) 174, 442n44
   Nîmes (1096) 83
   Toulouges (1027) 43, 50, 57, 58, 60, 62n23, 80
   Toulouges (1041) 43, 58, 80
   Toulouges (1064 × 66) 43, 58, 80
   Toulouse (1056) 80, 82
   Toulouse (1119) 77n1, 80
   Toulouse (1229) 169, 172, 174, 191, 192, 196, 197, 274, 276, 307, 308, 309, 408
creed/*Credo in Deum* 45n74, 72, 254, 274, 276–78, 284, 287, 290, 291, 313, 326, 330, 331, 333, 344, 380
cross 42, 48, 53, 62, 92, 99, 111–12, 134, 162, 165, 171, 182, 215–17, 221n72, 240, 244–47, 257, 258, 267, 268, 311, 324–25, 403, 447
   signing the cross 256, 264, 277, 350, 441, 443, 445, 459
   yellow crosses, penance for heresy 174, 197, 211, 343, 353–54, 356–58, 366

Devil/devils/demons 52, 63, 72, 124, 203, 208, 241, 270–71, 312–13, 319, 322, 351–52, 354, 359, 375, 441, 446–47, 452, 453, 459, 470, 484
Dominique Grenier, bishop of Pamiers 276, 289–91, 342–43, 346, 350, 456–57
Dominique Guzman (St Dominique) 121, 131–32, 136, 171
   see also Brothers Preacher
Duffy, Eamon 2
Durand d'Osca (/de Huesca) 122, 123, 171, 475n4, 482n33

Elne 29, 193, 220, 284
Étienne de Bourbon, OP 125, 317, 463
Étiennette de *Proaudo* 354, 355, 357, 360, 363
eucharist 53, 83, 111–12, 118, 167, 171, 172, 197, 220, 238, 252, 254, 257, 259–66, 268–69, 273, 278, 287, 318, 328, 427, 437, 439, 440, 455–56, 460, 466–67
   See also Christ; liturgy; mass
excommunication 52, 54, 77, 81n12, 85–86, 111, 120, 122n20, 164, 166, 167, 169, 177, 179, 182, 183, 192–95, 218, 220, 221, 266, 276n12, 279, 280n30, 281–82, 289, 290, 323, 326, 330, 351, 377, 387–88, 396, 398, 408, 464

Fanjeaux 11, 121n12, 125, 127, 239, 244, 275, 410–14
feastdays 28, 51, 53, 75, 99, 102, 109, 117, 151–53, 164, 167, 178, 179, 182, 183, 191, 193, 194, 204, 231, 238, 257, 276, 279, 284, 293, 294, 297, 299, 318, 325, 346, 348, 355, 374n123, 377, 391, 396, 397–98, 404, 411, 412, 414n103, 431, 444, 445, 449, 450, 461, 464
Fendeille 149, 217, 237, 411, 414
Feuchter, Jörg 235, 394, 476n5, 482
feudalism/feudal lordship 14–18, 26, 37, 57, 59, 63, 70, 170, 208, 372, 470
Figeac 50, 56, 58, 62, 131, 209
Foix 14, 27, 165, 331, 418, 422, 428, 481
Foucault, Michel 8–9, 336n6
Foulques de Marseille, bishop of Toulouse 168, 172, 182–83, 190, 309, 406
Foy, Sainte 11, 63, 66, 75, 93, 207, 209–10, 309, 325
   see also Conques
Francis of Assisi, St 132, 136, 316, 455
   see also Brothers Minor

Gap 10, 88, 109
gender 6, 236–37, 359, 415, 444–45, 481

Géraud Boffati, notary 239, 399–400, 417
godparenthood 276, 287, 395, 423–24, 432,
    437–38, 446, 463, 465, 466
Good Men (Cathar heretics) 119, 124–27,
    132–34, 136–38, 140–42, 145, 158, 168,
    172–74. 185, 203, 204, 207, 211, 220, 236,
    263, 274–75, 287, 292, 298, 306–7, 329,
    354, 359, 361–62, 364, 382, 384, 406,
    430–38, 440–44, 450, 451, 454–56, 460,
    461–65, 468, 475–85
Grandselve, Cistercian monastery 134n63, 135,
    185, 298
Gregorian reforms 3–5, 9, 14–15, 18, 28, 29, 49,
    64, 77–116, 118, 126, 133, 134, 163, 170,
    195, 385, 471
Gregory I ('the Great'), pope 251, 264n198, 285,
    299, 304, 315, 316
Gregory VII, pope 15, 77
Gregory IX, pope 173, 360, 409, 446
Grundmann, Herbert 3, 109n94, 133n60, 476
Gui Foulques/Clement IV 184, 283, 360–61,
    397, 453
Gui de Toulouse, OP 367–71, 378–79
guilds (trade) 219, 397–98, 406, 469
    see also confraternities
Guillaume IV, count of Toulouse 53, 213
Guillaume, duke of Poitiers 63, 67, 77n1
Guillaume Arnaud, OP, inquisitor 172, 364, 365,
    381, 485
Guillaume Durand, bishop of Mende 215n47,
    216, 217n51, 236, 251
Guillaume Bélibaste, Good Man (Cathar
    heretic) 430, 432–33, 437–38, 440, 441,
    448, 451–53, 455, 461, 463–66

Hamilton, Sarah 2n3, 52n98, 192n110, 274n4,
    338, 340
hell 72, 73, 312, 319
Henri de Lausanne 109–16
Henry I, king of England 135
heresy 9, 10, 11, 12, 20, 78, 109, 110–13, 117–19,
    120–25, 136, 138, 142, 145, 155n133,
    157n140, 165, 166, 168–69, 170–74, 182,
    185, 188, 191, 192–93, 197, 220–21, 247,
    253, 273, 275, 281, 288, 291, 307, 313,
    323, 326, 328–30, 333, 353–67, 376,
    381–83, 406, 415, 431, 432–43, 434,
    437–38, 443–44, 448, 451, 456, 461, 462,
    463, 464–69, 475–85
    see also Good Men; Waldensians
holiness 9, 55, 61, 110, 116, 127, 132, 136–46,
    155, 157, 158, 159–61, 201, 202–12, 226,
    260, 263, 267, 268–69, 379, 384, 469, 476,
    477, 478, 479, 485

Honorius III, pope 171, 407
Hospitallers (Knights of the Hospital of
    St John) 37, 53, 94–96, 105, 106, 107,
    126, 128, 136, 145, 156, 158, 183,
    330, 478
hospitals 28, 53, 92, 94, 97, 99, 104–6, 126–30,
    144–46, 158, 159, 183, 203, 214, 215, 247,
    299, 320, 384, 389, 402, 403, 413, 416,
    417, 423, 427, 432, 485
    see also lepers
Humbert de Romans, OP 139, 341

Innocent III, pope 133, 158, 162, 163, 168,
    172, 397n42
Innocent IV, pope 382n2, 408
inquisition into heretical wickedness 9, 10, 11, 14,
    19, 20, 119n5, 122, 125, 127, 131, 132,
    140, 141, 144, 145n99, 171, 172–74, 190,
    203–4, 211, 218, 219, 220, 221, 224, 235,
    253, 263–64, 266–67, 270n1, 274, 275,
    277, 281, 289, 298, 306–8, 313, 316,
    329–30, 332, 333, 334, 343, 353–67, 380,
    381–82, 387, 394, 408, 430, 436, 438, 440,
    442–43, 445, 449, 450, 451, 453, 460–61,
    463, 465, 468–69, 470, 476, 477, 480–85
    see also Bernard Gui; crosses, yellow; Good
    Men; heresy; Jacques Fournier; Pierre
    Cellan; Waldensians
interiority 4, 6–7, 197, 289, 318, 338, 355, 359,
    361, 380, 384, 445, 451, 459–60, 461, 467,
    469, 472–73
Islam/Muslims/'Saracens' 5, 8, 105, 111, 158,
    166, 175, 176, 178, 179, 266, 294, 309,
    323, 328, 396, 427, 428, 431, 448–49,
    451, 481

Jacques de Vitry 182, 300, 317
Jacques Fournier, OCist., bishop of Pamiers,
    inquisitor 218, 219, 224, 253–54, 266,
    329, 359, 364, 376, 387–88, 399, 430–31,
    432, 435, 436, 438–44, 449n67, 450, 452,
    455–67, 468, 483
Jerusalem 52n95, 73–74, 93, 99, 176, 273, 350
Jews 23, 111, 157, 159, 167–68, 170, 175,
    176–80, 182, 183, 184n82, 185, 196, 197,
    214, 220, 294, 295, 318, 320, 328, 364,
    396, 420, 431, 448–50, 452, 465

Katajala-Peltomaa, Sari 20n38, 447, 446n61
Kieckhefer, Richard 364, 452

Langmuir, Gavin 7, 180n66
La Roquebrussanne 227–32, 235, 239, 384
Laroque d'Olmes 33, 139n76, 232–36, 444, 447

INDEX

Lateran Council, II (1139) 163, 164n5
Lateran Council, III (1179) 165–66, 175, 177, 178, 182, 183
Lateran Council, IV (1215) 4, 113, 122n20, 131, 153, 163, 178, 185, 188–89, 191, 196, 197, 274, 279, 291, 299, 326, 338, 373, 470–71
Lauwers, Michel 42n62, 44, 49n91, 188n95, 215, 217n51, 220n63, 226–27
Lavaur 131, 171, 409–10, 417
Le Bras, Gabriel 3–4, 19
Le Goff, Jacques 145n101, 182, 471
legates, papal 77–78, 88, 119–20, 162, 166–68, 171, 175, 179, 189–90, 195, 341, 382, 408, 409, 485
lepers 94, 99, 104, 106, 113, 128, 130, 144, 154, 157, 187, 214, 309, 310, 332–33, 348, 417
 see also hospitals
Le Puy 10, 60–64, 93, 129, 131, 251
Le Roy Ladurie, Emmanuel 1n2, 219n61, 358n77, 376n130, 430
Lézat, monastery 17, 35, 36, 37, 48, 49n91, 63, 64–65, 67, 72, 81, 103, 187, 189, 222
lights, *see* candles; oil; wax
Limoges 56–58, 60, 62, 93, 131, 142, 165, 207, 293n66, 297n79, 309n116
Limoux 158–59, 223, 308, 366, 381–82, 384, 388–89, 410, 442n42
liturgy 34, 41, 45, 47, 48–50, 55, 78, 82, 85–86, 101, 107, 112, 116, 195, 197, 229, 236, 238, 239, 251, 253, 253–66, 268, 272, 293, 297, 302–4, 306, 308, 310, 343, 392, 396, 412, 449, 472, 478
 see also books, liturgical; mass; preaching
Lodève 29, 31, 68, 90, 92, 117–18, 131, 190, 193n117, 217, 257, 276, 284, 337, 386
Lombers 117–20, 125
lordship *see* feudalism/feudal lordship
Louis IX, king of France 162n4, 266, 283, 336, 407, 408
Louis of Toulouse, St 12, 210–11, 331–33, 435, 439, 441, 443, 446, 446n61, 454, 456

magic 347, 364, 450, 451–54
Magnani Soares-Christen, Eliana 65n33, 87, 94, 97n50
Maguelonne 29, 68, 86, 114
Manosque 10, 304, 337n7, 387
Marie Madeleine, Ste 102, 116, 128, 233, 239, 265, 293, 294, 311, 318, 324–25, 366–67, 435, 441
Marandet, Marie-Claude 223n80, 239n125, 308, 416, 418
marriage 29, 49, 53, 80, 111, 112, 118, 119, 153–54, 155, 156, 172, 255, 263, 278–79, 282, 283, 286, 322–23, 342n22, 351, 372n115, 373–74, 378, 392–94, 395, 396, 415, 417, 426, 427, 444, 453, 467n118
 see also women, marriage
Marseille 10, 13, 24, 33, 37, 47, 55, 60, 77, 131, 139, 149, 155, 171, 211, 212, 264, 268, 281, 286, 291, 294, 295, 326, 331, 364, 367, 383, 396, 402–4, 406, 434, 435, 446
 See also Benoît d'Alignan, bishop; Saint-Victor, monastery
Mary, Virgin 35, 52, 73, 74, 93, 94, 99, 100, 101, 156, 161, 191, 201–3, 208, 229, 238, 239, 241, 243, 244, 254, 255n169, 257, 283, 285, 293, 299, 307, 310, 311–12, 320, 321, 324, 330, 332, 336, 339, 375, 397, 398, 401–4, 407, 410, 411–14, 417, 431, 434, 435, 440, 445, 456, 458–59, 464–65, 470
 See also Rocamadour
mass 24, 30, 38, 40, 47n80, 48, 50, 51–53, 69, 73, 84–85, 98, 106, 107, 111, 112, 115, 142, 143, 154, 169, 187, 191, 195, 197, 204, 209, 211, 217, 218, 223n81, 227–28, 238, 239, 253–67, 293, 304, 305, 308, 310, 316, 318, 319, 322, 332, 340, 347, 351, 366, 387, 392, 393, 395, 398, 399, 402, 411, 412, 417, 418, 422–23, 426, 427, 428, 431, 433, 434, 439, 440, 444–45, 446, 447, 455, 457, 460, 469
 See also bells; books, liturgical; chalice; cross; Eucharist
Matfre Ermengaud 308, 314–16, 342, 346, 348, 350, 353, 370, 375, 376
Mazel, Florian 4, 18, 19n37, 78, 88–89, 98n51, 187n91, 190n102, 472
Meens, Rob 45n74, 52n98, 338, 340
Mende 10, 58, 60–64, 208, 216, 217n54, 220n66, 292, 442n44
mercenaries 164–69, 176, 208, 407
Meyrueis 152, 154–56
Milo, papal legate 166n11, 167, 168, 179, 195
miracles 50, 56, 62–68, 74–76, 121, 175, 201, 202, 205–10, 212, 255, 264–66, 268, 273, 285, 295, 300, 310, 315, 317, 319, 324–25, 330, 331, 351, 366–67, 375, 433, 434, 435, 443, 456, 458–59, 460
 See also pilgrimage; shrines; *various individual saints*
Mirepoix 131, 139n76, 224n85, 239, 288n54, 388, 389, 481n26
Moissac 24, 35, 36, 40, 52, 64, 69, 73, 82, 88, 101, 127, 147, 148, 149, 151, 153n127, 155n133, 171, 178, 240n130, 248, 305, 373n119

Montaillou 211, 377, 382n4, 430, 434, 447, 460, 462
Montauban 13, 122, 125, 127, 131, 147, 149, 159, 165, 235, 259, 263, 305, 394, 395, 398, 417, 436
Montcuq 122, 127, 152, 213, 251, 266, 387
Montolieu 385, 408
Montpellier 10, 99, 103, 106, 130, 131, 149, 166, 179, 184n82, 186, 203, 210, 270, 304, 318n149, 319, 321, 324, 418, 434, 440, 441, 445, 485
   See also councils of Montpellier (1195, 1215, 1224, 1258)
Montréal 121, 127, 231
Montségur 133, 139, 145n100, 480, 482
Moore, Robert Ian 110n97, 112–13, 118n4, 171n34, 185, 476–77, 484
Morlaàs 98–99, 108
Mundy, John Hine 13n25, 103n74, 130, 159n144, 238n119
Muret 187, 319, 323
Murray, Alexander 338n12, 340, 364

Narbonne 13, 24, 27, 29, 54, 55, 60, 68, 111, 120, 123, 127, 128, 130, 131, 149, 153n126, 162, 184, 186, 187, 213, 223, 307, 381, 383, 385, 396, 397, 403, 406–8, 441, 456–7, 482
   See also councils of Narbonne (990, 1043, 1054, 1055, 1227, 1243)
Nîmes 28, 29, 68, 72, 130, 131, 147, 166n11, 183n79
   See also councils of Nîmes (1096, 1252)

oblations 34, 40, 48, 52, 77, 80, 83, 84n23, 102n69, 106, 108–9, 111, 112, 175, 178, 183, 188, 212, 225, 254, 281, 384–400, 433, 446
   See also almsgiving; candles
oil 149, 387, 388
   for lights 48–49, 102, 211, 237–38, 239, 259, 268, 295, 391, 397–98, 414, 417
   holy oil 80, 390, 455
   see also candles; oblations; wax

Palazzo, Eric 239n126, 253, 256
Pamiers 122, 153n127, 250, 266, 276, 289, 290, 329, 342, 346, 387, 418, 430, 439, 458
   Statutes of (1212) 170n32, 172, 179, 188, 191, 407
parish, as administrative unit 33–34, 185–88, 194–95, 283, 400, 468
Pegg, Mark Gregory 18n34, 124n26, 139n77, 141, 361, 477, 479, 480, 482, 483

penance 20, 51–53, 72, 83, 86, 90–91, 93, 109, 111, 113, 119, 135, 137, 164, 165, 167, 168, 170n31, 171, 186, 191–93, 197, 204, 205, 208–9, 219, 270, 280–81, 283, 294, 295, 335, 337–53, 369, 378–82, 400, 442, 443, 444, 469
   For heresy 122, 204, 235, 353–67, 443
   see also crosses, yellow
   See also confession; restitution; sin
Perpignan 13, 32n22, 41, 115, 131, 147, 153n124, 154, 193, 194n118, 214–15, 219, 223, 239, 246, 250, 284, 305, 389, 396, 418, 419, 422
Peyrepertuse 31n19, 73, 91, 339
Pierre Autier, Good Man (Cathar heretic) 330, 354, 430, 434, 438, 440, 443, 460–61
Pierre Brun, OP, inquisitor 343, 354, 366
Pierre Cellan, OP, inquisitor 122, 125, 131–32, 137–40, 142, 235, 275, 394, 483
Pierre de Bruys 109–116
Pierre des Vaux-de-Cernay, OCist. 121, 167
Pierre Maury 266, 430–69
pilgrimage 13, 24, 33, 55, 73–74, 92, 94, 99, 128–29, 136, 164, 202–6, 235, 251, 265, 329, 331n193, 337, 343, 348–49, 350, 351, 353, 357, 389, 404, 413, 417, 435, 444, 448, 454, 469, 485
   See also women, pilgrimage
Pons de Léras 90–92, 109, 113, 116, 134, 136, 204, 205, 292, 316, 337, 339, 383, 479
   see also Silvanès
poverty, apostolic ideal of voluntary 92, 94, 110, 131, 133, 134–36, 145, 150, 156, 273
   the poor/socioeconomic poverty 39, 48n86, 53, 60, 68, 92, 99, 104, 105, 106, 128–29, 134–35, 143–45, 154, 157, 160, 222n75, 258, 270, 280, 294, 295, 309, 320, 322, 348–49, 400–5, 413, 414, 416, 417, 421–24, 426, 427, 428, 434
   see also hospitals; lepers
prayer 40, 50, 61–62, 72, 73–74, 75, 98, 108, 111, 112, 134, 138, 143, 144, 181, 183, 195, 197, 201, 203, 208, 210, 211, 212, 216–17, 219, 226, 237, 247, 254, 255, 256, 257, 259, 263, 274–76, 277, 283–86, 301, 302, 304, 312, 314, 321, 326, 330, 340, 351, 352, 401, 405, 435, 440, 441, 443, 444, 446, 454, 456, 458, 459, 467n118, 481
   Ave Maria 274, 276, 277–78, 286–87, 291, 312, 313, 321, 324, 330, 331, 344, 380, 402, 443, 458–59
   Pater noster 138, 217, 257n176, 274–78, 284, 286, 287, 291, 326, 330, 331, 344, 380, 402, 412, 443–44, 483

preaching 12, 51, 72, 92–93, 109–14, 120–21, 125–26, 132, 133, 136–41, 157, 171, 172, 176, 182, 191, 196, 207, 222, 255, 256, 264, 265, 270–72, 274, 281–82, 285, 291–301, 303, 304, 313, 315, 317, 319, 323–24, 330, 335, 341, 348, 351–52, 354, 355, 358, 359, 362, 366, 375, 376, 377, 432, 433, 434, 445–46, 456, 458, 462, 463, 465–67, 469, 479, 485
Privat, Saint 65–66, 208, 210
Puigcerdà 152, 240, 250, 410, 418–29, 437, 442, 449
purgatory 112, 224n85, 352

Quercy 165, 204

Raimon de Castelnou 311, 313, 315
Raimond V, count of Toulouse 67, 117, 152n122, 233n109, 305n100
Raimond VI, count of Toulouse 166–69, 170n31, 171, 175, 322
Raimond VII, count of Toulouse 18, 162, 168–69, 195, 408, 416
Raimond du Laburat 266, 330, 387–88
Raymond de Peñafort, OP 277n17, 341, 342, 345, 358n76, 361
religion, for laity 5–9, 19–20, 25, 197–98, 289, 318, 337, 380, 382, 384, 449–52, 469, 472–73
Remensnyder, Amy 66n37, 80
restitution 91, 92, 159, 182–83, 337, 343, 350, 353, 427
  see also confession; penance; sin
retables 228, 240–43, 250, 258
  see also antependium
Robert de Mauvoisin, archbishop of Aix 334–35, 452
Rocamadour 10, 11, 52, 129, 201–210, 407
Rodez 93, 129–30, 193, 222, 279, 281, 282, 284, 288
Rome 74n62, 93, 105, 203, 294, 308, 322n170, 381, 382n4, 413, 444, 447, 454
Rosenwein, Barbara 70, 88

sabbath, observation of 50–51, 61, 191, 227, 319, 346, 348, 380, 397–400, 464
Saint-Guilhem-de-Combret, rural church 32–33, 116, 256, 260–61, 302, 453
Saint-Lézat, monastery 37, 187
Saint-Marie-d'Aubrac, hospital 129–30, 203
Saint-Nazaire, Béziers, cathedral 84, 87, 177
Saint-Nazaire, Carcassonne, monastery 28, 232
Saint-Pierre-de-Mont, church 35, 36, 41, 48, 73

Saint-Sernin, Toulouse, monastery 23–28, 38, 46, 53, 69, 77, 81, 98, 99, 102, 298–99, 302, 304, 339, 353, 365, 383, 387, 403, 407
Saint-Victor, Marseille, monastery 24, 33, 34, 37–38, 47, 60, 77
sanctuary 42–44, 164, 404
Schenk, Jochen 134, 135
sermons, *see* preaching
sex 118, 154, 209, 218, 275, 282, 345, 359, 371–78, 438, 459
shrines 29, 50–1, 52, 55, 56, 60–62, 65–67, 74–76, 93, 99, 103, 107, 129, 160, 201, 202–12, 265, 268, 300, 317, 324, 325, 367, 384, 435, 440, 448, 458, 469, 485
  See also Compostelle; Mary, Virgin; miracles; pilgrimage; Rocamadour; *various individual saints*
Silvanès, monastery 90, 93–94, 101–2
  see also Cistercians; Pons de Léras
Simon de Montfort, count 18, 158, 159, 162, 165, 168, 172, 179, 188, 199, 397, 406, 407, 480
sin 7, 20, 52, 53, 67–68, 71–73, 90, 92, 94, 119, 137, 162, 164, 181–82, 184, 191, 203, 204, 209, 247, 252, 257, 266, 268, 272, 273, 278, 280–85, 301, 309, 312, 314, 315, 318–21, 326, 331, 335, 337–53, 356–61, 368–81, 405, 407, 432, 436–37, 438–39, 442, 443, 464, 465, 468, 469, 470, 472
  see also confession; penance; restitution; Ten Commandments
statues 56, 61, 66, 207, 229, 243–47, 434
  see also crosses

Tarascon 67, 131
Tarascon-sur-Ariège 329, 364
Templars, Knights 94, 96, 99–100, 105, 107, 126, 128, 134, 135, 136, 145, 158, 339, 401, 470, 477, 478
Ten Commandments 278, 280–81, 314, 345, 347
  see also sin
tithes 28, 34, 38, 40n51, 47n80, 48n88, 51, 52, 77, 79, 81, 83, 86, 101, 108, 112, 151, 188, 190, 195, 208, 212n40, 266, 273, 274, 281–82, 286, 314, 330, 346, 380, 385–91, 394, 395, 435–36, 469
Toulouse 2n2, 13, 23, 27, 53, 55, 63, 67, 77, 80–81, 93, 102, 119–20, 127, 128, 130, 131, 135, 140, 142, 147, 152, 158–161, 162, 165, 175, 182, 183, 184, 187, 195, 196, 205, 210, 211, 213–14, 215, 216, 219, 220, 221n72, 222, 232, 238, 247, 252, 277, 280–81, 289, 298, 300–1, 302, 307,